Operation Telic

The British Campaign in Iraq 2003-2009

Tim Ripley

Foreword by Andrew Gilligan

This edition published by Telic-Herrick Publications in 2016

Copyright © Tim Ripley 2016
The right of Tim Ripley to be identified as the author
of this work has been asserted by him in accordance with
the Copyright, Designs and Patents Act, 1988

All rights reserved. No part of this publication may be reproduced, stored in a retrieval system or transmitted, in any form or by any means, electronic, mechanical, photocopying, recording or otherwise without the written permission of the publisher.

Telic-Herrick Publications, 17 Fern Bank, Lancaster, LA1 4TT
www.operationtelic.co.uk

ISBN 978-0-9929458-0-0 (Kindle Edition)

Cover Design: Pagefast Print & Publishing Ltd, 4-6 Lansil Way, Caton Road, Lancaster, LA1 3QY, Lancashire, England

OPERATION TELIC

Waging Britain's Most Unpopular War?

The campaign in Iraq between March 2003 and June 2009 deeply polarised British politics, contributing to the fall from power of Prime Minister Tony Blair and seriously damaging the reputation, at home and abroad, of the British armed forces. Ten years on from the start of the war, it is now possible to put the British military campaign into a meaningful context and make sensible judgements about it. This book draws upon many new sources of information about Operation Telic, including:
- Contemporary official military documents from British and Coalition units that participated in the campaign.
- Internal British Army publications, giving first hand accounts of the campaign.
- Exclusive interviews with senior British commanders and military personnel.

Advance Reviews on Operation Telic

"This is the best I have yet read on Iraq."
Maj Gen Jonathan Shaw, commander British forces in Basra during 2007

"Thought provoking...I hope people will buy the book and debate the points its raises."
Lt Gen Robin Brims, Commander 1 (UK) Armoured Division during the assault on Basra in 2003

"Tim Ripley has done an amazing job piecing all this together - it is fascinating and has great pace and an engaging narrative."
Lt Col Nicholas Mercer, Chief Legal Advisor to British Forces in Iraq 2003

Tim Ripley travelled extensively in Iraq and the Middle East from 2002 to 2007 as a correspondent for Jane's Defence Weekly and The Scotsman newspaper, visiting British and US forces during the build-up to the war. Over subsequent years he travelled into Basra, Al Amarah and Umm Qasr and visited many of the key battlegrounds in southern Iraq. He now writes on defence for The Sunday Times and is a frequent broadcaster on military issues.

CONTENTS

Maps	5
Foreword by Andrew Gilligan	9
Writing Operation Telic	10
Chapter 1 Telic Tour	12
Chapter 2 The Commanders	22
Chapter 3 The Iraqis	30
Chapter 4 Planning the War	38
Chapter 5 To Kuwait	50
Chapter 6 The Battle Plan	65
Chapter 7 Across The Border	77
Chapter 8 Taking Down Zubayr	95
Chapter 9 Holding the Basra Canal	102
Chapter 10 Royal Marines vs T-55 Tanks	111
Chapter 11 To the Gates of Baghdad	119
Chapter 12 Fall of Basra	138
Chapter 13 Military Judgement	150
Chapter 14 Basra Summer	171
Chapter 15 A Mature Theatre?	191
Chapter 16 Street Fighting Summer	209
Chapter 17 Buying Influence	227
Chapter 18 The Trainers	239
Operation Telic Images, 2003 to 2009	253
Chapter 19 The Divorce	259
Chapter 20 RAF Against Insurgents	278
Chapter 21 Good Kit? Crap Kit?	292
Chapter 22 The Duel	310
Chapter 23 The Accommodation	333
Chapter 24 Charge of the Knights	360
Chapter 25 Time to Go	390
Operation Telic: Looking Back	396
Operation Telic Commanders, Headquarters and Major Units 2003 to 2009	409
With Thanks to	418
References	421
Bibliography	453
Glossary	460

MAPS

Iraq 2003 (US CIA)

Note: Large format/high resolution versions of these maps are available to view at http://www.operationtelic.co.uk

South Eastern Iraq and Northern Kuwait (U.S. Defense Mapping Agency Aerospace Center)

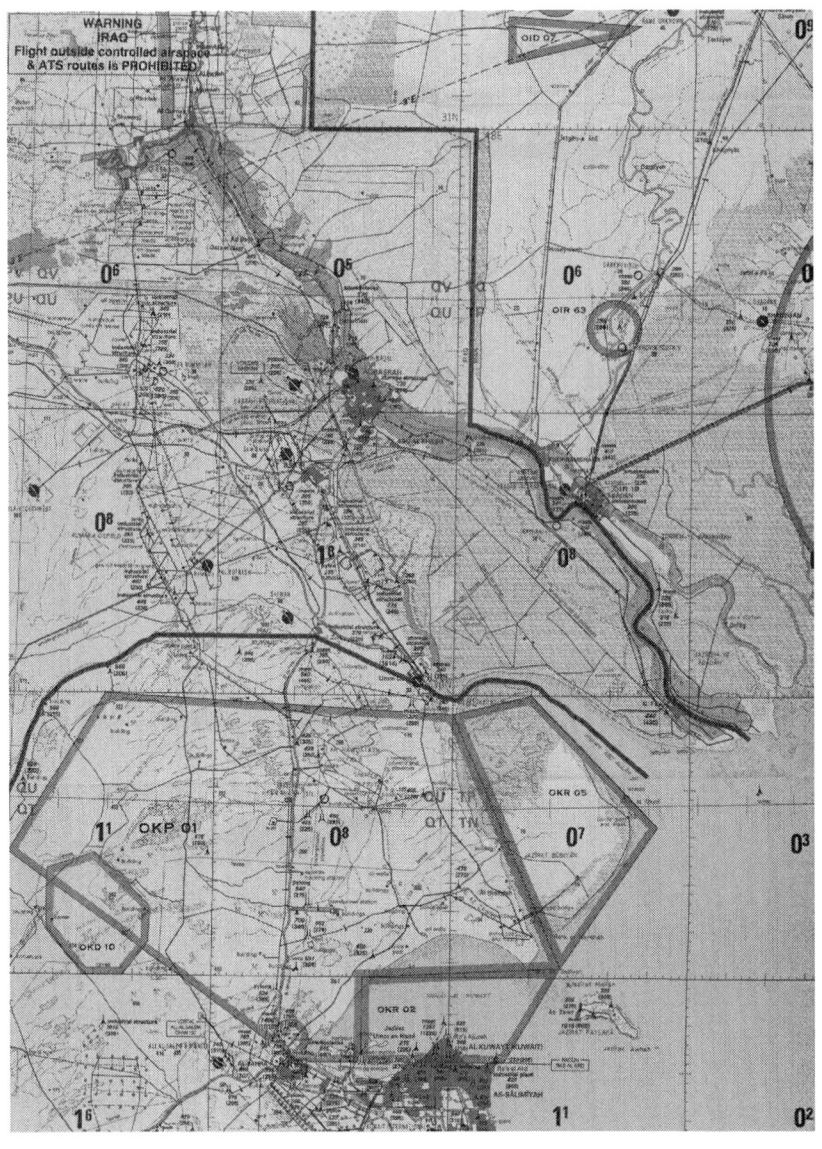

Al Amarah, Nasiriyah and Rumaylah (U.S. Defense Mapping Agency Aerospace Center)

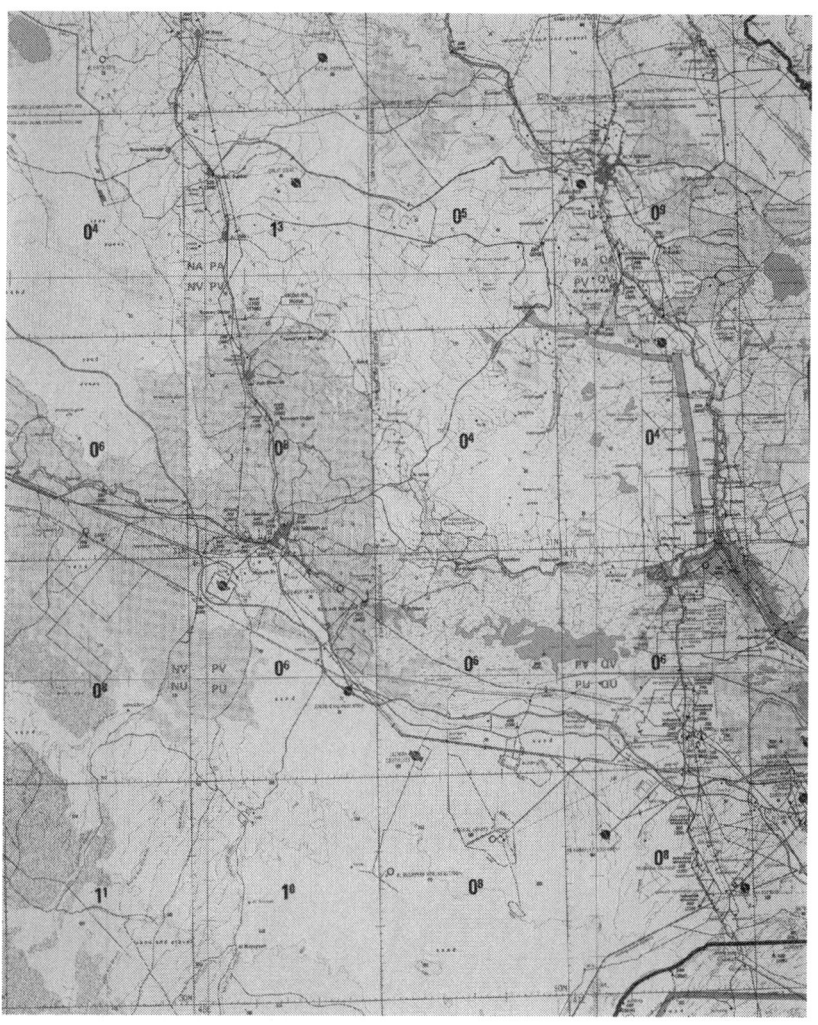

Basra City (US National Imagery and Mapping Agency)

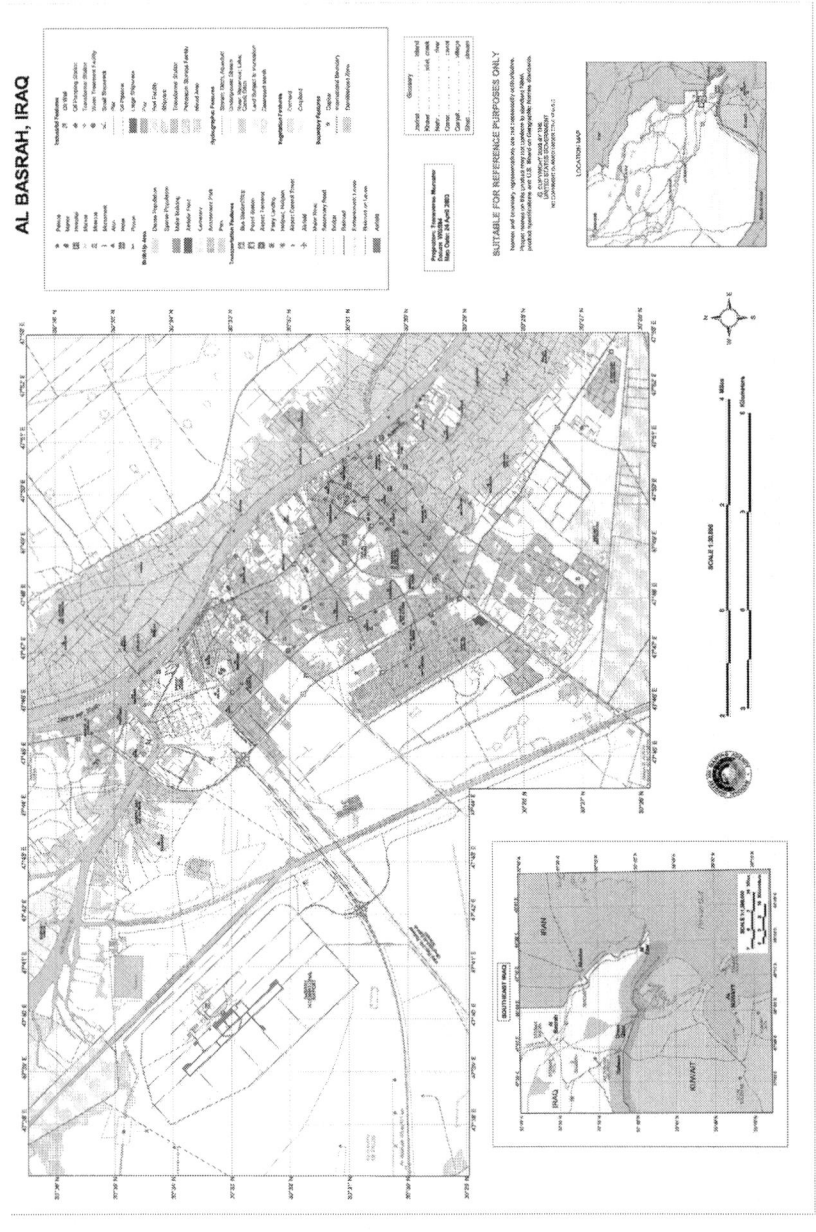

FOREWORD

By Andrew Gilligan

Iraq was a huge blow to Britain's moral and international standing. It changed, probably permanently, the relationship between this country's people and their leaders. But, less widely understood, it was also a military humiliation for the UK. In the debacle that was Operation Telic, one group of individuals - Britain's military leadership – got off too lightly.

For years, the top brass has been essentially exempt from the kind of criticism dished out to other public servants. The failings of Iraq are customarily blamed on conniving politicians or cheese-paring bureaucrats. Such people are not blameless, of course; but Tim Ripley's important book uses large quantities of previously unreported evidence to show why the blame must be more widely shared.

His is a nuanced portrait. It includes many accounts of good, even superb soldiering. It describes the frustrations felt by those on the ground at decisions from Whitehall, and tells the true, more complicated and fascinating story of Britain's failure to take on the Mahdi Army militia in Basra.But it makes clear, too, that many of the British Army's problems were self-inflicted. Senior commanders complacently underestimated the task. They failed to learn from their mistakes. And towards their political masters they seemed to act like "military toadies," in the striking phrase of one general quoted by Ripley, lacking the courage to speak truth to power about their real operational needs.Iraq, as Tim Ripley points out, is the war that everyone wants to forget. Many of the units which fought the hardest have been denied even battle honours.

The Ministry of Defence made strenuous efforts to obstruct the author's researches - always an excellent sign that you are on to something. But as we witness the West's response, or lack of it, to events in Syria and now Ukraine, Iraq is starting to look like a war we cannot avoid remembering.

It is starting to look like the misconceived, ill-executed operations of Iraq and in Afghanistan have caused a strategic watershed in the West, where political and public will to deal with egregious violations of international norms simply no longer exists. That is the real importance of this book. If we are to recover the confidence to stand up for civilised values, we must understand the truth about how we failed to do so in Iraq.

Andrew Gilligan
April 2016

WRITING OPERATION TELIC

On a stormy November night in 2002, I stood on the Kuwait-Iraq border looking into Saddam Hussein's domain. A few yards away a large sand berm or rampart could be seen, and beyond it a run-down Iraqi border post. A handful of very bored Kuwaiti border guards said no traffic had crossed for several days. There were no lights on the Iraqi side, which gave the scene a certain unreality. This did not seem like the place where a global international crisis would come to a climax. Yet only four months later, columns of British and American tanks would stream across border and head north for Basra and Baghdad.

For much of the first decade of the Twenty-First Century, my professional life and work was dominated by the war in Iraq. After covering the build-up for war in Kuwait and Bahrain during 2002 and early 2003, I worked at the media centre of US Central Command in the Qatari capital Doha during the invasion phase of the conflict. Later in the year, I travelled into Iraq to visit British forces in al Amarah, Basra, al Faw, Majar-al-Kabir, Umm Qasr and Zubayr, as well as visiting Royal Navy warships patrolling off the coast. The first signs of the insurgency that would rack Iraq for the next decade were clearly in evidence. The names of the places I visited would soon became tragically familiar to the British public as they featured in news accounts of the deaths of 179 servicemen and women, until the summer of 2009, when the British combat troops finally left the country.

Over the past decade, during visits to British military units in the course of my work as a correspondent for Jane's Defence Weekly magazine, I met hundreds of servicemen and women who had spent time in Iraq. They were keen to talk about their experiences. The stories they told were remarkable. I listened to tales of bravery, tragedy and in some cases crass stupidity.

After this, people started to let me see official briefings, operational reports and other military documents from the Iraq war. The story they told was even more powerful. Many people had long suspected that the government of Prime Minister Tony Blair, the Ministry of Defence and parts of the British Army had put an enforced positive spin on what was happening in Iraq. Events that did not fit the agreed narrative were not publicised, even within the British armed forces, for fear of leaks to the media or political opponents. Given that the Iraq war was deeply unpopular in Britain, it was not really surprising that the-then government would try to marshal facts to support its case.

From my reading of the documents from the conflict and my conversations with veterans, it was very clear that the planning and execution of Britain's military campaign in Iraq left a lot to be desired. Key decisions were made on the basis of incomplete information, by politicians, diplomats, senior civil servants and military commanders who had little understanding of Iraq and the forces fighting British troops. Meanwhile British troops had to live, fight and die in extreme conditions, which were little appreciated or understood by the public at home.

The British armed forces have developed their own language, jargon and bureaucratic procedures, which makes it far from easy to make sense of documents from the Iraq war. While the documents I have seen -commanders' diaries, operational orders, intelligence summaries, situation reports, post-operational tour reports, as well as operational maps and graphics showing troop positions - are rich in detail of many aspects of the British campaign, I am aware that they do not tell the whole story. At key points in the campaign, events on the ground were moving so fast that commanders had to make decisions on the fly during radio conversations, mobile phone calls or video conferences. Often these were not fully recorded at the time. Also some issues were so sensitive that commanders and staff officers were reluctant to record them in writing.

Another important source of information for this book is the journals of the British Army regiments that deployed to Iraq between 2003 and 2009. Although public documents, these journals have limited circulation and are aimed at internal regimental audiences. They give officers and soldiers a chance to talk about their experiences. While they are invariably upbeat about their tours of duty in Iraq, as the war progressed and casualties mounted, these publications became more sombre in tone, as page after page was devoted to obituaries and reports about the progress of wounded comrades. British army regiments are close-knit communities and as casualties mounted the concern and worries of senior officers and other regimental personnel were recorded in considerable detail in these journals.

While the battles of the British Army in the Basra region dominated reporting of the campaign at the time, I am crucially aware that the Royal Navy, Royal Air Force and Special Forces played important roles. On many occasions their influence on the British campaign was disproportionate to the number of their personnel deployed.

Up to now, media reports and historical accounts of the Iraq campaign have been dominated by the roles of Prime Minister Tony Blair and other senior government ministers. Very little attention has been given to the influence of senior military commanders, many of whom have very low public profiles. Their influence on the course of the campaign has up to now not really been examined in any great detail. I hope to rectify this.

The British armed forces fought hard in Iraq, but the outcome left many of the soldiers, marines, sailors and airmen who served in the country feeling that the campaign did not end on the terms they would have wanted. While it was not a crushing defeat along the lines of the humiliating surrender to the Japanese in Singapore in 1942, it was not a resounding and clear-cut victory, in the mould of the 1982 Falklands or 1999 Kosovo campaigns. The promise of easy successes that seemed within its grasp in the heady days of April 2003 eventually eluded the British military. This book tells that story.

Tim Ripley
April 2016

Chapter 1
TELIC TOUR

"It just was Operation Telic at first, not Telic 1, 2, 3 or 4 – that came later," was how Lieutenant General Robin Brims, who commanded the opening assault on Basra in 2003, looked back on the Iraq campaign.[1]

For the 140,000 or so British service men and women who were deployed to Iraq between 2003 and 2009, which Operation Telic tour, or six month period of duty, they served on defines their experience. It established all their points of common reference - who were their commanders, who their contemporaries were, the bases where they served and what major events occurred, particularly when and where any comrades were killed or injured.

Each six-month Operation Telic tour was given a numerical designation, and this was to become shorthand slang for the period of duty. Commanders, soldiers and their families used it, and the term peppered official documents. It set both the start date for the tour, and the date at which the troops went home. The Operation Telic number also crept on to mementoes and memorabilia, such as unit t-shirts.

The six-month tour of duty for British personnel in Iraq also shaped how the war was fought, how commanders and troops conducted themselves and had a major influence on the outcome of the campaign. "I didn't join the army to spend a year away on operations, we just don't do it, it's not in our culture," was how General Sir David Richards, Britain's Chief of Defence Staff between 2010 and 2013, responded to criticism of the relatively short tour lengths of British troops in Iraq, compared to the year-long tours experienced by US soldiers.[2]

Although almost all British army and air force personnel who eventually served in Iraq had been on operations in the Balkans during the 1990s, hardly any had fought in a war before they deployed to the Middle East. The soldiers who served during the invasion period in March and April 2003 had the 'full on' war experience for almost two weeks, fighting battles involving tanks, artillery and air strikes. At the time it was felt by troops that nothing could, in professional terms, be more fulfilling than this. The subsequent occupation of southern Iraq, they felt, could only be an anti-climax. It was not just the soldiers, but politicians and media in London who felt that after the initial invasion phase it was all over, bar the shouting.

Iraq was to dominate, in one way or another, the professional lives of almost every British soldier and a large part of the Royal Air Force (RAF) for most of the subsequent decade. The operational 'tour plot' or deployment schedule for army units was set one or two years in advance, so soldiers had a fairly clear idea that they were heading to Iraq.

Getting a regiment on the operational tour plot was a source of great competition in the British Army, as operational experience was seen as a key factor in recruiting both soldiers and officers. A good war tour ensured a regiment got media exposure both nationally and in local recruiting areas. At the same time, for serving soldiers, non-commissioned officers and officers, successful participation in operational tours was essential for promotion. The imperative to participate in operational tours was raised considerably in 2004, when the Ministry of Defence announced several infantry regiments and battalions would be disbanded as part of a package of budget cuts. Units not on operations were perceived as being more likely to be disbanded.

A major feature of Operation Telic was the dominance of line infantry regiments in troop rotations to Iraq. While the Parachute Regiment and Royal Marines played a major part in the 2003 invasion, apart from a couple of rotations as 'surge' battalions in 2004 and 2005, these elite units of the British armed forces played little part in the Iraq campaign. Infantry regiments recruited from the north of England, Scotland, Wales, the Midlands and the West Country bore the burden of the Iraq campaign, with some units cramming in three Operation Telic tours between 2003 and 2009.

Which units were selected for operational tours was the responsibility of the army's second most senior officer, the commander-in-chief Land Command. His staff made recommendations based on a unit's level of training and brigade assignment. The army policy said that brigade commanders deploying to Iraq would routinely take the units assigned to that brigade in peacetime, but Operation Telic brigades were routinely reinforced with additional units, and senior officers would lobby on behalf of their unit to get them on these tours.

The need to secure good promotion reports from operational tours ensured that army officers and senior non-commissioned officers were keen to volunteer for service in Iraq. For company and battalion commanders, a good report from an operational tour was essential for promotion to the next level of command. This was particularly the case with commanding officers, because an unofficial quota system existed for selection to attend the army's higher command and staff course. Brigade commanders are only usually able to recommend one of the unit commanders for this course, which opened the door to promotion above colonel. Without attending this course, an ambitious officer's career was effectively over, so not getting their unit on an Operation Telic tour could be a career breaker.

For the rank and file, the prospect of seeing combat was often enough to keep young men flowing into recruiting offices. As the Iraq war dragged on and units started to begin returning for their second and third tours, it did start to have an effect on the number of soldiers leaving the army early, fed up with spending too long away from home. By 2006, almost every infantry battalion was several dozen men short of full strength, and some units that had undertaken multiple tours in Iraq were up to 100 men short.

Morale of troops in Iraq was always difficult to gauge. The relentless pace of activity meant that few soldiers had much time to dwell on the reasons why they were there. Many were veterans of multiple tours in Kosovo, Bosnia and

Northern Ireland and treated their time in Iraq as just part of the job. A group of soldiers from the Royal Dragoon Guards in 2005 tried to raise morale by creating a spoof video of the hit song, Amarillo, which then went viral on YouTube. The circulation of the video across the Ministry of Defence computer network overloaded and crashed the system. Fortunately, the army hierarchy saw the joke and realised it was good for morale to show its troops having fun amid the mayhem in Iraq.

Commanding officers structured their battalion's training and promotion plans around the forthcoming tour, so soldiers would be grouped together with the comrades with whom they would work in Iraq. Six to eight months out from the deployment, units would begin to conduct formal training exercises, tailored for Iraq specifically by the army's Operational Training and Advisory Group (OPTAG). This was made up of instructors, alleged experts on the situation in Iraq, and the training was supposed to prepare soldiers for what they would face on the ground in Basra. The pace of this training would rapidly accelerate from small scale activity to larger exercises, often involving live firing and complex tactical scenarios that the instructors thought the troops would face on the ground in Iraq. For the first few Operation Telic tours, OPTAG training was pretty basic because of a lack of knowledge across the army about the situation in Iraq. As more soldiers served in the country, the quality of pre-deployment training improved considerably.

Getting to Iraq involved a complex and time consuming process managed by the Royal Air Force and the army's Royal Logistics Corps (RLC). British soldiers invariably complained that this experience was specifically designed to make Iraq seem welcoming. It started with being bussed to a reception centre at South Cerney in Wiltshire to wait for several days, before spending interminable hours at the departure terminal at RAF Brize Norton in Oxfordshire. A nine hour flight on a charter airliner or RAF Tristar jet to the giant US airbase at al Udeid in Qatar, was then followed by a wait of several hours or even days in large tents, which the RLC movements staff termed the 'transit accommodation'.

The onward movement to the huge British base at Basra International Airport was dependent on a night-time landing slot being available for the RAF C-130 Hercules shuttle flight. All movements by passenger-carrying aircraft into Basra took place under the cover of darkness, to protect them from insurgent anti-aircraft missile or anti-aircraft machine gun attack. Regular insurgent rocket and mortar fire on the airport played havoc with the schedule so flights were often delayed for days on end, with backlogs of personnel and cargo. Casualty evacuation flights took priority, and this further contributed to the precarious nature of what the RAF termed their 'air bridge'.

Arrival at Basra in the middle of the night was a chaotic experience as arriving passengers were shepherded in darkness across the exposed runway to the airport terminal. A RLC or RAF senior non-commissioned officer was usually in charge of the welcoming committee, giving a briefing on the latest threats to the airbase and directing the new arrivals to their accommodation.

Over the next week newly arrived soldiers would undergo what was described as the Reception, Staging and Onward Integration (RSOI) training package. This included an element of fitness training to acclimatise them to the 40 degree temperatures, and more, experienced during the Iraqi summer. At least two of the 179 servicemen who died in Iraq succumbed to conditions attributed to heat, so this was not taken lightly.

As the ROSI training was under way, unit commanders and other key personnel were in the midst of preparing to take over bases and tasks from the unit they were relieving. Newly arrived soldiers progressively began to move out of the airport into their homes for the next six months.

This change over of units was known as the Relief in Place or RIP, and was a complex exercise and a huge logistical challenge potentially involving up to 20 battalion sized units, comprising some 16,000 troops, arriving and leaving within the space of a month to six-week period. Through the use of helicopters, armoured vehicles and further C-130 flights the troops were moved across Southern Iraq and up to Baghdad. The logistical effort was substantial and very disruptive to day-to-day operations.

Troops began to conduct join patrols with their predecessors to get a feel for what the insurgents were doing in the neighbourhood. Equipment would be handed over and the lessons and key experiences of the past six months exchanged. The chronic lack of information technology (IT) and the critically under-developed software meant that often key intelligence, such as files on known insurgents or maps of enemy positions, were often not in a structured format and were lost at the end of unit tours.

Eventually a ceremony would be held at battlegroup or battalion headquarters to formally lower the flag of the outgoing unit, and the new unit's flag would be raised. With this over, the new arrivals were on their own. The departing unit's soldiers invariably looked exhausted and at the same time exhilarated to be going to home in one piece.

Home for the next six month for British soldiers would be one of around a dozen large bases spread across southern Iraq. These were sprawling installations with scores of air-conditioned tents for troops to live in. Contract workers, mainly from the Indian sub-continent, but also many locally recruited civilians, cooked food, laundered clothes, removed rubbish and ran sewage plants. These bases became progressively more comfortable as internet cafes, video rooms and satellite television sets proliferated. In the first years of the occupation the majority of British troops spent most of their time out of their bases, manning check points, on foot patrols, training Iraqi troops and police or conducting hearts and minds projects with local civilians. Often troops would set up temporary bases in neighbourhoods and villages to work and live side by side with locals. As the insurgency developed, troops increasingly got pulled back into their bases, firstly to reduce their vulnerability to attack and secondly to put 'an Iraqi face' on security to minimise the visibility of British troops.

At the same time, the fortification of bases was dramatically up-scaled to reduce their vulnerability to attack. Sangars or guard points were re-built in concrete to defeat drive-by-shooting and suicide bomb attacks. Key buildings, such as command posts, were provided with reinforced concrete roofs. Bomb shelters were built around the bases and warning sirens installed. In some bases soldiers were provided with so-called 'concrete coffins' so they could sleep in safety during mortar and rocket attacks.

When British troops pulled back to the airport in 2007 and abandoned their bases in downtown Basra, one British general described the base as being akin to a "battleship in the desert". The base was provided with C-RAM Gatling guns removed from Royal Navy frigates to shoot down in-coming insurgent rockets, and a battery of AS-90 self-propelled howitzers to strike back at rocket firing points pin-pointed by radar detectors. There was so much electronic equipment operating at the base that it was causing 'electronic fratricide,' and a stand-down had to be ordered to allow experts to work out how to make the electronic jamming equipment work at the same time as the army's radios.[3] While many of the soldiers involved in improving the protection of the air base were very proud of their endeavours, others complained that at this point British influence in southern Iraq was at its lowest.

The six months of a unit's tour would pass rapidly as officer and senior NCOs served up a relentless stream of activity for their troops. Day after day troops would participate in strike operations or raids into insurgent-held neighbourhoods to capture enemy fighters, convoy-escort road moves, and patrols in areas local to bases. There were training courses for Iraqi army recruits, repairing and maintaining vehicles and equipment, hearts and minds projects with local civilians, and interminable guard duty known as 'stags' in watch towers around bases. Insurgent rocket, mortar, gun and improvised road side bomb attacks (IEDs), came at random, and added to the unpredictability of soldiers' lives in Iraq. Although defences and fortifications meant that direct casualties from insurgent attacks on British bases were relatively minor over the course of the six-year long campaign, the corrosive impact of loss of sleep and jarred nerves was significant. Some British soldiers attributed many of the casualties incurred during operations outside bases to mistakes and misjudgements caused by lack of sleep and stress.

There was a hierarchy of popularity of the type of tasks undertaken by British troops in Iraq. By far the most popular were strike operations into the heart of insurgent controlled territory. These raids were very prestigious within the army and units measured their reputation by the number and complexity of strike operations they undertook during a tour. They were difficult to plan and organise, as well as being highly risky, but the kudos from successfully pulling them off was huge. The participants were happy to be taking the fight to the enemy, rather than just being on the receiving end of hostile fire while hunkered down in fortified bases.

The next most popular duty was with the brigade surveillance company, which carried out covert surveillance of insurgents. This work was seen to be pseudo-special forces in nature, and it was viewed by ambitious soldiers as being a stepping stone to joining the elite Special Air Service (SAS) or the Special Reconnaissance Regiment (SRR).

Patrol operations along the long border with Iran were also popular because they were one of the few times soldiers got away from the congested, polluted and smelly Iraqi towns and cities. For several weeks troops lived in the desert and could move around largely free from the threat of ambush and IED strikes. The border region was the nearest thing in southern Iraq to the classic Arabian desert of T.E. Lawrence and Thesiger legends. Troops went on patrol in stripped-down Land Rovers, and were re-supplied by RAF helicopters or airdrops from Hercules aircraft. Commanders and soldiers loved being out of big camps, and away from the petty bureaucracy that ruled in them.

Less popular were duties escorting supply convoys or guarding bases, because not only were they very dull, but they made soldiers passive victims of insurgent fire or IEDs. During late 2006 and into 2007, British convoys were coming under increasing attacks in downtown Basra and the escorts became large and complex tasks involving several hundred troops at a time.

To sustain the British garrison in southern Iraq required a huge logistic effort that was very manpower-intensive. At British bases in southern Iraq and around the Gulf, thousands of army, air force and navy logistic personnel worked to prepare vehicles, aircraft and ships for action. This was far from easy work, carried out in basic facilities in high temperatures. For those working in Iraq, insurgent rocket and mortar attacks added to their problems, while those outside Iraq still had to endure months away from home. Once the Afghanistan campaign geared up in 2006, the pressure on British logistic personnel increased as they were duel-tasked to support the war on two fronts. The guidelines or harmony rules that governed time between deployments were often broken for many RAF and RLC units and personnel in 2006 and 2007. The RAF Hercules force, for example, was heavily in demand to run the shuttle between al Udeid and Basra, while at the same time sustaining a similar shuttle around British bases in Afghanistan. Aircrews and ground crews were spending two months in Iraq, two months at home and then two months in Afghanistan. This inevitably meant that to keep this tempo up, Hercules crews had to make short notice deployments to fill gaps in units, often meaning they could not plan their affairs and had to leave behind families or sick relatives at no notice.[4]

The training of local Iraqi troops was never a popular task for British troops, for a variety of reasons. A separate training centre was established within the US base at Tallil, some 200 kilometres to the west of Basra, where a couple of hundred British troops conducted the training. Language and cultural barriers made it difficult for British soldiers to interact with their Iraqi counter-parts. The British approach to training Iraqi troops, which did not include attaching or embedding mentoring teams into Iraqi units after their troops had been through basic training, meant that British troops had little attachment or interest in the progress of Iraqi recruits. Churning recruits through training courses became an end in itself. For troops assigned to be instructors these training sessions were very dull and undemanding, with the most complex activity being running a rifle range. Iraqi soldiers appeared to lack many of the qualities that British troops aspired to, and British troops often found it hard to take their trainees completely seriously.

The troops committed to training Iraqis were the British soldiers who had the most contact with locals during their tours of duty. At the peak of the British deployment to Iraqi in 2005-06, probably only half of the British troops had jobs that took them out of their fortified bases and had regular contact with ordinary Iraqis, either civilians or members of the security forces. The British military became progressively less engaged with local people as the insurgency gained momentum. Only in the honeymoon period of the summer and autumn of 2003 could British troops mingle freely with the local population. As the insurgency took off, force protection measures meant the troops progressively took to driving around in heavily armoured vehicles or large convoys.

In 2006 and 2007, the most common way soldiers came into contact with locals were during night-time strike operations when British troops were breaking in the doors of their homes, and dragging off their male relatives into detention, or performing 'mortar base' patrols to mitigate the threat of mortar or rocket attack. It was not a situation that was in anyway likely to make the citizens of Basra like or respect British troops. In turn, British troops had little opportunity to strike up any sort of relationship with ordinary Iraqis. A siege mentality quickly took hold, and was turned into reality in 2007 when the British garrison withdrew behind the concrete and steel ramparts of Basra airport.

The most brutal way British soldiers inter-acted with Iraqis was when they were on the receiving end of the insurgent direct fire or improvised explosive devices. It was rare for a British regiment to suffer more than one or two combat fatalities during a tour. Many regiments that went to Iraq suffered no combat fatalities during their tours, and even during the war fighting phase in March and April 2003, more than two-thirds of the 33 casualties were due to accidents or friendly fire. Less than half a dozen were due to enemy action.

Just under a third of all British fatalities in Iraq between 2003 and 2009 were caused by accidents, friendly fire or natural causes. The proportion of non-battle injuries among British forces was even higher with only 315 of 3,283 admissions to the UK field hospital in Iraq being due to battle wounds. Of these just under 2,000 were serious enough to warrant evacuation back to the UK for further treatment. The causes of non-battle injuries and sickness were varied, including road accidents, bio-mechnical injuries from the challenge of carrying heavy kit across challenging terrain, heat exhaustion and a large number of very serious vomiting and diarrhoea cases caused by exposure to southern Iraq's unsanitary water system.

When soldiers were killed in action during the subsequent insurgency, it was a sudden and violent event. Corporal P.R. Barnes was a member of a vehicle patrol of the 1st Battalion, The King's Own Scottish Borders (1 KOSB), which was ambushed at Ali Ash Sharqi in August 2003.

" 'Stop, stop, stop' came the [officer's] order and we screeched to a halt," he recorded in his regiment's journal.

"I stopped and turned off the [Land Rover] engine, somewhat surreally placing the vehicle in gear. I placed my rifle on my lap and was alone. Two yards away Fusilier Russel Beeston appeared dead, a round having hit him in the chest, having first shattered his arm on its deadly journey. I ran for my life, instinct expecting another round to take my head off. I tasted blood, it was an expectation rather than fact. I found cover behind my Land Rover. Private Jim Ford came running past screaming 'I've been shot, I've been shot.' His voice full of disbelief, I grabbed him and dragged him to the ground to administer first aid to his wrist: we staunched the flow of blood and laid him behind [the Land Rover]."

The Scottish troops returned fire and neutralised the enemy.

"Suddenly the air was alive with someone shouting, 'Beasty's dead, Beasty's dead'. I thought this is real, this is not Salisbury Plain. Lance Corporal Mark Lawrie [was] kneeling astride his body pounding his chest, screaming at him to come back, covered in blood, working in vain to save a life already gone. Except for the howls of dogs there was silence. Death had come, visited in an instant and moved on. I fully expected to die that night as eight others had done in the 1 KOSB [area of responsibility] in the previous two months, and yet I live, the randomness defeats me. It was an experience I would never wish to repeat, although I'm privileged to say I was there. (Everyman thinks badly of himself for never having been a soldier). If there are such things as heroes in battle, the only one I saw that night was Fusilier Russell Beaston – Beasty, who died quickly and quietly with dignity in the service of a friend."[5]

It was only in 2007 that casualties from enemy fire started to escalate. Combat operations were of such prolonged intensity that few British soldiers had experienced such fighting since World War Two or the Korean War in 1950-53. Lieutenant-Colonel Patrick Sanders, and his men from the 4th Battalion The Rifles Battlegroup, spent nearly three months under siege in Basra Palace under daily mortar, rocket, small arms and rocket propelled grenade attack in the summer of 2008. He described to the Royal United Services Institute in March 2009 how his troops were attacked by 1,800 mortars and rockets, suffered 85 IED strikes and lost count of the number of small arms rounds fired at them. The battlegroup took 71 casualties or 10% of its strength, including 11 dead and 16 who required immediate evacuation for life-saving treatment.

At the time this intensity of combat was unprecedented, until the fighting in Afghanistan over the next five years made such things routine.

The British campaign in Iraq was also fought under a level of media scrutiny that was unprecedented. As political arguments raged at home over Prime

Minister Tony Blair's decision to go to war, and the subsequent death of the Ministry of Defence scientist Dr David Kelly in the summer of 2003, the government moved progressively to restrict media access to British troops in Iraq, to prevent its opponents using any information to discredit the prime minister. Visits by journalists were reduced in number and duration, in an attempt to close down the issue and limit access to information about what was happening in Iraq. Troops were routinely warned not to speak to visiting British journalists without permission of senior officers, and report all contact with the media immediately to unit media officers.

If British journalists were frustrated by this stone walling strategy, it was mild compared to the attitude towards Iraqi and regional Arab journalists. There were long periods when the British press information centre at Basra airport had no Arabic speakers or translators assigned to it to inter-act with Arab media. For the British troops on the ground in Iraq, this closing down of media coverage added to their feeling that they were the forgotten army, and when journalists did make it to units in Basra, they were assailed with complaints about why there was no reporting on how hard the soldiers were working or their successes against insurgents.

Soldier's six month tours of duty was broken by two weeks rest and recuperation, or R & R leave, that had to be taken in the middle four months. While families back home appreciated seeing their relatives, it was not universally popular. It effectively meant that all units had up to 5% of their troops absent at any point of the tour, which increased the workload on those left behind. Soldiers also complained it broke their concentration and distracted them. When the IED threat was at its peak in 2006 and 2007, this could be fatal if soldiers left their patch for R & R and lost their understanding of what devices the insurgents were using how, where and when. In the hours and days it took to get back up to speed with the battle situation, they would be vulnerable.

The precarious nature of the RAF air-bridge also added to the unpopularity of R & R, because any aircraft and airport delays at Basra, al Udeid or Brize Norton were deducted from the soldier's time at home. Some unlucky soldiers could end up spending only a handful of days at home, and more time languishing in airport transit accommodation wondering if it was worth the trouble. A consequence ordinary soldiers accumulated a great deal of 'negative feeling' towards the RAF, whilst many army commanders lacked trust in the abilities and attitude of the RAF.

The fixed six-month tour length policy had other negative impacts on the British campaign in Iraq. Senior army commanders were keen not to drive their troops to their physical limits by longer tours. They were also desperate to avoid what was termed 'breaking the army'. Not only was it important not to increase separation times from families, army chiefs were worried that longer tours would prevent officers and soldiers participating in promotion courses and damage their career prospects. This was seen as a line that could not be crossed, according to senior officers. The pre-deployment training requirement was substantial and delivered at a high tempo, meaning that the five to six months before the tour commenced did not allow much time at home with families, and few sacrosanct weekends. This was a further contributory factor in exhausting the troops.

In Iraq, the six month tour policy created a mentality of 'short termism' or, as it was called, 'roulementitus' by senior officers. Commanders and soldiers at all levels saw their operational tour in Iraq as a chance to make their mark, and get a positive confidential report to get the vital tick in the box for promotion. Huge efforts were exerted training their troops for the up-coming tour, and once in Iraq commanders wanted to be involved in as many high profile activities as possible. Bases were rebuilt, new training schemes for Iraqi soldiers introduced, and strike operations were ramped up. The problem was that when the next unit arrived to relieve them, their commanders wanted to do something different and introduced their own round of changes.

For the Iraqis, this was a bewildering situation and it seemed like the British army was lurching from strategy to strategy every six months. Even the ordinary Iraqi and insurgents were confused. The short-termism even stretched to a failure to keep accurate records on suspected insurgents, and rotating battalions rarely had the necessary IT equipment, architecture, training and processes to allow intelligence to be passed on to their successors. When one British unit raided an Iraqi house to arrest a suspected insurgent in 2006, they faced the wrath of their target's mother who was complaining violently about being woken up in the middle of the night, and having her front door being smashed in, when her son had been arrested by the British Army over a year ago and was languishing in the British prison at Shaibah Logistic Base.

As the end of tours drew nearer, unit commanders began to plan how they would manage the transit of their troops from combat back to normal life in Britain or Germany. During their tours, soldiers came to rely implicitly on their comrades to stay alive and the fear was they would not be able to re-adjust to new social or work environments. Also, some soldiers had lost comrades in violent incidents, and the pressure to keep up the tempo of operations meant they did not have a chance to grieve for dead colleagues. The answer was dubbed 'decompression,' and it involved gathering a unit together for up to a week in a safe location where they could play sports, clean equipment, lounge around, drink beer, swap war stories and adjust to not being on operations. Decompression took many forms.

In April 2003, all units of 3 Commando Brigade were brought together at a disused factory complex south of Basra for 'collective down time' before leaving Iraq. As the campaign progressed, decompression became more elaborate, involving time at the recreation facilities at the US air base at Al Udeid or on the British bases in Cyprus. On their return home, a first duty for many soldiers was to visit the grave of comrades killed in action in Iraq. Soldiers could rarely be spared from duty to return to the UK for funerals, so it was only at the end of a tour could they properly pay their respects to their fallen comrades.

Chapter 2
THE COMMANDERS

Operation Telic is often described as 'Tony Blair's War,' by critics who want to pin responsibility squarely on him for Britain's most unpopular foreign conflict since the 1956 Suez debacle.

The generals, as well as senior officers of the air force and navy who waged the Iraq war, were instrumental in the formulation of the plans and policies that went wrong between 2003 and 2009. Little attention has been paid to the role of the British military establishment in the Iraq campaign, and many senior officers are largely unknown outside the British armed forces.

In the popular consciousness, army generals, admirals and air marshals are dynamic figures, who spend their time masterminding dramatic actions in foreign battlefields. The reality was that in 2003 some two thirds of the 480 or so officers above the rank of brigadier, or equivalent, were employed in the Ministry of Defence Main Building head office, in NATO staff jobs or equipment procurement. Their speciality was the formulation of what was termed "politically aware military advice" for senior civil servants, diplomats or government ministers. This is something the British military prides itself on being very good at. While many officers saw these jobs as ticks in the boxes that they had to do before returning to proper soldiering with real troops, others liked it and specialised in this work.

At the top of the military chain of command is the chief of the defence staff, or, as he is known around Whitehall, the CDS. He is the professional head of the armed forces and the prime minister's senior military advisor, with the right to face-to-face audiences in Number 10 concerning the issues of war and peace, as well as the well-being of the armed forces. In 2003, the CDS was Admiral Sir Mike Boyce. He was a former nuclear submarine commander, who had taken his attack boat on daring missions close to Soviet naval bases at the height of the Cold War.

Although undoubtedly a very accomplished naval officer, Boyce was clearly uncomfortable with being a public figure and did not come across well during public speaking events. His specialisation was marshalling the Ministry of Defence's huge bureaucracy, and he won plaudits for overseeing Britain's involvement in the 2001 Afghan campaign. Alistair Campbell's diary contains several references to Boyce making what Blair's infamous spin doctor described as public relations gaffes, but after the event it is clear the Admiral was only stating the patently obvious. Speaking truth to political leaders is never popular, but is an essential quality for a successful CDS.

Admiral Boyce set off a chain of events that would subsequently entangle Blair in a web of controversy over the legality of the Iraq war. He firmly requested written confirmation from the prime minister in January and March 2003 that the coming conflict was legal. The subsequent paper trail of legal advice engulfed Blair in accusations that he had put undue pressure on government law officers to bend the legal opinion in favour of war. As a result of his insistence of having written legal authority to go to war, the mild mannered Admiral inadvertently provided critics of the Iraq war with some of their most powerful arguments to deploy against Blair.

Boyce's successor, General Sir Mike Walker, was a more complex figure. An urbane figure, he epitomised the loyal professional army officer. Although his military career had been shaped by the Cold War and Northern Ireland, he had also led NATO peacekeeping troops in Bosnia in 1996. His period as CDS from May 2003 to the spring of 2006 covered the start of the Iraqi insurgency. Unfortunately this coincided with a major spending review across Whitehall departments, which forced Walker and his fellow service chiefs to devote almost all their time and political capital to protecting their budgets from attack, by the cost-cutting then-Chancellor of the Exchequer, Gordon Brown. Walker was a firm exponent of the concept known as mission command, and put great faith in his commanders on the ground, so he rarely overruled advice from senior commanders or staff recommendations from headquarters in Iraq.

In April 2006, Walker was replaced by Air Chief Marshal Sir Jock Stirrup, and his time as CDS saw Britain's campaign in Iraq brought to an end. Stirrup had a reputation for ruthlessness and for not taking fools gladly. He was able to look at an issue, decide the solution and then issue clear instructions to sort it out. Anyone who got in his way would be dealt with severely. It was not a command style that made many friends, but in the bureaucratic labyrinth that was the Ministry of Defence in the first decade of the 21st century it was pretty revolutionary. Soon after his arrival in the Main Building, the ministry was placed on a war footing. That this occurred only three years after the start of the Iraq campaign was a surprise to many outsiders.

In the British system, the military advice the CDS presented to the prime minister was created collectively by a group know as the Chiefs of Staff Committee (Operations). Here the heads of the army, air force and navy formulated a common view on military strategy and operational issues. It was the job of the Deputy Chief of Defence Staff (Commitments) to prepare all the briefing advice for the chiefs to consider. Once a view had been taken it was his job to record it, and pass on instructions to subordinates. The DCDS (Commitments) was an incredibly powerful position in the Whitehall bureaucracy, because he would accompany the CDS to meetings with the prime minister and would also often lead negotiations, on behalf of CDS, with other ministries about military operations. The early discussions about Iraqi war planning in 2002 were led by the-then DCDS (Commitments) Lieutenant General Sir Anthony Pigott. He was very much a soldier of the Cold War, and as a Royal Engineer he had never commanded a large number of troops in action.

Pigott was replaced by Lieutenant General Rob Fry of the Royal Marines in the summer of 2003. Considered the most able Royal Marine of his generation, Fry had just left the Permanent Joint Headquarters (PJHQ) at Northwood in west London, where he had been the second most senior officer and had overseen the invasion of Iraq. His period in post coincided with the run up to the commitment of significant number of British troops to Afghanistan in early 2006. This controversial decision proved a turning point in the Iraq campaign.

Fry was replaced by Vice Admiral Charlie Style, and he lasted in his post for little over a year. He did not get on with Stirrup and he was made to take the blame when 15 Royal Navy personnel were held hostage by Iranian Revolutionary Guards in the spring of 2007. Style was replaced by Lieutenant General Peter Wall, who had been intimately involved in the Iraq campaign since 2002. The well-built Wall had led the team that established the first British headquarters in the Middle East at the US Central Command base in Qatar. He then moved to command the 1st (UK) Armoured Division in Basra for six weeks in May and June 2003, coinciding with the deadly incident at Majar-al-Kabir when six Royal Military Policemen were killed. After returning to Germany, he was responsible for preparing troops for service in Iraq, until he took up the number two job at PJHQ in the spring of 2005.

This was the period when the British troop strength in Iraq was at its peak and key decisions on the campaign were made. Wall was DCDS (Commitments) when the Iraq campaign reached its dénouement and he is the most constant figure in its military direction.

At PJHQ the commander of joint operations, or CJO, was the man responsible for the day-to-day direction of British overseas military operations. The CJO is at the heart of British military operations, but his powers are in theory limited by tight rules, so he does not step on the toes of the individual service chiefs. His job is to command deployed forces but he has a more limited role in the formulation of military policy, and crucially is not a member of the Chiefs of Staff Committee (Operations). As a result his job is nominally to carry out instructions, not develop policy or strategy. The role of PJHQ is also considerably constrained when British forces are placed under the operational command of US, United Nations or NATO headquarters. In these circumstances, the CJO loses his role to control day-to-day operations and in effect becomes the default 'red card holder', only intervening to stop the participation of UK troops in operations that do not chime with British government policy.

The CJO in 2002 was Lieutenant General John Reith, and he played an instrumental role in the deployment and conduct of British forces during the initial invasion of Iraq. Reith stretched his job description to the full during the build up for Operation Telic, often because of the absence of clear direction and leadership from elsewhere in the Ministry of Defence. His tight control and firm direction of deployed commanders led his team in PJHQ to be nicknamed the 'Third Reich' by those on the receiving end of his firm instructions.

His successors, Air Marshal Glenn Torpy and Lieutenant General Nick Houghton, found their room to influence events in Iraq considerably constrained as British troops by then had been firmly integrated into the US-led Multi-National Forces (MNF) set up. Air Marshal Torpy was a RAF Tornado pilot who had flown Scud hunting reconnaissance missions during the 1991 Iraq war, but he was an accomplished 'Whitehall street fighter,' who could hold his own against senior army officers in policy arguments. After running PJHQ, Torpy went on to head the Royal Air Force. His successor, General Houghton, was a very different character, who had no public profile, hated giving media interviews and liked to be a back room operator. He subsequently was appointed Chief of Defence Staff in July 2013, after serving as the vice chief.

There was only ever a forward deployed overall or joint commander of all British air, land and sea forces in the Middle East for five months in the first half of 2003. Air Marshall Brian Burridge had this role during the invasion, and worked side-by-side with the US Central Command chief, General Tommy Franks, in Qatar. The RAF officer was a former Nimrod anti-submarine aircraft pilot, and commandant of the British Joint Services Command and Staff College. His role was abolished a few weeks after the fall of Baghdad.

On the ground in Iraq from May 2003, the top military commander was on paper the Senior British Military Representative (SBMR) in Baghdad. He was also the deputy commander of all coalition military forces within Iraq, working for the US General controlling all US forces in the country. The three star SBMR was a post of considerable influence in the coalition military campaign, but had limited direct control over the British forces in southern Iraq. In theory, the direct tactical control of the British-led Multi-National Division South East (MND-SE) was vested in the three star, US MNF Corps commander and was one step removed from the SBMR.

The SBMR's most effective means to influence events in the coalition military bureaucracy was his control of the British special forces contingent deployed in Baghdad, as well as its supporting RAF detachment. This had great prestige with the American high command and gave the SBMR considerable clout. Lieutenant General Graeme Lamb, the SBMR in 2006 and 2007, became instrumental in the US surge campaign against Sunni insurgents in central Iraq.

Control of British troops in southern Iraq fell to the general officer commanding (GOC) of MND-SE. Over the six years of the British occupation, some 11 British Army and two Royal Marine major generals led the campaign in southern Iraq. These men were pivotal figures in the British campaign because they had considerable powers and discretion delegated to them by London and PJHQ. Major General Robin Brims, for example, said he had almost total freedom to direct the fight for Basra in March and April 2003. These delegated powers were progressively reined in as the campaign progressed, but the GOC was still a powerful player.

Although the British government issued general political guidance for its troops in Iraq between 2003 and 2009 it was never able to formulate an over arching strategic document describing the campaign's aims, and then setting out the details of how these were to be achieved. Several incumbents have described how before they headed for Iraq to take over in Basra they were issued with verbal guidance of the government's intent by the prime minister's security advisors. This strategic lack of direction meant that the GOC had considerable freedom to formulate his plans and conduct operations in southern Iraq. This situation did not really change until mid 2006 when Air Chief Marshal Stirrup begun issuing very clear instructions on timelines to wind down the Iraq operation.

The generals and brigadiers who took charge in Basra between 2003 and 2009 were some of the best of their generation, and as a cohort they were promoted at a far faster rate than their colleagues who remained at home. In the British Army during the first decade of the 21st century a brigadier had a one in four chance of making it to major general, yet only two of the 18 brigadiers to lead their troops in Basra were not promoted. While, during the same period, a major general stood a one in four chance of making it to Lieutenant General, yet only two of 13 Basra GOCs did not make it to three-star rank. Only Brims fought and directed what could be called a conventional battle. He won plaudits for his confident handling of the battle for Basra in 2003, and later rose to three-star rank and retired as commander of the field army back in the UK.

All his successors found their role was increasingly to manage the politics of the unfolding insurgency. Their job was to deal with internal UK politics within the British government and military, the coalition link to the US military command in Baghdad, Iraqi politicians in Baghdad and local leaders in Basra. Lamb's time in Basra became deeply controversial after the outbreak of riots in August 2003 and the murder of an Iraqi civilian in British custody. His special forces background came more to the fore during his subsequent time as SBMR in Baghdad.

Major General Andrew Stewart was in charge at the height of the Sadr revolt in the summer of 2004. His time was characterised by considerable tension with the Americans in Baghdad. He was succeeded by Bill Rollo, an aristocratic officer from the Blues and Royals who had led an armoured brigade during the 1999 Kosovo crisis. Major General Jonathon Riley headed up MND (SE) into 2005, and he had a reputation for being one of the most aggressive British generals of his generation. Jim Dutton of the Royal Marines took over from Riley just as Basra erupted during the Al Jamiat police station crisis in September 2005.

A ramping up of the British campaign against insurgents began under Major General John Cooper in late 2005. The Scottish general had to deal for the first time with rising opposition to British military operations from Iraqi politicians. After a period in Baghdad overseeing the ending of the British presence in Iraq, he retired from the army in 2009. Richard Shirreff's time in Iraq was the high-water mark of the British campaign. His aggressive drive against Basra's militias under Operation Sinbad saw fighting in the city escalate dramatically. The cavalry officer later rose to be NATO's deputy supreme commander. But perhaps the most controversial general in Basra was Jonathan Shaw, who oversaw a deal with insurgent leaders in the city, to allow British troops to pull out of Basra palace without a shot being fired in September 2007.

He was replaced by Major General Graham Binns, who as commander of 7 Armoured Brigade in 2003 had led the fight for Basra. He continued Shaw's policy of talking to insurgents. British participation in the Iraqi-led offensive that took back control of Basra from the militias was controlled by Barney White-Spunner, a very urbane Household Cavalry officer. White-Spunner went on to be commander of the field army and retired from the army to head the Countryside Alliance lobby group. The sun was clearly setting on British interest in Iraq by this point, and Major General Andy Salmon of the Royal Marines was the last British GOC of MND (SE) until he left Basra in the spring of 2009.

Tactical control of British troops in southern Iraq was the job of the brigade commander in Basra. While the GOC controlled British and multi-national troops across the four provinces of south-east Iraq, Basra city was the focus of the British brigadier. This was a really testing job for the brigadier and his staff, because they had to co-ordinate on a minute-by-minute basis the response to insurgent attacks and their bloody aftermath, as well as being as pro-active as possible, militarily and politically. It was full on work, with the commander and staff managing multiple contacts and incidents, whilst also dealing with complicated political machinations. Their soldiers were at risk, and they held the means to save their lives in their hands, such as directing casualty evacuation helicopters to recover casualties. Often this was a very lonely position, with a crisis breaking when their superiors at Basra airport, Baghdad or Northwood were absent or out of communications. John Lorimer had to lead the rescue of two SAS soldiers kidnapped by militia in Basra, with little or no guidance from London. While Julian Free in March 2008 found himself alone, as the major turning point in the war in southern Iraq unfolded with his GOC away on his R & R.

Many in the British Army considered the job of Basra Brigade commander far more demanding than being GOC, and the holders of the post have risen to high command, including some of whom who held in key leadership positions in Afghanistan. Two, Nick Carter and Adrian Bradshaw, have been deputy commanders of the International Security Assistance Force (ISAF) in Kabul, and Carter was selected to be the next chief of the general staff to take over from General Wall when he retires in 2014.

Senior Royal Navy and Royal Air Force officers also filled key command appointments during the Iraq war. Command of the multi-national naval task force providing security around Iraqi off-shore oil export terminals, was shared in rotation between the UK, US and Australia, with a Royal Navy commodore and his staff taking turns to control the warships and patrol boats in the Northern Arabian Gulf for four months at a time. The Royal Air Force senior officers served continuously from 2003 to 2009 in the US Air Force-led Combined Air Operations Center (CAOC), which co-ordinated all coalition air activity over Iraq. Initially based at Prince Sultan Air Base (PSAB) in Saudi Arabia, the CAOC moved to al Udeid airbase in Qatar in the late summer of 2003.

An RAF air commodore and a team of several dozen RAF officers served at the CAOC integrated into the USAF organisation. The Americans treated the RAF as equal partners on the CAOC floor, choreographing air operations across Iraq each day, including allowing them access to many highly secret activities, including the operation of MQ-1 Predator and MQ-9 Reaper unmanned aerial vehicles or drones. The duty air commodore also had responsibility for control of RAF assets across the Gulf directly supporting Operation Telic. These reached a peak in 2006 and into 2007 when Air Commodores Baz North and Clive Bairstow were in charge, and they had to motivate their air and ground forces to operate at a very high tempo to support both Iraq and Afghanistan. In September 2006 a Nimrod MR2 patrol aircraft based in Oman crashed in southern Afghanistan, leading to the fleet being grounded and placing a huge strain on other RAF reconnaissance aircraft during their absence. This was a major leadership challenge for RAF officers in the CAOC command team, who had to play their part restoring morale among Nimrod crews who were urgently needed back in the air over Iraq and Afghanistan to protect troops under fire.

On the ground in Iraq, the burden of leadership fell on the commanding officers of the battlegroups on the streets of Basra and al Amarah. Lieutenant Colonel Tim Collins of the Royal Irish Regiment remains the most high profile commanding officer of the Iraq war, for his rousing pre-war speech to his troops and his subsequent fall from grace following allegations of abuse. Perhaps the next most well-known regimental commander was Lieutenant Colonel Jorge Mendonca of the Queen's Lancashire Regiment (QLR), who was in command when an Iraqi waiter called Baha Mousa died in custody. Mendonca subsequently faced court martial, and was acquitted of negligently performing a duty and five of his men were also cleared of other charges related to the incident. One of his soldiers was sentenced to a year in prison and dismissed from the army.

The only other battalion commander who achieved any significant media prominence was Lieutenant Colonel Patrick Sanders of the Rifles, who oversaw the withdrawal from Basra Palace in 2007. Commanding officers were usually in the early forties, and were considered the most talented officers from their regiment at that point in time. Their period of command was the pinnacle of their military careers and every British Army commanding officer viewed their time in Iraq as an opportunity to show what they were made of. Most commanding officers had served the bulk of their career in their regiments and personally knew all their unit's officers and senior non-commissioned officers, as well as a fair number of ordinary soldiers. This created a conflicting pull towards mission success that might risk casualties, and a desire to protect old friends and comrades from death and injury.

Although their public pronouncements were generally up-beat and on message, in their classified end of tour reports a steady stream of commanding officers made pessimistic assessments of the progress, or lack of it, in the Iraqi campaign. Lieutenant Colonel Matt Maer, the commanding officer of the

1st Battalion, The Princess of Wales's Royal Regiment (PWRR), who was led his battalion through fierce fighting in al Amarah during the 2004 Sadr revolt, complained in his post tour report of a failure of the Foreign Office and the Department for International Development to help his troops win over the restive population.

"There is no military solution to Maysan's problems and until wider UK government interest is shown and is physically present in the Province the threat of failure will remain."

It was not surprising that the document was marked, "Secret – UK/US Eyes Only", given that the British government was at the time proclaiming steady progress in Iraq.[1] Many of the commanding officers of the Iraqi campaign are now senior officers, with several commanding brigades in Afghanistan or holding other important appointments. The likes of James Cowan of the Black Watch, Patrick Sanders of the Rifles and Gordon Messenger of the Royal Marines are rising stars. It remains to be seen if the lessons learnt in Iraq made a difference in Afghanistan. No British general or senior officer resigned in protest during their service in Iraq. One commanding officer, Lieutenant-Colonel Nick Henderson, famously wrote a scathing letter to a national newspaper complaining about a lack of resources to fight the war in Iraq and lack of support for troops from senior officers.[2] While Brigadier Paul Gibson, after he had retired, lambasted the conduct of the war by senior British officers, blaming them for not responding fast enough to the insurgency and for allowing the militias to take control of Basra.[3]

The British Army's Byzantine career planning system meant that many senior officers would never have been promoted anyway, so it was no surprise that not all the commanders from Iraq were promoted. These officers could see the writing on the wall. There were also a number of talented officers who had very successful tours in Iraq, and even thought they had good career prospects, but left the army anyway. Often they felt let down by their political masters and senior commanders and simply no longer believed in the cause of being a military man.

"Being a general for the sake of it is not all it is cracked up to be," commented one retired British general.

"At home you have little power or influence on big decisions, in many cases even no influence on small issues, so coming back from operations is always an anti-climax, and I am not surprised that people came back from Iraq and said it's all downhill from now on."

Chapter 3
THE IRAQIS

Many westerners view the Iraq war entirely through their own cultural references that are shaped by the sound bites of the media, or the positioning of politicians and spin doctors trying to shape agendas or push the given line. This entirely superficial approach has succeeded in pigeon-holing Iraqis, either as sadistic henchmen of the evil dictator Saddam Hussein, downtrodden victims of the so-called Republic of Fear, or fanatical Islamic terrorists bent on destruction and martyrdom. The reality is, of course, more nuanced and far more complex than the western media image of the country.

From analysis of British military documents, interviews with veterans and my own visits to Iraq, it is very clear that British political, diplomatic and military leaders often had a very fragmentary and confused understanding of the situation in southern Iraq. Understandably, this was far more acute prior to British troops entering Iraq in March 2003, because of a lack of physical contact with the country for more than a decade, due to the UN sanctions regime and the absence of a British embassy in Baghdad to provide information on Saddam's domain. British military intelligence was equally blind-sighted about important aspects of the forces that were facing them across the Kuwaiti border in the spring of 2003.

To understand Iraq, a basic appreciation of the religious and ethnic background of the country's main communities is essential. The country's population in 2003 was estimated to be some 24 million, of which 80% was Arab in ethnicity, with some two million more ethnic Kurds populating the north. In turn 65% of the population is Shia Muslim and the remainder largely Sunni. The majority of Shia live in the southern half of country, although they form over half the population of the capital Baghdad, after significant migration to the city in the 1960s and 1970s due to industrialisation drives. The Sunni minority is concentrated to the north and west of Baghdad, although there are significant Sunni communities in Shia areas. The 300,000 or so population of Zubayr, to the west of Basra, is overwhelmingly Sunni because the governing regime in Baghdad favoured Sunnis for jobs in the Iraqi state oil company that ran the nearby Rumalyah oil field and its pipeline infra-structure across southern Iraq.

The religious divide between Iraq's Shia and Sunni communities proved to be the great driver of conflict after the demise of Saddam in 2003. Little understood by westerners, the Shia-Sunni divide was the country's critical fault line. When the British created Iraq in 1920 they corralled a Shia minority into a state that was nominally ruled by a Sunni governing class. This unequal power relationship remained essentially unchanged until the fall of Saddam. Iraq's Sunnis see themselves as true Arabs and shared the interpretation of Islam practised by the majority of their neighbours in the Arabian Peninsular. It is the majority denomination within Islam, but within Iraq Sunnis are in a minority. The Shia or Shi'ite population of Iraq were followers of a version of Islam that is centred on the role of prophets and their descendants. Iraq is the cradle of Shia Islam and its cities contain some of the most holy Shia shrines. American politicians often accused Iraq's Shia of being surrogates for Iran. The toxic history between the Tehran Islamic regime and Washington made it all too easy for every incident involving Iraqi Shia to be portrayed as an Iranian plot by US politicians, diplomats and military chiefs. The reality was far more complex.

In the 1950s and 1960s, the Ba'ath Party rose to power in Iraq on the back of a wave of radical nationalism across the Middle East. Like its contemporaries in Syria, Egypt and Yemen, the Iraqi branch of the Ba'ath Party was committed to driving out British and western imperialism from Iraq. In its early years, the Ba'ath Party had been a largely secular organisation, and it attracted recruits from all communities in Iraq as it strived to build a neo-socialist paradise on the back of the country's oil wealth. Investment in education and health care soared, as well as in state owned industrial enterprises that employed a significant section of the adult population. It was a very east European model and not surprisingly the Soviet Union became a strong ally of revolutionary Iraq in the 1960s and 1970s.

The Ba'ath Party was also an instrument of control in much the same way as was the old Communist Party of the Soviet Union. After Saddam seized power in 1979, he brutally purged the Ba'ath Party of opponents and filled its upper and middle echelons with those whom he could rely on totally. These were mostly members of his clan from Tikrit, a small town to the north of Baghdad. They were all Sunnis. Over the next 24 years the higher echelons of the Ba'ath party were filled with Sunnis loyal to Saddam, and the Shia became Iraq's second class citizens. Shia areas got less state funding for infra-structure, education and health care, while Shia party members, state officials and army officers rarely rose to high office.

The Shia uprising of 1991 after the failed invasion of Kuwait made Saddam view them as the gravest threat to his regime, even more dangerous than a military coup led by his generals. The ease with which the Shia mutineers from the army had seized control of Basra and other cities across the south made Saddam convinced that he had to keep them on a tight rein. This in turn led to a ratchetting up of monitoring by the secret police of Shia religious and political leaders. The south also received almost no funding to rebuild infra-structure destroyed by American bombing in the 1991 war, and in the subsequent uprising. American and British intelligence were right to suspect that the Shia of Iraq might be willing to rise up against Saddam, but they had no idea who where the leaders of the Shia community or what their aspirations were.

As the insurgency unfolded in the summer and autumn of 2003, British commanders and troops found themselves facing growing unrest from Iraq's Shia population and this proved an increasingly challenging prospect with which to get to grips. In the build up to the formal launch of Operation Telic in

March 2003, British troops in Kuwait and around the Middle East were provided with crystal clear photographic imagery of Iraqi military installations and other strategic installations.

This was the result of over a decade of intensive surveillance of Iraq by the US Air Force and RAF. American satellites, along with US U-2 Dragon Lady and RAF Tornado GR1 reconnaissance aircraft, had photographed every airfield, dockyard, army barrack block, tank park, intelligence base, communications tower and presidential palace in Iraq, along with every piece of civilian infrastructure that might have a strategic importance.[1] American and British eavesdropping planes and listening stations had also been focused on Iraq. The primary focus of this effort was to try and determine if the Iraqi leader was breaching UN arms control resolutions banning him possessing poison gas, nuclear weapons, biological poisons and long-range rockets.

The side effect was when signals intelligence or SIGINT product was combined with the imagery database, as it enabled an incredibly detailed order of battle of Saddam Hussein's military forces to be complied. When British commanders opened the American intelligence assessments, which laid out the position of every Iraqi military unit in the country, they were initially impressed, but this soon turned to concern. Satellite imagery and SIGINT could not provide any insight into how well maintained Iraq tanks were, or whether their crews would fight for Saddam's regime. The collapse of Saddam's regime in just over two weeks of combat was a great surprise to the British commanders and troops who advanced in Iraq in March 2003. They feared that in the death throes of his regime, the Iraqi dictator would resort to his stocks of illicit chemical weapons as his elite Republican Guard troops fought to the last round in the ruins of Baghdad and other cities. It was all an illusion.

An exhaustive search of post war Iraq in 2003 and 2004 by the US, British and Australian Iraq Survey Group concluded that Saddam had in fact dismantled all his illicit weapons of mass destruction (WMD) in the immediate aftermath of the 1991 war. But he wanted to maintain the fiction that he still retained some to deter the Iranians from attacking Iraq, and to provide a back stop of terror to cow his civilian population from rising in revolt, for fear of a repeat of the Hallabjah incident in 1988. This was when a Kurdish town had been attacked with nerve gas and up to 5,000 civilians killed. Post war debriefs of Iraqi military officers also revealed that many of them also still believed that Saddam had retained stocks of gas and other special weapons.[2]

"It was a failure of intelligence, Saddam bluffed on WMD and kept up the pretence of having WMD," recalled Lieutenant General Robin Brims, who commanded the opening assault on Basra in 2003. "It was an elaborate hoax."[3]

The Iraqi leader in fact proved to be the US-led coalition's best ally. His paranoid delusion method of political control fatally handicapped the ability of the Iraqi military to put up any effective resistance to US and British forces. Saddam's paranoid and brutal regime has been well documented, but his influence on the planning and conduct of the war in 2003 is less well known. In the aftermath of the war, the US military launched a systematic effort, dubbed the Iraqi Perspective Project, to collect and analyse hundreds of thousands of captured Iraqi military documents and to interview Iraqi military personnel – both in coalition custody and retired – to build up a detailed picture of the 2003 conflict 'from the other side of the hill'.[4] This exercise and intelligence material gathered by British forces in Basra paints a far more different picture than that portrayed at the time by western governments and media.

The overriding impression from the Iraqi Perspective Report is that Saddam's military was paralysed by fear of its president. His plans and actions were in turn driven by a world view that is scarcely believable to westerners. According to Iraqi documents and the fallen dictator's generals, his main pre-occupation was neutralising internal threats. His enduring priority in all his military planning was to prevent any of his armed forces being able to successfully launch a coup d'état against his regime. This was even the case as American tanks were driving through the streets of his capital in April 2003.

The main way to stop the army and other military units, such as the supposedly elite Republican Guard, from launching a coup was to terrorise their officer corps with regular executions and arrest of any military personnel who displayed disloyalty or independence of action. Officers who even reported bad news or suggested changes to Saddam's orders were arrested. The lucky ones languished in jail for a few years but many were executed, after being brutally tortured. After more than 20 years of this the Iraqi military had any vestige of independence or sensible judgement squeezed out of it. Senior officers even gave up holding social gatherings with colleagues just out of fear of being suspected of plotting a coup.

This meant that as coalition forces were gathering in Kuwait in the winter of 2002, the Iraqi military was ill-placed to organise an effective defence because Saddam told his top commanders that the Americans would not have the stomach to risk a drive on Baghdad. He was convinced that the Americans were corrupt and spineless. Every time the US Air Force launched an air strike in retaliation for infringements of the no fly zone, it reinforced Saddam's view that they could not muster the will to fight Iraqis on the ground. He was reportedly very taken with the Hollywood film *Blackhawk Down,* based on a 1993 engagement in Somalia, in which 19 US soldiers are killed by Somali gunmen. That the US then withdrew from Somalia after loosing a handful of casualties made Saddam believe little had changed since Vietnam, when the so-called body-bag factor made the Americans retreat from South East Asia in 1975. For Saddam, his defining experience as a war leader was the Iran-Iraq war in the 1980s, when the Iraqi army had suffered more than a million casualties, and driven off superior Iranian forces by what at the time appeared to be sheer will-power.

The 1991 war over Kuwait provided Saddam with his next lesson on how to be a successful war leader. In the aftermath of the defeat of Iraqi troops in Kuwait, the Shia population of southern Iraq and the Kurds in the north both rose in revolt. For a few weeks in March 1991 it appeared that Saddam's days were numbered. However, he was able to rally units of the Republican Guard who turned the tables on the rebels, and by the summer he was securely back in control of Iraq, except for a small Kurdish enclave in the north protected by US, British and French air patrols.

As a result, Saddam set his defence priorities in late 2002 as first, preventing an internal revolt by Iraq's Shia majority, secondly a defence against Iran, and lastly dealing with the US threat. If the Americans did attack, Saddam convinced himself that the US would rely on air and missile attacks and would not dare launch a ground invasion to take Baghdad. The worse they would do was prompt a revolt by the Shia and Kurds. This latter eventuality reinforced Saddam's view that his overriding priority must be the internal security of his regime, not defence against external threats. The crushing of independent thought inside the Iraqi military meant no one was willing to risk challenging this delusion.[5]

Iraqi preparations to defend their country were pitiful. It was only in December 2002 that Saddam began taking seriously the threat of war with America. Apparently he created his own plan to defend Baghdad based on four concentric defence lines, manned by Republican Guard divisions. The regular Iraqi Army was assigned the job of holding a defensive line in the north against the Kurds, and deterring Iranian incursions in the south. The top priority was given to preparations to put down uprisings or coups, so the military chain of command was summarily replaced by a crisis control system, with four regional commands each led by a trusted political ally of Saddam. They all reported via the political hierarchy of the Ba'ath Party direct to the Iraqi leader. All army units were put under the direct control of these regional commands and the general staff in Baghdad was effectively sidelined. The air force was ordered to disperse and bury its aircraft to preserve them. Only the air defence command had the priority to directly confront any US-led assault.

The Iraqis Perspectives analysts could find no evidence that Saddam ordered any preparations for the insurgency that subsequently ravaged Iraq after the US-led invasion. For Saddam this would have been seen as an admission of defeat. Likewise, he instructed that Iraq's oil fields not be sabotaged or set on fire because he would need the revenue they generated after the current crisis was over. In southern Iraq, security preparations were in the hands of Ali Hassan al-Majid, also known as Chemical Ali because of his role in the gassing of Kurds during the 1980s. He had no formal military training and his speciality was political repression of the most brutal fashion.

In 1991 he had crushed the Shia and Kurdish revolts by rapidly seizing key buildings, and then ordering the public execution of captives to spread terror among the local population. On his arrival in Basra in late 2002, he set about mobilising Ba'ath party officials across southern Iraq, and distributed arms to Saddam loyalists throughout Basra and neighbouring provinces. The Ba'ath Party's own Quds militia was mobilised to provide manpower to augment the army, but in the Shia south, this meant this organisation was a mirage and only a few hundred people, mostly Sunnis living in the region, answered the call to arms.

During January 2003, the threat of war was growing, so defence preparations against an uprising across Shia-dominated southern Iraq were stepped up. Ammunition and other supplies were ordered to be distributed from depots to schools, hospitals and other locations under Ba'ath Party control where they would not be bombed by US aircraft. Units of the ultra-loyal Fedayeen paramilitary force were moved from Baghdad to Basra to provide a rapid reaction force to put down any sign of revolt.

Chemical Ali also had under his control the army's 225th Missile Brigade equipped with FROG-7, ASTROS and ABABIL-100 missiles, which could reach targets in Kuwait from launch sites around Basra. The Iraqi navy also provided Chemical Ali with between two and five Chinese made Seersucker cruise missile launchers, with 88 missiles. These were moved out of their barracks to prevent a surprise US attack knocking them out before the start of any war.[6]

In February 2003, Saddam at last realized that the Americans might be serious, and he ordered plans be prepared to defend the main urban areas. Saddam approved the dispersal of regular army and Republican Guard units out of their barracks to field locations to protect them from coalition air attack. Units of the 51st Mechanized Division were sent to man a series of border watchtowers along the Kuwait border, and it troops set up a series of strong points around Zubayr and Basra city. The 45th Infantry Brigade was sent to hold Umm Qasr, the 704th Infantry Brigade was ordered to protect the Rumaylah oil fields and navy marines guarded the al Faw oil terminals. Further north, the 6th Armoured Division was held in reserve around Al Qurnah with its tanks and artillery hidden under date palms and in industrial buildings.[7]

While the officers of the Iraqi army units in the south were professional soldiers with many years service, their rank and file were all conscripts recruited mainly from the south of Iraq. These soldiers were treated with great suspicion by Chemical Ali and his associates. Spies and informers were planted across the region to monitor the loyalty of both officers and ordinary soldiers. The Iraqi army had been heavily influenced by the Soviets during their long years as rivals, and its military system was very similar to the Red Army and other eastern European armed forces. The officer corps were all long-term professionals and they had extensive experience of the Iran-Iraq and Kuwait wars. There was no professional non-commissioned officer cadre, so officers performed most technical tasks in military units, such as operating air defence systems or radios. Promotion and postings in the Iraqi army at below divisional level was still largely depended on merit, unlike in the Republican Guard where political loyalty or clan affiliation was the determining factor in progression to senior ranks.

Like in eastern European armed forces, the Iraqi military provided housing and medical services for officers throughout their lives and pensions when they retired from active service. The Iraqi army was a social organization in its own right and service remained prestigious, even after the fall of the Saddam regime. Several Saddam-era generals from the Iran-Iraq war were viewed as patriots, even among the Shia community of the south, and rose to prominence in the post-2003 Iraqi military. Within Iraqi army units, the rank and file were filled by conscripts doing two years compulsory military service. Once they had completed their service, they in theory could be called back to uniform in time of crisis, but in the decade since the end of the Kuwait war the call-up system had fallen into disuse.

The international arms embargo and sanctions on oil exports imposed after the Kuwait war had crippled the Iraqi army. What money for training, new equipment and spares there was went to the Republican Guard. Regular army units still had their 1970s vintage T-55 tanks and BMP armoured personnel carriers, but had received almost no spares since 1991. They were lucky if 10% of their equipment was fully operational, although up to half of tanks and other vehicles could be made to work after a fashion.[8]

Lack of money for fuel and spares meant that by 2003 Iraqi units rarely carried out large-scale field training exercises. Iraq battalions became little more than recruit training depots, churning out a diet of basic training of small arms and low level infantry tactics to poorly paid and motivated conscripts. In southern Iraq this meant that almost all the adult male population had a basic level of military training but little loyalty towards their regime or motivation to fight for it. For the officer corps, this low level of activity was tremendously demotivating, and the poor state of their equipment made many military professionals despondent about their chances against the modern US and British armies. In the Iraqi Perspective study there are numerous references to Iraqi army officers expressing the view that they hoped any war would be over quickly, to avoid destruction and suffering among their troops, while prospects of emerging victorious were considered hopeless. That is not to say they were all queuing up to surrender to the first US or British tank that crossed the border.

Professional honour and the presence of Chemical Ali's brutal henchmen in southern Iraq meant they would need to put up some resistance. By March 2003, Saddam's defence plans assumed that US and British troops would launch direct attacks on Basra, and other cities, to allow them to be used to rally the Shia against the regime in Baghdad. The Iraqi leader was convinced the coalition would not advance on his capital but consolidate their hold over the south and north. They would then prompt uprisings across the country in a bid to install a pro-US regime.[9]

In the south, this meant the role of Fedayeen paramilitaries became increasingly important. As the most loyal force at Chemical Ali's disposal, and as well as being on hand to move quickly to crush uprisings, they were given the job of carrying out sabotage attacks on enemy forces. The Fedayeen had few heavy weapons, but relied on 4 x 4 pick-up trucks converted into 'technicals' by the installation of heavy machine guns. Criminals and street thugs were all drafted into the Fedayeen on the promise of loot and plunder when the war broke out. Hardly any of this made its way into US and British intelligence assessments. Saddam's plan for the defence of Baghdad was detected but preparations in the south were almost entirely misread.

The post-Saddam Iraq proved to be very different from the one envisaged by US and British intelligence before the March 2003 invasion. The county proved unwilling to be moulded in the way that US and British political leaders envisaged in the aftermath of the fall of Baghdad. The overnight collapse of Saddam's regime led to a proliferation of political leaders, political parties, as well as their allied armed militias. This explosion of political freedom and expression also led to Iraq becoming rapidly ungovernable, as the country's rival parties, religious communities and ethnic groups vied for dominance.

While the generalities of the Sunni-Shia divide were well known to the British and Americans, how they might play out after the fall of Saddam's regime was a big unknown. A March 2003 UK Defence Intelligence Staff (DIS) briefing document, prepared for troops and commanders heading for Basra, could not provide any insight or information on any of the Shia leaders who had remained in Iraq after the 1991 uprising.[10] The DIS analysts predicted that the Shia dominated DIWA party and Supreme Council of the Islamic Revolution in Iraq (SICRI) would return from exile in Iran, and vie for power in southern Iraq as British troops drove into Basra. There was no mention of the Muqtada al Sadr and his militia who were waiting in the shadows, biding their time until the end of Saddam's regime. Also lacking was any appreciation or even awareness of the tribal politics of southern Iraq and the importance of the town of al Amarah in the heart of Maysan province.

The existence of Sadr's underground movement and that of the tribal militias in Maysan province came as a big surprise to the British Army when they entered southern Iraq. These groups almost immediately became the main challengers of British rule. Their political leaders and networks were able to mobilise support through the region's mosques. Most importantly, they established a political narrative that challenged the legitimacy of the British presence in the region. From the day after Chemical Ali fled Basra, the British were foreign occupiers, who had no right to tell Iraqis how to run their country. In al Amara itself, tribal leaders and their militia were able to take control of the town after Saddam's troops fled and before British soldiers arrived. The legend of the self-liberation of al Amarah was born and for the next three years the British Army would struggle to retain a toe hold in Maysan province.

As British commanders scrambled to prepare their troops for deployment to Kuwait in January 2003, they devoured every book and newspaper article they could about the situation inside Iraq, but even the media and many think-tank analysts had little knowledge about the real players in the south. The British Army was standing on the edge of a void.

Chapter 4
PLANNING THE WAR

Alistair Campbell, Tony Blair's head of communications and so-called 'spin doctor,' recounts in his diary that in October 2002 a delegation from the Ministry of Defence, led by the Defence Secretary Geoff Hoon and Chief of the Defence Staff, Admiral Sir Mike Boyce, went to present their options for British military involvement in the US-led invasion of Iraq to the Prime Minister. The military top brass laid out the pros and cons of the various packages of forces that could work alongside the Americans. Campbell commented that Blair could not make up his mind what he wanted.

"[Blair] said it was not no, but it was not yet yes," recorded the spin doctor.[1] At the end of the meeting no one seemed to know what had been decided or what was to happen next. This was 'sofa government' in action. Hoon's senior civil servant running Iraq policy, David Johnson, at this time commented, "the more fundamental decision-making seemed to be handled in an incredibly informal style."[2]

The vignette sums up perfectly the period in the run up to the start of the war, as increasingly frustrated military planners tried to discern the political intent of the government and then translate it into action. Many opponents of the Iraq war have created complex conspiracy theories surrounding Blair's decision to join the US invasion of Iraq. For those tasked with actually planning the UK military campaign the reality was less impressive, with words like "confusion", "muddle", "shambolic", "chaotic", "amateurish" and "sub-optimal" proliferating. The launching of Operation Telic seems an abject lesson in how not to prepare to go to war, according to many of key players involved. Hoon was unrepentant, telling Johnson, "if we had started all our preparations as early as some wanted us to, we would have had the best prepared non-operation in history, because the Government would have lost Parliament."[3]

By 2002, Blair was already well versed in directing military campaigns, after his involvement in the 1999 Kosovo crisis, the interventions in East Timor and Sierra Leone and the 2001 toppling of the Taliban regime in Afghanistan, which made his faltering start in Iraq even more perplexing for Britain's military leadership. During the late afternoon of 11th September 2001, only a few hours after the collapse of the twin towers in New York, Britain's diplomatic, military, intelligence, security and police elite had gathering in the basement of the Cabinet Office, off Whitehall. The gathering was meant to be a means for the professional leadership of the British security establishment to co-ordinate their responses to the unfolding disaster in the United States. The meeting in the Cabinet Office briefing room, or COBRA as it is known, was soon brought to silence by the arrival of the Prime Minister. He gave a rousing speech in which he declared that America was under attack by enemies of civilisation and Britain would stand side-by-side with the US in this crisis. A few days later he made his famous 'shoulder to shoulder' comments and the dice was cast. British troops joined the Americans in the attack on Afghanistan. One senior British officer, who later went on to command troops in Iraq, was present at the COBRA meeting and recalled it set the tone for the next six years of British military co-operation with the Americans.

"The direction of travel was clear, the rest was just sorting out the details," he commented.

"Sticking with the Americans became the one constant in British strategy in both Afghanistan and Iraq. We were never sure if Blair really believed in the cause or just wanted to keep a seat at the top table with Bush, but it was clear from that day that we had to be up there with the Americans come what may."[4]

For most of 2002, the senior leadership of the British armed forces were suspended in a sort of paralysis, as Blair appeared torn between his gut instinct to support Bush and his uncertainty if the Cabinet, Parliamentary Labour Party and the country would back a war against Iraq. The Prime Minister's attitude meant it would not be until the last days of 2002, that firm instructions would be issued to the commanders and troops who would participate in the invasion. At the same time Blair ordered a news blackout on any aspect of preparations for war, which went so far as to prevent the notification of specific units that they were being earmarked for deployment. This was to stop leaks to the media. Blair and Hoon were convinced they could not trust the military not to leak what they were doing. Johnson summed up the mood at the top of government, "[limited distribution] circulations don't work anyway because the [Ministry of Defence] is full of leakers, and they are usually too senior to be sacked."[5]

Crucially, the Ministry of Defence was prevented from ordering new equipment or spare parts from hardware suppliers and even to begin hiring ships to transport equipment to the Middle East. For most of 2002 military planners were limited to developing "options" or "concepts" and "scoping troop packages". This was a long way from issuing the necessary orders to start troops moving out of barracks, ships cruising out of port or aircraft taking off.

Senior British military officers became aware in early 2002 that their American counterparts were working on war plans for Iraq. The British armed forces had several hundred officers attached to US headquarters and units working as exchange or liaison officers. British defence chiefs were very proud of this 'early warning network' which gave them an unprecedented insight into the workings of the US military machine. A team of British staff officers at the US Central Command (CENTCOM) headquarters in Tampa in Florida picked up the first hints of the US planning in January and February 2002. They reported these to their direct boss, the Chief of Joint Operations, Lieutenant General John Reith, who passed it up to the Ministry of Defence in London. Other officers in the Pentagon also got indications that something was happening that might drag in the UK and starting telling their colleagues back home.[6]

Blair was invited by Bush to visit his ranch at Crawford in Texas in April of that year, and to prepare for this he called in his senior political, military and diplomatic advisors to Chequers. This included Boyce and his deputy for commitments, Lieutenant General Sir Anthony Pigott.[7]

Then, over the summer months, Piggott and Reith both headed up small teams of planners who examined the options for British participation in any US-led invasion. Participants in this planning recall that this was a sort of 'continuous meeting' with few conclusions being made. These issues were hammered out in Chief of Staffs Committee (Operations), which contained all the heads of the armed services and Pigott but not Reith. This was the forum where the Chiefs hammered out their collegiate position, which Boyce and Pigott would then put to the politicians. Boyce was very careful to keep his service chiefs on side, and he invariably waited until he squared them away before moving forward on issues.

"I don't see the justification for this stately process, which gives the single service chiefs of staff the prerogative of the harlot", commented Johnson.

"I am a firm believer in [Orders] Groups. What the CDS of the day does to square his Chiefly colleagues is a matter for consenting adults behind closed doors. It should not waste everyone else's time."[8]

Once a collegiate view was agreed, then Boyce would next have to persuade Hoon. The defence secretary, with Boyce or Pigott, would lead delegations to Downing Street or Chequers to brief Blair and his senior staff. Firm decisions were rarely taken on the spot and it would take a couple of days for Downing Street to get back to the military with its view. Nothing was happening fast. This military planning was taking place against a background of the unfolding diplomatic crisis as the American and British governments ramped up the pressure on the Iraqis. President Bush ordered accelerated military preparations in the autumn to allow US forces to be ready for action by the end of the year. The British officers working with the US military picked up these preparations and reported back to London, prompting Reith to press Boyce and his colleagues to get ministerial approval for him to start active preparations for any operation against Iraq.

The recurring theme in all options and scoping being carried out at this time was the view by senior military officers that to gain influence over the American planning, the British needed to offer them up either forces with unique capabilities – special forces, photographic reconnaissance aircraft or precision, long-range Storm Shadow cruise missiles – or a large mass of troops that could make a significant contribution to any land battle. This was an age old maxim of coalition warfare, that the only way to gain influence over how the campaign was run was to bring something of importance to the table. When Boyce and other senior officers pitched this line to ministers, they repeatedly stressed that contributing significant air, land and sea forces was the best way to fulfil the government's over arching aim of gaining influence with the Americans. This also had the subsidiary benefit of ensuring that each of the British armed services got a piece of the action and a share of the credit.

On 13th September, the Chiefs heard from Reith on his recommended force packages, and the exercise came to a head ten days later when Hoon led another delegation to brief Blair on the status of the war planning.[9] He was told that American war planning was moving ahead rapidly, and if the UK was to play its part then it would have to accelerate its preparations. The timing was unfortunate for Blair. The Labour Party conference was a few weeks away and it was expected that his opponents would use this as a venue to denounce Blair's alliance with Bush. Delicate negotiations with the Americans, French and Russians were also underway to get them to back a new United Nations Security Council resolution, so Blair did not want to appear to authorising active military preparations.

Blair approved the designation of operational or component commanders who could begin active discussion with their US counterparts, but with the caveat that the UK was not committed to any specific action. Air Marshal Brian Burridge was designated as the UK national contingent commander to work alongside the head of CENTCOM, General Tommy Franks.[10] The land forces were to be led by Major General Robin Brims, the air force contingent was to be led by Air Vice Marshal Glenn Torpy and the maritime force was led by Rear Admiral David Snelson. The Director of Special Forces, Brigadier Graeme Lamb, headed up planning with his American counter-parts.[11]

These officers and their staff headed to the Middle East and the US to establish links with their American counterparts and find out the status of their planning. They were constrained in their conversations with the Americans by caveats imposed by Blair, who insisted that they were unable to make any firm commitments on participation in any operation until he had made up his mind. Hoon and Boyce went to see Blair again on 17th October, and briefed him on the proposed force packages for British involvement in the US-led invasion.

Package 0 was purely made up of special forces, Package 1 was a minimal involvement of so-called enabling forces, such as spy planes, air-to-air refuelling and use of bomber bases at RAF Fairford in Gloucestershire and on the British Indian Ocean Territory of Diego Garcia. Package 2 was a significant air, naval and special forces involvement, which was projected as costing £1 billion. The bigger Package 3 also included the addition of major land forces of 20,000 plus troops, at a projected cost of £2 billion.[12] According to Blair's chief of staff, Jonathan Powell, Admiral Boyce pressed Blair to approve the participation of a divisional-sized land force, saying the army's morale would be undermined if had to sit on the sidelines while the air force and navy took a leading role.[13]

The meeting was not very conclusive, as Campbell recorded in his dairies.[14] Although Blair was content with the air, maritime and special forces contingents he would not make up his mind over the size of the land forces for several weeks. Blair was still unwilling to allow the military to issue orders for units to deploy to the Middle East, or for orders to be placed to buy new hardware from industry. The UK Joint Force Headquarters element were authorised to deploy to the Middle East state of Qatar in November, to work alongside the CENTCOM forward command post that was opening up to run the invasion of Iraq. Burridge himself was not cleared to travel to Qatar until the following month.[15]

A major complicating factor was that as the crisis with Iraq was unfolding, the Blair government was engaged in a bitter industrial dispute with the Fire Brigade's union, which soon led to some 19,000 British military personnel being deployed on fire-fighting duties between October 2002 and March 2003. While it did not divert troops from the first phase Iraqi operation, it did soak up a huge amount of the Ministry of Defence's senior leadership time at a moment when they would rather have been concentrating on the Iraq crisis. The fire-fighting operation, however, did prevent the first follow-up formation, 19 Mechanised Brigade, preparing properly for its mission in the summer of 2003. The war planning was now accelerating as British commanders and staff started to get more information from their American counterparts. The RAF and Royal Navy were ahead of the game, because they already had planning staffs and units already in the Middle East enforcing no-fly zones and naval embargoes against Iraq. British air force and navy officers already worked in the US hi-tech headquarters in Bahrain and Saudi Arabia, and they were soon working side-by-side with their US counterparts on the war plans.

The main potential role for the RAF was to contribute a sizeable element of the air strike force, involving Tornado GR4 and Harrier GR7 jump jets armed with smart weapons. The Tornados were also envisaged as flying the major part of aerial reconnaissance missions with their RAPTOR systems. The RAF Tornado force had been constantly on duty in the Middle East since 1991, flying patrols over southern Iraq as part of the no-fly zone enforcement operation. Its crews were aware of the location of the main Iraqi air defence missile batteries and radars, as well as being highly experienced in working and flying alongside their American comrades.

The RAF's Tornados and Harriers had all been upgraded since the Kosovo conflict in 1999, which had exposed significant shortcomings and prompted Air Marshal Burridge to describe this operation as a "debacle".[16] Bomb damage assessments data leaked to the media revealed that during the 78 day Kosovo bombing campaign, the Tornado GR1 strike missions achieved only a 65% hit rate with 454kg (1,000lb) Raytheon Paveway II laser guided bombs (LGBs), used in combination with Ferranti's Thermal Imaging Airborne Laser Designator (TIALD) pod. Only 53% of targets were hit with the bigger 2,000lb Paveway III weapons, which was nowhere near the requirements of the 'smart' weapon era. Only 40% of the Hunting RBL755 cluster bombs hit their targets, the reports said, and 4% of 454kg (1,000lb) unguided bombs with impact fuses, with only 2% being confirmed as hitting their targets, where bomb damage analysis assessments were made after the war.[17]

The excruciating media coverage of the RAF's performance in Kosovo meant that funding had been found to buy the GPS variant of the Paveway bomb, which would allow them to be employed in bad weather or cloudy conditions. The Storm Shadow long range cruise missile, equipped with penetrating warheads, was also now ready to be employed on Tornado GR4s. Air Vice Marshal Torpy, who as air officer commanding (AOC) the RAF's No 1 Group was the designated UK air component commander, if Britain should join the US attack on Iraq.

"One of the big lessons from Kosovo was that we did not have enough all weather precision guided munitions and targeting pods to do close air support (CAS)," commented the Air Vice Marshal.

"So when I was appointed AOC 1 Group I put a lot of effort into getting targeting pods, more laser guided bombs, or LGBs, and Enhanced Paveway so we could drop in bad weather. We also strengthened relations with the British Army. CAS became a core task of the Harrier, Jaguar and Tornado forces. Up to then the Tornado force had concentrated on strategic strikes, but I saw no reason why the Tornados should not do CAS - they had a crew of two so were a good platform for CAS."[18]

A top priority mission for the US air commander, Lieutenant General Michael 'Buzz' Moseley, was to prevent Saddam Hussein launching Scud ballistic missiles from western Iraq at Israel, in a bid to split Arab opinion from the coalition, in a repeat of the tactic tried in 1991. Moseley's air command, based at Prince Sultan Air Base (PSAB) in Saudi Arabia, was to co-ordinate all the air and land operations in western Iraq against the Scud threat. US intelligence believed the Iraqis had ten mobile Scud launcher vehicles and 40 al Hussein missiles for them, which could reach all the main Israeli cities, possibly with chemical warheads.[19]

A team of RAF and British Army officers worked closely with the American planners to develop the plans to provide round-the-clock air surveillance of western Iraq, involving RAF Canberra PR9 photographic spy planes, and Nimrod MR2 patrol aircraft fitted with video cameras, backed up by US missile armed MQ-1 Predator drones. RAF Harriers and US Air National Guard F-16s were to be put on call to bomb any Scuds that the air surveillance had spotted. To try to flush out the Scuds, British and American special forces ground patrols were to be launched into western Iraq from Jordan and Saudi Arabia. The whole operation was to be co-ordinated by mission planners onboard RAF E-3D Sentry AWACS radar aircraft. Senior RAF officers were keen to praise a young army officer, Major Gus Fair of the Light Dragoons, for pulling the operation together in matter of weeks and having it ready to go in early December 2002.[20]

The Royal Navy believed it was in a good position to get involved in the US war planning. For over a decade they had been working alongside the US Navy to enforce sanctions, sending a frigate on a weekly basis up into Iraqi coastal waters to board ships suspected of breaching the UN oil and arms embargo. This gave both navies a very clear understanding of the Iraqi coast and its treacherous tidal waters. A high priority for the US Navy was to secure access to Iraq's only port, Umm Qasr, which was at the mouth of the Khawr al Arab or KAA waterway. The first version of the planning for this operation called for British minesweepers to clear the channel of underwater mines, while a company of Royal Marines from 40 Commando cleared the shores along the waterways so shipping could safely enter Iraq's only sea port.[21]

Then US and British planners began to realise that Iraq's offshore and on shore oil infrastructure had to be secured to prevent Saddam attempting to sabotage it, causing an ecological disaster by releasing oil into the Gulf or setting fire to the wells. The US Navy Special Forces – the famous SEALs - were given the task of launching a series of raids to seize the key parts of the oil infrastructure, including the pumping manifolds on the bottom of the al-Faw peninsular and the off shore, Khawr al Amaya Oil Terminal and al Basrah Oil Terminals, known respectively as the KAAOT and ABOT.[22]

The al-Faw terminal was surrounded by a large garrison of several hundred Iraqi marines and army troops, backed by tanks and artillery. A major operation would be required to take this facility. Rear Admiral Snelson and his planners in Bahrain saw this as an opportunity to dramatically increase the role of the Royal Navy and Royal Marines in the coming operation. With the backing of Admiral Sir Alan West, the head of the Royal Navy, Snelson offered the Americans the services of 3 Commando Brigade, backed by an amphibious task force, to provide the bulk of the forces to act as a protective screen for the SEALs around the al Faw peninsular. General Reith and his senior planners at PJHQ were not keen on this idea because it would divert resources, particularly RAF Chinook transport helicopters, from the big drive that was then being proposed through Turkey to open the so-called 'northern' option.

The Chief of Joint Operations flew down to Bahrain at the beginning of December, to tell Snelson that the commando brigade option was a no-go. In a very strange meeting between Reith, Snelson and the US naval commander in the Middle East, Admiral Tim Keating, the very junior British admiral refused to accept the cancellation of the 3 Brigade operation and openly defied Reith, requesting his American ally support his view. Surprisingly, the US Navy chief backed his British naval counterpart and said that 3 Commando Brigade were essential to the US operations. Reith had to gracefully accept that 3 Commando Brigade were still in the plan.[23]

"At first there were mine sweepers and infantry companies for force protection," observed Air Marshal Burridge.

"This [operation] grew incrementally and gained cumulative risk. This was mission creep by planning until the risk was levelled out."[24]

American war planners were increasingly focused on taking Baghdad as the way to bring about the collapse of Saddam's regime in a matter of days or weeks. They did not want to have their troops tied down in street fighting in towns and cities across southern Iraq, and proposed to screen them until they could be dealt with after the fall of Baghdad. It was felt that once Saddam's regime was removed from power, the periphery of the country would fall without a shot being fired after the iron grip of the Ba'ath Party was removed. As US

Marine Corps commanders became aware that their British counterparts were taking part in the mission to seize the oil infra-structure, it was suggested that they then take on the task of screening the city of Basra, while the bulk of the US land forces headed towards Baghdad. In effect, this envisaged 3 Commando Brigade, with its two battalion-sized main units, securing the terrain that the whole of 1 (UK) Division would eventually occupy in March 2003.[25] This was not viewed as sensible or prudent by senior British commanders.

"As the plan stood in December 2002, 3 Brigade would not have been able to do the job," said General Brims.

"The Americans envisaged going early and very light. It was a vague and wholly inadequate plan. It was a plan made with the forces to hand, if they had to go then. It was just the first version of the plan".[26]

For the RAF and Royal Navy, the preparations for war were relatively straightforward, because of their existing close working relationships with their American counterparts; but for the British Army the possibility of becoming involved in the Iraq operation was more problematic. On 31st October, Hoon and Boyce went to see Blair again to try to get him to make his mind up over the land package. According to Alistair Campbell, Boyce told Blair that the Americans were threatening to cut the British out of land operations planning because of a lack of willingness to consider contributing a significant land force.[27] Blair gave the go-ahead for the planning for Package 3 to begin. Reith then produced an option paper that included four main options, first the northern front, then joining either the US Army or US Marines during the drive on Baghdad, or providing a screening force throughout southern Iraq to protect the American's flanks.[28]

The army leadership were still keen to take on a high profile role to ensure they would be taken seriously by General Franks and his colleagues. There was little appetite to join the Americans in the main push on Baghdad from the south, because of the logistic challenges of being involved in intense battles in the Iraqi capital against the remnants of Saddam's elite Republican Guard. The next most attractive option seemed to be joining the Americans in an attack through Turkey into the Kurdish region. Some six to eight Iraqi divisions were deployed there to cordon off the Kurdish safe haven, and the Americans wanted to pin them down and then destroy them, to prevent this strong Iraqi force helping in the defence of Baghdad.

This had a major attraction because the proposed British contingent of 1(UK) Armoured Division, with 7 Armoured and 19 Brigades, would be roughly equal in size to the main US combat formation, the 4th Infantry Division, and this would potentially give London an equal say in how the battle in the north would be fought.

The troops would also be fighting in a temperate region that would not require expensive desert modifications to be made to their tanks and vehicles. Also the Kurds were known to be friendly to the British and would provide secure lines of communications to the Turkish border.

There were two major problems to be overcome. First, the long supply lines from ports on the Mediterranean coast would stretch the capabilities of the Royal Logistic Corps to deliver fuel, ammunition and other supplies to the frontline in Iraq. More importantly, the Turkish government was dead set against any war in Iraq, and insisted on putting its involvement to a vote in its parliament. In a telling contrast to the Arab monarchies and dictatorships who provided facilities for the US and British along Iraq's southern border, the Turkish parliament would subsequently vote against the opening of the northern front from its territory.

In October and November, the British chose to let the US take the lead on securing transit rights from the Turks. London turned down an American request to provide the British-led Allied Rapid Reaction Corps (ARRC) Headquarters because of issues concerning freeing it from NATO tasks.[29] The senior leadership of the British armed forces threw their weight behind the northern option, despite growing indications that it might not happen.

The UK Defence Intelligence Staff (DIS) in November warned that the Turks were going to veto the US plans but Hoon was not yet willing to pull the plug. Huge amounts of time and effort were spent trying to work up the northern option almost to the exclusion of other contingencies. Brims and his staff in Germany spent several weeks working up the details of moving their troops into Turkey. The General was able to get several of his key units exempt from fire fighting duty to allow them to continue operational training.[30] Troops from 7 Armoured Brigade, the famous Desert Rats, were in the middle of what was termed a training year, in preparation to becoming the Army's high readiness brigade in 2003, and this work continued. The Challenger 2 main battle tanks of the Royal Scots Dragoon Guards, for example, were undergoing a period of intense field firing to bring all their crews up to speed for combat.

The deception measures to prevent media leaks went into high gear with any officers involved in the planning being ordered not to talk about their work even to superior officers. The commanding officer of the helicopter regiment earmarked for the Turkey mission was not even allowed to tell his brigade commander, who knew nothing about the proposed operation.[31] During the first days of November, Reith dispatched Major General Albert Whitley to Kuwait to be the Senior British Land Advisor to the American land component headquarters, along with a team of 17 British officers. Whitley was a very level-headed Royal Engineer officer who would soon be a key player in the operation to invade Iraq. His job was to provide Reith with a ringside seat to the US Army land forces commander Lieutenant General David McKiernan's planning for the invasion. They were old friends from working together during the NATO peacekeeping force in Bosnia five years before. The US general gave Whitley free rein in his headquarters and used him as a sounding board, even on issues that were not really the business of a British officer.[32] Whitley quickly became aware that the preparations for the northern front were not going well. Not only due to the problems with the Turkish government, but also because General Franks was having difficulty co-ordinating the operation with his counterparts in US European Command, which was responsible for American forces in Turkey. The Americans were getting ready to pull the plug and turn the northern front into little more than a diversionary operation using just special forces and air power.

Reith and other British planners began advising Ministers and the Chiefs that if the government wanted to play a major role in the land war, they had better begin working up options to operate from Kuwait alongside the main US invasion force. Whitley also made it clear to Reith that the Americans were aiming to be ready to go to war in February 2003, which meant that Ministers needed to start making active preparations in a matter of days, or the British Army might miss the start of the war.[33] Reith headed to London to brief Hoon in mid-December, to try to get some firm decisions on hiring cargo ships to carry the army division's equipment to either Turkey or Kuwait, the mobilisation of thousands of army reservists including most of the doctors and medical staff needed in war time, as well as the purchase of urgent operational requirement (UOR) modifications for equipment.

The Chief of Joint Operations told the Chilcot inquiry, "[Hoon] said to me, 'You have been telling me, you know, week by week, that we have to do this, and now you are telling me you are giving me another deadline'.

I said, "This is the deadline".

He said, 'You know, we need to keep our options open', and I said, 'Well, actually, if we don't go to trade [to hire ships] by the end of this week, then we don't have any options, we are not going'. [Hoon] then went to the Prime Minister and we were then authorised to go to trade. But it was - there was a reluctance, as I say, to have any form of committal and anything that was public at that stage."[34]

On 18th December Hoon had to announce to Parliament that he had begun the process of chartering shipping as this could not be kept secret. Through December it was becoming increasingly apparent to senior British officers and Ministry of Defence officials that the northern option was just not going to happen. Even as the diplomacy at the United Nations was looking increasingly unlikely to bring results, and the Americans were becoming committed to action in the next few weeks, Blair, his minister and military chiefs were still refusing to make firm decisions.

The Chief of the General Staff, General Sir Michael Walker was now the main proponent of the northern option, which he termed a 'winning concept'.[35] He was concerned about the congestion of troops in Kuwaiti ports becoming a highly vulnerable target for Iraqi chemical weapons. While the northern option had secure lines of communications through Turkey and the intervention of British troops in Kurdistan could have a decisive effect on the war. As a result the Chiefs of Staffs Committee (Operations) could not come to an agreed way forward, and Boyce was unable to marshal his colleagues behind a single course of action that they could recommend to ministers. Although no decisions had been made, during December Hoon relaxed on some of the restrictions on the passage of information to the wider military, to allow some initial preparations to be made by units. He also authorised initial approaches to be made to industry for UOR equipment to be prepared, although not many contracts could yet be placed because there was not any decision on the northern or southern options. A planning conference was then held at PJHQ.

Across the army, rumours were rife about the preparations for war and commanders began to make their own unofficial contingency plans in case their units were included. The commanders of 7 Armoured, 3 Commando and 16 Air Assault Brigade were warned that it was likely they would participate in the operation. They in turn were authorised to inform their battalion and regimental commanders, as well as a few selected staff officers.[36]

The 16 Brigade staff were first tasked by PJHQ on 15th December to co-ordinate with their counterparts in the US Army's 82nd Airborne Division, who were planning a series of dramatic operations to seize Baghdad and other cities in Iraq in the event of what was termed 'regime collapse' before the war started. According to 16 Brigade's post operational tour report, "initial concept of operations, arrived at after consultation with US planners, saw five potential tasks: air assault operations at Kirkuk, H2, Baghdad International Airport, Baghdad, or in the southern Iraqi oilfields." These were classic air manoeuvre operations involving parachute drops and air-landing assaults from C-130s to capture Baghdad airport ahead of rapid moves to take control of key government buildings, oil fields and most importantly alleged weapon of mass destruction sites. Not surprisingly, senior Parachute Regiment officers were enthusiastic about being at the centre of offensive operations against Iraq.

In Germany, 7 Brigade had already been working up its troops on live firing exercises and command post drills, to build up their skills levels for the northern option. More focused preparations were now made, including on the immunisation of the troops against Anthrax, which was believed to be in the Iraqi arsenal of weapons of mass destruction.[37] The Colchester-based 16 Brigade had up to this point not been in the forefront of war preparations, except for 3 Regiment Army Air Corps, which was warned that it could be joining the British division deploying from Turkey. The Brigade had also been raided for equipment for other units that been earlier earmarked for participation. Only a small number of its Lynx helicopters had been modified to enable them to receive upgrades to allow them to fly in desert conditions.[38] In early December it had been ordered to hand them over to 3 Commando Brigade for its mission on the al-Faw, so when the news came that 16 Brigade could participate in the war, rapid plans had to be made to convert more helicopters to the desert configuration, delaying their deployment and training of crews.

Some of the Brigade's specialist communications equipment was also transferred to the Special Forces who were at the heart of British war planning at this stage. Four of 16 Brigade's major units were also committed to Operation Fresco, as the fire fighting mission was called, and a large number of its vehicles had been left behind in Afghanistan in the spring and had not been replaced. All of this combined to leave 16 Brigade in a difficult position when the final order to deploy to the Middle East was given. Vital operational training and the requesting of specialist equipment and ammunition had to be done in a matter of days, with the intensive planning required conducted over the Christmas period. At the end of December, the British military was still awaiting orders and had little idea if it would ever become involved in the coming war.

According to Hoon's senior advisor, Johnson, "perhaps the down-side of our organisation is a tendency to be a bit too clever, to see too many options, to over-intellectualise and to over-complicate."

"The excruciating saga over the so-called Northern Option was a case in point. We convinced ourselves that this was the best role for our land forces, and (therefore?) that it was 'strategically essential'. It became apparent pretty quickly that we had painted ourselves into a corner, but we were incapable of changing our mind without the catalyst of [Hoon] going to Ankara some months later [on 8th January]. Those around at the time will remember what a blight this uncertainty cast on our planning (and consequently how it abolished Xmas 2002!)"[39]

Chapter 5

TO KUWAIT

At the end of 2002, the British military deployment appeared stalled. Prime Minister Tony Blair had yet to get parliamentary approval for military action against Iraq, and the leadership of the British armed forces had yet to come to any definitive collective conclusion about the best course of action. A consensus was emerging among the service chiefs that the southern option, via Kuwait, was the best option for the deployment of the British land contingent. Even before the northern option was formally ruled out, military chiefs began initiating a series of enabling activities to ensure their forces were well placed to react if the government did give the go ahead for the southern option.[1]

The Royal Navy and Royal Marines were ahead of the game, because their role in the proposed operation to seize Iraqi oil infrastructure was a relatively stand alone activity that was not dependent on other decisions about the participation of the large force of army troops. In the final days of 2002, the Royal Navy was at an advanced stage of getting its amphibious task force ready, led by the carriers HMS Ark Royal and Ocean, to sail for the Mediterranean with 3 Commando Brigade and its equipment onboard. This was still being described as part of a "routine pre-planned exercise" by Hoon in a bid to dampen down speculation that it was preparation for war. Royal Fleet Auxiliary store ships began docking at the Royal Navy Ammunition Depot at Glen Douglas in Argyll just before New Year to take on artillery shells and other ammunition.[2] In Devon, 3 Brigade's personnel were already painting vehicles and other equipment in desert camouflage ready for operations in Iraq.

In the first days of January, the commander of 3 Brigade, Brigadier Jim Dutton, and his senior officers headed to Camp Pendleton in California to take part in a co-ordination conference with the leaders of the 1st Marine Expeditionary Force (I MEF), who were to lead the drive into south eastern Iraq.[3] Dutton was one of the most talented Royal Marine officers of his generation. He had been the UK's chief military liaison officer in the Pentagon in the months after the 9/11 attacks, and during the opening months of the Afghan war. He later went on to command British troops in southern Iraq in 2005 and be deputy commander of the NATO troops in Afghanistan. While Dutton had some idea of the scope and scale of US war plans from his time earlier in the summer, working in the Pentagon as the CDS's chief liaison officer to the US Joint Staff, his staff and battalion commanders were stunned by what they heard from the I MEF commander, Lieutenant General James Conway and his staff. Major Jim Hutton, the second-in-command of 40 Commando, listened as he heard for the first time that his unit in a matter of weeks could be making a night-time helicopter assault direct on to heavily defended Iraqi positions. In the midst of the briefing Hutton recalled how he turned to Dutton and said "this is bloody serious, sir!" Dutton replied, "Yes!" According to Hutton, the planning team returned to the UK with "mixed feelings of excitement and dread".[4]

In Portsmouth and Plymouth, navy personnel were preparing 17 warships and 14 auxiliary ships of the task force to sail, with some 9,000 personnel. On 8th January, Hoon announced the deployment of the amphibious task force, and over the next nine days it set sail with 40 Commando onboard, as well as the Commando Helicopter Force and other support units. Later in the month, the task force carried out an amphibious landing exercise on the British Sovereign Base Area on Cyprus. The media campaign to persuade the public that the deployment was not a preparation for war had an unintended consequence, when the station commander at RAF Akrotiri refused to cancel training flights by the Red Arrows aerobatic display team to make room for the Royal Marines exercises. The phone lines to London hummed and the hapless RAF Group Captain was put in the picture about the importance of the commando brigade's mission.[5]

The task force then set sail for the Suez Canal, and then headed to the United Arab Emirates, where another amphibious training exercise took place. Brigadier Dutton's advanced headquarters party flew out to Kuwait on 12th January to set up shop next to the US Marine Corps headquarters at Camp Rhino. The brigade headquarters was complete in Kuwait at the end of January, and a few days later 42 Commando had also flown out to Kuwait. The amphibious task group was off the coast of Kuwait on 15th February, three days ahead of their designated date for initial operating capability.[6]

The Commando Brigade had deployed with two of its battalions or commandos: these were 700-strong light infantry units who were trained to make amphibious or heliborne assaults from ships. Supporting the Brigade were its specialist units, which were also trained in operating from ships and moving ashore across defended beaches. Its fire support was provided by the 105mm Light Guns of 29 Regiment Royal Artillery which could be flown ashore by helicopter. Armed Lynx AH7 and Gazelle AH1 helicopters were on hand to scout out targets and engage enemy armour with TOW wire-guided missiles. The Royal Marines operated their own fleet of landing craft, fast patrol boats and hovercraft to allow it to bring men and equipment ashore, as well as to conduct offensive operations in coastal waters and river estuaries. Backing up 3 Brigade was the Commando Logistic Regiment, which was trained and equipped to deliver supplies to front line Marines by helicopter, truck or landing craft. The flexibility of this logistic regiment gave Brigadier Dutton multiple options for putting his troops ashore on the al Faw. The next most potent unit in Brigadier Dutton's formation was the Brigade Reconnaissance Force, which could operate well ahead of the main body of 3 Brigade on foot, in helicopters or in heavily armed Land Rovers. It was supported by the eavesdropping specialists of Y Troop, who were able to monitor enemy radio communications.

Brigadier Dutton was placed in an invidious position by the British government's precarious political situation. Blair had yet to secure full Cabinet and parliamentary approval for participation in the war, and so British commanders in the Middle East were ordered to participate in planning and preparation with their American allies, but were not allowed to make firm commitments to joining any offensive operations, ahead of a final decision in London. With the American preparations for war rapidly accelerating, US military commanders needed to firm up their plans and commit units to specific tasks. 3 Commando Brigade was assigned a potentially crucial role in the first hours of the war, but the ambiguous nature of the British commitment became more of an issue as the start of the war drew nearer. The closer to the start of the operation, the less possible it was for the Americans to fill the gaps left by any British decision not to commit its forces to action. As more units began arriving in Kuwait, more and more British commanders and staff officers found themselves facing the same dilemma.[7]

Air Marshal Brian Burridge, the UK's national contingent commander, who now had his headquarters up and running alongside General Tommy Franks' in Qatar, recalled that the uncertainty over political 'top cover' for the mission did not at this stage impact on the flow of forces to the Middle East.

"We were doing what we were doing until someone told us to stop," he said.

"We were already sailing stuff. If the Prime Minister said "hold", the force, then we could have pulled that lever. It was not politically difficult, but it was frustrating."[8]

At the beginning of January, the service chiefs and ministers in London had still not made up their minds between the northern and southern options. The southern option was now looking like the preferred solution, but no final decision had been made. In anticipation of this, the chiefs of staff ordered the commander of 1 (UK) Armoured Division, Major General Robin Brims, to report to Lieutenant General John Reith in Northwood to receive orders to prepare to execute the southern option.[9] Reith's man in Kuwait, Major General Albert Whitley, penned a brief memo to his boss on 5th January, saying "that any opportunity for worthwhile UK involvement of land forces in the North has come and gone."[10]

He recommended that the headquarters of 1 (UK) Armoured Division, 3 Commando and 16 Air Assault Brigades, along with the necessary logistic support be committed to Kuwait, to work with the US Marines in southern Iraq. He said decisions were "imperative".

"The effect of timely decisions on our own ability to successfully conduct operations and on our US allies cannot be underestimated" he wrote to Reith.

Air Marshal Burridge was in a meeting with General Reith on 6th January at PJHQ when General Franks telephoned.

"I was in CJO's office and Franks told Reith that the northern option was off and we should re-plan for the south," recalled Burridge.[11]

Action needed to be taken to demonstrate that the northern option was a no-go, despite the claims by senior British officers and officials that it was still in play. Defence Secretary Geoff Hoon flew to Ankara on 8th January to speak to the Turkish government and get a definitive answer. The importance of this mission was gauged by the fact the Hoon took his top civil servant, the Permanent Secretary Sir Kevin Tebbitt, with him. Tebbitt, who had previously worked in the British Embassy in Ankara, and spoke Turkish, thought he could swing the deal. Despite the high-level British delegation, the Turks said no, but it took another ten days for the British government to make up its own mind.

"This was a period of wishful thinking," said Air Marshal Burridge.

"We were trying to construct a new 'winning concept' [for the southern option] which led to the notion of the Basra Box as the UK land area of responsibility. On this basis, we had a 'winning concept' that would allow British participation at acceptable level of risk."[12]

In the first week of January, Brims had accelerated his own preparations. He called together all his brigade commanders and their senior staff officers at his headquarters in Germany to conduct what he called a "monster estimate" of the situation they would face in Iraq. Whitley flew in from Kuwait to brief the assembled officers on the latest situation and status of the American war plans.[13]

Brims and his officer's brainstorming session lasted several days as they worked over issues involved in deploying and employing their forces as part of the American invasion plan. They worked out the list of units needed, ammunition requirements and the proposed sequence of deployment, and then reported back to PJHQ. This planning resulted in Brims deciding not to take any of his division's Multiple Launch Rocket Systems or MLRS because they would cause too much collateral damage in civilian areas of Basra. The general also asked for as many Phoenix unmanned aerial vehicles that could be spared to maximise the number of surveillance flights that could be flown over enemy territory.

"Time was short" recalled Brims.

"We created the basic plan and back briefed it to PJHQ and [army] Land Command [who would have to generate the required units and equipment]."[14]

Events were moving fast now, and on 15th January Hoon and the Chief of the Defence Staff, Admiral Sir Mike Boyce, and the other chiefs of staff hosted Blair and his senior advisors in the Ministry of Defence Main Building to brief them on the commitment of British forces. The Prime Minister was asked to confirm the southern option and give the formal go ahead to start moving troops and equipment.[15] Reith and Brims then flew to Kuwait on 15th January for discussions with the CENTCOM chief General Tommy Franks, and Conway, of the I MEF, and on how British forces would be used and its tasks matched to US requirements. Brims made an immediate impression on his American allies.

One US Marine Corps officer commented that the British general, "who was tall, thin, articulate, approachable, and full of energy. He was the kind of soldier Americans did not meet every day. There was a trace of old-school eccentricity in his official biography, which described him as 'single, a cricket fanatic, Newcastle United supporter, and outdoor enthusiast whose specialty area is bonfires.' It was a trait that made him all the more attractive to US Marines, whose values sometimes seem to be from another era. In this he was not unlike [1st Marine Division commander] Major General James Mattis, with whom he was to forge a good working relationship."[16]

Brims said that US plans were still "fluid" but the Americans were clear they wanted the British division to cover their flank to free up troops to allow them to concentrate on Baghdad. Reith and Whitley supported the view that this was the best way to employ the British division, and passed their recommendations back to London. At this point in the build up to war, with the effective closing of the northern option, there was little possibility of the British division playing a more prominent role in the coming campaign.

According to a classified study of the war prepared on the orders of British army chiefs in the summer of 2003, "the lack of political committal also caused serious difficulties for UK planners in US headquarters. Although the UK military could see serious shortcomings in aspects of the campaign plan, they were unable to influence US decision-makers until UK committed major combat units – by which time the campaign had essentially been planned. PJHQ were politely excluded from key CENTCOM planning for much of September and October 2002. Furthermore, it was difficult to plan significant roles for UK forces when the US was unsure whether those British forces were going to arrive in time. In retrospect, the UK should have considered the possibility of Turkish refusal to allow [the northern option]. This would have permitted earlier consideration of a southern attack from Kuwait, rather than looking at it for the first time in January 2003. Earlier closure of this strategic option caused considerable short-notice planning, and resulted in the selection of a force package based on what could be deploy to theatre in time, rather than what was needed to accomplish the mission."[17]

General Walker told the Chilcot inquiry that "I would have preferred to have six months build up for the operation."

"But if you end up with a period that is shorter than that, everybody works twice as hard," he said.[18]

On 17th, Blair confirmed the plans and the next day the British got permission from the Kuwaitis to allow their troops to land in the Emirate. Two days later the deployment was announced by Hoon.[19] Reith and his team now moved into over-drive to make the deployment happen. He promised his American counterparts that the British division would be ready for action in the Middle East by 24th February, when it was assumed that the war would be well under way. The critical factor that could make this happen was the availability of chartered shipping, and it was due to come available at the end of January. There was now not enough time, or shipping, to lift two heavy brigades to Kuwait to meet the expected start of the war. So 19 Mechanised Brigade was now formally dropped from the plan and 16 Brigade, the army air manoeuvre formation, which was trained and equipped to move by aircraft and helicopter, was given to General Brims for the upcoming operation. This brigade took up less shipping and could be ready for action as soon as it got to Kuwait. Once in place, 16 Brigade would also give British commanders several important options. US commanders were worried that the Iraqi regime might collapse suddenly if Saddam fled or was killed in a coup attempt. It was all wishful thinking, but the US and British military planners had to go through the motions. British Parachute Regiment officers had already been working on elements of this planning for over a month.[20]

The commander of 16 Brigade, Brigadier Jonathan or 'Jacko' Page had commanded a platoon of 2 PARA during the 1982 Falklands war, and then a tank squadron in the 1991 Iraq war. He was considered the most innovative tactician ever to have commanded 16 Brigadier, as well as having a reputation for being hyper-active and being able to survive on only three hours sleep a day for weeks at a time. Not surprisingly, considering his background, he had little time for staff processes and military bureaucracy. He was subsequently to command NATO forces in southern Afghanistan at the height of fighting against the Taliban in 2007.

Once 16 Brigade got the formal word to deploy on 20th January 2003, pandemonium ensued at its bases in Colchester, Wattisham and Canterbury. Quartermasters began requesting huge quantities of desert uniforms and boots, body armour, extra vehicles, specialist communication equipment and nuclear, biological and chemical (NBC) protective suits. 3 Regiment's helicopters had to be modified with sand filters allow them to fly in desert conditions, and have defensive systems fitted to defeat shoulder launched surface-to-air missiles. All this equipment was in very short supply, and not all of it was ready by the time the Brigade moved into the desert at the start of the war in March.

The delays in authorising the Brigade's deployment and the short time frame before deployment, meant all this preparatory activity had to be done in a few days, to allow the 1,800 vehicles, thousands of cargo containers and 22 helicopters to be loaded onto cargo ships at Marchwood military port near Southampton, for the three week long voyage to Kuwait. All of 16 Brigade's heavy equipment had to be moved by ship because there was no spare air transport capacity.

When the ships carrying the Brigade's equipment arrived in Kuwait, the docks were full with US and British ships unloading cargo. It took weeks to sort out whose containers belonged to whom, and this process was not complete by the time the war started on 19th March. Equipment shortages meant that when the war started, some 20% of the Brigade soldiers did not have body armour, nearly half did not have desert boots, anti-malaria tablets quickly ran out and, most worrying, its chemical weapons detection equipment only had enough spare filters to last two weeks of continuous operations in a contaminated environment. This left many members of the Brigade wondering if the British government was really serious about going to war.[21]

16 Brigade deployed to Kuwait with two Parachute Regiment battalions, 1 and 3 PARA, the 1st Battalion, The Royal Irish Regiment, in the air assault

role and 3 Regiment AAC, which was designated an aviation battlegroup. The PARA and the Royal Irish battalions each mustered around 700 soldiers, equipped as light-role infantry. They each had four infantry companies with around 120 soldiers. The three battalions all bought a couple of dozen DAF four ton trucks with them to Kuwait, and these proved the main means of moving their infantry companies around the desert, leading to the paratroopers jokingly nicknaming them 'Deliverers of Airborne Forces' or DAFs.

In addition to their infantry, the three battalions boasted support companies, containing 81mm mortar, general purpose machine gun, Milan anti-tank guided missile, sniper, reconnaissance and assault pioneer platoons. These platoons were all mounted in Land Rover or Pinzgauer 4 x 4 vehicles, and provided their battalions with hard hitting mobile strike forces, dubbed Mobile Support Groups (MSGs), that spearheaded the invasion of Iraq. These drew their inspiration from World War Two Long Range Desert Group patrols that packed heavy fire power with high speed desert mobility. 1 PARA was designated as an airborne task force (ABTF) and it took all its parachutes and drop equipment to Kuwait. A detachment of four RAF Hercules transport aircraft deployed to a US Marine Corps airstrip in the Kuwaiti desert, to be ready to launch the ABTF.

The aviation battlegroup contained a mix of Lynx AH7 helicopters armed with TOW wired guided missiles, Lynx AH9 liaison helicopters which were used as airborne command posts, and Gazelle AH1 scout helicopters. It was usual to have a company of Paras or Royal Irish infantry attached to 3 Regiment to provide protection for forward arming and refuelling points, or to hold ground. The Brigade's Offensive Support Group (OSG) contained the bulk of its long range fire power, including four batteries of 105mm Light Guns of 7th Parachute Regiment Royal Horse Artillery (7 RHA), augmented later in the Iraqi campaign by two batteries of AS-90 155mm self-propelled howitzers. Crucially the OSG also contained all the Brigade's surveillance systems to find targets and groups of artillery, and forward air controllers (FACs) who were qualified and equipped to call in artillery fire and close air support. All these teams were connected to a firepower control centre within 16 Brigade's headquarters, so artillery and air support could be rapidly massed against targets. Three new, Swedish-made, MAMBA mortar and artillery locating radars from 5 Regiment Royal Artillery were attached to 16 Brigade for the Iraq mission. Electronic eavesdropping teams and Phoenix unmanned aerial vehicles were also assigned to the OSG, so 16 Brigade could look for targets dozens of miles behind Iraqi lines.

The Forward Observer Officers (FOO) and Tactical Air Control Parties (TACPs), who went looking for targets in heavily armed Land Rovers, were also supported by two specialist units of the Brigade. The Pathfinder Platoon was a forty-strong group of reconnaissance specialists mounted in heavily-armed Land Rovers. D Squadron, The Household Cavalry (HCR), was the only armoured unit assigned to 16 Brigade. It had 20 Scimitar Combat Reconnaissance Vehicle (Reconnaissance) (CVR(T)), lightly-armoured scout vehicles, which had specialist night-vision equipment fitted to help their crews find targets at night. Both the Pathfinders and HCR were lavishly equipped with communications equipment and contained a large number of personnel trained as FOOs and FACs to call down artillery fire and air strikes. The final element of the OSG was the assignment of a US Marine Corps ANGLICO (Air Naval Gunfire Liaison Company) unit, which provided the vital link to 3 MAW's airpower. ANGLICO teams worked in 16 Brigade Headquarters and other teams were assigned to each of its four main battlegroups and the OSG. They had highly secure satellite radio links to 3rd MAW's headquarters, and US Marine Corps aircraft on patrol above the UK sector, to allow strike aircraft and helicopter gunships to be directed to emerging targets in a matter of minutes.

In Germany, 7 Brigade's commanders and troops were also going through the same process as their colleagues in 16 Brigade. Their readiness state had been raised just after New Year and training regimes for troops had been stepped up. Troops were sent out to conduct field firing camps in their vehicles on ranges around northern Germany in freezing winter conditions. The internal organisation of regiments and battalions was tweaked, and the re-grouping of companies and platoons took place to bring units up to war establishment levels. Regimental Quartermasters started requesting spares, war stocks of ammunition, as well as modifications to vehicles and other equipment. These were all returned with the answer that peacetime waiting periods of at least six weeks still applied, as the Iraq operation had not yet been formally authorised and a budget set aside to pay for logistic support.[22]

This all changed on 20th January when Hoon announced the deployment of 7 Brigade. There was considerable consternation because the troops heard the news via television and radio broadcasts rather then from their commanding officers. Apparently, paranoia in Whitehall about media leaks meant Hoon did not want news to emerge from soldier's wives telephoning the media. Officers of the Royal Scots Dragoon Guards complained that this resulted in relatives finding out about the deployment before their soldiers. Some of these officers had served in the 1991 Gulf War, and a major 'lessons learned' study by the army had recommended that this less than perfect situation be not repeated.[23]

The commander of the Desert Rats, Brigadier Graham Binns, was a no-nonsense Yorkshire infantryman who had few airs and graces. On one exercise he had volunteered to serve as a tank radio operator to get an idea of what it was like to fight inside a tank. He had already led his brigade on peacekeeping duties in Kosovo and was well known across the army for his common sense and calmness in a crisis.[24] He had already agreed with his divisional commander, Brims, that 7 Brigade would be reinforced for the coming mission, up from three to four battalions or battlegroups, each containing two squadrons of Challenger 2 main battle tanks. The brigade boasted 116 of the 62 ton tanks. Brims and Binns wanted the Desert Rats to be able to handle themselves in a crisis.

The four battlegroups of 7 Brigade – the Royal Scots Dragoon Guards, 1st Battalion, The Black Watch, 1st Battalion, The Royal Regiment of Fusiliers and 2nd Royal Tank Regiment - were all built-up in a standard configuration. This was of two squadrons of Challenger 2s and two armoured infantry companies mounted in Warrior infantry fighting vehicles. The Challengers had only entered frontline service with the Royal Armoured Corps four years before, and boasted 120mm cannons that could devastate any tank in the Iraqi inventory with depleted uranium rounds. They also had a state of the art night vision and sighting system that allowed the tank to engage targets while it was on the move, at night or in bad weather. Additional armour packages made the Challenger 2 immune to any weapon in the Iraqi arsenal.

The Warrior was equally heavily protected so it could deliver an eight man infantry section into the heart of enemy territory. It did not have as much firepower as a Challenger, but the Warrior was battle-proven in Bosnia and the 1991 Gulf War, giving crews great confidence in it.

Each battlegroup had a full complement of supporting arms, including a battery of eight Royal Artillery AS-90 155mm self-propelled guns and a number of Warrior observation post vehicles to enable artillery spotters to keep up with the frontline tanks and infantry. Like 16 Brigade, the Desert Rats grouped their firepower into an OSG to allow concentration of fire to be bought to bear quickly. The next most important support unit in each battlegroup was the armoured engineer squadron, which had specialist armoured bulldozers and bridging vehicles to improve main battlefield mobility. When logistic, maintenance, medical, administrative and military police elements were added, each battlegroup mustered just over 1,000 troops, to complete a highly potent self-contained combat force.[25]

The Brigade's units had just over a week to conduct more field firing before their vehicles had to be packed up and loaded onto ships for the three-week voyage to Kuwait. The battlegroup command staff were each rotated through the army's computer simulation centre at Sennelager to prepare them to lead their units. Before the vehicles were dispatched to Emden port to begin loading on 6th February, mechanics began applying coatings of desert camouflage paint. It took just under two weeks for all the 6,000 or so vehicles of 1 (UK) Division to be loaded on ships at Emden. These were followed by almost 6,800 cargo containers and 15,000 tons of ammunition.[26] As the flow of ships loaded with equipment got under way, a small team of officers flew out to Kuwait to take over tented camps that contractors were building across the north of the Emirate. The Kuwaiti desert was being transformed into a huge encampment to hold more than 28,000 British and 200,000 American troops massing for the invasion. During February the bulk of the British land forces started arriving at Kuwait International Airport on commercial airliners, and they were then bussed to their desert camps. This led some officers to complain that the troops were not being toughened up enough to live in the desert and fight a war. This attitude received a sharp jolt when the first of several dust storms engulfed the British camps in the Kuwait desert in the run-up to the war. The dust from these storms penetrated inside armoured vehicles and tents collapsed under the weight of sand deposited on them.

The ships with the bulk of the vehicles and equipment for 7 Brigade arrived between 6th and 8th March, but one did not arrive until 13th March because of congestion in the Suez Canal. This meant there was less than a week to prepare the fourth battlegroup of the Brigade, The Royal Scots Dragoon Guards, for action before the war started.[27] There was considerable confusion and chaos as the ships arrived at Kuwait's Shuwaikh port, which was overwhelmed with vessels arriving with war supplies for the US and British forces. The British cargo tracking systems broke down and logistic staff lost track of where large amounts of their supplies were.

According to the commanding officer of the Black Watch, Lieutenant Colonel Mike Riddell-Webster, "in the end, most of what we needed was actually somewhere in theatre – the problem was getting it where we needed it."[28]

A huge consignment of ration packs went astray, and the British Army had to borrow thousands of US Meals-Ready-to-Eat packs. Regimental quartermasters went on 'raiding missions' to use unconventional methods to 'acquire' vital supplies, such as body armour and chemical protection suits. For a few days, the drinking water was rationed until supplies could be built up, and ablution activity was limited. With war approaching, unit commanders did not want their troops to lack life-saving protection and turned a blind eye to these activities. This chaos meant the 7 Brigade had very limited training opportunities once it got to Kuwait.

While the infantry companies were able to carry out small arms training, the tank squadrons were pre-occupied with getting their vehicles ready for action, including spending several days fitting upgraded armour packages and other UOR equipment. These included the US-made Blue Forces Tracking real-time combat position monitoring system. The most advanced training the tank squadrons received was a week of field firing to zero their main armaments, and practice firing the depleted uranium rounds that were only issued to British tank crews when they faced the prospect of going into action for real. The infantry also received UOR kit, including Minimi 5.56mm light machine guns and 40mm under-rifle grenade launchers. They had little or no time to train on these weapons before they went into action.[29]

The biggest shortfalls were in the delivery of nuclear, chemical and biological (NBC) protective equipment, such as NBC filters for Challenger 2s, replacement gas mask filters and perishable suits, and Enhanced Combat Body Army (ECBA) hard plates. The ECBA plates were particularly sought after because they provided potentially life saving protection from enemy snipers and small arms fire. There were not enough ECBA plates to go around because of the delay in placing UOR orders during the build up to the war in 2002. So in the days before the troops crossed into Iraq, they were re-distributed to frontline infantry units.

According to a briefing on Operation Telic logistics by 7 Brigade's deputy chief of staff, Major Peter Langford, the main combat battlegroups only had enough ECBA plates for between 50% and 80% of their troops at the start of the war.[30] The brigade made some 1,898 requests for new equipment and stores after it was notified of its deployment to Kuwait, yet by 19th March some 25% of them were still outstanding. But this was better than the 1 (UK) Division performance, that saw only 10% of logistics demands met during the war. A post-war army report said troops resorted to theft, sanctioned by their officers, to rectify short falls. One battlegroup had half its sleeping bags stolen from its vehicles, said the report, which concluded that "theft appears to have been a significant problem in most major operations, which the British Army has conducted, including [the 1991 Gulf war]."[31]

Small arms ammunition, NBC filters for Challenger tanks, morphine, malaria tablets, spare AS-90 howitzer barrels, desert camouflage uniforms and lightweight desert boots were also in short supply. The lack of personnel equipment was proving to have a major impact on morale of the troops gathering in Kuwait. The commanding officer of the 1st Battalion, the Royal Regiment of Fusiliers, Lieutenant Colonel David Paterson, wrote in his regimental journal from Kuwait that "the minimal official warning time for this deployment has been reflected in the logistic support, which has caused endless frustration and the Quartermaster's Platoon and [company quartermaster sergeant majors] feeling as through they have failed to provide their services. All ranks know they have worked like Trojans and have done their best in extremely difficult circumstances."[32]

Brigadier Binns put the logistics problems and training restrictions that faced his Brigade into perspective, commenting that its previous year's intensive training to prepare it for high readiness meant it was "ready to go" and faced no "great surprises".

"The logistics of deploying were complicated by our failure to take decisions in advantageous time, time to reduce logistic risk, it was rushed," he said. "We carried additional operational risk as a result."[33]

In his post-operational tour report, Brigadier Binns commented, "never again must we send ill-equipped soldiers into battle."[34]

As the main British land deployment got underway in Kuwait, the RAF deployment around the Middle East also gained momentum. Unlike the army, the RAF already had a strong footprint in the Middle East, in supporting Operate Resonate to enforce no-fly zones over northern and southern Iraq. At the turn of the year, the famous 617 Dambusters Squadron was taking its turn on no-fly zone duty at Ali al Salem airbase in Kuwait, and flying daily sorties over southern Iraq in its eight Tornado GR4 bombers. At Prince Sultan Air Base (PSAB) 111 Squadron was flying air supremacy missions in its six Tornado F3 fighters. Flying from Muharraq airport on Bahrain were Tristar air-to-air refuelling tankers.

Wing Commander Dave Robertson, the commander of the 617 Squadron detachment in Kuwait in early March described the type of missions being flown over Iraq.

"It is not a benign environment, we get shot at on a daily basis," he said.

"We have been lucky to date. The Iraqis are constantly firing anti-aircraft artillery and surface-to-air missiles. Some come very close to our aircraft, less then 100 metres away and detonating."[35]

In response to being engaged, the US and British aircraft were allowed to retaliate against Iraqi anti-aircraft batteries. If possible, they could respond with bombs or anti-radar missiles against the Iraqi forces that fired on them. In many cases this could not be possible, so air commanders were handed a menu of what were termed 'response options' that they could execute. These involved bombing the radar sites or command posts believed to be directing air defence operations in the vicinity of the engagement, and could be executed several days after the incident.

"We know when Iraqis make claims of civilian casualties," said Wing Commander Robertson.

"On occasions in the past when I know no weapons were released on a target, they claim we were bombing, it was a blatant lie. I tell my wife don't believe anything you read in the newspapers, and only half what you see on TV."[36]

The RAF eventually deployed 8,000 RAF personnel to nine main operating bases in an arc from RAF Akrotiri on Cyprus through Jordan, Saudi Arabia, the Gulf States and down to Oman. Some 112 fixed wing combat, reconnaissance and transport aircraft were eventually in place by early February, together with 27 helicopters. RAF officers in the Middle East had been drawn into US planning for the air campaign against Iraq for several months. Air Vice Marshal Torpy called a conference at RAF Lossiemouth in Scotland on 21st January, to brief the commanders of squadrons designated to participate in Operation Telic on the US and British air plan.[37]

The RAF deployment was also heavily influenced by the Turkish decision to refuse to open its bases and airspace to British and US forces. Out of some 1,396 sorties planned for the opening night of the war, some 102 of the sorties in the initial wave of aircraft were intended to come from the north, compared to 119 from the south.[38]

"The original plan emphasised the importance of the northern axis to fix Republican Guard Divisions in the North [of Iraq]," recalled Torpy, who was commanding the UK air component.

"As the Turkish position became more difficult, the northern option disappeared – causing significant problems, particularly for the air component."[39]

According to Air Marshal Burridge, this meant in the end only 770 sorties were flown on the opening day of the air campaign, with just 125 sorties in the initial southern wave.[40] After being denied access to bases in southern Turkey, the RAF was forced to find alternative bases for Tornado GR4 and Harrier GR7 aircraft that had been intended to support the offensive on the northern front. Lieutenant General Buzz Moseley, the USAF senior commander in the Middle East, proved extremely helpful in negotiating basing in the south for RAF aircraft, said Torpy. Soon PSAB and Ali al Salem Airbase in Kuwait were groaning under the weight of hundreds of US and British aircraft that were flowing into the theatre.

Fortunately, the Americans agreed to find space for RAF Tornados at their huge base at al Udeid in Qatar. They took off from RAF Lossiemouth in the middle of February, but the Qatari government took more than a week to make up its mind to approve the move and the RAF aircraft had to hold in Cyprus for a week, awaiting permission to move forward.[41]

The short notice switch from the north to the southern option had a significant impact on the RAF's air transport operations, requiring more sorties to flown in a very compressed time frame by the service's new C-17 Globemaster aircraft, as well as its veteran C-130s, Tristars, VC-10s and chartered airframes. "The RAF's contribution and the complexity of deploying the UK Air Component to nine air bases across the region, in very short timescales were exacerbated by the need to move the Land Component, including the Royal Marines, into Kuwait simultaneously" said Torpy.

Most of these deployments were to bases in the Gulf region, but the most diplomatically sensitive element in the RAF lay-down was the activation of Azraq airbase in Jordan, to host the Harrier GR7 close air support aircraft, Canberra RP9 photographic reconnaissance aircraft and Chinook HC2 transport helicopters. This was the first time RAF combat aircraft had operated from the Hashemite kingdom since the 1950s, and King Abdullah demanded that all details of the mission be kept out of the news media for fear of sparking unrest among his largely pro-Iraqi population.

The RAF contingent was to act in direct support of a US, British and Australian Special Forces task force that was planning to operate in western Iraq to neutralise Scud missiles threatening Israel. Already many of the special forces and RAF units participating in the counter-Scud operations from Jordan, as well Tornado GR4 crews from II Squadron, had been to Nevada for two highly secret exercises to rehearse the counter-Scud mission. The importance of this mission to the US war plan can be gauged by the fact that General Franks took the time to fly to Nevada to address the troops during one of these exercises in January, telling the assembled British and US aircrew and SF operatives that the "threat of use of weapons of mass destruction was very real."[42]

The Jordanians were acutely sensitive to being seen to be openly on side with the British and Americans against Iraq, and kept putting back agreeing to allow the RAF Harriers to operate from Jordan until the end of the first week of March. This resulted in 3 (Fighter) Squadron only being able to fly out of RAF Cottesmore on 9th March, which added to the worries of senior RAF officers about meeting the deadline to be ready for the war.[43] As Tornado F3 fighter, Tornado GR4 strike and Harrier GR7 aircraft arrived at the Middle East bases, they were cycled through missions patrolling the no-fly zones over Iraq. This gave the crews a chance to familiarise themselves flying into Iraqi surface-to-air missile (SAM) 'rings,' to experience getting locked on to, and then dodging in-bound missiles. The crews also got experience flying with their American colleagues, and an understanding of how their operators on E-3 AWACS radar control aircraft choreographed the flow of aircraft in and out of Iraqi air space.

Air Vice Marshal Torpy was keenly aware that the type of missions flown during no-fly zone patrols were very different from those expected to be required during the coming war.

"I knew that close air support (CAS) would be in heavy demand during the campaign so we placed significant emphasis on CAS training during the build up," he said.[44]

When the time came to strike at Iraq, the RAF aircrews would be fully integrated into the US Air Force operation, leading to the RAF being jokingly nicknamed the "USAF's 51st Wing". The senior RAF commander at the US run-CAOC, Air Vice Marshall Torpy, was so trusted by his US counterpart, Buzz Moseley, that he allowed him to sit in on video conferences involving Tommy Franks and President Bush.[45]

"The RAF tanker force ended up delivering some 40% of its fuel to the USN/USMC aircraft during the operation, our tactical reconnaissance asserts (Harrier, Tornado, Canberra PR9) and the E3D all made the vital contributions to the coalition air effort," said Torpy. "These were all capabilities that the USAF needed – they were not there just to make up the numbers!"

The British Army's logistics problems led to one incident that entered the mythology of the war, when a soldier's standard-issue combat boots melted in the Kuwaiti heat. He promptly wrote to complain to his parents, who in turn contacted a tabloid newspaper, which splashed it on its front page, alongside reports that the troops did not have enough toilet paper. This then played into a rare comic moment during a visit to 16 Brigade by the then Leader of the Conservative Party, Iain Duncan-Smith. It proved a rare chance to see one of the Labour government's spin doctors humiliated. The government was paranoid about negative publicity concerning troops not having enough equipment in the run-up to the war, and was trying to limit media contact with the troops. Duncan-Smith had supposedly agreed not to hold any 'political events' during his visit and Blair's press advisor Alistair Campbell classified this as including press conferences. When the Conservative leader started holding a press conference at one of 16 Brigade's camps, Simon Wren, a MOD spin doctor accompanying Duncan-Smith, telephoned his boss in Downing Street for instructions and was told in no uncertain terms to the stop the event happening. Wren turned to a group of paratroopers and ordered them to stop the press conference. One of the giggling soldiers replied, "what do you want us to do mate, shoot them?"[46]

The preparations for the media war were given considerable attention by Campbell and he was working with the Ministry of Defence, the Pentagon and the White House to build a co-ordinated UK-US media management machine.

This was to be a repeat of the organisation set up during the 1999 Kosovo and 2001 Afghan campaigns. Campbell had already been living and breathing the Iraq issue, as the Prime Minister had been trying to win over opinion in the UK and internationally, so the war itself was an extension of this effort.[47] Campbell's main effort was to ensure the military media relations organisation was fully under his control and no information was released that was 'off message'.

A cadre of spin doctors, loyal to Campbell, were assigned to the main press centres in Kuwait city, at the British divisional headquarters in the Kuwaiti desert and at the US Central Command headquarters in Qatar. A team of experts in 'political narratives' in Downing Street generated reams of 'lines to take.' There were briefing notes for the various spokesmen in the UK and Middle East, so they were all using the same message.

The heart of Campbell's media strategy was the embedding of some 150 British journalists, camera crews and radio technicians with British forces to report on frontline action. Every major army unit, RAF base and Royal Navy warship had embedded journalists attached, but the Ministry of Defence had complete 'shutter control' over all copy and images. Allegedly this was for operational security reasons but it also allowed Campbell and his media control organisation to switch coverage on and off to suit their agenda of the moment. On 15th March, the embedded media pool arrived in Kuwait on an aircraft chartered by the Ministry of Defence. They were then dispersed to their units, and many soldiers in the desert joked that they knew war was imminent because the press had arrived.

Chapter 6
THE BATTLE PLAN

What the British land force would do once it actually got to Kuwait was still a matter of great debate. Throughout February, Major General Robin Brims' staff worked closely with their counterparts in the US 1st Marine Expeditionary Force (I MEF) to fine-tune the war plans. These were tested in a series of war games and role-playing exercises. There was no time to conduct a major field exercise because 7 Armoured Brigade's vehicles did not start arriving until the first week of March. This meant the troops had to concentrate on low-level tactics and firing their small arms.

The main war plan was largely in place, with the capture of the oil infra-structure on the al Faw peninsular by 3 Commando Brigade now the UK's initial main effort. This operation was to begin at the start of the assault on Iraq. This would take place simultaneously as the main US land force crossed the border to secure a vast area of southern Iraq stretching from Basra to Nasiriyah, as a jump-off point for their drive on Baghdad. This land assault was intended to take place a day after the huge 'shock and awe' US and British air offensive to neutralise Baghdad's air defences.[1]

The Royal Marines were now under the direct command of 1 (UK) Division after its headquarters arrived in Kuwait at the beginning of February. To assist the commando brigade, the 4,000-strong US 15th Marine Expeditionary Unit (MEU) was placed under its temporary command. While the SEALs and 40 Commando, reinforced subsequently by 42 Commando, were tasked to assault the oil facilities on the al Faw, the 15th MEU would drive across the border from Kuwait to seize Iraq's main deep water port at Umm Qasr. In the initial planning, it was envisaged that 40 Commando would be flown by helicopter on to its objectives from the amphibious carriers HMS Ark Royal and HMS Ocean, with supporting units coming ashore by landing craft. The Royal Navy high command in London were looking forward to the service conducting its first major amphibious landing since the 1982 Falklands war.

As this attack was unfolding, the US I MEF would then storm across the border from Kuwait to capture the Rumaylah oil field complex and then turn east to screen Basra, to allow the US Army's V Corps to start its drive on Baghdad. In the wake of I MEF, 7 Armoured and 16 Air Assault Brigades were then to take over job of screening Basra and preparing to take on the Iraqi 6th Armoured Division, which was based to the north west of the city up the Euphrates valley. Brigadier Graham Binn's 7 Brigade was ordered to move to the outskirts of Basra, to take over the front line along the Shatt al Basra Canal from the US Marines and then await developments. There were a number of scenarios that might involve a move into Basra but it was made clear to General Brims by his direct superior officer, Lieutenant General James Conway, that he should avoid getting involved in street fighting that might result in the British troops getting bogged down or requiring the assistance of US troops. The 1 (UK) Division staff developed a series of decision points that would trigger a move into Basra.[2]

"Orders were to approach Basra and see what happens," recalled Binns.

"The US intent was not to enter urban areas. In order to achieve our mission we did not have to enter Basra. It was not important to drive into Basra to protect the flank of US forces advancing in Baghdad. Our plans to enter Basra were not very well developed. It was a case of reconnaissance by fire. We did not really know what elements of the Iraqi army would be left in Basra, whether they would fight, what would the reaction of the population would be. These are all things we discovered in the course of the operation. Fortunately we had time to do it while the US advanced on Baghdad."[3]

The focus of 1 (UK) Divison was the so-called 'British Box' or 'Basra Box', which encompassed the south-east corner of Iraq, running from Umm Qasr up along the Iranian border to al Amarah in Maysan province.

16 Brigade was tasked with taking over security of the Rumaylah oil field, which contained most of Iraq's oil reserves, from the US Marines and holding off the Iraqi 6th Division, who were north around al Qurnah. This area was criss-crossed with oil pipelines that could not be crossed by the heavy armoured vehicles of 7 Brigade without causing huge damage to the pipelines. At the same time, 16 Brigade was to hold its airborne task force, based on 1st Battalion, The Parachute Regiment (1 PARA), in reserve as the British armoured division's 'contingency force' to respond to unexpected events, such as a sudden collapse of the Iraqi regime, which might trigger a move out of the Basra Box towards Baghdad. This force was also told to be ready to mount a helicopter-borne assault of Qalat Sakir airfield. This was located to the northern edge of the box, and any assault could help protect the flank of I MEF's columns as they headed for Baghdad from counter attacks by an Iraqi armoured division based at al Amarah, to the east of the airfield.

The option was known as the 'northern expansion' in 1 (UK) Division's planning. Once the airfield was secured, a forward arming and refuelling point was to be set up to enable the attack helicopters, C-130 Hercules and Harrier jump jets of the US 3rd Marine Air Wing (MAW) to support the drive on Baghdad. The Qalat Sakir operation was by no means a certainty. It depended on the success of 7 Brigade around Basra and how the Iraqis reacted. The sensitivity of moving out to the edge of the box to take Qalat Sakir was such that it would have to be approved by the Prime Minister in London.

Confidence was high in 16 Brigade that the Iraqi resistance would collapse as soon as the first US and British troops crossed the border. Preparations were accelerated for the Qalat Sakir air manoeuvre and air drop operation by 1 PARA. Eight RAF Chinooks were allocated for the mission once they had completed landing the Royal Marines on the al Faw. US Marine AH-1W Cobra helicopter gunships were to fly close escort for the RAF helicopters, to neutralise any threats to the mission. 3rd MAW had promised lavish fixed wing air support from F/A-18 Hornet bombers and AV-8B Harrier jump jets. RAF and US C-130 Hercules were ordered to stand-by to fly Tactical Air Land Operations support for the mission after the helicopter-borne troops had secured the Iraqi airfield. Brigadier Jacko Page, 16 Brigade's commander, decided he would fly in behind the assault helicopters to set up his tactical headquarters to direct the battle against the Iraqi armoured division based in al Amarah.

The 1 (UK) Division commander, General Brims, was concerned about how the battle would develop and whether the Iraqis would use their much vaunted chemical weapons. Despite the media controversies over so-called 'dodgy dossiers' prepared by the Blair government, to justify the war, and the uncertainty over the state of Iraqis' chemical weapon arsenal, meant the British military acted as if they existed. In all the intelligence assessment and orders distributed to UK forces in Kuwait in the run up to the war, the Iraqi chemical threat was taken very seriously.

"We made assessments of Iraqi plans," recalled Brims.

"Kuwaiti [army officers] told me that the Iraqis always deployed their troops in the same places, to fight the Iranians, and we would be coming from a different direction. We thought Saddam would fight us a bit and then chuck in some chemical weapons. [Coalition troops crossing] the Euphrates River would be the trigger. The [Iraqis] would suck us into [bloody fighting] in urban areas [resulting in heavy civilian casualties] and then world opinion would end the war."[4]

"We were clear that we had to assume as the most dangerous option that Saddam had the potential to use tactical chemical weapons," said Air Marshal Brian Burridge, the UK national contingent commander in the Middle East. "We had studied the BBC coverage and other media reporting of the 1988 attack on Hallabja. We seriously believed he still had chemical weapons plus the intent to use them. We had watched the Al Kut military site where we believed we would find tactical, battlefield WMD tipped-artillery rounds, ready for out-loading and firing within about 45 minute of the order being given. This was an entirely plausible deduction but was not related to the claim in the infamous dossier that Cyprus was under threat of WMD attack. I have no knowledge of the evidence that led to that deduction."[5]

To counter the Iraqi chemical weapon threat, the British deployed some 600 personnel from the tri-service Joint NBC Regiment to the Middle East, including mobilised Territorial Army soldiers. The unit had teams of monitoring experts attached to each army brigade, as well as at RAF bases and with special forces detachments. H Squadron, of 2nd Royal Tank Regiment, was attached to the US Exploitation Task Force to participate in the hunt for Iraqi weapons of mass destruction. Some 100 personnel, including a mobile field laboratory from the Porton Down chemical weapons research centre, Defence Intelligence Staff experts, interrogators and forensic teams, were attached to the squadron. It mission meant it would operate throughout Iraq and was one of the few British units to reach Baghdad.[6]

H Squadron was expected by Downing Street and the senior leadership in the Ministry of Defence to play a major role in justifying the British participation in the Iraq war. Once WMD were found, plans were in place to helicopter a group of British journalists direct to the site to film the scene for rapid broadcast. This pool of journalists from the coalition press information press centre in Qatar were provided with NBC protective suits and placed on alert to be ready to deploy into Iraq.[7]

For the armoured forces of 7 Brigade, the focus was on preparing for fighting around Basra against heavily-armed Iraqi tank units. They were the only Iraqi units that were visible on what the intelligence officer of the Black Watch battlegroup, Captain Michael Williamson, termed 'the front of the hill'. There were indications about the presence of Fedayeen and other irregular forces in Basra but the assessment was that 7 Brigade would have to fight "conventional forces that had the ability to use unconventional weapons [nerve gas]". Iraqi conventional forces were not expected to put up strong resistance but they were equipped with powerful weapons, such as long-range artillery and rockets, that could inflict casualties and inhibit coalition operations.

"The front of the hill had been expected – now we were to find out what lay behind," recalled Williamson, of the mood immediately prior to crossing the border.[8]

While the US and British had very effective photographic reconnaissance aircraft and drones fitted with video cameras to beam live imagery to command posts, there was a major lack of information on the intent of Iraqi commanders and units around Basra. British commanders were not taking anything for granted and extreme caution governed their plans for entering Iraq. The intelligence void made them unwilling to risk their forces in the streets of Basra, until they had gained a firmer understanding of the situation. To help them in this task, a contingent from D Squadron of 22 Special Air Service Regiment was attached to 1 (UK) Division.[9] It was equipped with locally purchased pick-up trucks so they could move around southern Iraq and not be immediately identified as British forces. Their main task was to range ahead of the British division and verify a "ground truth" of the situation in Basra. British battlegroups were issued with identification photographs of the special forces vehicles in an attempt to prevent friendly fire incidents. A US Army special forces detachment was also attached to 7 Brigade with a similar mandate and also boasted a small contingent of hand-launched mini-drone aircraft.[10]

The American Central Intelligence Agency (CIA), assisted by operatives from the British Secret Intelligence Service, had been trying to penetrate southern Iraq for several months to recruit agents and other human intelligence sources. They distributed handheld Thuraya satellite telephones to tribesmen who claimed to be willing to offer intelligence.[11] In the immediate days before the war, the CIA ordered its paramilitary teams into Iraq to activate their agents. They began reporting back that the Iraqis were waiting impatiently to be liberated and Saddam's soldiers would not resist the invasion. British commanders, such as Brims and Binns, took this with a serious pinch of salt.

"I saw no evidence that made me believe that," commented Brims.

Air Marshal Burridge was equally skeptical, describing the CIA's belief that there would no resistance, as "wishful thinking."[12]

However, General Brims' operations orders for the invasion included detailed instructions on how the special forces could negotiate ceasefires with Iraqi troops.[13] This was to avoid the American approach to prisoners of war (POWs), which was either to let them go, or allow them to stay in their own barracks. The American proposals were deemed by the UK to be fraught with legal risk because they would have made the British legally responsible for feeding and protecting any prisoners. Local ceasefires would ensure that the Iraqi troops remained as combatants and would avoid these problems. The British orders envisaged two ways of implementing local ceasefires.

"Firstly the special forces who are forward and working to gain contact with Iraqi units would inform the Special Forces Liaison Element at Division Headquarters that they have established contact, and that the Iraqi unit wishes to negotiate a local ceasefire," said the orders.

"[The negotiators] will endeavour to get as high up the [Iraqi] chain of command as the local situation allows, in order to bring the maximum number of units under the agreement. The actual negotiation will be ideally done by the special forces escorting the Iraqi commander to the [British] Division or Brigade headquarters. The second way it could develop would be through a direct approach on the ground. Whenever the opportunity exists, local ceasefires should be established rather than accepting a formal surrender. This is in order to limit the scale of the prisoner of war problem and ease the transition to stability."

The al-Faw peninsular and the off-shore oil installations were the subject of a major strategic US intelligence-gathering operation. Real-time monitoring by Predator drones and signals intelligence was put in place to provide warning of an Iraqi attempt to sabotage the facilities. This meant the Royal Marines were provided with incredibly detailed photographic target packs, showing the position of oil infra-structure and Iraqi defensive positions. This was not foolproof and two Iraqi infantry company positions around the Al Faw oil terminal were not detected until after the Royal Marines landed.

Over more than a month, the Royal Marines and US Navy SEALs had rehearsed their operation in the Kuwaiti desert. It was an incredibly complex mission, involving air, land and naval forces all operating in the same battlespace, while artillery, naval gunfire, close air support and Tomahawk cruise missile were thrown into the mix. Commanders and their staffs needed to be sure their communications were able to cope with this complex environment. To help smooth the way forward, the US Navy provided the Commando Brigade headquarters with access to its secure email chat room, so British and American commanders could exchange messages in real-time.[14]

There was divergence between the British and American marines over how much effort had to be put into planning and preparing this operation, prompting a US officer to comment, "one British planner, Lieutenant Colonel James Hutton, Royal Marines, could not believe all of the time he spent at planning meetings with his American counterparts, especially the U.S. Navy Sea-Air-Land (SEALs) personnel, who, he thought, tried to plan for every last possibility. It was, he said, "mind-numbing" and inhibited flexibility. He added the thought that the Royal Marines might appear slack by comparison, but they also felt they had more leeway to react to situations as they developed."[15]

During the second week of March, Kuwait was engulfed by huge sandstorms that played havoc with the coalition invasion force. The storms were unlike anything that British troops had ever experienced before. Tents collapsed under the weight of sand, training exercises had to be cancelled and air operations reduced to non-essential tasks. The sandstorm appeared to heading out into the northern Arabian Gulf threatening the ability of Royal Navy helicopters to fly 40 Commando off HMS Ocean and Ark Royal. It was decided to pre-position 40 Commando ashore in Kuwait, much to the chagrin of the Royal Navy high command in London and Portsmouth.[16]

"In the end 3 Commando Brigade carried out a land to land air assault" commented Brims.

"It was the easier thing. There was no need to do it from ships. I was aware [of the pressure to do a full amphibious assault] and I told Jim Dutton [at the time], 'we are not here to make points, we here to do the right thing to get the job done, so do not play those cards'.

"The [Royal Marines] did a land-to-land air assault in RAF and US helicopters. It was entirely a land-based operation. I went to a conference after the war where a senior Royal Navy officer described the [assault] as an amphibious operation and I told Dutton who was sitting next to me that people were trying to re-write history."[17]

The 16 Brigade staff and main battalion command groups spent most of February taking part in a series of planning exercises or rock drills with the I MEF and 3rd MAW staffs to work out their role in the invasion. Close co-operation was established with the 5th Marine Regiment who would initially capture the Rumalyah oil field before handing it over to 16 Brigade. Once the Brigade's vehicles started arriving, two field exercises were held to test driving and navigating long distances in the desert.

For Brigadier Binns, the delays in bring all his equipment and vehicles ashore meant 7 Brigade's plans had to be re-jigged in the final hours before the war started. The Royal Scots Dragoon Guards (RSDG) had been selected to be one of the brigade's first battlegroups to cross into Iraq. This now looked unlikely because the Scottish regiment's tank crews and mechanics were still fitting the enhanced armour package to their vehicles. When the Scots soldiers finally got their tanks in working order morale improved dramatically.

"We test fired all weapon systems, including 120mm Depleted Uranium, giving us the confidence to know that everything was ready to go" said one RSDG squadron leader.

"We were certainly ready to take on the challenges facing us as we entered Iraq."[18]

The RAF were also now involved in making final preparations for their role in the US-led air offensive. British aircraft, backed by Tomahawk cruise missiles fired from Royal Navy nuclear submarines, were integrated into every aspect of the air campaign. Tasks included countering Iraqi ballistic missiles and supporting special forces in western Iraq, strategic attacks against regime targets in Baghdad, the neutralisation of the Iraqi Integrated Air Defence System and support to US and British land forces. This was a highly ambitious and enormous undertaking, with coalition aircraft scheduled to fly some 2,000 sorties on the first day of the war alone. This meant that the old rules of engagement (ROE) that had been used for no-fly zone (NFZ) operations since the end of the first Gulf War in 1991, were just not really practical any more and would need to be replaced.

"During NFZ operations target approval went back to PJHQ and the MOD," recalled the air component commander, Air Vice Marshal Torpy.

"Then we had the time to do it. Brian Burridge and I argued that this process would never keep pace during this operation. We couldn't have all target approvals remaining in the UK. We needed a mature level delegation to the in-theatre commanders. These arguments won the day and he and I were given delegated authority to clear specific target sets for attack."[19]

During the first two months of 2003, US Central Command considerably reduced the time allocated in its war plan for what it termed "Phase 2 shaping operations" by air power to devastate Iraqi ground units before US and British land forces were committed to battle. In Operation Desert Storm, it had taken almost two months of air strikes to inflict 50% attrition on the Iraqi army in Kuwait. In the original US plan, some 16 days were allocated to Phase 2 shaping operations and this was to be followed by four months of ground combat.

"This was much shorter than in Desert Storm, but was felt to be just adequate," said Torpy.

"However, the plan was being continuously developed and by February Phase 2 was down to five days. At that point the air component was facing concurrent tasks and potential resource issues. By March Phase 2 was reduced to only two days because of concerns about securing the Southern Oilfields, the vulnerability of Land Component in Kuwait and a feeling that a swift, integrated attacked would have maximum chance of dislocating Saddam's regime.[20]

This reduced time for Phase 2 raised concerns amongst senior US commanders about their ability to prepare the battlespace for the land invasion and, as a consequence they began to think about how the NFZ patrols could fulfil this task. The ultra-hawkish US Defense Secretary Donald Rumsfeld even made public statements enthusing about this. Rumsfeld wanted all Iraqi air defences totally neutralised, and any Iraqi ballistic missiles that were driven out of their barracks were to be considered hostile and bombed. London ordered Burridge and Torpy not to participate in these strikes, and limited RAF air strikes those that conformed to current UK rules of engagement, which only allowed RAF aircraft to hit air defence systems threatening aircraft enforcing the no-fly zone.[21]

There was also concern in London that an overly aggressive posture might undermine attempts to bring things to a peaceful conclusion. An example of this was when the US wanted to fly B-52 heavy bombers into the NFZ 'to send a message to the Iraqis'. "We vetoed it as being too aggressive," recalled Torpy.[22]

Rumsfeld then caused a very public 'wobble' with London on 11th March when he suggested in a media interview that British troops might not have to participate in the opening moves of the up-coming operations, and could only join in the peacekeeping phase after the war was over. Blair and Hoon were incensed and feared it would undermine their effort to win parliamentary support for the invasion, by giving the opponents of the war a way to avoid British troops joining in it.

The preparations for impending combat were taking up the majority of commanders' and soldiers' time in Kuwait, but there was still concern about what would happen in Iraq after the fall of Saddam's regime. These so-called 'soft power' issues would have major consequences once the fighting was over. Brims and other officers in 1 (UK) Division headquarters were becoming increasingly aware that their preparations for dealing with tens of thousands of POWs were not ready.

"POWs was a central major lesson from Operation Granby in 1991 but Operation Fresco [the fire fighting mission in the UK] limited the force available [to me for POW handling]" recalled Brims.[23] Lieutenant Colonel Nicholas Mercer, Brim's chief legal adviser, warned him that the situation was "legally amber".[24]

The Ministry of Defence and PJHQ initially did not give much attention to questions flowing up from Kuwait on the need for a dedicated guard force to look after the POWs.

"The US plan was just to let POWs go free," said Brims.

"Legally you can't do that. You have to look after them. It took some time for London to understand that you just could not by-pass them."[25]

Brims was eventually given a part of an infantry unit, the 1st Battalion, The Duke of Wellington's Regiment, to act as the POW guard force. This unit went through a period of being on and off the Operation Telic order of battle, due to the requirement to provide troops for firefighting duties. The General also re-designated the Regimental Headquarters of the Queen's Dragoon Guards to command his POW handling organisation, and its commanding officer was promoted to a full colonel to give him more clout with his American counterparts.[26] This allowed preparations to be made to receive POWs, but the Kuwaitis refused to allow the British to bring any captured Iraqi soldiers onto their territory, so a POW camp could not be physically built before the border had been crossed and enough territory secured to allow construction to begin. This would all have to be put in place once the war started.

The so-called 'day after question' had been vexing minds across the higher echelons of the British armed forces for almost a year. As the count-down to war quickened, the issue became more pressing. Many senior officers recorded their concerns and communicated them to the highest reaches of the British government and military chain of command. These ranged from concerns about humanitarian assistance to the civilian population to how to maintain public utilities. The main point of concern was the lack of any coherent political plan for the establishment of national and local administration to replace the Ba'ath Party regime. Without a plan to rapidly set up a new government a political vacuum could develop that would spiral out of control.

Major General Tim Cross, who had been appointed at the turn of the year to be the senior UK representative in the Pentagon's organisation that was being set up to administer post-war Iraq, was so concerned about the lack of preparation for so-called Phase IV operations that he went to Downing Street to brief both Blair and Campbell in March 2003. Major General Whitley in Kuwait also made his views know, as did other officers working in the CENTCOM headquarters in Qatar. The US land commander, General McKiernan, shared Whitley's concerns and made him his 'deputy for Phase IV' to try to increase the importance of the issue.[27] Brims raised his fears in January 2003 when he was doing his 'monster estimate' to develop his plans for the war.

"At that point I said there was no plan for Phase IV" he recalled. "I put that in writing."[28]

The British planning for the post-war occupation of south-eastern Iraq did not envisage a strong force remaining in the country after the end of combat operations. It was hoped other nations could be persuaded to provide forces to reduce the size and cost of any British occupation force.

"I was told before I went out [to Kuwait] that when we did phase IV it would be with a single brigade," said Brims.

"It was to be 7 Brigade and it would then be replaced by another force of the same strength. I was told this by General Sir Mike Jackson [head of Land Command and then Chief of the General Staff from 1st February 2003] and [the Chief of Defence Staff Admiral Sir Mike] Boyce.[29]

It is now apparent that all those officers who raised the 'day after question' did not receive substantive answers from their political and military masters in London. The fate of post war Iraq would lie in the hands of the Americans who were providing the dominant military force and who were aiming to capture the Iraqi capital. Those in Washington who had control of this issue just were not interested in the concerns of the British. But other factors were in play. David Johnson, who worked in Hoon's office in London, summed up the mood at the time.

"I do think we [in the government] collectively devoted insufficient effort to it, and with insufficient urgency. It is inevitable that people dealing both with planning for war and planning for the post-war give the priority to the former, which is always more pressing. Personally I must confess that in Autumn 2002 anything to do with Phase IV was always the last task of the day, and the one most likely to split into the next day, and so on….."[30]

He highlighted that although billions of pounds were set aside to pay for the invasion no money was allocated by the Treasury to pay for rebuilding southern Iraq.

"Once we are well down the planning route and tea and medals are in sight, we are too keen to get on with the war to disturb Ministers with the unwelcome thought that we should not proceed further without setting aside large sums for reconstruction," he recorded in a document released by the Chilcot inquiry.

"I reckon money has also been the biggest crippling factor in our efforts to exert any kind of influence on US decision-making [for Phase IV]."[31]

The count down to war gathered momentum in the middle of March when US President George Bush declared that the UN diplomatic route had run its course. General Franks gathered his senior commanders in Qatar in 14th March, including the top British commanders, for a planning conference to set the timetable for the start of the war. The scene was set when Franks played the Russell Crowe "On My Command, Unleash Hell" sequence from the Hollywood movie *Gladiator,* kicking off the briefing.

It emerged that Bush was going to gather coalition leaders in the Azores on 17th March to issue an ultimatum to Saddam and his sons to leave Iraq within 48 hours. Then the war would start on 21st March with the 'Shock and Awe' opening air bombardment of the Super Missile Engagement Zone around Baghdad. The following day the ground offensive would begin.[32]

Later on 14th March, the commander of I MEF, General Conway, held a morale-boosting parade for British troops in a desert camp under arches made from artillery gun barrels. In an exercise in psychological warfare 1 PARA made a parachute drop – while wearing full NBC protective clothing - to deceive the Iraqis into thinking thousands of British paratroopers would soon be descending onto strategic locations. Bush's decision placed Blair in a dilemma as the British prime minister had yet to secure parliamentary backing for going to war. A vote was called on 18th March and there was great uncertainty if the government would win enough votes. One cabinet minister resigned, another was wavering and other Labour MPs were in open revolt during the marathon nine hour-long debate.

In Kuwait and around the Middle East, senior commanders could only watch the tense debates in the House of Commons in disbelief. Their troops were still making frantic preparations to get their equipment ready for action and complete last minute training. During the day, the 2nd Royal Tank Regiment's Challenger 2 tanks drove into a Kuwait barracks to beginning 'bombing,' or loading their war ammunition, including their Depleted Uranium rounds.[33]

Although American commanders repeatedly said they understood the British predicament, at this late stage the prospect of British forces not joining in the invasion would have caused a serious breakdown in relations with the UK's major ally. British troops had been allocated key roles in the opening phases of the US war plan and if the government lost the vote, the Americans would have to make last minute changes to replace British troops, potentially causing a delay in the start of the war and putting other US soldiers at risk. The British forward troops were only a few kilometres from Iraqi artillery positions and at risk if war broke out around them.[34]

Sitting in his tent in the 1 (UK) Division headquarters in the Kuwaiti desert, Brims recalled watching the war debate on satellite television and wondering what he would do if the government lost. He admitted not having any idea how to deal with an unprecedented situation.

"What would I and my 25,000 friends in the Kuwaiti desert have done?" he mused.

"I remember watching the proceeding [in the House of Commons] from my command post in Qatar, wondering how I would explain a defeat of the Government to my US counterpart," recalled the overall UK contingent commander Air Marshal Brian Burridge.

"The proceeding Sunday's anti-war demonstration in London of almost a million people, with shades of Suez about it, had already given us all food for thought. But with the benefit of hindsight, it is also a fact that the intelligence on Iraq's real capability and, more importantly, Saddam's real intention was dubious. Hence the debate itself took place on a shaky premise."[35]

In the end Blair carried the day, with 412 votes to 149. British troops were going to war. After President Bush declared on 18th March that the Iraqis had not met his demands to disarm, all coalition forces in Kuwait were placed on a heightened alert. The readiness of British troops in Kuwait was raised to 12 hours notice to move and they were alerted to an increased threat of Iraqi gas attacks. British commanders now moved quickly to square away their last minute preparations and get their troops ready to move. Brims asked his brigade commanders if they were ready to move forward into Iraq. 3 Commando and 16 Brigades were well placed but 7 Brigade was still getting its tanks and other armoured vehicles ready. The 7 Brigade commander was confident that three of his four battlegroups were fit to go to into action, with all their tanks and armoured vehicles in fighting shape, with their upgraded armour and full ammunition loads. So he replied positively to Brims.

"My judgement was proved right" recalled Binns. "In many ways we over insured."[36]

General Brims explained, "sometimes you have to be positive . . . you are dealt a hand of cards . . . you would like to have 52 cards in the deck… But, in this case, we had actually declared readiness with 46 cards."[37]

In desert assembly areas, the commanding officers gathered their troops together for morale boosting speeches. There were a spattering of veterans from the 1991 Gulf conflict, but the majority of the officers and troops had never been to war before. Lieutenant Colonel Paterson of the Fusiliers stood on top of a FV432 armoured personnel carrier in front of a thousand troops of his battlegroup. According to the Fusiliers regimental journal, "he left all ranks in no doubt that if opposed we would provide devastating fire onto the enemy, but that we were not at war with the Iraqi people and must behave decently at every stage."[38]

Chapter 7

ACROSS THE BORDER

Operation Telic formally began at 6pm (Iraqi time) on 19th March 2003 when the rules of engagement for RAF aircraft patrolling the no-fly zones were changed, to allow them to conduct offensive missions throughout Iraq.[1] However, 22 hours earlier British ground troops had already entered western Iraq, as part of a covert mission to pre-empt any attempt by Saddam Hussein to fire Scud missiles at Israel. US intelligence said there were 10 Scud launcher vehicles armed with 40 missiles somewhere in western Iraq.[2] As darkness fell on 18th March the first patrols of 22 Special Air Service (SAS) Regiment crossed from Jordan into western Iraq. The move was choreographed to take place after the House of Commons vote to authorise military action against Iraq.

"It was minutes after the vote in the House of Commons," recalled Air Marshal Brian Burridge, the UK Joint Commander in the Middle East.

"They would not have gone if the vote had gone the other way."[3]

The 60 troops from B Squadron, SAS, headed in a north-easterly direction towards the town of Al Qaim in central Iraq. They met no resistance from Iraqi troops in the gloom as they drove across an empty desert.[4] A few hours later in the early hours of 19th March, US Delta Force operatives crossed into Iraq from Saudi Arabia on a similar mission and US Army Special Operations Forces pushed over the border from Jordan. The idea was for the British and US special forces to be inside Iraq and ready to strike when war was publicly announced by President George Bush, so they could catch the Iraqi missile batteries as they were moving into their firing positions.

During the evening of 19th March a 'noisy insertion' along Iraq's western and southern border began with US special forces MH-6 Little Bird helicopter gunships launching a series of co-ordinated rocket and machine gun raids to destroy 31 Iraqi border forts. Simultaneously, a US Air Force F-15E Strike Eagle directed a GBU-28 laser guided bomb to destroy the Iraqi air defence operations centre at H-3 airfield inside Iraq, across the Jordanian border.[5] In the space of a few hours the Iraqi early warning network across the west of their country was blinded. On the ground, additional columns of British, Australian and US special forces driving heavily-armed trucks and Land Rovers pressed into Iraq after blowing holes in the sand 'berm,' or rampart marking the border. Their mission was to find and destroy Iraq's arsenal of Scud ballistic missiles to prevent a repeat of the episode in 1991, when Saddam had tried to fracture the US-led coalition by firing the missiles at Israel.

This repeat of the so-called 'Great Scud Hunt' was far better prepared than the 1991 version, with dedicated close air support and reconnaissance aircraft being sent to Jordan to work hand in hand with the ground element.[6] Crucially, the command of the mission was placed in the hands of the US Middle East air commander, Lieutenant General Buzz Moseley. The British component of this mission, dubbed Operation Row, would eventually draw some 200 Royal Marines of 45 Commando and more than 100 RAF personnel from II Squadron RAF Regiment, operating across western and central Iraq in support of some 400 SAS and Special Boat Service troops.[7]

Further south in Kuwait, US special forces, Central Intelligence Agency (CIA) paramilitary units and British SAS teams were also moving into Iraq to provide 'eyes on ground' to coalition commanders and to try to negotiate the surrender of Iraqi generals and units. Operating in civilian pick-up trucks would allow them to weave past Iraqi border posts and then blend with the local population. A few dozen soldiers of D Squadron of 22 SAS headed into Basra, Zubayr and onto the al Faw peninsular to begin collecting what was termed 'human intelligence.' A handful of Special Intelligence Service or MI6 operatives went with them in a bid to establish links with local Iraqis opposed to the Baghdad regime. This was a vital mission as the British government and military commanders had no idea about the 'political landscape' of the region they would soon have to police.[8]

At this point, British and US commanders still envisaged that the main shock and awe air offensive against Baghdad to win air supremacy would not start until the night of 21st March, followed by the deliberate land invasion the next day. But during the evening of 19th March, the US CIA received information that Saddam was meeting key subordinates at a place called Dora Farms to the south of Baghdad. President George W. Bush was persuaded to launch a pre-emptive air and missile strike in a bid to kill his Iraqi counter-part. He authorised an air strike by F-117 stealth fighters and Tomahawk cruise missiles on the farm, but it later emerged that the intelligence was faulty and the Iraqi leader was nowhere near the location.

The air strike meant the Iraqis might start retaliating against targets in Kuwait at anytime, so General Franks decided to completely re-jig the sequence and timing of his main land attacks. He moved his land assault forward to the night of 20th March but the shock and awe air offensive was too complicated to move, so it would go in as scheduled on the evening of 21st March. Just after dark on 20th March, US Army and Marine Corps columns were to start bulldozing lanes through the sand ramp or berm along the Iraq-Kuwait border to open routes northwards. By dawn thousands of US armoured vehicles were to be heading towards Basra and Baghdad.

Simultaneously with the US land assault, 3 Commando Brigade's planned attack on the al Faw to capture Iraq's oil installations would go ahead. The main objective of the operation was to secure intact a number of key oil installations to prevent their sabotage and the release of crude oil into the northern Arabia Gulf. This was considered a strategic objective by US military commanders and as a result a large contingent of US Naval Special Warfare forces were given the task of actually seizing the oil installations themselves. 3 Brigade was then to begin to seize the Al Faw area to prevent any Iraqi attempt to regain control of the facilities and to secure the right flank of the main coalition land force, which was to advance northwards from Kuwait to secure the southern Iraqi city of Basra.

As the British special forces were driving across the largely empty western Iraqi desert looking for trouble, in Kuwait the 26,000 strong main British land forces was mustering from its tented camps and preparing to move forward into southern Iraq. The western desert had all the classic features of an Arabian desert – wide open spaces, soft sands, few roads and towns, complete with nomadic Bedouin tribes. Southern Iraq was the exact opposite, with a combination of urban sprawl, decaying industrial infra-structure, river systems and marsh land. This terrain would prove to be a significant challenge for the advancing British troops and determine the nature of the battle to control Basra.

On the eastern edge of the British area of responsibility was the Al Faw Peninsular and its oil infrastructure. Although called a peninsular, it was little more than a salt marsh with the Shatt-al-Arab waterway to its north and the Khawr Ahd Allah (KAA)/Khaw az Zubayr (KAZ) waterways to its south. This was the access route to Iraq's only deep water port at Umm Qasr. The peninsular was completely flat and bare, giving no cover to troops except for palm groves along the southern bank of the Shatt-al-Arab. The KAZ was then connected to the Basra canal that ran along the western edge of the city. These waterways provided a natural line of defence for the city and road traffic to reach the al Faw had to travel almost into Basra city before being able to get on the Peninsular. Basra itself was a huge sprawling city of over a million people, although no one was really sure of its exact population. It was a mix of old Ottoman, British colonial buildings and 1980s high-rise apartment blocks.

To the west of Basra were the smaller towns of Zubayr and Rumalyah. These were the main towns where workers in the Rumalyah oil field lived. These were some of the few Sunni Muslims in southern Iraq and many had been implanted by the Ba'athist regime in Baghdad to ensure the key oil industry remained loyal.

This area was criss-crossed by elevated oil pipelines connecting oil storage sites around Rumalyah with a large pumping station at al Faw, which sent more than half of Iraq's oil exports to two off shore terminals, known as the Kahr al Amaya and Mina al Bakr or the KAAOT and MABOT, where oil tankers could take on the black gold. These pipelines were a major obstacle to movement by vehicles except through a handful of crossing points. Mobile bridges were needed to allow vehicles to cross these pipelines. To the north of the oil field, the al-Hammar canal provided a west-to-east obstacle that blocked routes north into Maysan province. North of the al-Hammar canal was the southern reaches of the River Euphrates, which in turn flowed into the Shatt-al-Arab north of Basra.

Maysan encompassed most of the famous marshes that were flooded by the Baghdad regime in the 1980s and 1990s to deny sanctuary to rebellious tribes. The region's towns and its capital, al Amarah, were now protected by a series of earth works and water was diverted into a network of irrigation canals.

It was only possible to move around central Maysan by road or helicopter. The east of the province along the border with Iran turned into more open desert, but it was blighted by old bunkers, earth works, trenches and minefields left over from the Iran-Iraq war in the 1980s.

The Iraqi army and security forces historically had been positioned to defend the region from Iranian attack. One division was based in al Amarah defending Maysan, another was positioned around Basra and an armoured division was positioned in the centre of the region near al Qurnah, ready to launch a counter punch against any incursion. Apart from a line of watch towers, manned by poorly-trained conscript soldiers, and the sand berm on the Kuwait border, it was not defended in any serious way. The oil infrastructure was protected by small detachments of troops but they were only really protecting them from looting or civil unrest.[9] Across the border were the massed forces of the US 3rd Army, with the army's V Corps and the 1st Marine Expeditionary Force (I MEF), containing some 100,000 combat troops, with several hundred M1A1 Abrams tanks, Bradley fighting vehicles and AH-64 Apache helicopter gunships.

The surprise US air attack on the Dora Farms also caught the British and American forces in Kuwait unawares. During the night senior commanders spend hours re-jigging their attack plans, issuing new orders and monitoring the progress of the complex logistic preparations needed to get everything ready to attack 24 hours sooner than expected. Working in the Combined Air Operations Centre in Saudi Arabia, Air Vice Marshal Glenn Torpy said this prompted a period of frantic activity.

"The opening phase of the war re-sequenced in short order," he recalled. "This blindsided everyone, including us".[10]

In the Kuwaiti desert, 7 Armoured and 16 Air Assault Brigades had moved out of its tented camps during the night of 19th/20th March to a number of tactical assembly areas to reduce their vulnerability to Iraqi ballistic missile and rocket attacks. In the middle of the morning of the 20th, the Iraqis fired two ballistic, and one cruise missile at the Kuwait desert prompting US troops to don their full chemical warfare protective equipment on several occasions. Royal Tank Regiment and RAF Regiment experts from the Joint Nuclear Biological and Chemical Regiment had set up area monitoring gear across 1 (UK) Division's bases in northern Iraq. They quickly realised these missiles were not fitted with deadly chemical warheads, so no British troops were ordered to don their full chemical warfare suits for extended periods, according to the regiment's commanding officer, Lieutenant Colonel Patrick Kidd. US troops who did not have this equipment spent nine days in the uncomfortable protective suits.[11]

The Iraqi 225th Missile Brigade was well prepared for its attack, and had managed to position its launchers around southern Iraq undetected by coalition intelligence. One of its Seersucker cruise missile launchers was even able to be positioned at the southern tip of the Al Faw Peninsular to enable it to fire at coalition bases in northern Kuwait during 20th March.[12]

An Ababil-100 launcher in a suburb of Basra took two shots at Kuwait during the morning of 20th March, and was spotted by an SAS team working in the city. The team followed the launcher as it drove from its firing point to a secret hide under camouflage nets strung up between houses. They radioed the US Marines to dispatch an air strike to take out the missile launcher.

A pair of Marine F/A-18 Hornet fighter bombers were scrambled from Al Jaber airbase in Kuwait to hit the target. When they arrived over the target they established contact with what one of the airmen, Captain Ed Bahret, called an 'SAS agent'. According to the pilot, the SAS team did not have a laser designator to 'paint' the target and generate a precise co-ordinate. The airmen said their rules of engagement prevented them attacking a target in a populated area without precise laser guidance.[13]

"We ended up leaving the area, and the target was never serviced," recalled Bahret.

"I know the SAS operative was more than a little frustrated, as he had eyes on the launcher. He had no laser designator, so we would have been forced to self-designate. In order to do this with any accuracy we had to be able to see the target with our sensor, which we could not – even after six passes over Basra."

The US Marine and British command was sent into crisis during the afternoon after a CIA agent reported that he had seen Republican Guard T-72s heading south through Basra to confront the Americans as they crossed the border. Hours were spent warning troops of the threat and re-organising the attack plans. When aircraft were sent to look for the mystery column, they found no sign of the tanks but the incident just added to the tension as the moment came to join battle.[14]

In the early evening of 20th March, the US assault force literally rolled over the border. Helicopter gunships, Hornet bombers and artillery batteries devastated the Iraqi watchtowers, before the tank columns moved north. The 105m Light Guns of 7th Royal Horse Artillery fired in support of their US Marine counterparts as they blasted Iraqi border defence posts. The Iraqi brigade positioned south of Zubayr and Rumalyah was decimated by the extreme violence unleashed on it. Hundreds of soldiers fled their posts and others wandered the deserts offering to surrender to the passing American columns.

While the US Army's V Corps turned north-west and headed for Baghdad, via Nasiriyah, the US Marines drove north to seize the Rumalyah oil field to prevent it being sabotaged. Accompanying the Marines were teams of British civilian oil experts, who were to assess any damage caused by Iraqi demolition charges, or to help advise on how to defuse any explosives. Chemical warfare specialists from G Squadron, 1st Royal Tank Regiment (1 RTR) also moved forward with the US Marines.[15]

By early morning the Marines had secured all their objectives across southern Iraq, capturing the Rumalyah oil fields with minimal resistance. A handful of oil fires had been lit by the Iraqis to try to blind coalition thermal night vision sights but the arriving troops found no systematic attempt underway to destroy the vital oil field.

The Marines' 5th Regimental Combat Team (RCT) was assigned to secure the oil fields and to the east, 7th RCT had captured Basra International Airport and positioned other troops along the length of the Basra Canal to secure the western access to the city of Basra. The Iraqi army seemed to have melted away, but there were numerous skirmishes with irregular fighters dressed in civilian clothes, who fired at the Marines from moving cars around Zubayr and at the canal bridges. In one of these incidents the British television journalist Terry Lloyd was shot and killed by the Marines.[16]

The first wave of the assault saw US Navy and Polish special forces delivered by US Navy and US Air Force special forces helicopters on to two offshore oil terminals. More US Navy special forces were at the same time being landed by USAF MH-53M Pave Low special forces helicopters on the al Faw, to secure the manifold metering station and two pipeline heads that flowed out to terminals. They captured several Iraqi troops and a quantity of explosives but the oil sites had not been rigged for demolition. There appeared to be no evidence that any orders had been sent to them to commit deliberate sabotage.

As this was happening, follow-up waves of troops from 3 Commando Brigade were preparing to move by air, land and sea into the upper reaches of the al Faw to shut off any Iraqi counter-move against the initial assault force. The first wave of troops would be provided by Lieutenant Colonel Gordon Messenger's 40 Commando. A highly dashing and charismatic figure, Messenger gave off an aura of total confidence that many of his troops thought he would walk away from the coming battle without a scratch. He would need all his powers of leadership over the next two weeks, as his troops soon found themselves in some of the toughest fighting ever experienced by the Royal Marines since the 1982 Falklands war.

To control this complex operation 3 Brigade's commander, Jim Dutton, and his headquarters had to establish extensive communications links to the US Naval Special Warfare Group's headquarters at Kuwait's naval base, supporting air forces, and frigates proving naval gunfire support. One unique feature of the operation for British forces was the arrival in the headquarters of US liaison teams, to provide real-time video downlinks to intelligence, surveillance, targeting and reconnaissance assets, such as the MQ-1 Predator drone and P-3C Orion maritime patrol aircraft. In the crowded airspace above the al Faw the de-confliction of aircraft providing close air support, support helicopters moving troops and supplies, artillery fire and naval gunfire support would be a particular challenge for Brigadier Dutton and his staff.[17]

The old military maxim that 'no plan survives initial contact with the enemy' certainly applied to the al Faw operation. The assault had originally been conceived as a surprise coup de main, but President Bush's decision to authorise an air strike on Saddam Hussein in Baghdad ahead of the main attack denied

3 Brigade the element of surprise. The initial commando raids by the US and Polish special forces achieved their objectives with little resistance, and they then called in follow-up troops of 3 Brigade. The landing zones for 40 Commando soon came under fire but no British helicopters were hit.

"The air assault on the al Faw peninsula was unique - I've never seen helicopters used so aggressively in a plan," said Wing Commander David Prowse.[18] As commander of the RAF's 18 (Bomber) Squadron, Prowse led the first wave of Boeing Chinook HC2s through sand storms in the opening hours of the operation.

"All our aircraft and people came out unscathed," said Prowse.

"When I first briefed my inner circle on the plan there was stunned silence, after two months training everyone was ready for it. The plan changed very little, it flew as briefed to me. We knew the risks, that gave us a high confidence level."[19]

Squadron Leader Steve Carr was nominated to plan and lead the first wave of five Chinooks that were to land the commandos during the opening hours of the conflict. The veteran Chinook pilot was flying the Squadron's helicopter, with the call-sign Bravo November, which had seen heroic service in the Falklands campaign. It was consider a lucky mascot by ground crew of 18 (B) Squadron and it invariably was picked to fly the most dangerous missions.

"I was flying Bravo November on the first wave," recalled Carr.

"I am not sure if it was a total coincidence but the engineers might have arranged it."[20]

"Visibility was down to 1,000 to 1,500 metres," said Carr.

"It was very dark, there was low cloud and the air was full of dust thrown up by artillery fire and northbound American tank columns. Our night vision goggles were not much use. We were flying at a hundred feet or lower and then we descended to fifty to seventy feet when we entered Iraq."

"Each aircraft had 42-45 Marines on board and their war bergens [large rucksacks], each weighing in at around 60kg! We had removed all the seats, so the troops were all stood up, holding on to ropes that we had strung across the cabin roof – it was just like on the London Underground at rush hour. Once we'd been cleared into the landing site, the aircraft went in in three waves, two pairs and a singleton, each element about one minute apart. The Marines must have been pumped up, as they were out of my aircraft in 12 seconds. Within two minutes 215 Marines were on the ground."[21]

Carr and his colleagues returned to the assembly area in Kuwait to pick up support vehicles and underslinging them for the flight to al Faw.

"On the second run we were in a fire fight, with tracer all over the place. Fortunately, all of it seemed to be outgoing."

The Chinooks were not the only aircraft in the air over al Faw, and the 18 (B) Squadron pilots had to carefully co-ordinate their missions to prevent accidents.

"You know it is for real when you are talking on the radio to two American AC-130s Spectre gunships in orbit above you engaging some Iraqis who are firing at the Marines from entrenched positions" said Carr.

"It was quite exciting. It was a busy piece of air space."

On the ground Colonel Messenger's troops were soon in position around the oil pumping station, and were rounding up 230 hapless Iraqi conscripts. This phase of the attack went like clockwork, so much so that the Reuters news agency embedded journalist Peter Graff embarked on the Royal Navy carrier HMS Ark Royal, was able to file his story about the assault, based on a pre-war planning briefing without having to change any details.[22]

Back in northern Kuwait, a wave of 26 US Marine Corps CH-53 Sea Stallion and CH-46 Sea Knight helicopters were being marshalled in the desert next to 42 Commando's base to make the short hop across the KAA waterway to drop Lieutenant Colonel Buster Howes' Royal Marines in blocking positions. Howes was an intense officer with a reputation for running a very tight organisation. He had fought with the US Marines during the first Gulf War in 1991 across the same terrain and later rose to lead the Royal Marines.

At the same time as the helicopter assault would go in, US Navy LCAC hovercraft were also preparing to carry an armoured column of the Queen's Dragoon Guard's (QDG) across to the al Faw. US Marines of the 15th Marine Expeditionary Unit (MEU) had also started their land and helicopter assault to seize the port of Umm Qasr to open routes into the al Faw by river ferry. The opening of a secure land supply route depended on 1 (UK) Division seizing bridges over the upper reaches of the KAA. These moves were considered essential to protect the lightly armed troops of 40 Commando being vulnerable to an Iraqi armoured counter-attack out of Basra city.

The next phase of the operation unravelled when a CH-46E carrying elements of 3 Brigade's Reconnaissance Force crashed in a sand storm, killing all on board. The US helicopter crew appeared to lose control of their helicopter in the storm as hundreds of horrified Royal Marines of 42 Commando watched. Four US Marine aircrew and eight Royal Marines from the Brigade Reconnaissance Force died in the crash. Subsequent US and British inquiries could not agree as to whether the cause was pilot disorientation in dust or a technical problem with the helicopter.[23] Until the weather cleared, the US Marine aviators refused to continue the insertion of 42 Commando.

For more than six hours the troops on the al Faw were unsupported, until Brigadier Dutton could organise more RAF Chinooks and Puma HC1s of the Joint Helicopter Force, held in reserve in Kuwait, to be brought forward and carry 42 Commando into action. Colonel Howes' men ended up making their air assault onto the southern shore of the al Faw in daylight but fortunately there were no Iraqi troops near their landing zone. This insertion was given added importance, after the first QDG's light armoured vehicles could not come ashore from their LCACs after US Navy SEALS found the landing beach was mined, frustrating plans to bring armoured support to 40 Commando.

Meanwhile the 15th MEU took far longer than expected to clear Umm Qasr, delaying the opening of overland supply routes to the al Faw. Its battles in the port were broadcast live on Sky News for several hours on 20th March, much to the chagrin of British officers in the 1 (UK) Armoured Division and 3 Brigade headquarters. They lost count of the times the US Marines claimed to have secured the town.[24] With Umm Qasr still disputed, the Royal Marines on al Faw had to rely on helicopter re-supply to bring in reinforcements and supplies from the amphibious task group off shore. In the first 72 hours of the war, 355 under-slung loads of ammunition, water, rations and medical supplies were hooked onto helicopters from the amphibious warfare ship HMS Ocean in the northern Arabian Gulf.[25] The guns of 29 Commando Regiment remained on the Kuwaiti Bubyan island to provide covering fire in case of an Iraqi counter-attack. Royal Artillery Phoenix drones flew scouting missions up the peninsular to look for any signs of enemy troops, and overhead Royal Navy Sea King ASAC7 radar helicopters flew continuous patrols to detect movement by Iraqi tanks. Early on the morning of 22nd March, a relief helicopter was on its way from HMS Ark Royal to take over from the on-station Sea King, when they collided over the Northern Arabian Gulf. A navy inquiry failed to find any explanation why the helicopters flew into each other, with the loss of six Royal Navy and one US Naval aviator.[26]

On al Faw, 40 Commando moved to expand its bridgehead overnight on 21st/22nd March by mounting a company sized assault into al Faw town, to seize the Ba'ath Party headquarters and neutralise local leaders loyal to the regime in Baghdad. Two Royal Marines were injured in the attack when a household cooking gas bottle exploded, setting them on fire. By the early hours of 22nd March, the US Marines had made enough progress in Umm Qasr to allow C Squadron of the QDG to be shuttled across the KAA in landing craft of 539 Assault Squadron. According to the regimental history of the QDG this journey was far from straightforward, and it showed the precarious nature of the 3 Brigade position on the al Faw.

"A number of the vehicles bogged in at the landing point due to an unfortunate appreciation of the tide state, including one of the command vehicles, which were carrying the ANGLICO [US Marine Corps artillery and air control] team," said the account of the regiment on Operation Telic.[27]

"The crew learnt new evacuation drills escaping through the commander's hatch when the vehicle sank in an uncharted channel. Those of the squadron ashore on dry land then advanced along Route Stonehouse, and joined up with 40 Commando. To complicate matters further as the tide went out, the crews of the bogged vehicles realised that the landing point was in fact a prepared minefield and anti-tank mines surrounded them. Sergeant McDonnell and the Engineer Reconnaissance Sergeant cleared a safe lane through the mud, allowing the crew to leave their stranded vehicle. As the squadron advanced East along Route Stonehouse, Guided Weapons Troop and [3 Commando Brigade] Lynx missile helicopters, working with the Squadron, destroyed unoccupied but intact bunkers, artillery and anti-aircraft positions along the way. A very close shave was had by Corporal Armstrong who was patrolling on foot near his vehicle when he felt a trip-wire around his neck. His operator cut the wire and traced it back to an anti-personnel mine. In the early hours of the 24th March the Squadron's lead troops linked up with 40 Commando's forward positions."[28]

The arrival of the QDG was relief to 40 Commando, but this line of communication was very precarious. The tides meant the 539 Squadron landing craft ferry was only open for two hours a day. This was a major problem when it came to delivering fuel to drive the QDG's Scimitar light tanks and the Land Rovers of the Royal Marines' Brigade Reconnaissance Force, which were engaged in a cat and mouse battle with Iraqi tanks hidden in palm groves along the Shatt-al Arab waterway. The Commando Logistic Regiment had to resort to hitching 2000 litre fuel bladders to Chinooks and flying them direct to the QDG when they were on the verge of running out of fuel.[29]

In northern Kuwait, the troops of 7 and 16 Brigade could only wait until the US Marines decided they were ready to be relieved by the British. During the afternoon of 21st March, the Marines signalled they were ready to begin the relief in place, or RIP, with 1 (UK) Division. This was a complex manoeuvre involving British troops moving forward and then taking over the positions held by the Marines. Then the American troops would in turn advance northward across the area held by the British and head to Baghdad. The potential for confusion and friendly fire was immense, so staff officers and liaison teams were swapped between the Americans and British to make sure things went smoothly and safely.

According to Major General Robin Brims, the commander of 1 (UK) Division, the mission of his troops had not changed since the start of the war.

"We were to secure the [American] flank and secure oil fields, that was our mission," he recalled.

"There was never any intention to go into Basra city."[30]

For a day, the British Army waited in their assembly areas for the Americans to secure their objectives in southern Iraq. During the evening orders were issued for 16 Brigade to move forward and Royal Engineers of 51 Field Squadron began bulldozing a breach in the Iraqi berm in the early hours of 21st March. Scimitars of the Household Cavalry crossed into Iraq during the evening of 21st March to link up with the 5th Marine Regiment, which had secured the Rumalyah oil field complex. Iraqi resistance had been swiftly overwhelmed by the US Marines and they had captured the oil field before the elements loyal to Saddam Hussein had time to conduct any sabotage.[31]

The Royal Irish under the command of the well-known Lieutenant Colonel Tim Collins, were the first to conduct a RIP with the Americans and soon afterwards 3 PARA moved through the breach to take over security of the northern part of the oil field complex. As this was happening, 3 Regiment AAC began dispatching aviation reconnaissance patrols northwards to the Rumalyah bridge over the al-Hammar canal, to try to give warning of a counter-attack by the

Iraqi 6th Armoured Division, which was based to the north of the canal. At first there was little sign of enemy activity. Although the oil field infrastructure was secured intact, the whole of the 16 Brigade area was littered with the remnants of an Iraqi mechanised brigade that had been rolled over by the US Marines. Paratroopers and Royal Irish patrols fanned out to round up the prisoners, make contact with the local population and set up a security perimeter to stop any Iraqi counter attacks. The size of the security zone was so big that helicopter patrols by 3 Regiment were the only way to monitor it all and give any kind of early warning of any Iraqi forces massing nearby.[32]

As this clear-up and security operation got underway, the Brigade got the first taste of occupation duties. Power and water supplies in Rumalyah town needed to get back in operation and rumours began circulating that undercover insurgent groups were still at large. Iraqi Ba'ath party loyalists, dubbed Fedayeen, were the core of these groups and they were said to be preparing arms caches ready to launch guerrilla-style attacks on British and American troops. And while 16 Brigade was mopping up in the Rumalyah oil fields, 7 Brigade was moving north towards the outskirts of Basra. Its experience was very different.

Brigadier Graham Binns' Brigade had to enter Iraq through a very narrow sector about 25 miles north west of Umm Qasr. At 1.30am on 21st March, AS-90 self-propelled howitzers of 3rd Royal Horse Artillery and 81mm mortars of 1st Battalion, The Royal Regiment of Fusiliers (1 RRF) began a 90 minute barrage to suppress suspected Iraqi positions around 7 Brigade's breach of the border berm. Then Combat Engineer Tractors of 39 Armoured Engineer Squadron began bulldozing the berm to allow giant Challenger bridging tanks to come forward to put in place a metal bridge across the six metre wide anti-tank ditch just behind the berm. Covering this crossing operation, troops of 1 RRF had set up firing positions on top of the berm. The troops could hear the crump of artillery fire from the north, where the Americans were fighting around Basra and Umm Qasr. Small arms fire was seen from a nearby bunker and Lance Corporal Cardell of the 1 RRF Milan Platoon loosed off a missile at the target. It misfired and veered off into the sky. A second missile demolished the target.[33]

As the engineers set to work opening the breach and launching the bridge, Fusiliers said the ground was shaking from the exploding British artillery just inside Iraq. As the commander of the 1 RRF Drums Platoon, Warrant Officer Olly Campbell, said, "finally we reached the large berm, and scrambling up two metres of sand, we reached the top and, heaving for breath in the heat and (under our) sheer weight of ammunition, we had our first glimpse of Iraq. The feeling was strange, no Medina division [Republican Guard], no screaming hordes of Saddam Fedayeen, but a peaceful landscape exactly the same as the other side of the border."[34]

The crossing operation was complete in 10 minutes, and columns of 1 RRF Warriors and Challenger 2 tanks of its attached armoured squadron, from the Queen's Royal Lancers (QRL), were heading north into Iraq and spent the day expanding the bridgehead. During 22nd March the 1 RRF battlegroup headed north along the main road to Basra to link up with the US Marines. The northward advance of 1 RRF allowed the three remaining battlegroups of 7 Brigade to move into Iraq. The Fusiliers were followed by the 1st Battalion, The Black Watch battlegroup, which crossed into Iraq in the early hours of 22nd March. By the afternoon, D Company of the Black Watch had linked up with the US Marines holding an oil refinery outside Zubayr, known as the 'Crown Jewels' because of its key place in Iraq's oil export infrastructure. Other companies of the Black Watch began securing other oil facilities around the town. The Royal Scots Dragoon Guards (Scots DGs) battlegroup followed in their wake, and set up a regimental laager in the desert ready to respond calls to action. The B Squadron Leader, Major Chris Brannigan, described the 100 kilometre drive to the outskirts of Zubayr.

"The scene to us would have been familiar to any invading army" he recalled.

"A population with a dazed expression, plumes of smoke on the horizon and destroyed and abandoned enemy vehicles by the roadside. From the turret, commanders could see where defensive positions had been constructed at every junction and at every dip in the ground. The Iraqi forces obviously had a plan and the question at the back of one's mind was why they hadn't stuck to it? What we did not see were large collections of prisoners or large numbers of destroyed vehicles. There seemed to be something of a vacuum which made us wonder where were the enemy".[35]

The movement forward by 7 Brigade, even though it was not yet in contact with any serious Iraqi resistance, was hazardous. US convoys were moving across the British northward axis of advance in an east-west direction and there were several close shaves as British and American columns nearly opened fire on each other. One British artillery unit came close to opening fire on a QDG column outside Basra.

But these deconfliction problems, as previously mentioned, were predicted and the Americans had provided the British with its Blue Forces Tracking systems, which transmitted the position of units via the GPS satellite navigation systems, and Royal Signals units had been sent forward with the main US Marine Corps headquarters to provide direct communications between commanders. In a brief ceremony at Basra airport, Lieutenant Colonel David Paterson of 1 RRF formally took charge of the airport and the Basra canal from the US Marines. His troops were already planning to seize the main bridges over the Basra canal. Reconnaissance troops of A Squadron, QDG had led the move forward and set up a scouting screen watching the bridges ahead of the arrival of the main battlegroup.

A series of deliberate attacks were launched by Z and Y Company in their heavily armoured Warrior infantry fighting vehicles during the night of 22nd/23rd March. Lieutenant Chris Rees-Gay described the scene as "like a Vietnam film, with a dark evening sky from oil fires in the city."[36]

American Cobra attack helicopters were called in to hit targets ahead of the Fusiliers dismounting from their Warriors. Rees-Gray's platoon was accompanied by a team of SAS men in a white pick-up truck following up behind his three Warriors. As they raced to Bridge 4 over the canal, the assault force was engaged by an Iraqi T-55 tank firing 100 mm shells at them. Iraqi machine gunners joined in the battle from buildings at the edge of the bridge. The Fusiliers dismounted from their Warriors, some started returning fire with anti-tank rockets and others charged into the buildings to clear them. A Challenger 2 arrived and destroyed the Iraqi tank, allowing the Fusiliers to seize the bridge. A team of Royal Engineers searched it, and disabled demolition charges planted underneath its span. The Fusiliers had little chance to celebrate their success before inaccurate Iraqi artillery and mortar rounds started landing around them, forcing them to dive for cover.

C Squadron of the Queen's Royal Lancers led the assault on Bridge 3, which was equally swift and violent. Two troops of Challengers drove straight up the road to the bridge, avoiding marsh-land either side of it, and started to engage dug-in T55s on the far bank of the canal. A platoon of Fusiliers came up behind them and started to clear out Iraqi infantry around the bridge. In a 45 minute battle, the Lancers and Fusiliers destroyed four Iraqi tanks, two BMP armoured personnel carriers, an anti-aircraft gun, and killed two dozen Iraqi infantrymen. Again the Iraqis showed their displeasure, and after dawn a squad of Fedayeen paramilitaries staged an attack on the Lancers as they were dismounted from their tanks, refuelling and re-arming them. The Lancers returned fire, and then pursued the retreating Iraqis in a Spartan armoured command vehicle, eventually capturing six of them.[37]

Y Company took longer to relieve US Marines deployed around Bridge 2 than its comrades, and was only able to begin its attack at 7am. This, however, gave the Fusiliers time to organise artillery fire to soften up the defences before their Warriors moved forward. The artillery fire did its job, keeping the Iraqis' heads down until the Fusiliers were onto the bridge, and they could dismount to begin clearing demolition charges.

But the Iraqis on Bridge 2 were well organised, and were soon raining highly accurate mortar fire onto the Fusiliers. Supporting Challengers came up and engaged Iraqi tanks and BMPs across the canal. The presence of the tanks and heavy fire from the Fusiliers forced back the Iraqis, and in forty-five minutes the bridge was secure. Again, the Fusiliers and Lancers had little chance to rest before mortar and artillery fire started to land around their vehicles.

Further up the canal, B Squadron of the QRL found Bridge 1 undefended, and by mid-morning on 23rd March, 1 RRF was in control of the Basra canal. Iraqi troops remained in place on the eastern bank, and traded fire with the Fusiliers, regularly bringing up T-55s to shoot at the British. On one occasion they even mounted a company-sized attack backed by several T-55s. The presence of the Lancers tanks supporting the Fusiliers was decisive, and every time the enemy tanks broke cover they were hit by fire from the Challengers.

As the battles to control the bridges was underway, A Squadron of the QDG was edging past the airport to scout out a route across two small rivers and a swamp to allow British troops to cut the main road out of Basra to al Amarah and Baghdad. The reconnaissance troops found a route passable and set up a forward position overlooking the road, and the Shatt-al-Arab waterway at a site known as Nick 1004.[38]

The last battlegroup of 7 Brigade, 2nd Royal Tank Regiment, entered Iraq later in the morning of 22nd and advanced northwards to take up positions around the south-west fringes of Zubayr. During the early hours of 23rd March the Black Watch soldiers started to take fire from snipers in Zubayr. An effort by Royal Engineers to move into Zubayr, to make safe an abandoned Iraqi ammunition dump, ended in a hasty withdrawal when they came under a barrage of rocket propelled grenades (RPGs). The town was now clearly becoming a major thorn in the side of the British, lying behind the line the Fusiliers had set up along the Basra canal.

That evening a tragedy unfolded in Zubayr, when a Royal Engineers explosive ordnance disposal (EOD) team were driving past the town on a ring road when they were ambushed. They were driving in two unarmoured Land Rovers and took a wrong turn, leading them into a Fedayeen strong point. Survivors made it to safety at nearby British positions and reported two soldiers were missing. A rescue mission was immediately ordered. Two platoons from D Company were scrambled to recover the lost sappers, but soon ran into a hail of RPG and machine gun fire on a road that was soon nicknamed 'RPG Alley.' The Warriors pressed on and soon found the two Land Rovers. One was burned out and overturned. While under fire, Black Watch soldiers dismounted to examine the wreckage but there was no sign of the missing soldiers.[39] Over night, the Black Watch and 2 RTR was ordered to set up a series of checkpoints surrounding Zubayr to try to control the movement of Fedayeen fighters in and out of the town. Intelligence was received from friendly locals that the two missing soldiers were being held in the home of a leading Ba'ath Party official in the centre of Zubayr.

"People were starting to talk to us at checkpoints" said General Brims.

"They pointed out where the enemy where, where their headquarters were. They told us where our two missing soldiers were and the Black Watch launched a raid."[40]

Just as the events in Zubayr were unfolding, the Scots DGs were moving to exploit the opportunity created by the QDG scouting sortie to the north of Basra. In a daring night move, the Challengers and two companies of infantry from the Irish Guards weaved along narrow roads between marshes and inundated fields. None of the tanks or Warriors slipped off the levee roads, and during the evening they reached the forward position held by the QDG. The reconnaissance troops had spent the day being mortared, machine gunned and sniped by Iraqi troops lurking in farm land and nearby buildings. The relieved QDG troops beat a retreat, and left the newly-arrived troops on their own for several hours under unpleasant harassing fire. The tank crews remained closed down in their vehicles, as the Guardsmen tried to clear out pockets of resistance in fields and hamlets along the road. A platoon of Guardsmen was sent to clear a bunker complex, and as they retreated back into their vehicles after completing the task, four Iraqi soldiers attempted to rush the Warriors.

Major Ben Farrell, their company commander described the Iraqis as "very brave" but said they were "duly cut down by our [Warrior] 7.62mm chain guns."[41]

As dawn started to break, 7 Brigade sent an intelligence report to the commander of the Scots Dragoon Guards, Lieutenant-Colonel Hugh Blackman, that a brigade of Iraqi Republican Guard T-72 tanks were heading their way. The brigade commander, Brigadier Graham Binns, ordered Blackman to pull his troops back across the Basra canal as fast as possible. The Challengers and Warriors swivelled and started moving back along their precarious route. It turned out that the report was just a repeat of the same CIA sighting of the T-72 column that had played havoc with the US Marine advance into Iraq on 20th March. In the vehicles, the tank crews and Guardsmen were less than happy at being made to retreat.

"In hindsight we could have held our position as the Republican Guard failed to materialise", commented one of the Irish Guard's company commanders, Major Farrell.[42]

Binns recalled that he was worried that bridges would not last. "There was the possibility the battle group would get isolated" he said.

"It was an armoured battle in close country. Faced with that evidence, I took the decision to tidy things up and pull back. At the time it seemed sensible. With hindsight I would have left them there to have another option to enter Basra. A Challenger 2 battle group would have decimated a Republican Guard division. The reason we put them north of Basra was to exploit north, and with that option reduced we had no need to have an armoured battlegroup there. I wanted to preserve them for main effort, the eventual attack on Basra."[43]

While the three British brigades were going firm in their frontline positions, a huge logistic effort was launched to build up the supplies needed to sustain the British force inside Iraq. The old RAF station at Shaibah to the north of Zubayr was selected as the site for 7 Brigade's administrative area, complete with fuel stores, ammunition dumps, helicopters landing pads and vehicle repair shops. Brigadier Binns moved his forward headquarters to the site and important divisional artillery assets, including launch vehicles for Phoenix unmanned aerial vehicles and AS-90 self propelled guns, were also moved in. A seemingly non-stop flow of supply convoys shuttled to the base from Kuwait for the rest of the war. General Brims, however, left his headquarters in the desert of northern Kuwait near to Camp Rhino. He said it was close enough for him to visit the forward units and moving the hundreds of his vehicles of his headquarters in Iraq would "just have given the enemy another target".

One aspect of the logistics build-up which was not going smoothly was the plan to build a prisoner of war camp for a projected 14,000 Iraqi soldiers – half of all the enemy troops around Basra - that the British expected to capture. An ad hoc POW Handing Organisation (PWHO), had been pulled together in the weeks before the invasion, headed up by the Regimental Headquarters of the QDGs, a re-roled air defence battery, a squadron of Gurkha engineers and elements of the 1st Battalion, the Duke of Wellington's Regiment.

The latter unit had been flown out from Germany with no vehicles or equipment, beyond what the soldiers could carry in their rucksacks, to be the guard force for the POW camp. In total some 1,200 troops, 270 vehicles and all the material needed to build the camp had to be cobbled together in the few days before the war started.[44] The refusal of the Kuwaitis to allow any Iraqi POWs to be brought into their country meant that the proposed site of the camp was to be outside Umm Qasr, 10 kilometres over the border from Kuwait. The plan was for the camp to be up and running 48 hours after the start of the invasion, but the 15th MEUs five-day battle to capture Umm Qasr meant that the PWHO organisations' move into Iraq did not go smoothly. The convoy carrying the main body of the PWHO and its equipment had waited for a full day for clearance from the US Marines to move through the border.

"Finally ordered by a frustrated Commanding Officer, Lieutenant Colonel Gil Baldwin, to 'get on with it', [the QDG second-in-command] faced down the resolute US Sergeant blocking the border" recorded the QDG regimental history.

"Progress was made but soon halted by a series of Iraqi obstacles and a vicious firefight that developed around them. The only way out of the firefight was for the Adjutant to task Corporal Rees to unload one of the bulldozers and remove the obstacles. And here the surreal scene unfolded when a Royal Logistics Corps officer demanded to see Rees' licence to drive a bulldozer, as tracer bullets arced overhead. The reply, understandably, was short and to the point and Rees completed his task in quick time."[45]

Even before the British camp was open, the US Marines in Umm Qasr declared they were leaving and said they would hand over 500 captured Iraqis. This placed the British in an invidious position. The American high command said it was not concerned about the rank and file Iraqi soldiers it captured, and said they should be released to walk home. This was not an option open to General Brims and other British commanders, who had been advised that under the Geneva conventions they were legally obliged to look after and protect prisoners. The war was still raging across Iraq, and any released prisoners would be left to their own devices in an active battlefield, at risk from coalition and Iraqi fire, reprisals from civilians or regime forces.[46]

Elsewhere in the 1 (UK) Division area, hundreds more Iraqis had been handed over by departing American units or captured by British units. On Al Faw alone there were more than 230 prisoners. The first wave of British troops had no rations, water or shelter for these prisoners. There were several who were seriously wounded. The Kuwaitis included the wounded in their ban on Iraqis being brought into their country, but British Army doctors ignored these restrictions to evacuate several seriously injured prisoners to the main 1 (UK) Division field hospital in Kuwait. It took two more days for the PWHO to charter a fleet of 25 civilian buses in Kuwait to begin shuttling the prisoners held in the British area back to the prison camp at Umm Qasr. The description of the site as 'a camp' was a bit of an exaggeration. It consisted of six barbed wire enclosures with little shelter, food or sanitation at first.[47]

Eventually, more than 3,000 Iraqis were held by the PWHO and soon tempers flared in a series of riots and mass escape attempts. On 2nd April the British were holding some 230 officers, 2,353 soldiers and 1,172 civilians – Ba'ath Party officials and paramilitary fighters –in the camp. The International Committee for the Red Cross visited the site during the last week of March and made a formal complaint to the British government about the treatment of the prisoners by interrogators. This was potentially embarrassing, given that British government ministers were at this time extolling the coalition's humane treatment of POWs, compared with the Iraqi regimes' breaches of the Geneva convention by the parading of captured US soldiers on television.[48]

There was great relief when the camp was handed over the US Army's 800th Military Police Brigade on 8th April, and it was soon renamed Camp Bucca, or the Theatre Internment Facility. Little did the British and American commanders realise at the time, but the treatment of prisoners would become a major source of resentment among Iraqis. It would lead to a series of incidents that would play an important part in the discrediting of the whole Iraqi occupation to a significant part of domestic opinion in the UK and around the world.

Meanwhile the abduction of the British Engineer EOD team in Zubayr and strong resistance put up by the Iraqis along the Basra canal, prompted General Brims to reconsider his options. Reports were also starting to come in from the US Marines who were facing heavy resistance from irregular fighters in Nasiriyah. American convoys were being ambushed by heavily armed irregular fighters, dozens of Marines were killed or injured, and several US Army soldiers were missing, presumed captured. It appeared that consolidation was needed. For the first three days of the operation, senior British commanders had run the war from their headquarters in northern Kuwait, so as to to be close to their communications links with neighbouring forces. Co-ordinating the handover to the US Marines was their main preoccupation. With the handover complete, senior officers began to move forward to see for themselves what was actually happening, to get the 'ground truth' before making decisions on future operations, and judging the morale and physical condition of their troops.

"At the beginning I did not go forward, I needed to let the brigades find their feet," said Brims.

"Three to four days later I started to visit because I wanted to smell and feel the battlefield. I wanted to talk to the troops and see how much fuel they had left in their petrol tanks."

"We where we needed to be - my general impression was the need to hold our gains," recalled Brims.[49]

"We were getting less resistance from formal Iraqi forces and more from the Fedayeen. There was a need to hold where we were and consolidate what we won. I ordered our troops to concentrate into strong points and to begin a hardening of our logistic arrangements. The intention was not to leave isolated sites that might be vulnerable to attack. This was my initiative, there was no pressure from headquarters above me."

More than 400 troops, including two squadrons of Queens' Dragoon Guards Scimitar reconnaissance vehicles, and an armoured infantry company from 1 RRF, were also diverted to provide rear area security, garrisoning villages on the British supply lines or escorting supply convoys to forward bases. For the next week the British division would concentrate its effort on holding the ring around Basra, while the town of Zubayr was dealt with.

"We were holding the line, with Zubayr behind. My focus was on Zubayr," said Binns.[50]

Chapter 8

TAKING DOWN ZUBAYR

The first full week of Operation Telic found 7 Armoured Brigade fully committed to containing remaining Iraqi forces inside Basra and Zubayr. This was not a full-fledged military siege, with British troops forming a solid cordon around these two urban areas. Brims, the senior British land commander, was loath to engage in a tight siege. His superior, the US Marine Lieutenant General James Conway, did not want the British to become bogged down in street fighting until the outcome of the US drive on Baghdad was clear, in case British troops were needed to help in the decisive battle of the war. The UK Joint Commander in the Middle East, Air Marshal Brian Burridge, did not want a tight siege to be imposed because he did "not want to create a humanitarian dependency" which might force British troops to have to intervene to deliver aid to the population.[1] General Brims also wanted to give the hard-line regime loyalists in the city the chance to flee to Baghdad.

British commanders were well aware that the predominantly Shia population of Basra had little love lost for the Saddam regime, and could potentially become a fifth column against Chemical Ali and his loyalists running Basra. They thought the civilians should be allowed to go about their lives as normally as possible, and be 'educated' to support British forces, so General Brims ordered his troops to allow civilians where possible to move freely through their lines.[2]

What unfolded became a loose cordon with British troops setting up a series of checkpoints along the Basra canal and around Zubayr to use as bases, from which to launch targeted raids against pockets of resistance in those urban areas. On the relatively unpopulated al Faw peninsular, the Royal Marines had to fight a more conventional battle against Iraqi tanks and artillery. Great uncertainty surrounded how this battle would unfold, but General Brims wanted his troops to be able to move quickly to seize Basra should an opportunity present itself. He drew a boundary, or line of exploitation for his brigades, that ran up to the Basra canal and the outer fringe of the southern edge of the city. His brigade commanders were to move their troops up to this line as quickly as possible but not to cross it without his permission.

A big problem for British commanders and troops was actually working out what was happening around them, where the enemy was and what their intentions were. Although 7 Brigade ran into a stiff fight when it engaged the Iraqi defences along the Basra canal on the night and morning of 22nd/23rd March, elsewhere across the area to the west of the city the Iraqi army had apparently fled. The bases and battle positions of the two Iraqi brigades based in and around Zubayr, some 20 kilometres to the west of Basra city, were found abandoned, with hundreds of tanks, artillery pieces and vehicles just left behind by their crews. Large ammunition bunker complexes were also left unattended.

7 Brigade's commander Graham Binns recalled that "until we met resistance it was impossible to make decisions".[3]

The blunt-talking Yorkshireman was happy to take advice from his four battlegroup commanding officers through the course of the battle. They were the men on the ground, who had the pulse of the fighting. Binns spent almost all of the next 10 days travelling from one battlegroup to another seeing for himself what was happening and making decisions. He then left his headquarters staff to make the necessary co-ordinating measures to translate his intent into action.

"When you were in brigade headquarters you were blind," he recalled. "[The job of the staff] was really just to deconflict activity, [the headquarters was] not a place for making decisions. The only way to do that was face to face dialogue with battle group commanders, by being forward alongside them."[4]

"This was not only reconnaissance by fire, but decision-making by fire" said Binns.

"Decisions were taken when evidence presented itself. The enemy were just too disorganised to be able to predict with any certainty what they would do. We had to weigh up the balance of risk until we had more resolution about what was happening in Basra."[5]

The town of Zubayr had a population of around 300,000, and was the only Sunni majority town in southern Iraq, so it was expected to be a hotbed of regime support. Its population made their livings either working in the oil industry, or at the army bases in the town, so there was a strong cadre of Ba'ath Party supporters among them. Many were serious hardcore believers in the cause of the Iraqi regime in Baghdad.

For the first couple of days resistance was limited to sporadic machine gun and rocket propelled grenade (RPG) fire on British convoys, travelling up and down the ring roads that skirted the fringes of the town.

The deadly ambush on 23rd March that left Staff Sergeant Simon Cullingworth and Sapper Luke Allsopp of 33 Engineer Regiment missing changed the British view of the town. It was now home to a serious threat to British operations. The two engineers had been dragged from their bullet-riddled Land Rovers, and were then filmed being tormented by a mob of Iraqis. The footage was broadcast on the Qatari-based satellite television channel al Jazeera. They were then summarily executed on the orders of senior leaders of the Ba'ath party at a secret police base in the town. Their fate remained unknown for almost two weeks, when a shallow grave containing their bodies was discovered.[6]

With the events unfolding in Zubayr, Brims spoke to the commander of 7 Brigade during the evening about "the changing nature of our understanding of the conflict". The two officers agreed that there "was not to be a solely conventional battle" and proposed that they each spent some time doing studies, known as estimates or appreciations in military jargon, to work out how to defeat the resistance in Basra and Zubayr. Brims went away to work on Basra and Binns studied Zubayr. The two came to similar conclusion that direct frontal assaults would be counter-productive, generating large numbers of civilian casualties that would play into the Baghdad regime's propaganda narrative. They resolved to make extensive use of heavy armour – Challenger 2 tanks and Warrior infantry fighting vehicles – to launch surprise raids on Iraqi strong points. This would unhinge the Iraqi defence and convince the civilian population that the Iraqi regime's days were numbered. This would set the conditions for the final collapse of Iraqi control and it was hoped that British action would create a 'tipping point' that could be exploited without a bloody and destructive battle.

"Aggressive patrolling in armoured fighting vehicles was the decider," said Binns. "It gave us protection in case we met defence in depth. It also gave the enemy the opportunity to disappear."[7]

With two soldiers missing in the town, the commanders of the British force based on its outskirts were going to throw every resource they had into getting the sappers back. Leading the effort to secure Zubayr's northern and eastern outskirts was the 1st Battalion, The Black Watch, led by Lieutenant-Colonel Michael Riddell-Webster. Although quietly spoken, slightly balding and wiry, Riddell-Webster's appearance was not to be misjudged. He was a highly aggressive and determined leader of his battalion. The Black Watch, recruited from the Scottish cities of Perth and Dundee, was one of the toughest and best trained in the British infantry. The coming week would see a tough battle unfold for control of Zubayr and the loyalty of its people.

When US and then British forces took control of the huge oil facilities situated around the town, the leaders of the local Ba'ath party formed the core of resistance after army officers fled. While the Iraqi army units in the town had largely evaporated in the face of the American advance, several hundred Fedayeen fighters – who wore distinctive black pyjama uniforms - backed up by secret policemen from the feared Mukhabarat, and armed members of the Ba'athy Party meant it was a nest of resistance. The Iraqis used a network of safe houses away from government buildings to hide their arms, ammunition and other supplies. This made it very difficult for British commanders to get a good picture of what was happening.

Captain Mike Williamson, the Black Watch's intelligence officer described the irregular forces holding Zubayr as the 'new enemy' because it was largely unforeseen during pre-war planning. He called the enemy a 'network' that dressed in civilian clothes, merged with the local population and ensured its loyalty through a mix of intimidation and propaganda.[8] Identifying and locating these networks was a pressing need for Williamson and his colleagues from the Black Watch. He said that the Scots soldiers soon realised that the Iraqi irregular fighters could not react quickly to fast-move armoured raids. Initially local people were reluctant to provide information on the location of regime forces, he said.

"Successful operations against key strongholds changed the situation," he recalled.

"Local confidence in the British soared as they saw the Saddam Fedayeen and local Ba'ath members being targeted. Consequently the required information [was] gained quickly in detail and substance."[9]

On the southern and western fringes, the British 'encirclement' of Zubayr was completed by the 2nd Royal Tank Regiment (RTR) battlegroup. Its two squadrons of Challenger tanks were augmented by soldiers from the Light Infantry in Warriors. But the first full day of operations against Zubayr did not start well. At an RTR vehicle check point, a crowd of angry Iraqis approached a troop of Challengers and the situation escalated, after the Iraqis started throwing stones at the three tanks. One of the Challenger commanders, Sergeant Steve Roberts, was checking cars when the stones were directed at him, but as he tried to defend himself with his 9mm pistol it jammed. One of the tank crews responded by opening fire with a 7.62mm machine gun. An Iraqi and Roberts fell to the ground. When the Iraqi got up and started hitting the prone British soldier, the attacker was cut down by machine gun fire.

However, the incident later attracted attention because Roberts turned out not to be wearing Enhanced Combat Body Armour, which had hard plates to defeat high velocity bullets. A pathologist told the inquest into Robert's death that hard plates would have saved his life; but not enough sets of plates had been delivered to Kuwait before the war started. Being a tank commander, Roberts thought he was not a priority for body armour, and he gave up his set of plates so they could be re-distributed to frontline infantry soldiers. The tragic nature of the situation was made worse when it emerged at the subsequent inquest that Roberts had actually been killed by a burst of British machine gun fire.[10]

The Black Watch by now had split its efforts, with one infantry company and an attached Challenger 2 squadron from 2 RTR securing Bridge 4 across the Basra canal. The balance of the battlegroup was positioned around Zubayr in a series of platoon-sized vehicle check points, each reinforced with a troop of three or four Challengers to provide long range firepower and night-vision surveillance. These check points were engaged on an almost hourly basis by Iraqi snipers and machine gunners, trying to provoke the British into launching raids into the town. The Fedayeen were clearly trying to set up ambushes and the British only launched raids on their terms. The Light Infantry, working with the 2 RTR battlegroup, began to employ their own snipers at the check points to shoot back at the Iraqi snipers. The British snipers became very aggressive, infiltrating at night to take shots at Fedayeen commanders and bases.

During the late morning, Colonel Riddell-Webster launched the first of a series of armoured raids into the heart of Zubayr. A troop of the Royal Scots Dragoon Guards (Scots DGs) led a column of Black Watch Warriors down the main street into the heart of the town. Driving past shops and market stalls, the Scottish soldiers progressively noticed the civilians were disappearing from the streets. Armed men began to appear in side streets. When a man walked out of a shop and aimed an RPG at a Challenger the shooting started. Scores of RPGs were fired at the British vehicles as they pressed on through the town, with rockets coming from rooftops, street corners and ditches. Pickup trucks, with improvised 12.7mm heavy machine-gun mounts, known as 'technicals,' started taking pot shots at the British column from side streets. The Challenger tanks rotated their turrets and fired their main armaments at the four-by-four pickups with devastating results.[11]

By the time the column had passed through the town and was back in the safety of open land, the three Challengers in the column had fired more than 4,400 rounds of 7.62mm co-axial machine gun ammunition, exhausting their on-board supply. The Challenger and Warriors' crews were exhilarated by the sheer violence of the experience and at the same time relieved that they had come out of it unscathed. When the US Army tried this tactic in the streets of Baghdad a week later, it would be dubbed a 'Thunder Run'.

Within hours, tragedy would hit the Black Watch battlegroup, after a group of FV432 armoured personnel carriers from the regiment's mortar platoon was driving back from Bridge 4. They were headed to the main battalion base on the fringes of Zubayr to carry out repairs and resupply their vehicles. Fedayeen fighters caught the vehicles in a RPG ambush in narrow streets. Lance Corporal Barry Stephen, a long serving Black Watch soldier, tried to engaged the attackers with the 7.62mm machine gun in his commander's cupola but took a direct hit from a rocket. The force of the impact threw him out of the vehicle as the British vehicles sped away from the scene.[12]

When Riddell-Webster heard the news over the battlegroup radio net, he ordered an immediate rescue effort to bring back Stephen. The Colonel gathered together a platoon of four Warriors, backed up by three Challengers of the Scots DGS, and set off into the town to find his missing soldier. The approach to the last known position was relatively quiet, and then the Black Watch men swept the scene until they found the dead soldier. It was a trap. As the troops mounted up and moved out, the departing vehicles were sprayed with machine gun and RPG fire as they tried to escape from the narrow streets of Zubayr.[13]

While the Black Watch had got their man back, the hunt was still on for the two missing sappers. Royal Artillery Phoenix drones were patrolling over the town for long periods. One was shot down by Iraqi gunners. Two Gazelles from 662 Squadron Army Air Corps joined the patrols around Zubayr looking for suspicious activity, such as snipers climbing onto roofs, technical vehicles dodging British patrols, or Fedayeen fighters stockpiling supplies. SAS troopers joined this effort, moving around the fringes of Zubayr in their civilian pickup trucks in an effort to get intelligence on Fedayeen bases and movements. Some promising information pointed to a building, where a high-ranking Ba'athist, linked to the attack on the two missing soldiers, lived. It would the job of the Black Watch to deliver the SAS to their target later that night.

Driving through the night, the convoy of Warriors surrounded the target's six foot high compound and the company commander's vehicle smashed through the walls surrounding the building. The SAS assault team dismounted and attempted to blow a hole in the front door. Small arms and RPG fire erupted and the escorting Black Watch soldiers returned fire. One SAS man and a Scots soldier were injured in the firefight. Eventually the SAS troops managed to knock down the door and within five minutes they had the target apprehended. He was unceremoniously bundled into the back of a Warrior, but there was no sign of the two captured British soldiers anywhere in the building. There then followed a hair-raising extraction, as the Black Watch had to run a gauntlet of sustained small arms and RPG fire from roof tops as they drove out of Zubayr.[14]

The next day, the Black Watch upped their game when its D Company and the Scots DGs pushed into the town centre and seized its prison. Scottish soldiers swept into the building and cleared out a few pockets of Fedayeen fighters. A huge quantity of ammunition was captured. But this time the Black Watch were not going to retreat. It became the first British base inside the town. In a new tactic, the Black Watch sent a column of trucks carrying aid into the town to start giving out food and other supplies to civilians. A Fedayeen RPG attack brought this event to an abrupt end, but it set the scene for the next couple of days.[15]

The SAS and US Special Forces continued to work around Zubayr, looking for suspected Fedayeen bases and de-briefing local civilians who might be able to give useful intelligence. On 26th March the SAS reported that they had identified the main Fedayeen headquarters. Dubbed Objective Bain, this target was to receive special treatment. The US Marine Corps laid on a F/A-18 Hornet to drop a 2,000lb satellite guided Joint Direct Attack Munition (JDAM) on the building. On cue after the blast, a column of 2 RTR's Cyclops Squadron arrived on the scene to mop up the mess. The militia had gone. Later in the day the RTR heard that the militia had returned to the site and they set off to attack it again. This time the Fedayeen were up for a fight, and rained RPGs on the approaching Challengers. Another running battle developed, with the British tanks blasting RPG teams. The RTR column returned to its base without any casualties.[16]

This days' fighting proved decisive. More 'raid and aid' missions were carried out by the Black Watch, and received an enthusiastic response from the local population. An attempt by the Fedayeen to storm the prison and drive out the Black Watch was repulsed by Scottish snipers, 30mm cannon on Warriors, MILAN anti-tank missiles and SA-80 rifle fire.[17] Over the next three days patrols of the Black Watch and Light Infantry pushed into more neighbourhoods and received significantly reduced levels of resistance. On 31st March, the Scottish soldiers rescued two Kenyan truck drivers who had been part of a convoy heading to the US base at Umm Qasr when they got lost. A tip-off from local people led to the raid and they freed the Kenyans, who had previously been paraded on al Jazeera television. Another tip from local people led to a dawn raid on 1st April by the SAS and Black Watch, on two Ba'ath Party officials linked to the deaths of the two missing British engineers. The targets were apprehended without a shot being fired. Ten days later the bodies of the two British soldiers were found in shallow graves at a government building in Zubayr. They were found to have been killed at close range by multiple gunshots.[18]

The 1st April also saw the Black Watch taking off their helmets, and putting on their distinctive 'tam o' shanter' hats with the red hackle. Zubayr was still a dangerous place but hardcore Fedayeen and the local Ba'ath Party leadership had been killed, arrested or fled. General Brims said the JDAM attack on the Fedayeen headquarters on 26th March had a decisive impact.

"For over a week we were outside Zubayr and eventually we got in" said Brims.

"Most of the enemy had gone by then. We think they left on buses [for Basra], dressed as ordinary people. Zubayr was a highly significant and successful operation. We could have gone thundering in but there would have been a blood bath. We had the time, so we tied up behind our lines. That was our focus."[19]

Binns described the raids into Zubayr, and later Basra, as an effective way to build up the combat experience of their troops. "For many of us this was our first war, we were not sure what would happen" he said.

"So we rotated people into the fight on raids, to get people used to fighting. We thought bigger things were to come [after Basra]."[20]

Chapter 9

HOLDING THE BASRA CANAL

At 5am on 26th March, Major General Robin Brims convened a commander's conference at the 7 Brigade forward headquarters at Shaibah, to discuss the resistance being put up by the Iraqis and how the battle for Basra would unfold. Brigadier Jacko Page, of 16 Air Assault Brigade, attended the conference and recorded in his war diary that several plans to take the city were proposed by the three brigade commanders.

"One involved the attacking and seizing of two lodgements near the Shia [flats] neighbourhood to force [an] uprising," recorded Page.

"[Brims] would not commit to anything. His priorities remained "supporting the [US] 1st Marine Division and [oil field infra-structure] security. The staff at 1 (UK) Division headquarters were tasked to conducted a new study to set out firm plans for future operations. Clearly, the time was not yet ripe."[1]

General Brims talked about his "more cunning way" to defeat the Iraqis in Basra, but would not commit to a specific deadline to take the city. He laid out his plans for a series of deep operations by special forces, reconnaissance patrols, armoured raids, artillery fire, helicopter missile strikes and precision air raids on regime targets. Brims' divisional headquarters was to set the day-to-day objectives of this operation, but the 7 Brigade headquarters would co-ordinate the execution of each specific attack. More efforts were to be made to build up a detailed picture of what was happening in Basra to help frame any future decision to move into the city.

"Basra has UK/US Special Forces well embedded and they are keeping 7 Brigade well informed of what is happening," recorded Brigadier Page.[2]

The limitations on relying on under 30 SAS men to monitor what was happening in a city, with a population of well over a million people, was highlighted the night before after the undercover soldiers reported back to the British division that they thought an uprising was underway in Basra.

According to Air Marshal Brian Burridge, the British national contingent commander in the Middle East, this amounted to only six to 12 policemen in Basra who he said "started a demo".

"Our special forces guys had eyes on and saw them," recalled Burridge.

"The policemen did not like the regime and called for a popular revolt. It created a lot of interest but then the Fedayeen came along and shot them. That dulled enthusiasm."[3]

Before the final details of the incident had been confirmed during the evening of 25th March, the British chief of staff at the coalition headquarters in Qatar, Brigadier Peter Wall, gave a briefing to the media claiming the population of Basra were starting an uprising against the regime. When the uprising did not materialise it raised accusations that the British were engaging in a propaganda exercise.[4] It also showed up that the British had little visibility on what was happening across the Basra canal. Debriefing teams with translators from the Intelligence Corps were moved up to the canal bridges to try to get information on Fedayeen and Iraqi army positions from civilians coming out of the city.

"We had no real idea what happening in Basra more than 1.5km from main roads," Brigadier Graham Binns recalled.

"The intelligence, surveillance, targeting and reconnaissance (ISTAR) priority was elsewhere [in theatre]. It was difficult to sense from air what was going on the ground."[5]

After the special forces, the Royal Artillery's Phoenix drones and the Mamba locating radar were the main means 7 Brigade had to find enemy artillery and mortars that were conducting a steady stream of attacks on British troops positioned along the Basra canal. The drones had many successes finding Iraqi tanks and other pieces of equipment moving around the city and their role was praised by General Brims, who said "it gave my subordinates real-time information on what was happening over the hill, situational awareness."[6]

The Iraqis were not unaware of the role played by the Phoenix, and on several occasions they successfully engaged the British UAVs with anti-aircraft fire, bringing down at least half a dozen air vehicles. 32nd Regiment now began to move into its battle rhythm, launching air vehicles around the clock for the next three weeks to support British troops around Basra, from launch and recovery sites at Shaibah and Basra airport. Phoenix flew 133 sorties during the war fighting phase, and some 23 air vehicles were lost or damaged beyond repair, with only some half a dozen being attributed lost to Iraqi anti-aircraft fire.[7] Daily planning meetings in 1 (UK) Division headquarters allocated air vehicles and ground control stations to meet the requirements of General Brims' battle plan. Areas of interest were allocated for Phoenix to watch for extended periods of time. This often required launch vehicles and ground control stations to move forward close to the frontline to provide the necessary coverage and endurance over the required areas of interest.

Co-operation with the Mamba radars of K Battery also soon became a well-oiled procedure, according to Major Charles Barker, second-in-command of 32nd Regiment. Once Iraqi mortar fire was detected, Phoenix could be re-tasked to identify and confirm their location, before directing AS-90 fire to destroy the target. Baker said this type of engagement was routinely completed within seven minutes of the Iraqi mortar opening fire and being detected. The use of 'shoot and scoot' tactics by the Iraqis meant that Phoenix was a key way of tracking Iraqi gun batteries as they tried to move to safety after firing at the British.[8]

To try to minimise civilian casualties, a no-fire list with up to 1,000 locations, such as hospitals and schools on it was compiled. But the proximity of civilians made General Brims loath to loosen rules of engagement that required 'eyes on' a target, by a human observer on the ground or via a Phoenix live video feed before targets in the centre of the city could be engaged by artillery fire. A final check on artillery fire into Basra was imposed, with all requests for fire having to be approved by senior artillery commanders in divisional headquarters. Iraqi battlefield surface-to-surface missile batteries operating in the area of northern Basra were becoming a major irritant for the coalition, because they were firing missiles into Kuwait on an almost daily basis. US Air Force Predators and British Phoenix were regularly tasked to patrol suspected missile launch 'boxes'. Barker described how three Iraqi FROG missile launchers were discovered by a Phoenix, and two USAF A-10A Warthog attack jets were tasked to take out the missiles.[9]

The use of airpower within Basra's city limits was also tightly controlled. General Brims's troops could call in and control close air support against Iraqi forces directly attacking British troops, but the divisional headquarters had to get permission from the UK national contingent headquarters in Qatar for attacks, which Air Marshal Brian Burridge described as having "strategic significance".[10]

RAF Harrier GR7 aircraft attacked several targets in Basra, including strikes on snipers firing on British troops, but they also helped 7 Brigade's efforts by acting as 'eyes in the skies'.

"When we had a jet over our troops we would talk to them, telling them where more targets were," recalled one Harrier pilot.[11]

There were several complaints from British army officers that more RAF aircraft were not committed to supporting operations around Basra. This led to some RAF and US Marine Corps officers working in the British divisional and brigade headquarters to be critical that their British Army counterparts did not really understand the planning process needed to pre-programme aircraft to appear over Basra. The main problem for the British Army was that the US Air Force controlled all air power in theatre, and allocated aircraft, including RAF Harrier GR7s and Tornado GR4s, according to strategic priorities. During this phase of the war, the drive on Baghdad was the priority and the fighting in Basra was a lesser priority. On the ground along Basra canal, 7 Brigade confronted the Iraqi garrison of Basra, and its battlegroups were fighting their own battles to win intelligence on the Iraqi resistance.

A series of strongpoints were set up along the canal, controlling the key bridges. In the centre of the 7 Brigade front at Bridges 3 and 4, B Company of Black Watch held sway, while further north the Fusiliers were in charge. The canal was separated from Basra's suburbs by almost three kilometres of open land, a combination of scrub and marsh land. The Iraqi defenders set up a rival series of strongpoints in large industrial buildings and blocks of flats on the other side of the open land, opposite the British positions. This set the stage for a week-long duel between rival snipers, artillery batteries and tank gunners. Both sides traded fire and manoeuvred for advantage across what was soon dubbed no man's land. From his battlegroup headquarters at Basra International Airport, the Fusilier's commanding officer, Lieutenant-Colonel David Paterson was determined to take the fight to the enemy.

"The CO's intent was clear, he wanted the Fusiliers to dominate no man's land, or in his own words we were to 'take it to the enemy,'" recalled Major Paul Nanson, commander of 1 RRF's Y Company.[12]

Each Fusilier base along the canal was reinforced with Challenger tanks of the Queen's Royal Lancers (QRL), their own MILAN anti-tank missile teams, British artillery observers, US Marine Corps forward air controllers, and a small detachment of US Army special forces equipped with hand-launched unmanned aerial vehicles. These mini drones beamed live television pictures from their camera to a laptop sized control console that Fusilier officers could watch in their frontline command posts.[13] The next week developed into a grinding routine as the British and Iraqis traded fire across no man's land with their full range of weaponry. The population of the city regularly came out during lulls in the fighting to approach the British checkpoints. They came to escape the city, search for food and medical assistance, or in some cases to pass on information to help the British. British and American special forces operatives at the bridges took a great interest in them, and passed on the intelligence to 7 Brigade units to help them plan raids across the canal.

The Fusiliers launched nightly raids across the canal, with small foot patrols covertly scouting out Iraqi positions, capturing prisoners or ambushing the enemy. Artillery, US Marine Corps Cobra helicopter gunships, Phoenix drones and Warriors were on hand to cover the extraction of patrols if they got into trouble. The first couple of days patrolling saw the Fusiliers penetrate deep across no man's land and start operating around the industrial waste land on the fringe of Basra. The Fusiliers began to build up a detailed picture of the enemy forces arrayed against them. Imagery from the US drones allowed the Fusiliers to plan their raids in great detail and keep them safe from enemy ambushes. On one raid on 27th March, the Fusiliers were able to seize an Iraqi fighter and return him across the canal for interrogation.[14]

The Iraqis were not waiting passively for the British to attack, and mounted their own patrols to launch RPG attacks on the Lancers tanks guarding Bridge 2 and 3. They used drainage ditches to crawl up towards the British positions before emerging to fire on the tanks. On the night of 29th March, the Fusiliers sent their own ambush party into no man's land to turn the tables on the Iraqis but it returned empty handed. However, as they extracted back to the canal, the patrol spotted an Iraqi base in an industrial complex, including seven BMP armoured personnel carriers and a multiple-barrelled rocket launcher. This was the core of Iraqi defence in area, and Colonel Paterson ordered an immediate raid by armoured vehicles to destroy the position. A platoon of Warriors and a troop of tanks set off to attack just after dawn on 30th March.

Major Nanson used the American drone to plan the routes to the target and AS-90 155mm artillery fire was brought in to 'prep' the target. A Royal Engineers Combat Engineer Tractor (CET) came along to try to douse a fire from a fractured oil pipeline near the target, which was belching out noxious fumes.

As the artillery barrage kept the Iraqis head down, the Challengers and Warriors moved to their attack positions and started to engage the enemy. Dismounted infantry cleared several bunkers and engaged Iraqi soldiers as they fled the scene. The British tanks blasted several Iraqi positions and blew up the rocket launchers. Meanwhile the engineers were under heavy Iraqi fire, and the oil blaze was threatening to engulf the CET. Major Nanson decided his raid had done enough damage for one day, and he ordered his troops to pull back across the canal.[15] Y Company now rotated frontline duty with Z Company, and it continued the aggressive patrolling agenda set by its predecessors. The troops soon spotted a regular shuttle of trucks arriving at a warehouse complex just across the canal. An infantry raid was ordered, supported by tanks, and within minutes the Fusiliers found themselves in control of Basra's main food supply. The site was known to Iraqis as the Breadbasket, because it was the main warehouse of the UN Oil for Food programme in southern Iraq. The Fusiliers were ordered to stay put.

Resistance to the Fusiliers was weakening by the day, and on 3rd April, Brigadier Binns approved the battlegroup's most aggressive raid to date. A troop of Challengers from B Squadron QRL and 12 Platoon from Z Company, in broad daylight, drove down the main dual carriageway road into the centre of northern Basra to a large road junction, known as the Loop. They were literally putting British tanks on the Iraqis front lawn.

As the column approached the large traffic island, Iraqi fighters, backed by tanks, started to emerge from cover to engage the British force. A T-55 that broke cover engaged the Warriors. One of the Fusilier's vehicles fired off six rounds of 30mm cannon at the tank with no effect, then a Challenger came up and devastated the T-55 with a depleted uranium round, blowing its turret off. The Iraqis now backed off and resorted to mortaring the British for an hour. During this time, British tanks were sent on scouting forays around north Basra to check out Iraqi positions and the status of key infrastructure. With its job done, the British now pulled back to the canal.[16]

The next day the Fusiliers and C Squadron of the QRL were ordered into the city again, to demolish a four metre-high statue of Saddam Hussein. Again the column moved effortlessly into the city, and swiftly put a mortar team who engaged them out of action. Once at their objective, the crew of a Challenger armoured recovery vehicle dismounted and attached a heavy duty steel chain around the statue. An ITN news crew filmed the spectacle, which got off to an inauspicious start when the chain snapped. At the second attempt, the Iraqi leader's image was a pile of rubble. This raid suggested that the Iraqi defence of Basra was failing.[17]

B Company of the Black Watch had the job of holding Bridge 4 during this crucial period, backed up by Challengers of the RTR and Scots DGs. Bridge 4 was the main road route into Basra and the British troops holding it had to deal with a huge number of civilians who were trying to leave or enter the city. Their position was also well known to the Iraqis and the Scottish soldiers were routinely shelled and mortared. This fire was very accurate and several soldiers were wounded.

"Gunners were soon using warning bursts from the Warrior to move civilians from the artillery target area, whilst sections became experts at dealing with refugees under indirect fire," recalled a Black Watch soldier who served at the bridge.[18]

At night, the Black Watch led their own raids across the canal to try to scout out Iraqis positions around the large Basra technical college compound, where the main enemy force in the area seemed to be based. In one raid they discovered a large Al Samoud ballistic missile abandoned in its grounds. On the night of 25th March, a tank gunner of Egypt Squadron of 2 RTR, attached to B Company at Bridge 4, misidentified Challenger tanks of the QRL at Bridge 3 some two kilometres up the canal in the 1 RRF area of responsibility. There was confusion over the position of the neighbouring units in the day after the Black Watch company took over Bridge 4 from the Fusiliers. The RTR tank fired on the QRL vehicle and two soldiers were killed.[19]

Three Lynx helicopters of 662 Squadron were called forward from 16 Brigade on 25th March, to set up a forward operating base at Shaibah airfield to support the possible offensive by the Black Watch into the city after reports of an uprising in Basra.

"We received reports that Basra was falling," was how it was recorded by 3 Regiment Army Air Corps's (AAC) war diary. "Upon arrival, there were no specific missions for the aircraft."[20]

In the early hours of the following morning, the Lynxes staged a raid on Iraqi troops occupying a factory complex, described as a Ba'ath Party facility, destroying four buildings, an ammo dump and a water tower with TOW missiles. Later that evening the compound was attacked again by the British helicopters. The 662 Squadron detachment remained at Shaibah for several more days, and was increasingly drawn into the battle for Basra.[21]

The AAC helicopter crews began to find that the Lynx's TOW missiles had several limitations, including a tendency to 'hang-up' when the missile's rocket motors failed to fire, and drop down below the helicopter, spooling out the guidance wire. Unless these wires were immediately cut, they could become entangled in the helicopters tail rotors. Firing the TOW missiles also required the helicopters to either hover, or to fly straight and level towards their target. In the industrial wasteland on the fringes of Basra this made the AAC helicopters very vulnerable to Iraqi fire. The profusion of high tension power cables and telephone lines made the outskirts of Basra a nightmare for helicopter pilots, particular if they were flying at speed to dodge enemy fire.

A pair of Lynx made their first successful attack on Iraqi T-55 tanks on the afternoon of 27th March, despite receiving incoming mortar and small arms fire which forced them to return to base.[22] When trucks armed with mortars and machine guns were spotted firing on civilians trying to leave the city in the early hours of 28th March, two 662 Squadron Lynx were scrambled to take them out.

A US Marine Corps forward air controller directed the final stage of the attack, bringing the helicopters into the hover only 1,800 metres from the target. It still took time for the crews to positively identify the targets, and they eventually destroyed two of the vehicles.[23]

But the Iraqis defenders still had plenty of fight left in them, and remained dangerous opponents. On the night of 28th March, A Squadron of the Scots DGs got a very nasty surprise when their hide location, just behind Bridge 4, came under sustained fire from a multiple barrelled rocket launcher. Rockets started hitting the squadron, catching the tank crews sleeping in the open. Three soldiers were injured by shrapnel fire as the Scots DGs raced for cover inside their tanks, and then drove out into the desert to escape the killing zone.[24]

The Scots Dragoon Guards mounted the largest armoured raid of the war next day into the heart of Basra. At dawn on 29th March, the tank column, with a platoon of Warriors carrying Black Watch and SAS soldiers, drove over Bridge 4 and headed for the centre of city. Fedayeen fighters tried to engage the column with machine guns and RPGs but it was moving too fast to have any impact. The tanks pulled up outside the city's main television transmitter tower. As the dismounted troops attacked and cleared a nearby Fedayeen base, the Squadron Leader's Challenger took aim at the tower with its 120mm main armament. The gunner was on target and the tower crashed to earth, filmed by the BBC. The Scots DG then took time to demolish a statue of Saddam before returning safely back to Bridge 4.[25]

The two-man SAS team with the tank column wore Arab robes over their British uniforms and they were dropped off close to a large industrial complex opposite Bridge 4. Their job was to stalk a highly mobile Iraqi mortar team who were responsible for bringing down very accurate fire on the Black Watch base at the bridge. It was hoped that the noise and mayhem created by the raid would force the mortar team to break cover. They were picked up by the retreating Challengers later in the day and reported a successful outcome to their mission.[26] Meanwhile other SAS teams were operating across the city, dressed in Arab clothing and driving old civilian vehicles in a bid to blend into the population. Their top priority was finding Ali Hassan al-Majid, 'Chemical Ali,' who was believed to be leading the defence of Basra.

The small US Army special forces team attached to 7 Brigade were not having such a successful time, because Brigadier Binns would not let them move forward across the canal into the city with the SAS. This caused considerable friction between the Americans and British, which came to a head when a 7 Brigade tank crew reported seeing what they thought was a US air strike in Basra. It turned out not to have been requested or approved by any British headquarters, so Brigadier Binns confronted the Americans and directed them to leave his brigade area.

"I remember having a conversation with US special forces at Basra airport," said Binns.

"I did not regard it as significant. I commanded an armoured brigade with 116 tanks. I was concentrating on co-ordinating with others. The action of a small group of SF constrained my ability to act. They did not have blue forces tracking [real time position marking system], no communications [with us] and no sure access to fire support."[27]

By the first days of April battlegroups of 7 Brigade had been in continuous combat for almost 10 days. The troops were incredibly tired. Soldiers were saying that only adrenalin was keeping them going. The frontline infantrymen were surviving on two or three hours of sleep a night, with little hot food and no chance to wash. The tank and Warrior crews spent days in their vehicles, often sleeping in their seats. Commanders were getting worried that troops would start making fatal mistakes, so units began to be rotated back from along the canal to be given a chance to sleep in disused hangers at Shaibah airfield. The Scots DG battlegroup was brought up from their reserve position at Shaibah to take over from the Black Watch at Bridge 4. The Duke of Wellington's Regiment was moved up to Zubayr from the Umm Qasr prison camp to free up the troops who had fought in the town for over a week. Colonel Riddell-Webster's men had earned a rest at Shaibah.

When the newly-arrived Scottish tank crews and their supporting infantry from the Irish Guards took over the Bridge 4 position, it was being mortared on an hourly basis, and was strewn with abandoned and wrecked Iraqi vehicles. It stank of human excrement and burning buildings. The new battlegroup got little respite, and was soon into a cycle of mounting two or three raids a night up the main road into Basra to hit back at the Iraqis, and gather information about the situation in the city centre. The technical college complex was the main target of these raids in an attempt to thwart the mortar attacks on Bridge 4. It was suspected of being the headquarters of the Iraqi 18th Infantry Division, which was the last regular army unit still putting up resistance in the city.

The Iraqis continued to greet the arrival of the British raiding parties with barrages of machine gun, RPG and mortar fire from roof tops, trenches and barricades. In turn, the British armoured vehicles responded in kind. The protection of the British Challengers and Warriors prevented serious casualties but the Iraqis paid in blood. One British tank commander recalled that his gunner was traumatised when he saw a dog pick over the remains of an Iraqi soldier he had just killed with machine gun fire, the animal then darting off carrying the unfortunate man's hand in its mouth.[28]

Later, on 29th March reports came into 1 (UK) Division headquarters from special forces teams in the city that a group of two hundred Fedayeen fighters were gathering in a building in north-east Basra. After getting approval from the UK national contingent headquarters in Qatar, General Brims requested that US Marine Corps air controllers, attached to the British headquarters, use their secure radio communications to order up a pair of US Air Force F-15E Strike Eagles to attack the target. The jets dropped two laser-guided bombs and flattened the building. Senior British and US officers at the coalition headquarters in Qatar claimed 200 Iraqi fighters were killed in the attack. When British troops visited the site after the fall of Basra they detected a strong smell of decaying bodies, suggesting the strike was successful.[29]

General Brims described the attack as very significant. "I think it shook the Fedayeen and the leadership," he said.

"It also encouraged the locals that we meant business and had the capability to back it."[30]

The attack coincided with another effort by the 1 (UK) Division planning staff to look "in earnest at a Basra Entry plan and also Phase IV plans," recalled Brigadier Page.[31]

Two days later, the division planning group convened and General Brims was distinctly upbeat, telling the assembled senior officers, "we are winning."[32]

However, US Army and US Marine Corps commanders had just told General Brims that they did not yet consider the time right for the British to move into Basra. The British division was ordered to continue to protect the oil fields and the western flank of the US Marine Corps. Ideas for moving into Basra were discussed, including a soft push by a single battlegroup or a larger-scale operation on a broad front, including drives by 3 and 16 Brigades to the north and south of the city, respectively. General Brims was holding his nerve at the moment.

"Do as we do – no change," was the order.[33]

Chapter 10

ROYAL MARINES VS T-55 TANKS

South of Basra on the exposed al Faw peninsular, the Royal Marines of 3 Commando Brigade were fighting a very different type of battle. They had no heavy armour, precarious supplies lines and the marshy terrain split the Brigade's area of responsibility in two parts, severely hampering its ability to move its forces across the battlefield. On top of these challenges, the heavy casualties suffered by US forces around Nasiriyah on 23rd March prompted the American high command to ask for the 15th Marine Expeditionary Unit (MEU) to be returned to them on 25th March. Although this had been expected, it happened at a very unfortunate time for Brigadier Jim Dutton. At a stroke a third of his infantry strength was withdrawn and a significant part of his combat power, including his only main battle tank unit and 155mm artillery battery, as well as a Cobra gunship squadron.

"We were content to let 15 MEU depart because that was in the original plan and they had other tasks to perform back with 1st Marine Expeditionary Force (I MEF)," recalled Major General Brims.

"The timing of that decision was ahead of us encountering the Abu al Khasib resistance."[1]

During 22nd March, the Brigade Reconnaissance Force (BRF) was re-organised and re-united with its Land Rovers, and was sent up the al Faw to set up a blocking position outside the town of Abu al Khasib. The Land Rover-borne Royal Marines raced up Route 6 along the banks of the Shatt-al-Arab waterway, passing scattered groups of Iraqi soldiers who were more than happy to surrender and pass on intelligence about troop positions further north. Two days later they were outside the town and set up a series of observation posts in palm groves, with MILAN anti-tank missiles set up to deal with the suspected Iraqi amour based in and around the town.

C Squadron QDG managed to get up to support the BRF during the night of 23rd March, and by dawn its Scimitars and other vehicles were positioned along the screen ready for action. Daylight allowed the Royal Marines and Cavalrymen to start identifying what was described as an "extensively prepared defensive position" for what appeared to be a multi-battalion-sized force of Iraqi troops.[2] Royal Navy Sea King ASAC7 radar helicopters spotted the Iraqi force mustering in the dark and preparing to attack. Royal Artillery Phoenix unmanned aerial vehicles arrived overhead to help find targets. US Marine air controllers in 3 Brigade's headquarters began mustering fixed wing strike aircraft, or 'fast air' to hit the armour. During the coming battle 36 US jets would be 'flowed' over the battlefield.

"Initial attempts to call in Close Air Support were unsuccessful for two reasons - the pilots were unable to identify targets and once identified were unwilling to drop due to fears of collateral damage" recorded the QDG regimental history.

"However, in the west, 3rd Troop was busy dealing with a T-55, which engaged the Troop Corporal, narrowly missing his head. The Troop further identified defensive positions supported by armoured vehicles and dug-in infantry, so a vehicle from Guided Weapons (GW) Troop was tasked in support, receiving artillery and mortar fire along the way. The GW vehicle then pulled over and proceeded to destroy a T-55, bunker system and a watchtower before withdrawing to reload. Returning to 3rd Troop, the GW vehicle was contacted by Iraqi soldiers mounted in a civilian vehicle, and when the vehicles' machine gun failed, 3rd Troop were called to assist, subsequently destroying the vehicle with 30mm High Explosive rounds."[3]

An Iraqi armoured battalion was on the move, with an estimated 50 tanks bearing down on the lightly armed British troops. Air support from fast jets and Lynx AH7s of 847 Naval Air Squadron soon arrived. A US Air Force F-16 Fighting Falcon arrived overhead, and was directed to drop a 2,000lb satellite-guided (Joint Direct Attack Munition) bomb onto a bunker complex surrounded by T-55 tanks. A huge fireball engulfed the Iraqi positions and the Iraqi attack seemed to stall. Pairs of Lynx helicopters joined the battle engaging the Iraqi tanks with wire-guided TOW missiles. The Royal Navy helicopter crews spotted red and white taxis shuttling around the Iraqi positions dropping off and picking up armed men dressed in black. Soon Brigadier Dutton changed the rules of engagement of his helicopter crews, to allow them to engage the taxis if they spotted them.[4]

British and Iraqi artillery traded fire across the battlefield as the fight raged all day. Royal Navy Gazelle AH1 helicopters flew forward to scout out targets for their TOW-armed Lynx colleagues. Iraqi artillery and tank gunners traded fire with the Lynx helicopters, which were very vulnerable when they were about to fire their missiles. The Lynx crews had now spotted plenty of targets and started working as airborne forward air controllers for the 'fast air.' First they pin-pointed targets for a pair of US Air Force A-10 Warthog ground attack pilots and talked them on to their targets, who proceeded to make a series of bombing runs against the Iraqi tanks. 1st Troop of QDG was now being engaged by Iraqi tank main armament, recalled the QDG history.

"These rounds initially fell short, but became progressively more accurate. The Troop withdrew to a prominent hill where one of the Squadron's Forward Air Controllers (FAC) joined them and brought in two A-10 Warthog aircraft that destroyed all the enemy tanks. Sergeant McDonnell, the FAC and the officer commanding the US Air Naval Gunfire Liaison Company (ANGLICO) team proceeded to control back-to-back close air support (F/A-18's and A-10's) accurately into enemy armour, transport, bunkers, and infantry for the remainder of the day. Until the air kill box closed several days later, they continued to coordinate sustained aviation fire and reconnaissance in the area, pausing only to eat and shave. Sergeant McDonnell even took control of two A-10's mid shave."[5]

US Marine Cobras then joined the battle and by end of the day some 20 Iraqi tanks and around 40 other vehicles were burning on the battlefield. A huge sand and rain storm swept across the al Faw over the next 24 hours bringing fighting to a halt, giving both sides a chance to re-organise for the next phase of the battle.[7]

Further south, 42 Commando was helicoptered off the al Faw to Umm Qasr to take over from the 15th MEU. Their commanding officer, Lieutenant Colonel Buster Howes, set about putting Royal Marines on the streets of the town to finally make sure that it was clear of Iraqis, and began building relations with its newly liberated citizens. He then used troops and assault boats, landing craft and hovercraft of 9 and 539 Assault Squadrons to clear the upper reaches of the Khawz-al-Zubayr (KAZ) waterway.

The upper reaches of the KAZ formed a large marsh area that effectively blocked movement between 7 Brigade units positioned along the Basra canal, and 40 Commando over on the eastern bank of the Shatt-al-Arab. Hundreds of Iraqi troops had fled to the region in the wake of 7 Brigade and 40 Commando's advance. These included special forces units and the naval missile batteries that had been firing Ababil 100 rockets and Seersucker cruise missiles at Kuwait. This area also offered the Iraqis a route to infiltrate southwards to strike at the main supply lines up from Kuwait, or to push down the al Faw behind 40 Commando. Without this tidying up exercise, 3 Commando Brigade would not be in a position to strike into Basra when the time was right.

For the eight days after it landed in Umm Qasr on 25th March, 42 Commando mounted a series of company-sized operations across the region, acting on tips from local people or signals intelligence picked up by listening posts manned by 3 Brigade's Y Troop. Brigadier Dutton also moved his headquarters to Umm Qasr to be closer to his troops.

On 27th March, 42 Commando sent its first water-borne patrols up the KAZ against known enemy positions, while a position occupied by 30 Iraqi troops was attacked without loss on the southern bank of the waterway. Meanwhile the remainder of the Commando Group secured a large waterworks further up the KAZ at Umm Khayyal.

Royal Marine landing craft and patrol boats pushed deeper up the KAZ, occasionally becoming engaged in fire fights with armed Iraqi boats, with Gazelle and Lynx helicopters of 847 Naval Air Squadron scouting ahead to look out for enemy positions. In one of these patrols a crewman was killed by accident, when another Royal Marine unit opened fire and badly damaged his boat with a MILAN anti-tank missile.[8]

The work of 42 Commando took on more importance as the Commando Logistic Regiment moved to the Zubayr port, on the banks of the KAZ, to set up a brigade administrative area to support the drive through the al Faw. A sprawling warehouse complex was soon filled up with supplies, fuel dumps and a rest area for troops to be ferried from the al Faw to have a break away from the fighting. A field kitchen and portable showers were brought up to provide 3 Commando Brigade personnel with some form of creature comforts. Soon Brigadier Dutton moved his headquarters to the site and 847 Squadron set up its forward operating base there.[9]

The site was far from secure and came under Iraqi mortar fire on a nightly basis, and on 30th March a Seersucker missile landed just outside its perimeter, sending hundreds of Royal Marines diving to dodge flying shrapnel.[10] Over on the eastern bank of the Shatt-al Arab, 40 Commando was fighting a very different type of war. The small town of Abu al Khasib was still firmly in Iraqi hands and intelligence from listening posts suggested that an Iraqi armoured regiment was massing to strike at Colonel Messenger's men. His troops started describing their exposed position as 'Custer's Land' because of the apparent mismatch in their fighting power, compared to the dozens of Iraqi tanks and 2,500 troops based only a few kilometres away.[11]

This was the largest concentration of Iraqi troops in the Basra region, and they seemed in no mood to surrender. The men of 40 Commando had been living out of rucksacks and eating ration packs for a week. Almost all of their supplies, particularly essential water and ammunition, had to helicoptered up to their position. This supply operation, combined with the sustained mission of 42 Commando up the KAZ, swallowed up nearly all the transport helicopter capacity of the British force in Iraq.

General Brims was worried that 3 Brigade had a large area of responsibility to hold with little armour and few logistics vehicles. US airpower had kept the Iraqi armour at bay on 24th March, but if bad weather grounded the jets during a future attack 40 Commando's infantry would be in some peril.

"I was concerned that 3 Commando Brigade would over expose themselves," recalled Brims.

"The QDG reconnaissance squadron working with the brigade could not deal with Iraqi armour. My concern was that the [lightly armoured] vehicles of the QDG lacked the protection for the task. I did not want to get in an armoured bash-up."[12]

Staff officers in Brims' headquarters and senior Royal Marine officers set about working how to reinforce Colonel Messenger's over-exposed positions.

"I decided to send the commandos a squadron of tanks," said Brims. "The Challengers had protection and anyway could stand off and attend to any counter attack if we did not get the air support."[13]

In the meantime, during the evening of 26th March, armed reconnaissance patrols of Lynx AH7 from 16 Air Assault Brigade were ordered to fly to southern Basra to engage the 70 Iraqi tanks suspected to be threatening the Commandos. In the gloom they could not find any tanks and successfully engaged a Ba'ath Party compound on the southern fringes of Basra.[14]

During the night of 26th March, C Squadron of the Scots DGs was detached from 7 Brigade and sent to reinforce the Commandos. But getting the fourteen 75-ton Challenger tanks across the KAZ was easier said than done. The tanks set off at night from their base at Shaibah airfield to link up with a Royal Engineer bridging squadron equipped with M3 ferries. In darkness each of the tanks was ferried across the 250 foot wide river in an operation that took nearly four hours. The crossing position was several miles from any friendly forces, and on top of that none of the tank crews had ever manoeuvred their Challengers onto the ferries, down a muddy river bank, before. None of the tanks came unstuck and the Territorial Army Engineers – who had also never put a Challenger tank on any of their ferries before – eventually got C Squadron onto the al Faw.[15]

After a 22 mile drive along narrow roads through the marshes, C Squadron approached Abu al Khasib as dawn was breaking. The plan was for the Scottish tanks to swing onto the dual carriageway road that skirted along the southern edge of the town, in a west-east direction, for just over ten miles to get to the forward reconnaissance screen held by the Royal Marines Brigade Reconnaissance Force and the QDG. The town was teeming with Iraqi troops and tanks and the Scots DG were expected the enemy to try to intercept their manoeuvre.

Cruising like a naval squadron with its turrets swung out to the left to point at the enemy, the Scots DG picked up speed as it hit the metalled road. The daring move initially took the Iraqis by surprise but a few minutes later Iraqi T-55s emerged from the town to engage the British tanks. Firing on the move, the Challengers hit seven T-55s, six MLTLB tracked troop carriers and two bunkers in the mayhem. Scores of Iraqi infantry were machine gunned as they tried to approach the tanks, and one Scots DG tank commander even found time to fire his cannon at a giant mural of Saddam Hussein by the road.[16] The squadron's commander tried to radio ahead to warn the Royal Marines that they would soon be emerging from Iraqi-held territory, and that they should not open fire on the British tanks. In the space of a few minutes, the Iraqi defences in the town had been dealt a heavy blow.

Abu al Khasib remained a major thorn in 3 Brigade's side, protruding into the al Faw and giving the Iraqis a jump-off point to infiltrate southwards. Brigadier Dutton was worried that without clearing out the town, his Royal Marines would not be in a position to strike into Basra. His solution was Operation James, a full Commando-sized deliberate attack, reinforced with support from the Scots DGs, the QDG and almost every unit of 3 Brigade. The operation was named after the famous secret agent, James Bond, and the objectives for the assault teams were code-named after Bond girls and villains, including Objectives Pussy Galore and Blofeld.

"This operation was proposed by 3 Commando Brigade as they judged that they could control the district and prevent the enemy 'popping back up'," said General Brims.

"I agreed to the timing because we were in something of a consolidation [phase] elsewhere and 7 Brigade's artillery could support (by range and priority) the 3 Brigade operation."[17]

Having got clearance from General Brims during 28th March, Dutton was keen to get the attack under way before the Iraqis could recover from the rampage of the Scots DGs. His Brigade Reconnaissance Force had already been mounting night-time raids into the town to keep the Iraqis off guard, while gathering intelligence. The attack would go in during the early hours of 30th March, and Dutton's troops would have less than 24 hours to make their preparations and get into position to strike.

Dutton's aggressive plan called for 40 Commando to move during cover of darkness to a series of attack positions along the southern edge of Abu al Khasib. Then four infantry companies – three from Messenger's unit and one from 42 Commando, which was helicoptered up for the assault – would advance along a ten kilometre front to clear the town from south to north. A troop of Challengers was attached to each Royal Marine company for the sweep northwards into the town, towards the Shatt-al Arab waterway. The QDG and the Brigade Reconnaissance Force protected the attack force as it moved into position and then staged noisy diversions at the eastern and western edges of the town to deceive the Iraqis into thinking the attack was coming from these directions.

Some participants compared the build-up to the attack to an exercise assault, like those against the British Army's Copehill Down Fighting in Built-Up Areas training centre on Salisbury Plain. Others likened it to the Vietnam war movie, "Full Metal Jacket," because for the first time in living memory the Royal Marines would be launching an attack with main battle tank support, just like the US Marines in the battle for Hue in Vietnam in 1968.[18]

The Royal Marines of 40 Commando's B Company had to march 14 kilometres through knee-deep mud to get to their start line. To ease the burden quad bikes with trailers carried their heavy body armour and ammunition. Fortunately, they had formed up ready to attack, and put on their body armour and helmets minutes before H-Hour, or the planned time for the start of the attack. But as they did so, the guns of 29 Commando Regiment started to fire air burst shells onto B Company's position for two minutes. Eight Marines were seriously injured and only escaped death because of their body armour and helmets. A subsequent board of inquiry blamed the friendly fire incident on the rush to plan the operation, which prevented proper co-ordination of the fire plan by 3 Brigade staff officers. Prompt action evacuated the casualties and the attack soon got going.[19]

Throughout 30th March, the 40 Commando companies swept forward into the town clearing houses of Iraqi defenders. When heavy resistance was encountered, the Royal Marines would summon up a Challenger or TOW-missile armed Lynx AH7s to blast the target. Close-quarter fighting with Iraqi regulars and Fedayeen fighters raged all day. Fires burned through the town as the British troops moved through palm groves, walled compounds and the town's low-rise buildings.

The Scots DG Challengers stalked the occasional Iraqi T-55 that tried to fight back through the town's streets, to stop them interfering with 40 Commando's assault. When A Company of the Royal Marines moved to clear a palm grove they ran into 14 T-55s spread out in a defensive ring. Their supporting Challengers soon knocked them all out, but they turned out to have been abandoned by their crews.

Four Iraqi MLTB troop carriers tried to stage a counter attack, when they were spotted by 847 Squadron, and destroyed at two kilometre range with TOW missiles. The Royal Navy aviators were airborne throughout the battle supporting their Commando comrades. They fired a total of 22 TOW missiles during the day, scoring 17 confirmed hits on targets, including two T-55 tanks.[20]

While returning from a mission over Abu al Khasib, one of the Royal Navy helicopters spotted an Iraqi artillery battery hidden in a desert fort right in the middle of the al Faw peninsular. It has been by-passed by Colonel Messenger's advancing spearhead. The Iraqi battery poised a serious danger to all British bases in southern Iraq, so two gun batteries of 29 Regiment Royal Artillery was tasked to bring down fire on the Iraqi gunners, devastating the position.[21]

The sheer size of Abu al Khasib meant that Colonel Messenger's troops were still fighting into the evening. The companies paused on several occasions to allow replenishment of ammunition, water and food to be brought up to sustain the Royal Marines. Civilian cars and trucks full of armed men started to be observed making a quick exit from the town towards Basra.

For the Scots Dragoon Guards, the fight was not yet over. The tank troop supporting A Company was soon involved in a bitter battle to recover one of their Challengers that had rolled on its side, off of a raised road. The other tanks formed a protective ring around the stricken vehicle as a recovery tank was called for. At this point more than 50 Fedayeen fighters tried to rush the position to seize the wounded tank. They were beaten back but soon were pouring down withering machine gun and rocket propelled grenade fire on the recovery team as it tried to extract the tank. It took three attempts by two recovery tanks to pull the stranded tank out, and for almost all of the nine hours it took the Scottish tankmen they were under heavy enemy fire. One tank took 14 RPG hits. The Fedayeen were denied their trophy.

It was a matter of great pride to the Royal Armoured Corps soldiers that a British tank had not yet been abandoned in battle since the Korean war, and the Scots DG were not going to be the first to lose a Challenger. The QDG also had a Scimitar immobilised with a lost track during the battle, and the crew ignored orders to abandon it before successfully recovering the vehicle.[22]

By dawn on 31st March, 40 Commando were in control of Abu al Khasib after a battle that had lasted some twenty hours. Hundreds of civilians started to emerge from the houses to talk to the British troops and survey the state of their town. The troops set up improvised bases throughout their newly liberated territory and took stock. After the biggest battle of the Iraqi campaign, 40 Commando and the QDG were to be kept in reserve and allowed to recuperate.

The troops were exhausted. They were soon being rotated through the Commando Logistic Regiment's newly opened rest centre, while at the same time sustaining a presence in Abu al Khasib to deliver humanitarian aid and provide security against small groups of Fedayeen fighters who had not been able to flee during the battle.[23]

42 Commando was flown forward to an assembly area to the west of the town on 5th April, to at last seal up the gap between 7 and 3 Brigades. A squadron of the 2nd Royal Tank Regiment was sent to join it to provide it with the firepower needed to counter any surviving Iraqi armour. The scene was set for the dénouement of the Battle for Basra.[24]

The advance of 40 Commando up the al Faw Peninsular was a major success. It was the biggest battle fought by the Royal Marines since the 1982 Falklands war. Surprisingly, given the intensity of the fighting, 40 Commando suffered no fatalities during the battle and few serious casualties. Some two hundred Iraqi soldiers were captured, including several senior officers. Dozens of Iraqi tanks and armoured vehicles were abandoned around the town.

A major factor in the success of the operation was the leadership of Colonel Messenger of 40 Commando, and the physical endurance of his troops.

General Brims commented, "Gordon [Messenger] was and still is a star!"[25]

Chapter 11

TO THE GATES OF BAGHDAD

While the bulk of 1 (UK) Armoured Division was engaged around Basra during the final days of March and into April, other British units were operating across Iraq in support of the American drive on Baghdad. At the time, these operations had little public or media profile as senior commanders and government ministers sought to focus attention on Basra. It was easier to explain the fight in Basra and the participation of British forces along side the Americans raised all sorts of complications, over rules of engagement, treatment of prisoners of war, intelligence co-operation and the involvement of highly secret special forces units.

Also within the British armed forces there was not a settled view on whether the main focus of their effort should be along side the Americans in Baghdad or concentrating on the specific British area of operations in south east Iraq, which became known as the "Basra box". These debates ebbed and flowed through out the British involvement in Iraq over the next five years. During the war-fighting phase in April and March 2003 the arguments in favour of a Basra-centric strategy won the day and set the course for the remainder of the British campaign, although on several occasions the desire by some commanders to swing resources towards the American effort in the Baghdad regime reared its head.

The leading proponents of going to Baghdad, before the war, were in the Airborne Forces and the Parachute Regiment. During January and February, the commander of 16 Air Assault Brigade, Brigadier Jacko Page, was involved in contingency planning with Americans to develop options in case of what was termed 'regime collapse' in Baghdad and Saddam Hussein decided to leave the country or was overthrown as a result of the US threat of invasion. In the chaos of Saddam's premature demise, the American and British airborne forces envisaged a rapid assault to capture Baghdad airport, thus to allow troops to fan out to take control of key buildings in the capital and sites connected to Iraqi weapons of mass destruction. It all proved illusionary, but exposed Brigadier Page and his senior officers to ambitious US plans to seize Iraq in a blitzkrieg offensive. They were excited by the daring and imaginative nature of their American counterparts thinking, and were keen to join them in the decisive battle of the war.[1]

On the eve of the war in early March events had moved on. US commanders had given up on the idea of a coup de main to seize Baghdad. Their main effort would be the armoured thrust up from Kuwait by the US Army's V Corps and the I MEF. The British division was given the task of screening the eastern flank of the American advance. A important part of British planning for this mission was an option known as 'northern expansion', which would push British troops up north past Nasiriyah, to set up a strong blocking position to stop the Iraqi 10th Armoured Division based in al Amarah pushing westwards into the flank of I MEF.[2]

Brigadier Page's brigade was given this job and he proposed launching a daring helicopter-borne assault by the 1st Battalion, The Parachute Regiment (1 PARA) to capture the Iraqi airbase at Qalat Sakir, some 200 kilometres northwest of Basra and almost half way to Baghdad. Once the first wave of paratroops had seized Qalat Sakir, they intended to turn it into a forward operating base and move up 105mm guns of 7th Royal Horse Artillery (7 RHA), as well as Lynx AH7 and Gazelle AH1 helicopters of 3 Regiment Army Air Corps to dominate Maysan province and a large swathe of central Iraq.

For five days, 1 PARA sat in its assembly area waiting to get the order to launch the Qalat Sakir strike, before the operation was cancelled at 5.30am on 26th March. The American advance on Baghdad was bogged down north of Nasiriyah and the drive on the capital was temporarily on hold until the I MEF firmed up its plans. As this was unfolding, the 16 Brigade staff were looking at other potential missions – such as securing bridges in Nasariyah. An air assault seizure of the North Rumiayah Bridge was debated but ultimately discounted, according to brigade officers.[3]

Senior British commanders in Iraq were still keen to try to help their American allies, and lobbied hard to get the Qalat Sakir operation reinstated. On the morning of 26th March, it was back on. Preparations were accelerated, air support organised and the RAF Chinooks of 18 Squadron were issued with orders for the mission, which was to launch during the night of 27th March.

US Marine Corps Hornets carried out reconnaissance flights over the airfield, and reported the presence of Iraqi anti-aircraft missile batteries. At the RAF-led Joint Helicopter Force (JHF) base in Kuwait the reports caused great unease among the RAF Chinook and US Marine Cobra pilots. They estimated at least one Chinook would be shot down, with the loss of dozens of paratroopers. Protests were made to the 16 Brigade and 1 (UK) Division headquarters. The operation was placed on temporary hold as senior commanders debated what to do. By the late afternoon, General Brims gave the go-ahead and the operation was scheduled for that evening. In its assembly area, 1 PARA began final preparations and the Chinooks, with their escorting Cobras, were winding up to fly forward from Ali Al Salem airbase in Kuwait to pick them up.

Just as darkness was falling, news came in that the US Marine Corps forward arming and refuelling point outside Nasiriyah, where the helicopter force needed to refuel to be able to reach their objective, was under sustained Iraqi artillery and mortar fire. The troops and helicopter crews were stood down. A few hours later US Marine Corps troops heading for Baghdad approached the Qalat Sakir from the south and found it undefended. 16 Brigade's Qalat Sakir mission was cancelled and would never be resurrected.

"Three hours before the operation we got reports that helicopters were under fire at Nasirayah" recalled Brims.

"Group Captain Andy Pulford, the commander of the JHF, called and told me he could do the operation, but there was a chance a helicopter could be hit. I took the decision. Although there was value to targeting Qalat Sakir, the strategic nature of the proposition to lose a helicopter with troops in it, at this stage in the operation, meant I cancelled it. Everyone was content, no one complained."[4]

Brigadier Page subsequently expressed his displeasure at the cancellation of the mission in his post-operational tour report, commenting "ultimately, the operation was stood down less than two hours before its execution following a flurry of pre-dawn telephone calls, without any formal command group gathering and as a result of an undefined [intelligence] assessment. In hindsight, the criteria for a GO/NO GO should have been determined during the planning stage, agreed by the Division and then delegated down to the lowest appropriate level. Support helicopters, placed under tactical command to the executing commander, should have deployed as ordered. A disciplined decision process, rather than an informal telephone briefing, would have proved more robust in the face of the uncertainties that bedevil any military operation."[5]

One unforeseen side effect of the Qalat Sakir operation was that G (Mercer's Troop) Battery of 7 RHA had been moving by road via Nasiriyah, to support the assault on the airfield, when it got caught up in the heavy street fighting in the city between US Marines and fanatical Fedayeen fighters loyal to the Baghdad regime. The Iraqi guerrillas had set up positions dominating two key bridges over the Euphrates River, and were raking US convoys crossing them with rocket propelled grenade and machine gun fire. The British gunners set up their 105mm Light Guns 1,500 metres from the bridges, and as the US convoys raced over the bridges they laid down a barrage of fire on the insurgent positions. The 105mm guns could switch fire in under two minutes, compared to the eight minutes it took the US Marines 155mm howitzers to engage new targets, so the American commanders attributed their British allies with saving scores of their troops' lives. After a day in action in the middle of Nasiriyah, the British divisional command to the east was increasingly worried about the battery taking casualties and ordered them to pull back to Rumalyah.[6]

The Pathfinders had also been ordered to move by road, via Nasiriyah, but they got through the town before the Iraqis started to put up major resistance to the US Marines. They passed through it without meeting any opposition, and started to drive north towards Qalat Sakir, when they ran into a group of Fadeyeen fighters and killed around fifty of them until extracting themselves to safety.[7]

As they drove through the night, Iraqi Fedayeen fighters in pick-up trucks opened fire on the Pathfinder's Land Rovers. Then they tried to block their escape route. Sergeant Nathan Bell led his patrol off into the desert to escape the attention of the fanatical Iraqi militiamen. Manning the General Purpose Machine Gun in the front of his vehicle, Bell shot up several Iraqi positions as they headed south towards friendly forces. For his bravery that night Bell was awarded the Military Cross.[8]

With its air manoeuvre operation cancelled, 16 Brigade was now ordered to focus on containing the Iraqi 6th Armoured Division north of the al-Hammer canal. The Household Cavalry Regiment, the Pathfinders, the Mobile Support Group of 3 PARA and Armed Reconnaissance Patrols of 3 Regiment were ordered to probe along the canal to find the centre of Iraqi resistance, and then called down artillery fire and air strikes. Artillery commanders huddled over television screens in the Brigade headquarters to look at live video feeds from Royal Artillery Phoenix UAVs trying to find targets. Other intelligence analysts used eavesdropping equipment to monitor Iraqi radio communications to try to find more targets.

For over a week, this battle grew in intensity as 16 Brigade pushed its reconnaissance forces further north from the al-Hammer canal towards the Euphrates River, and the main defensive positions of the Iraqi division. The terrain between the al-Hammer canal and the Euphrates River alternated between palm groves and marshy ground, so there was plenty of opportunity for the Iraqis to hide their positions. Around the clock, the reconnaissance teams were calling down artillery fire from the 16 Brigade's Offensive Support Group (OSG) against Iraqi bunkers and tanks. 3 Regiment's Lynx joined the battle engaging targets with TOW missiles or calling in artillery fire. US Air Force A-10A Warthogs and US Marine Corps Harriers made daily forays over the battlefield, striking at targets identified by 16 Brigade troops. They were also looking for Iraqi ballistic missile batteries that were still firing at Kuwait from palm groves along the Euphrates.

A flight of Lynx and Gazelle helicopters led by Captain Richard Cathill arrived overhead to give fire support to Scimitar armoured vehicles of the Household Cavalry Regiment (HCR). With visibility obscured by sand thrown up by the Iraqi fire, Cathill manoeuvred his Lynx to behind the Scimitars so he could line up his helicopters to fire along the path of 30mm tracer rounds fired by the HCR vehicles. He spotted the muzzle flash of an Iraqi self-propelled artillery piece and guided a TOW missile onto its targets. This required him to fly his helicopter straight and level as shells exploded around it. This bravery won Cathill the Distinguished Flying Cross.[9]

This was by no means a one sided battle, with the Iraqis making extensive use of their own target location systems to control their return artillery fire. British Lynx pilots on an hourly basis had to dodge Iraqi tank and artillery fire that was aimed at their helicopters, and if they got too close to Iraqi infantry, volleys of rocket propelled grenades could be expected. Iraqi artillery spotters tried to infiltrate 16 Brigade positions on several occasions, including trying to surrender to troops of the HCR before opening fire. For 16 Brigade's artillery fire spotters and forward air controllers the attention of Iraqi artillery was very unwelcome, and the best defence was a rapid withdrawal out of range in their vehicles, before they would re-group and try to find another way to approach their targets. The British reconnaissance teams often dismounted to move forward to occupy covert observation posts to watch their Iraqi opponents for days on end, relying on secrecy for protection. Occasionally, if targets presented themselves MILAN guided missile firing posts were brought forward under cover to launch surprise attacks on the Iraqi positions.

In a major success the Brigade identified the 6th Division's headquarters in Ad Dayr, and directed a US Marine Corps jet to drop a satellite-guided Joint Direct Attack Munition (JDAM) on the site.

In effect, a few hundred members of 16 Brigade were playing a deadly game of cat and mouse with several thousand Iraqi defenders, who had by no means given up the fight. The 6th Division conducted a professional defensive operation, and gave as good as it got on many occasions. Fortunately, US airpower meant the Iraqis were pinned in their defensive positions and could not risk their tanks breaking cover. At the same time, the 16 Brigade reconnaissance teams had freedom of movement, to pull back to safety, and to re-group.

The Iraqis were firing back with their South African made G5 155mm howitzers, which out-ranged 7 RHA's 105mm guns, so 16 Brigade's OSG staged a series of artillery raids. The regiment's 105mm batteries were raced forward to firing points close to the al-Hammer canal to engage the Iraqis, before they rapidly withdrew when it was feared the Iraqis had identified their positions and were directing artillery fire against them. Heavy self-propelled AS-90 155mm guns were then called forward to counter the big Iraqi guns, and through the Royal Engineer mobile bridging capability were placed on rafts and floated across the al-Hammar canal to take up position. Officers of 7 RHA attributed its success in its battle with the longer-range Iraqi artillery to the new MAMBA radars, which allowed it to rapidly pin-point enemy batteries and bring down effective counter-battery fire. The MAMBAs were responsible for over 40% of the fire missions fired by 7 RHA.[10]

In one of these artillery duels, the gunners of 7 RHA's I Battery moved forward to engage the Iraqis when they came under fire. To cover their withdrawal, F Battery moved up to engage the Iraqis. It too came under fire from the enemy. As the gunners dived for cover, the battery commander, Captain Grant Ingleton, realised his men's best defence was to keep firing to neutralise the in-coming fire. He defiantly took his helmet off and replaced it with his maroon paratrooper's beret, and walked around the gun position to encourage his men back to their weapons. The citation for his subsequent Military Cross said Ingleton's "infectious sense of humour and selfless leadership drew the men back to their guns, where they maintained their rate of fire and allowed the other battery to withdraw safely without casualties".[11]

During this period the bulk of 16 Brigade's infantry battalions were not engaged en masse, and stood guard on the oil complexes. A couple of small-scale attacks were mounted by 3 PARA to mop up resistance around the Rumalyah bridge, but the bulk of the action was controlled by the OSG. In the course of this battle 16 Brigade claimed the destruction of 86 Iraqi tanks and scores of enemy artillery pieces.[12]

All through this battle 16 Brigade was very lucky, and its reconnaissance teams managed to avoid taking any casualties. But on 28th March, a patrol of the Household Cavalry Regiment came under attack by USAF A-10As. The patrol was strafed twice by the American pilots, leaving one Household Cavalry soldier dead, and four wounded, before they were called off. The day after this incident, 16 Brigade's commander went to the divisional headquarters for a planning conference. Brigadier Page then had a meeting with Colonel Chris Vernon, General Brims' media spokesman. Brigadier Page, like many special forces veterans, was very wary of the media, and unlike many other senior army officers in the Middle East was not comfortable engaging with journalists.

The Brigadier complained that "small skirmishes are being reported as ferocious battles," and embedded media on the medical recovery ship, RFA Argus, were interviewing wounded soldiers from a blue-on-blue incident "with no control".

"The soldiers were fresh out of field and nobody is screening it," recorded Page in his brigade's war diary.

"The press interviewing wounded soldiers is bad because it captures raw emotion. Comments were made [by a wounded soldier] that did not really help coalition resolve when the rest of [the unit concerned were] very much on side and accepted the blue on blue [attack on the HCR] as an accident."[13]

Four years later the two USAF pilots were ruled to have unlawfully killed a soldier of the Household Cavalry Regiment in this incident.[14] The war diary then records that Brigadier Page raised what he called an "extraordinary story" with Colonel Vernon, concerning at least two of his soldiers who were refusing to fight because they did not believe in the war's morality, and felt they would be killing civilians. Page said he believed the soldiers were from 13 Regiment Royal Logistic Corps. One of the soldiers had a troubled family background and a psychological weakness, recorded Page. One of the soldiers was seen by a medic and deemed fit, and was sent back to Colchester but there had been no legal repercussions yet, and he had received no formal warning for [disciplinary] orders from his commanding officer, he wrote.[15]

A few days later when newspapers back in Britain started running stories about the two soldiers, the Ministry of Defence initially denied it was true, saying there was no evidence to prove the claims.[16] 16 Brigade also continued to support the US Marines during this period, and the Pathfinder Platoon was also inserted deep behind Iraqi lines by RAF Chinook to watch routes towards Baghdad that the commander of I MEF was considering using. The teams were successfully extracted and were debriefed by senior US Marine Corps officers before the big US attack on Baghdad.[17]

The battle against the Iraqi 6th Division was a very innovative battle, that was fought without the Brigade's infantry battalions actually being engaged, relying instead on artillery and predominantly US air power. For the British

Army this was a revolutionary form of warfare, and the skills honed in this battle would be put to great use three years later in Afghanistan. The shortage of helicopter lift capability in the UK armed forces meant resources had to be prioritised, and 16 Brigade was not considered the main effort by 1 (UK) Division, with the majority of helicopter support being given to sustaining 3 Commando Brigade on the al Faw peninsular. Also, the lack of long-range surveillance and artillery capabilities meant that when the Brigade was given the chance to mount an air manoeuvre operation against Qalat Sakir airfield, it had to be cancelled because threats could not be confirmed with any certainty. The guns of 7 RHA had insufficient range to hit the suspected enemy air defence site blocking access to the airfield. There was a feeling that 16 Brigade had not really cut its teeth in Iraq, and left plenty of unfinished business.

General Brims said he recognised the frustration.

"16 Brigade were itching to do things. Their job was to hold the oil fields, which was US Defence Secretary [Donald] Rumsfeld's major concern and I was constantly being asked if they were secure. Soldiers want to do things but they did not need to do any more than necessary. My purpose was not to satisfy troops with tasks but to do the military solution. They did just fine, they did not need to do more."[18]

Out in Iraq's western desert, another British force was embarking on what would turn out to be an operation that would impact significantly on the outcome of the US drive on Baghdad. A constant nightmare for the US and British governments was the possibility of the Iraqis repeating their Scud missile attacks on Israel, which had caused so many problems during the 1991 conflict. The risk that the Iraqis might be able to provoke the Israelis into retaliating in response to the missile attacks, threatened to fracture support for the US and British war on Iraq across the Middle East. Popular outrage in Arab countries that were providing vital bases for the US and British might have forced these countries' governments to withdraw support, just as the war was entering a critical phase. Attacking Israel was seen as a way for the Iraqi dictator to turn Arab opinion into diplomatic action that could have seriously de-railed the US and British war.

Not surprisingly, a major effort was devoted to neutralising this threat. The US air commander in the Middle East, Lieutenant General Buzz Moseley, was heading up the new iteration of what became known as the 'Great Scud hunt.' Unlike in 1991, when the counter-Scud campaign was improvised in a matter of days after the start of the war, this time around considerable effort was put into preparing the operation for several months ahead of the start of hostilities.

By mid March, several thousand British, Australian and US troops were positioned in Jordan and Saudi Arabia to begin the counter-Scud effort. The British component of this mission, designated Operation Row, involved just over 1,500 personnel. These were drawn from 22 Special Air Service (22 SAS) Regiment, M Squadron of the Special Boat Service (SBS), 45 Commando Royal Marines and II Squadron of the Royal Air Force Regiment. A strong RAF contingent, led by Wing Commander Bob Adlam, was dispatched to Azraq airbase in eastern Jordan to support the special forces teams that would conduct operations inside Iraq. This included Chinook HC2 transport helicopters from 7 Squadron and Hercules transports from the Special Forces Flight of 47 Squadron. Also at Azraq were Harrier GR7 jump jets of 3 (Fighter Squadron), and high-flying Canberra reconnaissance aircraft of 39 Squadron, as well as protection and operational support teams from the Royal Auxiliary Air Force's 504 Squadron. The latter unit was made up of mobilised reservists.[19]

A considerable chunk of the RAF aircraft deployed to the Middle East was dedicated fulltime to supporting Operation Row. These included four Nimrod MR2 patrol aircraft, fitted with thermal imaging video cameras, of 120 Squadron and four E-3D Sentry AWACS aircraft of 8 and 23 Squadrons. These big aircraft operated out of Prince Sultan Air Base (PSAB) in Saudi Arabia. At Ali al Salem several Tornado GR4 strike jets of II (Army Co-operation) Squadron were dedicated to fly Scud hunting patrols over western Iraq.[20]

General Moseley created a special team within the Combined Air Operations Centre (CAOC) at PSAB to direct the Scud hunt. In an unprecedented move, the overall US commander in the Middle East, General Tommy Franks, put Moseley in direct command of the special forces teams operating on the ground in western Iraq so their operations could be seamlessly integrated with his air power.[21]

The ground element of the new Scud hunt was controlled by the US 5th Special Force Group's commanding officer, Colonel John Mulholland, who had led the US special forces campaign in northern Afghanistan in the days after 9/11. He set up a Combined Joint Special Operations Task Force – West in Jordan to co-ordinate the Australian, British and US special forces patrols.[22] The British sent Brigadier Adrian Bradshaw, a suave cavalry officer from the King's Royal Hussars, who had previously served in the SAS, to work with Mulholland as his deputy.[23] Leading the British special forces contingent in Jordan and Iraq, which was dubbed Task Force 14, was the commanding officer of 22 SAS, Lieutenant Colonel Mark Carleton-Smith, a former Irish Guards officer.[24]

The operation in western Iraq was considered so strategically important that the charismatic Director of Special Forces, Brigadier Graeme Lamb, flew out from London to supervise things from the US Special Operations Forces headquarters in Qatar. This was the biggest British special forces operation since the 1991 Gulf War, and almost everyone wanted to be part of the action. Lamb was one of the few members of an SAS force that operated in western Iraq in 1991 who was still serving, and he was keen to avoid repeating the mistakes that consigned the ill-fated Bravo Two Zero patrol to disaster.[25]

Moseley's planners and US, British and Australian special forces officers had studied the 1991 Scud hunt in great detail, pulling archived patrol reports from US and British troops who had entered Iraq at this time. They also looked at UN weapon inspection reports and aerial imagery from reconnaissance aircraft and satellites, as well as missile plume heat signature data from space surveillance systems. They built up a detailed picture of where the Iraqis had launched Scuds from in 1991, potential hiding places for missile launchers and missiles, as well the bases of Iraqi troops across the western desert. This allowed them to build a concept of operations that would not repeat the mistakes of 1991, when no Scuds had been confirmed destroyed by either coalition aircraft or special forces teams on the ground. During the early 1990s UN weapon inspectors visited all the sites where the US and British claimed to have destroyed Scuds, but found no evidence of destroyed missiles or launchers. Moseley and his team were determined to do better this time around.[26]

Western Iraq was to be placed under round-the-clock aerial surveillance by the RAF Canberra and Nimrods, as well as by US MQ-1 Predator drones, E-8 Joint STARS radar aircraft and U-2 Dragon Lady spy planes. The U-2s and E-8s used their moving target indicator radars to monitor road movement across western Iraq, and if suspicious activity was spotted a Nimrod or Predator would be dispatched to provide a positive identification. The Canberras would meanwhile fly daily surveillance missions to take high detail stills pictures of suspected Scud hiding places, which would be studied by analysts for any signs of suspicious activity.

On the ground, the big lesson from 1991 was that special forces units needed to be highly mobile, and heavily armed, to avoid the fate of the SAS Bravo Two Zero foot patrol that had been inserted by helicopter. It had been compromised and then run to ground by Iraqi troops, with all its members being killed, captured or forced to flee to Syria. This time the special forces would be used to patrol along the main roads of western Iraq in heavily-armed Land Rovers, in trucks and on quad bikes, to stop the Iraqis using the roads to move their Scuds around. At the same time other patrols would be used systematically to visit all the suspected Scud facilities within firing range of Israel. In turn, these ground patrols would be cued, in real time, to intercept any Scuds that were detected by air surveillance.[27]

These ground patrols would have their own dedicated air protection provided by the RAF Harriers, armed Predators, a squadron of US Air National Guard F-16C Fighting Falcons based in Jordan, and the RAF Tornados. Moseley's planners created a permanent flow of jets over western Iraq to ensure that aircraft would be in the air over the special forces constantly, in case they came under attack and needed air support for protection. The 3 (F) Squadron RAF Harriers, led by Wing Commander Stu Atha, flew mainly in day time, while the USAF F-16 and II (AC) Squadron Tornados had the night shift. For the pilots, the bad weather that engulfed western Iraq during March 2003 created a nightmare because it meant they could not fly at medium and high altitude to spot targets. The only way to put bombs on target was to drop to low level, making their jets vulnerable to Iraqi anti-aircraft guns and shoulder-launched anti-aircraft missiles.[28]

For the Special Forces patrols this on-call air power was their 'ace in the hole' that would allow them to defeat superior Iraqi forces, but the fluid and mobile nature of the battlefield meant considerable effort had to be put into ensuring that strike aircraft could differentiate between friendly and enemy forces. Operating far behind enemy lines, the risk of being attacked by accident by coalition jets was immense. All the US, British and Australian special forces vehicles were fitted with an electronic tracking device known as Blue Forces Tracking. This linked the GPS navigation system that allowed officers in the special forces headquarters in Jordan to monitor in real time the position of every patrol. In turn, a co-ordination system to divide up western Iraq into 'kill boxes' was set up. If a special forces patrol was in a specific ten kilometre square box then it was classed as closed, and strike aircraft could only attack ground targets if they were in radio contact with the ground troops, who could see the target. 'Open' kill boxes were those clear of friendly troops and pilots could make their own decisions to attack.[29]

According to Squadron Leader Harvey Smyth, who flew many of these missions as a Harrier pilot in 3 Squadron, the high-level of co-ordination between the air and ground forces in western Iraq allowed more than 100 'danger close' close air support missions to be successfully conducted, with no instances of blue-on-blue. These were missions where the friendly troops calling in air support were so close to the enemy they risked being injured or killed by their own side's bombs, illustrating the intensity of the fighting in western Iraq.[30]

At the centre of the air and ground operations were the RAF E-3D Sentry aircraft, which flew continuous orbits over western Iraqi throughout the war. They were in radio contact with the special forces patrols, the surveillance aircraft, the special forces headquarters, the US Army Scud missile launch detection and warning network, and the CAOC at PSAB. The aim was to speed the reaction time to a Scud being discovered by any of the players, and the dispatch of forces to deal with the threat. It was hoped that any Scud launcher could be hit in a matter of minutes of it breaking cover.[31]

After pushing into Iraq on the night of 18th/19th March, the British, US and Australian special forces teams fanned out to establish themselves in their respective patrol zones. For the next week, there were a series of short engagements as the special forces patrols, backed by air power, took on the isolated Iraqi detachments in the towns of the region.

A pair of Harriers, Tornados or F-16s were in the air over the SAS on a constant basis, with air-to-air refuelling being used to allow the jets to fly nine-hour long missions. They were in action on a daily basis repulsing Iraqi counter-attacks, artillery positions firing at British troops and anti-aircraft sites defending key bases. The actions of 3 Squadron in the western desert became legendary in the RAF, with the commander of the Harrier unit winning the Distinguished Service Order. A pilot won the Distinguished Flying Cross, and another won the Air Force Cross.[32] "One of the things that made the Western Desert operation so successful was the level of practice undertaken by the participating forces," said the British air component commander, Air Vice Marshal

Glenn Torpy. "This included several exercises in the US, where the procedures and techniques were developed and practiced – it was a key lesson."

Top priority was given to seizing half a dozen Iraqi air bases in western Iraq to neutralise the threat to British and US aircraft and helicopters. The hardened shelters and bunkers at these bases were also suspected of being used to hide the dreaded Scuds. US troops swept into these bases, H-2 and H-3 airfields, and easily captured them. The British SAS were assigned the sector to the north of these airfields, stretching along the Syrian border towards the town of al Qaim. This town was home to a garrison of Republic Guard troops who were suspected of protecting a chemical weapons storage site.[33]

As the SAS vehicles patrols penetrated the border berm on the night of 18th/19th March, an SAS assault force from D Squadron was flown by RAF Chinook up to the outskirts of al Qaim to try to launch an attack on the chemical weapons store. After a fierce firefight with the Republican Guard, the SAS troops pulled back into the desert to join up with their vehicle-borne colleagues of B Squadron.[34]

The Americans had in the meantime captured H-1, H-2 and H-3 airfields in western Iraq, and were turning them into forward operating bases to support the Scud hunting patrols. Helicopters and vehicle refuelling points were set up at them and a prison camp was also built to house the hundreds of Iraqi soldiers that were now being captured.

Royal Marines of 45 Commando and the RAF Regiment gunners of II Squadron moved into Iraq with them to set up the British forward logistics base at H-2. They patrolled the surrounding desert, guarded the base, processed prisoners and provided airborne reaction forces for the SAS teams scouring the desert for Scuds.[35]

Providing the eyes and ears of the Scud hunt were the 44 year old Canberra spy planes which were flying continuous patrols over western Iraq, taking photographs of 17 areas of interest which were suspected of being the most likely Scud launch sites.

The-then officer commanding 39 Squadron, Wing Commander Ken Smith, recalled how his aircraft flew three nine-hour long patrols a day over western Iraq. The crew then used a digital datalink to download digital pictures of targets to a ground station at Azraq airbase in Jordan.

"The photo interpreters then scoured the images for Scuds," he said.

"Then they burnt the images on to a CD and then they were taken by bike to the transmission point on the other side of the airfield. We also had a phone to the CAOC if we found anything. The network wasn't there [to email the images direct to the CAOC]." [36]

The vintage British aircraft proved to be one of the few airborne surveillance assets that could operate below the low cloud ceiling over western Iraq.

"The western desert weather was abysmal so the US was not expecting to get any imagery, but we went below the clouds and sand storms to use sensor differently and got images," said Smith.

"The U-2 couldn't go down fast and low."[37]

RAF Tornados crews' low-level flying skills also came into their own flying nightly missions over western Iraq using their TIALD thermal imaging targeting pods and side ways looking infra-red sensors of the Tornado Infrared Reconnaissance System to look for Scuds. On their first mission on the night of 19th/20th March, a II (AC) Squadron found what the crew thought was a Scud launcher hiding under a bridge, and made repeated low level passes to try to get a good enough look to positively identify it.[38]

Both the Tornados and Harriers flew daily sorties and dropped weapons when called into action by British and US vehicle patrols, which had set up hides to watch key road junctions and suspected Scud hides.

While the bulk of the special forces patrols were pre-occupied with this operation, commanders were beginning to think about expanding their area of operations to drive the Iraqis back towards Baghdad. The idea was to convince the Iraqis that a large coalition tank column was advancing on their capital.

The leaders of the British special forces had bigger ambitions: they wanted to push M Squadron of the SBS through western Iraq and up towards the Kurdish region around Mosul, to establish communications with the Iraqi 5th Corps, which MI6 and the CIA said was on the verge of surrendering.[39]

The Land Rovers and quad bikes of M Squadron were flown by 47 Squadron C-130s into H-2, and then they were cross-loaded into 7 Squadron Chinooks for a night-time flight deep into Iraq, leap-frogging over the Euphrates to within striking distance of Mosul. With only two Chinooks available for the mission, it took three nights to shuttle all the Squadron's vehicles to its drop-off point.

After driving across the desert towards Mosul, the squadron was compromised by a large force of Iraqi regular troops and Fedayeen fighters in a fleet of pick-up trucks on 27th/28th March. The Royal Marines were chased across the desert for a night before many of their vehicles became stuck in a muddy wadi. They scattered into three smaller groups that were pursued relentlessly by Iraqis. One group of SBS troopers called up air support to help it break contact with the Iraqis, and to allow it to make a dash for a helicopter pick-up point. A pair of US Air National Guard F-16s responded to the call for help and made repeated low level passes to intimidate the Iraqis. The pilots said they could not differentiate between the British and Iraqis, so it was too dangerous to drop live weapons for fear of hitting the spread-out SBS troops. The intervention did the trick and the British Marines were soon heading for safety, but not before they had several more brushes with the Iraqi pursuit force.[40]

Two Chinooks were now in-bound to pick up the scattered British troops. A pair of RAF Tornados appeared over the battlefield and made a series of low level passes to keep the Iraqis' heads down, while the Chinooks landed and picked up the isolated British troops. One group was surrounded by Iraqi tanks and only just had time to scramble on board the helicopters. They had to leave demolition charges in their vehicles before escaping. The other two groups had more luck, and one was even able to bring out its vehicles. In total 58 SBS men were rescued. All were exhausted but none were seriously injured. Two men were missing, though, and RAF helicopters flew several search missions along the Syria-Iraq border over the next two weeks to try to find the men. It later emerged that they had successfully escaped to Syria, and both men were handed over to Foreign Office minister Mike O'Brian in Damascus in April.[41]

The American, British and Australian special forces were now staging daily raids closer and closer to Baghdad, dropping by parachute and helicopters onto airfields and other strategic targets. On one airfield, they flew in a detachment of M1A1 Abrams main battle tanks to add to the impression that an armoured force was advancing from Jordan. The ruse worked spectacularly well. When American tanks of the 3rd Infantry Division advancing from Kuwait seized Baghdad International Airport on 4th April, Saddam Hussein and his inner circle were convinced it was a feint to distract them from the main attack from Jordan. According to the Iraqi Perspective Project, which studied captured Iraqi documents and interviewed former Iraqi generals, Saddam now made a crucial mistake. He ordered his last Republican Guard reserves to move out to the west to counter the force coming from Jordan, rather than sending it to set up a last line of defence at the airport. It sealed the fate of his regime. Within days the Iraqi dictator was on the run in his own country.[42]

Into this maelstrom, Brigadier Lamb and a small contingent of D Squadron of 22 SAS flew to Baghdad airport to help infiltrate an MI6 team into the city. They wanted to establish contact with old sources, who might have leads on the location of Saddam and his weapons of mass destruction. This was becoming a more pressing issue because so far none had been found.[43] Out in the western desert, there had been no sighting of Scuds or even any attempts to fire them.

"We found no Scuds, we found mock-ups that were subsequently destroyed" recalled Wing Commander Smith in late 2003.

"We put so much effort into finding the Scuds that we created the effect desired and scared them off".[44]

Air Marshal Burridge described the counter-Scud operation as "an elegant piece of operational art", which had been first demonstrated during an experiment in the Nevada desert.

"It was led by the air component, as the supported commander," he said,

"No Scuds were fired at Israel. Saddam saw a lot of activity in the west. The military intent was to give him so many problems he would not be able to interpret it."[45]

However, a few months later experts of the Iraq Survey Group concluded that the intelligence saying the Iraqis still had Scuds was wrong and that they had destroyed all their Scuds in the 1990s. Operation Row had been a wild goose chase.[46] "To ignore the threat would have been irresponsible," commented Torpy.

The next most significant British contribution to the American drive on Baghdad was provided by the RAF Tornado and Harrier forces based in Kuwait and Qatar. The Iraqi air defence forces around Baghdad had been devastated during the 21st March 'shock and awe' air strikes around the Iraqi capital. RAF Tornado GR4 from the Ali al Salem combat wing were involved in both of the large 'shock and awe' strike packages, launching the new Storm Shadow long-range cruise missile and ALARM anti-radar missiles.

The Storm Shadow missions were led by Wing Commander Dave Robertson, the commander of the RAF's elite Dambusters 617 Squadron. His formation of four aircraft came under Iraqi gun and missile fire as they approached the so-called 'super missile engagement zone' or Super MEZ around Baghdad, but they all launched their weapons and scored 100% direct hits on a series of Iraqi air defence command bunkers.

Over the next three days, General Moseley and his air planners swung the bulk of US, British and Australian air power to supporting the drive on Baghdad by the US Army and the US Marines. As the American tank columns weaved through Nasiriyah and then pushed north into central Iraq they were hit by increasingly fanatical resistance from Fedayeen irregular fighters, and elite units of the Republican Guards. A spate of sand storms hit central Iraq at this time reducing visibility to a few dozen metres and dropping huge quantities of sand on top of vehicles and tents. This prompted American commanders to pause the advance to clear up the battlefield, bring up fuel and wait for the clouds to clear. When the sand storms cleared the drive on Baghdad resumed. For the RAF commanders, pilots and ground crews in Kuwait and Qatar, the drive on Baghdad saw them ramp up operations dramatically, with each of the 32 Tornados and 12 Harriers flying two missions each day. There was great rivalry between the pilots who flew the small jump jet and the crews of the bigger two-engine strike bomber. The Harrier crews considered themselves the RAF close air support specialists and were all qualified to work with army forward air controllers (FAC). Almost all of those deployed to Kuwait had seen action in the 1999 Kosovo war. Their commander at Ahmed al Jaber airbase, Group Captain Mike Harwood, was an aggressive leader.[47] He declared he had a "mind of doom" and he focused his pilots and ground crews on inflicting maximum damage on the Iraqi army. His pilots from 1 (Fighter) and IV Squadrons were equally up for the operation and were soon relentlessly pounding the Iraqi Republican Guard.[48]

"After the pause we became really efficient, really took them apart," recalled one of the Harrier pilots.

The Tornado crews at Ali al Salem in Kuwait and Al Udeid were almost all veterans of more than a decade of no-fly zone patrols over southern Iraq, so took the move to all-out war in their stride. They were heavily involved in the shock and awe campaign and ranged far and wide attacking strategic targets. The RAF crews were experienced at dodging Iraqi air defences, and had worked routinely with the US air-to-air refuelling tankers, E-3 AWACS radar and other surveillance aircraft throughout the Middle East theatre. Precision strategic air attacks were the specialisation of the Tornado crews, so when the focus of the air campaign switched to supporting the armoured drive on Baghdad, they had to rapidly switch to working with FACs to attack targets close to friendly ground troops. The Tornado would prove well-suited to close air support because of its two man crew: there was an extra pair of eyes to look for targets and the bigger jet could carry more weapons than the smaller Harrier.

The pause came as a major surprise to US ground commanders, and they turned to air power to open the way to Baghdad, according to RAF Harrier pilots. The FACs on the ground with the armoured columns were ordered to take more risks. The rate of destruction of the Republican Guard tank force had to be dramatically increased. When a US Army AH-64A Apache attack helicopter brigade was devastated by Iraqi anti-aircraft fire, with every helicopters taking hits and one being shot down, leading to the capture of the crew, fixed wing air support was ramped up even more.

Air Vice Marshal Torpy and a team of RAF planners were working in the operations centre in Saudi Arabia as part of General Moseley's command team. Each day they were overseeing the planning, launch and conduct of more than 2,000 US, British and Australian aircraft across the Middle East. The CAOC was a highly computerised command centre with large screens displaying in real-time the position of every aircraft airborne over Iraq and neighbouring countries. The British and American staff controlled all the aircraft operating against Iraq via virtual 'chat rooms' linked to the airborne AWACS aircraft, and email to airbases around the region. The key tool was a giant spreadsheet known as the 'Air Tasking Order,' which listed the flights of every aircraft in the theatre, including its target, weapon load, radio call sign, route, take off and landing times, as well as the crucial time on target.

"The CAOC and ATO was a machine that delivered 2000 sorties a day," said Torpy.

"It was a well proven process."

Moseley, Torpy and their senior advisors met every late afternoon to approve the next days ATO.

"In general, we did not have to get involved in individual target selection, we had a very experienced and efficient staff to undertake the detailed planning," commented Torpy.

"There was just not enough time for senior commanders to get involved in that level of detail.

The speed of the advance on Baghdad surprised everyone," he said.[49]

"The US transitioned from pre-planned counter air sorties to focusing on close air support very quickly. The pace of the operation dictated that pilots got used to taking-off with a general idea of where they were going, and then receiving detailed guidance once airborne from AWACS or forward air controllers (FAC)."[50]

RAF pilots said that in the first week of the war, the US organisation for controlling air support was not working well.

"The ground forces before the war said they could handle fifty pairs of aircraft, but it turned out they could only handle three pairs," said a Harrier pilot based in Kuwait.[51]

"The American air and army commanders did not see eye to eye but in the end they were told by General Franks to get their shit together and change attitudes."

Overseeing things from Saudi Arabia, Air Vice Marshal Torpy had a different perspective. "The issue here was not a difference of opinion between land and air commanders but rather a difference in expertise between the [air operations centre] supporting [US Army's] V Corps and the US Marine Corps [air operations centre] supporting the Marine Expeditionary Force. Because of the highly integrated way the USMC operate – where aircraft are used to supplement artillery – they are highly efficient in the way they control and use air power. The same was not true of the [US Army's air operations centre] - certainly at the start – they improved over time."

At first, senior US Army commanders were very cautious about opening killing boxes, to allow strike jets to hit targets without referring to a FAC on the ground for clearance to attack. This procedure was designed to prevent friendly fire incidents, or the accidental targeting of civilians, but it meant that targets out of sight of friendly ground troops could not be hit. Frustrated Harrier pilots recalled flying over fields full of Iraqi tanks and artillery dug-in in revetments but not being allowed to attack them.

"[Fixed wing] air was not being given open kill boxes" said another pilot.

"At the start of the war, the ground forces were moving so fast they were not able to control opening and closing kill boxes. For about three days 80-90% of sorties came back with bombs still on. Once the Apache brigade took a beating then a decision was made to use airpower deep."[52]

The US Air Force and Marine Corps began sending up F-15E Strike Eagles and F/A-18 Hornets to act as airborne forward air controllers (AFAC), who would patrol above kill boxes, monitoring the situation on the ground and then handing off targets to other jets. Known as "traffic cops" by the Americans, the AFACs dramatically increased the efficiency of the air support operation because the majority of pilots did not have to waste time and fuel looking for targets. Soon the tank kill rate went up dramatically, and some 700 attack sorties a day were being flown over Iraq, with the majority of these hitting targets between Baghdad and Nasiriyah. The RAF was flying nearly 100 of these sorties each day, with many jets dropping all their weapons. Some 85% of the weapons involved were precision laser or satellite guided weapons, and hit rates of more than 95% were recorded for the 600 weapons dropped by the RAF. This was a systematic effort to destroy resistance.[53]

RAF VC-10 and Tristrar tankers were now flying deep into Iraqi air space to pass fuel to British and US jets, so they could remain on station over the kill boxes for longer. This meant there was a near constant flow of jets over the Republican Guard, adding to its misfortune.

According to Harwood, "the result in the end was the decimation of the regular army, Republican Guard and Special Republican Guard. Their combat effectiveness was reduced to almost zero. Air power destroyed organised military resistance".[54]

"The majority of pilots took off not knowing their target", he said. "When they got over the battlefield they spoke to someone who had an idea about what was going on on the ground, and they would tell the pilots what to attack. Decision making took place in the cockpit by the pilot. A very big part, was that they had to understand the rules of engagement, politics, law of armed conflict. They briefed to death. In a single seat aircraft like a Harrier, the pilot became a lawyer, accountant and media man. Tactical actions have strategic effect."[55]

Once the pause ended, the RAF Harriers spent five days hitting the Republican Guard's Medina and Baghdad divisions, while the US Marine Corps Harriers focused on hitting the Iraqi 6th Armoured Division north of Basra.

"We gave them a real hammering," said an RAF Harrier pilot.

"The Republican Guard was well dispersed in revetments. Most targets I found were cold after sunset – indicating the crews abandoned them at night when they thought they would be attacked. Only on one occasion did we see tanks gathering in a square. Over 60% of all tanks in Republican Guard Divisions were destroyed by RAF and US air attacks."[56]

"When we interviewed Republican Guard commanders after the war they said the bad weather in the Baghdad region led to a pivotal event in the war," commented Air Marshal Burridge. "The Iraqis assumed that they would be safe to manoeuvre and began repositioning their divisions from north of Baghdad to the south of the capital to defend against our approach through the Karbala Gap. Their rationale was that we would not be able to see them in bad weather. However, we launched 750 counter-land sorties that day, directed by moving target indicator radar on the US E-8 Joint STARS surveillance aircraft. The Iraqis could not understand how we saw them, as they did not understand the capability of Joint STARS. They got whipped. They were convinced someone inside their organisation was giving away information and that broke their morale."[57]

The Harrier pilots said they used all types of the weapons in their inventory, including 50% laser guided Paveway bombs, 15-20% Maverick television guided missions and 5% satellite-guided Enhanced Paveway. The remainder were 'dumb' or unguided 500lb bombs, and the controversial RB755 cluster bomb, which were withdrawn from RAF service in 2008 when the British government signed the international ban on cluster weapons.[58]

"We used the cluster bombs if we saw tanks in the open quite close together" said a Harrier pilot.

"Most others were in individual berms so we used precision-guided munitions. We had to ask guys on the ground to clear us to use cluster bombs because army guys would have to pass over the ground at later date. We used precision weapons all the time. On one occasion I dropped four weapons in the space of 20 minutes and took out four targets."[59]

Crews in the Tornado combat wings had similar experiences in the later phases of the war, but unlike their Harrier comrades they ranged far and wide across Iraq including striking targets in western Iraq, as well as supporting Kurdish fighters and US special forces in the north of the country. This took the Tornados into areas patrolled by US Predator drones, and for the first time RAF aircrew were directed to hit targets by the operators of robot aircraft.

During the first days of April when US troops entered Baghdad, the need for close air support increased exponentially as the heavy street fighting broke out across the city. US air commanders set up an 'Urban CAS Stack' over the city, which was constantly being topped up with fully-armed and fuelled jets ready to be called into action by FACs. The idea was to have bombs on target in a matter of minutes of getting the call from a FAC.[60]

The Harrier squadron sent two pairs of jets a day to do urban close air support, armed predominately with Enhanced Paveway bombs, which had a fuse that could be adjusted by the pilot to detonate the bomb at variable altitudes from the ground.

"We tried to get a vertical impact of the munition inside buildings or between buildings," said a Harrier pilot.

"We had every weapon in our inventory on our aircraft so we had the right weapon for the job."[61]

To try to reduce collateral damage when dropping bombs in urban environments, the Tornado crews began experimenting using inert training bombs, which lacked an explosive warhead.

"It was difficult and war was not what we expected," recalled Harwood.

"We expected an air tasking orders for 48 hour cycles [of pre-planned operations], but it was more dynamic. We had to respond more quickly and it was down to guys in the cockpits."[62]

Other parts of the RAF force in the Middle East were increasingly being drawn into supporting the US advance on Baghdad. The US Marine Corps had opened a series of forward air strips in central Iraq to bring in supplies by C-130 Hercules. Four RAF C-130s had been forward deployed to Kuwait International Airport, and a desert airstrip built by the US Marines to support 16 Air Assault Brigade. But once the Qalat Sakir air assault was cancelled, these aircraft were made available to participate in the air bridge to I MEF advance columns.

Two 70 and 47 Squadron Hercules flew the first night-time mission to Jalibah, as part of a joint formation with US Marine C-130s on 26th March. The airfield had recently by captured by American troops and was shrouded in smoke from burning buildings, prompting the aircrews to have to wave off landing at first, until a gap in the smoke cleared. Four days later 30 Squadron joined the air bridge, flying the new C-130J model of the Hercules on its first combat operation. The aircraft flew into Iraq at 300 feet before landing at Tallil airbase.[63]

When the Iraqis started firing Seersucker cruise missiles at American bases in Kuwait, there was an urgent need to help beef up the air defences of key strategic locations. One of the missiles landed only 400 metres from the I MEF Headquarters at Camp Commando, which was located a few kilometres south of the Iraqi border. This prompted the RAF to order its Rapier anti-aircraft missile battery at Ali Al Salem to be rushed forward to defend the nerve centre of the US Marine Corps in the Middle East.[64]

President George Bush and Prime Minister Tony Blair's rationale for going to war was the refusal of the Saddam Hussein to dismantle his weapons of mass destruction (WMD). It was a matter of the highest priority that these be found, and paraded to the world, to prove the case for war. The Pentagon created a dedicated task force of intelligence experts, scientists and a force protection unit drawn from the 75th Field Artillery Brigade to lead the hunt for the WMD. They were dubbed the 'Exploitation Task Force,' or XTF. They were to act on intelligence from informers inside Iraq or reports from advancing ground troops about WMD, in what were designed Sensitive Site Exploitation (SSE) missions.

If there was the chance to seize WMD inside Iraqi-held territory, then elite US special forces operatives known as Task Force 20 (TF20) would lead the way and set up a cordon to allow scientific experts to be flown in to secure the prize. Operating in the wake of the advancing land forces, it would then be the job of the troops of the 75th Brigade to secure the site.[65]

The strategic importance of this mission resulted in Britain sending its own personnel to be part of the XTF. Its contribution was grouped around H Squadron, 1st Royal Tank Regiment, under the command of Major Jonathan Billings, and eventually rose to some 100 personnel. These included a mobile field laboratory manned by scientists from the chemical weapon research centre at Porton Down, Defence Intelligence Staff experts, bomb disposal personnel, a satellite communications team, interrogators and forensic experts.[66] The XTF and its British contingent advanced north towards Baghdad, stopping first at Tallil airbase during the pause before continuing the advance.

H Squadron was the first non-special forces British Army unit to enter Baghdad a matter of hours after the fall of Saddam's regime, and went on to help secure the British Embassy until follow-on troops arrived from Basra.[67] The lack of WMD was a major disappointment for the Blair government in London. Elaborate plans had been developed to fly a media pool of journalists from the coalition press centre in Qatar to the site of any confirmed WMD, so the results could be broadcast immediately to the world. The rapid pace of the advance on Baghdad meant that US troops did not stop to carry out in-depth investigations of suspected WMDs until they had captured the Iraqi capital. The good headlines would have to wait.[68]

Chapter 12
FALL OF BASRA

During 4th April, Abrams tanks of the US Army's 3rd Infantry Division drove onto the runway of Baghdad International Airport. The following morning an American tank column cruised through downtown Baghdad to carry out the first 'Thunder Run.' Iraqi Republican Guards put up fanatical resistance, but their weapons were no match for the US Army M1A1 Abrams tanks, and a trail of devastation was left in the wake of the American armour.

When the head of the Iraqi information ministry, Muhammed Saeed al-Sahaf, appeared at a press conferences in the capital to declare the imminent defeat of the US Army, he soon picked up the nickname 'Comical Ali.' Saddam Hussein's regime was on its last legs. Iraq's army would soon collapse.

In the south, the British Army's mood changed noticeably over this period as commanders and troops began to feel a noticeable trailing off in resistance to their raids into Basra. Air Marshal Brian Burridge, the UK national contingent commander in the Middle East, flew by helicopter up to major General Robin Brims' headquarters in northern Kuwait, to brief him on plans for what were termed Phase IV operations after the fall of the Ba'athist regime.[1] With Baghdad teetering, it seemed likely that British troops would soon be taking full control of Basra. The Air Marshal briefed the General that London and Washington had agreed that the UK would be eventually responsible for the four most southern Iraqi provinces and that 1 (UK) Division needed to be ready to occupy this areas.

"The four provinces decision was cleared by London at a strategic level," recalled Burridge. "This notion was entirely in keeping with our legal responsibility as an occupying power. While force density was always going to be a challenge, at the time, it seemed do-able."[2]

Although the media coverage of fighting in Baghdad seemed to suggest that the Iraqi regime's days were numbered, not everyone in the British forces were convinced the war would be over any time soon. On 2nd April, General Brims' intelligence team generated a summary of the state of Iraqi forces facing British forces. While the analysts were upbeat about the damage being done to Iraqi armour and artillery, it concluded that the local population in Basra was not ready to rise in revolt and was still hedging its bets.

"Until the population is convinced of the resolve of the coalition to stay, resistance will continue," said the analysis. Although the regular army units were "increasingly challenged" to maintain a conventional defence, the analysis predicted the Iraqis would keep fighting, continue to fire ballistic missiles and launch asymmetric attacks on coalition rear areas. There was no prediction of imminent collapse.[3]

General Brims and his senior officers were now thinking about how to deliver the coup de grâce to Ba'ath Party rule in Basra. At the heart of the

General's thinking was the launching of a simultaneous concentric attack on the city from the west and north to overwhelm the Iraqi resistance. This attack was not intended to be launched until the morale of the Iraqi defenders had reached rock bottom, so the mere appearance of British tanks would have the Fedayeen running for their lives.

The final phase of the Battle for Basra was code-named Operation Sinbad, but General Brims considered its execution still to be some days off. The General and his staff were confident that Operation Sinbad would succeed, but they wanted to have a few more days to build the right conditions. He issued a fragmentary order to his brigades on 2nd April predicting that they were considering launching an offensive into Basra, but that it would not kick off before 8th April. During that day General Brims set out on a tour of his brigades and battlegroups to get a feel for the situation on the ground to help him plan the operation.[4]

"I had complete freedom to do this at the right moment" recalled Brims. "I was never under pressure to get into Basra [from commanders above me]. The only people pressuring me were my subordinates, I was resisting until circumstances were right to do it in a less bloody way."[5]

The first major element of Operation Sinbad was to be a move by 16 Air Assault Brigade to push across the Shatt-al Arab north of Basra at Ad Dayr, to cut the main road to Baghdad. This would isolate Basra from reinforcement as well as defeating a major group of irregular fighters that had been identified in the town.

Orders were issued to 16 Brigade to begin positioning its attack force during the afternoon of 7th April, to be ready for the operation to kick off at 1am on 8th April. The first iterations of the plan called for the Warrior-borne armoured infantry of the Black Watch to lead the assault, because the Scottish regiment had been placed in reserve to recuperate after its heavy fighting engagement at Bridge 4 and Zubayr. The plan was then changed, with a Challenger squadron from 2nd Royal Tank Regiment, backed by 1st Battalion, The Parachute Regiment (1 PARA), 1st Battalion, The Royal Irish Regiment and by batteries of AS-90 155mm self-propelled howitzers, slatted to lead the push forward. They were to set up a blocking position on the east bank of the Shatt-al Arab.[6]

On 3rd April senior British officers began to think that events might be moving faster than expected. Early that morning the Royal Scots Dragoon Guards battlegroup raided the Technical College complex opposite Bridge 4 and found the site empty, where as previously it had been a hotbed of resistance. During the Scots DG raid Lynx helicopters flying top cover were engaged by a man-portable surface-to-air missiles, forcing the helicopters' pilots to violently break formation to avoid the incoming missiles.[7]

The battlegroup was ordered to take the college over as their forward base. Later in the day the 1st Battalion, The Royal Regiment of Fusiliers and the Queen's Royal Lancers (QRL) raided 'the Loop'. (as described in Chapter 9). The ease with which the QRL's Challenger's were able to cruise around Basra's roads and seemed to swat away any resistance impressed senior officers at brigade and division headquarters. When the QRL's B Squadron Leader, Major Giles Harrison, returned to his base on the western bank of the Basra canal he would find the exploits of his troops had already reached General Brims and Brigadier Binns.

"That evening, the GOC and the Brigade Commander congratulated the Squadron on a job well done, and Staff Officers stopped saying that Basra would not fall until after Baghdad," recalled the Major.[8] This later comment was a reference to the orders of General Conway, the overall US Marine Corps commander in southern Iraq, that the British division was not to get bogged down in Basra until Baghdad was secured by US armoured columns. The buzz in the British division was that they could now finish off Basra before the Americans took Baghdad.

In his warning order to 16 Air Assault Brigade on 4th April, Brigadier Jacko Page said that regime and Ba'ath Party paramilitaries in Ad Dayr were coercing Iraqi regular troops to keep fighting. The aim of his Brigade's coming offensive would be to target irregular fighters to create the conditions to allow the soldiers of the 6th Iraqi Armoured Division to be able to surrender to the British. 16 Brigade's reconnaissance teams had closed up to Iraqi positions outside Ad Dayr and Al Qurnah, and were engaged in skirmishing with well-camouflaged and apparently determined Iraqi troops during 4th and 5th April.

During the morning of 5th April, 16 Brigade received word that the plans for attacking into Ad Dayr would not go ahead until after Basra fell. According to the Brigade's war diary, General Brims "continued to express that the timing is wrong and that we will not move until the timing is right."[9]

On the southern edge of Basra, Brigadier Jim Dutton was also re-organising his brigade to participate in Operation Sinbad. The relatively fresh troops of 42 Commando were brought up to the eastern edge of Basra by RAF Chinook helicopters on 5th April, to a take over point from 40 Commando, which had just finished its tough two day-long battle to take Abu Al Khasib.[10]

Meanwhile, on the Basra canal, Brigadier Graham Binns was also stepping up his preparations for the launching of Operation Sinbad. A warning order was issued by the Headquarters of 7 Brigade on 5th April that it would hold an orders group for the senior officers on 7th April for the drive into Basra, that would not take place before 8th April.[11]

The Scots DG's battlegroups daily raids down the main road into the city, the so-called Red Route, continued. The troops reported that resistance appeared to be getting significantly less organized and effective, although individual Iraqi soldiers and paramilitaries were still fighting fanatically. Major Chris Brannigan, who led B Squadron of the Scots DGs on the raids recalled, "they were utterly determined and their courage in the face of our onslaught was commendable. They never faltered in their commitment to their cause, and inevitably increased their losses by their resolute and tenacious defence against such overwhelming odds."[12]

The raids were also giving the Scots tank crews a chance to familiarise themselves with the city's road system, and the extensive network of barricades and trenches build by the Iraqis on the main routes into Basra.

They also allowed the small contingent of SAS troops attached to the British division to gain access to more and more of Basra. The special forces soldiers were dropped off from the back of Warriors during night-time raids.

Then they moved around the city trying to find the headquarters of Ali Hassan al-Majid - the infamous Chemical Ali – who was reputedly still leading the defence against the British. Although the chaotic and uncoordinated nature of the resistance put up by the Iraqis made many British officers wonder if he was in fact their best ally during the battle: he appeared to have completely sidelined the few competent regular army officers in Basra who might have put up a better fight.

Chemical Ali's Fedayeen fighters, Ba'ath Party loyalist militias and a network of secret policemen seemed to spend most of their time trying to stop the Shia population of Basra rising in revolt. According to the Pentagon's post-war Iraqi Perspective Report, the British tactics around Basra convinced Chemical Ali and Saddam Hussein in Baghdad that they were winning the war. By their reckoning, every day the British did not enter Basra was a victory, with the invaders scared away by the bravery of the Iraqi defenders. Even as American tanks approached Baghdad, the Iraqi dictator was being buoyed by reports from Basra that British tank columns were being chased out of the city on a daily basis. It did not register with Chemical Ali that the British were retreating after their raids of their own accord.[13]

The Iraqi chief in Basra had ordered his fighters and loyalists to disperse around the city to set up small bases in each neighbourhood. This prevented US and British aircraft targeting them for fear of hitting civilians, as well as ensuring they could continue to keep control of the population. Attacks on the British were launched for propaganda reasons, to convince the population that the regime was still in charge. The longer the British stayed outside the city, the easier it was for the Ba'athists to convince the Shia population that they were going to be abandoned to their fate, as had happened in 1991 after the Shia revolt.

To motivate his loyalists, Chemical Ali regularly called them to meetings which proved his undoing. During the late afternoon on 4th April, an SAS team detected a large gathering of Ba'athists at a house in the centre of Basra. The Ba'athist leader was seen entering the building with his entourage of bodyguards.

This was too good an opportunity to miss. General Brims, alerted by the Special Forces Liaison Element in his headquarters, was determined to hit the building with an air strike to decapitate the leadership of the Ba'athist resistance in Basra. The General described the intelligence produced by the SAS teams inside Basra as "vital".[14]

The location of the target in the middle of the densely populated centre of the city meant his rules of engagement required him to get permission from Air Marshal Brian Burridge's headquarters in Qatar before he could execute the attack. A Phoenix unmanned drone was sent over to make sure that the Ba'athist fighters and leaders were still in the building, and provide reassurance that it would not cause mass civilian casualties.[15]

"The special forces had eyes on and were 98% certain that Chemical Ali was in building," said Burridge.

"I was having supper when Brigadier Peter Wall came to me and said he had cleared the target 10 minutes ago. As the commander and an airman I decided to re-clear the target. I did so in 10 minutes. I did not refer to PJHQ [in the UK]."

Now something of a race developed between the RAF and USAF to get jets over the target to attack what could be a highly prestigious target.

"Two Tornado GR4s were on the way," said Burridge. "The F-16s got there first."[16]

At 4am on 5th April, a pair of American F-16s were scrambled from al Jaber airbase in Kuwait to bomb the building. One of the pilots, Lieutenant Russ Piggott, of the 524th Fighter Squadron, had used the delay to study satellite photos of the target and when they were overhead he immediately recognized it. Then things started to go wrong. The two pilots each dropped a GBU-12 500lb laser guided bomb. One went rogue and did not guide to its target, exploding two streets away from the target.

"[My] bomb entered the building on the second floor street side and exited through the back porch, leaving a gaping hope in the front and a huge plume of dust in the back yard – it was dud! I was so pissed, " recalled Piggott.[17]

The two pilots circled around and re-attacked. This time Piggott's bomb was spot on and the side of the building collapsed in the explosion. His wingman's bomb again was off target, landing 300 metres over the canal in a civilian neighbourhood. The jets attacked again and put in two more bombs, completely collapsing the building. The SAS team asked for one more attack just to be sure and Piggott put a fourth bomb on target, completing a twenty-minute long pummeling of the Ba'ath Party leadership in Basra. When they got back to base Piggott's wing man studied the video from his thermal imaging targeting pod, and observed a man running out of the building just before the second bomb hit.

In the 1 (UK) Division headquarters frustration was rising in the run up to the attack.

"It took ages to execute, then there was a blind [dud bomb]," recalled Brims.

"I don't known the full facts [about Chemical Ali's fate but] the perception was that he was killed."[18]

When the strike was reported up the chain of command to Qatar later in the day, the British team in the press briefing organization were keen to get the news out to the international media in a bid to undermine Iraqi resistance.

During the evening of 6th April they staged a series of media briefings, boasting of Chemical Ali's demise, and within hours it was running as a major story on satellite news channels.[19]

"The people of Basra convinced themselves it was Chemical Ali, with a little help from the special forces," said Burridge.

"Until you make a DNA match you cannot prove anything. It was part of our information operations campaign not to say exactly what had happened."[20]

However, Saddam's henchman escaped unharmed and was not captured until August 2003. British commanders in southern Iraq were soon aware that Chemical Ali had not died, but was on the run, and only two days later on 7th April launched an SAS-led raid on to the eastern bank of the Shatt-al Arab to try to capture him.[21] Not surprisingly, no effort was made by the British and American military spokesmen in Qatar or Basra to row back on the hype about Chemical Ali's demise. When a British Army officer in Basra confirmed to a newspaper journalist in May that Chemical Ali had escaped the air strike, he was unceremoniously put on a flight home to the UK for speaking to the media without authorization.[22]

At 7 Brigade's headquarters, Brigadier Binns and his staff were now trying to gauge the impact of the attack.

"Perhaps we attached more importance to the attack at the time than it really had," recalled Binns.

"It possibly had more effect on us, than the enemy. Did resistance collapse because of it, I don't know? Was there any [organised] resistance anyway? He was not killed anyway. It gave us the confidence and was a catalyst for us to press on."[23]

The Scots DGs continued to push into the city during 5th April, and smashed through a huge barricade across the main road dubbed 'Red Route' by the British. This attack culminated in the only tank-on-tank engagement of the war in which the Iraqis managed to hit a British Challenger with a T-55 main armament. An Iraqi crew had managed to get a previously abandoned tank working, and they tried to surprise the Scots DG as they demolished the barricade. The Iraqis managed to get off a single 100 mm shell at a Challenger but the tank's Israeli-made reactive armour on its front hull defeated the round. Several British tanks simultaneously fired at the T-55 and it evaporated in a huge fire ball. The Scots DG commanders reported back that the road into Basra was open.[24]

During the afternoon of 5th April, Brigadier Binns asked General Brims if he could step up the tempo of his raids. The 7 Brigade commander asked for the Black Watch to be released to him to launch a simultaneous raid with the Scots DG on the morning of 6th April.[25]

At 7.30pm in the evening, the plans for the two-pronged raid were confirmed, and the Black Watch commanders started issuing orders for the move up to Bridge 3 from Shaibah, where the Scottish regiment was resting and refitting after nearly two weeks of continuous combat. H-Hour for the new attack was set for 5.30am on 6th April.[26]

Lieutenant Colonel Mike Riddell-Webster told his troops before the start of the raid, that they "were going in to test the water. If it was cold, they were going to stay on. If it was hot, they were getting out of there. If it was just right, they were going to wallow around for a while."[27]

The troops participating all knew the coming day could be decisive to the outcome of the campaign, after hearing radio reports on the BBC World Service about the American successes in Baghdad. Morale was high and the excitement seemed to compensate for lack of sleep. As the Black Watch column waited on its start line an officer started playing 'Scotland the Brave' on his bagpipes.

The two battlegroups pushed forward along the main roads into Basra and immediately ran into what seemed like fanatical resistance, but proved to be only a 'thick outer crust'. Four US Marine Cobra gunships flew top cover over each armoured column, firing missiles and cannon shells at Iraqi fighters in the apartment blocks on the western edge of the city, some three kilometres down the road from Bridge 3. One of the helicopters took a direct hit and the crew had to make an emergency landing next to the Black Watch. The Challengers, of Egypt Squadron of 2 RTR, at the front of the armoured columns, returned heavy fire at the Iraqis, destroying a string of bunkers.

After a few minutes Riddell-Webster's men had crashed through the first line of barricades on the road and by 9am they were five kilometres inside Basra and meeting rapidly diminishing resistance. The Colonel called up his reserve force of armoured infantry, and Challengers from the Scots DG's A Squadron to reinforce his success.[28]

Riddell-Webster and his Scots DG counter-part, Lieutenant-Colonel Hugh Blackman, were riding in the front vehicles of their columns and began reporting early good progress to Brigadier Binns. They strongly recommended that he reinforce their success. In the space of a few radio conversations, the Brigadier spoke to General Brims and they agreed this was the time to accelerate Operation Sinbad.

"There was no set plan" recalled Binns.

"It was like twelve phase rugby, you run to locate a gap. When a gap appears you see to go through. When it appears it is unpredictable. I relied on the intuition of the battlegroup commanders to keep pushing to find the gaps."[29]

"During the morning my Chief of Staff [Major Chris Parker] woke me up to say that the Black Watch were 1.5 km in Basra and asked 'did I want to commit 2 RTR [the brigade reserve]?' I had a [radio] conversation with my three battlegroup commanders. The Black Watch kept pushing for us to reinforce. I committed the reserves because of the initiative of battlegroup commanders."[30]

The Brigadier radioed Lieutenant-Colonel David Paterson of the 1 RRF at Basra airport at 6am and told him "Basra was ripe for the taking".

He asked Paterson if he could have his battlegroup moving forward by 9am. A two minute long discussion followed and the battlegroup was committed.

The Fusilier's infantry companies and its attached tanks from the Queen's Royal Lancers were spread over a large area, patrolling rear areas, guarding the canal bridges and resting at Basra airport. They were called over the radio to drop what they were doing and concentrate at Bridge 2 as soon as possible.[31]

On time, the Fusiliers battlegroup crossed the Basra canal along the two northern bridges in two columns, each containing a Fusilier company in Warriors with a squadron of Challengers leading the way. They were to sweep up to the Shatt-al Arab to capture the naval academy, the bridge over the Qurmat Ali waterway, Al Najabir power station and the old Basra airport. When C Squadron of the QRL found a line of mines across its route, the lead tank opened fire with its machine gun and 120mm main armament to blast a safe route through. As the columns passed, individual Iraqi tanks and RPG teams tried to take shots at the passing British troops. The QRL took out the handful of T-55s that tried to engage them and small teams of Fusiliers dismounted from their Warriors to take them on.

General Brims was monitoring the situation closely, and when the armoured columns reported that they were not receiving the usual level of fire, he spoke to Brigadier Binns about expanding the scope of the British commitment into a full scale attack to seize the city.

"Binns said he was ready and after he did a few checks I gave radio orders at 11am, setting a mid-day H-Hour. 7 Brigade were to attack into Basra from the bridges and 3 Commando Brigade were to come from the south."[32]

The appearance of the General on the divisional radio net set the tone for the day and it was the only way he could keep control of events. His staff had twice tried to generate written orders for the division during the morning, but events were moving so fast that by the time they were produced and distributed, both sets of orders were out of date.[33]

Brims said 16 Brigade was also "itching to go" and they were already attacking Ad Dayr where the Iraqi irregulars had a headquarters.

The Brigade was scheduled to launch its major operation to neutralise the 6th Division in two days time, and then launch a drive towards al Amara. During the night of 5th April, as regime loyalists fled from Basra through Ad Dayr heading towards Baghdad, the morale of the Iraqi 6th Division began to waver. At this point, Lieutenant-Colonel Tim Collins, of the Royal Irish Regiment, sent friendly tribal leaders across the lines in an attempt to persuade the Iraqis soldiers around Al Qurnah to flee. Outside Ad Dayr, Brigadier Page and some of his staff made contact with local leaders to try to broker another peaceful withdrawal. Both attempts worked and by the following morning, 16 Brigade found the 6th Division had disbanded itself and its soldiers had fled.[34]

"The first reports we got was from 16 Brigade in Ad Dayr was that white flags were flying in town," said Brims.

"Basra was ripe. So when Binns went in he met no resistance. We were ready. I wanted to attack Ad Dayr at the same time, to attack everywhere at the same time. Do a knock out blow and go in on all angles. I left the back door open so they could get away."[35]

In Basra city, the Black Watch had fought their way nearly to the Shatt-al Arab by midday and resistance was faltering. On Red Route, the Scots DGs were having a tougher time at the College of Literature near the symbolic Basra Gateway road junction. As the column drew up on its objective it started taking fire from more than 30 bunkers. One Iraqi charged a British tank in a forlorn attempt to drop a grenade inside it. The attacker did not get very far before being cut to pieces by machine gun fire from several tanks. A pair of Cobra gunships were called up to engage two Iraqi armoured vehicles in the grounds of the College of Literature.[36]

A Challenger tank broke down the college gates and infantry from the Irish Guards fanned out to clear the complex. Just as they were moving to clear away several dead bodies, the corpses suddenly rose and started firing at the British with RPGs. One of the attackers was blown apart with a 120mm HESH round, and another crushed under a wall when a Challenger drove over it. For several hours the Irish Guards fought room to room with foreign fighters from Tunisia, Egypt and Morocco occupying the college. The passports and return airline tickets of the fighters were discovered by Guardsmen as they swept through the remains of the college.[37] This was the only group of foreign fighters discovered by British troops during this phase of the war.

The 1 RRF battlegroup was now close to its objectives near the Shatt-al Arab and the Fusiliers were sweeping them on foot. Several fire fights broke out with small groups of Iraqi troops. One Fusilier was killed in a confused incident during this time, and a coroner's inquest three years later concluded he was killed by machine gun fire from a QRL Challenger.[38] By the end of the afternoon the battlegroup had secured all its objectives.

The second wave of British forces were now up with the forward troops. The Challenger tanks and Light Infantrymen of the 2 RTR battlegroup passed through the Black Watch and swung southwards to move up to the fringes of the city centre shouk region, securing the Basra Ba'ath Party headquarters and central police station. The British troops were now moving down narrow city streets lined with parked cars and crowds of civilians were watching their progress. There were some cheers and children ran up to the troops to try to beg for food.

An additional squadron of Scots DG Challengers were brought up from reserve by Colonel Blackman to push past the Basra Gate, allowing his B Squadron to return to base to replace its almost exhausted ammunition.

Further south, at 12.30pm 42 Commando, with the Challengers of Falcon Squadron of Royal Tank Regiment leading the way, began moving towards the city centre. They too faced little resistance. A troop of Challengers lead each Royal Marine company through the narrow streets of the southern and eastern suburbs of Basra. Only M Company met any resistance from Iraqi troops during the afternoon. Civilians started to come out to greet the British troops as they occupied Saddam Hussein's palace on the banks of the Shatt-al Arab, and the city's main water treatment plant.[39]

As dusk approached, there was fighting still going on throughout the city but it was now very sporadic. Civilians were starting to emerge from their homes to approach their new rulers. They were generally friendly and seemed happy to have seen the back of the Ba'athists. British units throughout the city were ordered to go firm on their objectives during the night to allow ammunition, water and fuel to be brought up to allow the advance to continue during the following day. In the gloom two Iraqi fighters rushed the back of an Irish Guards Warrior parked in the grounds of the College of Literature. They sprayed the inside of the vehicle with AK-47 fire, killing two Guardsmen and wounding two others. In the confusion, the gunmen escaped despite a search by their comrades and a team of the Special Boat Service attached to the Scots DG battlegroup.[40] The incident meant British troops throughout Basra had an uncomfortable night nervously watching movement around their improvised defensive positions in case of further attacks. As well as the dangers of surprise attack, British commanders were starting to realise that Basra's environment posed other threats to their troops' health. All around the city were huge piles of rotting rubbish that had been dumped in the open in 40 degrees of heat for more than a month, and that Basra's many canals and other waterways were little more than open sewers. A few days later diarrhoea and vomiting sickness would sweep across British units in the city, incapacitating hundreds of soldiers for days at a time.[41]

The British had pushed through most areas of Basra except for the oldest part of the city, known as the shouk, which was a maze of narrow streets and alleyways. The coup de grâce was to be delivered by fresh troops brought in to reinforce 7 Brigade. Earlier in the day, 3rd Battalion, The Parachute Regiment (3 PARA), had been warned to be ready to move into Basra city to join the attack. Lynx anti-tank helicopters of 622 Squadron were also ordered to Shaibah airfield in support. The paratroopers set off for Basra in a convoy of four ton DAF trucks, which they had sarcastically nicknamed "deliverers of airborne forces" in a dig at the lack of helicopters in the British forces in Iraq.[42]

In the early evening the convoy passed Bridge 4 and stopped a kilometre south of the College of Literature. They then marched up to join the tanks of the Scots DG to spend the night waiting to attack.

"Over night, all the enemy disappeared" recalled General Brims.

"It was the same story all day."[43]

At 10am, 3 PARA started to move forward with the tanks of the Scots DG in support, expecting to have to clear some 200 hard core Fedayeen fighters from the shouk. The paratroopers would not have fought a major battle during their time operating around the Rumaylah oil field, and were keen to see some action, and show the supposed non-elite, or non-airborne units of 7 Brigade what they could do.

In the event it was an anti-climax. The Ba'athists had fled and the main problem was clearing a route through the crowds of civilians as the Paras and tanks cleared the final section of the city. General Brims and Brigadier Binns drove into the city centre to soak up the atmosphere. The General was amazed, "So many people were welcoming us."[44]

An officer of 3 PARA's A Company commented on the scene, "we were not met by bullets but crowds of elated and cheering civilians. This reception symbolised to us that we had been part of something deeply significant in Iraq. Despite press cynicism over the term 'liberation' we saw it in Basra and it was real."[45]

Through the rest of the city, other units of 7 Brigade were continuing to expand their foot print, moving into government buildings and other sites to deal with possible resistance. Apart from occasional gunfire from isolated groups of Iraqi soldiers there was no one left to fight. A report that Chemical Ali had been sighted in a village just over the Shatt al-Arab prompted a raid to be rapidly mounted by the SAS, supported by troops from the Light Infantry and 2 RTR Reconnaissance Troop. The mission failed to find the infamous Iraqi, after crowds of cheering civilians slowed its move through the city and over the bridge over the waterway to a snails' pace.[46]

During the day the British troops started to see the population of Basra taking their revenge on their rulers. Statues of Saddam, Ba'ath Party and government building were all attacked and anything of value was looted. There we no Ba'athists to be found inside the buildings. The cheers and applause from the local population were echoed back in Britain and further afield as the British forces were praised for their success in capturing Basra with apparently minimal civilian and military casualties. Out of the 31 British military fatalities up to 7th April, only half a dozen could be attributed to enemy action. The remainder had fallen victim to friendly fire, road traffic accidents or natural causes.

Pre-war predictions of hundreds of dead and thousands of wounded had proved wrong. There had been no chemical weapon attacks and the Iraqi defences were chaotic, with little discernable organisation and planning.

In London, senior government ministers and service chiefs could breathe easy, and there was lots of congratulatory back slapping that the British armed forces appeared to have pulled off a notable victory again, and even beaten the Americans in capturing Basra before Baghdad. It seemed like the Kosovo experience was being repeated, with a grateful population welcoming the British as liberators. The British Army's equipment appeared to have worked well, with its Challenger tanks, Warrior armoured vehicles and body armour proving very reliable, providing superb protection against Iraqi weapons and contributing significantly to the minimal casualties suffered by the units of 1 (UK) Division. The ability of the British troops to switch from war fighting in helmets, to peacekeeping in soft berets was praised by many senior officers and media commentators alike. If there was any criticism, it was that the British had been too cautious and had hung back for too long outside Basra, rather than sweeping in and crushing resistance in the first days of the war.

General Brims said there were "remarkably few [British] casualties, it was astonishing", and said that "this led to false lessons being learnt from that".[47]

Brigadier Binns put the apparent slow pace of the advance up to and into Basra to the "sheer friction" of moving so many troops and units up from Kuwait.

"Co-ordinating the big beast of an armoured brigade in close terrain – it was an industrial not a desert landscape - took a lot of time. It was just not possible to roll over the Iraqi defences."[48]

In the first days of the war, the mindset of General Brims and his senior commanders, such as Brigadier Binns, was undoubtedly very cautious. They were conscious that the battle for Basra was part of a bigger operation. Predictions of the level of resistance ranged from the Central Intelligence Agency's claims that the Iraqi army would surrender as soon as British and American tanks showed themselves, to US Central Command planners who predicted the Iraqis were preparing to fight for more than a hundred days.

"What would have happened if we had driven straight into Basra?" asked Binns.

"Driving into the centre of Basra would not have been as significant or have ended the campaign as the US drive into Baghdad did. The coalition did not want to get bogged down entering urban areas unless it wanted to. What would have happened if the Brits had got bogged down and the US had had to divert resources from Baghdad?"[49]

Keeping their options open and not getting bogged down in Basra were important considerations in this environment.

"Even if there was token resistance in Basra we did not know it would be token," said Binns.

"Then there was possible weapon of mass destruction use in the background, along with resistance of the Republican Guard, suicide bombers and Nasariyah fighting. It created a natural caution. We credited the Iraqi army with an ability to do much more than it did."[50]

On 7th April, just over 5,000 British troops from six battlegroups were in the heart of a city with a population of around one and half million people. This was the high point of British troop strength inside the limits of the city. Never again would a British commander in Basra have so many troops at his disposal, but also, never again would the British military be so popular with the city's population. This was the high water mark of British rule in Basra.

One Fusilier officer commented, "we thought we had reached an end point, but discovered very quickly that we were now just at the start of a bigger job."[51]

Chapter 13

MILITARY JUDGEMENT

'Use your military judgement' is a phrase that litters British Army documents from the first days of the occupation of Iraq in April 2003. It is military short hand for 'do what you think best,' or use your common sense. Army officers usually employ the phrase in the absence of definitive orders about what to do. Given the near lack of orders, instructions or even guidance from the government in London, or US military commanders in the Middle East to British forces in southern Iraq it is not surprising that 'military judgement' was in such strong demand at this time.

British officers and soldiers in southern Iraq had been thinking about what they would do once they captured Basra for several weeks before the city fell. These musings had all been speculative, and there were few detailed contingency plans for what was referred to as Phase IV of the operation to depose Saddam Hussein's regime. Commanders in Iraq were provided general advice on the requirements under the Geneva Convention as occupying powers, including providing limited humanitarian aid, securing prisoners, helping locate administrations and providing law and order, as well as proposing that British troops be responsible for looking after the areas they would be in control of at the end of the fighting. There was little other guidance as to what type of regime was to be put in place of the old order, or the process by which the Iraqis would form a new government.

Before the war started the British government had recognised that there would be a need to provide occupying troops until a new Iraqi government could be set up.

Approval was secured from the Treasury to fund the deployment of around 8,000 troops to Iraq for a year, including a brigade made up of four battlegroups, as well as a divisional headquarters. It was hoped that other countries could be persuaded to send troops to beef up the British division.[1] The Ministry of Defence wanted to dramatically reduce the 46,000 strong British deployment in the Middle East as soon as possible after the end of the demise of Saddam Hussein's regime. Military chiefs hoped to bring home 3 Commando and 16 Air Assault Brigades almost immediately, to leave 7 Armoured Brigade to look after southern Iraq, until a brigade that was to carry out the first full six-month tour of occupation duty could be dispatched.[2]

The longer-term political and economic recovery of Iraq was to be left to the US government, which would have overall control of the country. Many senior British military officers and diplomats had expressed concern that the American plans for the rebuilding of post-Saddam Iraq were not ready, but there was a faith across Whitehall and in British headquarters in the Middle East that once Washington swung into action with its huge financial, material and human resources Iraq would be 'sorted.' British planning for the post war situation had been hampered by the delay in selecting the 'southern option' until January 2003. There then ensued a frantic rush to get 1 (UK) Armoured Division to Kuwait, which meant the commanders and planners were pre-occupied with the logistics of the deployment and preparing to fight the war.

"Preparations for after the war always seemed to be the last thing on the list of things to do," recalled one senior staff officer in the British division.[3]

Once the war started, fighting and winning it dominated commanders and staff officers' days. This started to change only once American tanks reached Baghdad on 3rd/4th April, and the outcome of the war seemed certain. Major General Robin Brims toured his brigades in the first days of April, and started to discuss how the situation would pan out after the fall of Basra. Permanent Joint Headquarters (PJHQ) at Northwood had just confirmed to Brims that he would have to ultimately take over responsibility for the four south-eastern provinces of Iraq. This followed discussions between US Central Command chief, General Tommy Franks, and the British Chief of Defence Staff, Admiral Sir Mike Boyce.[4] General Brims' discussion with his brigade commanders were inconclusive because no one in the British army in southern Iraq had any firm idea what would happen when the Ba'athist regime fell, how the population would react or what the British would find once they got into the heart of the city. This was just uncharted territory for everyone on the British side.

"Battlegroup headquarters began considering our actions on entry into Basra before we left Kuwait," recalled Lieutenant Colonel David Paterson, commanding officer of the 1st Battalion, The Royal Regiment of Fusiliers (1 RRF).

"Our problem was that we had no idea what the city would be like and where we would end up."[5]

The abrupt departure of Chemical Ali and his acolytes from Basra on 5th April caught the British by surprise, and although some of the 7 Brigade battlegroup commanders were keen to launch an all out assault on the city, General Brims was less sure and at first only authorised a limited incursion for the morning of 6th April. This then ran its course and by the end of the day, the British had secured most of the city.[6] Subsequent events at first reminded British commanders and troops of the liberation of Kosovo, as cheering crowds mobbed the advancing units of 7 Brigade. There had been expectation of some type of revenge attacks on any vestiges of the old regime, but the outbreak of looting was a surprise. Even on the afternoon of 6th April, as fighting was still taking place throughout the city, crowds of Iraqi civilians surged into recently abandoned government buildings and stripped their interiors bare. 1 RRF were the first British unit to experience this phenomenon when they arrived at the Shatt-al-Arab Hotel, to find a mob had just stripped it bare in the two hours since its caretaker and guards had fled.[7]

British units elsewhere in the city fortunately got to the power station and sewage works before they could be attacked, but many Ba'ath party headquarters, police stations, hospitals, army barracks, schools, local government buildings and large commercial premises were systematically looted. The police, local bureaucrats and other key workers just went home, abandoning their places of work to the mobs. The power and water supplies across the city just stopped working. Looting and sabotage was suspected, but it was later discovered that the creaking public utilities in Basra had been starved of money and refurbishment for decades by the regime in Baghdad and were only just kept going by their managers and repair staff. When their staff went home the utilities simply ground to a halt.

After the 3 PARA swept into the old shouk on the morning of 7th April the looting continued. At first the British troops tolerated this looting and did little to intervene.

General Brims described the early disorder as "civilised looting".

"It was a form of collecting what they were due," he recalled.

"They trashed a few things, Baa'thist buildings and bases. I thought there would be a lot more blood-letting. Looting was better than bloodshed and getting even."[8]

In Basra city there were few attempts at serving up rough justice for members of the former regime, because most had fled with Chemical Ali, but further north around Al Quernah troops of the 1st Battalion, The Royal Irish Regiment had to rescue four unfortunate Ba'athists from angry mobs.[9]

During the day, British troops were deployed throughout Basra to set up checkpoints and mobile patrols. They wanted to reassure the population that the Ba'athist regime was gone, and to try to find out as much as possible about the state of the city infra-structure, requirements for humanitarian aid and the location of possible bases for British units. General Brims was keen to find local people who could assume positions of leadership, in a sort of local council that would help get the city's administration, police and utilities working again. Intelligence operatives from MI6 had been circulating in the city under the protection of teams of heavily armed members of M Squadron of the Special Boat Service. They thought they had found an influential tribal leader who could help set up the Basra council.

"I got in touch with local people who we could start working with to run Basra," said Brims.

"Through good officers we identified Sheik Muzahim al-Tamimi as our first point of contact. On the night of 7th April I met him in a tent in the middle of nowhere. It was bizarre. I spoke through an interpreter, although he spoke English."[10]

"He was very charming and we sat down on the floor drinking tea," said the General. "He gave me a lecture on the Geneva convention in English. He was spot on. He knew what he was talking about. I asked him to help us run it [Basra] and asked him to get other Iraqis to help do it. He agreed to meet us in two days and we did. We had our first meeting in Basra and he introduced me to twenty people and we started to do business. The meeting was a bit chaotic, then we stopped to have something to eat and they pulled back a curtain revealing a huge feast. Bizarre considering all that had gone on just a few days before."[11]

The Battle for Baghdad was still unfolding on the 8th and 9th April, so the British command was still unsure if it could focus its efforts fully on occupation tasks, or if its units would be needed for combat operations elsewhere in Iraq. General Brims held a conference of his divisional command group on the morning of 8th April to try to map a way forward. His brigade commanders presented requests for resources for aid projects, guidance about how they were going to treat the population and the deployment of civilian advisors to their units.

The commander of 16 Brigade, Jacko Page and his colleagues left the meeting rather frustrated. Page's brigade war diary recorded that he considered this a "very unsatisfying meeting".

"The brigade has no firm guidance, because our area of operations is unknown in size and breadth of area, civilian population involved, whether there is war fighting yet to be done or whether it is time to completely focus [on reconstruction and stability]" recorded the diary.

" [General Brims] would not say one or the other – not his fault really because he doesn't know either."[12]

Page requested the attachment of civil servants and diplomats to his brigade to allow it to conduct sustained reconstruction and stability operations.

"Although not spoken, we are going into phase IV [reconstruction and stability], said the diary. [Brims] currently had no plan. Regime needs to be removed and security put in place."[13]

The British faith in the US to come to the rescue was apparent, with the meeting of senior officers being told by General Brims that the US-led Office for Reconstruction and Humanitarian Assistance (ORHA) was "straining at the leash" to begin work in Iraq. It was said to have a "huge budget but no plan". OHRA turned out to be poorly led, under-manned, did not know how to spend its budget and within weeks was disbanded.[14]

The meeting did, however, give the British brigade commanders some general guidance on how General Brims envisaged the British zone being patrolled. In Basra city, 7 Brigade would continue to run things. While the Royal Marines would remain on the Al Faw Peninsula and in Umm Qasr, they would also expand their area of responsibility to take over the security of the Rumalyah oil fields, to possibly release 16 Brigade to move north to al Amarah in the heart of Maysan province.

There was some good news for the British troops: the government in London seemed to be keen to run down the size of the force in southern Iraq very quickly, with 3 Brigade going first, followed by 16 Brigade, although nothing was confirmed yet. The next several days saw dramatic changes in Iraq as the Ba'ath regime in Baghdad collapsed, the Iraqi army evaporated and fighting died down across the country. General Brims moved his headquarters up to Basra International Airport to be at the heart of the British controlled region of Iraq. The General's staff were busy trying to formalise a long term plan for British military operations in the country. General Brims' immediate US superior, the US Marine Lieutenant General James Conway issued orders to the British division setting out its occupation zone. PJHQ in Northwood also confirmed the intention of the British government to draw down the strength of the British force to the originally proposed single brigade-sized force. The OHRA organisation was also in the process of moving from Kuwait to Baghdad and had begun issuing instructions to coalition forces across Iraq.

Drawing on all these things together, the British division staff generated an operations order for Phase IV or stability operations on 22nd April.[15] It would formally come into effect once the American command declared the end of combat operations, but with the fighting already effectively over in the south, British units started putting it into action immediately. It crucially laid out the time line to have all of 1 (UK) Division's brigades and units out of Iraq by the end of June, or in two month's time. Some units would be gone in a matter of a few weeks.

General Brims set his division the mission to "conduct security and stabilisation operations in order to set the conditions for Iraq becoming a stable, self-governing state". His orders then laid out how British troops would deploy across southern Iraq, work with the civilian population, establish local administration, deliver humanitarian aid and promote economic activity. The operations order is littered with references to how OHRA will eventually take over responsibility for huge swathes of the Iraqi state's functions. This left the impression that much of Iraq's fate was just left hanging, with no decisions or likelihood of decisions being made soon.

In his operations order, General Brims laid out the centre of gravity of the British mission in Iraq. This is military jargon for the mission's vulnerable point, or what would cause it to fail. He identified "the Centre of Gravity for Phase 4 as the positive support of the Iraqi population for Coalition Operations".

Brims raised the prospect of anti-coalition forces trying to undermine the population's support for the coalition by attacking what were referred to as critical vulnerabilities, such as the water supply, equitable distribution of Iraqi wealth, control of housing and supply of medical assistance. This was an early recognition that the future Battle for Iraq would be fought for the support of its people, although the ground would ultimately be very different from that envisaged by General Brims and his team.

Iraq's second city and its environs were to be the main pre-occupation of Brigadier Graham Binns and the 8,000 troops of his brigade until late June. The heart of the city was patrolled by the 1st Battalion, The Black Watch, reinforced with troops from the Irish Guards. They took over a string of police station and public buildings across the city as their bases. In the north of the city, the Fusiliers set up base at the Shatt-al-Arab hotel and also controlled the Basra power station and the Camp Breadbasket depot that was the city's main source of food. 45 Commando remained at Saddam's Basra Palace on the banks of the Shatt-al

Arab waterway, and patrolled the south of the city, until 7 Brigade's Headquarters took over the sprawling site.

With looting and general lawlessness continuing, there was a need to get more troops out on the streets, so several specialist British units were rapidly re-roled into infantry. Less than half of 7 Brigade's 8,000-person strength was made up of infantrymen, so drastic action was needed to get more troops on the ground in Basra. Tank regiments, artillery gun batteries, air defence units and the joint nuclear biological and chemical defence regiment were put through a five-day long crash course in infantry skills so they could be sent out on patrol.[16]

The daily diet of operations were mobile patrols around the city, as well as guarding public buildings, controlling riotous crowds at water distribution points, controlling traffic, responding to crime, negotiating neighbourhood disputes, clearing up war debris and administering medical assistance.

This was relentless work with soldiers working 12 to 16-hour shifts out on the streets in 40 degrees of heat. The troops were already exhausted from the war, and many were vulnerable to illness due to lack of sleep. There was growing concern among the British officers about the health of the troops in southern Iraq. The majority of the troops in the heart of Basra city were living and eating in their vehicles or in ruined buildings, with no running water or toilets. Many troops were involved in burying corpses and processing prisoners of war, which added to health problems.

An officer in the Scots Dragoon Guards, Major Tim Brown, described the situation in the city as his squadron of tanks set up check points at important road junctions.

"We endeavoured to maintain some sort of law and order amongst the looters," he recalled.

"We endured some of the most unpleasant living conditions we were ever likely to see. When someone referred to Basra as the Venice of the Middle East, we had not realised that many of the so-called canals are in fact open sewers. In no time our own hygiene became an issue and people were suffering from diarrhoea and vomiting (D&V)."[17]

The commander of the Scots DG battlegroup, Lieutenant-Colonel Hugh Blackman, estimated that on most days at this time 20 percent of his 800-strong battlegroup were afflicted with D&V and effectively out of action.[18] To try to improve the living conditions of its troops, 7 Brigade ordered its units to consolidate in a few locations that could be better supplied with water and centralised cooking facilities to be set up. The old RAF base at Shaibah, outside Zubayr was turned into a logistics hub and several units, including the Scots DGs were withdrawn back there. They then launched daily vehicle patrols in Land Rovers into the city. The Royal Marines did the same thing at their logistic hub at Zubayr port, but 16 Brigade would soon be on the move so its logistics were less well organised.[19]

These measures had little impact and Shaibah was described by Major Brown as a "health nightmare, as flies passed around D&V at an amazing speed."[20]

By 18 April, 7 Brigade's major units were each reporting ten to twenty new cases of D&V a day. In the brigade headquarter two or three of the 15 key staff officers were out of action at any one time with the infection. Even the British division's main medical facility, 34 Field Hospital was hit with a major outbreak. The debilitating effects of the outbreak were felt by every unit in the brigade, just as they needed every man out on the streets of Basra to maintain order.[21]

Across 7 Brigade, battlegroups moved to re-role personnel into civil military co-operation, or G5 teams, to help get infrastructure, health services, humanitarian aid and local administration up and running in their areas of responsibility. The same thing happened in the 7 Brigade headquarters, where senior officers and their staff were set to work on the higher levels of Basra's administration. The teams were all invariably manned by well-meaning and enthusiastic amateurs who had little expertise in the areas they were put in charge of.

"Phase IV needed different resources than were at my disposal," said General Brims.

"I had to make do with what was at hand. Fortunately among the army reservists were a lot of people who knew a lot of stuff, a lot of experience started being used."[22]

The Black Watch's G5 efforts were typical. They set up a five strong team of officers and senior non-commissioned officers to run its G5 operations. They immediately became immersed in the problems of Basra. They identified years of neglect after the 1991 Gulf War, UN sanctions and looting over the past month, rather than war, as the main issues that needed to be resolved, and fast. Mains power and electricity were restored by the Royal Engineers, and the engineers from the US company Bectel on 28th April but this did not solve Basra's power problems. The looters continued to strike at power transmission lines and sub-stations to steal copper at a rate of more than 500 tons a day across southern Iraq, according to the Black Watch G5 team. Power cuts plagued the city of Basra for months and crucially they hit the water pumping stations hard, limiting the supply of water to homes. The water treatment works were not up to European standards anyway, and the Black Watch G5 soldiers were surprised the city was not swept by cholera.[23]

To try to overcome the water shortage in the summer heat, the British organised the shipping of drinking water from Kuwait with 30 tankers a day making the journey into Basra. This was nowhere near enough to meet demand and there were frequent scuffles with Black Watch soldiers at distribution points. The water convoys started being hijacked by armed men so they had to be guarded by British troops. Then the Iraqis tried to break into the water mains to divert supplies, further reducing the quantity available to the people.

The British battlegroups had limited funds for what were termed quick impact projects (QIPs) to rebuild schools and carry out minor works on local utility infrastructure, such as painting schools. The UK Department for International Development (DFID) made £2 million a month available to the British Army for QIPs, which was not enough to carry out the major infrastructure projects.[24]

The biggest problem identified by the G5 teams was the lack of local people with management experience to take over the running of the local infrastructure and utilities. The Black Watch medical officer visited a Basra morgue and found several dead bodies decomposing inside because there was no one to organise their identification, so they could not be buried.[25] In late April, the UK national contingent commander, Air Marshal Brian Burridge, and his chief of staff, Brigadier Peter Wall, made a series of visits to Basra to Baghdad to try to get ideas that might kick start economic regeneration.

"We thought we had got to a plateau," recalled Burridge.

"Electricity and water were back to pre-war levels and a pipeline was now pumping water from Kuwait up to Basra. In terms of fabric of life and feel for the place, it was at a plateau. This was deeply frustrating. Ideas we put up included rebuilding the power station and dredging the port but we could not get lift off."[26]

General Brims was keen to get the local schools open again to get Basra's children back into their class rooms, as a means to restore normality. British units made a concerted drive to help secure and renovate schools. Most of them opened in time for the start of the next term. The biggest help to the British came from OHRA in Baghdad who managed to dispatch several pallet-loads of cash found in old regime buildings down to Basra. This money was used to pay the salaries of government employees and de-mobilised soldiers. This did a lot to help local people buy food and other necessities.[27] These initial aid projects were run by British soldiers in the south or via OHRA. There was a conspicuous lack of DIFD experts or Foreign Office diplomats in Basra.

"What we needed was diplomats and people who showed up to make things happen, not soldiers," said Brims.

"The latter did not turn up. I was astonished that no ambassador and no consul general had been appointed, and was ready to be back-filled behind us immediately once the fighting finished. It was not until July that Jeremy Greenstock was persuaded to stay on for six months longer, to be ambassador in Baghdad. The same with Hilary Synott in Basra, who did not arrive until later in the summer. I thought the Foreign Office would have found these people much earlier."[28]

Pervading the city was an air of lawlessness caused by the rapid collapse of the old regime. What began as spontaneous revenge attacks on the symbols of power of the hated Ba'ath Party accelerated to include schools, private business and vital public utilities.

An officer in 1 RRF battlegroup said the looters "did so with great verve".

"They stole everything imaginable from grand pianos to air conditioning units, to front doors," he said.

"By the end of the frenzy, they were taking things simply because they were there."[29]

Generally the presence of British troops was enough to scare away looters but another Fusilier officer recalled, "small pockets of armed resistance appeared occasionally during the first few days, and while robust action was taken against armed looters, that option was not really available against women and children stealing books."[30]

For several days large crowds were roving the city looking for loot, and on 8th April, the British were becoming increasing exasperated that they could not contain the problem. That day Brigadier Jim Dutton, the commander of 3 Brigade, asked the divisional headquarters if his troops could shoot looters on sight. The request was turned down and the senior British legal advisors in the headquarters, Lieutenant Colonel Nicholas Mercer, sent out guidance on how commanders should deal with the problem. He recommended increased patrolling to deter looters but said the principles of minimum force should apply because the looters were civilians and not combatants. The troops were allowed to arrest looters, but Colonel Mercer recorded in a memo issued to units that there was as yet no plan or procedure to deal with anyone who was arrested for looting, and it was a matter for the discretion of the local Royal Military Police (RMP) as to whether they were to be detained beyond arrest.[31]

By the end of April, the mass looting seemed to plateau, but some British soldiers suggested that this was only because there was nothing left to loot. The British tried to prevent a future outbreak of looting by reforming the Basra police, using money seized from government buildings to pay their salaries. The RMP were given the job of helping infantry battlegroups set up and advise the local police. The offer of pay prompted several thousand policemen to return to work, but they were an indifferent, poorly-equipped force with no police cars, police stations, jails or weapons. In conjunction with the British military lawyers, the judicial capacity of Basra province was gradually restored with the opening of the courts and the appointment of a new judiciary.

The economy had collapsed. Most of the population had no work and those with government jobs had not been paid for months. Crime became endemic as the population tried to scrape a living by what ever means possible. British bases became targets for gangs of thieves, many of them young children or youths, who tried to sneak in at night to steal food or anything of value.

There are several recorded instances of British troops becoming exasperated at this behaviour and coming up with their own 'street' punishments to try to scare off local trouble-makers. A group of Irish Guardsmen took to dunking captured looters in a canal but this ended in tragedy when one youth was later found drowned. The Guardsmen were subsequently charged with murder but were acquitted in 2005.

Three soldiers from 1 RRF were convicted of abusing suspected looters at the Camp Breadbasket food warehouse, which contained almost all of Basra's food supplies. Captured youths were made to carry their loot back to the warehouse, others were stripped naked and tied up to forklift trucks. The crimes of the Fusiliers only emerged after so-called 'trophy pictures' showing the incident were handed over to local police in Britain by a shocked assistant in a photo developing shop.

The issues relating to the abuse of civilians would dog the army throughout Operation Telic, with concerns about the discipline of British troops proliferating in official reports and documentation. In a major lessons learned report published in 2006, Major General Bill Rollo said these incidents had the potential to "create operational or strategic reverses, and have a political impact at home which extends to Army retention and recruiting."[32]

He reported that "'since the start of major combat operations to 12 January 2006, there had been 191 investigations into all types of incidents. Some 171 of these investigations have been closed with no further action, of the remainder, four investigations were still ongoing but the remainder resulted in military or civilian prosecutions. There are five cases which could be classed as deliberate abuse, two of which have been dealt with by General Courts Martial,'" reported General Rollo.

In the heart of the city, the Black Watch was starting to come under sporadic small arms attack, and the first improvised explosive devices appeared, although they were poorly designed and caused no serious injuries. The Black Watch decided that it would stage a series of raids to try to capture what were described as "various local hoodlums."

This was part of a US-ordered clampdown in the carrying of small arms by civilians, dubbed Operation Claymore.

"Despite 'reliable' sources, these raids would often prove fruitless and turn into a hunt for weapons", recalled one Black Watch soldier. One Black Watch soldier was wounded during one of these raids when he was shot through a door with an assault rifle. Private Tabua's body armour saved him from serious injury, but it illustrated that Basra had a far from benign security environment.[33]

Many British officers were sceptical that search and raids would make much difference because firearms were so prevalent in southern Iraq. They concluded the few that could be collected in such raids would make no difference to the anarchy of Basra, while the raids would just antagonise the local population. During April, the Fusiliers and Black Watch discovered three caches of IEDs around Basra. There were no more than 20 crude devices but they were the first examples of the weapons that would subsequently cause so much grief for the British over the next six years.[34]

The increase in shooting incidents and civilian fatalities was raising concerns in the British headquarters at Basra airport. Lieutenant Colonel Nicholas Mercer, the top legal staff officer in the division, was pressing for more rigorous investigations by the Royal Military Police (RMP). He was questioning the rise in what he called "unexplained deaths" in custody. Colonel Mercer issued urgent guidance to UK troops, known as FRAGO 152, re-iterating advice on the legal standards required for the handling of prisoners and pointing out the legal risk for those who breached the Geneva Conventions.[35]

These resulted in a number of prosecutions for murder against British soldiers, such as the Irish Guardsmen mentioned earlier. Several paratroopers from 3rd Battalion, The Parachute Regiment, were also brought to court martial, but acquitted, for the murder of an Iraqi civilian at a vehicle check point.

General Brims was worried that the increasing number of Iraqi civilians being arrested and held in the US-run prison at Umm Qasr, known as Camp Bucca, would damage relations with the local population. On the advice of the military lawyers, the British division set up a system of monitoring by senior army officers who would review detention cases every ten to twenty days, with the final decision resting with the General Officer Commanding. This had terrible shades of the internment exercise in Northern Ireland in the early 1970s. That saga was seen as a 'recruiting sergeant' for Irish Republican groups because of the lack of legal process involved. Officers of Brims' generation knew how emotive this could be become, and felt it could stir up discontent against the British. The General wanted to have a judge or other senior legal figure, separate from the British military chain of command, to be sent out to Basra to set up a sort of court to rule on requests to hold civilians in custody.

"I proposed the UK should send out a legal figure to take decisions [on detainees]" said Brims. "He needed to be a lawyer, independent of the chain of command to oversee the whole delicate issue. I put this to people from London on visits. They seemed to take this on board and they came back to me saying they would not do it. I was told, 'Brims, just get on with it'. I regret I did not challenge that. Some of the problems we had subsequently might not have been as aggrieved to the extent they were."[36]

One security challenge that was never really resolved was the clearing up of old Iraqi military bases, and the safe disposal of thousands of tons of arms and ammunition.

"Everywhere you saw Iraqi military hardware lying around," said General Brims.

"There were tanks with ammunition and machine guns in them just parked up. In a compound in Shaibah we found 60,000 155mm rounds of artillery ammunition supplied by [the British company] Royal Ordnance."[37]

While British recovery teams did manage to salvage some of the tanks and weapons abandoned in Basra city centre, most were stripped bare by looters. Out in the desert there were several huge ammunition storage compounds, each containing more than 200,000 individual items, that would have required hundreds of troops to guard. There were just not enough troops to spare to do this and they were just abandoned. Bulldozers were used to bury many of the arms bunkers under sand, but once the troops had left the looters returned and started to tunnel into the sites.[38]

Occasionally Explosive Ordnance Disposal (EOD) teams were sent out to blow up items at the compounds, but even by September 2003 there were still thousands of abandoned munitions littering the sites. Accidents were commonplace as looters tried to scavenge scrap metal. A huge explosion rocked the ammunition compound outside Al Quarnah in April, badly injuring several looters. Most of these looters were children who used primitive tools to try to smash open artillery shells to strip off the copper elements. The result was a steady stream of injuries to Basra's hospitals.

There were increasing fears that the abandoned ammunition and explosives would find their way into the hands of people with malicious intent, particularly after the looting started to appear to becoming more organised and systemic. One RAF EOD operative recalled being tasked to go to dispose of a site supposedly made up of ten ISO containers full of ammunition, but when they arrived everything, including the containers had all disappeared. It seemed as if explosives and ammunition were being horded for future use.[39]

A major drive got underway in May to engage with the local political leaders and political groups that were emerging all over southern Iraq. Almost every city district in Basra or town and village in the countryside set up a governing body to try to bring order to the looting, and get local services up and running. British commanders across southern Iraq started to meet these groups, who it was hoped would help with efforts to stablilise the region. General Brims had already started talking to a group that eventually grew into the Basra Provincial Council. Other brigade, battalion and company commanders made similar contacts. At first these were meetings were positive and progress seemed to be made.

Across Basra more than 50 political parties were formed and exiled groups returned to re-establish their organisations. Demonstrations became a daily occurrence as the population got its first taste of street democracy. This brush with democracy was doomed to be still-born by the arrival in Baghdad of the new head of the US-led Coalition Provisional Authority, or CPA. This was Paul Bremer. The new organisation was to replace the discredited OHRA and give the occupation of Iraq a distinctive neo-conservative feel. In a matter of weeks in May and June 2003 Bremer issued a string of decrees that had a profound impact on the course of the occupation of Iraq.

He famously disbanded the Iraqi army, and launched the de-Ba'athification policy that banned anyone who had been a member of Saddam Hussein's ruling party from holding public office. He put off the setting up of a new Iraqi government for 18 months at least. The US government was determined to rebuild Iraq in the way it wanted and was not really interested in what the people of the country actually thought about their future.

In southern Iraq, the disbanding of the army was largely irrelevant because it had effectively disbanded itself. Bremer's political measures soon had a profound impact and changed the political mood. The Americans and their British allies were now seen by significant parts of the population as no longer liberators but occupiers, who seemed to have little interest in leaving.

"Sheikh Muzahim al-Tamimi was OK but he regularly lost his temper" recalled General Brims.

"Charlie Bird, my embedded Foreign and Commonwealth Office advisor became Muzahim al-Tamimi's right hand man. Charlie was an Arab speaker and I sent him to calm him down in a crisis. Things were going quite well with this and I heard there was going to be some event of a similar type in Baghdad. Then Paul Bremer and his people turned up [to set up the Coalition Provisional Authority] and said they knew best."[40]

"I left Basra in mid-May and back in England I heard on the BBC that they had disbanded the Iraqi army and set the Ba'ath Party exclusion line" said Brims.

"I was astonished about the de-Ba'athification. Muzahim al-Tamimi was excluded even though he was a Shia. I told Jack Shaw when he was in Kuwait in April that Muzahim al-Tamimi was not a real Ba'athist even if he had a Ba'ath party card but this made no difference."[41]

While General Brims was unhappy that the Sheikh had been excluded from the Basra Provincial Council, his many political rivals saw it as an opportunity. Basra was a hotbed of political intrigue as rival politicians, tribal and local leaders and religious figures jockeyed for position. Given the then anarchic situation in post-Saddam Iraq, it was no surprise that all these aspiring leaders had armed bodyguards. Most also had links to unofficial militias that were gathering their strength. And as the British Army was moving into Basra at the end of the first week of April, the US Marine Corps was driving towards al Amarah in the heart of Maysan province. This had originally been a British objective in pre-war planning and the US command directed the British to administer it after the conflict.

A battalion of Task Force Tarawa, from the US Marines, approached the city of 500,000 people from the west on 8th April, and proceeded to establish several check-points around its outskirts. The Iraqi division in town had melted away after its barracks had been bombed by US jets and large groups of soldiers were seen walking out of the town, apparently heading home to Baghdad. Rebel groups and tribal militia fighters then fought a series of running street battles with Ba'ath Party loyalists and secret policemen. The rebels then approached the US Marines and declared their city had been "liberated" and invited the Americans to enter the provincial capital. All over Maysan the Ba'athist state apparatus fled, leaving local people in control. This created a very different political dynamic, which became known as 'self liberation' and it made the people of Maysan very suspicious of foreign troops and political interference. There was another dangerous side effect of the brief power vacuum in al Amarah. In Maysan province alone, British commanders estimated that enough small arms and heavy weapons to equip two army divisions was looted from army barracks over the two-day period of the liberation. This huge arsenal just disappeared into the back streets of the town and was hidden away for future use, or put up for sale.[42]

The US Marines wanted the British to take control Maysan very quickly so they could establish control of the border with Iran. The commander of 16 Air Assault Brigade, Brigadier Page, flew up to al Amarah on 10th April to look the place over, and co-ordinate the hand over from Task Force Tarawa.

The scale of the task was enormous, Maysan is the size of Northern Ireland and boasted a population of nearly a million people, although no one was really sure. It geography was challenging, with its marshes limiting road movement in the centre of the province.[43]

Brigadier Page was to take all of his brigade, including two battalions of paratroopers, the Royal Irish Regiment battlegroup, an army air corps helicopter battlegroup and the Challenger tanks of the 2nd Royal Tank Regiment. According to one of Page's staff officers, the Brigadier thought having tanks "would be good – the Iranian presence will need to be held at bay, they understand firepower!" A full squadron of the Special Boat Service were also sent to help monitor the Iranian border.[44]

16 Brigade began moving into Maysan on 12th April, and Page told his senior officers and staff the day before that the "next phase [of the operation] will be more complicated and intellectually challenging than the last". He also stressed that "if we assist in the process of getting the situation right now it will go a lot further to shorten the requirement for forces in theatre".[45]

When the Brigade's troops started to fan out across Maysan they found a very different situation to that around Basra. The region was fertile, and although there had been some looting in the larger towns after the fall of the Ba'athists, most communities were well organised and relatively self-sufficient. Apart from bomb damage to the main army barracks in al Amarah itself the region was largely untouched by the war. Delegations of local community leaders invariably met arriving British troops with courtesy and were keen to discuss how the British could provide humanitarian aid. The politics of Maysan confounded the image popular in the western media, where the famous draining of the region's marshes by Saddam Hussein created the impression that its population would be keen to reverse his controversial project. The province was divided with much of the population keen to keep the canals and drainage systems set up by the old regime because they prevented flooding and allowed agriculture to flourish. Meanwhile the famous Marsh Arab tribes were viewed by Maysan's urban population in much the same way as gypsies are in much of Europe. Overlaying this were strong tribal and family ties to the Shia slums of Baghdad's Sadr City suburb, which meant it was soon a hotbed of radical Shia unrest.[46]

The first weeks of 16 Brigade's stay in Maysan were relatively uneventful and soon its troops were counting down the days to when they would go home. There was a daily routine of road accidents, occasional shooting incidents and the provision of medical assistance to local people injured by unexploded ordnance. During the second week of May, the newly appointed Chief of the General Staff, General Sir Mike Jackson, flew out to Iraq to see for himself how British forces were doing. He made a brief foray up to Baghdad to visit the British Embassy, which was then being guarded by a detachment of paratroopers, and to meet the American military leadership in Iraq. The Iraqi capital was still being convulsed by rioting and looting, overwhelming the ability of the US Army to secure key buildings and infra-structure in the city.

General Jackson was asked if the British Army could send a brigade of infantry to Baghdad to augment the Iraqi police force. The idea was to put 'boots on the ground,' or at least on street corners, so that the looting could be brought under control. As the British Army's most famous and high-ranking Parachute Regiment officer, Jackson immediately volunteered 16 Air Assault Brigade. It contained two battalions of paratroopers who were well trained in urban warfare and could be moved up to Baghdad by air, with minimum logistic support. Also it would propel the British Army into the heart of the Iraqi crisis in a very high profile operation. Jackson had commanded the NATO mission in Kosovo in 1999 and knew how coalition operations worked.

"Unless you are prepared to put your troops into the heart of the operation you will have limited influence on how the senior player – the US in this case – directs the campaign" recalled a close advisor to Jackson. The move of the Paras would also be great publicity for the regiment, which up until this point in the campaign had not played a very prominent role. General Brims and his staff considered the idea and on 19th May alerted 16 Brigade to the possibility of going to Baghdad. The brigade staff swung into action and started writing deployment orders and loading schedules for aircraft.

"I said Ok, I could do it," recalled Brims. "It went up to the Chiefs of Staff [operations committee] in London, who said 'no thanks'."[47]

Air Marshal Burridge says that there was also a proposal to send the British-led NATO Allied Rapid Reaction Corps to Baghdad to form a kind of civil-military cooperative dynamic with the American OHRA. Then the idea of a British presence in Baghdad was vetoed by the new UK Chief of the Defence Staff, General Sir Mike Walker. 16 Brigade stood down on 22nd May. General Jackson was not happy. He described the political mood as not being positive, saying, "we have done what we said we would do. We are in the south and that's where we going to stay".[48]

He described the view of his collages as "a bit myopic", and said the UK should have been "looking at the campaign as a whole" not just Basra. General Walker was not keen on the idea and did not think sending 3,500 troops from 16 Brigade to Baghdad would make any difference, commenting "I did not think they were going to alter the price of fish, to be honest."[49]

And for the men and women of 16 Brigade the news that they were not going to Baghdad came as a great relief. "We were exhausted and just wanted to go home," commented one of the Brigade headquarters staff.

This decision not to deploy British troops to Baghdad is one of the great 'what ifs' of the British campaign in Iraq, and effectively meant that for the next six years the main effort of the British would be confined to Basra. The Service chiefs in London were acutely aware that Prime Minister Tony Blair's government was keen to rapidly draw down the British force in Iraq, and try to draw a line over the conflict, which had poisonously polarised political opinion in the country. An expansion of the British commitment in Iraq by a major deployment to Baghdad ran counter to the government's political narrative. One senior British officer who worked in the Ministry of Defence at the time said a difference of opinion between Jackson and Walker played a big part in killing the Baghdad plan. Both officers had served in Bosnia under NATO in 1996, and had developed very different views on how to influence the Americans.

"Jackson was up front and wanted to get alongside the Americans showing them how we do things" said the officer.

"Walker, who claimed to have many friends in the top ranks of the US Army, thought a group of arrogant Brits turning up in Baghdad saying "here is how we did things in Belfast" would just get up the Americans noses.[50]

The one thing the Blair government was keen to push on with was the hunt for Iraq's weapons of mass destruction (WMD), which was its rationale for going to war. Britain's contribution to the WMD hunt was the 100 personnel of H Squadron of 1st Royal Tank Regiment, which comprised British Army, RAF Regiment and civilian experts and scientists. As part of the US-led Exploitation Task Force, the British WMD experts moved into the Abu Ghraib Palace close to Baghdad International Airport at the end of April, to begin the hunt for Iraq's secret weapon programmes. They were assisted by agents from the Secret Intelligence Service or MI6, and protection teams from the special forces, who were scouring Baghdad trying to find Saddam's weapons scientists, and regime insiders who might know where the WMD were hidden.

The British search teams became progressively convinced they were participating in a wild goose chase, with RAF Regiment Flying Officer J Weekes, who served with the team in Baghdad, described it as the "search for the dribbling water pistol".[51] The teams toured Iraq making what were termed Sensitive Site Exploitation (SSE) visits, searching for documents, interviewing witnesses, surveying WMD sites and excavating for hidden material. This soaked up a huge amount of resources, particularly scarce interpreters and intelligence analysts. In the British sector alone it involved several major operations, tying up hundreds of troops at a time. The Black Watch spent several days guarding an SSE that involved digging up a huge area inside a large steel works in central Basra. In 16 Brigade's area, two SSE operations involving ground-penetrating radar were carried out. Nothing was found. All over the British sector Iraqis civilians were reporting hidden WMD caches, raising expectations that something was there. The commander of an Irish Guards company in Basra, Major Ben Farrell, commented at the time, "we have a constant stream of people providing us with information regarding the location of WMD – it's only a matter of unweaving Saddam's intricate web."[52]

Flying Officer Weekes described the "quality and accuracy" of the intelligence in the WMD hunt as "varied". The most positive finding was the discovery of chemical plants that might have had dual use but at other sites there was "no evidence of an anything to do with chemical, biological, radiological and nuclear [material], the Iraqi military or the regime." He described being sent to visit a suspected Iraqi Atomic Energy Commission site, which turned out to be a Baghdad Hotel in which a meeting of two hundred tribal chiefs was in full swing. They invited the WMD experts to discuss the future of Iraq over a soon-to-be-slaughtered lamb. He concluded that "we never actually found the "Smoking Gun" in all our time".[53]

This was of course not what the Prime Minister was expecting to hear. The WMD search was extended and a new contingent of soldiers, spies and experts was sent out to Baghdad at the end of June to replace H Squadron. They would serve in the newly formed US-led Iraq Survey Group, which would eventually report in September 2004. Detachments from the SAS, and other special forces units that had participated in the western desert operation, now moved into central Iraq to help the Americans capture senior leaders of the old regime. Brigadier Graeme Lamb was still running this operation, and he was reporting directly to General Reith in PJHQ, with Brigadier Adrian Bradshaw as the senior British representative in the US Joint Special Operations Task Force based inside western and central Iraq.[54]

An RAF Chinook crew involved in moving prisoners captured by British special forces troops near Baghdad on 13th April to an American-run 'black' prison camp in western Iraq for interrogation, were so shocked when one of the prisoners died after being violently restrained while being loaded on board their helicopter, that they reported the incident to their superior commanders for investigation. One of the prisoners was an old man who had artificial legs. Documentation about the incident emerged in the media several years later, but military legal authorities were never able to establish the cause of the death of the prisoner or who was responsible for the incident. The prison camp to which prisoners were taken was never revealed to the International Committee of the Red Cross as required under the Geneva conventions, so it was never inspected by the respected humanitarian organisation. No mention of the camp, dubbed Station 22, ever emerged in any of the documentation on British prisoner of war policies, that was published in the Baha Musa inquiry into prisoner abuse in Basra.[55]

At the end of May Blair visited Basra and Baghdad in a triumphant tour to see the newly-liberated Iraq. Army commanders in Basra tried to press Blair on their problems, the mess the US were making of the political situation, and the failing of the aid effort by DFID and the Foreign Office. However, the Prime Minister's visit was overshadowed by a broadcast on the Radio 4 Today programme alleging Downing Street had "sexed up" the September 2002 dossier on Iraqi WMD. For the next six weeks Blair's government would be engulfed in crisis because of the WMD claims, and it got worse when a MOD biological weapons expert, Dr David Kelly, who was at the heart of the BBC story, committed suicide. Downing Street would not be focused on events on the ground in Iraq for several months.

Although the British had sent 46,000 service personnel to the Middle East on the eve of the war, by the end of May more than half the force was back home, and within a month they all were.

"We went in on the strategic assessment that we go early, go light and then get out," said Generals Brims.

"The strategy was to reduce force levels so the Iraqis would take control of their own destiny. I am not sure why they [London] thought that, but they did. They said 60% of Iraqis were Shia and that they should be able to take control of their country. But you could wonder if that was the case, why had they not got rid of Saddam before. Also the Shia were split among themselves, fighting among themselves."[56]

"I was told before I went out that when we went to do Phase IV, it would be with a single brigade, 7 Brigade. I was told this by Admiral Sir Mike Boyce, the Chief of Defence Staff and General Jackson. So it was not a surprise that PJHQ and Lieutenant General John Reith were enacting this. No one was objecting to thinning out [troop numbers]."[57]

The way the drawdown of forces was organised undermined the operational effectiveness of the residual force, by creating considerable disruption and command confusion. Over the space of 11 weeks, the British force across southern Iraq changed on a weekly basis. First, 3 Commando Brigade took over the security of the Rumaylah oil fields to release 16 Brigade to move into Maysan. In turn, the Commandos moved back to the UK at the end of April, so 7 Armoured Brigade had to move south and take over responsibility for 3 Brigade's area. By late May, the bulk of 16 Brigade was heading home too, and it handed over Maysan to 1st Battalion, The Parachute Regiment (1 PARA) in the first week of June, which worked directly for the divisional headquarters. Within the brigades the number of battlegroups and major units was also progressively drawn down, so unit boundaries had to be changed and moved on a weekly basis, while all the time the number of troops available to commanders was decreasing.[58]

Administratively these re-organisations were relatively straightforward for the units and staffs concerned to conduct, but it meant that the 'British face' presented to the Iraqis was changing almost by the day, as a different set of commanders and troops would turn up to meetings with locals. British officers said this led to confusion and hindered the building up of trust, while lasting relationships were hindered considerably. While troops on the ground had often just got to known their particular patch of territory and its people, they would be told to pack up and move somewhere else or go home.

It was not helped that the senior leadership of the British force in southern Iraq was also shuffled around, with the British going through three divisional commanders in the space of eight weeks. These officers had only one-or-two day handovers to their successors. General Brims left in mid-May to be replaced by the newly promoted Major-General Peter Wall, who was gone by early July to hand over to the 3 (UK) Division commander, Major General Graeme Lamb. While the command of 7 Armoured Brigade, which controlled the centre of Basra, also switched with Brigadier Graham Binns being replaced by Brigadier Adrian Bradshaw in the last days of April. Both Brims and Binns had been due to move to other jobs just before the start of Operation Telic, and had been extended in their posts to lead their troops into Iraq.

So it was no surprise they were moved, but it was unfortunate that they did so at a delicate time as the British occupation was just finding its feet. The cumulative impact of the troop drawdown and the change over of commanders was to hinder the ability of the British in Basra to develop a coherent approach and strategy. Confusion in the British chain of command would play an important part in the tragedy at Marjar al Kabir at the end of June.

As 1 (UK) Armoured Division's tour of duty was drawing to a close, an event occurred that convulsed the British operation in southern Iraq, and fuelled political and public disquiet about the campaign. In Maysan province, 156 Company of the RMP, had launched a mentoring operation to help the province's police force. This involved visiting police stations in towns and villages to assess their performance, as well as the need for future training and equipment requirements.

At the same time, 1 PARA who had been the only major unit in the province since the departure of the rest of 16 Brigade at the beginning of June, had been running a weapons amnesty to try to get local people to hand in their firearms. This was part of a nation-wide scheme, and it was a singular failure. The US command in Baghdad then ordered a tougher approach, involving house searches to seize weapons. Known as Operation Claymore, it resulted in 1 PARA launching a number of house searches in Marjar al Kabir on 22nd June. The town's population of 90,000 was outraged and the Paratroopers were stoned and shot at, forcing them to retreat from the town. A deal was done with town elders being promised that the searches would end.[59]

Two days later a six-strong RMP patrol was visiting the town police station, while two patrols from 1 PARA arrived in a different part of the town. Confusion between the leadership of 1 PARA and 156 Company meant neither knew what the other was doing. The result was tragedy. The Paratroopers came under attack and had to retreat from the town. Local people were furious, thinking that the British were reneging on their agreement to stop house searches. The armed civilians then turned on the RMP patrol in the police station and they were all brutally killed by a mob, after the soldiers ran out of ammunition. Meanwhile, the Paras on the edge of the town had called for reinforcements, and an RAF Chinook helicopter flew a Quick Reaction Force from 1 PARA's headquarters outside al Amarah.

The Chinook was raked with machine-gun fire as it approached a landing zone and had to return to base to drop off several seriously wounded paratroopers. A column of reinforcements led by 1 PARA's commanding officer, Lieutenant-Colonel Tom Beckett, eventually arrived and stabilised the situation, but it was only when an ambulance driven by a local doctor delivered the bodies of the dead 'Red Caps' to the British checkpoint outside Marjar al Kabir did 1 PARA realise that the RMP patrol had been in the town. Colonel Beckett decided to withdraw his troops back to al Amarah so he could find out what had happened, and try to de-escalate the situation. [60]

The incident was over in couple of hours, and soon the Ministry of Defence (MOD) in London was fully aware of what had happened. Senior officers tried to brief the Prime Minister but he was out of London at a summit. Downing Street banned the MOD from issuing details of the incident until the Prime Minister was fully in the picture, leading to a several hour-long period when rumours were swirling around about what had actually happened. This in turn fuelled accusations that the MOD was running a cover-up, so as to avoid embarrassing questions about the failures that led to the deaths of the soldiers.[61]

The incident would eventually became a running sore for the Prime Minister, with the father of one of the dead military policemen standing against Blair in the 2005 general election. Within the British command in Iraq, the incident highlighted divisions about what the way forward was, and weaknesses in its ability to understand what was happening outside the gates of their bases. An official army Board of Inquiry into the incident concluded that British commanders had no reason to expect that the searches of 22nd June would prompt a violent response. There were so few troops – 800 troops of 1 PARA - on the ground in Maysan province that the British intelligence gathering capabilities were severely limited and meant commanders had only a tenuous grip on events.[62] After the incident, a squadron of Special Air Service troops led by Major Richard Williams was dispatched from Baghdad to reinforce 1 PARA, which was preparing to launch a deliberate battlegroup-sized operation into Marjar al Kabir.

On 28th and 30th June, the SAS troops mounted brief forays into the town to try to find the killers of the six RMP soldiers. This incident later prompted several of the town's policemen trying to sue the SAS men in British courts, claiming they were physically assaulted during questioning.[63] General Wall ordered the SAS to call off its efforts to apprehend those involved in the deaths of the RMP team. The last thing he wanted was the incident spiralling out of control and sparking major unrest across southern Iraq.

The hope amongst senior officers in Basra was that Marjar Al Kabir was a 'one off' and not the start of a trend. As the last troops of 1 (UK) Division headed home over the next two weeks, they had mixed feelings. The war-fighting phase had gone well, with two Iraqi divisions being defeated and Basra city being occupied with minimum casualties. Forty-three British servicemen died during Operation Telic 1 between March and June 2003, of which only five were due to enemy action in the war-fighting period up to 8th April. Except for the six military policemen, the remainder lost their lives in road and air accidents, friendly fire incidents, accidents with abandoned munitions and to natural causes. The liberation of Basra and the warm welcome by the city population, as well as the pitiful living conditions, made the bulk of the British contingent feel positive that they had participated in a just war.

The mixed execution of the Phase IV operation in the aftermath of the fall of the Ba'athist regime sowed the seeds for subsequent rotations of British troops. The control of the political agenda in Baghdad by the Americans made the British military leadership concerned that they were not masters of their own fate. The lack of political engagement by the government in London, particularly its aid agency DFID, was a source of great concern. And then the killings at Marjar al Kabir made many British soldiers and officers wonder if the Iraqis really wanted the British to stay in their country. General Brims' identification of the consent of the population as the centre of gravity of the British mission would be proved right, with tragic results.

Chapter 14

BASRA SUMMER

"Upon landing [at Basra International Airport] we were thumped, square in the chest, by a great wall of heat - like nothing we had felt before," was how one officer described landing in Iraq in June 2003.[1]

The experience was debilitating for many of the soldiers arriving to replace the troops who had spearheaded the invasion of Iraq in March and April. It took several days of acclimatisation, at a camp in the Kuwaiti desert, before they were fit to move north to Basra city and Maysan province. The situation they would find there turned out to be very different from the one they had trained and prepared for a few weeks before. Even before the new troops were fully established in place, the killings of the six Royal Military Policemen at Marjar al Kabir signalled that the honeymoon period for the British Army in southern Iraq was over.

Heading up the new British Army units that were making for Basra to take over from 1 (UK) Armoured Division was the newly promoted Major- General Graeme Lamb. He had just finished a tenure as Director of Special Forces, and had been heavily involved in directing special forces operations in western Iraq and Baghdad. The 50 year-old Scotsman, who had commanded the Queen's Own Highlanders, led 5 Airborne Brigade and served with the SAS on three tours, was already scheduled to take over command of 3 (UK) Division on his promotion. He had overseen special forces operations in the wake of the 9/11 terrorist attacks and during the 2001 invasion of Afghanistan, with both British politicians and senior military officers identifying Lamb as one of the military stars of his generation who could rise to the very top of the armed forces.

Like many officers who had served in the SAS, Lamb projected an air of confidence and undoubted charisma. He had a familiar, blokeish turn of phrase and peppered his conversations with a near-constant stream of profanities. His SAS background meant soldiers and officers who had not served in the special forces were almost universally in awe of him, while his former comrades from SAS days were considered part of his own personal band of brothers.

He headed to Iraq supremely confident that he was the man to sort out the situation, recording in an interview prepared for an internal army post-tour debrief report in February 2004, that he "was fully up to speed with what was going on", "was pretty comfortable with Arabs" and had " a good feel for the cultural differences [in the Middle East]."[2] He took most of May off, on leave after his time with the special forces in Iraq, and left the preparation of his division for the upcoming operation to his chief of staff, Colonel Richard Barrons. The colonel had been left to run the division headquarters largely by himself since its previous commander had left in February. Lamb arrived at its headquarters in Bulford on Salisbury Plain in June, and a couple of weeks later flew out to Basra.

He told the army interviewer, "I was comfortable in the theatre [Iraq] and that comfort was born out of the experiences and education that I have accrued from my somewhat unorthodox but interesting career. I have done shed loads of staff courses; Higher Command and Staff Course, Royal College of Defence Studies, Joint Services Command and Staff Course and I felt I had been hugely well prepared to tackle most things. I did not have any advisor but I did know where to go whenever I wanted advice."[3]

The General was not keen on staff paperwork and bureaucracy. He banned computer-generated Powerpoint slide shows from his staff conferences, and declared "as soon as you start writing you slow down your thought process". He wrote one command directive for his division before he deployed and then ran everything though a series of daily conferences and personal visits to units, local leaders and allied headquarters. Operation Telic 2 needed "a broad approach" with "fine tuning", said Lamb.

The next most senior British officer in the new contingent was Brigadier Bill Moore, the commander of 19 Brigade, which would have day-to-day control of tactical operations in Basra city and Maysan province. As a character, Moore was the exact opposite of his direct superior, General Lamb. He was a master of detail, deliberate, methodical and was very much a military technician. One officer who served with Moore in Iraq said he was totally lacking in ego, and a "thoroughly nice gentleman". As an artillery officer who had commanded 7 Royal Horse Artillery, the British Army's airborne artillery regiment, Moore wore the maroon beret of the airborne forces. During this period of his career he had served with Lamb in 5 Brigade; unlike General Lamb, who had only commanded 3 Division for a matter of weeks, Moore had held his command for more than two years and had, during 2002, taken his brigade to Canada for a series of armoured warfare exercises. The relationships and friendships built-up among the 19 Brigade staff and battlegroup commanders would be the bedrock of the coming tour in Iraq.[4]

The mission set to Lamb and Moore by the UK Permanent Joint Headquarters (PJHQ) at Northwood, which controlled the Iraq mission, was "an improved security situation, more self-confidence among the Iraqi people and better services will allow coalition forces to draw down", according to the mission statement in 19 Brigade's formal orders for Operation Telic.

"We are to create an environment where it will be safe to draw down our forces, and in which the Iraqis will become increasingly responsible for their own security."[5]

Lamb and Moore were told by Lieutenant-General John Reith, the head of PJHQ, that he wanted the 9,500-strong British forces reduced by almost a half by the end of September 2003, with two of the four battle groups in 19 Brigade being sent home before they had completed their six-month tour. Reith envisaged only one battlegroup each being responsible for Basra and Maysan provinces respectively, and the 19 Brigade headquarters was to be moved out from

Basra Palace to the international airport, as part of a plan to merge the British brigade and divisional headquarters into a single organisation.[6]

The mobilisation of 19 Brigade for its mission in Iraq was a far from straightforward exercise, and it shared many of the delays and problems faced by British units that participated in the invasion phase of Operation Telic in March and April. Although it had been part of the original planning for the so-called 'northern option' through Turkey, it had been stood down in January 2003 when the British land force was diverted to Kuwait. Then the brigade's units were sent off to participate in fire fighting duties as part of Operation Fresco in response to the national fireman's strike. They were involved in this until into April. The Brigade headquarters were dispatched to Sierra Leone for February and March to run a peacekeeping operation, because PJHQ's rapid deployment headquarters had been sent to work in Qatar as part of the UK National Contingent Headquarters for Operation Telic.

Even though the army 'ring fenced' 19 Brigade as the follow-on force for 1 (UK) Division and 7 Armoured Brigade in Basra, it was unable to make any serious preparations until near the end of April, when Brigadier Moore was formally notified of his Brigade's new mission.

The diversion of the Brigade and its major units into these diversionary tasks prompted the Brigadier to conclude that his "units were therefore not as well prepared for Iraq as they should have been."[7] On subsequent Operation Telic tours, units usually had more than one year's warning time to prepare for deployment, compared to the just eight weeks for 19 Brigade.

His staff had less than a month to get their vehicles and heavy equipment ready to be loaded on ships for the three-week long voyage to Kuwait. Brigadier Moore then ordered that the training period be curtailed by two weeks, to allow the troops two weeks of pre-deployment leave because of the time everyone had spent away from their families on Operation Fresco and in Sierra Leone. Training was thus limited to low level weapons drills, first aid and basic tactics. There was no time for major field exercises for the troops, or even for a command post exercise to prepare headquarters staff. The troops complained that the so-called experts from the army's Operational Training and Advisory Group, known as OPTAG, knew next to nothing about the situation in Iraq. Senior officers went to Iraq in May on a reconnaissance trip but when they returned only a few weeks later everything had changed.

The brigade was being augmented by nearly 1,000 compulsorily-mobilised Territorial Army reservists, but they had little time to train with their new units before leaving 19 Brigade's Catterick garrison. Many only found out what they would be doing when they actually arrived in Iraq.[8]

There was not enough time to deliver much of the new equipment that had been provided to the previous British contingent on to 19 Brigade, such as grenade launchers and light machine guns, prompting the Brigade to have to collect them off the units they were replacing in Basra. When they got there, this equipment in turn was found to be worn out, and in need of extensive repair before was it fit for action.

The officers and soldiers of 19 Brigade were all keen to get to Iraq. Morale had slumped when the brigade was dropped from the invasion force in January. On the announcement in April 2003 that 19 Brigade was committed to Operation Telic 2, excitement picked up across Cattterick garrison, but the news that only some 4,000 troops of the 6,000 soldiers in the Brigade were deploying under Brigadier Moore meant many in the Brigade would not be going. This hit the infantry, cavalry and artillery units of 19 Brigade hard, as many of their officers and senior NCOs were keen to participate in an operational tour to help with their promotions. An operational tour would also help to maintain recruiting levels.

The leadership of the 1st Battalion, The King's Own Scottish Borderers Regiment (1 KOSB) took the news that they would not be going very badly, and their regimental colonel, Brigadier John Cooper, who was a senior officer in the army's Land Command headquarters at Wilton near Salisbury, was asked to intervene to get the decision reversed. He was successful in this lobbying effort.[9] Meanwhile the leadership of the Royal Artillery were keen to get 19 Brigade's artillery regiment included in the Iraq tour in the infantry role, to ensure it had a chance to get operational experience.

19 Brigade's troops began flying out to Iraq and Kuwait in mid-June to begin the relief in place, or RIP process. The stifling heat led to the brigade having to spend 12 days in a large tented camp in the Kuwaiti desert acclimatising. For the first four days, the troops had to stay inside tents and drink large quantities of water to prepare to go out into the 60 degree heat. There were many heat casualties during this training period, and to provide recovery facilities a fleet of air-conditioned buses were hired to be parked next to training areas in case soldiers collapsed from heat-related conditions. The extreme climate would severely impact on 19 Brigade's operations over the next six months, with 150 soldiers having to be evacuated back to the UK hospitals with heat-related injuries, while one soldier died from heat related causes.[10]

The actual transfer of authority took place from 7 Brigade to General Moore on 28th June, and General Lamb took over the reins from Major General Peter Wall two weeks later. General Lamb described the outgoing 1 (UK) Division as "exhausted" after the war fighting phase, and said the handover between the incoming and outgoing headquarters staffs "was not done well". Too many staff officers had just a day or so to hand over their posts and files, with the General saying "a great deal we had to start from scratch".[11]

"The environment was still one of turmoil following the removal of the Regime and HQ 1(UK) Armoured Division handed over a militarily stable area of operations, but a potential political and environmental powder-keg", Lamb recalled in his post operational tour report.[12] He said his over-arching aim was to build security by helping the population improve its lot.

"If we did not improve the quality of life for the local people it was my opinion that we would lose," he said.

"It was not about killing people but denying [terrorist groups] freedom of action while you get on with the task of delivering fuel, water, food, sanitation, governance and basically a better life. Don't kill the enemy : kill his courage."[13]

General Lamb and his troops barely had time to settle into their new bases before the rapid pace of unrelenting events just enveloped them.

"Day one the Iranians cross the border, day two the electricity supply fell over and day three the temperature went through the roof," Lamb recalled.

"There was no one else in theatre but the military and so I worked on first principles. My priorities were to deliver operational success, allocate from within the resources I had been provided, dissemble the problem, reassemble the solution and crack on. The condition that I therefore set the Division was that in all matters "adequate was good enough".[14]

The Marjar Al Kabir incident and a spate of attacks on British forces across southern Iraq prompted Brigadier Moore to reassess how he would operate.

"The planning in UK was focused on the requirement to conduct a Peace Support Operation" he recalled in his post-operational tour report.

"On arrival it quickly became evident that we had to refocus our efforts to peace enforcement, verging on conflict operations on occasions."[15]

Only two days after taking over command, Brigadier Moore had command of a major operation in Marjar al Kabir, involving his own troops and elements of 1st Battalion, The Parachute Regiment (1 PARA), who were due to fly home in the first week of July. Two companies of paras, a Warrior company from the 1st Battalion, The King's Regiment (1 KINGS), Challengers of Royal Tank Regiment and infantry from the 1 KOSB, backed by US Marine Corps AH-1W Cobra gunships swept into the town and carried out a handful of searches for weapons. The idea of General Wall and Lieutenant Colonel Tom Beckett, the commanding officer of 1 PARA, was to provide a demonstration of overwhelming force to deter further attacks on British troops. Major Chris Frazer, the commander of B Company of 1 KOSB, whose troops subsequently garrisoned Marjar al Kabir for the next six months tour concluded that Operation Swordfish did not have the desired effect.

"The operation ran smoothly, the local population were made aware of the firepower available, however, the subtlety of the British response was lost on the local population who expected rapid and severe retribution and interpreted the response as a sign of weakness – this created many problems later for B Company," recalled Frazer.

"The [troops] were elated, however, but with the benefit of hindsight the weapons cache find was not as significant at all by Iraqi standards, and as we later were to find out paled into insignificance such is the proliferation of weapons throughout the country."[16]

General Lamb's force had fully taken over from the departing units of 1 (UK) Division at the end of the first week of July, although the General did not formally assume command until 11th July. The major units took over the main bases and areas of responsibility from their predecessors. The heart of 19 Brigade's operation was the centre of Basra city, where the 1st Battalion, The Queen's Lancashire Regiment (1 QLR) was based in the ruins of the old security headquarters. The north of the city and the east bank of the Shatt-al Arab waterway was run by 1 KINGS from the Shatt-al-Arab Hotel. South of the city, 40 Regiment Royal Artillery controlled the port of Umm Qasr, the al Faw Peninsular and the Rumalyah oil fields. Maysan Province was the responsibility of 1 KOSB and its attached support units.

The size of the areas given to the units were enormous. Maysan was the size of Wales, with a population of more than 800,000 people – most of whom had access to some sort of firearms, including assault rifles - but 1 KOSB had just under 1,000 troops. 40 Regiment had less troops at its disposal but again its area of responsibility was huge, similar in size. This left Brigadier Moore with around half of his 4,000-strong Brigade to work inside Basra city, which had a population of between 1.3 and 1.5 million people; but no one was sure of its exact size. There were two reconnaissance squadrons of the Light Dragoons and a Challenger 2 main battle tank squadron in the brigade, but they worked mainly in Maysan, supporting 1 KOSB.

There were another 4,500 British troops in southern Iraq but they were mainly logistics, communications and administrative personnel, and thus not available to field commanders for combat deployment. Some 500 of these were RAF specialists running and guarding Basra International Airport. A further 3,000 of them were logistic troops driving supply trucks, repairing equipment and running supply dumps. The remainder were based at Basra airport working in the divisional headquarters, or operating the British communications network across southern Iraq.[17]

The ability of British units to generate manpower to put out on patrol or operations was heavily impacted by the decision to begin giving each soldier two weeks rest and recuperation, or R 'n R leave during their six month tour of duty in Basra. This effectively left each infantry battalion 50 soldiers short during most of their tour. On top of this, a third of each battalion were administrative and logistic specialists, leaving some 400 combat infantrymen to deploy on the streets. So out of the 9,500-strong British force, it was lucky if on a daily basis 1,600 troops could be operational. If they were allowed to sleep this would push the numbers of deployable manpower down to around 1,200, in an area the size of England.

The environment in southern Iraq further affected the combat capability, with the British division suffering 1,227 heat casualties between July and November 2003, and 5,199 cases of gastrointestinal disease in the same period. The heat casualties were blamed on the lack of air-conditioned accommodation, and units reducing acclimatisation times below the recommended length, according to General Lamb's post tour report. This document blames the diarrhoea and vomiting on lack of hand-washing facilities and the use of untreated water for washing. Some 150 heat casualties were so severe they had to be evacuated back to the UK, and no replacements were sent out to take their place. The impact of all this was to keep even more troops off duty.[18]

When General Lamb and Brigadier Moore toured their new command it was very obvious that their troops were spread hopelessly thin and would be sorely pressed in a crisis. The big hope for the British was that allied contingents would arrive soon to fill out the division in southern Iraq. As a result the division was re-named Multi-National Division (South East) or MND (SE). It was also hoped that Iraqi police and paramilitary units could be set up to fill the security vacuum, but the police were still in chaos and only a few hundred military personnel were under training. In July 2003 these developments seemed a long way off, with the only significant allied contribution being the arrival of a Danish battlegroup of 450 troops who were working to the north of Basra city.

To get more troops would have required the head of PJHQ, General Reith, to sign off on it, and then recommend the decision to government ministers. Sending extra troops back to Iraq only a few weeks after some 17,000 troops were withdrawn would have been a hard pitch for senior officers trying to persuade ministers, but officers like General Lamb appeared not to want to even try. Lamb told the 2009 Chilcot inquiry into the Iraq war that he did not immediately ask for more troops after he arrived in Basra, "what I did not want to do in those very early days was just ask for more forces."

"Because somehow in effect we would just throw them into a set of circumstances which were, to me, at that point in time, one was struggling to understand as to how to combat this escalation of violence and the sense of falling into a situation which was becoming less and less stable."[19]

"What I needed to do was be absolutely clear of what I wanted these forces for, rather than just saying 'send me more'", Lamb told the inquiry.

"It is very easy to ask for more, but actually you have to know what you are going to do with these young men and women who are coming in. That took a little bit of time. My view was not to rush to failure. I [did] know how to get there."[20]

Out on Basra's streets, 19 Brigade was beginning to realise that it was facing a challenge of a scale that the British Army had not faced since Northern Ireland in the 1970s. The tempo of operations was unrelenting. During July incidents ranged in scope and seriousness from full-blown fire-fights with dozens of armed men, to riots involving hundreds of people. Amid this mayhem the city's population were getting increasingly restive at the slow pace of their city getting back to normal. Each British battlegroup was dealing with ten or twelve major incidents a day, and often units found themselves responding to multiple events simultaneously.[21]

The first week of July was typical. It started off with Basra's doctors going on strike to demand improved security after one of their colleagues was kidnapped. In a village south of the city, a mob stoned an elder and he had to be rescued by 40 Regiment. A 1 KINGS patrol was attacked by four men armed with rocket propelled grenades and AK-47s. One was shot dead and two arrested by the British troops. On another occasion a car full of heavily-armed men rammed a 1 KINGS vehicle checkpoint. This type of incident became a daily occurrence.

The RAF Regiment found a grenade rigged to a trip wire in the city's water treatment plant. Crude improvised explosive devices (IEDs) started being thrown at British vehicles. In an attempt to bring some sort of control to the situation, 1 KINGS and the men of the Queen's Lancashire Regiment started to search vehicles at check-points, and had soon amassed a considerable haul of assault rifles, machine guns, grenades, rifles, pistols and ammunition. The two Basra-based units then launched four platoon-sized raids on several houses to seize weapons and ammunition.

A building collapsed in the centre of Basra, prompting the QLR to organise a rescue effort to dig out the trapped victims. The British units in the city also become involved in distributing back pay to former Iraqi army soldiers. To try to stop the looting of public buildings the British set up a series of guard forces but they were of indifferent quality. One of these guards opened fire on a QLR patrol and was shot dead. British military and civilian contractors' convoys began to be attacked. A convoy of contractors, from the US company KBR, formerly called Kellogg, Browne and Root, was bringing in material to build British camps when it was attacked with machine guns. A large crowd almost overwhelmed a British convoy outside Basra palace and was only disbursed after the soldiers fired shots in the air. The following day, 150 men ambushed a Royal Military Police convoy. The Danes to the north of Basra started to come under attack, and on two occasions fired 80 to 100 rounds in response. Such a tempo of operations became routine for the rest of 19 Brigade's tour.

Maysan province remained largely quiet until late July, when two KOSB vehicle check-points were attacked. In one of these incidents 200 rounds of fire was returned at the attackers who escaped. Two KOSB patrols were fired upon by heavily-armed men and significant firefights developed. A group of 20 men attempted to storm the al Uzayr police station and they were not driven off by the Scottish soldiers inside until reinforcements were flown from al Amarah by RAF Chinook helicopters.[22]

Meanwhile efforts to re-build Basra's utilities were progressing slowly. The attacks on convoys and small British units prompted heavily armed escorts to be assigned to units helping the local population, and training the Iraqi police. This in turn further reduced the re-building effort to a snail's pace. Senior British officers in Basra were getting exasperated by the non-appearance in southern Iraq of aid experts from the Department for International Development (DFID), and diplomats and civil administrators from the Foreign and Commonwealth Office. These civilians were dubbed the other government departments (OGDs) by the soldiers in Basra and soon there was contempt for the "civvies", who were accused of hiding in safety in London, Kuwait or the heavily-fortified Baghdad Green Zone. The US-led Coalition Provision Authority

(CPA) in Baghdad was equally loathed as being next to useless. Army officers had to step in to the breach and they spent endless hours in seemingly fruitless meetings with local politicians or in organising aid projects.

"At times it felt as if the Ministry of Defence (MOD) was receiving little support from UK OGDs, and was left facing these challenges on its own," commented Brigadier Moore in his post-tour report.

"While the work of the officers and soldiers involved should be seen as a success, the drain on military capability had significant impact on our ability to conduct counter-terrorist operations. The link between failure to deliver essential services and increasing civil unrest (thus creating conditions to support insurgency) was understood at all levels, yet finding civilian experts to deliver results seemed beyond the capacity of the CPA. For most of the time the Brigade was responsible for just about everything that the Coalition did or did not do in both Maysan and al Basrah Provinces. We were let down by UK OGDs who now need to establish some sort of expeditionary capability alongside that of the MOD." [23] The commanding officer of 40 Regiment, Lieutenant-Colonel Richard Nugee, recalled "there were no civilian experts to help us at battlegroup level so we had to do the best we could. It was not unlike 1950s colonialism, where no standing civil service existed and the military had to do everything themselves."[24]

One of the few tools the British did have was a small cash budget for aid projects, known as the Commander's Emergency Response Pool, or CERPs, which was used to fund Quick Impact Projects, or QIPs, such as painting schools, digging wells for drinking water or the installation of generators to restore power in remote villages. These were only worth a few hundred thousand US dollars but made the locals feel that British troops were actually improving their lives.

Lieutenant Colonel Ciaran Griffin, the commanding officer of 1 KINGS described them as using "money to buy effect", which he compared to the "way we use indirect fire to achieve effect on the battlefield."[25]

Brigadier Moore described these projects as "'buying' short-term security". But he complained that "as the tour progressed ever greater constraints were placed on the discretion of commanders' to use these funds. This unnecessary penny-pinching did not reflect the importance of QIPs, in particular, to maintaining working relations with tribal leaders and the ordinary people. It also inhibited work to generate the Iraqi security organisations. The effect of this bureaucracy was particularly evident with the CPA failing to deliver."[26]

Efforts to build up the Iraqi police and army were just not gaining any traction either.

"In the realm of Security Sector Reform (SSR) grandiose plans were made with scant regard for their adequate resourcing," commented Moore.

"This situation was gripped on the return of the Division Deputy Chief of Staff, but by then the chance to make the necessary preparations had been lost. Frantic activity by Division and Brigade logistics staff made the best of a bad situation, but there was a real danger of the Brigade failing to deliver the resources needed by the various SSR organisations. It cannot be assumed that the logistic assets, funds and resources will simply appear to support any plan."[27]

At the end of July temperatures soared, tempers frayed and Basra's creaking infra-structure fractured even more. The troops of 19 Brigade were hit hard.

"At their peak, temperatures rose into the high 50s, compounded through August with the southerly winds bringing extreme humidity," wrote Moore in his post tour report.

"We suffered a high rate of heat casualties early on in the tour, many of whom were evacuated to the UK and did not return to theatre, which depleted force levels. Sustaining prolonged operations in the heat of the day was very challenging if not dangerous, and while night operations gave relief from the worst of the conditions, the lack of enough air-conditioned accommodation made sleep throughout the day difficult. Troops at all levels were exhausted and most lost considerable amounts of weight in a short space of time."[28]

There was an immediate and pressing need for rapidly deployable infrastructure to support operations in an extremely hostile and unforgiving climate. The primary need was for cooled accommodation where soldiers could rest when not working. The US company KBR, a subsidiary of the US oil industry infrastructure company Halliburton, had been contracted by the MOD to install pre-fabricated buildings and tents, dubbed 'Theatre Deployable Accommodations,' or TDA. Attacks on convoys and the sheer scale of the task meant this was slow work.

"The aspiration to provide at least one air-conditioned cooled tent or room at each location across the Brigade was not achieved in anything approaching a reasonable timescale," according to the 19 Brigade post operational tour report.

"One of the last locations to get a respite facility was the Stadium in al Amarah shortly after the death of a soldier from heat injury."[29]

If the British army was having a tough time in the August heat, the people of Basra were suffering even more. There was still no permanent power to keep air conditioning going, running water supplies were intermittent and of very poor quality. More than 80% of the population was out of work, and even those with government jobs had not been paid for months. Crime was rife and only those with guns could feel secure. This was a tinderbox, and the spark was a five-day city-wide break down in power supplies, followed by the institution of petrol rationing after the city's oil refinery stopped working because of the power cuts.

Basra was less than thirty miles from one of the world's largest oil fields and the city's people were just exasperated that the British could not get petrol supplies right. General Lamb said local people blamed the British army for "incompetence" and said it was "losing consent of the Iraqis".[30]

This tinderbox burst into flames on 10th August in huge riots across Basra. A British Army truck was caught by a mob, and the vehicle was looted and set on fire.[31] Crowds gathered at petrol stations and started stoning troops from 1

KINGS and 1 QLR. An angry mob of former Iraqi soldiers mobbed 1 KINGS soldiers distributing back pay at the Rashid Bank. Gunmen started to open fire on QLR patrols and they returned fire with baton rounds. In the north of Basra, a mob attacked a 1 KINGS' patrol with rocket-propelled grenades, and then tried to climb up on the soldier's Warrior armoured vehicles. One Iraqi was shot by a vehicle commander as the rioter tried to pull him from his turret. When a Warrior opened fire with its 30mm cannon the crowd pulled back.

The rioting spread to al Amarah, Zubayr and the al Faw. In the capital of Maysan province mobs overturned cars and set them on fire. KOSB troops were shot at with small arms, and two 40 Regiment vehicles were overturned in Zubayr, while an injured soldier had to evacuated by helicopter. A mortar round was fired at the British base at al Faw.

What troops could be spared – 120 men from the RAF Regiment at Basra airport and three troops of 80 men from 40 Regiment – were mustered and sent into Basra to help the QLR. Detachments of troops were sent to guard petrol stations and other public buildings. They were routinely stoned and sniped at over the next week. The troops were out in the August heat in full body armour and helmets for hours at a time; heat casualties started to mount. Two serious cases had to be evacuated to hospital and one of them subsequently died.

An IED was thrown into a 1 KINGS base on 12th August, but the device did not explode and more serious attacks continued. A rocket propelled grenade was fired at a QLR Saxon armoured vehicle on the morning of 14th August, but the weapon ricocheted off the road and exploded three metres from the armoured vehicle, injuring three soldiers. That evening 19 Brigade suffered its first combat fatalities when an unarmoured QLR ambulance was hit by an IED when it was tasked to respond to soldiers injured in another incident. A remote controlled IED destroyed the vehicle, injuring the crew, while the commander, a QLR captain, was killed. Five days later Brigadier Moore's Landcruiser was attacked by an IED, and the windows of his protection team's vehicle was blown out by the blast.[32]

The unrest was getting out of control. Attacks on British troops continued and fire was returned on a regular basis. A Danish soldier was shot by accident by his comrades in a melee, when their patrol tried to intervene and stop looters stripping a civilian lorry. The QLR launched three raids on houses and 13 suspects were arrested when arms and document forgery equipment was found. Power pylons were reported destroyed outside Basra city, adding to the air of crisis. General Lamb and Brigadier Moore made desperate efforts to try to calm things down. A fleet of military and civilian fuel tankers were dispatched to Kuwait to start shuttling petrol to Basra's petrol stations. $5 million was paid out to oil, electricity, power, education, transport, water and port workers.

"Sensing a serious risk to the mission", General Lamb ordered the MND(SE) main effort be switched to essential services and a £127 million Strategy for Essential Services in Southern Iraq was developed by Royal Engineers, using money from DFID and the CPA. Work kicked off a few weeks later and General Lamb said it "probably saved coalition lives".[33]

General Lamb's dynamic personality came to the fore in knocking heads together, and generating action from his staff officers and civil servants across in the British government and in the CPA in Baghdad. He told a debriefer in February 2004 about his style of leadership in the August Fuel crisis.

"All you need to be able to do was conduct an estimate, realise the importance of time and space, work out the effect you want to achieve and then sort it out. Once you knew what you needed to do you then dispatched the nearest captain with the "find me a hundred trucks…. order and it all worked. It didn't need a suit with a 2/2 [degree] in Civilian Affairs to do that."[34]

A call was now made for extra troops to bring some relief to 19 Brigade's hard-pressed units in Basra city. With images of the rioting being broadcast on satellite news channels, General Reith was quickly able to secure government approval for 150 men from C Company of the 2nd Battalion, The Light Infantry (1LI) to be flown from Cyprus to Basra. These 'surge' troops were PJHQ's Middle East Reserve and had the benefit of being fully acclimatised so could be sent into action immediately they landed in Iraq. They only arrived just in time to stop 1 QLR being overwhelmed.

"The civil unrest of August in Basra fixed the Brigade in the protection and delivery of essential services," recalled Brigadier Moore.

"This resulted in the battlegroups being spread too thinly over a wide area and unable to concentrate combat power to deal with an increasing insurgent threat."[35]

"The fuel crisis required Basra-based battlegroups to conduct public order (riot control) operations", said the Brigadier.

"Battalions were required to quell several separate situations simultaneously in Basra over a period of three days. This pushed 1 QLR to exhaustion and required the employment of a surge company to take over the area of operations for twenty four hours and allow the battalion to recuperate. The Brigade did not have the manpower resources to contain prolonged widespread public disorder. The nature of public order [riots] in Iraq is also significantly more violent than our previous experiences had prepared us for. Use of small arms, grenades, rocket propelled grenades and improvised explosive devices were the norm. The Info Campaign at the command level was the key to preventing and quelling the riots, (as was restoration of fuel delivery and essential services), and this could not have been achieved by force alone."[36]

The call now went out from Basra for more reinforcements, with the balance of 2 LI arriving in early September and then 1st Battalion, The Royal Green Jackets (1 RGJ), which was the British Army strategic reserve unit, or Spearhead Lead Element (SLE), followed soon after. Both units were split up among 19 Brigade's existing battlegroups to free up troops to conduct offensive operations and try to kick start the training of Iraqi troops.

"The commitment and resource implications of training a credible Iraqi security organisation were underestimated," said Moore.

"The deployment of the SLE for this task was essential. Their task was, however, hampered by financial bureaucracy that limited the availability of equipment, vehicles and weapons with which to equip the [Iraqi security] force."[37]

The rush of reinforcements and efforts to placate the population of Basra seemed to have some effect, and by late August, the streets of the city had calmed considerably. A drop in temperature helped a lot to ease tension. Stability was a relative term, because gun and IED attacks on British troops were now routine on a daily basis, and British vehicles were routinely stoned by local children. Three Royal Military Policemen were shot dead in an ambush on their Landcruiser in Basra on 23rd August. The attack had all the hallmarks of a professional assassination. Later that day, a 1 KOSB operation to arrest a tribal leader, suspected of being behind attacks on British troops, ended in tragedy when the British convoy returning from the night time mission was ambushed by a large and well armed force of Iraqis at Ali Ash Sharqhi. One of the soldiers was killed and a number wounded, before the British force could extract itself to safety.[38]

The terrible day was concluded when a Royal Logistic Corps sergeant was killed in a firearms incident at Shaibah Logistic Base outside Basra, involving another British soldier. At a subsequent trial and inquest, it emerged that the soldier who fired the weapon was one of 2,000 from the Operation Telic 2 contingent who had failed his personal weapon test before deploying to Iraq.[39] In the space of 24 hours, General Lamb lost five of the eight British soldiers to die on Operation Telic 2.

General Lamb was now determined to use the arrival of the reinforcement troops to begin offensive operations. He wanted to put opponents of the British presence in Basra on the back foot, and reassure local people he was doing something to counter the rampant criminality in Basra. In September 1 QLR and 1 KINGS began a series of rolling raids against houses across Basra, in a bid to find those behind the spate of gun and IED attacks on British forces.

In Northern Ireland, this was the kind of specialist task that would first involve close surveillance by highly-trained Intelligence Corps operatives before the elite strike teams from the special forces would conduct the assault on the target. These resources were not available to Brigadier Moore – the SAS were committed to strategic operations in Baghdad and they considered Basra to be a bit of a backwater – so he gave the job to his two Basra battlegroups. Royal Artillery target observers from 4/73rd Battery were re-roled to act as surveillance troops, watching potential targets for extended periods and providing the strike teams with photographs of them. This was all very improvised, because of the need to put the entire plan together very quickly.[40]

Nightly, during September, the strike teams raided a string of houses around Basra. Brigadier Moore liked to accompany the raids to get a feel for what was happening and to boost the morale of the soldiers. Participation in the raids was popular with the troops from 1 QLR and 1 KINGS, who at last felt they were at last striking back at their hidden enemies.

It was during one of these raids, dubbed Operation Salerno, on 14th September, that four Iraqis were arrested by 1 QLR in a Basra hotel. In one of the most infamous incidents of the Iraqi war, the prisoners were violently abused at 1 QLR's main headquarters and one of the men, Baha Mousa, died of the inquiries he received. Seven soldiers involved in holding the prisoners were tried in 2006, and one was sent to prison after admitting inhumane treatment. The other six were acquitted. Lieutenant-Colonel Jorge Mendonca, the commanding officer of 1 QLR, was accused of dereliction of duty but acquitted. He subsequently resigned from the army, even though he had been awarded the Distinguished Service Order for the leadership of his battalion, in Basra. The unsatisfactory outcome of the army legal process led to a torrent of criticism in the government, media, parliament and in the upper echelons of the army. A public inquiry reported in 2011. It accused soldiers of 1 QLR of being responsible for Baha Mousa's death and reported that they had been involved in other abuses of Iraqi civilians.[41]

The whole incident tarnished the reputation of the QLR, the British Army and the Iraq mission. At the time the incident was not revealed to the media, and it only started to emerge in the spring of 2004. News of the incident emerged in the midst of the continuing public, media and parliamentary outcry over the failure to find weapons of mass destruction and claims that Prime Minister Tony Blair launched the Iraq war on a false prospectus. Popular support for the Iraq campaign reached what appeared to be a new low.

During September and October, General Lamb and Brigadier Moore continued their raids and other offensive operations. The General secured the services of the US 13th Marine Expeditionary Unit for a number of days to help him launch Operation Sweeney, designed to clamp down on illicit fuel smuggling along southern Iraq's waterways. The first phase of Operation Sweeny netted 39 alleged smugglers arrested, six loaded barges were impounded, seven empty barges impounded, eight oil boats and 14 road tankers and seven fuel pumps confiscated. The next phase's haul involved 48 smugglers being arrested, and the impounding of nine loaded barges, seven empty barges, eight oil boats, six road tankers, seven fuel pumps and nine pick up trucks.[42]

"The deployment of the over-the-horizon reserve from Cyprus (2LI) was the key to unfixing the Brigade, and allowing us to conduct offensive operations to counter the Former Regime Loyalists (FRL) or Extremists (FRE) as they latterly became known" recalled Moore.

"The ability to surge combat power in support of battlegroup operations enabled the Brigade to gain the initiative by late October, and hand over a far more stable situation to 20 Armoured Brigade. The lack of individual reinforcements to backfill casualties, however, degraded battlegroups capability throughout the tour."[43]

By the end of October, 20 Brigade's troops started to arrive in Iraq to take over from Brigadier Moore's troops. A month later, General Lamb handed over to Major General Andrew Stewart. As he departed Iraq, General Lamb issued a farewell message to his troops.

"Operations are what we live and die for, Iraq has been no exception. You have made a real difference here, touched people who had never been shown a shred of decency and made their lives significantly better. What we do in life is the foundation of our humanity. We place ourselves in harm's way, in facing terror and intimidation, in standing up for those ideals of service and sacrifice, we stand apart from others. We are a band of brothers who do not seek fame but quiet solitude in doing a difficult job well. I am immensely proud to have served alongside you. Keep doing what you do so well, keep safe but if you need to march to the sound of gunfire do so without hesitation or fear of failure. Life has taught me that courage is not a gift, merely the brutal application of will power; be strong. Much done and much yet to do, failure is not likely – it is quite simply not an option."[44]

"[My experience in Iraq] has reinforced the complexity of modern operations, the importance of those old fashioned ideas of service and sacrifice," Lamb wrote in his end of tour report.

"It has tested our people and their training, provided an insight into how we need to organise our effort across the [MOD]. Overall it has been good for us and reminded me of the sheer quality of our people, soldiers, NCOs and officers and the overriding importance of retaining them."[45]

Brigadier Moore was equally upbeat about his Brigade's time in Iraq, calling it a "cracking tour".

"This was a highly successful deployment and operational tour for the Brigade," he wrote in his end-of-tour report.

"We were extremely well supported by both PJHQ and Land [Command] throughout, and the foundation for our achievements can be traced back to the Training Year [in 2002]. The cohesion, trust and interaction gained in [Canada on exercise] are difficult to quantify in pure financial terms, but there is no doubt that these score very highly in the case of operational effectiveness. The commanders and soldiers performed exceptionally well in a very complex, dangerous and volatile environment, and their professionalism when coupled with a healthy slice of luck prevented more casualties. Theirs was by far the largest contribution to the success of the tour."[46]

And what of the aim of stabilising southern Iraq to allow the size of the British force to be nearly halved by the end of September? The directive given to General Lamb and Brigadier Moore turned out to be hopelessly optimistic. General Lamb in his end-of-tour report concluded that his force was effectively two battalions bigger by November 2003. He asked for a "modest increase in the UK order of battle" in Iraq to make the effort to build up the Iraqi security forces in time for the proposed formation of a new sovereign Iraqi government in June 2004. Then he anticipated that troop levels could drop again. Iraqi sovereignty, which the CPA chief Ambassador Paul Bremer had announced in the autumn of 2003, was now the British exit strategy.[47]

Eight years later, General Lamb gave a less upbeat assessment of his time in command in Basra to the Baha Mousa inquiry.

"The situation in the south of Iraq deteriorated rapidly during Operation Telic 2. At the point of taking over from 1 (UK) Division there was optimism, tinged with concern about how things might turn out. In fact, things started to unravel quickly. In July it became evident that the social fabric and infrastructure of southern Iraq was breaking down and by August we started to face massive unrest, and open hostility on the streets. No longer was our presence generally tolerated."[48]

IEDs, small arms and rocket propelled grenade attack meant British troops could not travel freely around southern Iraq, without detailed planning and protection measures, said the General. Failures to rebuild Basra's infra-structure and economy were blamed on the British.

"Our troops increasingly found themselves having to operate in an extremely dangerous security environment, in adverse physical conditions, and at full stretch," said Lamb.

"It was absolutely uncompromising. We were facing a deteriorating situation of enormous complexity, and we were so far short of being able to solve the problems that we were operating at full capacity in difficult and crude conditions. For six months I personally slept on the steel frame of a bed without a mattress, rarely having more than two or three hours of uninterrupted sleep a day. From my perspective, at command level, the demands of the situation were so great that we were constantly on the back foot, and being pushed backwards, responding to events. There was simply no time to get everything in order."[49]

He told his de-briefer in February 2004 about the precarious nature of the Basra mission, saying it required "a crippling amount of the commander's will power to keep the damned show on the road."[50]

The Operation Telic 2 tour was a real shock for the British Army. For a brief period in August, 19 Brigade was almost overwhelmed by a tide of anarchy. The British Army had prided itself at doing peacekeeping well, yet it seemed to have badly misjudged the Iraq situation. It raised serious questions about whether senior British military commanders really understood what was happening on the ground in southern Iraq, and had good intelligence about who was trying to undermine the British campaign. General Lamb was convinced his intelligence organisation was as good as it could be and he had a good idea of what was happening on the streets of Basra.

"[Our] intelligence came from a combination of strategic assets down through human intelligence (HUMINT) (a skill which the British Army is in danger of losing) and down to the commanders and soldiers speaking with the local community," General Lamb told a debriefer in 2004.

"Within six months I had an intelligence picture in Basra that was a match for the picture which had taken thirty years to produce in Northern Ireland.

Every two days I met all the key intelligence players to fine-tune what they were doing, what effects they were delivering and how we needed to adjust the intelligence direction."[51]

However, many British officers in southern Iraq were not convinced that their intelligence-gathering operation was up to speed or relevant to the situation in Iraq. The British were never able to penetrate Iraqi militia groups to the level they had achieved in Northern Ireland where both Republican and Loyalist extremists groups had been systematically compromised with agents and informers. In Northern Ireland, the British Army had a reasonable working understanding of the leadership, weapons inventories and operational capabilities of most extremist groups, which meant they were able to devise and execute responses that over time severely disrupted the Provincial IRA and its Loyalist counterparts. Despite General Lambs' boasts, the British Army in southern Iraq seemed blind for long periods about what its opponents were doing, or even who its opponents were.

Senior British intelligence officers in Iraq were extremely concerned that there was too much reliance on HUMINT, which according to post operational tour reports from MND(SE) and 19 Brigade accounted for more than 85% of all intelligence received. The British Army's Phoenix unmanned aerial vehicles could not fly in the thin summer air and for most of the Operation Telic 2 tour, there was no operational radio eavesdropping capability in southern Iraq, making the British almost totally dependent on HUMINT.[52]

The operation in southern Iraq to gather this was run by two Field HUMINT Teams (FHT), who worked directly for the head of intelligence in the MND (SE) Headquarters. These were manned by twenty-four agent handlers, translators, intelligence analysts and interrogators, who toured southern Iraq interviewing prisoners, 'walk-ins' to British bases, potential recruits to the Iraqi security forces, local political or tribal leaders and anyone else who might have useful information. Another third team interrogated prisoners in the US-run prison at Umm Qasr.[53]

One of Brigadier Moore's two senior intelligence officers, Major M Robinson, was very critical of the way the FHTs operated in Iraq in the summer of 2003, and said they were not very good at targeting the people suspected of actually attacking British troops. He wrote in the 19 Brigade post-operational tour report, that "the Division [intelligence] collection plan guided FHT collection and failed to deliver the required tactical information, concentrating on background detail rather than pinpointing specific information to target the threat and deliver an effect."[54]

"FHT's dogmatic approach to collection was based on Northern Ireland experience and failed to take into account the mission or Iraqi culture," wrote Major Robinson.

"The FHT concentrated on developing sources with long-term penetrative value, at the expense of debriefing known Iraqi personalities, politicians, religious and tribal leaders with access to information that could deliver immediate results. The majority of these personnel held significant information and had access to a large pool of sub-sources. The FHT sources of long-term penetrative value were able to provide corroborative or background information but were rarely able to provide information to drive the targeting process due to limited access. [Our] Brigade's inability to task the FHT direct meant that a significant gap in intelligence began to develop."

The divisional staff were very keen to act on FHT information, but Major Robinson said it was often of poor quality.

"For the reasons of force protection this often led to operations being run on single source information and the information often proved to be inaccurate," he wrote.

"Division level operations were generally task-driven as directed by CJTF-7 [the US command in Baghdad]. On a number of occasions [arrest] and kinetic operations were developed to target a group or achieve an effect without the intelligence to support the initiative. The intelligence was then fit to meet the task. This diluted collection against the actual threat, misdirected valuable collection assets and invariably led to missions of limited impact or success."[55]

The whole British intelligence-gathering effort in southern Iraq was severely hampered by old computers and networks. Staff officers said the thing was dependent on a few self-taught PC hobbyists in headquarters and battlegroups who kept the thing going. The Ministry of Defence-supplied computer system and supporting network was hopelessly slow and could not be modified to meet the needs of intelligence experts in Iraq. It did not have the capacity to send high resolution pictures or video imagery to the battlegroups who needed it to plan raids. Paranoia about computer viruses meant officers could not use USB data sticks to download intelligence information to distribute information to battlegroups. The biggest shortfall was the lack of an intelligence data base, identifying potential terrorists or insurgents that could be accessed easily by battlegroups. Each battlegroup ended up trying to build its own, which could not be used in conjunction with other data bases in other headquarters in southern Iraq. When prisoners were captured or documents, computers and mobile phones were seized in raids, the British were unable to exploit any intelligence they might hold because of a lack of interpreters or computer experts.

"The collection and processing of documentation was greatly hampered and the Brigade was forced to rely on favours from Iraq Survey Group (ISG) to exploit documents," commented Major Robinson.

"The ISG is an over-resourced organisation that has had limited impact in theatre. The ISG performed a necessary role but was over populated with valuable UK and US personnel that would have better suited to resolving the immediate issues of security and force protection. A large number of the document exploitation and HUMINT personnel working with ISG would be better employed with the under-resourced [integration teams] where documentary information can assist the debriefing/interrogation process. The ISG should also re-role immediately to Counter Terrorism (CT) to mirror the current threat."[56]

Many of the problems with IT, data bases and translators were repeatedly raised by in post-tour reports by British units over the next six years, and many officers who served in Iraq said they were never solved, severely affecting intelligence gathering and analysis. After HUMINT, the next best source of intelligence was the huge number of meetings between British officers and local political, tribal and social groups that happened each day as part of efforts to set up local administrative councils or improve the running of public utilities. This gold mine of information was not exploited to the full because of a lack of interpreters, either British military personnel or locally recruited.

Many British officers complained that the Iraqi interpreters often made local civilians suspicious about passing on sensitive intelligence. The fear was that the local Iraqi interpreters had split loyalties. One Arab speaking British officer who served as General Wall's interpreter recalled how he was present when an Iraqi was translating for the General, and became concerned that the local interpreter was giving a deliberately misleading account of the conversation.[57]

British military intelligence seemed to be one step behind the Iraqis, and it was not until near the end of 19 Brigade's tour that it tried to monitor radio traffic in Basra.

"The lack of an Electronic Warfare (EW) capability proved particularly detrimental", commented 19 Brigade's Chief of Staff Major E.A.Fenton.

"The belated Mobile Electronic Warfare Technology trial demonstrated the utility of the equipment and identified the use of Motorola [handheld radios] by extremist groups to monitor coalition forces movements. The equipment was not able to pinpoint exact locations of indigenous forces but highlighted their capability and forced a change in [our] modus operandi."[58]

If the British military intelligence was struggling to get a handle on the situation in southern Iraq, then questions must also be asked of the assessments drawn from the limited raw intelligence information available. Senior officers, such as General Lamb and Brigadier Moore, spent many hours each day meeting political leaders and tribal chiefs while they travelled around southern Iraq, and this played a major part in shaping their views of the situation on the ground and the political climate. They could see for themselves the wretched living conditions of Basra's population. They, however, were totally reliant on their intelligence staff to work out who was attacking British troops or planning to attack British troops.

Internal British army documents from the summer and autumn of 2003 make great play of what are termed former regime loyalist or extremists (FRE) being behind the majority of small arms, rocket and IED attacks on British troops in southern Iraq.

General Lamb made this assessment when he left Iraq in November 2003, that "there is a consistent level of [IED] attacks at 5/6 weekly and it is anticipated that this threat will continue. It is further likely that FRL Groups will try to increase their level of attacks through surges in activity. Their tactics are evolving in response to coalition force actions and this clearly indicates that coalition operational activity is being monitored. There is increasing reporting about threats from outside the [British area] in form of large IEDs."[59]

This clearly mirrored US fears that the remnants of forces loyal to Saddam Hussein were behind the growing insurgency that was engulfing Iraq. There were regular requests from the US command in Baghdad to the British in Basra to raid the hideouts of suspected Ba'athist insurgents. While at the same time many Shia leaders in the south were also keen to blame Sunni Ba'athists from central Iraq for any attacks on British troops, because it suited their agenda.

But the reporting of incidents from British troops pointed to local Shia being in the forefront of attacks. Many of the most dangerous incidents in Basra city involved gunmen and bombers using willing crowds of civilians during the August riots as cover to attack British troops. The two deadly attacks on British troops in Maysan province during the summer of 2003 took place in overwhelmingly Shia towns and villages, and required the active co-operation of the local population. It was stretching credulity to suggested that Ba'athists played any part in these incidents. British military intelligence seemed to be playing down the growing sophistication and scale of attacks by armed Shia groups on British troops – or was not properly aware of them.

The formation of the first battalion of the Mahdi Army militia, which was loyal to the radical cleric Muqtada al Sadr, in Basra in October attracted little interest from the British. The cleric and his senior lieutenants deliberately avoided meeting representatives of the British in Basra, so they were not considered "players".

By the end of 2003, the British Army's was struggling to understand what was happening in southern Iraq. Its intelligence-gathering efforts were hampered by technical shortcomings and it appeared to be heavily influenced by the US view of the Sunni/Ba'athist threat in Baghdad. This did not bode well for the coming months when the Shia of southern Iraq would rise up in active revolt against the British occupation.

Chapter 15

A MATURE THEATRE?

In November 2003 the newly-arrived troops of 20 Armoured Brigade had settled into the bases across southern Iraq. The handover or relief in place (RIP) from 19 Mechanised Brigade went relatively smoothly, and senior British officers started to think a corner had been turned. They began to talk about Iraq being a "mature" theatre of operations. The British Army was also beginning to get its collective mind around how to sustain its contingent in Iraq for the foreseeable future, and better organise the training and deployment of future troop contingents for their six-month long operational tours. An exit strategy of sorts had emerged and the intention was to further reduce the size of the British contingent in Iraq during 2004.

Central to the British military campaign were decisions made by the US President George W Bush and his administrator or 'viceroy' in Iraq, Ambassador Paul Bremer. After being appointed head of the Coalition Provincial Authority (CPA) in May 2003, he had laid out a two-year long plan to create a western style democratic constitution for Iraq, followed by a referendum and national elections. Barely four months later, as central Iraq was ravaged by insurgency and US casualties spiked, President Bush ordered a rethink to try to head off accusations from Iraqis that the US wanted to permanently occupy their country.

The new plan was that the CPA, which nominally governed Iraq on behalf of Britain and the US, would wind up in June 2004 and hand over sovereignty to an appointed Interim Iraqi government. Then this new body would create a constitution and hold Iraq's first democratic elections in the spring of 2005.

Once the new Iraqi government was formed and its security forces were able to sustain it, then US, British and other coalition troops could rapidly draw down. Coalition forces could drop from 150,000 at the end of 2004 to less than 50,000 by 2005, according to one Permanent Joint Headquarters (PJHQ) projection, potentially reducing the British commitment to a single battalion to train the future Iraqi military.[1]

For the British government this provided its exit strategy and also the political top cover for an increasingly unpopular military commitment. Continuing controversy over the failure to find weapons of mass destruction in Iraq, the inquiry into the death of the Ministry of Defence (MOD) scientist Dr David Kelly, rising British casualties and accusations of mistreatment of Iraqi civilians by British troops was sapping the will of the government to sustain Operation Telic. Iraq was rapidly becoming a toxic issue. With a route to Iraqi sovereignty on the table, Blair could point to light at the end of the tunnel and at the same time keep his word to President Bush to keep British troops in Iraq as long as US troops remained on the ground.

For the British military, this tentative timeline provided the basis for their planning of the Iraqi commitment over the next two years. The British Army moved into campaign mode and kicked in its proven processes to train, generate, deploy and sustain forces on overseas operations. Its experiences in the Balkans and Northern Ireland shaped how the army would operate in Iraq : this was very much its default mode.

The first priority was to bring some order to the rotation of army brigades to Iraq, so unlike the troops of 19 Mechanised Brigade, in future units would arrive properly trained and equipped for their six-month long tours of duty. The troops of 20 Armoured Brigade, for example, were notified in July 2003 that they would deploy, which gave them almost four months to train for their Iraqi mission. The subsequent formation, 1 Mechanised Brigade, had nearly six months to get ready and preparation time progressively increased. Some troops who returned from the Operation Telic 3 rotation, or roulement, were told they would be heading back to Iraqi in two years time on Operation Telic 7.[2]

Lessons from 19 Brigade's tour were also being learnt quickly about the unique and unforgiving nature of Iraq. Future RIPs were timed to take place in the spring and autumn to avoid the oppressive summer heat incapacitating hundreds of newly-arrived troops. The summer of 2003 also produced a cadre of Iraqi veterans who would provide valuable experience and advice to subsequent units heading in-theatre.

The troops in Iraq were being steadily provided with pre-fabricated buildings, known as Theatre Deployed Accommodation (TDA), to live in at their bases, along with welfare packages like satellite phones and internet cafes to contact their families back in Britain.[3]

Although they was now a commitment to keep British troops in Iraqi until 2005 at least, there was still strong pressure from the MOD and Treasury [finance ministry] to reduce, or at least contain, the huge cost of the British presence, which was now projected to run at nearly £1 billion a year.

Just like in the Balkans, civilian contractors were hired to provide catering, sewage, fuel supplies and other camp services, as well to provide a commercial standard internet and telephone communications network, dubbed Synergy, to link together British bases across Iraq.[4]

Hundreds of white sports utility vehicles (SUVs) were bought so soldiers could travel around Basra in an unobtrusive manner and reduce the need for military vehicles to be deployed in the city. A drop in violence during late 2003 had allowed the tank and armoured infantry units to put their Challenger 2 tanks and Warrior vehicles into temporary storage at Shaibah Logistic Base. Almost every infantry, artillery and armoured unit was re-equipped with armoured Snatch or open-top unarmoured Land Rovers.[5]

There was also a constant pressure to reduce troop numbers. The big ambition for 2004 was to co-locate and then merge the British-led divisional headquarters at Basra International Airport with the British brigade headquarters at Basra Palace, allowing hundreds of soldiers to be sent home. The divisional headquarters itself was, from November 2003 onwards, to be formed on an ad hoc basis, rather than to use one of the army's two existing deployable divisional headquarters. This allowed fewer personnel to be deployed and was less disruptive to the peacetime training of the army back in Germany and the UK, but it meant Basra headquarters took time to get up and running. It also created the impression that the British Army was using its B Team rather than one of its properly manned and trained headquarters.[6]

As all the paraphernalia of logistics infrastructure began to flow into Iraq, so did the British Army's peacetime bureaucracy. The Synergy network and Skynet satellite ground stations connected headquarters and units in Iraq to the Ministry of Defence's administrative email system. Staff officers were increasingly deluged in paper work and form filling, as PJHQ and the MOD in London demanded more and more information from Iraq on what was happening or not happening. A new development was the video telephone conference, an early military version of Skype, which was increasingly being used, and added a new dimension to micro-management of overseas operations by the MOD.

The projected two-year time horizon of the British military presence in Iraq, however, led to an attitude of "short-termism" across the MOD, Treasury and PJHQ. Only just enough money would be spent to keep the operation ticking over, but no more. The TDA was supposed to have a life of nine months but it would have to make do until the final drawdown, whenever that would be. The reluctance to make investments in new equipment would be come more of an issue when British troops came under sustained attack in 2004 and 2005.

The military bureaucracy governing troop rotations also kicked in with a vengeance, with the divisional and brigade commanders in Basra soon having little say in the number of troops or even the units they could take with them. The number of British troops in Iraq was governed by a bureaucratic process, dubbed the Force Level Review or FLR. Every six months a team from PJHQ went out to Iraq to assess what the troops were doing and whether they were really needed. It was the military equivalent of a 1970s time and motion study. Their recommendations were then used by the head of PJHQ to pitch for troops, equipment and money from the MOD and Treasury for the next year ahead.

The divisional commander would add his recommendations to each FLR but his voice was not the dominant one in the process. Once the head line troop numbers had been agreed by government ministers, then PJHQ would ask the frontline commands of the three armed services to offer up troops and units. In the case of the army, Land Command at Wilton, in Wiltshire, had the deciding say on which brigade and its constituent units would deploy to Iraq. In 2003 and 2004, the British force in Iraq contained many surge units and battle groups augmented with extra personnel and sub-units, over and above those normally assigned to each brigade, so senior officers were keen to pitch to get their regiments or sub-units included in the next rotation to Iraq. The kudos of participating in an operational tour was an immense help to officer's careers and was seen as the best way to generate positive publicity to recruit soldiers to individual regiments. Until the ramping up of the British deployment to Afghanistan was expanded in 2006, there was intense competition across the army to get to Iraq.[7]

This force generation cycle, however, was out of synchronisation with the appointment of the divisional commander. They were rarely appointed until three or four months before RIPs, so the commander's ability to select and train his forces was limited. Beyond appointing a few senior staff officers and re-arranging the layout of his headquarters, the prospective divisional commander had little influence on picking the troops and units he would command in Iraq. He would have to play the hand he was dealt by others.

Another significant element of the British campaign in Iraq was the relationship of the Basra division with the US headquarters in Baghdad. The Iraq mission was run by the Americans and in 2004 the British division was under the operational command of Lieutenant General Ricardo Sanchez's headquarters. A British Lieutenant General was assigned to be Sanchez's deputy, with the grand title of Senior British Military Representative in Iraq.

The Royal Air Force contingent, except for battlefield helicopters, was controlled by the US Air Force-run Combined Air Operations Centre (CAOC) at Al Udeid Airbase in Qatar. The Royal Navy warships protecting Iraq's off shore oil installations reported to the US Navy Middle East headquarters in Bahrain, and the Special Forces contingent in central Iraq was assigned to work with the US Joint Special Operations Command at Balad Airbase, north of Baghdad. Britain also had a strong contingent of experts working in the US-led Iraq Survey Group, which was spearheading the hunt for Saddam Hussein's weapons of mass destruction.

British staff officers worked inside all these American headquarters, and it was hoped they would provide an important way for the UK to influence the overall direction of the campaign, as well as providing advance warning of changes in US strategy or controversies, such as the Abu Ghraib prisoner abuse scandal. The British air, naval and special forces contingent commanders at the turn of 2003/4 all had good working relationships with their US counterparts, but the relationship between Baghdad and Basra was difficult and fraught. General Sanchez was so overwhelmed by the wave of violence engulfing Baghdad and the so-called Sunni Triangle that he paid little interest to Basra. It was almost a policy of benign neglect, according to British officers who served in Basra at the time. As long as nothing was going wrong, Sanchez just ignored Basra, only visiting the city once between November 2003 and June 2004. When he wanted something to happen in Basra, Sanchez just issued diktats. This exasperated the British divisional chief of staff, Colonel J.K.Tanner, who recorded that "despite our so-called 'special relationship,' I reckon we were treated no differently to the Portuguese."[8]

"The whole system was appalling" Tanner told an army debriefing session after he returned from Iraq.

"We experienced real difficulty in dealing with American military and civilian organisations who, partly through arrogance and partly through bureaucracy, dictate that there is only one way: the American way. I now realise that I am a European, not an American. We managed to get on better…with our European partners and at times with the Arabs than with the Americans. Europeans chat to each other, whereas dialogue is alien to the US military… dealing with them corporately is akin to dealing with a group of Martians. If it isn't on the Power Point slide, then it doesn't happen."[9]

This disconnect in the most important military relationship for the British was exasperated by a personal and political tension between Bremer and his British deputy, Sir Jeremy Greenstock. They had fundamental differences on major issues, which were never really resolved. Added to this potent mix was the fact the Bremer and Sanchez also had a poor relationship. The leadership of the coalition campaign in Iraq until June 2004 was essentially dysfunctional and resulted in several poor decisions that had a serious detrimental effect on the course of the campaign.

The British General who stepped into the Iraq maelstrom was Major General Andrew Richard Evelyn De Cardonnel Stewart. He was a cavalry officer, who had commanded 7 Armoured Brigade in Bosnia in 1997 and then spent two years working in PJHQ as assistant chief of staff for operations between 1999 and 2001.

General Stewart was described as a "safe pair of hands" and "a master of the MOD process" by one of his army contemporaries and not someone who was noted for innovative thinking or unnecessary risk taking. His time in the Balkans and PJHQ had made him very aware of the political sensitivities in Whitehall and Westminister of complex military operations in the modern media era. Given the Blair government's nervousness about Iraq in 2004, his appointment to the Basra command was not a surprise.

In June 2004, Stewart handed over to Major General Bill Rollo, who was a very different character. Although he had the outward appearance of a university don, he was very charismatic and radiated an aura of confidence, even in high stress situations. As an officer in the Blues and Royals, he was very well connected and respected across the higher echelons of the British Army. He had led 4 Armoured Brigade into Serb-occupied Kosovo in June 1999 and this experience had brought him into contact with many of the senior US officers, who by late 2004 were serving in Baghdad. These relationships would be very beneficial during his time in Iraq.

Running the day-to-day operations in Basra during the coming year were three brigadiers who all had their careers shaped by operations in the Balkans in the 1990s. The commander of 20 Armoured Brigade for the first three months of its tour, David Rutherford-Jones, had led his regiment, the Light Dragoons, in Kosovo and then took 20 Brigade to the southern Serbian province in 2001. His time in command came to an end at the middle of his brigade's Iraq tour, and unusually he was not extended in post. The situation in Basra was considered benign enough to allow command to be handed over in the middle of the brigade's tour, with Nick Carter coming in for its final three months in Basra.

Brigadier Carter was very much seen as a rising star in the army, who was judged to be able to handle taking over a brigade in the middle of an operational tour. He was the former commanding officer of 2nd Battalion, The Royal Green Jackets, who had served during the Mitrovica rioting in Kosovo in spring 2000. Outwardly self-confident, Carter had a cool head in a crisis and was not someone who was flustered or panicked by unexpected events.

Carter handed over in turn to Andy Kennett, who was not as confident in front of the media as his predecessor but considered very competent. Kennett was a bullish Parachute Regiment officer, who had a reputation for being very competitive and tactically aggressive.

When it deployed in November 2003, 20 Armoured Brigade found southern Iraq outwardly calm. The drop in temperature since the summer appeared to calm tempers. By the late autumn, the CPA had also managed to get its organisation in Basra up and running. Its team of diplomats, civilian administrators and technical experts, assisted by Royal Engineers and US civilian contractors, had succeeded in patching up Basra's 1970s era public utilities. More importantly, the CPA team had taken over responsibility for the branches of government ministries and state-owned enterprises in Basra, and had managed to begin paying the monthly wages of the hundreds of thousands of people who were on their pay-rolls. As the Iraqi state controlled almost every commercial activity it meant a majority of the adult males in the southern Iraq was dependent on this money. The hundreds of millions of dollars the CPA paid out in wages each month was a central element of what British officers termed their strategy of 'buying consent' of the population. It was hoped that by pumping money into southern Iraq, it would head off armed resistance or civil unrest.[10]

The 'buying consent' strategy was already fraying at the edges even before the end of 2003. By effectively channelling money largely through the old structures of the Ba'athist state, the British and the CPA were reinforcing the perception among the majority Shia population of southern Iraq that they were not getting a fair share of the country's economic spoils. Large parts of southern Iraq had been excluded from the Ba'athist economy by Saddam Hussein as a punishment for their participation in the 1991 uprising.

This large Shia underclass, which was drawn from the tribes of Maysan province, had been carefully cultivated by the 29 year-old cleric Muqtada al Sadr during the final years of Saddam's rule and he was poised to make a push for leadership of Iraq's Shia majority. Many established Shia clerics and middle class Iraqis, both Shia and Sunni, were deeply suspicious of Sadr and his movement, which was seen as anarchic and a threat to public order. He threatened revolution.[11]

Sadr was the son of one of Iraq's leading Shia clerics who had been murdered by Saddam's secret police. He had stayed in Iraq during the 1990s and been under house arrest for most of this time, which gave him immense credibility with the disposed Shia underclass, particularly the young men who had been denied jobs by the Ba'athist regime or been rounded up in mass arrests by the secret police in Basra and al Amarah. The key to Sadr's success was a network of local Imans across southern Iraq whom he used to distribute welfare money to the families of arrested or economically disadvantaged Shia. After the fall of Saddam's regime, Sadr moved quickly to build up his organisation across southern Iraq and in the Sadr city slums of Baghdad, where over a million Shia from Maysan province had moved during the 1970s and 1980s. His supporters began participating in the local councils set up by the British across southern Iraq and Sadr began funding these councils. Sadr was also trying to 'buy the consent' of the population.

Like many other Iraqi politicians, Sadr set up his own militia, known to the British as the Mahdi Army or Jaish al-Mahdi (JAM). The first units were set up in Basra in October 2003, and they were soon a familiar sight in their distinctive black pyjama uniforms. Sadr himself was based in the Holy city of Najaf, and never ventured into the British zone around Basra and al Amarah. He relayed his instructions to his supporters and lieutenants by couriers and via sermons delivered by friendly imans, which made it very difficult for the Americans and British electronic eavesdropping organisations to monitor his communications, leaving them largely blind about his intentions and even his location. The American National Security Agency hit upon the idea of trying to listen in to the mobile phones of wives and relatives but the scheme never yielded much actionable intelligence.[12] Bremer never understood why Sadr was so popular among Iraq's Shia, and in August 2003 arranged for a US-appointed Iraqi judge to issue a secret warrant for his arrest. But on that occasion his advisors managed to persuade the US diplomat not to put the plan into action.

The organisation set up by Sadr aimed to mirror that of the Lebanese Shia Party of God, or Hizbollah. His political wing, based around regional headquarters in major towns, was known as the Office Muqtada al Sadr or OMS, while the JAM had a parallel command structure. The British, who had little exposure or understanding of Hizbollah, inevitably started to refer to OMS as Iraq's Sein Fein, in a comparison to the political wing of the Provisional Irish Republican Army. Closely allied with Sadr was the Islamic Virtue Party or Fadhila Party, which many British observers considered to be a front organisation for the firebrand cleric's movement, allowing it gain covert control of local and national level government institutions.

Sadr was vehemently opposed to foreign interference in Iraq, and refused even to meet representatives of the US and British occupying forces. This made it even more difficult for the US and British military and diplomats to understand Sadr and his militia.

The JAM militia were also very secretive, and British military intelligence at first did not pick up the threat it posed. Through late 2003 and into 2004, the JAM began a campaign of low level attacks on British troops in Basra and intimidation of civilians working for the occupation authorities. Locally recruited

CPA civilian staff were targeted for assassination during the first weeks of 2004. Shops selling alcohol were ransacked by Sadr's supporters and women intimidated into wearing Islamic dress. Schools and work places were forced, under threat of attack, to introduce rigid separation of men and women.[13]

This rising tide of attacks was set against a background of growing unrest across southern Iraq because of lack of jobs, as well as continuing poor provision of power and water. The proliferation of political parties, with more than 50 operating in Basra alone, prompted an inevitable jockeying for power ahead of the transfer of sovereignty and subsequent elections. Iraqi politics has long been a brutal and violent business and the spring of 2004 was no different. Political assassinations and violent demonstrations was a perfectly acceptable modus operandi for many aspiring Iraqi political leaders.

Maysan province became the epicentre of this unrest during the spring of 2004. It lay on the fault line of much of the unrest across the south of Iraq. Sadr's organisation had strong roots in the region. The local population believed they had liberated themselves so the continued British presence was viewed as an illegitimate occupation. Rival politicians and tribal chiefs were manoeuvring for advantage, with a vengeance.

Meanwhile the British troop presence in Maysan was also very weak, with only one battlegroup, built around the 1st Battalion, The Light Infantry (1 LI), with its 1,000 troops spread across a province the size of Northern Ireland. Also the CPA civilian administration was nowhere near as well developed or efficient as its counterpart in Basra city. For most of the last three months of 2003, the CPA office in al Amarah consisted of little more than the quixotic British diplomat Rory Stewart and a satellite telephone.[14]

The day 1 LI took over from the King's Own Scottish Borders in Maysan, the province was plunged in chaos by the assassination of its police chief. Since the days of Lieutenant-Colonel Tim Collins in April 2003, the British army had backed a warlord, Kareem Mahood al-Muhammadawi, aka Abu Hatim. He was nicknamed the Prince of the Marshes by the British, who supported him as the leader of the local provincial council and one of his close allies, Abu Rashid, as the provincial police chief.

On 24th October Abu Rashid was shot dead in broad daylight at a public meeting. His relatives wanted revenge on the Sadrists whom they accused of murdering the police chief, and they in turn kidnapped two leading supporter of the cleric. Across al Amarah rival supporters were trading fire, until the Warrior armoured vehicles of the Light Infantry and the Scimitar light tanks of the 9th / 12th Royal Lancers were deployed to quell the fighting, which left scores dead. The CPA managed to broker a peace deal but the incident set the stage of a power struggle amongst al Amarah's political and military groups that would play out over the next four years.[15]

The JAM militia were determined to become the dominant force in Maysan, to open the way for supporters of Sadr to take control of the province's political and security institutions. Central to their political narrative was resistance to the British occupation and only a few days after their arrival a 1 LI Land Rover taking a company commander to a meeting in al Amarah was attacked by an improvised explosive device (IED). The weapon failed to detonate properly so caused no casualties, but it was a clear indication that the JAM intended to challenge British control of Maysan. The arrival of the 1 LI company to take over the police station in Majar-al-Kabir was greeted by a mortar attack on their base.[16]

In downtown Basra, the Queen's Royal Hussars (QRH) and 1st Battalion, The Royal Regiment of Wales (RRW) battlegroups were responsible for security across the city. Both these battlegroups pushed out around-the-clock patrols to set up vehicle check points in an attempt to intercept illegally-held arms and deter movement by armed men. They also launched regular house searches to try to seize illegal arms. The CPA allowed each house to hold an AK-47 and enough ammunition for self defence, but anything over and above this was liable for seizure. Huge quantities of weapons were seized, with one company of the Light Infantry working in the city reporting that they always needed a four-ton truck to accompany them on raids to take away the haul of booty.[17] In mid December, the QRH battlegroup had to deploy en masse to damp down a serious outbreak of fighting in northern Basra between two tribes. The fighting lasted three days and the QRH troops fired several thousand rounds of ammunition during the incident, with the regiment's Challenger 2 tanks firing their heavy machine guns.[18]

General Stewart was keen to push ahead with training of the Iraqi police and the paramilitary Iraq Civil Defence Corps (ICDC), which were touted as eventually being able to take over from the British after the Iraqis regained sovereignty. Each British battle group was given the job of training several ICDC companies, and to continue this effort the two surge infantry battalions deployed in September 2003 were eventually replaced by new battalions on six month-long tours of duty. At the start of 20 Brigade's tour the plans to train up the ICDC, police and numerous other local security agencies were already behind schedule, with only half the required number of recruits under training across the British sector. By December, Brigadier Rutherford-Jones was realising that a revamp was needed if the target for forming a new Iraqi army division in southern Iraq was to be achieved. There were still problems building training centres and barracks for the new Iraqi military, equipment and weapons were in short supply and large number of translators needed to be recruited to help the British instructors pass on their wisdom to the Iraqi recruits. To try and break through the bureaucratic inertia the regimental headquarters of the QRH was re-roled to take over running the training of the ICDC and police.

More than half of the British force in southern Iraq was now involved in training the ICDC and a significant chunk of its logistic resources were also involved in building and supplying the new training centres. Across southern Iraq every British battlegroup was now running some sort of training programme for Iraqi personnel.[19] There were also ambitious targets to build up the new Iraqi police force, but their training and re-equipping was formally in the hands of the CPA, international police trainers and US contractors. Its training was way behind schedule. British troops were drafted in to boost this effort, led by the Royal Military Police.

Al Amarah was still boiling, and in January the city was rocked by rioting for two days after a protest about unemployment got out of control. Iraqi police started shooting rioters, so the Light Infantry stepped in to begin controlling the riots. They used rubber bullets and snatch squads to try to disperse the rioters who were throwing petrol bombs at them. This resulted in members of the Light Infantry meeting out 'street punishment' beatings to several of the rioters whom they apprehended.[20] This caused a scandal in 2006 when a video of the incident was made public. The Light Infantry staged a series of raids across Maysan province in bid to try to begin to whittle down the huge holdings of arms and ammunition among the population.

A raid on a compound in the town of Quaat Salih in the south of Maysan went wrong on 5th March, and a small contingent of British troops found themselves under attack by hundreds of heavily armed tribesmen, outraged that their homes were being searched. The incident had shades of the Majar-al-Kabir massacre in June 2003 but on this occasion a heavily-armed quick reaction force was able to intervene and rescue the beleaguered troops. Over the next three weeks there were two radio controlled IED attacks on 1 LI vehicles in al Amarah, indicating an improvement in the skills and capabilities of the British Army's opponents.[21]

The first three months of 2004 rolled on in much the same fashion with public disorder, political violence and attacks on British troops on a daily basis. At the end of March, units of 20 Armoured Brigade began handing over to their replacements from 1 Mechanised Brigade. The soon-to-depart regiments thought they had a successful tour and crucially had not lost any soldiers to enemy action, although seven had been killed in accidents. Events elsewhere in Iraq would soon throw the British-controlled zone into chaos.

US forces in central Iraq were facing an increasingly sophisticated insurgency drawn from the Sunni population around the capital. Convoys were being ambushed, bases attacked and helicopters shot down on a daily basis. Bremer was getting increasingly frustrated at the lack of political progress to set up his interim Iraqi government, and vented his fury on a Sadr supporting newspaper, which he accused of inciting attacks on US troops. He ordered US troops to close down the newspaper on 28th March. Sadr threatened that there would be "hell to pay" if the newspaper was not re-opened. Bremer was unmoved and ignored the threats. The timing was dreadful.

Three days later an SUV driven by four US contractors working for the security company Blackwater took a wrong turn and drove into the Sunni insurgent-controlled town of Fallujah. The Americans were shot and dragged from their vehicles by a mob, then set alight. Their charred bodies were strung up from a bridge and video was soon being broadcast by Arab satellite news networks. President Bush was outraged. He issued orders that the US Marines were to immediately storm Fallujah. Heavy casualties among the civilians in the city inflamed Iraqi opinion after the Al Jazeera network broadcast pictures of football pitches it claimed had been turned into grave yards. Hundreds of Iraqi troops refused to join the battle and mutinied.[22]

Sadr now decided not to back down in his duel with Bremer. On 2nd April he issued a sermon to be read out at Friday prayers, attacking the American occupation and even praising Osama bin Laden and the 9/11 attacks on New York. Bremer was enraged and the next day ordered the arrest of one of Sadr's top lieutenants. This was not the time to show weakness, claimed the US viceroy. Within 24 hours, southern Iraq and Sadr city were in flames. It would also trigger the biggest breach in UK-US relations since the start of the Iraq operation.

Sadr's militia launched a co-ordinated offensive across the Shia areas of Iraq, seizing police stations, ICDC bases, municipal buildings and other institutions of the occupation. In the centre of the country, coalition troops from the Ukraine, Spain and El Salvador withdrew to their bases rather than resist the militia attacks. The last thing the home governments of these troops wanted was for them to become involved in a war. CPA compounds in Najaf, al Kut and Nasiriyah were besieged and subsequently had to be abandoned in hasty retreats under fire. US troops in Sadr city found themselves fighting prolonged street battles with heavily-armed JAM fighters. In Najaf, Sadr militia men took up positions around Shia holy shrines. US troops were dispatched from Baghdad to pick up the pieces left by the virtual collapse of the Polish-led Multi-National Division Centre. The appearance of US troops outside Najaf enraged Shia opinion and bolstered support for Sadr. In a matter of days, Bremer had succeeded in uniting Iraq's Sunni and Shia communities against the occupation. According to Lieutenant Colonel Philip Napier, commanding officer of 1 RRW in Basra Palace, the attitudes of people changed rapidly, with his battalion's situation changing "from a benign to a difficult one overnight".[23]

In the British controlled-zone events spiralled out of control rapidly. Not surprisingly al Amarah was the first city in the British sector to be hit by unrest. Pro-Sadr riots swept through the capital of Maysan. All of 1 LI's three British companies based in the city were deployed on riot control duties in their Snatch Land Rovers. They were soon stretched and Lieutenant-Colonel Bill Pointing, the Light Infantry commanding officer, called back into al Amarah his second Warrior unit, C Company of 1 RRW, from a patrol along the Iranian border. The RRW Warrior column entered the city late in the afternoon, after which it had to run a gauntlet through 17 carefully planned ambushes, by fighters heavily armed with rocket propelled grenades (RPGs). Every vehicle was hit by RPGs and one Welsh soldier was wounded by AK-47 fire. It took most of the night for the Warriors to escort the Snatch patrols of the Light Infantry back to Camp Abu Naji, to the south of al Amarah.[24]

The Iraqi interim governing council building in Basra was soon overrun by JAM fighters on 5th April. Within hours, the leaders of the OMS in the city were filmed by Al Jazeera parading through the ransacked building. A patrol of 1 RRW was sent to investigate and confirm that the symbol of the fledging Iraqi government's control had in fact been occupied. Bizarrely the troops managed to get close enough to knock on the door, before being told to go away in no uncertain terms. The British proceeded to surround the building, as a crowd of several thousand local people gathered to show their support for the JAM fighters. A RPG was fired at one of the 1 RRW Warriors and the Welsh troops returned fire with small arms and machine guns from their vehicles.[25]

In Baghdad, Bremer had seen the television reports of the incident and demanded that General Sanchez order that the British Army immediately storm the building. General Stewart at Basra airport was not having any of it. He did not want the situation in the heart of Basra to escalate into all out battle in which thousands of civilians would be at risk. It would also provide a propaganda gift to Sadr, so Brigadier Carter was sent to negotiate an end to the stand off.[26] As this was happening, 1 RRW was ordered to concentrate its troops and prepare them for a deliberate assault on the JAM-held building if the negotiations should fail. This came as something of a surprise to the Welsh soldiers who were in the process of packing up all their equipment and preparing to ship home their vehicles as the end of their six-month long tour in Basra approached. Preparations for the strike moved quickly and orders were issued to company commanders, before the troops were put on hold only 12 hours before the regiment's attack was due to go in.[27] Fortunately, Brigadier Carter's negotiations culminated in the Sadr fighters handing the building peacefully back to the Iraqi authorities.

In Baghdad, Bremer was less than impressed. In an interview with a British Army debriefing team, General Stewart described this as a "sticky" situation.

"As the world's only superpower [Americans] will not allow their position to be challenged," he commented to his debriefer. "Negotiation is often a dirty word."[28]

The American viceroy was enraged by Stewart's outright refusal to follow his directive.

"This resulted in the UK being demarched by the US," said Stewart.

"This, however, was conducted by Bremer through [the Department of State] to the UK Ambassador in Washington. The US military was mortified as this having happened, recognising that I was trying to neutralise Sadr through the use of local Iraqis and succeeding. I was also fully supported in the UK by [General Sir Michael Walker] Chief of the Defence Staff and [Lieutenant General Sir John Reith] Chief of Joint Operations who were content that I was operating to the same intent as the US but in a different way to achieve it."[29]

The rising tension with the Americans was quickly detected in London and the deputy chief of the defence staff for operations, Lieutenant General Rob Fry, telephoned Stewart to warn him of the growing disconnect with the UK's major ally. If Bremer was not happy with the way General Stewart was running things in Basra, the British in Basra were not happy that the US viceroy had picked a fight with Sadr without giving them any warning.

Brigadier Carter, in a de-briefing interview commented, "when the situation deteriorated in April, as a direct result of the American arrest of one of Sadr's lieutenants, it was not co-ordinated with us and no one had been told that it was to happen. Had we known we would have at least been able to prepare the ground. The arrest of a Shia religious figure had an impact on the whole of the Shia South with the consequence that my whole Area of Operations went up in smoke. This was as a result of Coalition operations that were out of my control or knowledge and proved to be the single most awkward event of my tour."[30]

The fissure in UK-US relations was not just limited to those between Bremer and the British military in Basra. The Prime Minister Tony Blair's special representative in Baghdad and Bremer's nominal deputy, David Richmond, was greatly concerned that the stand off at Fallujah and proposed US assault would unite all of Iraq against the British and American occupation. After consulting the British government in London, he formally warned Bremer that he should call off the coming attack on the insurgent-held city. Senior UN diplomats also made their views known to Bremer and, crucially, the American-devised Iraqi interim government baulked at supporting an attack by foreign soldiers on their own people. On 9th April, President Bush stood down the US Marines outside Fallujah until political support could be built to take on the insurgent-controlled sanctuary only 40 miles from Baghdad.

Back in Basra and al Amarah, the opponents of the British seemed to be multiplying by the day. As a result of Bremer's arrest of Sadr supporters and attack on Fallujah, the rival political parties, armed militia and tribal warlords in the south all seemed to be content to co-operate or at least acquiesce with attacks on the British military. Sadr's uprising transformed the political dynamics of southern Iraq. Sadr's lieutenants seemed to be in ascendant across the region and few political or tribal leaders would criticism them. Now the vast majority of the armed groups in the south began attacking the British in solidarity with their countrymen in Najaf and Fallujah. Even if there was not much evidence of formal co-operation or co-ordination between armed groups in the south, the fact that so many groups were launching attacks at the same time, and in quick succession, created major problems for General Stewart and his men.

The Light Infantry and RRW in al Amarah came under sustained attacks for several days. Camp Abu Naji and the British base inside al Amarah, the CIMIC House, and next door CPA headquarters, came under repeated mortar and rocket attack. Patrols into the city centre were now only conducted in heavily-armoured Warriors because of the proliferation of RPG ambushes on the main roads. Two Welsh soldiers were shot when they temporarily dismounted from their Warrior.[31]

Colonel Pointing tried to negotiate a reduction of tension with local political and tribal leaders but the attacks on British troops continued with a vengeance across Maysan. An RRW patrol around Camp Abu Naji's perimeter was attacked by a large group of fighters and three soldiers were shot, although their wounds were not serious.[32]

The Light Infantry were in process of being relieved by the 1st Battalion, The Princess of Wales's Royal Regiment (PWRR), which meant that briefly there was a surge of reinforcements into Maysan, which helped to stabilise the situation a little. Towards the end of April, 1 LI and C Company 1 RRW had to head south to Basra before heading home. The movement of troops south through Maysan was a magnet for insurgents and several of the withdrawing unit's convoys were ambushed.

Across Basra, British bases were now coming under mortar, grenade, RPG and small arms fire on daily basis. In five attacks on its main city centre base at the Old State Building, 1 RRW's A Company was hit by six RPGs and five mortars in the last weeks of April. The company in turned responded with 24 raids on the homes of suspected insurgents.[33]

Tension and anger remained high across the city, which boiled over on 21st April with multiple suicide car bomb attacks, believed to be Iraqi Sunni in origin, on Iraqi police stations and co-located British bases. Two police stations in the Asher district and one in the old city were rocked by suicide bombs, killing some seventy-four civilians and police, as well as injuring more than a hundred others. RRW troops who arrived to try to assist with the rescue and recovery operation were attacked by a hostile crowd, protesting that the British had failed to protect them. The Welsh troops were ordered to withdraw back to base rather than inflame the crowd.[34]

On the outskirts of Zubayr the base of the newly arrived 1st Battalion, The Royal Welch Fusiliers was the victim of two suicide car bomb attacks in the space of two hours. The first attacker tried to drive his car through a chicane at the base's main gate before he detonated his bomb, killing three policemen, injuring six more and slightly wounding two British soldiers. As Iraqi and British personnel moved out to rescue the wounded, another car was spotted driving directly at the scene of the carnage. Many of the rescuers tried to take cover but the bomb detonated, killing several Iraqis and seriously injuring three British soldiers.[35]

The other major concern for General Stewart at this time was the deteriorating situation in the Italian sector, which was part of his Multi-National Division. In the chaos of April, Sadr fighters had besieged the CPA compound in the centre of Nasiriyah. Italian troops reluctantly rescued the small team of CPA diplomats from the city but the Rome government was not keen to get involved in a serious fight and initially ordered its soldiers to remain at their camp in the desert outside Nasiriyah.

Under heavy pressure from the Americans, General Stewart put 1st Royal Horse Artillery (1 RHA) on standby to drive to Nasiriyah and reassert control of the city from the 600 JAM fighters holding sway there. The RHA had just arrived in Iraq to take over from the QRH in running the training of Iraqi security forces, when it was hurriedly re-roled for the Nasiriyah mission. Operation Able involved the setting up of an ad hoc battlegroup comprising a squadron of Challenger 2 tanks, a Warrior mounted infantry company and two infantry companies in Snatch Land Rovers. The gambit worked and within days of hearing about General Stewart's plans, the Italians changed their minds and ordered their troops to move into Nasiriyah and chase out the JAM fighters. The Operation Able battlegroup was stood down on 18th May.[36]

By the end of April all of 20 Brigade's troops were relieved to be out of Iraq. The continuing heavy fighting across southern Iraq forced General Stewart to reconsider the protection of his troops. Two of the newly arriving squadrons of the Queen's Royal Lancers (QRL) were told to drop plans to operate in Land Rovers and start breaking out Challenger 2 from storage at Shaibah Logistic Base. There was also a pressing need for more Warriors so General Stewart requested that when one of the surge infantry battalions that was training Iraqi troops came to the end of its tour in July, it should be replaced by an armoured infantry unit.

The RRW were to leave their vehicles and heavy equipment at Shaibah for the new unit to take over.[37] This was considered the quickest way to get reinforcements to Iraq as the unit set to replace the RRW, 1 PWRR, was in the process of deploying with its own vehicles. While effectively doubling the number of armoured infantry companies in Iraq, it was a recognition that training the local security forces would have to be put on the back burner while the threat to British troops was so high. 1st Battalion, The Black Watch received their warning order to deploy on 27th June.

One company was on the ground in Iraq in three weeks, and the bulk of the battalion flew out from the UK on 15th July. The battalion was to be General Stewart's divisional reserve, and the original plans envisaged it being based in Nasiriyah to allow it to operate across southern and central Iraq. It was also earmarked to support the US Army in central Iraq.[38]

The new units of 1 Brigade had to take over their new bases and responsibilities under fire. They spent a week or so working with the outgoing units, before being left to get on with it. In Maysan province, 1 PWRR found itself fighting determined resistance from the JAM and its allies for almost every day of the next six months. The commanding officer, Lieutenant Colonel Matt Maer, formally took over from Colonel Pointing on the morning of 18th April, and later that day was himself taking cover and returning fire after his Land Rover was ambushed by heavily-armed fighters in downtown al Amarah. Two soldiers were injured, one seriously, in the incident.[39]

This dynamic commanding officer of the PWRR was determined to regain the initiative and prevent Sadr's militia dominating the city. Iraqi police were either actively co-operating with the insurgents or too scared to venture out of their bases. On 7th May, the battlegroup launched Operation Pimlico in southern al Amarah, which involved a large cordon being put in around a neighbourhood suspected of harbouring insurgents and several houses were then raided, with nine prisoners being seized, along with what was described as "significant" quantities of arms and ammunition.[40]

The situation was still nowhere near calm with almost daily mortar and rocket attacks on the PWRR's bases. To resupply the CIMIC House required large convoys that were invariably ambushed. During one of these re-supply operations on 1st May a PWRR Warrior came under repeated RPG attacks. Its driver, Private Johnson Beharry, would subsequently be awarded the Victoria Cross, Britain's highest gallantry award for coolly driving his damaged vehicle out of the ambush and saving the lives of his crew. Beharry repeated his bravery a month later in a similar incident, prompting his award of the first VC since the 1982 Falklands war.[41]

To try to clear out the militia RPG and mortar teams Maer ordered a major sweep of the city. Dubbed Operation Waterloo, almost all of the battlegroup was involved, backed in the air by RAF Tornado GR4 bombers, RAF Nimrod MR2 spyplanes with night vision video cameras and US Air Force AC-130 Spectre gunships. On the ground were two companies of Warriors and a squadron of QRL Challenger tanks. The aim was to capture the OMS headquarters in the heart of al Amarah, show up the weakness of the JAM and allow Iraqi police to take over security in the city.[42]

The armoured columns moved into the city from multiple directions under the cover of darkness, and attracted the inevitable mortar and RPG fire. Overhead the Nimrod was able to spot several militia mortar teams moving into position and guided the AC-130 to deliver devastating fire down on them. At dawn, Maer ordered the final assault on the OMS building where some 16 tons of arms, including 120mm mortar rounds, mines, 107 mm rockets, anti-tank missiles and thousands of rounds of AK-47 ammunition, was seized. A crowd gathered and it started stoning the British vehicles as the search was under way, which soon escalated into a barrage of RPGs. A series of low passes by RAF Tornados over the city prompted the crowds to disperse and by the afternoon Maer was pleased to be able to report that Iraqi police were starting to move out of their bases on patrol. The respite for Maer's men was very brief.

Six days later a major incident occurred outside Majar-al-Kabir in the south of Maysan after a patrol of the 1st Battalion, The Argyll and Southerland Highlanders in Snatch Land Rovers was ambushed by a group of more than a 100 tribesman and militia fighters. They had dug a series of trenches and firing positions near a police checkpoint, known as Danny Boy to the PWRR, which gave the incident its nickname. The small contingent of Highlanders found themselves outnumbered and outgunned but responded aggressively. They were soon pinned-down by Iraqis and called for help, via a convoluted satellite telephone conversation routed via the MOD switch board in London.[43]

A quick reaction force from C Company, 1 PWRR, arrived and joined the attack to clear out the enemy firing positions. At one point they charged into the militia trenches with bayonets fixed on their SA-80 rifles. Warriors and QRL Challenger provided covering fire, before the militia fighters fled. At the end of the battle the PWRR claimed to have killed 20 enemy fighters and captured nine. Other participants in the battle claimed that more enemy fighters had been killed, with the QRL tank squadron saying that up to 70 enemy fighters had died. Brigadier Kennett in Basra ordered that the bodies of dead fighters be removed for identification, in case any of them were implicated in the killing of the RMP soldiers at nearby Majar-al-Kabir a year earlier. The bodies were loaded into the back of a Warrior and returned to Camp Abu Naji.[44]

The aftermath of the Battle of Danny Boy was the subject of a major judicial inquiry in London, with the families of the dead Iraqi fighters claiming they were captured alive and subsequently executed at the British base outside al Amarah. Almost every British participants in the battle disputes this version of events and the inquiry eventually came down on the side of the soldier's view.

A day after the battle, the British handed the bodies back to their families. It sparked an upsurge in fighting across Maysan after Abu Hatim claimed the prisoners had been executed by the PWRR. The fighters had come from his tribe, and tensions were high when the bodies were examined in the Majar-al-Kabir mortuary. The Prince of the Marshes' brother, now the governor of Maysan, arrived and tried to whip up the crowd into a frenzy of anti-British feeling. When the police chief of Majar-al-Kabir, who came from the rival political party, tried to calm tension by suggesting that they had been killed in the fighting, Governor Riyadh pulled a pistol and shot him dead. The politics of the extreme were now dominant in Maysan.

In Basra city, the 1st Battalion, The Cheshire Regiment bore the brunt of the JAM's attempts to drive out coalition forces. The regiment took control of city from the 1 RRW on 23rd April and immediately had to deal with a daily diet of mortar, RPG and small arms attacks on its bases and patrols. This culminated on 8th May, the same day as Operation Waterloo, with the Cheshires fighting an eight hour-long battle with the JAM in the centre of Basra. This resulted in the Cheshire's A Company being ordered to launch an advance to contact into the al Halaf district from the Shatt-al-Arab headquarters.[45]

According to the Cheshire's commanding officer, Lieutenant-Colonel John Donnelly, the battle involved 15 major contacts or individual engagements involving rocket propelled grenades and heavy machine guns. He said the Cheshires accounted for 15 dead and ten wounded militia men, describing the incident as his regiment's "first significant blooding".[46]

The violence in Basra during May and June was not on the level experienced in Maysan and Iraqi army units based in the city did not experience the huge desertions experienced around Baghdad. Some 30% of the ICDC deserted across southern Iraq, according to US military reports, but the British army was pleased that the units in their sector remained largely intact. The police were a different matter, and they largely avoided getting involved in British operations that might have forced them to choose sides. A significant number appeared to help the militia.

In June, Sadr decided to call a cease fire after a call for negotiations by Iraq's pre-eminent Shia cleric, Grand Ayatollah Ali al-Husseini al-Sistani. The transition of sovereignty on 28th June was rapidly approaching and the cleric and other aspiring political leaders were looking to position themselves ahead of coming elections. This ceasefire was a relative term, particularly in Maysan, where attacks on British troops continued largely unabated. The intensity of this fighting can be gauged by the list of weaponry fired off by PWRR during the first month of its tour. This included 16,000 rounds of 5.56mm, 5,000 Warrior chain gun rounds, 24 under-rifle grenades, 270 51mm and 81mm mortar rounds, 75 30mm Warrior cannon rounds and one 120mm Challenger round. This was in response to 72 shooting attacks, 54 RPG attacks, 53 mortar attacks, 18 IED attacks and 15 rocket attacks.[47] The British army suffered heavily in the attacks, with the PWRR alone taking 28 soldiers wounded in combat between 17 April and 16 June. Remarkably, given the intensity of the fighting no British soldiers were killed in what became known as the First Sadr Uprising.

The intense fighting and bravery shown by the troops in al Amarah went largely unreported in Britain at the time. Government ministers and army chiefs were desperate for any sign of progress. US commanders in Baghdad were also desperate for any good news, with the British division's war diary recording, "[the US Corps commander in Baghdad] General [Thomas] Metz's drumbeat campaign has begun. Each evening the Division is required to pass good news stories to Baghdad. The intent is to provide unclassified headlines of Corps significance; in order to both brief General Metz on progress, and to ensure that the Corps' key messages on progress are continuously disseminated, Operations Support Branch will action."[48]

Media visits to British forces in Iraq were tightly controlled by army 'spin doctors' and military personnel who spoke off message faced disciplinary action. Stephen Grey, one of the few British journalists to actually visit al Amarah, reported a bizarre encounter with Colonel Maer, writing in May 2004, "'reading some media reports, anyone would think we are in some kind of war zone out here!'" [Maer] scoffed. Flanked by two press officers, Maer was breezing utter normality. It was all "'rather dull'", he said."[49]

Subsequently, General Stewart confirmed in a debriefing after he returned home that the army and the government were deliberately trying to put a positive gloss on what was happening. It was no accident that the Ministry of Defence did not want the public in Britain to know what was happening in Maysan.

"I believe there is one area that is hurting the morale of deployed soldiers," recalled Stewart.

"The UK press and media decided that the invasion of Iraq was unjust. Thus there has been nothing but criticism of events in theatre. Nothing good was reported. I saw no point in trying to sell good stories to the UK because I soon discovered they were ignored. And telling the story of what was happening in Mayson would have been difficult politically because it would have reinforced the public view that things were going badly. As a result deployed troops found their families only heard down-beat messages on the news and at some times their significantly brave actions were not being reported."[50]

Chapter 16

STREET FIGHTING SUMMER

The militia commanders on the ground in Basra and Maysan, as well as their tribal allies, at first seemed to go along with the cease-fire. Tension began to ease and the British forces began to return to their pre-uprising posture. Commanders ordered training of local security forces to be moved back up to the top of the agenda. To free up manpower for training the Iraqi army and the police, the Queen's Royal Lancers' (QRL) Challengers were returned to the vehicle parks. The Princess of Wales's Royal Regiment (PWRR) switched two of their companies to training the local army. In Basra, the Cheshire's focused its efforts to building up the Iraqi police. The regiment pulled out its troops from small bases in a number of police stations, including the former Ba'ath Party headquarters, which had been home to the Cheshire's C and Support Companies. In a bid to reduce tension, the PWRR's Warriors were kept out of town centres across Maysan and off Basra's streets. Major General Andrew Stewart, the British divisional commander, was concerned that plans made before the uprising to pull back British troops into a handful of bases would leave them vulnerable.

"As we pull back into the four UK camps, and our force posture becomes less visible outside them, it is inevitable that these large fixed locations will become targets," he recorded in the divisional war diary.[1] The three southern locations have been attacked fourteen times since the beginning of April. An options paper on Theatre Force Protection was sent to PJHQ on 15th June. [Stewart said he] considered that Tier 1 – Do Nothing is not an option; but recognised that none of the other three are particularly attractive. We await direction from PJHQ."

The term 'ceasefire' was only relative, and militia groups and tribal fighters across the south of Iraq attack continued to attack British troops with improvised explosive devices (IEDs) and small arms attacks. Basra airport also started to be rocketed, and an RAF C-17 airlifter had to abort its landing and return to the UK. The rise of IEDs was an ominous development with two British soldiers being killed by weapons during the year. British bomb disposal and intelligence experts began to suspect that Jaish al-Mahdi (JAM) militia was receiving expert assistance in IED design and manufacture by Iran or the Lebanese Hizbollah.

IED attacks on a 1st Battalion, The Royal Highland Fusiliers (RHF) Snatch Land Rover on 28th June killed one soldier and another later in August killed the driver of a Black Watch Warrior. At the time the main impact of these deaths was on public opinion back in Scotland, fuelling criticism that Scottish regiments were bearing a disproportionate burden of casualties in Iraq. During 2004 three Scottish infantry regiments and the Scots Guards served in Iraq, with the Black Watch being sent back to Iraq just a year after serving as part of the initial invasion force. This all played badly in Scotland, particularly as it emerged during the summer of 2004 that one of the six famous Scottish infantry battalions was to be disbanded. The London government's political troubles would undoubtedly have been worst had the full circumstances surrounding the deaths of the two Scottish soldiers been made public as the time. More than a year later it emerged at soldier's inquests and boards of inquiries that the vehicles they had been travelling in were not fitted with electronic counter measures (ECM) to jam the radio controlled detonators for IEDs. Fusilier Gordon Gentle, died because an administrative mistake meant his Land Rover had not been equipped with ECM by the time he went on patrol.[2] The Black Watch soldier, Private Marc Ferns, was killed while standing exposed in open hatches of a Warrior. The Warrior's armour was considered good enough by the army that it had not yet planned to fit the vehicles in Iraq with the electronic jamming defences.[3]

In the latter part of June and into July both the British and JAM militia worked to prepare for what was openly being talked about as "round two". The hand over of sovereignty to the Iraqi Interim Government only served to increase political tension and rivalry between the country's emerging political leaders. Sadr's men re-stocked their arsenals with the purchase of arms from tribal hordes held in the villages of Maysan province, and they began to receive assistance and advice from the Iranian Revolutionary Guards elite Quds Force. A senior Quds Force officer was reported by US intelligence to be in Najaf acting as Sadr's top military advisor.[4]

The JAM commanders in Basra and Maysan, Ahmed al-Fartosi and Ahmed al-Gharawi, set about co-ordinating their plans to take on the British. They were both outraged by the ease at which the OMS head in Basra, Abdul Sattar al-Bahadili, had been persuaded by the British and the Baghdad government to pull out of the governing council building in Basra in April. Fartosi in Basra, in particular, hoped to score a big success by killing British soldiers or humiliating the occupying forces. His rival in Maysan had seen his prestige soar after the heavy fighting in al Amarah, so Fartosi wanted to make the British bleed in Basra. He was a veteran and skilled underground operative after participating in resistance to Saddam's rule in the 1990s, and spending time with Hizbollah in Lebanon.

A recruiting campaign was launched by the JAM in Basra, training sessions extended and commanders began planning for ambushes. Supporters in the police were recruited and waverers intimidated.[5]

While the British also absorbed the lessons of the fighting in May, Colonel Maer's 1 PWRR in al Amarah recognised the key role played by air support during Operation Waterloo, and were planning to repeat the extensive use of airpower if the JAM staged another major uprising.

July also saw the arrival in Basra of Major General Bill Rollo to command the Multi-National Division. The new General had to deal with a very different situation from his predecessors. The British forces were no longer legally occupiers, but were now officially 'guests' of the sovereign Iraqi government, so Rollo's skills as a soldier diplomat would soon be put to the test. Offensive operations were now supposed only to be possible with the permission of the Iraqi government. New rules of engagement (ROE) negotiated with the new Baghdad government meant British commanders and troops now operated in a very different political and legal environment.

"The major changes are that with effect from [28th June], except with regards to routine re-supply and reaction and self-defence patrolling, no patrols will be conducted without Iraqi Security Force (ISF)" recorded the British division's war diary.

"Detention, except in extremis hereafter, will also be conducted in conjunction with ISF. We are trying to demonstrate that we are no longer an occupying power; and that a change has taken place. It will require a major change in our mindset, and our approach to operations."[6]

However, General Rollo had also to work within orders given to him before he left for Basra by Lieutenant General Sir John Reith at Permanent Joint Headquarters, calling for the British operation in southern Iraq to be significantly reduced by the end of the year.

The spark for the second round occurred in Najaf on 31st July when a top Sadr lieutenant was arrested by Iraqi police, acting on the orders of the new Prime Minister Ayad Allawi, who was keen to undermine Sadr in the run up to elections in January 2005. Sadr supporters then kidnapped several policemen. On 2nd August, JAM militia men and US Marines patrolling on the outskirts of Najaf exchanged fire. This soon escalated into a major battle, that was broadcast live on al Jazeera to audiences across the Middle East. Shia viewers in Iraq were outraged that American troops appeared to be bombarding some of their religion's most holy sites. Sadr decided to exploit this wave of popular opinion across southern Iraq to order his militia to seize control of the region. At this point, the Grand Ayatollah Sistani declared he was ill and flew to London for medical attention. The scene was set for a bloody show down.

Not surprisingly, in the British zone, al Amarah was the first flash point. The CIMIC House and Camp Abu Naji came under sustained mortar and rocket attacks on 5th August. Helpfully, the local police chief telephoned the British beforehand to tell them that the JAM had ended their ceasefire. The insurgents were very confident. The following day Sadr militia and their tribal allies attacked police stations across the city. Al Amarah's police put up only token resistance and four stations were soon under militia control. They let 65 prisoners out of the city's main jail.[7] The troops of the PWRR, backed up by reinforcements from the Black Watch, the Royal Welch Fusiliers and Queen's Royal Lancers, traded fire with the JAM across al Amarah for days in some of the heaviest fighting yet experienced by British troops in Iraq. The CIMIC House became the focus of the fighting, with militia mortar teams, backed by more than 300 heavily-armed fighters, making life very difficult for the British troops holed up inside. British snipers on the building's roof duelled with

Operation Telic | 211

militia mortar teams for hours on end. The base would be effectively besieged for the remainder of the month.

Colonel Maer rushed back to Maysan from Britain, where he had been on R&R leave, to organise a meeting of the local political leaders in a bid to patch together a cease-fire. General Rollo flew up from Basra to try to bolster the peace bid but with US Marines and the JAM fighters battling in the streets of Najaf, there was no appetite for peace.[8]

During the night of 8th/9th August attacks on the CIMIC House spiked again and were only dispersed when a US Air Force F-15E Strike Eagle made high speed passes over the building at a hundred feet, prompting a respite of attacks for 12 hours.

In a bid to put a lid on the fighting, Colonel Maer organised another major battalion-sized operation in al-Amarah. Operation Hammersmith was a bigger version of the previous May's Operation Waterloo, with columns of heavily-armoured Warriors and Challengers, backed by strong airpower pushing into the city down its main roads. A company of the Black Watch were detailed to move to the police headquarters, where a small force of the PWRR was holed up.[9]

The result was a series of running PRG ambushes against the British columns as they pushed into the city on the night of 10th August. Several British vehicles were hit by multiple rocket propelled grenades, with a platoon of the Black Watch being hit by a barrage of 14 of them, which seriously injured the commander of one of their Warriors when shrapnel cut into his neck, above the collar of his body armour. Air support from Spectre gunships was on hand, and they hit several enemy mortar teams with devastating effect.

By the following morning, the British columns had driven back the insurgents from the main roads to the CIMIC House. This was only a temporary respite, as the JAM fighters re-organised and re-engaged. During the day the PWRR recorded 155 individual engagements with insurgents. British armoured vehicles were sent to patrol along the main roads in a bid to flush out more of the fighters.[10] Attacks on the CIMIC House continued to escalate as the JAM made a determined effort to drive out the hundred or so defenders. Overnight on 14th/15th August, 49 mortar rounds were fired at the building and 37 attacks on British troops across the city took place. The PWRR defenders called in US F-16 jets to make low passes over the centre of the city, which gave them a brief respite. The divisional commander in Basra delegated to Colonel Maer authority to use close air support inside the city limits. The risk to British troops was such that concerns about collateral damage and civilians casualties had to be put to one side.[11]

During the early hours of 16th August, an F-16 on station over the CIMIC House was able to identify one of the JAM mortar teams and was rapidly cleared to engage it with a 500lb bomb. Six insurgents were claimed killed in the air strike and attacks on the British base ceased for seventeen hours.

This was only a temporary break for the near-exhausted defenders of the CIMIC House, who were manning firing positions on the heavily-damaged building's roof. The vehicle park was rapidly filling up with damaged Snatch Land Rovers and Warriors from the unrelenting mortar fire. Food and ammunition were running low. General Rollo was beginning to wonder if it was worth holding on to the base. Colonel Maer protested that retreating from the position under fire would hand a propaganda victory to the militia. The general relented as long as the PWRR commander could guarantee he could continue to supply it.[12] A relief column managed to get into the building on 17th August and bring in fresh troops and supplies, with A Company of the Royal Welch Fusiliers providing many of the reinforcements.

A week later another major operation needed to be launched after two soldiers in the base were seriously injured and had to be evacuated. The battle of the CIMIC House continued until the end of August when the fighting in Najaf ended. The commander of the PWRR company in the base, Major Justine Featherstone recorded the scale of the fighting. Some 760 mortar rounds and 57 RPGs were fired at the base during 309 separate attacks. Nine of the defenders were seriously injured and needed to be evacuated. One soldier was killed when the base's gate fell on him. Two Snatch Land Rovers were destroyed in the base, with four others, a Warrior and two assault boats damaged by mortar fire. The troops fired 31,000 rounds at their attackers. When the dust settled, the defence of the CIMIC House entered the folklore of the British Army as being akin to the heroic defence of Rorke's Drift during the Zulu wars.[13]

While the British troops in Maysan were fighting for their lives, a bigger and more significant battle was unfolding in Basra city. As in al Amarah, the JAM militia planned to strike at the British presence in Basra by seizing a swath of police stations across the centre of the city. The humiliation of the interim government and its police force was a key objective, to allow Sadr's allies to seize the political agenda. The British troops in Basra had not yet faced such a determined and co-ordinated militia offensive before. While the Najaf crisis set the scene for the fighting in Basra, the immediate trigger was the arrest of three OMS members by the Iraqi police on 3rd August. The following day the leaders of the OMS in the city demanded the release of their operatives.

The Old State Building base in the centre of Basra was rocketed and mortared during the night. Three other British bases were attacked, with 12 vehicles damaged and two soldiers being wounded. This was followed by a wave of attacks on the police across the city culminating in the capture of the old Ba'ath Party Headquarters, close to the Old State Building. General Rollo ordered British troops to stay out of the city centre and minimise road movement. On 8th August the Basra Council condemned the American attacks on Najaf and demanded that British troops pull out of Basra.

Across the city British bases were now being rocketed and mortared on a daily basis, while small groups of insurgents started sniping at the bases. The Old State Building was effectively under siege. General Rollo ordered British troops to begin hardening their bases to withstand mortar and rocket attacks, and warned his superior in Baghdad, Lieutenant General John McColl, that any all-out attack on Sadr in Najaf could spark fighting that might overwhelm the British troops in Basra and al Amarah.

The British division's war diary recorded that Rollo "has emphasised the difficulty of our position to [McColl in] Baghdad; we are not masters of our own destiny, and any decisive assault – especially with a US lead – could lead to a major upheaval across our area of operations. We would be hard pressed to contain simultaneous uprisings. Any contacts with senior US military officials should emphasise these concerns."[14]

Ominously, the Iraqi police were not getting involved in resisting the militia. The police unit assigned to defend the Basra Palace base deserted en masse. Only the Tactical Support Unit, an elite paramilitary squad was putting up any resistance. Arms, ammunition, uniforms, radios and police cars were looted by the militia from several police stations.

General Rollo was cautious about launching a major operation to take back the Ba'ath Party Headquarters and drive out the militia from other locations. He was concerned this would prompt heavy fighting and civilian casualties, playing into the hands of Sadr's propaganda machine.

So he started planning Operation Centurion to put in place the forces necessary to retake the city if the situation got worse.

The QRL's D Squadron were ordered to activate their 14 Challenger tanks that were in storage at Shaibah Logistic Base and move to the edge of Basra city. On 10th August, the tanks, backed by troops from 1st Royal Horse Artillery (1 RHA), re-roled as infantry, moved to set up three check points on the bridges over the Shatt-al-Basra canal on the western edge of the city. This was the same line that 7 Armoured Brigade had held during the siege of Basra in March and April 2003. Many of the QRL soldiers participating in Operation Centurion had fought in exactly the same positions a year earlier.[15]

The QRL tanks were used to provide an intimidating presence at the RHA check-points to stop more JAM insurgents moving into the city or receiving supplies. These check points were maintained for the rest of the month in searing 60 degree heat. Improvised bases were set up at the check points to allow the soldiers some creature comforts. Planning was meanwhile underway by 1 Brigade and the Cheshire Regiment for an offensive operation, dubbed initially Operation Centurion Phase 3, and then renamed Operation Clash, which envisaged the QRL tanks leading columns of Cheshire Regiment troops, with AC-130 support, into the city to relieve the Old State Building, capture the OMS Building and storm the Ba'ath Party Headquarters. The latter building was the centre of JAM resistance with an estimated 500 fighters suspected of occupying the former British base. The heavy fortifications built by the British, before it was handed back to the Iraqi police in June, were a major headache for officers working out how to attack and clear the base.[16]

Brigadier Kennett kept his forces ready to execute Operation Clash throughout August, even though it pulled troops away from holding bases and training Iraqi security forces. The situation was so tense that the option to strike had to be kept on the table.

"I have never been so convinced that we were about to go into action" commented Captain H.T Burton of the QRL. H-Hour for the operation was set to be on 24th August unless a political solution could be found.[17]

Inside Basra, the Cheshire Regiment soldiers holding the Old State Building were fighting a similar battle to their comrades in the al Amarah CIMIC House. The Cheshire's B Company put snipers on the building's roof to try to counter the militia mortar and RPG teams that stalked around the base during darkness. Fighting patrols were sent out into alleyways around the base to take the battle to the enemy, and ambush insurgents trying to set up mortar firing positions. The weight of fire from the militia was so heavy that Brigadier Kennett sent a platoon of Black Watch Warriors to reinforce B Company, and allow it to undertake more aggressive counter attacks. The Cheshire's own Saxon wheeled armoured personnel carriers just did not have enough protection to risk them being driven out of the base.[18]

JAM fighters had set up a network of ambushes around the British bases in the centre of Basra, and whenever vehicles moved they were engaged with varying degrees of success. On 9th August, a Snatch Land Rover patrol was ambushed near Camp Cherokee in the docks region of the city. To evade the attack the RHA soldiers in the vehicles ended up driving deeper into the city, and were eventually cornered near the Ba'ath Party Headquarters. A Warrior patrol, from the PWRR operations company supporting the Cheshires at the Shatt-al-Arab Hotel, was sent to rescue the RHA soldiers but was itself ambushed. A PWRR soldier proving top cover was hit by a bullet that penetrated the part of his body armour not protected by a hard ceramic plate. The trapped gunners were eventually rescued but two more British soldiers were seriously injured.

Three days later, the JAM ambushes tactics scored another success when a Black Watch Warrior operating from Basra Palace was hit by an IED. The crew were driving with their hatches open and the turret crew were exposed to get a better view when driving through the city streets. The driver was killed and the gunner was seriously wounded. This was one of several IED strikes on Warriors during the August fighting. Another, on 20th August, was so big the explosion could be heard two kilometres away but the crew were closed down inside the Warrior, and survived.[19]

Cheshire regiment patrols were now mounted on the outskirts of Basra to try to protect remaining police stations from being overrun. A Land Rover from one of these patrols in the al Hayanniyah district broke down and when the crew tried to repair the vehicle, they were attacked by a force of 70 militiamen and the soldiers were pinned down while they attended to two seriously injured casualties. The Black Watch Warriors at the Old State Building were sent to their rescue. They managed to secure the trapped soldiers and evacuate the wounded men but one subsequently died in the Shaibah field hospital. In the battle, the combined Cheshire Regiment and Black Watch force claimed to have killed 20 insurgents.[20]

These incidents were all traumatic for the soldiers involved, with the victims being seriously injured inside vehicles. Their comrades then had to extract them from the confined spaces of the vehicles, often while under fire or being stoned by mobs of civilians. In some three weeks of fighting, B Company of the Cheshire Regiment claimed to have killed 70 insurgents in the course of 40 large fire fights. Their base came under three rocket attacks that seriously injured two soldiers, while some 123 mortar strikes and 83 RPGs were fired at the base. B Company reported that they suffered 15 wounded, that most of their vehicles and large parts of the camp were destroyed.[21]

General Rollo's 'wait and see' policy continued for three weeks but his patience was running thin. Operation Clash was scheduled to be launched on 24th August. With four hours to go before H-Hour word came through to the British headquarters at the airport that there had been a diplomatic breakthrough. British intelligence had been keeping a close eye on Grand Ayatollah Sistani during his stay in London and out of blue they reported that he seemed to have made a dramatic recovery and was en route back to Kuwait. General Rollo immediately consulted with the British Ambassador in Baghdad about the implications and then stood down the assault troops. Operation Clash was cancelled.[22] Sistani drove through Basra, picking up a convoy of 500 cars as an escort from his supporters and headed to Najaf on 26th August. He met with Sadr in a Shia shrine and the two hatched a peace deal the following day. A ceasefire was called and almost overnight southern Iraq was quiet. On a visit to clerics in downtown Basra, General Rollo quickly picked up that this was a game-changing moment.

The Cheshire Regiment's commanding officer, Colonel Donnelly, recalled that there was a "sense of unfinished business on both sides" in Basra and his men were keen to go for the "home run" against their opponents.[23] British commanders were suspicious that JAM in Basra would not go along with the order to stop fighting. This was not without some justification, as the JAM operations commander in the city, Fartosi was furious that his fighters had been called off just as they were inflicting serious casualties on the British. The OMS political chief in city, al Basri, was also unhappy and issued a media statement declaring he was going to fight on. At first it seemed like bluster.

And at first the city remained peaceful, and on 1st September General Rollo ordered his units to standdown from warfighting mode and re-activate its training regime for the Iraqi National Guard (as the ICDC had been re-branded after the transfer of sovereignty, and police). The Iraqi Tactical Support Unit (TSU) moved back into the Ba'ath Party Headquarters unopposed on 4th September and four days later movement restrictions on British vehicles in Basra city were lifted. The CIMIC House in al Amarah was handed over to the Iraqi police. It seemed like business as usual.[24]

The TSU was loyal to the Shia political faction opposed to Sadr so it was one of the few Iraqi security units that was willing to take part in offensive operations against the JAM. It led another raid on another OMS building that netted the Cheshire Regiment a huge haul of weapons, ammunition and a cache of IEDs.[25]

The denouement of the Second Sadr uprising was to take place in the late afternoon of 17th September, when two British convoys driving past the main OMS building in the centre of Basra were fired upon with RPGs and small arms fire. One soldier was seriously injured by an RPG. General Rollo was away on his R&R, so Brigadier Kennett was in charge, and he immediately decided to act, using the 'hot pursuit' rules of engagement that allowed British troops to take offensive action, without consulting the Iraqis. In less than an hour, orders had been issued to the Cheshire Regiment to take the building.

Colonel Donnelly described the operation as a "come as you are" version of Operation Clash but with only four infantry companies, no armour or AC-130s. He rapidly mobilised every available soldier and vehicle in his battle-group headquarters for the mission. Columns of Cheshire Regiment troops led by Warriors of the Black Watch and the PWRR sped through the city from the Shatt-al-Arab Hotel base to surround the OMS building. Other troops moved by boat down the Shatt-al-Arab waterway to complete the encirclement of the militia base. The troops were engaged during their move into position and crowds of civilians tried to block the British vehicles moving through the narrow streets in the city centre.[26]

At 8.25pm a PWRR Warrior crashed though the OMS building's compound wall to allow C Company of the Cheshire Regiment to surge inside. The shock of the assault caught the defenders by surprise and they fled without putting up any resistance. A Royal Engineer search team swept the building and they eventually collected some 15 tons of arms and ammunition, including 89 107mm rockets and over 100 82mm mortar rounds. The British put a cordon around the building to allow the sappers and intelligence experts to do their work. For nearly 18 hours the troops held the line against a steady barrage of RPGs, sniper fire and crowds throwing rocks. Rushing to extract a group of Cheshire infantry pinned down by heavy fire, a Black Watch Warrior drove over a car. The troops were enjoying themselves. It felt good to be taking the fight to heart of the enemy. An hour-long mortar barrage in the morning was a less welcome event, prompting the soldiers to take cover inside the Warriors. Colonel Donnelly recorded that his troops had been attacked 114 times during the course of the operation.[27]

The morning heat proved to be too much for many of soldiers, and a shift system had to be set up to shuttle troops suffering from heat stroke back to the nearby Old State Building to recover. In the afternoon of the 18th September the search teams declared themselves to be happy and the TSU were called into take over, allowing the British to collapse their cordon, mount up in their vehicles and head back to base with a haul of booty. For Colonel Donnelly and his men the operation brought closure to the situation. The Second Sadr insurrection was over, or so the British thought. At first it seemed like a corner had been turned as Basra was strangely quiet. The Cheshire Regiment and its attached units were heading home in a few weeks time and they were elated. They had fired 50,000 rounds in 450 major contacts and killed 192 insurgents since April and not suffered any fatalities.[28]

For the next two months, Basra seemed to return to some sort of normality but the heavy fighting of the summer had changed perceptions. Normality was a relative term, with the rate of IED incidents rising from three a week in September to ten a week the following month, according to assessments by the British divisional headquarters in Basra. On one day in September there were three attacks across the city. There was an outbreak of tribal fighting that last three weeks and involved 200 policemen trading fire amongst themselves that left 11 of them dead.[29]

General Rollo was convinced that the JAM were behind the persistent attacks on his men, and ordered his staff to prepare a series of strike options, dubbed Operation Ballard and Banjo, to arrest the leaders of the organisation in Basra and Maysan. This work was ramped up after two RHA soldiers were killed in an RPG ambush on a Snatch Land Rover patrol on 28th September. The head of the OMS, al Basri was added to the arrest list after intelligence reports fingered him as ordering the deadly attack.[30] But these plans remained on file in the divisional headquarters at Basra airport. Now was not the time to stir things up with a provocative arrest of Sadr's top lieutenants. The Shia political parties of southern Iraq were now manoeuvring for the coming national parliamentary elections in January. Being Iraq, this included activities that in other countries would be considered gangsterism, such as the assassination of opponents, bribing of government officials and appointment of acolytes to key government jobs to guarantee influence and loyalty. The British were loath to interfere for fear of sparking a new uprising. Iraqi democracy was the British exit strategy.

This was General Rollo's call after he consulted with PJHQ and the other commanders of the multi-national troop contingents in the British-led division.

"The Sadr Uprisings in 2004 were dealt with by [our General in Basra] as they saw fit," recalled Major General Robin Brims who was co-ordinating Iraq operations at PJHQ.

"Ultimately [our troops] were under Coalition command but there was a UK view that we did not want to antagonise the Sadr community as we still had enough on our hands dealing with the other issues. The other nations in MND(SE) took a similar view. It was recognized at the time that Sadr and his supporters were a political issue and that it needed to be handled accordingly."[31]

The two Sadr insurrections had tested the British Army to the full. Unlike some other coalition contingents, the British fought hard and held their ground. They killed hundreds of insurgents, including nearly 200 in Basra alone, and more insurgents must have died in the heavier fighting in al Amarah. During its tour, 1 Mechanised Brigade suffered 99 battle casualties and five killed in action.[32] So what had the British Army achieved during its duel with Sadr and his militia? From the autumn of 2003, the main effort of the British campaign had been to build up the local Iraqi security forces. Against its own objectives, the spring and summer's fighting had left the British effort to build up the Iraqi security forces seriously behind schedule. It effectively ground to a halt as large parts of southern Iraq were turned into battlefields. A report by the Queen's Royal Hussars on its Operation Telic 3 tour concluded:

"...in April the steady improvements to Basra's security dissolved in the al Sadr rebellion. The tangible and destabilising influence meant that much of the improvements that the QRH had implemented throughout the security forces stagnated."[33]

The efforts to rebuild the police had proved fatally flawed, with almost all of the police siding with the JAM or just staying at home during the two insurrections. The seizure of police stations in August left many of them gutted and most of their equipment was looted by the militia. In his post tour report, General Rollo concluded "in August, the 'Shia uprising' instigated by Muqtada al-Sadr saw the police in Basrah and Maysan, the Southeast provinces most affected, effectively withdraw from the fray. The Iraqi Security Forces were neither capable nor committed to removing militia from the streets."[34]

Despite much bluster about the Iraqi National Guard (ING) being the jewel in the crown of the security sector reform effort in the August uprising, the British choose not to commit them to any of their offensive operations against the JAM. The eight ING battalions in the British zone were barely trained, lacked armoured vehicles and heavy weapons. General Rollo complained that much of their training was misdirected and too western in outlook, with too much time being spent on women's rights awareness training rather than basic military skills. They suffered a 30 percent desertion rate during the April/May uprising and the British command decided not to risk pushing their loyalty by suggesting they fight their co-religionists in the JAM.[35]

This was a big change from June when General Stewart was recording in his war diary that he was impressed with them, after inspecting a parade to mark the transition to Iraqi sovereignty at Basra airport on 30th June.

"The ING looked good" said the General. "They had a confidence about them that impressed; it was rewarding to see the product of six months' Security Sector Reform training marching with reasonable precision. The Commander - Brigadier Dhia - wants to get on with the job; we shall find out in the next few weeks just how much he can do."[36]

"The ING in the south east is quantifiably ahead of the rest of the country and has taken over parts of our area of operations," Stewart wrote in his end of tour report in July.

"Current progress does not mean that we should relax on security sector reform. It remains [our] main effort and is our ticket out of Iraq. Provided there is no really significant upsurge in violence and the Iraqis are still prepared to take our assistance (not a given) Iraqi Security Forces in the south east will have reached 'regional control' by the end of this year. The pragmatist tells me that we and the Iraqis will somehow muddle through. This would see multi-national forces being able (or asked) to leave with honour at the end of 2005 following national elections within Iraq, but before democracy as we understand it has taken root."[37]

Yet only a five months later, General Rollo recorded in his end of tour report that this ING training programme was over ambitious and the Iraqi troops were not ready to fight during the August uprising.

"601 and 602 ING Battalions were declared to be operational at [transition of authority on 28th June] and [British training] effort was reduced to monitoring" he wrote.

"The increase in militia activity in August 04 highlighted the weaknesses within the organisation, and it became apparent that the umbilical cord had been cut too soon and as a fledgling organisation they were not as robust as had been previously believed."[38]

He recommended investing even more time and resources in training the Iraqi army if the prized hand over to the Iraqis was to be achieved in 2005, writing, "the expansion programme in 2005 will see the size of the ING double, and it will be necessary to ensure that the training and mentoring bill is met and is robust enough to provide sustained cover over a period of time."

When 1 Brigade restarted training for Iraqi troops and police in September 2004 after the August uprising, it effectively meant five months training time had been lost. The fighting also put a halt to recruiting, further delaying plans to expand the local forces. Although the British government had emphasised that training the Iraqis was the main effort of the British forces, as soon as fighting started to threaten the British position across the south, the troops assigned to training were re-tasked for combat. Rarely did 1 PWRR manage to free up any of its companies to train the Iraqis during its tour because of the near continuous fighting. While in Basra, 1 RHA, the lead security sector reform battlegroup was regularly being diverted to take part in combat or contingency operations. The same thing happened to the QRL, which also had a big training role, when it was ordered to activate its Challengers. The Argyll and Southerland Highlanders, who had arrived as a surge unit in January 2004 to train Iraqis was replaced in July by the Black Watch, which was used constantly for combat missions.

The pressure to generate troops and resources to train the Iraqis was a symptom of the small size of the British force in Iraq. Out of the 8,900 British troops in southern Iraq, those not fighting the JAM in Maysan and central Basra were involved in protecting and sustaining the force. The Royal Welch Fusiliers, a squadron of the QRL and the Royal Highland Fusiliers, as well as their replacements, 40 Commando Royal Marines, had nearly 1,500 troops tied down securing the rural areas south of Basra and protecting the key British and US supplies from Kuwait into central Iraq.

A further 2,500 logistic and administrative troops were based at the divisional headquarters at Basra airport and at the sprawling Shaibah Logistics

Base. These huge sites had to be guarded by other troops and when they started to be rocketed more troops were diverted to hardening their buildings. This left less than 4,000 troops for frontline duty or training the Iraqis. Generals Stewart and Rollo had little spare capacity to cope with unexpected events and when push came to shove, force protection was a higher priority than training Iraqis.

In their orders for operations during the Sadr insurrections, British commanders stressed strongly that they were trying to achieve specific political effects. Colonels Maer and Donnelly, talked about their offensive operations being aimed at "improving confidence in the Iraqi police", "giving moderate voices a chance to sideline extremists", "force a return to co-operation with coalition forces", "bolster support for coalition forces" or "to dominate the streets and convince the Iraqi Police Service that the conditions were in place to allow them to carry out their own patrolling".

British battlegroup commanding officers during Operation Telic 3 and 4 were strongly influenced by what became known as the 'strongest tribe' philosophy that had been passed onto them by units that had participated in the final phase of Telic 1 and during Telic 2 in Maysan province. The view was that warlords, tribal chiefs, politicians and militia commanders they found on the streets of southern Iraq would only respect the British if they could demonstrate that they had the ability to apply overwhelming force, which was often characterised by the presence on the streets of columns of Challenger tanks and Warrior fighting vehicles. These vehicles with their near invulnerability made them the ultimate arbiter of political disputes in southern Iraq in 2004.

General Stewart reinforced this view, describing in his end of tour report how the "Iraqis saw me as the Sheikh of Sheikhs."[39] While Brigadier Carter, commented to an army debriefing team that "there are times the Iraqis appreciate military might."[40]

General Rollo played a subtle hand in Basra city, where he was trying to play off the Sadrists against other political factions less hostile to the British.

"By demonstrating restraint and actively limiting militia freedom of action, British forces prevented the militia from gaining any political or popular advantage from their attempts to dominate the streets," was how General Rollo described his wait-and-see tactics in August 2004 in his end of tour report in late 2004.

"By the end of August, when Sistani intervened to resolve the crisis in Najaf, British forces had emerged from an intense operational period with their reputation intact: the militias did not."[41]

The General commented that a "more heavy-handed approach could have led to a loss of consent and a much more serious and long term deterioration in the security situation".

It is apparent from internal documents and reports from the spring and summer of 2004 that the British army was engaged in a series of improvised and short-term measures to shore up its precarious position in southern Iraq. In a candid assessment at the end of his tour, General Rollo commented "when

[I] arrived [I] felt [I] was on a bike, going downhill, out of control and without brakes. All [I] could do was steer and hang on."

There was no long-term political plan to back groups or political parties favourable to the British. Bizarrely the man whom the British Army had originally backed – Abu Hatim, the famous Prince of the Marshes – in the summer of 2003 as a key power broker in Maysan province metamorphosed into their most implacable opponent during the Sadr uprisings. He became involved in a form of competition with the JAM militia to prove his tribal militia could kill more British soldiers.

Lieutenant-Colonel Philip Napier, who led the Royal Regiment of Wales in Basra during the first half of 2004, recalled that every operation had to be focused on achieving immediate impact and effect, telling a debriefing team, that "in a country like Iraq everything hinges on what the people are thinking, right now".[42]

The need for British commanders to constantly juggle the political impact of their operations weighed heavily on senior officers in Iraq in 2004, particularly after the Coalition Provisional Authority closed down in June, after the transfer of sovereignty to the Iraqis, and its administrators stopped working with local Iraqi leaders and power brokers. Colonel Maer was trenchant in his criticism of the British Foreign and Commonwealth Office (FCO) and Department for International Development (DfID) for not stepping into the breach.

In his end of tour report after leaving Maysan he wrote that, "no FCO nor DfID representation is based in the Province and little interest appears to be shown. Thus, the commanding officer and the battlegroup carries the responsibility for military, political and economic progress. A sergeant in the battlegroup placed $6.5m of water projects during the tour. Something for which he received no training and little guidance - this is unacceptable. There is no military solution to Maysan's problems and until wider UK government interest is shown and is physically present in the province the threat of failure will remain. Excuses that the area is not secure are false. The area will never be secure until economic development takes place and this, in turn, will never occur until more on-the-ground activity and interest is shown by UK Government departments who can create such conditions."[43]

The precarious nature of the British position in southern Iraq was made clear by General Rollo, who revealed in his end of tour report in December 2004 that the British presence was almost totally dependent on the intervention of Grand Ayatollah Sistani.

"In all probability our success will continue to depend upon the subtle intervention of Grand Ayatollah Sistani; having witnessed the transformation in August when he used his influence to retrieve the situation in Najaf, I am clear that he is the only man with the moral authority to persuade the majority to pursue a peaceful path. To that extent, we have little control over own immediate destiny."[44]

Keeping the rickety and precarious show on the road was hard work, with Lieutenant Colonel Julian Free, the commanding officer of 26 Regiment Royal Artillery, recalling that the "high tempo of operations surprised me, as did the shortage of planning time."[45]

Brigadier Carter commented that commanders had to juggle the minutiae of tactical decision-making with things that could have strategic impact, saying that "as you move into the peace enforcement stage of the campaign, the strategic through the operational to the tactical levels become significantly compressed."[46]

The Brigadier that said the commercialised Synergy radio communication network did not work properly and hindered the ability of commanders to operate effectively, commenting, "communications were appalling. If I was on the move I could only be contacted via mobile telephone."[47]

Brigadier Carter's chief of staff, Major AJ Aitkin, said, "there was no day in Iraq that was the same and there certainly cannot be a model for it. The pace of operations was so intense that there wasn't time to sit and take stock. Once we did force ourselves to take time out we were able to use our intelligence to much better effect as a decision-making tool rather than as a force protection measure."[48]

While British commanders were under intense pressure of events, they also had to deal with very imperfect information.

According to Major Aitkin, "our intelligence picture was somewhat fractured and we were looking too short-term. It was our comfort zone of decision-action to look 24 hours ahead and concentrate on arresting suspected terrorists. The information we received (the majority of sources were human intelligence (HUMINT)) verged from the frustrating to the plain inaccurate. Just when you thought you understood what was happening in the country something would happen that would shake your faith in it."[49]

General Stewart told his debriefers, "we do have a problem with intelligence. We have insufficient analysis and assessment. In fact I made nearly all of the assessments myself and on reflection perhaps I was best placed to do so. I had strategic intelligence coming in and was able to blend it with the tactical [intelligence]."[50]

Colonel JK Tanner, General Stewart's chief of staff, commented that the British headquarters was swamped, saying "huge quantities of information flooded in, but we received very little of use operationally from above."[51]

Lieutenant Colonel RD Marshall, the British division's intelligence chief for much of 2004, in a post-tour report said his staff were struggling to cope and things had little improved from the summer of 2003 when British intelligence experts in Basra had warned that their activities were hobbled by poor information technology.

"We cobbled together an intelligence system, often a database, which was unproven, unsupported, costly and largely ineffective," recalled Marshall. The colonel said the "thing that was really lacking was collection assets. We were often relying on single sourced un-corroborated information."[52]

The British division had no surveillance systems, such as unmanned aerial vehicles (UAV) or aircraft with video cameras, of its own to monitor insurgent activity and to provide early warning of their attacks on British bases. Iraq's summer heat meant the Royal Artillery's Phoenix UAV or drone could not fly between April and October, so the British had to ask the Americans to borrow their Predator drones or surveillance aircraft, which the US dubbed an intelligence, surveillance, acquisition and targeting (ISTAR) system. The US would only provide these scarce assets during major operations, such as Operations Waterloo and Hammersmith in al Amarah, but the British could not rely on them to be available.

The Sadr militia also did not use radio communications very much, so British signals intelligence (SIGINT) was not much use against them.

"SIGINT did not give a huge amount of intelligence and the Special Intelligence Service or MI6 were aimed at the strategic" said General Stewart.

"Because we had insufficient ISTAR the only decent intelligence that we got was through HUMINT and we really did need more Field HUMINT Teams (FHT)."[53]

HUMINT covered a multitude of sources from information passed by civilians to soldiers on foot patrols, tips from interpreters and local employees to the information by spies recruited inside Iraqi political parties and militias, which they dubbed "MX reporting". The latter were highly valued by the British Army, who from their experience in Northern Ireland were used to having agents in the higher echelons of both Republican and Unionist terrorist groups. It clearly came as something of a shock to senior British army commanders to find that such sources of intelligence were not available to them in Iraq.

General Rollo commented that in 2004 "approximately 80% of the Division's intelligence is derived from HUMINT, in particular MX reporting. MX is a primary driver in operations at brigade level. There is a need to achieve greater HUMINT penetration of groupings with an anti-multi-national force agenda, as there are gaps in our knowledge. This is caused partly by a shortage of handlers, and partly by the operational conditions under which the teams work, and partly by the inadequate level of training for these conditions."[54]

Other British officers were despondent that its agent penetration efforts were ineffective, with Colonel Tanner commenting, "it is not feasible to conduct covert operations in an Arab society like Iraq".[55]

The weakness of this intelligence effort in southern Iraq meant that the Sadr uprising, as well as its scope and intensity, caught the British by surprise and they were unprepared to react.

Colonel Tanner commented that "we never expected Muqtada al Sadr to have a go at us so severely,"[56] While General Stewart conceded that he "was surprised at the Arab preparedness to die".[57]

The British also under-estimated the tactical ability of Sadr's fighters, with Tanner saying the militia were able to devise tactics to exploit loop holes in the army's rules of engagement (ROE) that only allowed soldiers to open fire on armed men who were actually firing at the British. The Colonel said that "during the Sadr insurgency it became apparent that the militia knew our rules of engagement and how to exploit them."[58]

"On many occasions in al Amarah Muqtada Militia stood on roof tops from where they had fired in the past, with RPGs and small arms at their feet, thus not showing hostile intent" said Stewart.

"During the incident at Danny Boy, which resulted in 1 PWRR conducting a dismounted attack with fire support from a flank, it was not possible to take on a position in depth because anti-coalition forces started withdrawing and thus stopped showing hostile intent. Those who got away remained free to attack multi-national forces again later. The opportunity to make a severe dent in the opposition could not be taken."[59]

Colonel Marshall recalled that the insurgents were difficult to classify and this made it difficult to build up a detailed order of battle, listing units, commanders and their equipment, to allow his analysts to work out what was happening.

"We were fighting an insurgency where the enemy fought with a single RPG and AK-47 which he stashed under his bed, and then went to work in the morning, there was no enemy [order of battle]," he recalled.[60]

While General Rollo reported in December that the insurgents were growing in capability and tactical skills, "the ability of the enemy to establish a firing point, range, engage and depart is improving rapidly and is making taking the fight to him much more difficult."[61]

The British were also struggling to get a firm handle of who was behind the growing number of IED attacks on British troops in the summer and autumn of 2004. General Rollo commented in his end of tour report.

"The number of IED attacks in Basrah and Maysan increased during October with attribution being difficult for Basrah but probably a mixture of Sunni and Shia groups. In Maysan, intelligence showed that some were by the [JAM] and may have been related to the Relief in Place (RiP) of 1 PWRR. What is unclear is whether the level of Sunni activity has increased, as reflected in the increase in IEDs or whether other Sunni activity has been masked by the focus on the [JAM]. A marked reduction in the number of IEDs in November following the arrest of a Sunni gang outside Shaibah Logistic Base may represent a clue."[62]

General Rollo's assessment that the intervention of Grand Ayatollah Sistani was decisive in ending the Sadr uprising, was a telling admission that the British presence in southern Iraq was precarious. Sistani's influence was itself transitory, and powerful forces were at work in southern Iraq that was strengthening the position of anti-British groups. The fighting had inflicted heavy losses on the JAM and their allies. In Maysan, the summer's fighting proved an enormous boost to the pro-Sadrist politicians, tribal chiefs and warlords in the province. Moderate politicians were marginalised or forced to adopt an anti-British stance to keep on the right side of public opinion or just stay alive. In many parts of the province, the police were now almost extensions of the JAM or intimidated into supporting it. The British had pulled their base out of the centre of al Amarah and many parts of the province were effectively off limits to the British. Majar-al-Kabir now was a no-go zone for British troops.

In Basra the situation was less clear cut. The Sadrist and their Fadilla party allies were still being challenged by strong Shia parties. Sadr supporters had effectively set up a shadow government across Basra and his supporters were infiltrating local and national government institutions in the city in a bid to bring them over to their cause. The OMS and the JAM were heavily split by the decision of Sadr to call the August cease-fire. While the OMS politicians jockeyed for votes or organised the assassination of their political rivals, many battle-hardened JAM fighters drifted home embittered and determined to continue the fight against the British. Word came down from Sadr himself to his JAM fighters that they should continue their struggle against the British.[63]

He suspected the British would soon leave and a retreat under attack by his fighters would help boost his reputation as an opponent of the occupation. The tactic of choice for the JAM would now be the IED attack. During raids on JAM bases in August and September, British units seized hauls of sophisticated IEDs. These included command wire detonated weapons, radio controlled bombs and the first explosively formed projectile devices.[64]

Operation Centurion in August was a disconcerting experience for some of the British troops, including the tank crews of the Queen's Royal Lancers and the infantry of the Black Watch. They had led the assault on Basra in Operation Telic 1 and just over a year on from those battles, British forces were planning another operation, from the same start line, to seize back many of the same buildings that had been objectives in April 2003. While senior officers and Ministry of Defence spin doctors tried to put a positive gloss on the situation, it was harder to convince the ordinary soldiers that progress was being made.

The QRL moved to set up check points on the Basra canal bridges, just as the regiment had in March and April 2003. This led QRL Challenger tank commander, Captain Henry Burton, to comment, "many of D Squadron's troops had served on Operation Telic 1 and had spent many days the previous year on these bridges. As we pulled into position on Bridge 3 my ever cheerful driver, Trooper Upsher, muttered over the intercom his delight at being back on the 'bloody bridges'."[65]

Chapter 17

BUYING INFLUENCE

Fighting as part of a coalition is almost second nature to senior British military officers. Gaining the trust of allies and being able to influence their decision-making is a skill that British officers spend much of their careers working on. Since the Second World War, Britain's ally of choice has been the United States, and the relationship between the high-ranking US and UK officers has defined the military aspects of the famous 'special relationship.'

The British military has more than 70 years of experience of working with their US counterparts and at the time of the Iraq operations some 750 UK military personnel were working inside the Pentagon, American military units or US defence companies. Not without reason have some Americans described the efforts of the British Defence Staff in Washington DC as the "best espionage operation inside the US military".

During major military operations led by the Americans, the British have long traditions of sending senior officers to work inside US headquarters, as deputy commanders, chiefs of operations or other senior staff jobs. Their task was to find out what the Americans were doing, find out the views of their senior commanders and work out the best way to put British opinions on the top table. In the post Cold War era, this approach was followed in the 1990/91 Gulf war, Bosnia and Kosovo in the 1990s. In Afghanistan in 2001 this approach was repeated with a vengeance and a new generation of British officers, in the army, air force and navy, built up a network of contacts and friendships with US personnel who would eventually lead the war in Iraq.

When Prime Minister Tony Blair committed Britain to participate in the invasion of Iraq in 2002, one of his top priorities was getting a seat at the top table in the White House so he could influence President George W. Bush's decision-making. The British armed forces took their lead from this, and set about making sure they had people inserted in all levels of the US military operation in the Middle East.

After the fall of Baghdad, the British moved quickly to position staff officers and other specialist personnel in every military headquarters across Iraq and in neighbouring countries. Britain offered land, air, naval and special forces to help the US occupation, as well as diplomats, administrators and technical experts to help run the Coalition Provisional Authority (CPA). According to the well-worn rules of coalition warfare, the British realised that to get a position at the top table they had to contribute either large forces or very unique units and capabilities. This was seen as the way to get the Americans' attention. So as the second largest contributor of personnel, the British were able to put in a three star officer or lieutenant general into Baghdad as advisor to Ambassador Jeremy Greenstock, who was the deputy head of the CPA. This officer was also nominally the deputy to General Ricardo Sanchez, the US military supreme commander in Iraq.

The RAF offered a squadron of Tornado GR4 bombers, VC-10 tanker aircraft, Nimrod MR2 surveillance aircraft and Nimrod R1 electronic eavesdropping aircraft to the US Air Force component supporting the occupation. As a result, a senior RAF air commodore and several staff officers filled top posts in the US Combined Air Operations Centre at al Udeid airbase in Qatar. Similarly, the Royal Navy committed to sending a frigate to protect Iraq's off shore oil infra-structure in the northern Arabian Gulf as part of the US Navy-led security task force. This meant a Royal Navy commodore took turns with his US and Australian counterparts to run the security operation, from a warship in the Gulf and at the US Navy 5th Fleet Headquarters in Bahrain.

In Baghdad, similar situations applied, with the commander of 22 Special Air Service (SAS) Regiment being the deputy of the US Joint Special Operations Command (JSOC) task force that was running covert anti-terrorist operations. British personnel were also appointed as deputies within the Iraq Survey Group that was hunting down Saddam Hussein's weapons of mass destruction, and in the command set-up to oversee the rebuilding of the Iraqi police and army. The Secret Intelligence Service (SIS) also worked hand-in glove with its counterparts in the Central Intelligence Agency (CIA).

Through its network of officers in the US headquarters across the Middle East these British officers were designated 'red card holders'. They would employ this if the Americans tried to use British troops for things the government in London were not happy with. This was a delicate balancing act. The main way to get influence with the US was by the contribution of forces to do things, not by perpetually refusing to participate in their operations. By having capabilities on hand which the Americans considered useful, the British hoped to do deals and gain access to US support for their own operations.

An important part of the job of these staff officers was to give senior British commanders, and in turn government ministers, advance warning of American intentions so they could be ready and able to respond to any formal approaches. If British forces were committed to new operations with the American allies, advance warning would also allow more time to plan and prepare so British forces could take part in the most effective manner.

This command construct was also the vehicle for disagreements with the British government and military over the conduct of the Iraq war. Throughout the Iraq campaign there was a constant pull between those who felt that success would come from directly supporting the Americans in Baghdad, and those who favoured concentrating resources and effort on Basra. There were also major differences of opinion over how best to put British views across to the Americans. These debates ebbed and flowed over the six years of the campaign but rarely surfaced in public at the time. The politics of the Iraq war and its toxic influence on Tony Blair's position inside the Labour Party was a significant factor at play in these strategic arguments.

These arguments played an important role in the pre-invasion planning, with the-then head of the British Army, General Sir Michael Walker, pushing strongly for the so-called 'northern option' via Turkey so UK forces would be at the heart of the American operation. The commitment of 1 (UK) Armoured Division to the southern front in Kuwait led by default to the British ending up occupying the 'Basra Box' in south eastern Iraq. They were replayed again in May 2003 when proposals to send 16 Air Assault Brigade to Baghdad came to nothing.

UK-US military relations in Iraq during the summer and autumn of 2003 reached a pretty low level. The US commander in Baghdad, General Ricardo Sanchez, and his political master, Ambassador Paul Bremer, appeared to have little interest in their British allies and their concerns. The steady escalation of American casualties meant they were focused on dealing with the situation in central Iraq and the political fall-out back in the US. Sanchez had not served in a post where he worked with British troops before, and had little interest in cultivating his links with the junior partner in Iraq.[1]

A major British interest in Baghdad was the Iraq Survey Group and the hunt for weapons of mass destruction (WMD), which had been thrust into the limelight by the suicide of the Ministry of Defence scientist Dr David Kelly in July 2003. Leading the hunt for former regime WMD experts were SIS agents and SAS protection teams.

UK Special Forces were also becoming involved in operations by the US JSOC against former regime leaders who were suspected of master minding the Sunni insurgency. This operation was kept secret by the British government, but the death of a Special Boat Service soldier in October during a raid on an insurgent hide-out near Tikrit led to news entering the public domain. The deaths in a road accident in Baghdad of a major and sergeant serving in the SAS made it even more difficult for the government to plausibly deny British involvement in the fight in the infamous 'Sunni Triangle'.[2]

The sensitivity of the SAS participation in the US special forces campaign became all too apparent in April 2004 when the Abu Ghraib prisoner abuse scandal broke. The outrage caused by the publication of photographs showing US soldiers torturing prisoners shocked the world and public, media and parliamentary support for British participation in the occupation dropped to new lows. The British government was desperate to avoid any linkage between the SAS and the delivery of prisoners to American torturers. Extreme measures were taken to minimise any potential damage and restrictions were placed on how prisoners could be handled by the SAS. This all remained secret until 2006 when a former SAS soldier, Ben Griffin revealed at an anti-war event that two Pakistanis captured in Iraq by his unit in February 2004 had been handed over to the US and then transferred to a 'black' or secret prison at Bagram airbase in Afghanistan. This site was hidden from the International Committee of the Red Cross, and it was claimed that torture was routinely used on prisoners by US interrogators. So sensitive were these accusations that the government sought and received a court injunction preventing the soldier repeating them. In 2009 the British government admitted his claims were true, although it never lifted its injunction on Private Griffin.[3]

On the transfer of sovereignty to Iraq at the end of June 2004, both Sanchez and Bremer were replaced and UK-US co-operation seemed to recover. The new American commander, General George Casey, had served with NATO troops in Bosnia and had worked closely there with the British Army. Early in 2004, the US Army also sent a three star or corps headquarters to Iraq to provide an operational level of command, taking much of the pressure off General Sanchez. It also meant the British divisional commander in Basra did not have to deal with the overall American commander in Iraq but with his subordinate, Lieutenant General Metz. So in the build-up to the departure of Sanchez Anglo-US military co-operation began to improve considerably.

The outbreak of the Sadr uprising in April forced the British and Americans to increase their co-operation. Despite an inauspicious start after the initial spat between General Andrew Stewart and Sanchez over the occupation of the Office of Muqtadr al Sadr in Basra, the seriousness of the situation prompted British officers in Baghdad and at Permanent Joint Headquarters (PJHQ) in Northwood, to begin work on contingency plans to shore up the collapse of the coalition division to the south of Baghdad.

With Sadr's militiamen in control of a swath of cities across central Iraq and coalition troops from Spain, El Salvador, Italy and the Ukraine effectively surrounded in their camps, the Americans and British had to move quickly to stamp out the insurrection before it created 'political facts' on the ground and allowed Sadr to claim a political victory.

In the short term, the US created a series of ad hoc task forces around Baghdad and ordered them to move south to take back al Kut, Hillah and Najaf. The British stood up a battlegroup to reinforce the Italians in Nasiriyah.[4] During early May 2004, the British and Americans began looking at a more permanent solution to replace the Polish-led Multi-National Division Centre, which seemed on the verge of disintegrating as the majority of troop-contributing nations began to pull their soldiers out of Iraq. The US command in Baghdad approached the Senior British Military Representative, Lieutenant General John McColl, to explore the possibility of the UK-led ARRC Headquarters moving to Iraq to command all southern Iraq.[5]

In addition to this, it was proposed that the headquarters of 3 Commando Brigade would be sent to run Najaf province and take on the task of containing Sadr in the centre of the Shia faith. To provide some British muscle for its potential new commanders, the Warrior equipped 1st Battalion, The Black Watch, was earmarked to operate as a roving rapid reaction force across central Iraq, backed up by 40 Commando Royal Marines, which was also nominated to rotate into Iraq under a pre-planned deployment at the start of July.[6]

Senior British officers liked the idea because it would bring the main Shia areas of Iraq under the control of a single headquarters, run by a British officer,

Lieutenant General Richard Dannatt. With Sadr stirring up Basra from Najaf, this offered the opportunity for the British to take control of the solution to their troubles.[7]

"You have influence where you are and you do not have influence where you are not," General Stewart told an army debriefing team. "This is true of the Americans as well as the Iraqis. The UK had no influence in Najaf, for instance, we weren't there and if we wanted to influence events we would have had to deploy an additional brigade there."[8]

The plans rapidly gained traction during May, and Brigadier Barney White-Spunner, the head of PJHQ's Joint Force Operations Headquarters, was sent to Iraq to see if the mission was feasible.

"I did reconnaissance to Najaf to look at the expansion of our area of responsibility to take over from withdrawing Spanish troops," recalled White-Spunner. "The idea was to put in 3 Commando Brigade and I was asked to look at whether it was tactically possible. I was dropped off outside Najaf by UH-60 Blackhawk helicopter at a US headquarters in middle of the desert. The Americans thought it was a great idea. ARRC Headquarters was on-off-on-off all the time during this period."[9]

Bringing in the ARRC Headquarters into the command set up in Iraq had some support from the US Defense Secretary Donald Rumsfled.

"The 'Rumsfeld school' in the Pentagon still hankered after an Afghanistan [light footprint] model, whereby the US had done the 'invasion' and then left it to the Europeans to do the peace enforcement/rebuilding," said White-Spunner.[10]

In the first week of June the plans were briefed to the British Prime Minister and senior ministers. There was not a unified view from the military leadership and other government departments. While there were some benefits from being able to influence engagement with Shia leaders in Najaf, expanding the British zone would also come with a large cost for setting up base infra-structure and logistic support. Also Britain would become responsible for aid to the civilian population. The cost issues were considered too high and deployment of the ARRC and 3 Commando Brigade were put on hold.[11] The Black Watch deployment would go ahead because it would only be replacing an infantry battalion that was already in Basra training Iraqi troops.

The Americans eventually found a US Marine Corps unit to take over Najaf from the Spanish and the crisis died down when Sadr called a ceasefire in mid June. The arrival of the Black Watch in central Iraq in the middle of July gave British and American planners more options. Contingency plans were developed for the Scottish troops to operate from a base at Tallil, outside Nasiriyah, across central Iraq up to Hillah or Kut. General Metz suggested that they could even be sent to the Syrian border to interdict insurgent supply lines. Black Watch officers flew from Basra up to the American headquarters in Baghdad to work on the plans. By the end of July, Blair again vetoed the idea. According to the commanding officer of the Black Watch, Lieutenant Colonel James

Cowan, the cancellation of the new mission "was not all together surprising" because "the scope of the operation fell beyond the original intended by British ministers".[12]

The second Sadr uprising in August saw the Black Watch committed to action in the British sector, and then the battalion began counting down the days until its four-month long tour of duty was up at the end of October. During September and October, with the Sadr uprising over, the American command in Baghdad started to turn its attention to dealing with the Sunni insurgent stronghold of Fallujah.

The plans for the return home of the Black Watch were abruptly dropped when General Metz invited Major General Bill Rollo to Baghdad on 7th October, for informal discussions about Britain providing assistance in the forthcoming American offensive against the Sunni insurgent-held city of Fallujah. By later that evening General Rollo's staff had completed initial planning for the mission, warned off the Black Watch for the mission and contacted PJHQ to get political top cover.[13] The formal request from General Metz arrived two days later for a British battlegroup to replace a US battalion in North Babil province to free up American forces for the attack on Fallujah.

While PJHQ and ministers in London considered the high politics and strategic implications of the commitment, in Basra General Rollo and his staff worked furiously to see if it was feasible. The Black Watch had already sent 100 of its soldiers back to Britain ahead of its departure from Iraq, and the proposed operation would coincide with the RIP of 1 Mechanised and 4 Armoured Brigades, greatly complicating the logistics of moving the battlegroup up to central Iraq. Fortunately the Black Watch command team had already studied the technicalities of moving its Warrior armoured vehicles up to the Syrian border earlier in July so they had a good idea of what needed to be done.[14]

Senior British Army officers in Iraq were keen to back the move to help the Americans. The attack on Fallujah would involve more than 10,000 US troops and it was to be an overwhelming offensive to eliminate a pocket of nearly 3,000 fanatical Sunni insurgents who had held the city since April. Every US combat unit that could be spared in Iraq was being massed for the attack, so General Casey was looking for as much help from his allies as possible. The feeling was that this was the American's hour of need and the British needed to step up to the plate. According to Colonel Cowan, "British officers in Baghdad recognised that the British reputation for flexibility was at jeopardy unless the United Kingdom was prepared to assist her principal ally".[15]

According to Lieutenant General John McColl, the senior British officer in Baghdad during the summer of 2004, the fear was that unless the Fallujah boil was lanced soon, it would threaten the success of Iraqi parliamentary elections in January 2005.

"There were risks associated with [committing the Black Watch] and I was very conscious of those risks," he told the Chilcot inquiry.

"There were British soldiers involved, but it had to be set within the context of the risks to the rest of the [coalition] force, and the very important operation was going on to try and ensure the security for what was perceived as being the centre of gravity for the operation, particularly for the elections, which was Baghdad. It was an entirely reasonable request on behalf of Lieutenant General Metz, who was the corps commander, and, from a military perspective, I thought the judgment was sound that they should go."[16]

"There was a huge amount of discussion," recalled Air Marshal Glenn Torpy, then Chief of Joint Operations at PJHQ.

"We did the right thing. I was convinced by McColl, he said UK credibility rested on this and a refusal would impact on our relationship with the Americans. The US needed our help to do Fallujah properly. It was a discrete operation, time bounded, so we would not have our hand in the mangle."[17]

In Basra, General Rollo was pressing for an early decision because of the tight timetable to allow the Black Watch to move north in time for the opening of Operation Phantom Fury, as the Fallujah attack was code-named, in the second week of November. With its senior field commanders all reporting that some sort of assistance to the Americans was necessary, as the Fallujah campaign came to its dénouement, the service chiefs in London lined up in favour of joining the US operation. General Walker stressed to Ministers that the proposed mission of the Black Watch was a discrete operation, that could be time limited and could be done in such a way that it did not suck the British Army into a permanent commitment in central Iraq.[18]

"The UK government did not want to get involved in wider Iraq operations because of sustainability issues", said Air Marshal Torpy.[19]

Prime Minister Tony Blair and senior government ministers were loath to become involved in what could turn into a blood bath, that would be played out on national and international television screens. They did not want to overturn their decisions earlier in the summer to restrict UK operations to southern Iraq. There was also the possibility that the Americans might ask British special forces and RAF Tornado GR4 bombers to become directly involved in the battle for Fallujah.

"There were reservations amongst the UK leadership about the Fallujah operation," recalled Major General Robin Brims, who was the chief of staff for operations at PJHQ.

"The reservations led to the instruction that UK forces would not take [a direct] part in the Fallujah operation and this was managed by UK/US military people with the result that they did not take part."[20]

Lieutenant General John Kiszely, who had now replaced General McColl in Baghdad, and senior RAF officers in the Middle East, were instructed to advise the Americans that the British would do everything to support them except fighting in the streets of Fallujah. As a result, the senior US commanders did not formally ask for help from the SAS and the RAF so British officers would not have to use their 'red cards,' and risk a split with their American allies. It was a delicate way to get round a tricky issue.

When details of the warning order that General Rollo had issued to the Black Watch leaked to the media it caused an immediate furore, particularly about the involvement of the Black Watch. The fears of ministers about the unpopularity for the deployment proved well founded. Scottish Members of Parliament and newspapers attacked the commitment of the regiment as a sign that Scots units were bearing a disproportionate burden of the war in Iraq. The historic regiment was also facing disbandment or amalgamation in a looming round of defence budget cuts, so other critics attacked the Ministry of Defence for contemplating cutting a unit that was now at the centre of a high profile operation. Opponents of the Iraq war accused the government of widening British involvement, and risking more casualties for what appeared to be a lost cause. The timing of the request from the US military, only a few weeks before the November US presidential election also raised eyebrows and led to accusations that Blair was trying to help the re-election of George W Bush.

In an acrimonious session in the House of Commons on 18th October, defence secretary Geoff Hoon received unequivocal support from only one MP, a Tory back bencher, signalling the unpopularity of the proposed deployment.[21] Yet Blair felt unable to turn down a direct request from the UK major ally at a crucial point in the war, particularly after it had been recommended by its senior field commanders in Iraq, and the military chiefs in London. The Prime Minister did promise that the Black Watch would be back in Britain in time for Christmas.

On 21st October, Hoon announced that Operation Bracken, as the Black Watch mission was now code-named, would go ahead.[22] He however did not reveal that the government had taken some important moves to reduce British military involvement in the Fallujah attack. A squadron of SAS troops that was camped outside the city ready to join its American comrades from the JSOC in the assault never got orders to move forward and returned to its base.[23] RAF Tornado bombers did not participate in direct air strikes on the city, but replaced US aircraft on patrols elsewhere in Iraq.

In Iraq preparations were already accelerating for the move of the Black Watch. It had to be brought back up to strength with mortar teams and infantry from 40 Commando Royal Marines, as well as reconnaissance troops from the Queen's Dragoon Guards, and additional medical, communications and logistic specialists. RAF Puma and Army Air Corps Lynx helicopters fitted for airborne surveillance were also prepared to fly north.[24]

The road move was immensely complicated, involving 72 low loaders carrying the battlegroup's tracked vehicles and 86 trucks carrying cargo containers. They had to be safely moved some 673 kilometres from the relative safety of the British zone into the heart of the Sunni insurgency, along roads that were expected to be heavily seeded with improvised explosive devices. The British convoy would carry 42 days' worth of supplies to make the battlegroup self-sufficient for the duration of its mission. Colonel Cowan was only able to make one aerial reconnaissance, and a brief ground visit to the proposed area of operation and their proposed base at Camp Dogwood, on the banks of the Euphrates. It was very much a leap into the dark.[25]

Operation Bracken got underway on 27th October when the Black Watch advance party flew to Baghdad airport. The same day the huge convoy left Shaibah Logistic Base outside Basra. After overnighting at Tallil, near Nasiriyah, it began moving along the Euphrates to Babil province, escorting by a US mine-clearing task force. Their services were needed when five large daisy chain IEDs made from multiple 120mm artillery shells were discovered en route, but the first packet of British vehicles carrying the vehicles of the three Black Watch rifle companies arrived late on 28th October. Hundreds of other Scottish soldiers began arriving in American Chinook helicopters on the same day. Other elements of the convoy arrived the following day but tragedy struck when a Warrior rolled into a deep drainage ditch alongside a road, trapping the crew inside. One soldier drowned inside the vehicle before he could be rescued.[26]

The insurgents greeted the arrival of the Black Watch at their sprawling desert base with a salvo of 122mm rockets. Now Colonel Cowan and his men had to try to find out what they had got themselves into. Patrols were sent out across their area of operations to establish where they would have to put in blocking positions, to stop insurgents retreating through the Black Watch's zone when the American attack on Fallujah, some 60 kilometres to the north, started. The US 24th Marine Expeditionary Unit, which was controlling the area where the Black Watch was operating, had little detailed intelligence on the composition of insurgent groups, their weapons or dispositions. There appeared to be no Iraqi administration or security forces in area.

When the first British patrols pushed out of Camp Dogwood, they found the Sunni population sullen, resentful and in some case openly hostile. The bodies of several Iraqi policemen who had been executed by shots to the back of the head were soon discovered.[27] The insurgents had total control of the population and were expected to strike at their new visitors very soon. The situation was very different from the south, where the Shia population were relatively friendly and even the most determined JAM militia were prepared to negotiate and talk to the British when it suited them. The only dialogue with the insurgents in North Babil would be violence.

The Black Watch were ready to move out of their base to take control of their area on 3rd November, and the British Warrior-mounted patrols started to come under rocket and mortar attacks. All over the area large IEDs hindered movement. One Warrior was severely damaged in a huge IED strike and another was blown into a ditch by a rocket.[28]

The next day the troops began setting up vehicle check points in a bid to monitor and intercept insurgent movement. During the afternoon a smiling suicide bomber approached a checkpoint in a car and calmly detonated his device.

Three Black Watch soldiers and an Iraqi interpreter were killed outright and the eight other soldiers at the checkpoint were injured. Minutes later the devastated British position was hit by mortar fire. Reinforcements arrived in Warriors and began giving first aid whilst the mortar rounds were still falling. American helicopters evacuated the wounded, preventing more fatalities.[29]

The psychological impact of the first loss of British soldiers to suicide bombers in Iraq was immense. When the insurgents released a video of the attack on the internet, some sources suggested Tony Blair considered pulling back the Black Watch to the relative safety of Basra.

General Rollo commented in his war diary, "the calm and dispassionate manner in which the martyrs conducted themselves in their final moments is hard to comprehend."[30]

Over the next three days rocket and mortar strikes continued unabated, and then two more soldiers were seriously injured by another suicide bomb attack. A Warrior patrol and a bomb disposal team were investigating a suspected IED when a car approached and accelerated towards them. Before the soldiers had time to jump inside their Warriors and close the doors, the driver detonated his bomb as he gave a thumbs up sign.

To prevent further suicide attacks on their static vehicle check points, the Black Watch devised new tactics involving the firing of warning shots in front of cars to force them to stop some distance from the British vehicles. Some of the soldiers were reluctant to employ the new tactics in case it led to them being prosecuted by the army for injuring civilians, so Colonel Cowan went out to set up the first of the new style check points and demonstrated to his men how it should be done.[31]

Increased helicopter patrols were flown by the Pumas and Lynx to give early warning of suspicious car movements and to pursue any vehicles trying to speed away from British check points. One Lynx was raked by fire during such a mission and the pilot seriously injured but he managed to bring his helicopter safely back to base.

The Black Watch suffered their fifth fatality on 8th November when a Warrior drove over a huge IED that blew off six of the vehicle's road wheels and killed the driver, as well as injuring two crewmen. This incident coincided with the start of the US attack on Fallujah and throughout the day sporadic rocket and mortar attacks continued on British patrols.

A further four days of intense insurgent activity continued, until a helicopter patrol followed a car-borne group of insurgents, who had just attacked a Warrior with rocket propelled grenades (RPGs), back to a mosque. A follow-up operation surrounded the mosque and arrested two suspects, as well as seizing explosives and detonators. A further helicopter spotted a large arrow etched into the nearby sand pointing towards Camp Dogwood as an aiming mark for insurgent rocket teams. More searches turned up mortars, RPGs and IEDs. Colonel Cowan described the seizures as a "psychological turning point" and it marked the first of several seizures and arrests of insurgent suspects over the following week.[32]

In the early hours of 25th November, Colonel Cowan organised a battle-group-sized mission to simultaneously seize multiple insurgent bases and arms caches, using some 650 troops in 116 tracked vehicles. Operation Tobruk would be final battalion-sized operation ever conducted by the Black Watch before its possible amalgamation, and Colonel Cowan's men were fully aware of its significance. As the Warrior columns headed out of Camp Dogwood towards their objectives, the Regiment's pipe major performed with some gusto.[33]

The Black Watch wound up Operation Bracken at the end of November, and at 4am on 2nd December a convoy of 200 hundred heavy trucks and 100 armoured vehicles drove out of Camp Dogwood for the last time. The regiment's soldiers flew back to Britain by the middle of the month, in time to hear the defence secretary announce on 16th December the disbandment of one of the six Scottish infantry battalions, and the amalgamation of the remainder of the surviving units into a new "super regiment". The government had kept their promise to bring the Black Watch home in time for Christmas.

American officers were keen to praise the efforts of the Black Watch, telling Colonel Cowan that the "level of enemy activity in the Baghdad and Fallujah areas dropped considerably as a result of the blocking and disruptive operations that took place in North Babil".[34]

During the month-long operation, the battlegroup endured three suicide attacks, 25 large road side bombs, daily indirect fire attacks, totalling 120 serious incidents. Five Black Watch soldiers and one civilian interpreter were killed, and 17 wounded. Four Warriors and one Scimitar light tank were damaged beyond repair, with two helicopters damaged by ground fire.

"Incidents of enemy activity fell away considerably as the Black Watch began to dominate the ground – to the point where attacks virtually ceased in the last week," reported Colonel Cowan.

"Most significantly, the enemy failed to reinforce Fallujah, thereby contributing to a considerable operational success that drew the praise of a number of senior American officers. Strategically, the deployment reaffirmed the strength of a coalition based on British and American resolve."[35]

Government ministers in Britain were very relieved when the Black Watch got safely back to Shaibah. The American assault on Fallujah in the immediate wake of President Bush's re-election was portrayed in the media as a blood bath, and this image was not helped when footage was broadcast that appeared to show US Marines executing a wounded insurgent.

General Kiszely told the Chilcot inquiry that the assault on Fallujah was "quite a bloody affair". He estimated that "there were over 2,000 insurgents or civilians and -- I think they were described as "insurgents" -- were killed, over 85 Americans were killed and over 700 seriously wounded, and a number of Iraqi security forces as well." [36]

Senior British officers in Iraq were keen to praise the success of Operation Bracken, saying the Black Watch had suffered proportionately fewer casualties than neighbouring US units. In London, the reaction within the Blair government was more muted, as the damaging effects of of the Iraq war, for the prime minister, ramped up. Major General Robin Brims was the chief of staff for operations in PJHQ during 2004, and he described how the US request had prompted a big political debate in parliament and within the government.

"There was huge reluctance to allow the Black Watch to go and do this and huge US pressure for it to go ahead," he recalled. "This operation drained the 'political capital' [of the government to see the campaign through] even more."[37]

Early in 2005, General Brims was preparing to go to Baghdad to replace General Kiszely. "I asked the system what should I say if the US ask us to expand [British area of responsibility]" he said, "The answer [I was told to give] was not until after UK general election [in May]."[38]

Chapter 18

THE TRAINERS

Iraq's first election of the modern era took place without major incident on 30th January 2005. Across the country millions of Iraqis went out to vote with obvious enthusiasm for this first taste of democracy. In the south of the country, the predominately Shia electorate voted in larger numbers than elsewhere in the country.[1]

For the British government, this exercise in democracy was a huge boost and it was hailed as a turning point, signalling that its troops could soon be heading home. Apart from the obvious political progress, the elections were also a major test of the fledgling Iraqi security force, and British military commanders were able to report that their charges had performed pretty well. Although British troops had co-ordinated the whole exercise and provided specialist support, direct security at pooling stations and at street level across southern Iraq was in the hands of the local police, security agencies and the national guard.

Even in Maysan province, where only five months before troops of the Princess of Wales's Royal Regiment had been fighting for their lives in al Amarah's besieged CIMIC House, the population turned out in their thousands to vote. The Welsh Guards worked with the Iraqi police to secure the city. Major Charles Antelme, of the Welsh Guard's No 3 Company, recorded that weeks of preparation building up relationships with the police meant that on the day, "everything ran like clockwork".

"The Election Day proved to be a moving experience, as nascent democracy took its first hold," recalled Antelme.

"After the elections a post euphoric calm spread across the province and a collective sigh of relief was followed by a 'honeymoon' period of a month."[2]

It of course did not last, and the Welsh Guards' bases and patrols across Maysan were soon being mortared, rocketed and sniped at on a weekly basis. The level of violence was nowhere near as that experienced during the previous summer, which added to the feeing that a corner had been turned. The Welsh Guards were also able to send a large company-sized patrol into the Majar al Khabir for the first time since the spring of 2004, which went relatively smoothly without major violence.[3] During the whole of Operation Telic 5 tour, between November 2004 and April 2005 not a single British soldier was killed by hostile fire or improvised explosive devices in southern Iraq. Ten crew and passengers on a RAF Hercules transport aircraft were killed when it was shot down on a resupply mission to UK special forces near Baghdad, but the only two fatalities in the south were later judged at inquests to have been suicides.[4] This added to the feeling among senior British officers that the Iraq campaign was on the right track.

For an 18 month-long period up to the spring of 2006, the British Army's campaign in southern Iraq reached a plateau of sorts. Parliamentary and local provincial elections in January 2005 and a constitutional referendum the following October went relatively peacefully and seemed to suggest that Iraq was moving to democracy, if in a rather haphazard fashion. Attacks on British troops declined rapidly after the Sadr uprising ended in September 2004 and southern Iraqi seemed an oasis of stability compared to the mayhem unfolding in the American controlled zone around Baghdad.

This period was also characterised by the absence of what were termed "strategic shocks" outside the British-controlled area. There were no surprises lurches in US strategy or high level Iraqi political disputes to suddenly throw British operations off kilter. Although it was not apparent at the time, this period proved to be the last window of opportunity for the British army to pull off something that could be called a success in Iraq.

The British military presence was at its peak since the draw down after the invasion in the summer of 2003, with seven battlegroup or battalion-sized units deployed on the ground. British commanders were convinced they had the measure of southern Iraq after the successful defeat of the two Sadr revolts in the summer and autumn of 2004. Major General Bill Rollo's seemingly adroit handling of the second uprising in August and September, involving minimal use of firepower, or kinetics as it became known, was seen as the way forward. The way he managed to corral Basra's squabbling politicians in the aftermath of the collapse of Sadr's uprising was much praised in the higher ranks of the British Army and across Whitehall. There was also growing confidence that the US military leadership in Baghdad had at last a reasonably coherent campaign plan that the British could work to.

Several British units and senior officers who served on Operation Telic 1 were now starting to return on follow-on tours and many were shocked at the lack of progress. The squalid living conditions, lack of economic development and random violence were immediately obvious, as well as the overwhelming stench of raw sewage and unwashed humanity.

Air Chief Marshal Brian Burridge, who had led the British invasion force in 2003, returned to visit Basra during 2005 and recalled that the city's fabric of life for its ordinary people had not really changed.

"It looked the same – it was really depressing."[5]

Lieutenant David Rees of the King's Own Royal Border Regiment recalled when his troops arrived in Basra later in 2005, "it was plain to see this was an area struggling to get back on its feet, with poor living conditions, no sewer systems and a total disregard for litter on the streets. On a daily basis you could see people young and old scavenging the rubbish for anything of use. Flies were everywhere. In most cases you can make comparisons with places that you have been before, however, in this instance for the City of Basra this was not possible. Ask any member of [my] Company and the answer will remain the same, "'they have never seen anything like this before'."[6]

Iraq was still the British military's biggest on-going operation and soldiers of all ranks were keen to get a piece of the action. The prospect of an operational tour excited soldiers across the army. Even if the invasion of Iraq was very unpopular among the British public, the army saw the on-going operation as a chance to prove its metal and once again demonstrate its can-do credentials. Within the army, tours of duty in Iraq were seen as a way to boast regimental profiles, recruiting and careers. There was intense competition to get on the Operation Telic order of battle, as the list of units selected to deploy to Iraq was dubbed within the army.

Lieutenant Colonel Jonny Cray, the commanding officer of the Royal Dragoon Guards (RDG), wrote to his regimental colleagues of the pressure to get his unit selected to serve in Iraq in late 2004.

"Our place on Operation Telic was not in any way guaranteed," he wrote.

"The combination effects of force level reviews in the light of operation progress in southern Iraq, plus our relative lack of operational experience and credibility, meant that there was a very real chance of the RDG not making the cut for the Operation Telic 5 order of battle. In my view this would have been little short of catastrophic for Regimental morale and, while much lay beyond our control, one key factor was very definitely within our gift; it was vital to prove that the regiment was, in every sense, fit for operations; and then to live up to that promise."[7]

"The force package debate rumbled-on against the background of a very violent summer in Basra and al Amarah," he continued.

"The Regiment acquitted itself in training and earned a place on the order of battle for Operation Telic 5 with three company-sized sabre squadrons. Our initial task in Iraq was apparently unglamorous: rear operations. But no matter, it got us into theatre and what we did once we had got there was up for grabs in my mind – we just needed to be ready to seize what opportunities presented themselves."[8]

The Colonel's enthusiasm to get his troops to Iraq was a common feeling. A member of the Welsh Guards recorded the attitude of his comrades, commenting, "after the company commander's [reconnaissance] to al Amarah, in late August, where operations were seen to be of an even higher intensity, there was every reason to believe that Shiny Two [the Welsh Guards] would also be 'getting stuck in', in only a few weeks time. By the time the company deployed in October, there was a tangible air of expectation and excitement."[9]

Major Nick Wood, of the King's Own Royal Border Regiment, declared "frustration" at his company being assigned to work with the Danish battlegroup in what he thought was a backwater task at the sprawling Shaibah Logistic Base.

"Clearly this was a second rate job and one which was difficult to believe in", he recalled. "Thankfully the Brigade Commander saw fit to move [my company] to Basra and attach us to The Highlander's Battlegroup – time to be serious. After all, this was where it was all happening."[10]

The "can do" attitude of the army was widespread despite the uncertainty about what soldiers would have to do once they got there. Lieutenant Colonel

James Hopkinson, commanding officer of the 1st Battalion, The Highlanders described his unit's positive attitude.

"Regimental officers in [our battle group] headquarters found themselves in unfamiliar territory [when they got to Iraq] as they became responsible for elections, civilian military co-operation, operation support (information operations), security sector reform (SSR) and movement," he wrote in his regimental journal. "Despite having no formal training in these areas they, to a man, took to their complex bailiwicks like ducks to water."[11]

The upper ranks of the army also saw tours of duty in Iraq as a means to give senior officers the vital tick of operational command experience on their confidential reports to ensure progression up the promotion ladder. On Operations Telic 5, 6 and 7 between November 2004 and April 2006, five brigadiers were given the chance to command the Basra brigade, with four of them only having little more than three months in post before they had to hand over the reins to their successors. [12] This gave the impression that the army felt it had events so under control that it could shuffle its senior commanders without damaging the operation. If that was not the case, the army appeared to care more about senior officer's career planning than operational success.

"There was already, by this stage, some concern about this approach," commented a member of General Sir Mike Walker's staff.

"I recall making the point to the Chief of Defence Staff about the lack of continuity, but it wasn't his way to interfere with 'the staff', I'm afraid. The approach went, though, completely counter to the approach that we used for Northern Ireland. It was impossible to build up good working relationships at senior level in Basra on a three-month tour, and it showed. But it was almost as if the British Army was being driven by the Military Secretary [senior officers career planning officer], rather than vice versa."[13]

The way the British Army deployed across southern Iraq and operated during this period was driven by how it interpreted the US campaign plan, which was promulgated by the new senior American commander in Iraq in the late summer of 2004, General George Casey. His plan was centred around a concept known as transition, which envisaged the building up of Iraq's security forces to allow US, British and other foreign troops to go once the locals troops and police were ready to protect their own country.

"We were not running our own campaign plan, we were part of a wider [coalition] campaign," recalled Air Marshal Glenn Torpy, who as Chief of Joint Operations between July 2004 and April 2006 was Chief of Joint Operations at Permanent Joint Headquarters (PJHQ).[14]

The campaign plan had been developed by a team of US and British officers in Baghdad, including Brigadier Jonathon Riley, who served in the Iraqi capital during 2003 as part of the coalition military advisory and training team, which subsequently became the security transition command.

In November, the newly prompted Major General Riley arrived to command the British division in Basra, and he put into place the concepts that had been developed during his time in Baghdad.

"Jonathon Riley came up with the transition plan. What we did prompted the Americans to follow us," said Torpy.

"Riley's transition plan was adopted by the US. It envisaged us handing over to the Iraqis four brigade areas. Then we would step back to Basra and then move to Kuwait as strategic reserve. It was completely realistic. The times lines were flexible. Riley put stakes in ground to get momentum. We fudged when transition would take place."[15]

This in turn was part of an Iraq-wide plan to transition provinces in an orderly sequence. In early 2005 the four British controlled provinces had a far more benign security environment that American-run provinces in central and western Iraq. Hence the southern Iraqi provinces were in the frame for transition near the start of the process, while within the British divisional areas Muthanna and Maysan provinces first, followed by Dhi Qar and Basra. The later two were also lower down the schedule for Iraqi control because they sat across the main US Line of Communication from Kuwait to Baghdad.

Riley and his successors adopted four themes, or lines of operations to drive the campaign. These included providing security through both the building up of Iraq's own security forces and joint operations with local forces, improving the governance of Iraqi state institutions, improving economic development and communicating with a wide range of Iraqi society. The specifics of this campaign were fine tuned by each commander of Multi-National Division (South East) at the start of their six month tour but the direction of travel was never challenged.

On the ground in Iraq this translated into a very distinct and British style of operation. At the heart of the operation were ground holding or framework battlegroups. The term "ground holding" came to be the more popular term as it was easier to explain to Americans, who originated it. "Framework" was the original British description, which came from the Balkans where a whole generation of British infantry officers and non-commissioned officers had spent the past decade on peacekeeping and humanitarian duties. The success of British operations in Bosnia and Kosovo had reinforced the view that 'people friendly' framework or ground holding operations were the way forward in Iraq.

"One of the first things I did was to get an Iraqi divisional commander appointed in the south and give him an office next to mine in our divisional headquarters," said General Riley.

"As the Iraqi division headquarters built up, we were thus able to travel together, develop things together and exchange staff."[16]

In southern Iraq in late 2004 and into 2005, the British army deployed three ground-holding battlegroups and their operations were the divisional main effort throughout this period. One battlegroup was in Basra city, while the other was operating in the rural areas to the south of Basra. The Basra rural north battlegroup was under Danish command and was the only significant contingent of coalition troops in Basra province. A Third British ground holding battlegroup was under divisional command in Maysan province. An Italian/Romanian brigade was operating in Nasiriyah, and a Dutch battlegroup was in Muthanna province until early 2005 when it was replaced by a combined Australian and British force. General Riley kept a divisional reserve battlegroup, and gave a battlegroup with two large Territorial Army and three regular companies to the British logistic commander, making him responsible for all rear operations including guards and escorts. This freed up the ground-holding/SSR units for their main tasks.

The over riding priority of these ground holding battlegroups was the driving through of SSR. This was the building up of Iraq's army, police service and other security agencies. In practice this activity came to dominate the day-to-day work of more than 5,000 of the 8,000 British troops, in frontline and support roles, in Iraq at this time. Only a few hundred of the remaining troops were involved in combat or direct security operations against militia fighters across southern Iraq. The balance of the British garrison were logistic troops or RAF personnel running the airport.

Patrolling was not our main effort on arrival," recalled Major Andrew Speed, of the Scots Guards' Left Flank Company. "[As well as being divisional reserve], our main task was working up the 605 Iraqi National Guard Battalion. The job was a very important one and was on the Divisional main effort. It is clear that in order for Multi-National Forces (MNF) to extract from Iraq, the Iraqi security forces must be credible and effective. It is important also to maintain the consent of the people. We must convince them that their security forces are capable to take over from us, thus showing them that MNF are not a permanent occupying force."[17]

This approach to SSR overlaid every aspect of British operations in the south from how the division headquarters worked to the patrols of the lowest infantry section, or multiple, as the smallest British tactical unit was dubbed. In late 2003 and early 2004, the focus had been on basic training of police and army recruits, but this phase had now evolved and the emphasis was on what was termed "mentoring" and "monitoring" of Iraq forces as they went about their day-to-day work. By mentoring the Iraqis it was hoped that British advisors would pass on their skills and expertise, and monitoring was aimed at keeping Iraqis under observation to ensure they were up to the required standard.

Senior officers from the British division and brigade headquarters topped off this operational construct with 'engagement' activities among senior local Iraqi politicians, police chiefs and military commanders to secure what was termed as "improving governance," to "guide" them in a positive direction and ensure their subordinates co-operated fully with British-led SSR efforts. General Riley's plan for transition to the Iraqis taking full control of their country's security, included concepts known as 'tactical overwatch' and 'operation overwatch'. These were intended to guide the hand-off transitions to Iraqi forces and envisaged that British and US troops would be progressively stepping back as the locals became more capable. American planners created a large 'conditions matrix' and explained it to visitors on a very long Microsoft Power Point briefing.

"Some people never understood what Overwatch was and how it worked – and still don't," said Riley. "It was really about the level of cover we would provide, when, and where, as Iraqi capabilities developed. In its final form, overwatch is what the Americans provide for Taiwan: watching their strategic back."[18]

While the theory sounded very good and visiting politicians from London were usually suitably impressed, the situation on the ground was more complex and increasingly became very messy. The scale of the task was made clear by Major Speed, of the Scots Guards, as he described in grim detail what happened after he and his troops arrived to train the 605 Battalion in November and December 2004.

"Sadly, on first inspection, 605 seemed far from the desired end state," he recalled. "There was no Commanding Officer as he had been sacked by [the British], along with the Headquarters Company commander, during the August violence for collaboration with the enemy. Both characters had failed to leave the Battalion. Indeed both of them had gone to Baghdad to speak to various relatives and had come back promoted!"[19]

Speed said the soldiers lived in squalid conditions and there were many complaints about corrupt officers and poor food.

"There were no functioning ablutions and therefore the perimeter fence became the de facto defecating area" said Speed. "Rubbish was strewn everywhere and there was little pride in the camp or its maintenance. There was also a rumour that the Battalion was to be redeployed closer to Baghdad which sent a collective shiver down the spines of most of the soldiers."

The Scots Guards set about running basic training courses for the ordinary soldiers in tactics and weapon handling and Speed's sergeant major organised a tidy drive in the camp.

"So what success have we had?" said Speed. "Initially we found that attendance was good. However, by the end of the first week their enthusiasm had begun to dwindle. At the initial muster parade on day one we had approximately 200 men. By the end of the week this had dwindled to 50. Fortunately after much cajoling and tea drinking sessions we managed to persuade the [Iraqi] Adjutant that this was unacceptable. At the same time a new Commanding Officer arrived who really got stuck into the Battalion. Gradually the attendance increased until we were back up to the original 200. We found that theory training was not well received. There was no shame. If a student was bored there was no attempt to hide the body wracking yawn."

By early 2005, when the Scots Guards had to move to preparing for election security operations, Speed said "we cannot claim that we have turned 605 [battalion] into the best counter insurgency battalion ever seen in the country. What we can claim is that we have raised their standards and, in conjunction with their new Commanding Officer, developed them into a unit that is capable of operating in a more professional and effective manner. There is a long way to go. There seems to be a much improved atmosphere across the Battalion, dare I say it a little more pride. The ING across Iraq are an ongoing project."[20]

The British brigade headquarters in Basra took the lead in many aspects of the SSR campaign and it was assigned a SSR battlegroup, of some 300 troops, based around a Royal Artillery regiment to work with the leadership of the Iraqi police in Basra province, as well as with branches of central government security agencies based in the city.

SSR had become something of a Royal Artillery specialisation since April 2003, and the Gunner regiments that had rotated through Basra since then had taken on this task with some gusto. Without targets to fire their big guns at, SSR offered a good way to keep the Royal Artillery at the centre of the operation in Iraq and on the Operation Telic order of battle. The Royal Artillery had carried out a similar role in Bosnia and Kosovo, where it specialised in what was loosely termed "warring factions" liaison and mentoring with local military, paramilitary and militia forces.

Lieutenant Colonel Iain Harrison, commanding officer of 3rd Regiment Royal Horse Artillery, who led this effort in Basra in late 2005, said this encompassed 13,357 Iraqi Police Service (IPS) officers, including 4,898 in the city of Basra and 8,459 in rural areas, working from 70 police stations. While the 300 strong SSR battlegroup concentrated its efforts on mentoring and monitoring the Basra chief of police and his headquarters staff, the three ground holding battlegroups took on looking after police stations across the city, as well as police elements, such as the 580-strong paramilitary Tactical Support Unit, which had a province wide remit and was essentially the Basra governor's bodyguard and enforcement squad.[21]

The Basra city battlegroup was the largest ground-holding unit, and it had the most politically sensitive and high profile role looking after Iraqi police in the main residential areas of the city. The rural battlegroups also had responsibility for looking after local units of the 5,000-strong Directorate of Border Enforcement (BDE), which manned border crossing points on the Iranian and Kuwaiti borders, as well as Umm Qasr port and a nascent civil passenger terminal at Basra International Airport.[22]

Maysan province was the responsibility of a separate British battlegroup, dubbed Task Force Maysan, and its commanding officer ran all the governance and SSR activities that were carried out by the brigade in Basra but with fewer staff officers and only 1,200 troops. There were some 3,000 IPS, 940 DBE and 4,000 Facilities Protection Service (FPS) personnel in Maysan in mid 2005, as well as an army brigade of some 3,000 troops.[23]

In March 2005 after the withdrawal of Dutch troops, British troops also took on responsibility for al Muthanna province and 600 strong Task Force

Eagle began engaging with the local political and security organisations in this largely desert region that included a long section of border with Saudi Arabia. As well as the core IPS service, there was a plethora of other police bodies operating in Basra, including the 7,000 strong FPS, as well as Scientific Support, Serious Crimes Unit, Department of Internal Affairs (DIA), Central Investigations Unit (CIU), Auxiliary Police (APF), Courts Police (CP), City Reaction Force (CRF), Permanent Vehicle Checkpoint Police (PVCP), Schools and Colleges Police (SCP), Banks Police (BP), Governorate Guard (GG) and the Traffic Police (TP). The leaderships of these organisation, which controlled some 12,000 armed men, had to be monitored by the SSR battlegroup, further complicating its work.[24]

The basic training of all these Iraqi police and civilian security organisations was the responsibility of civilian contractors, funded by the US government. Other US civilian advisors were hired to work with the senior Iraqi police leadership and the Foreign and Commonwealth Office (FCO) dispatched a contingent of serving and senior retired police officers from Britain to help the training effort. The American and British police advisors had diametrically different views on how their Iraqi charges should be trained, mentored and monitored, effectively leaving the British Army leadership in Basra to come up with their own ideas and put them into action. Many senior officers were aware this was a far from optimal situation and the results would be mixed.

"No one else was available to train the police, so the army had to step into try to do it," said Torpy. "The British Army can train other armies.

We were not good at training the police." [25]

General Riley made a rather blunter assessment, describing the police training as "a shambles".

"It was a shambles because it was given to the FCO to run," he recalled, asking "how can the FCO be responsible for such a thing? He said the Home Office might have been more appropriate but British policing and legal models did not fit Iraq's Roman/continental/paramilitary police model. "The correct lead nation for police training should have been the Italians, via the carabinieri," he said. "In the event, the military gradually took the lead as the mix of contractors, UK civil policemen and Americans simply did not do the job".[26]

The bulk of the mentoring and monitoring work involved British and Danish troops making daily visits to Iraqi police stations to see what was happening, strike up relationships with local police commanders and rank and file cops, as well as going out on joint patrols. The later idea was to give British troops a chance to pass on low level skills to the police. Colonel Hopkinson of the Highlanders, explained that most of the IPS had gone through basic training run by previous British forces in Iraq, saying, "the most effective way to [build up police] was training through operations as that all the [patrols], when they visited stations, encouraged the IPS out on patrol with them." [27]

The scale of this undertaking was immense, as on any day, more than 1,500 troops across southern Iraq would be out making visits to police stations, conducting joint patrols and helping the police carry out specific operations. Two or three times as many troops were involved in making this happening, repairing vehicles, manning command posts, providing medical support and operating helicopters in support.

There were plans to dramatically expand the Iraqi Army, which had previously been the Iraqi Civil Defence Corps and then Iraqi National Guard, in the south after the declaration of sovereignty in June 2004, with the aim of ultimately having a division of troops in place around Basra. By mid 2005, the 10th Division Headquarters had been set up in Basra, and four subordinate brigades established in each of the four southern provinces, but it had not been possible to recruit and train enough soldiers to expand the number of battalions from six to the required 10 battalions.[28]

Training of the Iraqi army took place at two levels, with recruits undergoing basic training at the regional training centre at Talill airbase, outside Nasiriyah. This was run by a combined Iraqi, US, British and Australian staff. Once recruits reached their units in Basra and Maysan province they received more training from visiting British army trainers, detached from the ground holding battalions, while British officers visited the Iraqi battalion commanders to see how they were getting on.

The British concept of engagement with Iraqi police and security forces was based on a system of visits, rather than co-locating or embedding, as it subsequently became known, small contingents of troops to live and work with their Iraqi counter-parts. The killing of six Royal Military Police soldiers in Majar al Kabir, in June 2003, made British commanders very wary of leaving small detachments of troops on their own inside Iraqi bases.

"There was an institutional reluctance in the senior echelon of the British Army to doing embedding," said Air Chief Marshal Torpy. "Maybe it was the Majar al Kabir effect. The army thought there was undue risk in embedding."[29]

There was also a fear that the Iraqi police would come under attack just because they had British troops inside their bases. Senior officers in Iraq and back in the UK thought that co-location would make the Iraqis over reliant on British advisors, and they would never have any incentive to stand on their own feet.

"They had to stand on their own feet, and we could not act as a crutch or they would never make progress," said Torpy.[30]

At the time, the embedding policy was not controversial and only became an issue in late 2007 and early 2008, when Iraqi units really did have to operate on their own. As a result British troops lived in large main bases that were relatively easy to protect, with officers and troops on engagement tasks who would commute to work in small convoys. The favoured mode of travel was the Snatch Land Rover and the ground holding battlegroups were re-organised to operate these vehicles to their best advantage to provide security during monitoring visits around Basra. Throughout this period the basic British infantry unit was a 12-strong squad known as a multiple, which would operate from three Snatch Land Rovers. This formation was lifted straight from Northern Ireland.

Each multiple had enough troops to carry out basic tasks, such as setting up a vehicle checkpoint, cordoning a building during a search operation or providing security to move small groups of passengers around Basra.

Despite all the effort to build up the Iraqi police in Basra, it was soon clear to British officers and soldiers involved in the SSR campaign that it was producing distinctly mixed results.

"After working with the Iraqi Police Service for a short while, we soon established that they were ill-equipped, undisciplined, untrained and lazy, the Iraqi Army on the other hand were badly equipped but were keen to improve and performed in a far more professional manner," recalled one officer of the RDG involved in the SSR.[31]

"The problem is that the Iraqi Security Forces are like an elastic band", commented Major Johnny Austin, of the 1st Battalion, The Royal Regiment of Fusiliers (1 RRF).

"You can stretch them so far through training but as soon as you let them go, they'll revert back to their normal shape and size. Culturally, they're very different than us and it was hard to impress upon them the importance of certain things. They were very impressed by new pieces of equipment but they weren't necessarily impressed by new pieces of instruction or new information."[32]

The police was considered almost beyond redemption by almost every British soldier who came into contact with it during 2004 and 2005. At one point the army and police were even fighting each other. Lieutenant Colonel Ben Bathurst, who led the Welsh Guards to al Amarah in November 2004, described how when he arrived in Maysan the Iraqi police and army "were barely on speaking terms and frequently fought each other".[33]

Colonel Hopkinson said when his Highlanders visited police stations around Basra during late 2005, it was a struggle to get the police to go out on joint patrols, commenting, "for the multiples this was a frustrating experience as they sought to winkle out reluctant policemen who were only too happy to sit in their stations doing nothing."[34]

The main leverage the British had over the police, was the promise of new equipment and weapons and the visits to police stations often turned into prolonged bargaining sessions. A Royal Dragoons Guards soldier described the attitude of senior Iraqi police officers, who recalled, "the hoarding of Gucci equipment (soldier's term used to refer to decent military kit) by the senior representatives of different Iraqi organisations is a simple reality in a country built on mistrust and riddled with corruption. The commanders want the equipment either as a status symbol, to sell on the black market or as an incentive or perk for those below them to work to their methods, i.e. you do this dodgy job for me and I'll give you a nice new shiny pistol."[35]

Major Wood, of the King's Own Royal Border Regiment, described how after a few weeks of visiting police stations in central Basra, "it became obvious that most of the low level policemen were an acceptable standard. They were clearly not going to be the Cumbrian Constabulary but at least they had grasped the rudiments of keeping their districts safe as possible. Whereas the 'bobby on the beat' was keen and enthusiastic, their commanders were not."[36]

The cultural issue of authority, power, knowledge and privilege began to make progress very difficult, commented Wood, who identified influence by competing political parties as a major issue preventing the development of the police.

"With no concept of routine patrolling, community policy, delegation and planning this weakness started to exasperate itself which in turn prevented us from taking significant steps to guaranteeing security," he said.

"Coupled with this was the inherent corruption – to be an officer in the Police one to had to be part of one of the religious parties that were dominating the city. So without authorisation from their masters, the commanders would do nothing and made the premise of jointery a farce. Many a times the boys would arrive at a police station ready to conduct a joint patrol, and be faced with at best blank faces, at worst down right refusal to co-operate, So off we would go alone, at all hours of the day, frustrated and a little unsure of why it was we were here."[37]

The same issues were prevalent in Maysan, according to Major N.M Niblett of the 1st Battalion, The Staffordshire Regiment.

"Whereas the Iraqi Army and Tactical Support Unit (TSU) were far more receptive and grateful for the investment in their training and equipment, this was not so with respect to the police" he recalled.

"Their overwhelming concern was the acquisition of equipment and investment in their infra-structure. Furthermore, the police were also most sectarian in terms of tribes, local politics and their support for SCIRI and Badr [political parties]. The TSU were reported to be infiltrated – mainly by Office Muqtada al Sadr supporters. All of these various allegiances (led by their chain of command) had a direct impact on whether these organisations were co-operating or otherwise with the [coalition forces] or indeed with each other."[38]

Through the spring and summer of 2005, the feeling was gaining momentum in the higher reaches of the British government and military, that the UK had done enough to prepare the Iraqis. It was now time to kick off the process of handing over to them as a precursor for a rapid withdrawal of British troops. The big hope of the British was the Iraqi army with many officers being upbeat about its prospects.

"One has to hope that its bright future shines through and overcomes less positive aspects to this potentially wonderful country," said an RDG officer in 2005.

"The Iraqi army is perceived by the local populus to be less corrupt and more effective that the police in combating crime and terrorism. The army would appear to be less susceptible to bribery and act more effectively on local intelligence. The army certainly forms the backbone in enforcing and maintaining a secure environment in southern Iraq."[39]

Major General Jim Dutton described the Iraqi army as the "Jewel in the Crown" of SSR effort when he handed over command of the British division in Basra in December 2005, but warned that "sustainability and depth is wafer thin" in his end of tour report.[40]

The training efforts with the Iraqi army started to show some improvements during 2005, and by the summer the British were increasingly confident about the qualities of the new force, even if the police were universally considered a lost cause. In September, the prospective leader of the SSR battlegroup, Colonel Harrison, told a briefing of officers heading to Iraq on the Operation Telic 7 tour later in the year that the local army units were performing well on patrols directed by the British brigade.

"They have had huge success recently in operations," he said. "The SSR drive had reached a plateau and this was as good as it was going to get."[41]

Fry's self confident manner and command of his brief – he had been chief of staff at PJHQ during the 2003 invasion - ensured the military's view was heard in the corridors of power. With positive feedback coming from Iraq in the spring and summer of 2005, Walker and Fry began to develop plans with General Riley in Iraq to accelerate the draw down of troop numbers and to move from British control of security to a position of overwatch, with the Iraqis stepping up their role.

This was in line with the view from Baghdad, where General Casey was starting to generate proposals to begin significantly ramping down US troop numbers, and was soon pushing for the UK to begin following suit to keep in step with their ally.[42] Fry told the Chilcot inquiry that the intention was for the British force in Iraq to be significantly reduced by the end of 2006 to allow a build up of troops in Afghanistan. A series of draw-down planning options were developed, to allow the Army's Land Command headquarters in 2005 to start planning future rotations of troops to Iraq and Afghanistan. The most optimistic plan envisaged that there would only be a 1,000 strong battlegroup in Iraq at the end of 2006, acting as a reserve force for the Iraqi army and police, from a base at Basra airport. It was proposed that Maysan and Al Muthanna would be handed over to Iraqi security control in March 2006, Basra would go in July and the Italians were to leave Dhi Qar in the summer of 2006.[43]

In September 2005, Colonel Harrison told the Iraq-bound officers that Maysan was to move to tactical overwatch in November 2005, and remote small bases through the province would be closed the following month, with Camp Abu Naji outside al Amarah being closed in January/February 2006. Overwatch would see British troops standing back in Basra or patrolling in rural areas to re-intervene if the Iraqis lost control. He predicted that this "should have minimal impact on the province".[44]

The Iraqi army's 4th Brigade in Maysan was well equipped, organised and trained with less influence from tribal organisations, he said. They had completed brigade level exercises and had approached the British to join them on counter-insurgency operations, led and planned by themselves. This proposed arrangement was "not too much of a problem, really" said the Colonel.

Muthanna was also progressing well and the IPS in the desert region were assessed to be at a suitable level for a move to overwatch at the target date of 30 October 2005, along with the army battalion in the province, said Harrison. The positive gloss on things from London and Baghdad was not shared by commanders on the ground in Basra, and they often hedged their bets about the prospect of accelerating transition. Even in November 2004, the British commander in Basra, General Riley, refused to set specific deadlines for any handover to Iraqi control and withdrawal, citing the need for it to be condition based. Things moved on at a pace during 2005.

Despite the optimistic view from London and some in Basra, it seems some senior British officers were still not ready yet to make a firm prediction when Basra's security would be judged ready to begin transition to Iraqi control. Air Marshal Torpy urged caution in a letter to Dutton in Basra in August 2005, describing the timelines for Maysan and Muthanna overwatch as "informed guesses" but hoped it would induce a "mindset of eventual drawdown and to initiate the required detailed staff work". He described a proposed timeline for the handover of Basra's security to the Iraqis in July 2006 as "tentative," and dependent on political conditions. However, the six-monthly force level review in August 2006 set in train the drawdown of British troop numbers, with proposals that some 1,000 troops be cut from the size of the Operation Telic 8 tour that was due to start in May 2006.[45]

General Dutton's tour of command in the summer and autumn of 2005 was meant to set the conditions for the withdrawal.

"We were really quite optimistic about what was happening in Iraq, certainly in southeast Iraq, at that period in 2005," he told the Chilcot inquiry. "I can remember being told actually, in my briefings in the Ministry of Defence, that my job was to go there for six months and make sure nothing went wrong because things were going right and, you know, just keep the thing ticking over and we will be okay. There will be the referendum, there will be the elections, there will be a government and all will be well."[46]

OPERATION TELIC IMAGES, 2003 TO 2009

Video imagery of Basra from a Phoenix unmanned aerial vehicle, March 2003 (BAE Systems)

16 Air Assault Brigade arrives in the Rumaylah oil field, March 2003 (US Combat Camera)

7th Royal Horse Artillery open fire on Iraq, March 2003 (BAE Systems)

RAF Tornado GR4 aircraft at Ali Al Salem airbase in Kuwait, March 2003 (Tim Ripley)

Jubilant Iraqis greet British troops in Basra (private collection)

1st Battalion, The Royal Regiment of Fusiliers cross the berm into Iraq, March 2003. (Coalition PIC pool image)

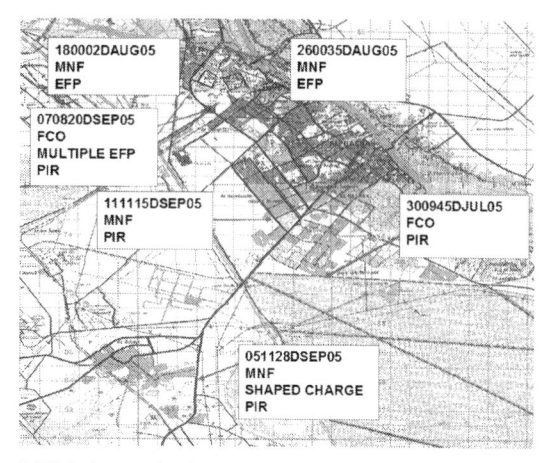

Militia improvised explosive device attacks, September 2006

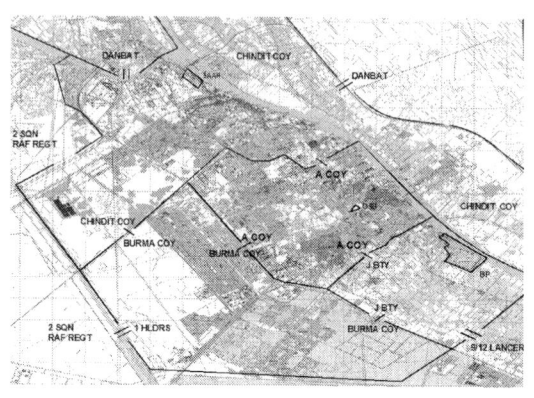

Basra City Brigade area of operations, March 2006 (bottom)

Air Vice Marshal Glenn Torpy, UK Air Component commander March 2003 (Tim Ripley) (left); Air Marshal Sir Brian Burridge, UK National Component Commander in Middle East March 2003; (Tim Ripley) (centre); Brigadier Adrian Bradshaw, deputy commander of special forces task force in western Iraq March 2003 and then commander 7 Armoured Brigade in Basra (NATO) (right)

Lieutenant General John Reith, Chief of Joint Operations March 2003 (Tim Ripley) (left); Major General Robin Brims, commander 1 (UK) Armoured Division March 2003 (US DoD) (centre); Brigadier Graham Binns, commander 7 Armoured Brigade, March-April 2003 (US DoD) (right)

Brigadier Jacko Page commander 16 Air Assault Brigade March 2003 (Tim Ripley) (left); Rear Admiral David Snelson, UK Maritime Component commander March 2003 (Tim Ripley) (centre); Brigadier Peter Wall, Chief of Staff of UK National Component Headquarters March 2003 (Tim Ripley) (right)

The strike operation on the Al Jameat police station, September 2005 (private collection)

British troops move out into Basra for a night-time strike operation in Snatch Land Rover in early 2006. (UK MOD/Crown Copyright)

The impact of explosively former projectile on a Snatch Land Rover (private collection)

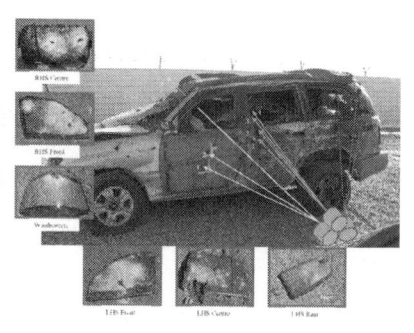

The impact of explosively former projectile on a Foreign and Commonwealth Office armoured SUV (private collection)

EFP Find 20 Jul 05

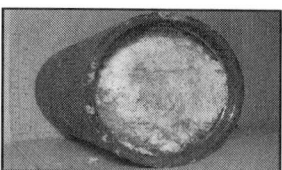

EFP Find 16 Sep 05

Explosively formed projectiles captured by British troops in 2005 (private collection)

Basra's police was notoriously poorly trained, corrupt and heavily influenced by Shia militias. (Tim Ripley)

A Muqtadr al Sadr propaganda poster in Basra (private collection)

The tented accommodation at Shaibah Logistic Base in 2005 (private collection)

Militia graffiti in Basra designed to undermine the morale of British troops (private collection)

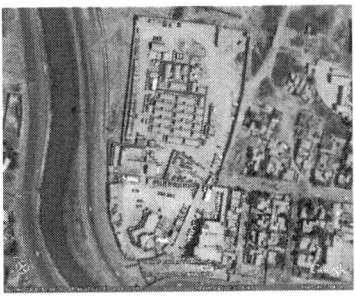

A Google Earth satellite image of the British base in the Old State Building seized from a militia safe house in 2005 (private collection)

The introduction of the new Mastiff Mine-Resistant Ambush Protected (MRAP) in 2007 transformed the protection available to British troops in southern Iraq. (UK MOD/Crown Copyright)

A British Army patrol with a Snatch Land Rover in the back streets of Basra in 2005. Commanders said the vehicle was ideal in such terrain. (private collection)

Major General Jim Dutton, commander Multi-National Division South East June 2005 (NATO) (left); General David Petraeus, commander US forces in Iraq January 2007 and Brigadier Nick Carter, commander 20 Armoured Brigade March 2004. (NATO) (right)

Major General Graeme Lamb, commander Multi-National Division South East July 2003 (Tim Ripley) (left); Major General John Cooper, commander Multi-NationalDivision South East December 2005 (US Army) (centre); Brigadier Bill Moore, commander 19 Mechanised Brigade July 2003 (Tim Ripley) (right)

Major General Barney While-Spunner, commander Multi-National Division South East January 2008 (Tim Ripley) (left); Major General Jonathan Shaw, commander Multi-National Division South East
January-August 2007 (right)

Chapter 19

THE DIVORCE

The January 2005 Iraqi election introduced a significant new dynamic into the situation that the British could not control. Iraqis voted in large numbers for politicians and parties who were implacably opposed to Britain's presence in their country. This set in train a series of events that would eventually lead to British withdrawals from Maysan, and then Basra, under conditions that would look like retreats under fire. Militia commanders would claim to have driven out the British.

The parliamentary and provincial government elections across southern Iraq returned to power candidates from parties hostile to a continued British presence. The provincial councils in both Maysan and Basra were dominated by Shia parties, and they in turn elected governors with impeccable anti-British credentials. In Maysan the governor, Adel Mahudar Radi or al Maliki, was a former Jaish al-Mahdi (JAM) or Mahdi army militia commander, and the governor of Basra, Mohammed al-Waili, was a leading member of the Fadhilla party, which was a mouthpiece for Sadr's movement. They were demanding an immediate withdrawal of British troops from southern Iraq's streets.

The British Ministry of Defence hired an opinion poll company in 2005 to find out what the people of Basra thought, and it seemed to suggest the city's politicians had broad backing. The insurgents attacking British troops were given a 30% approval rating, 48% thought British troops should leave within six months and 84% felt that security should be provided by Iraqi forces alone. 91% felt safer when they saw Iraqi police, and 67% said they felt somewhat or much less secure when they saw British troops.

The quixotic British diplomat who had worked in the Coalition Provincial Authority in al Amarah, Rory Stewart, returned to Maysan after the January election to see the new governor installed in office.

"The Sadrist [governor] was elected with ninety percent of the vote [by the provincial council]. In his acceptance speech the new Sadrist governor deliberately avoided recognising the foreigners in the audience. Within a month he had sacked the old ministry directors, calling them Ba'athists, and replaced them with his own men. He announced he would no longer allow Iraqi police to patrol with coalition forces. The number of attacks on the coalition increased."[1]

For British commanders in Iraq the onset of democracy seemed to convince them that their exit strategy was working. Lieutenant Colonel Ben Bathurst of the Welsh Guards who led Task Force Maysan in early 2005, told Stewart, "the governor is a moderate, reasonable, intelligent technocrat. He campaigns against corruption. We are quite happy to go if they want us to leave."[2]

The British, however, were locked into keeping their timetable for withdrawal in sync with the Americans, and there was no prospect of speeding it up. Keeping on side with the US was the underlying objective of British policy, so this was not really a surprise. Prime Minister Tony Blair had declared that British troops had "entered Iraq as part of a coalition and would leave as a coalition". There would be no full withdrawal of British troops until the US forces in Baghdad had defeated the predominantly Sunni insurgency. The British army would have to stay in southern Iraq for some time yet, and it would be another year before the government in London decided to accelerate the withdrawal process.

"The issue was our credibility," recalled Air Marshal Glenn Torpy, then the Chief of Joint Operations, of the mood in early 2005.

"We went into the Iraq operation together with the Americans, so we said we would leave together. It was a sense of responsibility. It is not easy for the UK to leave unilaterally. That is why we have a unique relationship with the US. We not only delivered capability to the coalition but we are a reliable ally. That is vitally important when we want a favour from the Americans. If you want to have a long term strategic relationship, you have got to take the consequences of that. You can't just support the Americans when the going is good."[3]

For southern Iraq's Shia insurgents the last months of 2004, and the spring of 2005, were a chance to rebuild their strength after the heavy losses during the Sadr uprisings. Moqtada al Sadr's decision to call a ceasefire after the intervention of Grand Ayatollah Sistani was deeply unpopular among the rank and file of his JAM militia. Several of the most determined militia leaders formed their own breakaway groups to continue the resistance to the US and British occupation. Others opened up contact with the Iranian Revolutionary Guards Quds Force in a bid to secure new arms supplies. These groups included the Asaib Ahl al-Haq or League of the Righteous, which evolved into one of the most professional and deadly Shia militia groups to confront the British in southern Iraq.[4]

The two most high profile JAM leaders at this time were Ahmed al-Fartosi in Basra, and Ahmed Abu Sajad al-Gharawi in Maysan. They had learnt their trade as insurgents against Saddam Hussein's rule in the 1990s and were determined and effective leaders of their fighters. Their growing mystique, as a result of their successful attacks on British troops between April and September 2004, in turn prompted a steady flow of recruits into the ranks of their respective groups. Gharawi's fighters provided some of the British army's most determined and effective opponents. Their leader would never be captured by the British and he still remains a mysterious figure.

The insurgent leader apparently had excellent contacts with the Iranians, and in the spring of 2004 his fighters started to receive a new type of IED, known as the explosive formed projectile (EFP), which had very improved armour-piercing qualities. The EFP was essentially a shaped charge device that on detonation created a super-heated high pressure jet of molten metal that could cut through armoured plate. To work properly, the EFP required very fine engineering and manufacturing processes, which US and British intelligence soon determined could only mean that the latest versions of EFPs were coming from Iran. The JAM also fielded passive infrared detonator, or PID, initiation technology; this was triggered by the heat of vehicles' engines which enabled them to control the detonation of IEDs to allow them to target specific British vehicles in ambushes. The tactical emplacement of the devices was very well planned, including planting chains of devices to target more than one vehicle, the targeting of weaknesses of specific vehicles, and advanced camouflage and concealment techniques, such as the use of painted expanding foam around a device to make them accurately resemble rocks.[5]

The JAM had access to huge quantities of weapons and explosives, the vast majority of which had been looted from Iraqi army bases in Maysan province in April 2003. Much of this had been seized by Maysan tribes and was then sold or given to militia groups. The quantities involved can be gauged from the increasing size of arms-finds during 2004 and 2005. On one occasion, a joint British-Danish operation dug up an ISO container jammed full of explosives and small arms ammunition in a rural location north-west of Basra.[6]

In the city of Basra, Fartosi was a more flamboyant and higher profile figure. He was well-known around the city, and after he fled Iraq in 2008 to the safety of Beirut he gave a series of media interviews describing his role in the anti-British insurgency. He read reports on the British military intently and tracked the movement of specific regiments in and out of Basra, as well as using Google Earth satellite imagery to identify targets inside British bases for his rocket and mortar teams.[7]

Although nominally a leader of the JAM in Basra, Fartosi seemed to have influence over several other militia groups across Basra and could mobilise them for co-ordinated operations.

Major Austin, of the Fusiliers, described the JAM as the "most effective" opponent faced by the British Army in southern Iraq, and dismissed the next largest groups, the Badr brigade and SICRI militia, as little more than "background noise".[8]

According to Austin, the JAMs had mastered sophisticated methods of initiation for IEDs and very effective shaped-charge IEDs.

"The ones that detonated in our area appeared to be military grade as opposed to the homemade stuff that was out there," he said.

"The JAM was very efficient," said Austin. "Their IED attacks were second to none. If you think about the time between 2003 and 2006, they had made leaps that took the Provisional IRA 30 years to make. The sophistication and accuracy of some of their attacks were unbelievable. In the early stages [of our tour between November 2005 and April 2006], we didn't encounter too much small arms and rocket propelled grenade contact, but that certainly changed towards the latter stages. There was certainly at least one sniper operating in Basra and certainly one operating in Maysan, where another one of our battle groups was based further north. The JAM, because Moqtada al-Sadr had pretty much unleashed the dogs, were busy. Their intelligence-gathering capability was obviously pretty good. They knew where to hit vehicles. They'd obviously conducted a full operational analysis of where it was better to hit vehicles."

"Although they launched attacks on some of our Warriors, they weren't ever able to defeat them. In Arab culture, if you can walk away from what should be your death that sends quite a good message. Indeed, a couple of our Warriors in the city were hit by huge EFP devices and just drove off, much to the disgust of the bombers. That forced the JAM in the Basra area to look at attacking foot patrols with snipers and multi-weapon shoots, as well as going for your classic dug-in IEDs with huge weights of explosives. While we were there, although they incurred some damage, no Warrior was defeated, which was very reassuring for the soldiers."[9]

Sadr fielded candidates in the parliamentary elections in 2005, and his representatives and political allies helped form the coalition government that emerged in Baghdad in the spring of that year. At the same time his Sadrist allies dominated the Basra and Maysan provincial councils. His placemen and allies had a central role in national and provincial governments that in public had agreed to co-operate with US and British forces. But it appeared that Sadr's militia commanders were let off the leash to attack them. At worse it seemed that he was unwilling to stop them.

Throughout 2005 and into 2006, British commanders began to notice an increasing co-ordination between political demands from the Basra and Maysan provincial councils, and the upsurges in insurgent attacks on their troops. Getting to the heart of who was actually pulling the strings among the British Army's opponents was a major challenge.

"Battlegroup headquarters attempted to understand the operating environment," commented Colonel Hopkinson of the Highlanders."

"It became clear very early on that although there was a plethora of information there was little intelligence, and that trying to untangle the web of militia, criminal, tribal and political links would be nearly impossible."

The task was not helped by the very poor computer infrastructure, from the number of computers to their applications, with intelligence databases being a particular weakness. The consistent failure to record digitally where British forces had patrolled brought the re-emergence of hand drawn 'honesty' traces or paper maps at sub-unit level. The traces were a simple tool for commanders to assess if troops were showing predictable movement and to link this with insurgent activity. This was 'steam driven' attempt to allow British and enemy tactics to be assessed. On Operation Telic 6, the Brigade Headquarters went as far as identifying an officer with a strong computer hobby expertise to build a basic reporting tool for patrols, but it was not successfully fielded to units.[10]

Predictably, Maysan province was to see insurgents restart their attacks on the British Army. After a honeymoon of a month after [the January 05] election [in Maysan] rockets and mortars became regular, and it was more dangerous to patrol at night, said a Welsh Guards officer. His regiment handed over to the 1st Battalion, The Staffordshire Regiment in April, and the province's new governor was soon locked into a struggle of wills with the new regiment's commanding officer, Lieutenant Colonel Andrew Williams.[11]

Rocket and mortar attacks on the main British base outside al Amarah, Camp Abu Naji, as well as night-time ambushes on British patrols in the city's limits had been escalating against the Welsh Guards, but when the Staffords arrived, attacks spiked to a new high. It was becoming very dangerous to move around al Amarah to mentor the Iraqi police and army units. According to the Staffords' officers, "the situation was exacerbated by the assessment that elements within the [Iraqi] security establishment (including at the highest levels) were at best, aware of who the perpetrators were and possibly contained elements that were actually 'involved' in the planning and conduct of these attacks."[12]

The Staffords launched Operation Thunderbolt to put out nighttime patrols, backed by snipers, into al Amarah's streets to try to turn the tables on the insurgent mortar and rocket teams. On the night of 1st/2nd May 2005, the JAM in al Amarah hit back using their latest weapon. The PID initiated an array of multiple IEDs, devastating a Snatch Land Rover operated by a patrol from the Coldstream Guards attached to the Staffords. The device sent a shower of shrapnel over the vehicle and fatally injured one of the top cover soldiers, who was exposed with his torso out of the vehicle. Examination of the wreckage and the remains of the IED revealed that the PID device defeated the electronic counter-measures on the Snatch.[13]

Colonel Williams responded by launching a series of raids in a bid to capture the perpetrators of the attacks. The day after the body of the dead Guardsman was flown out from the airstrip outside Camp Abu Naji, the Staffords launched a battlegroup-sized search and arrest operation in southern al Amarah. Operation Titanium targeted two compounds and arrested at least one known insurgent leader, as well as thirty other suspects.[14]

On 29th May, another British soldier was killed in an IED attack on a Land Rover patrol of the King's Royal Hussars, near the Iranian border in the east of Maysan. This saw the first confirmed use of EFP-equipped IEDs, which also injured two other members of the stripped-down and unarmoured Land Rover's crew.[15] Fortunately the array of a number of IEDs had not properly activated and a bomb disposal team were able to disarm it. The subsequent forensic examination determined the devices had been manufactured to a high specification. These were unlike any previous EFPs found to date in southern Iraq. The repercussions of intelligence assessments that the weapons came from Iran would spread across Iraq and the Middle East.[16]

Majar al Kabir was identified as the centre of the JAM in Maysan, and the Staffords' B Company intensified patrolling to interdict the IED teams, while a detachment of Special Air Service troops was dispatched from Baghdad to spearhead the effort. Further reinforcements from the British divisional reserve, the 1st Battalion, The Royal Regiment of Wales, surged into Maysan for the operation. The town was in ferment and according to Staffords soldiers, every time one of their patrols entered it there was a riot. Operations into the town were now only mounted with British and American fixed wing air support.[17]

In mid June, a battlegroup operation was planned to raid a house in the town, where the JAM leader Gharawi was suspected to be hiding. The operation almost ended in disaster when a Royal Navy Sea King helicopter, carrying a strike platoon to seize Gharawi, crashed on take off at Camp Abu Naji, injuring several of the soldiers. One had to be flown back to Britain for treatment. The SAS men and Staffords continued the operation on the ground, but their target had gone by the time the assault troops got to their objective.[18]

The Staffords' summer tour in Maysan was turning out to be very different to that experienced by the Princess of Wales's Royal Regiment the previous year. There were scores of small scale contacts, including around 60 fire fights and numerous riots in the centre of al Amarah, but no big battles or set-piece engagements. The insurgents had learnt their lessons and did not try to face the British in a stand-up fight. They restricted their attacks to night-time ambushes, rocket and mortar attacks, which were designed to disrupt the sleep of British troops and cause nuisance damage, trying to prompt them into making mistakes and becoming vulnerable to IEDs. The main method of killing British troops would be the new EFPs.

This was a war in the shadows, with both sides using fleeting information to select their targets. The Staffords were convinced that local Iraqi employees and policemen were passing information to the JAM so they could target their convoys. The British, meanwhile, had little information to act on.

During the course of the summer, the Staffords came under repeated IED attacks. The Regiment's C Company in al Amarah suffered the largest British loss in a single incident in Maysan, since the June 2003 killing of the six Royal Military Policemen. A patrol in al Amarah on 16th July was the first Snatch Land Rover to be penetrated by the new EFP, killing three of the crew and seriously injuring two other soldiers.[19]

The psychological impact on the British troops in the city was immense, as their vehicles appeared to be no longer invulnerable. Lance Sergeant Sutherland, of the Coldstream Guards, was ordered to participate in a show of force in Warriors in the area of the previous night's attack on the Staffords' vehicle.

"As we were forming up at the guardroom we heard an almighty explosion; this, together with a threat warning suggesting that there was a Vehicle-Borne IED roaming around town, and the previous night's devastating events, immediately put my nerves on edge," he recalled.

"At this point it would have been difficult to speculate on the mood of the rest of my Half – Multiple; however all the quips, one liners and daft jokes Guardsmen are famous for seemed to have suddenly stopped. We then set off on the journey to the southern part of al Amarah; a journey which, though short in distance, seemed to take ages. I suppose at the time I had taken it for granted that, because I had done three operational tours of Northern Ireland and one of Bosnia, and never had to cock my weapon in anger, that this tour would be similar. It had dawned on me before I even deployed that this was a very different kettle of fish and there was a very real threat to life. However, my attitude has always been that this is what I agreed to do when I signed on the dotted line."[20]

Immediately, Colonel Williams ordered the light armoured Snatches off the roads of Maysan. In future all vehicle movement in al Amarah would be by Warrior. Major Mike Niblett, who commanded the troops who were killed in the 16th July attack, recalled that "two of the three fatal attacks were assessed to having been initiated using passive infra-red sensors for which we have no counter-measures. Following the attack of 16th July it was clear that it had become unfeasible for Task Force Maysan to operate outside our base other than in Warrior."[21]

The Challengers of the King's Royal Hussars now accompanied every major operation, including a major raid on Majar al Kabir on 6th August. Two weeks later the big tanks were out on the streets again, to help set up a cordon as part of an operation to defuse a 35 kilogram IED. More sophisticated IEDs came into play, including command wire and radio controlled devices, which were used against the Staffords' Warriors on two occasions in early August. Fortunately, there were no major injuries, and the electronic counter-measures on the Warriors defeated the radio controlled-IEDs in one of the attacks. The Staffords continued their cat and mouse game with the JAM IED teams for the remainder of their tour, but soon the crisis in Maysan would be overtaken by events in Basra city two weeks later.

An armoured four-wheel drive vehicle driven by a Foreign and Commonwealth Office (FCO) security detail, from the private company Controlled Risks Group, was targeted by an EFP on the outskirts of Basra on 30th July. The EFP passed straight through the vehicle's armour, killing one person and fatally wounding another.[22]

Lance Corporal Nicholas Wright, a medic with the Staffords, was one of the first British soldiers on the scene.

"The IED had been detonated on a stretch of road and dirt track that can only be described as desolate, overlooked on one side by desert and two hundred metres away on the other side by the al Quibla estate, separated by a dried lake of human waste. The vehicle had been travelling along at high speed when the EFP was detonated, but it had penetrated the vehicle's armour like a hot knife through butter. With the driver dead the vehicle travelled a further hundred metres before coming off the road, hitting a dune, flipping and coming to a halt facing the way it had come from."[23]

In the time it took the rescue party to get to the wreckage of the vehicle, the victim was stripped of his weapon, passport and wedding ring by looters, bringing home to the soldiers dealing with the incident the unforgiving nature of the fight they were in. Over the next six weeks the British Army and diplomatic vehicles were systematically targeted in Basra by the new improved IEDs. EFP attacks on 18th and 26th August damaged vehicles and wounded soldiers. Then on 5th September, two soldiers of the 1st Battalion, The Royal Regiment of Fusiliers were killed in a PID initiated EFP near Zubayr. Another FCO vehicle was targeted two days later with a PID EFP. Then an Intelligence Corps major was killed in another PID-initiated attack on 11th September.[24]

This escalating series of attacks did not go without a reaction from the British brigade in Basra. Its commander, Brigadier John Lorimer, was an aggressive Parachute Regiment officer with many tours of duty in Northern Ireland under his belt; he had also served as the commanding office of 3rd Battalion, the Parachute Regiment as part of 16 Air Assault Brigade in the invasion of Iraq. His chief of staff was Major Rupert Jones, who also had a reputation for decisive decision-making.

In the aftermath of the first EFP attacks hitting Basra, orders were given to start improving the fortification of British bases in the city and to restrict movement in high threat area to Warriors.

"There is no doubt that the presence of Warriors in the City saved men's lives," recalled Major Andrew Hadfield of the Staffords company in Basra.

"There is no certainty that Warriors would survive the largest devices used by the terrorists, but they had a better chance than the lightly armoured Land Rovers used by other companies. Conducting those operations with just fourteen Warriors left both men and machines very tired, and I sense that our trusty steeds were almost at the end of their serviceability when we were relieved by the Highlanders."[25]

Lorimer and Jones were, this time, determined to take the fight to the insurgents. Like many other British officers in Basra, they were convinced that the JAM bomb-making teams were getting inside help from the Iraqi police - either because they were followers of Sadr or had been intimidated.

"The JAM had definitely infiltrated the local security forces – not the army, but definitely the police," commented Major Austin.

"As such, the police were generally complicit in most terrorist actions."[26]

The British military and police leadership in Basra had already become exasperated with the Iraqi police in the city, and were already preparing lists of corrupt policemen or ones with links to insurgent groups. These had been passed to the Iraqi Interior Ministry in Baghdad, but the police in Basra were protected by their allies in the capital and the Basra governor's office. All attempts to sack the members on the list were rebuffed. Political protection for insurgent groups was now a growing issue, because the Shia-coalition government in Baghdad was dependent on the votes of Sadr supporters to stay in power. Prime Minister Ibrahim al-Eshaiker al-Jafari demanded a veto on all US and British arrest operations against senior political figures and insurgent leaders. A notable figure on the no-arrest list in September 2005 was the leader of the JAM militia in Basra, Ahmed Fartosi. He lived openly in Basra and seemed convinced that he was untouchable.[27]

The fatal EFP attacks prompted Brigadier Lorimer to take action. He had the power to overrule the orders of the Baghdad government if he thought

British lives were at risk. His immediate superior, General Dutton, was at this point on holiday in the south of France, and Lorimer had the authority to act on his own.

The Basra Brigade's Surveillance Company (BSC), led by Major James Woodham of the Royal Anglian Regiment, and a small team of SAS covert surveillance operatives, were tasked to keep a close watch on Fartosi and other suspected insurgent leaders, including a senior police officer, Captain Jaffar. They set about photographing their targets' homes from the air and the ground, to allow assault troops to carry out raids to capture them.

BSC troops used long-range cameras to photograph their targets, while the SAS operatives donned civilian clothes and drove local cars to get close to the suspects and get a street-level feel for the situation. They also called in Royal Navy Sea King HC4 helicopters fitted with night-vision video cameras, nicknamed Broadsword, to watch and trail suspects in real time as they moved around Basra.

With Fartosi positively located, Brigadier Lorimer gave the go-ahead for him to be captured on the night of 17th September. The local battlegroup, the Coldstream Guards, provided the outer cordon, while the Brigade Operations Company from the 1st Battalion, The Royal Anglian Regiment provided the inner cordon, and immediate support for an SAS detachment from Baghdad to conduct the arrest.[28] Fartosi was carried kicking and screaming from his home into the back of a Warrior, before being delivered to the Divisional Temporary Detention Facility at Shaibah Logistic Base. He famously has tried to sue the British government claiming he was mistreated during his arrest.

Events were now moving very fast, and the British commanders had little time to celebrate their success. During the morning of 19th September, two SAS surveillance operatives were out on task in western Basra trying to track down Captain Jaffar. Iraqi police spotted the two soldiers in their car and surrounded them. Before long they were overpowered, and taken to Captain Jaffar's Jamiat police station, where they were roughed up and filmed. Once the images were broadcast on Arab television channels it ignited a major crisis.[29]

In the police station, the local police lost control of the two hostages to officers loyal to the Department of Internal Affairs, who in turn were loyal to Sadr supporters in Baghdad. British troops were scouring Basra looking for the two missing men. Eventually they were located at the Jamiat and a stand-off ensued. A British negotiating team led by Major Woodham entered the police station, while Warriors and infantry from the Basra-based company of the Staffords ringed the building to stop anyone escaping. Reinforcements from the Coldstream Guards and Royal Regiment of Wales arrived, along with the Guard's commanding officer, Lieutenant Colonel Nick Henderson.

The Iraqi Basra City Reaction Force, a paramilitary police unit, then arrived to beef up the defences of the Jamiat. Large crowds were now harassing the British cordon, throwing stones and petrol bombs. In an iconic image of the day, one Staffords' Warrior was set on fire and the burning crew only just managed to escape from their vehicle. The British troops responded with rubber bullets. When the Iraqis opened up with RPGs, the British fired 127 rounds at their attackers. The Iraqi Police Service (IPS) reported that eight people were killed and 43 wounded in the rioting and subsequent gun battles. Two Staffords were badly burned and seven other British troops were seriously injured. Seven Warriors were badly damaged and two were beyond repair.[30]

At Basra airport, Brigadier Lorimer was running the operation, which was becoming highly complex, as he tried to get the government in Baghdad to free his men. At PJHQ near London, and at the Ministry of Defence, there was pandemonium as ministers and military chiefs struggled to work out what was happening and decide what to do. There were fears that if a gun battle developed between the British troops and the police, it would set Basra alight.

What happened next is controversial. In Baghdad, Lieutenant Colonel Richard Williams, 22 SAS Regiment's commanding officer, immediately dispatched a squadron of his troops to Basra when he first heard about the incident. They wanted to storm the police station but by the time they were ready, the hostages were in the process of being moved out of the police station. A Broadsword Sea King spotted the two soldiers being loaded into a car and tracked them.

Brigadier Lorimer now gave permission for the Royal Regiment of Wales Warriors, led by two King's Royal Hussars Challengers, to storm the police station, crushing through walls and driving over several British-supplied police cars. They secured the police station and recovered the SAS men's weapons and equipment.[31]

Elsewhere in Basra, the SAS squadron stormed the compound where their men were held, and released them without firing a shot. Their captors had abandoned them. Seven years on from this incident, it is not clear if the final SAS raid was authorised by Brigadier Lorimer or PJHQ, leading to accusations from within the SAS that ministers in London were prepared to sacrifice their men to buy peace in Basra.[32]

The incident provoked outrage among the pro-Sadr political leadership in Basra. Governor Waeli denounced the British as terrorists. He demanded Brigadier Lorimer's dismissal, and that British troops stay out of Basra and ordered the police to stop co-operating with the British. On the streets the insurgents continued planting IEDs and mortaring British bases, apparently with the backing of the city's governor.

In London, the government was looking for a response. The former Chief Constable of the Royal Ulster Constabulary, Sir Ronnie Flanagan, was dispatched to Basra to review plans to reform the Iraqi police and see if anything new could be done.[33] The troops were ordered to return to their SSR mission and a charm offensive was to be mounted to persuade Governor Waeli to relent.

For several weeks a stand-off ensued, culminating in the death of a Coldstream Guards Sergeant on 18th October, when he set off an IED while patrolling on foot after dismounting from his vehicle. There were clear hints that the IPS had been involved in reporting the movement of the Coldstream 'multiple,' or patrol, to ensure a successful attack by the perpetrators.[34] The Highlanders of Colonel Hopkinson were now in the process of taking over from the Coldstream Guards and Staffords as the Basra City Battlegroup. The colonel described the atmosphere as "tense, with little engagement" between the governor, provincial council, the IPS and the British Army.[35]

Major A.G.S Hutton, of the Highlanders' A Company, who operated in the city, described the governor of Basra as being "Anti Multi-National [coalition] Forces", who "relishes the opportunity to make such an order to bolster his apparent power within the various militia and political factions within the city."[36]

"The city was in the grip of a sustained IED campaign that was being waged against the Multi-National Force," recalled Hopkinson.

"We identified early on the need to rebuild bridges with the city, and in particular the IPS, and regain trust and the much needed consent to operate."[37]

This was easier said than done, as the IED threat continued to force the use of Warriors deep inside the city. This soaked up so many troops that there were few troops left over to re-start the liaison visits to police stations. There was no blanket ban on the use of Snatch Land Rover, because it would have effectively ground the British operation in the city to a halt. An extra company of Warriors was brought with 7 Armoured Brigade, crewed by soldiers of the Queen's Royal Lancers, in order to act as battle taxis, and General Dutton was able to temporarily secure extra helicopter flying hours to reduce the number of vehicle movements.[38] But not every commander in Basra was keen on using the big Warriors, because they were restricted to a few routes that could take their width and areas that could take their 30 ton weight.

"Ultimately this made the job of insurgents a bit easier, and in a short period from the start of our tour, three Warriors had been hit by roadside bombs, causing significant damage to the vehicles, but fortunately not to the occupants," recalled Major Jonny Crook, who led the Brigade Operations Company at this time.

"In contrast, we could take a far greater variety of routes in the more mobile Snatch vehicles but had really no inherent protection. This was a great concentrator of the mind and key factor in our constantly-evolving dynamic of tactical movement. It is a testament to our commanders that we did not experience a successful IED attack."[39]

"The early part of the tour of [my Warrior company in the city] was particularly difficult, as they bore the brunt of vital protection tasks to ensure that there was safe transit into the city from outside, "said Hopkinson.

"This entailed the clearance and securing of routes, which effectively prevented them from developing their area of responsibility for the first six weeks. We had sixteen attacks over the period, and in many cases were saved by the protection afforded in up-armoured Warriors."[40]

Another EFP attack left a Sergeant of the Fusiliers dead on 20th November, with Colonel Hopkinson reporting, "there was little doubt that there was

IPS complicity in the attack in that it occurred only some 250 metres from an IPS district headquarters station."[41]

British troops on the ground were not inclined to cut the IPS any slack, and openly regarded them as part of the insurgency, accusing them of tipping off their movements to the JAM by activating the horns and flashing lights on their police cars when British troops approached.

"Our soldiers were particularly wary when they saw police cars flashing their lights and generally stopped them and searched them," said Major Austin of the Fusiliers.

"We were fortunate in that we didn't have any deaths in our battlegroup from IEDs. I think that was because of the fact that we realized the police were rotten and we treated them the way that rotten police should be treated."[42]

The new divisional commander, Major General John Cooper, and the new brigade commander in Basra, Patrick Marriott, were both determined to continue taking the fight to the JAM, and had organised their troops to better execute intelligence gathering, and then strike operations, against insurgent bomb-making teams. Cooper had been a chief of staff in a brigade in Northern Ireland at the height of the Troubles, and was well versed in urban counter-insurgency tactics. Marriott was an urbane cavalry officer, who had been chief of staff to Major General Robin Brims during the initial invasion of Iraq in 2003, making him one of the first cohort of officers from that period to return to Basra in a more senior position.

The troops were up for the more aggressive stance and some thought the British strategy up to this point had been too soft.

"I wouldn't have pursued the strategy that we've been following since our initial invasion into Iraq," commented Major Austin, of the Fusiliers, who had participated in the invasion in 2003 and who was returning with his unit as part of 7 Brigade.

"We've got ourselves into a position now where we've distanced ourselves from the Iraqi population. I know that the plan was to transition to provincial Iraqi control, and that counter insurgency forces can be seen as more of a problem than a solution, but we allowed ourselves to be too politically correct, to allow the people in southern Iraq to have more determination than they really needed. As a result, we have these horrible in-fighting struggles."[43]

"I'm a great believer that Iraqis, when they step out of line, they need a smack," Austin told a US Army debriefing team.

"You don't have to go over the top, but if you can prove that you're stronger than them, they'll keep the lid on things – and that's something we lost after our first deployment. We allowed the conditions to change within the city to a degree where the insurgents felt able to operate with impunity. I don't think it was until we came back in 2005-2006 that major arrests started to happen. Clearly that was the result of intelligence being built up over time, but if we hadn't allowed that situation to be created, there wouldn't have been that situation in the first place. From the time I left Basra in June 2003 until I got back in

October 2005, I was shocked at how things had deteriorated. It was disappointing to me because I'd been welcomed with open arms, and I could do anything I wanted in the city in 2003. That wasn't the case in 2005. In my opinion, that was clearly because we were rushing things too quickly."[44]

Before deploying, Brigadier Marriott had stressed to his battlegroup commanders at a briefing in late September 2005 that they had to focus on rectifying problems with the British intelligence organisation in southern Iraq, which was still not configured for counter-insurgency. He said the intelligence effort "lacked unity" and so far the British had only a "limited penetration of insurgent networks".[45]

This meant Basra was "not like Northern Ireland," because covert surveillance was almost impossible to undertake and ordinary soldiers lacked the language skills necessary to pick up useful quantities of human intelligence from civilians. A briefing to the Brigade's Command Group at PJHQ by Foreign and Commonwealth Office officials left some officers concerned.

"At no stage in the hour's presentation did the officials address the crucial point of articulating what the objectives of Iranian influence in Basra were, because, like most things to do with Basra, they simply didn't know," commented a 7 Brigade staff officer.[46]

General Cooper emphasised to his troops that the best way to defeat the insurgent IED threat was avoid what he called "templated plans", varying the number of troops in units to make it difficult to predict deployments and to "make the enemy think twice" by using surprise and deception.[47]

The British Secret Intelligence Service, the US Central Intelligence Agency, SAS surveillance operatives and the British Army Field Human Intelligence Team (FHT) had stations in Basra Palace, and they were working hard to recruit agents in the militia. A platoon of Warriors from the Highlanders was put at the disposal of the 'spooks' to move them around central Basra, under the code name Operation Damask. This was slow work.[48]

To capitalise on what little intelligence was available, almost a battalion and a half of troops were dedicated to offensive operations in Basra city. Marriott's 7 Armoured Brigade had its own dedicated operations company drawn from the 1st Battalion, The King's Own Royal Border (1 King's Own Border) Regiment, and a expanded Brigade Surveillance Company (BSC), provided by the King's Own Border reconnaissance platoon and C Squadron of the 9th/12th Lancers.

Their focus was to react quickly to any intelligence tip-offs, and exploit them before the trail went cold. The BSC had the task of developing so-called 'target packs' so that the operations company could strike. The operations company was based at the Shatt al-Arab Hotel in Snatch Land Rovers, to allow a rapid reaction to intelligence and flexibility of methods to insert to and from target objectives, including by foot, Snatch Land Rover, Warrior, boat and helicopter.[49]

For bigger operations, the divisional reserve battlegroup, the 1st Battalion, The Royal Regiment of Fusiliers, was held on alert at Shaibah Logistic Base to strike. The mechanics of strike operations were explained by Major Austin, the battalion's operations officers.

"The methodology of the divisional and brigade reserve companies was that we were the bad boys" he explained to a US Army debriefing team. "The ground holding units would put in a cordon, and they would be the ones responsible for consequence management and for setting the conditions. We were the ones who went in there and seized people. We were purposefully more robust than the ground-holding battle groups, and that was on the brigade and divisional commanders' orders. It gave the ground-holding battle groups the opportunity to say, "If you play right, we'll carry on like this. If you don't play nice, the bad boys will come in, the Fusiliers, and do a strike. That worked very well."[50]

According to Austin, the presence of Warriors in certain parts of Basra was carefully minimized so when they were used they would have "a huge shock effect."

"A silent cordon would go in, and then either an armoured infantry company with seventeen Warriors or two companies' worth of Warriors would go into an area, sanitize the area and lift somebody," he said.

"That sort of effect wasn't well-liked by the population. As a result, people were more willing to give information [to the ground holding units] just to keep us out of the area."

"To be frank, the blokes loved [strike operations]," he said.

"The ground-holding battlegroup guys did all the hard work. We just followed the GPS [navigation device], got to where we were going, and they either used explosive entry for a hard knock or just kicked the door in. They lifted somebody, searched the place, got back in their Warriors and went home. It was a perfect day out for the troops. They got to be rough and take out their frustrations on people and the consequences were managed by others. It seemed to work very well. There was a genuine dislike of the divisional reserve companies being deployed and, as a result, the ground-holding battlegroups had a better time with it. The strategy paid off."[51]

The consequences of the stand-off between the British, Governor Waeli and the militia were spilling out into the streets. The IED campaign and threats of rioting forced the British to place large parts of Basra off-limits to their troops, unless as part of deliberate large scale operations.

"A month into the tour the multiples started during the day to patrol the infamous Shia Flats, a notorious slum area harbouring a strong support base for the insurgents," recalled Major Hutton.

"It was a real eye opener to some people who had not seen people living in such poor conditions before. The first few minutes of the patrol were fine but as soon as the multiples started getting deeper into the flats the crowds grew as word spread of patrols in the area. Then the rocks and stones would be launched and the Jocks quickly donned their helmets as the intensity of the stone throwing increased. The crowds continued to build and as it soon became apparent we were going to be unable to complete our patrol taskings without starting a major riot, the commanders decided to extract from the area."[52]

Mortar and rocket attacks continued to escalate across Basra with the Highlander's bases being hit 28 times during the tour. The Scottish soldiers became convinced that Iraqi staff were providing targeting information to the insurgents, culminating in a mortar barrage on the British consuls' Christmas Eve party.

"The event at the British Consulate in Basra Palace was curtailed by a number of mortar attacks: whilst the consulate staff took cover and wondered how the insurgents knew they were having a party. None of the local guests had arrived and all of the locally-employed staff had failed to turn up for work!" recalled a Highlander's officer.[53]

The Brigade surveillance and operations company troops spent most of the time in the center of city, preparing for operations, checking routes to targets and rehearsing missions. They worked closely with the Highlanders' companies across the city to try to understand insurgent activity in their areas. They began to build their own informal sources of intelligence through exploiting intelligence in mobile telephones, laptop computers, and forensic information from weapons and bomb components. Interpreters working with the two companies were an essential part of this effort allowing for 'hot analysis' of documents and mobile phones, so they could rapidly move on targets before they realised they had been compromised. They started to engage in psychological warfare with the insurgents, using seized mobile phones to issue them with threats or spreading rumours that militia men were informers or working for rival groups.

The value of the interpreters was considerable. "The company greatly valued the significant contribution of the interpreters towards our operations, with the value of a quality interpreter perceived as a force multiplier for our troops," commented a member of the brigade operations company.

"On strike operations, their insight and observations often produced more immediately exploitable intelligence. Principally due to one of the sergeant major's ability to inspire, cajole and mentor the interpreters we somehow managed to keep all five we had throughout our tour, despite the substantial threats they faced, although one was shot and wounded in the last month of the tour. It is sad to relate that since our return home, three have been murdered by the JAM as part of their callous targeting of locally employed civilians".[54]

Whilst the interpreters employed by the Danish contingent were looked after very well and subsequently offered Danish citizenship, the British dithered in their approach, which undermined the will of interpreters and other locally-employed citizens to work with British forces. The fate of the interpreters was later to become a political issue, which damaged both the British Government and the military, as they were shown to be lacking in resolve to act to protect people who had put their lives on the line to help British forces. But by the end of 2005, the combined intelligence-gathering efforts were starting to bear fruit, and the British had identified several high ranking Iraqi police officers as being in league with the JAM insurgents.

Governor Waeli and the provincial council had temporarily relaxed their non-cooperation policy in the run up to the 20th January 2006 parliamentary elections, but things got worse again at the end of the month. This culminated in the launch of Operation Shackleton to seize the rogue police officers, who included a number linked to the IPS intelligence agencies. Intelligence linked them to IED attacks on British troops, as well as the kidnapping and murder of local people, said Colonel Hopkinson.[55]

The Commanding Officer of the Highlanders was tasked with co-ordinating the operation that simultaneously hit four houses, each involving company-sized raids in three different battlegroup areas. He rejected an offer from special forces in Baghdad to lead the raids with helicopter assaults and Warrior-delivered strike teams. Colonel Hopkinson thought this too provocative and only likely to stir up unrest that might lead to a violent reaction. He decided to use locally-based troops and use low profile Snatch Land Rovers.[56]

Y Company of the Fusiliers lifted four targets in the Danish area in the north of Basra, and two other objectives were seized by the brigade operations company. The King's Own Border troops took a local agent with them on one of their raids to identify the target building. The troops then stormed the target with some gusto because of the prospect of arresting the men believed to behind the death of their comrades. "Private Robertson took great satisfaction in personally tackling the most wanted individual, with some forceful restraint techniques," recalled his company commander.

A significant amount of both small arms, IED components and heavy weapons were found in the raids, according to the strike troops. As news of the raids appeared in the local media, the repercussions were serious, with Hopkinson saying "we became victims of our own success after the Governor re-introduced the policy of 'non-cooperation'."[57]

General Cooper now decided to calm things down, to try to re-build some sort of dialogue with Basra's politicians. Strike operations were scaled back considerably, much to the consternation of senior officers in Brigadier Marriot's headquarters.

"We thought it would only take the arrest of twenty more senior commanders to break the back of the militia," commented one 7 Brigade officer.

"We had built up momentum with our strike operations, but General Cooper was more concerned about the politics and we were ignored. On one occasion we had pretty good intelligence on three Iranians in Basra with IED components, but the message that came back was to stand off, which was immensely frustrating and of course couldn't be related to the troops."[58]

"The [non-cooperation] situation with the Governor and Provincial council continued for the remainder of our tour and has effectively prevented any engagement or reform of the IPS," Hopkinson wrote in his regimental journal in April 2006.

"A lull followed in the immediate aftermath of this non-cooperation, as influence was brought to break this stance by the Governor but it failed and continued unabated. Effectively we 'sat on our hands' not wishing to give the Governor and Provincial Council any excuse to point the finger at us. This resulted in a tactical pause and we lost the initiative on the street; the vacuum was filled with the JAM and other unsavoury elements. After three weeks of drift we resolved to wrestle back the initiative, even if it meant unilateral action."[59]

In the meantime the JAM picked up the number of mortar and rocket attacks on the British bases in Basra, with attacks occurring pretty much every night, together with occasional day time attacks.

"The indirect fire attacks were a real nuisance, they interrupted precious sleep, they messed up the chronological aspect of planned operations, they destroyed equipment and materiel and had the potential to cause significant death and wounding, as the temporary building we had put up around the Shatt Al Arab Hotel, Basra Palace and Old State buildings had limited protection. By the grace of God, only injuries and not deaths were sustained from the indirect fire," wrote a 7 Brigade Officer.[60]

The British desire to go back on the front foot involved a surge in night-time patrol operations to dominate the ground, and try to interrupt rocket and mortar attacks on British bases. Major Crook and his operations company scored a major coup when they raided an insurgent EFP factory in Basra.[61]

Meanwhile the situation in Maysan mirrored events in Basra. The Royal Scots Dragoon Guards had replaced the Staffords, and they made little progress with the Sadrist-dominated provincial council in damping-down insurgent activity. One soldier was killed in a sniper attack and three others were killed in two EFP attacks on Snatch Land Rovers. When the Regiment left in April, the commanding officer, Lieutenant Colonel Ben Edwards, expressed some exasperation at the lack of progress. "I am sad to be handing over at the time of a ripple," he recalled.

"I am not talking directly about six key men in the Provincial Government, because after we arrested those thought to be involved in the [IED] attack on Richard Holmes and Lee Ellis, the chairman of the Provincial Council declared a boycott. It is a childish and naïve way to conduct business, but it is what we have been faced with throughout this tour. Quite apart from helping an inexperienced Provincial Council to learn how to grasp the needs of Maysan, we have tried to lead them towards coming to terms with political responsibilities. We are chipping away at the boycott, but some of the Provincial Council are not quite ready to talk face to face. It is a most tiring experience. I liken it to trying to catch one of the ponies when I was a child. You have to go to meet them with something they want, and you are often faced with pretending that you do not actually wish to talk to them, until suddenly you find you are. It is a sort of horse whispering move, in which one side sidles up backwards looking the other way."[62]

General Cooper told the Chilcot inquiry, "up until the divorce, so to speak, in September 2005, we and the police training teams had been able to get access to police stations in Basra. And the progress, I believe -- and clearly I was not there at the time -- I think had been quite good. By keeping us out of Basra, we then were unable to put our hands on the Iraqi police, and two or three things happened. At the grass roots level a lot of the training, a lot of the equipping that we had put in disappeared, and it also allowed, in terms of this struggle for political and economic power inside the police force, a series of murder squads and corruption to become endemic. And they were -- some of them were linked to political parties, others were merely gangsters. But that produced a climate of lawlessness inside the police, inside Basra. But because we were not allowed to go back into contact until May of 2006, it meant that we lost ground and we lost time. And it was -- one of the key issues when we did get back to Basra was the rebuilding of the Iraqi police service, which was really quite difficult and became an issue for the next several months."[63]

The optimists in the British government and military now had great difficulty putting a positive spin on events in Iraq. The plans to hand over Basra and Maysan to Iraqi security control had to be put on hold until things calmed down. A troop level review in early 2006 slowed down the handover process, and the summer target for handing over Basra had to be put back. In March, Lieutenant General Nick Houghton, now the senior British officer in Baghdad, gave a media interview in which he said the middle of 2008 was now the target date for getting British troops out of Iraq.[64]

The first months of 2006 were also instrumental in the evolution of the British contribution to the US campaign against Sunni insurgents loyal to al Qaeda in central Iraq. A British special forces squadron had been rotating through Baghdad continuously since the summer of 2003, conducting operations to arrest former regime leaders, assisting in the hunt for weapons of mass destruction, and joining the US Joint Special Operations Command (JSOC) against the growing insurgency.[65]

After the destruction of the al-Askari shrine in Samarra in February 2006, Shia-Sunni inter-communal violence was threatening to spiral out of control, prompting the JSOC commander, Major General Stanley McChrystal, to ramp up his operations against al Qaeda. His Delta Force and US Navy SEAL operatives were now launching nightly raids against al Qaeda, and the British Special Air Service (SAS) were soon operating at the same high tempo. This gave the UK SF teams a high profile role at the heart of US operations in central Iraq. While Prime Minister Tony Blair backed the SAS role, and was delighted when they rescued the British hostage Norman Kember from an insurgent hide out in Baghdad in March 2006, some senior officers in the British armed forces and the special forces themselves were less happy.[66]

Following two helicopter crashes in Baghdad, the head of the army's Land Command and the RAF's Air Command to launch a formal investigation that eventually criticized the command arrangements of the special forces helicopter detachment in Baghdad. [67]

There was also pressure from senior officers to switch the special forces main effort to Afghanistan, to support the growing British deployment there. The commanding officer of 22 SAS Regiment at the time, Lieutenant Colonel Richard Williams, was a keen advocate of supporting General McChrystal's mission in Iraq, and during 2005 and 2006 he had repeated arguments with senior officers over the diversion of special forces resources to Afghanistan. The high profile nature of the special forces mission, and the value placed on it by very senior US officers in Baghdad, meant Colonel Williams got his way and his troopers spent most of 2006 and 2007 launching night raids into the heart of the Sunni insurgency.[68]

The UK special forces mission in Baghdad, secretly code-named Operation Crichton, eventually cost the lives of 18 SAS, Special Boat Service, Royal Signals and RAF personnel between 2003 and 2008. This was some 10% of the total of UK fatalities during Operation Telic, where as the Special Forces never made up more than 3% of the total UK troop strength.

"If the overall UK objective was to be good allies to the US, then the special forces mission provided very good leverage for a relatively small personnel investment," commented a senior advisor to General Sir Mike Walker.

"But we never had these discussions, because we never really honed down the overall strategic objective nor tested our operations against it."[69]

Chapter 20

RAF AGAINST INSURGENTS

Throughout the Iraq campaign, RAF aircraft were airborne almost continuously over the country, flying offensive and reconnaissance missions. The vast majority of these missions were flown in support of US troops and British Special Forces fighting Sunni insurgents in and around Baghdad. For this reason the Ministry of Defence did not want the RAF contribution to have any publicity, in case it might prompt accusations of 'mission creep' and distract attention from the British Army's efforts in Basra.

After the fall of Baghdad in April 2003, the two RAF combat wings deployed for war were stood down, and 26 of their 32 Tornado GR4 aircraft and personnel returned home. To help secure Iraq's borders and deter intervention by the country's neighbours, a strong contingent of US and British airpower was maintained in the Gulf region.[1] The RAF contribution was in the shape of a detachment of six Tornado GR4 strike aircraft based at Ali Al Salem. Crews of 13 Squadron took on this task in May 2003 from II Squadron, and soon found their main activity was flying photographic reconnaissance missions, using the Vinten Digital Joint Reconnaissance Pod (DJRP) system.[2] The apparently peaceful nature of the time was highlighted by the fact that the British Army divisional headquarters in Basra reduced the manning in its air liaison cell to a single officer, working part time on other duties.[3] Offensive air support was not on the agenda. The presence of the RAF bomber force in the Middle East seemed an anachronism and few expected the aircraft would ever drop any bombs in anger on Iraq.

The commitment of the RAF Tornados was part of wider British efforts to gain influence with the larger US air force operating over Iraq. By offering up a squadron of Tornado GR4 bombers, VC-10 air-to-air refuelling tanker aircraft, Nimrod MR2 surveillance aircraft and Nimrod R1 electronic eavesdropping aircraft, to work as part of the US air component, it was hoped that the US would in turn make some of its extensive capabilities available to work with British ground forces in Iraq.

From the start the RAF operated as a fully integrated entity with the Americans, rather than limiting its aircraft to operating only in support of the British Army in south-eastern Iraq. The RAF and US Air Force, as well as the US Navy and US Marine Corps, when they had squadrons in the Middle East, set up a continuous shift system of fast jet combat aircraft over Iraq, with air-to-air refuelling enabling jets to remain on station for several hours at a time. This would enable aircraft to be directed to support incidents across the country and be overhead any troops in trouble in less than half an hour. Senior RAF officers judged this a far more efficient use of its Tornado. If a continuous air patrol was to be maintained just over the British division then far more aircraft and tankers would have been needed. This approach was often misunderstood by

British troops in Basra, who were often heard to complain that the RAF never seemed to be in the air when they called for air support. But it did mean that aircraft - even if on many occasions they were American - were always available when a call for help was made. During the two Sadr revolts in 2004, and in Operation Charge of the Knights, air support would have a decisive influence on the course of battle in Basra.

At the heart of the British air effort during Operation Telic was the handful of RAF officers working in the USAF's Combined Air Operations Centre, or CAOC, at Al Udeid air base in Qatar. The CAOC staff were then focused on the strategic direction of air operations across the US-Central Command area of responsibility, rather than micro-managing the release of individual weapons by individual aircraft.

"We look at the big picture, the strategic picture here" said Wing Commander Mason Fenlon, the Senior UK Representative in the CAOC in 2006.

"We are fighting two separate wars [in Iraq and Afghanistan], and within those theatres, each army division is fighting its own little war."[4]

Although almost all weapon release authority had been delegated to Joint Terminal Attack Controllers (JTACs) or forward air controllers on the ground with army units in Iraq and Afghanistan, the strategic direction of air power was needed to ensure the efficient allocation of resources – particularly scarce tanker, airlift and intelligence, surveillance and reconnaissance (ISR) assets - across the area of responsibility, said Fenlon.

"We deal with ground alert aircraft, tanker support and rules of engagement, that sort of thing".[5]

The CAOC was divided into a number of distinct sections, which all operated on a 24 hour basis. In a raised deck above the main floor of CAOC is a separate section dubbed the Battle Cab, where the CAOC Director and his senior staff and ground forces representatives monitored the progress of air operations.

"The offensive co-ordination guys are on the floor and they feed up here things that need decisions from the general or the duty lawyer," said US Navy Captain Bill Reavey, who was duty colonel running the Battle Cab in 2006.[6]

The main CAOC floor was dimly lit, and was dominated by large projected screens showing the real-time air picture in both Iraq and Afghanistan, showing the position of all military and civil air traffic. On either side of these maps were live feeds from General Atomics MQ/RQ-1 Predator unmanned aerial vehicles (UAVs) flying over Iraq and Afghanistan, as well as CNN television news. Next to the main CAOC building was the ISR Division or ISRD, where intelligence feeds from airborne sensors and collection platforms were monitored.

Before the Iraq war, in old style COACs, full motion video imagery from Predators and other ISR platforms could not be shared with ground units resulting in high-level decision-makers monopolising its use. CAOC staff said the development of Remote Operations Video Enhanced Receiver, or ROVER, technology, meant that suitably-equipped JTACs could now receive Predator imagery, and this has allowed authority for weapons release to be delegated to troops on the ground. Predator UAVs or aircraft equipped with Litening targeting pods, which were carried by RAF Tornados from 2007, were also be able to download imagery to ROVER equipped JTACs. The ROVER terminals used in Iraq were laptop sized and meant troops in combat zones had an unprecedented access to airborne imagery.

On the main CAOC floor, the director of combat operations controlled on-going activity, assisted by several rows of specialist staff who represented the main air force units in theatre. The director post was shared by three lieutenant colonels, including one RAF officer. It was the director's job to choreograph the execution of the daily air tasking order or plan. This was the daily plan, which saw 50 strike aircraft a day being flowed over Iraq, in six-hour time blocks.

"Things start with scheduling, [ground component headquarters] in Baghdad prioritise ranking of requests for air support," said a British CAOC staffer.

"The operations team here then generates the air tasking order (ATO) [or the daily air plan, with routes, patrol areas, refuelling details, call signs and radio frequencies]. We put our say in at that stage, saying if the task is appropriate to our assets."[7]

The dynamic nature of the battlefield in Iraq meant few targets were pre-planned. When army units reported that they had troops in contact, or TIC, the CAOC staff would then have to begin to juggle their assets. At this point aircraft were allocated to JTACs, who would then authorise weapon release, and ground alert strike aircraft were scrambled to provide additional fire power, tankers diverted to keep fuel on hand, and ISR assets moved to provide coverage of incidents.

Surprisingly the CAOC floor was very quiet, with almost all activity co-ordinated over internet-style chat rooms. Many staff officers had multiple computer screens to show all the messages that were transmitted over secure computer networks. High priority messages, such as requests for close air support for TIC incidents were highlighted and logged in red, as well as being projected on to the large CAOC maps, to aid decision making.

A large sign outside the CAOC building proclaimed its mission was to "enable the kill chain," and staff at the facility said their work was "all about supporting the land campaign, and the ISRD is no different - the air campaign is for the ground commander."

RAF officers complained throughout the Iraqi campaign that the British-led Multi-National Division (South East) or MND(SE) did not really understand the ATO process, or how to make air support requests to the CAOC.

"We repeatedly tried to push them to be pro-active," recalled an RAF commander. "We planned to have the twenty to forty minutes at the end of our Tornado sorties to Baghdad free to support British troops when we come back from working with the Americans."[8]

"We have the tasking ready but where the British Army falls down was on tasking to higher headquarters" said the planner.

"There was an initial reluctance in MND(SE) Headquarters to declare TIC or troops in contact. Then they will get CAOC support, then they will get whatever they want."[9]

The burden of the RAF offensive air effort in Iraq fell to the Tornado GR4 Force from RAF Lossiemouth in Morayshire, and Marham in Norfolk. At the end of the 20th Century, the RAF's Tornado Force was in turmoil, as it found itself heavily committed to operations in Kosovo and the Middle East, at the same time as the old GR1 aircraft were in the midst of a major mid-life upgrade. This effort to create the GR4 variant, which featured a new computer-drive mission system that would allow the integration of a wider range of 'smart' precision-guided munitions, using 'plug and play' style soft and hardware, was dogged by delays and cost overruns.

The need for this upgrade, which gave the GR4 the ability to employ satellite-guided weapons with an all-weather capability, was graphically demonstrated during the 1999 Kosovo campaign, when bad weather seriously inhibited the use of the older laser-guided weapons. This prompted Air Marshal Brian Burridge, the UK's joint commander during the opening phase of Operation Telic, to describe the Kosovo campaign as a "debacle" for the RAF.[10] Bomb damage assessment data leaked to the media revealed that during the 78 day Kosovo campaign the Tornado GR1 strike missions achieved only 65% hit rates with 454kg (1,000lb) Raytheon Paveway II laser-guided bombs (LGBs), in combination with Ferranti's Termal Imaging Airborne Laser Designator (TIALD) pod. Only some 53% of targets were hit with the bigger 2,000lb Pavaway III weapons, which was nowhere near the requirements of the 'smart weapon' era.[11]

After a lot of hard work, by June 2001 the GR4's new computer systems had been improved in time for the first aircraft to deploy to Ali Al Salem Airbase in Kuwait, to participate in no-fly zone (NFZ) enforcement missions, under the code name Operation Resonate (South). In October 2003, the Tornado Detachment, or TORDET as it was known, had to move from Ali Al Salem after major runway repairs started at the Kuwaiti airbase. It moved to Al Udeid, alongside the major USAF combat wing in the Gulf region, and remained there until the end of Operation Telic in 2009.

As has been explained in preceding chapters, the spring and summer of 2004 saw Iraq convulsed by heavy fighting, as rival Sunni and Shia militia took up arms against the occupation forces. Beleaguered US and British troop detachments started calling up air support to help them drive off insurgents surrounding their bases. The next six months in 2004 saw a huge build-up of US forces for the attack on the Sunni insurgent stronghold of Fallujah, to the west of Baghdad. While overwhelming US airpower was committed to the Battle of Fallujah, the RAF helped fill gaps patrolling over other Iraqi cities after the British government vetoed Tornados from dropping weapons on the city.

This climatic battle seemed to bring calm to Iraq, and relatively peaceful elections went ahead in January 2005, resulting in almost a year when the TORDET's aircraft dropped no weapons in anger until 25th December 2005. Then 14 Squadron dropped a 1,000lb bomb on an insurgent target.[12]

By 2006, the GR4 Force had settled into a routine to sustain the detachment at Al Udeid, with each squadron in the force spending two months at a time on duty in the Middle East. In 2006, the six jets of the TORDET provided an eighth of coalition offensive airpower in theatre. Each detachment usually consisted of seven or eight air crews and between 80 and 90 ground personnel. This was effectively 50% to 70% of a squadron's personnel and many units rotated their people during deployments, to share out the work load or allow them to gain operational experience.

Squadron Leader Andy Arnold, the executive officer of 31 Squadron, was the detachment commander in September 2006, and he said emphasis of operations had shifted to what was termed non-traditional intelligence, surveillance and reconnaissance or NTISR using their TIALD pods to monitor the situation on the ground.

"It is all about Non-Kinetic Effect – support to the army by presence overhead and shows of force (SOF)" he said. "Doing NTISR you have to look out for and interpret the situation on ground for the army commander."[13]

Typical tasking was to launch two pairs of aircraft a day, one for close air support/NTISR and another for close air support/Tac Recce. Although missions were usually tasked for three to four hours long over Iraq, the tactical situation usually meant they were to be extended by two or three air-to-air refuellings pushing the sortie length to up to eight hours, which Arnold described as "hard work" for the aircrew.

"Crews fly about four times a week and we can flex to surge if needed" he said.[14]

During NISTAR missions, GR4 crews looked for insurgent mortar teams, roadside bombs or improvised explosive devices and protected coalition convoys.

"We can look [with pods and binoculars] on the roofs of houses to see if people are on them or ahead of convoys," said Arnold.

"We provide available and visible deterrence, as well as escalatory responses. Army guys were able to hear that we are offering protection. First, we do SOFs – putting down noise, providing a visible menace to stabilise the situation, dispersing riots and deter people from firing. We don't want to kill people but to start to win hearts and minds. It is very rare that we go up the ladder. If you drop bombs you have lost."

"We concentrate [our operations] on Baghdad," he said. "Airpower can be over the top of an incident in ten to fifteen minutes. There is a constant presence, twenty-four hours a day. The majority of our work is with the US."[15]

The TORDET was also in demand to collect still imagery with its DJRP, because they were then the only Tac Recce asset in theatre, since the demise of F-14 TARPS [US Navy's aerial reconnaissance jet], said Arnold.

"DRJP is both highly used and valued. The Tornado is platform of choice for deep target analysis."

GR4 sorties during the insurgency were conducted in relatively benign environments, compared to the pre-2003 no-fly zone (NFZ) missions, when RAF crews faced Iraqi surface-to-air missiles and anti-aircraft artillery fire on a hourly basis.

"There are not the same risks as flying NFZ missions – the Iraqis are not firing missiles at you" said Arnold. "But [now] if you are on the ground [if your jet goes down] you face a greater danger if a terrorist group gets hold of you."[16]

Flight Lieutenant Kim Smith, a 31 Squadron NFZ veteran, said that by 2006, missions over Iraq were very different.

"In the old days the maximum sortie duration was two hours, you went into NFZ as part of a large package [of other aircraft] because of threat from Iraqis," he said. "Now there is no identifiable [ground-to-air or air-to-air] threat. Today it is a different role. We operate on our own. We have no pre-designated targets before we take off on our missions. You know roughly where you are going. Things are made up on the hoof as the situation unfolds. Before we throw weaponry at a problem we try to solve it by us just being there. Nine out of ten times the bad guys just melt away."[17]

During the first half of 2006, the Tornado Force began to look to replace its TIALD 500 pods with a more modern system. These had greater resolution, and a downlink to allow the live or real-time transmission of video imagery to ground-based forward air controllers, or Joint Terminal Attack Controllers, as the US military called them, equipped with early versions of the ROVER terminal. The 1980s vintage TIALD pod was designed to identify tanks and other large pieces of military hardware but was showing its age during the Iraqi insurgency, when ground commanders wanted aircraft crews to identify and track individual insurgents in complex and confused urban environments. Without the new equipment, the fear was that US ground commanders would not call upon the services of the Tornados, and the justification of the deployment of the TORDET would have been undermined.

An urgent operational requirement (UOR), for the purchase of a batch of Rafael Armament Development Authority Litening III advanced targeting pods, was given the go ahead in the middle of 2006. Arnold described the move to Litening III as a "quantum leap forward" because it would allow Tornado crews to identify specific weapon types being carried by insurgents, or IEDs.[18]

"We desperately needed it to track people and vehicles and send information direct to the ground controller" he said. "This will give us connectivity to US Joint Terminal Attack Controllers."

It fell to 14 Squadron to introduce the new pod to the Iraqi theatre in the first weeks of 2007. Flight Lieutenant Bryn Williams described the exercise.

"This process involved squadron aircrew being hands-on from a very early stage in the service life of the pod, introducing it onto the jet after only limited testing by the Fast Jet Operational Evaluation Unit, and then designing the standard operating procedures for use of this awesome new capability," he wrote in the squadron newsletter.

"Similarly, the squadron engineers have been heavily involved with integrating the pod from a ground perspective. Litening III supplements the TIALD pod, which has been in use for the last decade and a half, and gives the GR4 a major improvement in capability. Not only are the fidelity and definition of the images received by the aircrew (the pilot can now see the real-time images as well as the navigator) much improved, but the pod also has a data-link capability which allows the Forward-Air-Controller (FAC) you are working with on the ground, to receive the imagery, real-time, via a lap-top computer. This understandably speeds up the whole process of close air support (CAS) operations."[19]

According to Williams this made a big difference to the capability of the Tornado Force and increased its combat utility.

"The feedback we received from the FACs within theatre was very positive, and the quality of picture delivered by our new capability was the best from any fast air asset," he said.

"This fact, coupled with the flexibility that we offered, meant that we found ourselves in situations that we would have never previously been utilised in with the TIALD pod."

The introduction of the Litening III pod saw the Tornado Force in the forefront of combat operations during 2007, with the majority of the work being in support of the US surge around Baghdad. British troops in Basra also called upon the Tornado crews to cover their move from their headquarters in the centre of the war-torn city, and for weeks ahead of the withdrawal they flew missions along the escape route to spot insurgents trying to plant IEDs.

March and April 2008 saw the Tornado Force involved in its most intense period of combat operations, which overlapped with the handover of the TORDET at Al Udeid between 13 and 14 Squadrons. The RAF aircrew were in the forefront of providing offensive support to Iraqi, British and US troops advancing into the heart of Basra to drive out Shia militia fighters. Operation Charge of the Knights got under way on 28th March 2008, with US and British forward air controllers working closely with Iraqi infantry brigades, to bring down precision air strikes on militia strong points in urban areas, or on insurgent rocket and mortar teams trying to fire on coalition bases. A near continuous presence was maintained over the city by RAF Tornados, USAF Predator drones and US Navy F/A-18 Hornets. The close integration of air and ground forces was central to the success of the offensive that soon had the insurgents on the run. Not only did the RAF Tornado crews have to engage fleeting targets inside the city, but they had to operate in very congested airspace, de-conflicting their attack runs with Predator flights, as well as making sure they avoided coalition helicopters and kept away from out-going British artillery fire. Charge of the

Knights was a full blown battle, that saw the RAF Tornado crews tested in way not seen since the invasion phase of Operation Telic in March and April 2003.

Although the offensive against the Basra militias was over after little more than a week of intensive fighting, the TORDET remained on duty at Al Udeid until June 2009, when the last British combat troops finally pulled out of Iraq. The TORDET clocked up one more first in this time, with 9 Squadron operationally flying with the Dual Mode Brimstone anti-armour for the first time in December 2008, although none were fired in anger. The final flight by the TORDET brought to an end nearly 19 years of continuous presence in the Gulf by the RAF Tornado Force.[20]

Throughout the Iraq campaign, ground commanders had an insatiable appetite for support from surveillance aircraft to provide early warning of insurgent attacks or allow on-going incidents to be monitored in real-time, via downloaded video imagery. At the start of the Iraq campaign, the US Air Force was the dominant partner in this sphere and the RAF was desperate to catch up. The view was that the unless the RAF had its own state of the art overland Intelligence, Surveillance, Targeting and Reconnaissance (ISTAR) aircraft, the Americans would have little interest in sharing their assets with the British.

The RAF's eavesdropping Nimrod R1 spy planes were early visitors to the skies over Iraq after May 2003, flying missions to monitor hostile communications. Over the next six years, 51 Squadron worked to deploy one of its three aircraft to the Middle East for between three and six months a year. They divided up this duty with the USAF's RC-135 Rivet Joint spy planes to ensure continuous coverage.[21]

Efforts then focused on the RAF Nimrod MR2 force. It had participated in the US-led invasion of Afghanistan in October 2001 and March 2002 when it flew some 1,533 hours over the land-locked country; mainly to provide communications relay services for UK special forces teams on the ground. This operation also exposed the Nimrod force and their 'customers' in the special forces units to American Lockheed P-3C AIP Orions, equipped with high-performance electro-optical (EO) video systems. These allowed them to monitor ground activity from altitudes well over 10,000 feet. The long endurance built into the design of maritime patrol aircraft (MPAs), such as the Orion and Nimrod, meant that they could stay on station over an area of interest for up to ten hours at a time so their crews could build up intimate knowledge of what was going on the ground.

An UOR bid was made to equip several Nimrods with latest generation EO sensor systems, known as the Wescam MX-15, in a mounting under the aircraft's starboard wing. Four of the modified aircraft, from 120 Squadron in March 2003. They were to support the campaign to find and destroy Saddam Hussein's Scud ballistic missiles, believed to be aimed at Israel from Iraq's western desert. The task of the Nimrods was to provide an 'eye in the sky' for the coalition special forces taking part in the 'western offensive,' or Operation Row, as the UK contribution was code-named. The XXV detachment returned home to RAF Kinloss in April 2003 but the Nimrod force was soon drawn back into action in Iraq.

In June 2003, the UK SF teams were committed to a new mission, code named Operation Paradoxical, in Baghdad, to hunt down senior members of the old Iraqi regime who were suspected of directing the growing insurgency against the US-led occupation. In November, the Nimrod detachment that was based on the north ramp of Seeb International Airport, outside of the Omani capital Muscat, to conduct maritime patrol tasks over Middle East waters, was directed to start supporting the new mission in Baghdad.

At this point the RAF did not have any unmanned aerial vehicles (UAVs) of a similar capability to the USAF's General Atomics MQ-1 Predator, so the Nimrod force was given the job of providing the same type of real-time surveillance capability for US and UK ground troops. This mission was aided by the installation of a new piece of technology, the Enterprise Control System Longhorn data link, to allow troops on the ground to view in real-time full motion video images from the Nimrod's MX-15. This was an early version of the ROVER terminals that are then in widespread use in Afghanistan, but the Longhorn data-link only worked with a dedicated terminal, unlike the newer ROVER terminals that could receive imagery from a range of aircraft, helicopters and UAVs. The Longhorn-MX-15 combination transformed the utility of the Nimrod. Early versions of the Longhorn were notoriously unreliable, and it took a while for the Nimrod force and ground troops to get the best from them.[22]

The spring of 2004 saw the Nimrod force drawn deeper into the Iraqi conflict, after militia fighters loyal to the rogue Shia cleric Muqtada al-Sadr launched an insurrection across southern Iraq. A single Nimrod and a full aircrew, along with ground personnel from the Nimrod Line Squadron to provide first line maintenance, were now forward deployed to Basra airport to provide support for the British Army, as well as continuing to support the special forces in Baghdad.

British forces soon staged a series of offensive to clear out militia fighters from Iraqi towns and cities, with the Nimrod in close support. This culminated in Operation Waterloo in al Amarah town centre, and saw British troops stage a night-time assault on several militia positions. They were supported by a Nimrod and a USAF Lockheed AC-130 Spectre gunship. The RAF crew used the MX-15 to spot insurgents hiding in back streets and then relay their co-ordinates to the gunship for destruction.

The British commander in south east Iraq at the time, Major General Andrew Stewart, praised the Nimrod-AC-130 combination in his post operational tour report, commenting, "The very nature of the threat posed by 'militias' and the methods they use saw UK forces often unable to find, fix and strike effectively. The combination of AC-130 and MR2 was, on two notable occasions, a battle winner."[23]

The General was full of praise of the Nimrod's capabilities, which he saw as one of the few 'stellar' UK airborne ISTAR performers of this period.

"Dedicated UK airborne ISTAR assets have been a pretty sorry tale with availability described as fragile at best" he wrote. "For operations of this nature a stand-off covert airborne system is critical to success, and something close to 24 hour coverage is demanded. For the UK only Nimrod MR2 offers a truly covert capability and it has been superb for endurance over wide land areas. More of this sort are needed."[24]

During the later half of 2004, the situation in southern Iraq stabilised enough for the focus of Nimrod operations to move north to Baghdad again. The US and British special forces leadership in Baghdad was determined to ramp up the intensity of their strike operations, or raids, against the insurgents in an attempt to keep them off their guard, to turn the relentless tide of car bombing in civilian areas, sectarian killings and roadside bomb attacks on coalition troops. The UK special forces contingent was to launch at least one raid a night, and the Nimrod crew at Basra were soon flying on almost a nightly basis to support them. In 2004, the Nimrod force was flying just over 200 hours a month over Iraq, amassing more than 2,000 hours in the year.[25]

The raids in Baghdad were often launched with only a few hours' notice, after the receipt of intelligence tip offs, so there was often very little time for the army liaison officers to brief the Nimrod crews on the nature of their missions. Nimrod crews recounted how they would have to launch their aircraft with minimal target information, which sometimes would only come in during the flight north to Baghdad. The army liaison officers usually flew on the missions to receive the highly secret briefings over the radio, and help the MX-15 operators identify targets on the ground. One Basra veteran recounted a liaison officer once racing along the taxi way in his pick-up truck to catch up with the Nimrod as it was moving to take-off.[26]

The arrival of the MX-15 camera and the new overland ISTAR mission changed considerably how the Nimrod crews operated. The aircraft's three acoustic sensor operators, known as the 'wet team,' found themselves re-roled to operate the camera and they would take turns during the aircraft's nine hours on station. While the remainder of the crew found they had other roles too. The electronic support measures and Searchwater radar operators found they spent most of their time monitoring weather, and making sure that the aircraft was kept safe in the congested airspace over the Iraqi capital.

"We continued to fly as a full crew, there was no talk of thinning people out," said an Iraq veteran. "Everyone had a job too do and having more people on board meant we could pace ourselves better."[27]

Another Nimrod crewman with several Iraq tours under his belt, described the new role as "very different to our normal mission – very interesting".

The job of the mission controller, usually a squadron leader or an experienced flight lieutenant, on overland missions was also very different from his normal role of co-ordinating data from anti-submarine sensors, such as Searchwater radar contacts and acoustic tracks from floating sonar buoys. On Baghdad missions, the controller's master display would be filled with airspace control information and pre-loaded co-ordinates of target buildings to allow the tactical situation to be easily visualised.

A mission controller recalled that the "camera was not a surveillance system, it is an intelligence system, you need to know where to point the camera particularly when operating over a huge city like Baghdad or Basra. We would stake out a 'box' around targets and watch it. Some times we not even know what we are watching. Only the liaison officers on board would know details of what we were looking at."[28]

At the heart of the overland ISTAR mission was getting the aircraft in the right position to get the best images of the target. This is more complex that its sounds, because the aircraft often had to fly in 'stand-off' positions to avoid alerting the targets they were being watched. But it raised issues concerning shadow effects from buildings degrading the images. The position of the camera below the Nimrod's starboard wing also meant the aircraft had to fly in a pattern to ensure it could always see the target.

"On our jet [the camera] is on the wing and that has issues for how you use the camera," said a MX-15 operator, with six tours in Iraq under his belt. "You often couldn't fly straight over the target."[29]

The MX-15 sensor turret has three cameras - narrow band, wide band and infra-red. In the operator's position, the three camera's images are displayed in a strip along the bottom of the big screen. The operator then selects the best image to examine on the big screen. A feed from the KX-15 is also displayed on a small screen in the mission commanders' console in the middle of the aircraft. Next to the MX-15 operator's station was a display screen with a moving map display, that automatically put a cursor on the location of where the camera is focused.

"This a very potent capability and we did not have it when we first got the camera" said an MX-15 operator.

"Before we had this we had to calculate distances and locations by hand. People on the ground could pass me grid reference - I would plug it into the system and then it would slew the camera on to a target. In seconds, we can have eyes on target."[30]

"The Longhorn digital microwave data link allows the guys on the ground to see the imagery, so we are both looking at the same imagery. They would then direct me to look at targets," he said.

"The liaison officer sitting beside me would also look at the screen and bring out more information that is relevant to the customer. My job is to give the best image to the customer."

As operations in Baghdad evolved through 2006 and into 2007, the UK special force contingent gained more experience utilising the Nimrod, and started to use their own integral ISTAR assets, including the RAF Puma detachment with P4 camera pods, for close-in surveillance during the climax of raids.

"Our main thing became 'pattern of life' – watching what was going on the ground and building up a picture of long term activity around a target and we would then hand over to the other ISTAR systems as the assault team began their final preparations," said the MX-15 operator.

"We were an eye in the sky."

For the duty Nimrod crew in Basra, life was different from that experienced back home in Morayshire. The British base regularly came under insurgent mortar and rocket fire, and Nimrod detachment personnel had to carry their body armour with them at all times in case they had to dive for cover when rocket alarms sounded.

The small Nimrod Line Squadron team had what was described as "a small shed at the end of the runway", next to the aircraft to work from. Flight planning and Nimrod operations offices were located in the main airport building and the detachment lived at first in ten-man tents with "questionable air conditioning". Infra-structure steadily improved over time, and a purpose-built operations centre for all air units at the base was eventually opened.

The unpredictability of the situation in Baghdad meant that crews were regularly held at 45 minutes notice to get airborne. Crews had to stay together in their accommodation or the base NAAFI café, waiting for the call to go over a radio always carried by the crew captain. At night this was particularly interesting, because getting to Nimrod operations for briefings and starting up the aircraft had to be conducted in darkness so as not to attract the attention of insurgent rocket or mortar teams.

"We wore combat body armour on take off and landing from Basra because of the indirect fire threat" said a Basra veteran. "We couldn't wear helmets because of our headsets. Some guys got really used to the rocket alerts and started to sleep through them."[31]

By mid 2006, the rocket threat was getting far too dangerous to risk keeping a big Nimrod at Basra and the aircraft was pulled back to Seeb in Oman, to join the other Nimrods supporting the British operation in Afghanistan. This eased aircraft maintenance, and the rotation of personnel, but many of the Basra veterans commented that even though the Seeb deployed operating base accommodation was far superior to Basra, they missed the camaraderie of sharing hardships with their army comrades.

July 2006 saw the Nimrod force take on its most demanding mission to date when a 'surge' of aircraft and crews was ordered to support Operation Herrick in Afghanistan. Now RAF Kinloss had to generate four aircraft and four crews at any one time. British troops in Afghanistan were fighting for their lives in remote bases called Platoon Houses across war-torn Helmand province. The sortie rate of the deployed Nimrod force surged to nearly 3,000 hours in the year 2005-6, across both theatres of operation.[32]

The ramping up of operations in Afghanistan meant an increasing proportion of the 20 Nimrod crews would spend time in the Middle East. Crews spent eight weeks in theatre at a time but the heavy rotation schedule meant the Nimrod force was able to do little else except support operations and maintain its search and rescue commitment at RAF Kinloss.

"Approaching one quarter of the Nimrod force at any one time was deployed on operations overseas as well as being committed to operations back in the UK," said Group Captain Robbie Noel, RAF Kinloss station commander in 2010.[33]

"We went through an intense operations tempo. Every [Nimrod] aircrew and every ground crew deployed at some point. They contributed to life saving or detention operations in the wider geographic area."

Through 2007 and into 2008 the Nimrod fleet was beset by safety problems, related to the aircraft's air-to-air refueling piping, and hot air ducting following the crash of aircraft XV230 in September 2006 with the loss of all its 14 crew. As a result, in March 2009, the Ministry of Defence decided to put the remaining 11 aircraft through a modification programme to see them through to their out of service date in 2011. Even though the 'fix to fly' project was largely complete in the autumn of 2009, the Nimrod did not return to operations in Iraq or Afghanistan. Despite the Nimrod Force's successes, the veteran maritime patrol aircraft had severe limitations. It was expensive to operate, required a large amount of logistics to run, and it had limited communications equipment to allow video imagery to be downloaded from the aircraft.

In 2003, the US Air Force was ramping up its MQ-1 Predator operations in Iraq, to give US ground commanders a huge increase in video imagery. To try to get a share of this capability for British ground commanders in Iraq – both in the UK-led division in Basra and in the UK special forces task force in Baghdad – the RAF struck a deal with the USAF to send personnel to work in its Predator Force in return for UK ground commanders getting a percentage of the video output. UK headquarters could bid for Predator time and receive the full motion video (FMV) imagery, distributed via the US global satellite network or downloaded direct from air vehicles into ROVER terminals.

The RAF's UAV activities got under way when No 1115 Flight was formed in April 2004, as the UK contribution to the US-led Combined Joint Predator Task Force. The flight boasted some 40 personnel, including aircrew, engineering and intelligence specialists. They were fully integrated into USAF General Atomics MQ-1 Predator UAV operations, predominately at Creech Air Force Base in Nevada and in Iraq. Pilots, intelligence analysts and maintenance personnel worked both at the US remote operations site at Creech, controlling UAVs over Iraq via satellite and at Balad Air Force base outside Baghdad in the launch and recovery element.[34]

This gave the UK a wide exposure to how the US ran its UAV operations. A RAF UAV pilot fired a weapon from a UAV for the first time in August 2004, supporting US troops during the battle of Najaf in Iraq.[35] With a surge in demand for UAV support, the UK Ministry of Defence decided that the best way to rapidly get more UAVs into service was to expand its contribution to the US-UK UAV force. The more resources the UK put in, the more UAV time the UK could expect to receive from the joint force.

In 2006, it was decided that the RAF would get its own MQ-9 Reapers. The Reaper is almost twice the size of the older Predator, boasting a more powerful engine, more robust avionics and other new systems. The new UAV had a top speed of 260 knots compared to 117 knots for the Predator. This dramatically improved its ability to get to the scene of any action. The Reaper had a range of 5,900km compared to 3,700km for the Predator, and the Reaper could carry up to 14 Hellfire missiles on six hard points, or four Hellfire and two GBU-12 Paveway II laser guided bombs. The Predator could only carry two Hellfires on two hard points. And the Reaper was also fitted with a General Atomics Lynx synthetic aperture radar to allow it to find targets in bad weather.

Not surprisingly, the RAF opted to buy the more advanced Reaper to give its UAV force more range, speed and strike power. However, the Reaper was destined to go to Afghanistan, not Iraq, but RAF personnel continued to support US Reaper and Predator operations in Iraq as quid pro quo for continued access to their video imagery.[36]

In October 2008, an RAF engineer non-commissioned officer led a 37 strong team of ground personnel who deployed to Balad airbase to support USAF Reaper operations. The team set up a maintenance unit to take over from a group of contract engineers, provided by the air vehicle's manufacturer General Atomics, who had supported the Reapers entry into service in the Iraq theatre earlier in 2008.[37] The RAF UAV contingent in Iraq was invariably drawn into supporting US and UK special forces operations, rather than the UK-led division in Basra. As the strategic tasking of the special forces in Baghdad had a higher priority than routine framework patrols in Basra, the former had first call on Predator and Reaper output. This led to complaints from British commanders in Basra that they were not getting a fair share of the FMV product. This situation only changed in April 2008 when the US committed significant numbers of troops to Operation Charge of the Knights.

The Royal Air Force was at the heart of the US-led coalition campaign across Iraq from 2003 through to 2009. Its aircraft, intelligence experts and senior staff were involved in almost every aspect of the US campaign, flying and supporting American land operations across the length and breadth of Iraq. This gave the RAF a perspective of the campaign that was very different from their army colleagues in Basra. Although many army officers and soldiers in Basra routinely complained that RAF air support was nowhere to be seen, the RAF was fighting a very different war. Its heavy involvement with the US air campaign, meant that when British forces needed air support they invariably got it from Americans because of the leverage provided by the support the RAF was giving to the USAF elsewhere in Iraq. RAF officers claimed the support the Americans provided to the British Army in Basra was far in excess of what the RAF alone could have provided. "It was a good deal and we got a good return on our contribution to the coalition air campaign," commented one senior RAF officer. "The army never really understood this and they just complained when an American jet turned up over Basra rather than a RAF Tornado."[38]

Chapter 21

GOOD KIT? CRAP KIT?

Every war generates iconic weapons, for good or for bad reasons. The US Army in Vietnam turned the Bell UH-1 Huey helicopter into a legend, the Battle of Britain made the Supermarine Spitfire famous, and the Martini Henry rifle epitomised Britain's war against the Zulus.

For the British Army, the Iraq campaign did not produce any weapon that entered the public consciousness as a war winner. If anything, the reputation of the British Army's equipment and the Ministry of Defence's ability to procure new hardware was seriously damaged by the Iraq campaign. British military inadequacies in Iraq seemed to be summed up by the vulnerabilities of the Snatch Land Rover to improvised explosive devices (IEDs). After several of the vehicles were successfully penetrated by roadside IEDs and their crews killed or injured, their design appeared to be defenceless against the new militia weapons. Stories appeared in the media reporting that soldiers in Iraq had nicknamed the Snatch Land Rover's 'coffins on wheels'. This was a superficial analysis, exacerbated by inevitable exaggeration, but the Snatch story stuck in the minds of many journalists, commentators and parliamentarians.

The narrative of British Army's equipment in Iraq is far more complex and nuanced than the superficial media coverage but it is ultimately far from flattering to many in the army's senior leadership and the officials in the Ministry of Defence. Criticism of British Army's equipment is not a new phenomenon. In World War One the infamous "shell crisis," when artillery batteries on the Western Front allegedly ran out of ammunition, prompted the resignation of the Prime Minister H.H. Asquith. In World War Two, the poor quality of British tanks prompted debates in parliament. In the 1990s, the BBC Radio 4 Today Programme journalist Andrew Gilligan carved a niche for himself broadcasting reports about the shortcomings of British military hardware in the 1999 Kosovo campaign, including radios that did not work and hundreds of smart bombs that missed their target.

The then-Labour government deployed the full weight of its publicity machine against Gilligan to neutralise what would now be known as 'reputational damage' to the British military. His reports became known as "crap kit stories" and they took on a ritualistic flavour, with leaked documents revealing problems with equipment, and then lame rebuttals from New Labour spin doctors. This confrontational style of journalism ensured that Fleet Street journalists were very receptive to what became a never-ending series of stories blaming poor equipment for the death of soldiers in Iraq.

The invasion of Iraq in the spring of 2003 was to provide the first test of the British Army's latest equipment. While the army's tanks, vehicles and main weapons would work well, the rushed and chaotic deployment of the 1st (UK)

Armoured Division would expose serious problems with the British military's logistic support organisation in delivering equipment to frontline units.

Nothing characterised this more than the case of Sergeant Steven Roberts of the Royal Tank Regiment who was killed at a checkpoint outside Zubayr in March 2003. He had no body armour because his unit had been asked to hand it over to infantry regiments that appeared to have more need for it than tank crewmen, like Roberts.[1] The secrecy ordered by Prime Minister Tony Blair to cover the preparations for war throughout most of 2002 meant that orders for additional body armour, and what were termed urgent operational requirement (UOR) improvements, to existing equipment had to be put off until the last minute.

Only in December 2002 were orders allowed to be placed under UOR procedures and then everything had to be delivered in less than three months. On top of this, the decision to divert the main land force from Turkey to Kuwait in January added even more pressure on the supply lines and procurement organisation, as additional desert warfare equipment now had to be purchased.

The Defence Logistic Organisation's asset tracking system broke down in the chaos of Kuwait's overcrowded ports, resulting in hundreds of containers full of body armour, desert camouflage uniforms and boots, chemical warfare and defence equipment going missing on the eve of the war.[2] The then-Brigadier Dick Applegate worked in the Ministry of Defence's equipment capability or requirements branch at this time, and recalled, "we were not allowed to prepare [for the war]".

"We were not allowed to talk formally to industry [about UORs], but we did it anyway to see if they could do it [if we got the go ahead]. We were always on the back foot. The preparation was rudimentary but it was done by good people under huge time pressure and despite some simplistic thinking about how quickly industry could respond – it's not possible to simply pop down to 'Tanks R Us' and clear the shelves. The risk was just about managed and it did not turn out to be catastrophic. But it's not the way to prepare for a war."[3]

In the end, the big-ticket UOR items, such as armour upgrade packages for Warrior armoured vehicles and Challenger 2 main battle tanks were flown out by air, and were fitted just in time for war. These vehicles performed superbly and none of them were ever penetrated by Iraqi weapons during the invasion phase of Operation Telic. The only Challenger destroyed was the victim of what became known as friendly fire or a 'blue on blue' incident. The only soldiers killed inside a Warrior at this time fell victim to an ambush by an Iraqi who sneaked up on the crew while they had the vehicle's doors open and sprayed the inside with AK-47 fire.[4]

Eventually some £510 million was budgeted for UORs for Operation Telic 1 with some £400 million actually being spent by the end of combat operations in May 2003.[5] The Phoenix unmanned aerial vehicle or drone also performed well, spotting targets behind Iraqi lines, and the Mamba locating radar was credited with detecting incoming mortar and artillery fire in seconds thus allowing counter battery fire to be directed with devastating effect.

All these weapon systems had been designed in the 1980s and 1990s with high intensity combat in mind and so their excellent performance outside Basra was not really surprising. As the campaign moved into the counter-insurgency phase, the issues of equipment performance became far more pressing as army hardware found itself being used in circumstances for which it was not intended.

Eventually more than £1 billion was spent on UOR equipment during the course of Operation Telic and much of it undoubtedly saved lives and contributed to tactical success but controversy dogged the effort to provide the British Army with new equipment. Over the next five years those involved in bringing UOR equipment into service faced conflicting pressures and challenges as they learned how to make the UOR process work. Each piece of UOR equipment was different. Some went through the UOR process quickly with little technical difficulty. Other took longer due to bureaucratic issues within the military or civilian authorising chains. Some became highly political. All involved considerable 'friction' as the various players in the UOR process moved through the bureaucracy in London.

To order new equipment, commanders in Iraq initially had to raise what is termed an 'urgent statement of user requirement' (USUR), which was sent for endorsement to the UK's Permanent Joint Headquarters (PJHQ) at Northwood which controls all overseas operations; to the single-service staffs; and to the capability management staff in London. With those key approvals secured, MoD officials then approached the Treasury to secure funding from the government's financial reserve. Procurement officials in the Defence Procurement Agency (now the Defence Equipment & Support (DE&S) organisation) were then tasked to purchase the required items. Usually, discussions with industry took place informally at an early stage and ran in parallel, with the best companies willing to work before a contract had been agreed. "Trust between all parties was the bed-rock of this system", commented Brigadier Applegate.[6]

The traditional UOR rules, were set up during the Falklands War, dusted off for the 1991 Gulf War, and then redefined during the Bosnia and Kosovo campaigns. Under these, in order to gain access to the emergency funding from the Treasury commanders in the field had to prove the required equipment was demonstrably urgent, demonstrably needed, had a defined requirement and could be delivered with six months. This created numerous bureaucratic hurdles that needed to be jumped before UOR equipment could be purchased and delivered to Iraq.

Many of those working in UOR process were doing new things for which they had not been trained for. Replacing large amounts of equipment in the middle of a campaign, under considerable time and operational pressure was a new experience for almost everyone involved in the process. The British Army had never done this before on such a scale.

According to Colonel David Eadie, the head of the Equipment Branch in PJHQ at the height of the effort to purchase UOR equipment for Operation Telic between 2006 to 2009, many vital lessons were learned about the UOR process in Iraq and many of them were put to very good effect in Afghanistan subsequently.

In Iraq, the intensity of operations initially swamped senior commanders and their staff. They worked 18 hour days just keeping the mission on the road and this meant there was little prospect of diverting scarce time to work on detailed UOR paper work for a project that would not come to fruition anytime soon. During the first two years of the occupation, the headquarters in Basra did not have sufficient scientific, technical, weapons intelligence and administrative staff to make detailed assessments of equipment requirements and feed them up to PJHQ for approval – even though such an organisation had been a core element of UK's operations in Northern Ireland. This collective experience was ignored or considered irrelevant. Even at PJHQ, right up to the end of Operation Telic there was only one colonel and a couple of staff officers to turn UOR bids from Iraq around and send them up the Ministry of Defence and Treasury in London.[7]

"However, one of the most critical lessons was the definitive requirement for better technical education amongst the officer class at all levels," said Eadie. "Regrettably, it is not clear even now that this has been fully grasped by senior staff or by the Defence Academy, where the imperative to train officers in operational staff work still takes complete priority over technical training. Most senior commanders in Basra from 2005 onwards realised the desperate need to have technically educated staff embedded within their operational headquarters and PJHQ did their best to facilitate that. However, manpower shortages across the Army as a result of the operational demand and a lack of suitably technically trained officers meant that this was always going to be a drag on rapid process."[8]

Furthermore, senior officers involved in the UOR process reported that senior civil servants in the Treasury in many cases did not share the sense of urgency of those nearer the frontline.

"Technical staffs in theatre, at PJHQ, in the Ministry of Defence and DE&S worked ridiculous hours to ensure that soldiers in theatre were as well equipped as possible, but arcane rules and significant Treasury obduracy proved almost as much a block on progress as the lack of staff," said Eadie. "The Treasury, very tenuously, argued throughout the campaign that they had never turned down a UOR 'on cost grounds alone', but they did everything in their power to turn them down for any other reason they could dream up. We were tasked to justify, often several repetitive times, the number of equipments required, their capabilities, their functionality, their usability in other theatres and sometimes even on Health & Safety grounds. Trying to define something that was only usable in Iraq or was not dangerous to use in an operational theatre was virtually impossible and not a little frustrating. Even when it was obvious that lives could be saved by urgent deployment of the equipment concerned, that was sometimes insufficient to sway certain treasury mandarins. This was hugely frustrating and caused immense friction. Unfortunately it was invariably PJHQ and DE&S who took the blame, when it was beyond their power to influence. It often took weightily deployed arguments from very senior officers to break these unnecessary log jams at a time when they ought to have been able to concentrate on more vital operational concerns."[9]

The most high profile and controversial equipment issue during Operation Telic involved the provision of new armoured vehicles to counter the militia IED threat. The summer of 2003 saw British troops come under attack by large number of rioters throwing stones and using petrol bombs. This period also saw the first appearance of crude IEDs, which killed one soldier. As a crisis response, commanders in Iraq requested that Snatch Land Rovers be sent out to provide their soldiers with protection in riot situations. Eventually nearly 600 out of a fleet of some 950 Snatch Land Rovers would be sent to Iraq.[10] To deal with the IEDs initiated by electronic remote control, the army asked for the electronic counter-measures (ECM) equipment fitted on Snatch vehicles in Northern Ireland to be adapted to meet the threat in southern Iraq.

Experts at the Defence Scientific Technological Laboratories soon delivered a viable solution, and contracts were placed with those British companies that had made the highly specialised equipment for use in Northern Ireland. As the IED threat is by its very nature unpredictable and dynamic, it had been UK practice to develop key technologies up to a level of maturity that would enable rapid production in the event of the threat becoming real. This approach now paid great dividends and the work was conducted among a small group of trusted companies, scientists and users.[11]

Now promoted to be the army's head of land equipment requirements, as Master General of the Ordnance and a Major General, Applegate said the UK had a lead in counter-IED technology that was two years in advance of anything the US had.

"We felt comfortable. Because of Northern Ireland we were world leaders in dominating the electro-magnetic spectrum," he said. "Our solutions were incredibly responsive, light weight and tuneable so we could prevent attacks, rather than just absorb attacks on our vehicles."[12]

"In 2004, the Americans were in a desperate predicament because of the IED attacks around Baghdad and asked us to help them," he recalled. "We provided them with our technology and we sent people out to help them set up the counter-IED task force. Our Northern Ireland experts went to work with them. This collaborative effort helped bring the Americans up to speed quickly and they were very grateful. Our relationship became very special."

Details of this collaboration remained highly secret at the time and the Ministry of Defence could not use it to counter some of the simplistic criticism in the media. However, it went a long way towards cementing Anglo-US intelligence co-operation on future IED threats in Iraq (and Afghanistan later) and it speeded up the delivery of mine-protected vehicles when they were eventually ordered. A UOR to roll out improved ECM equipment for Iraq was issued in November 2003, launching what became known as Project Locksmith. This initially had a budget of £73 million and eventually evolved a suite of counter-measures that was designed to jam the radio and mobile telephone devices being used to activate IEDs. The suite of counter-measures was initially designed just to be fitted to Snatch vehicles, but the demand was such that the equipment was soon being fitted to other armoured vehicles and civilian SUVs used by Foreign and Commonwealth Office diplomats.[13]

British commanders and troops were enthusiastic users of ECM equipment and were full of praise about how it was instrumental in saving soldiers' lives. There were repeated requests for more ECM-equipped vehicles. In November 2004, a second larger tranche of Locksmith equipment was ordered under a £127 million contract. The importance of Locksmith can be gauged by the fact that it soaked up more than half of the total £380 million spent by the British government on UOR equipment between 2003 and 2005.[14] In a September 2005 briefing for troops heading to Iraq, an army Locksmith expert claimed that its "ECM Capability inhibits 95% of the current threat in Multi-National Division (South East)".[15]

The Sadr revolts of 2004 exposed British troops to a series of new threats and during its tour, 1 Mechanised Brigade issued requests for several new UORs, including a man-pack ECM device designed to detect IED command wires, which was known as Walrus. The armour protection of the Warrior was also identified as needing improvement to counter mass barrages of rocket propelled grenades (RPGs). By the time the Black Watch was dispatched on Operation Bracken to central Iraq in October 2004, its Warriors boasted what was dubbed 'bar armour.' This was essentially similar to the "armoured skirts" fitted to German tanks in World War Two to defeat shaped charge weapons – the precursors of the modern RPG. The first Warriors with ECM kit had also appeared by this time.[16]

The need for troops to remain within the protection of Warriors and Snatch vehicles during riots and cordon operations in the summer heat prompted requests for enhanced air conditioning systems for both vehicles. Some £27 million was spent on air conditioning upgrades to the Snatch fleet in 2004, and a further £22 million was spent on similar improvements the following year.[17] Snatch, which had been introduced for use in riots in Northern Ireland in the 1990s, continued to receive good reviews in unit post operational tour reports in 2004 and into 2005 on account of its mobility and protection against small arms fire.

This was not the case with the Saxon wheeled-armoured personnel carrier, about which 1 Mechanised Brigade was damning, saying its "General War Saxon deployed in theatre is not fit for role. The only 'top cover' is provided by the commander, who has to command the vehicle as well as provide 360 degree observation against RPG firers and an IED threat. This is unacceptable overload. It also lacks sufficient armoured protection against RPGs and, unlike Snatch, lacks speed and agility."[18]

The Brigade asked for the Northern Ireland version of the Saxon with a better turret to be sent to Iraq. All but a handful of the Saxons were soon withdrawn from use and the remaining vehicles provided with bar armour to allow them to be used as ambulances until 2006. Other vehicles, such as tank recovery vehicles, fuel tankers and supply trucks also ended up receiving bar armour and ECM.

Several British soldiers were also seriously injured during the heavy fighting over the summer of 2004 by sniper fire or shell fragments, caused injuries in areas not projected by their body armour. This prompted work to field the Kestrel and Osprey body armour with full chest and back plates, as well as neck and groin protection, which eventually entered service in 2006. "These solutions were 'pushed' from UK following identification of new insurgent tactics being used in Baghdad, outside of the UK sector", said Applegate.[19]

The threat from suicide bombers to troops manning checkpoints prompted a move to acquire a system called the Danger Light. This was a dazzling light mounted on a rifle that was designed to dissuade approaching motorists from continuing towards a checkpoint or road block. Officers involved in this project recalled it turned into a real struggle to persuade the Treasury to fund its purchase. "For some reason the Treasury decided they didn't like it and they (and the UK's Laser Safety Committee – a very dogmatic group of civilian doctors, with no real understanding of the military imperative, who refused to meet more than twice a year, whatever the circumstances) did everything in their power to stop the programme running," said one senior army officer. "In the end they thankfully relented and it was successfully fielded."[20]

The appearance of passive infra-red detonator (PID) initiated IEDs, and then explosively formed projectile (EFP) warheads in the summer of 2005, initially left the British Army struggling to respond.

It took several weeks to analyse the first batch of captured EFP warheads and PID devices. Their initial limited employment in Maysan province made commanders in theatre cautious about jumping to the conclusion that these weapons were a true game changer. The migration of the EFPs to Basra though was more significant. However, the army was not immediately able to switch to using Warriors due to the relatively low number held in theatre and even those vehicles were unable to withstand the full blast effects of the biggest IEDs. That coupled with the apparently continued effectiveness of the ECM equipment, meant that there was no immediate request for new vehicles to replace the Snatch from commanders in Basra.

There has been intense speculation that penny-pinching defence cuts by the-then Labour government was behind the lack of a replacement for the Snatch Land Rover. However, from contemporary documents it is clear that in the key period between August 2005 and July 2006 there were intense disagreements within the army in Basra over the whether the Snatch needed to be replaced. Many officers and soldiers shied away from using Warriors because their heavy weight and bulk channelled the vehicles onto a few routes and bridges, which could be easily seeded with IEDs. It was only a matter of time before the insurgents fielded bigger bombs to defeat Warrior. The Snatch, or even dismounted operations on foot, were a better way to keep troops safe by allowing them much greater manoeuvre options to avoid obvious ambush sites. From a tactical perspective, the Warrior could also not operate in much of Basra due to the city's narrow roads and alleyways. Snatch crews were ordered to drive close to Iraqi civilian traffic to make it more difficult for insurgents to specially target the British vehicles without killing their fellow countrymen; although on occasions this seemed not to bother them much as it was believed it would.[21] The main concerns of one unit that used Snatch in 2006 and 2007 was the lack of spare parts and maintenance time available to keep the vehicles roadworthy and the frustrating bureaucracy and outlook within the parts of the army responsible for repairing the vehicles.[22]

The British commander in Basra, Major General Jim Dutton, in his end of tour report in November 2005, assessed that the army "has never entirely defeated [the IED] threat but it is manageable, and I don't believe that it has a significantly deleterious effect on morale in the area of operations. South eastern Iraq remains at the lower end of any table of security incidents."[23]

Air Marshal Glenn Torpy, the Chief of Joint Operations until the spring of 2006, told the Chilcot inquiry that there was reluctance among senior officers to second guess the views of commanders in Iraq regarding the threat. "So, as always, there is a balance to be struck, and there's a risk balance to be taken, and the only person I believe who could take that is the commander on the ground," he said. "I would not wish, and I don't think an army officer in my position would want to be taking a different view to the advice that he's getting from the person on the ground."[24]

At the army's Land Command headquarters at Wilton in Wiltshire, General Sir Richard Dannatt and his staff were working up their own ideas for new protected vehicles, but their proposals did not gain any traction until the late spring of 2006. Dannatt was pushing for the purchase of the new Vector protected vehicle, which was an up-armoured version of the Pinzgauer 6 x 6 vehicle and he wanted to accelerate delivery of the new Bulldog vehicle, an improved FV432 armoured personnel carrier, to Iraq.[25] Except for a handful sent to work in Baghdad with the force protecting the British Embassy, the bulk of the Vectors ended up being diverted to Afghanistan, where it proved to have limited protection against IEDs and a serious problem with its front differentials.

In his Chilcot evidence, Air Marshal Torpy said that Ministry of Defence procurement experts had trouble finding a suitable replacement on the international defence market. "Everybody was working on this as an issue" said Torpy. "It was just there was not a solution which anybody could pull out of a hat at that particular moment."[26]

Up to June 2006, the British headquarters in Basra had not generated a USUR asking for a replacement for Snatch, which created a bureaucractic log jam that prevented anyone back in the UK moving forward with the purchase of new vehicles.

According to Lord Paul Drayson, the defence procurement minister and former biotech entrepreneur, the military chain of command could not agree on a requirement for a new vehicle or its specification. "The military found it difficult to reach agreement about what was required," he told the Chilcot inquiry.

"Overall, the procurement "system" reinforced the environment whereby the *process* was more important than the *end result*."[27]

Fatal attacks on the Snatch continued into 2006, with nine vehicles being destroyed with the loss of 11 soldiers.

"There was a general awareness that we needed to take this seriously," said Applegate. "The early IEDs were unsophisticated but we had now run out of the option of relying entirely on ECM. It was no longer possible to prevent attack, we now need to be able to absorb an attack."[28]

The shooting down of a Lynx helicopter over Basra in May added to the feeling that the insurgents were starting to overmatch British equipment in Iraq but there was still no firm plan for a way forward. The spring of 2006 saw intense media and parliamentary pressure for something to be done. General Applegate said "force protection had became a political issue, with huge newspaper headlines, and coroners inquests were criticising the army and all this cranked up the demand to avoid any casualties".[29]

With no agreement within the army on what do, Drayson decided to take matters into his own hands. He described in a statement to the Chilcot inquiry, how army commanders in Iraq, PJHQ and at Land Command headquarters could not agree on requirements for new vehicles. During the spring of 2006 Drayson "resolved to encourage the army to identify a requirement for an additional medium weight vehicle rather than a replacement of the light Snatch to avoid getting bogged down in resistance from the military."[30]

On 27th June, Drayson met with the defence secretary Des Browne and Armed Forces Minister Bob Ainsworth to try to push the issue forward. The military were asked to come up with something fast. A week later, the new Chief of Joint Operations, Lieutenant General Nick Houghton wrote to Drayson to confirm formally that there was now a requirement for a medium patrol vehicle. On 13th July Major General Applegate and the officer charged with staffing all requirements for ground vehicles, Brigadier Bill Moore, were tasked to find a solution. On 20th July, the Treasury was asked for money to buy 108 new heavily-armoured vehicles based on the wheeled American 6 x 6 Cougar chassis and the first of these new vehicles, now named Mastiffs, were to be ready for service by the end of the year.

Air Marshal Torpy confirmed that Drayson was the driving force behind the initiative, commenting in his Chilcot evidence that, "it took the Minister to say, "'We are going to do this'".[31]

"I was tasked by Drayson and Brown to find a solution" said Applegate. "There was a need to do something. I had carte blanche to cut through the process and it was politically crucial to do it quickly. The Force Protection Mastiff was the answer. Browne wanted it in Iraq before Christmas but there was a need to fit radios and ECM. I called in some favours with US Marine Corps and industry."[32]

The Mastiff had a V-shaped hull to deflect mine blasts away from the crew, as well as independent suspension and drive units so that if a wheel was blown off it could still be driven out of an ambush. The small company that designed and manufactured the vehicle was struggling to meet the huge demand from the US Marines and US Army at this point when the British decided they wanted to buy 108. The US Marines Corps agreed to give up vehicles from it own order and so the British took vehicles from their slots on the US production line. Other American officials ensured that the British gained access to the special materials needed for the Mastiff's enhanced armour and received the necessary export approvals.

"That was thanks to the help we gave them on IEDs and the relationships we had built up over time," said Applegate. "Our embassy in Washington also worked superbly to gain Congressional approval – the fastest ever, I believe."[33]

At the end of December 2006 the first vehicles were delivered to Iraq but Applegate said that his team had had to make a conscious decision not to wait for a full provision of spare parts on initial deployments in order to speed up the delivery.

"We took risk on availability - saving people came first", he said.

"Des Browne [who as defence secretary was Drayson, the procurement minister's immediate boss] deserves huge credit for pushing it through, to enable those who do to act, to cut through the crap" said Applegate.

"Not one single person was killed in Mastiff [in Iraq]. The crews survived EFPs and huge bombs – it was very survivable."[34]

The Mastiff decision was not the end of efforts to improve British armoured vehicles in Iraq. At the same time as Mastiff was announced in July 2006, Browne also ordered that an additional batch of 54 Bulldog tracked personnel carriers were to receive enhanced armoured protection. The Bulldog was an upgraded version of the 1960s vintage FV432 vehicle that was in process of receiving fleet-wide enhancements to their engines, transmission and electrical system. In late 2005, some 70 were already earmarked for deployment to Iraq but the project was expanded and accelerated in June 2006. A new armour package called ASPRO-HMT containing both passive and explosive reactive armour (ERA), and appliqué produced by Israel's Rafael Advanced Defense Systems, was installed, along with a protected machine gun cupola and ECM. This project was also accelerated and the first of 117 vehicles were delivered to Basra in September 2006.[35]

The heavily armoured Challengers and Warrior were also not immune to insurgent attacks. In August 2006 a Challenger was penetrated for the first time by an advanced RPG-29 anti-tank weapon, which has a duel shaped charge warhead. An EFP IED then badly damaged one of the tanks in an incident in April 2007. In response the 14 tanks in theatre were first fitted with new Dorcester (the successor to Chobham) frontal armour packs and then Rafael reactive armour packs appeared, as well as advanced ECM systems.[36]

Fatal attacks on Warriors in December 2006 and April 2007 led to a crash project to provide protection against upwardly angled IEDs. This project involved increasing the area coverage and protection levels of the Warrior's side appliqué armour and the first Warrior Additional Protection 2, or WRAP 2 as they were known, were developed in six weeks. The vehicles were also fitted with the Israeli ASPRO-HMT armour, which had been developed by Rafael to counter Hizbollah rocket propelled grenades in Lebanon. It was hoped that this Israeli made armour would give the British vehicles enhanced protection against rocket propelled grenades with advanced shaped charge warheads. The first of the new vehicles began arriving in Iraq in November 2007. Both the improved Warrior and Bulldog were the work horses of British units in Basra during 2007 and 2008 and their crews suffered few casualties.[37]

One of the most innovative UORs developed for the Iraq campaign was the fielding of the counter-rocket, artillery and mortar (C-RAM) systems at Basra airport. The British Army were not initially keen on the system due to an incorrect perceived potential for collateral damage. However, during 2006, as rocket attacks on the main British airbase escalated in the spring of 2007, a UOR was approved. This initially involved the leasing of five US Army Land-based Phalanx Weapon Systems for a six-month period through to late 2007. This allowed time for ten Royal Navy Raytheon Phalanx Block 1A anti-missile close-in weapon systems to be stripped from warships and converted for use at Basra airport.[38]

The Phalanx guns were designed to shoot down anti-ship missiles by spraying thousands of rounds of high explosive shells into the path of the inbound weapons. The US Army had adapted them to defend its bases in Baghdad from insurgents rockets and mortars and had developed a new ammunition that was programmed to explode in the air at a certain distance from the gun and therefore did not fall to earth in highly populated Iraqi cities.

To make the system work at Basra airport required a network of Saab Giraffe radars, which were set up to detect in-coming fire. Lockheed Martin provided its Indirect Fire Locator, Alarm and Intercept System (IFLAIS) that automatically reacted to the radar contacts and then activated a system of warning sirens at the airbase to allow troops to take cover in shelters. It was rapidly realised that the simple expedient of lying down on the ground dramatically reduced the chance of a soldier being hit by any shrapnel rising from a ground-detonating warhead, so these alarms were crucial and very effective. IFLAIS also automatically assessed if any aircraft or helicopters were in the template of the C-RAM guns before cuing the guns to engage the target, all within seconds of the target being detected. If aircraft were in the vicinity, the guns' arcs of fire would be inhibited accordingly.

The system was also linked to Royal Artillery 105mm and 155mm gun batteries at the airport to allow them to return fire at the insurgent firing points. The whole warning system was operated by personnel from the RAF Regiment and 16 Regiment Royal Artillery, backed up by Royal Navy maintainers who looked after the guns themselves. From their first activation in May 2007 to September 2008 the seven C-RAM guns took part in "over 100 successful engagements of targets in the defended area," according to Royal Artillery officers involved in the project.[39]

The British Army struggled throughout the Iraq campaign to provide its contingent in Iraq with unmanned aerial vehicles (UAVs) to monitor insurgent activity. Whilst Phoenix performed well in the invasion it proved less suitable during the subsequent insurgency. The air vehicle was often badly damaged on landing and as the Iraqi campaign dragged on, the Royal Artillery's inventory was progressively put beyond repair. Production had ceased in the late 1990s so Phoenix was clearly a time limited system.

By September 2005, there were only 84 air vehicles left in the British Army's inventory and it was predicted that half would be lost by the end of 2008. In 2005, Royal Artillery Phoenix batteries were restricted to taking 40 Phoenix air vehicles with them on six-month tours to Iraq, but even with the tight restrictions on flying the loss rate was just too high for the limited stock. The deteriorating security situation in Iraq made it increasingly difficult to recover damaged aircraft for repair because of the risk to troops of ambush by insurgents, but this was just at the time frontline commanders wanted Phoenix missions to be surged. The time was up for Phoenix after less than a decade in formal British Army service and by early 2006 there were just not enough air vehicles left to sustain a viable operational detachment in Iraq. It was decided that the system would remain in use for training in the UK and be officially retired in March 2008.[40]

22 Battery was the last ever Phoenix battery deployed to support Operation Telic. The final operational flight of Phoenix was conducted by Koehler's Troop in May 2006, at Camp Abu Naji near al Amarah. The departure of Phoenix left a major gap in the intelligence, surveillance, target acquisition and reconnaissance (ISTAR) capability of the British-led division in southern Iraq. After being lent some US-owned, Lockheed Martin developed Desert Hawk UAVs for a trial, the British Army purchased a quantity under UOR procedures. Although later versions of the hand-launched mini-UAV had been modified to overcome the interference problem with the local television network, it only had sufficient flying time to be able to operate close to British bases for an hour at a time, and its imagery could not be distributed beyond its small laptop-sized control unit. As a result, Desert Hawk was used almost exclusively to provide perimeter surveillance of British bases.

The RAF Regiment borrowed a small number of AeroVironment RQ-11 Raven mini-UAVs from the US Army in the autumn of 2006, to help its airfield defence squadron in Basra protect the city's airbase. The British Army then conducted a couple of further trials in southern Iraq. The Queen's Royal Hussars took a Raven system out into the desert around al Amarah for one of these trials, but when it flew into the side of an RAF Merlin HC3 helicopter parked next to their camp, the watching group of senior officers were less than impressed and Raven stayed as an RAF Regiment system.[41]

It was also hoped that the increase of RAF personnel assigned to the USAF Predator Task Force would result in enhanced availability of the operational level American UAV to British forces in Basra, but Baghdad remained a priority for the USAF and the British Army never had any certainty of when Predator would be available to support them.

The then-commander of British forces in Basra, Major General Richard Shirreff, was exasperated at the failure of the Ministry of Defence in London to generate a replacement for Phoenix. He later told the Chilcot inquiry, "it beggared belief that nearly three and a half years after the start of this campaign, we still [had] no UAV capable of flying in south-east Iraq, in the summer. I was told that no more staff effort could possibly be put in to deploying UAVs to southeast Iraq. I think [this was] just because the Ministry of Defence was incapable of generating the drive and energy to deliver them."[42]

The problem revolved around the contract for the Phoenix replacement, Watchkeeper, which was signed with the Anglo/French defence company Thales in July 2005, acting in a Joint Venture with Elbit Systems of Israel. Only enough money could be found by the Treasury to fund a slow rate of development to allow delivery of Watchkeeper to the British Army in 2010. Thales offered to lease the Ministry of Defence an interim solution, based around Elbit's Hermes 450 UAV, from which Watchkeeper was to be evolved, to cover any gap if Phoenix had to be withdrawn from service early.

This was turned down on cost grounds by the Treasury and Ministry of Defence. The British government at this point still believed that events in Iraq were moving in a positive direction and that the UK garrison could be reduced from its divisional strength to a battalion-sized force by the end of 2006. In this environment there was no appetite to spend large amounts of money on new equipment that would only be used for a few months. Inflexible UOR rules also meant that money could not be spent on equipment that could be used outside the existing operational theatres; this was the Treasury's way of preventing the army from trying to replace in-service equipment that would otherwise have to be replaced through the long term Equipment Plan.[43]

Events in Iraq and Afghanistan during the summer and autumn of 2006 would turn this situation around. In September 2006, an RAF Nimrod MR2 crashed in Afghanistan and immediately the aircraft, which provided a great deal of the UK's full motion video surveillance capability, was grounded for prolonged periods as safety problems were rectified.

By the end of 2006, additional UOR funding had been agreed for new UAVs for Iraq and Afghanistan. New batches of Desert Hawk III variants were ordered and a replacement for Phoenix was finally agreed. Thales was asked to dust off their plans to provide Hermes 450 systems. Within only six months, lease contracts were signed, crews were trained in Israel and hardware was delivered to Basra airbase.[44]

22 Battery returned to Basra in the spring of 2007 with their new Desert Hawks, and in June the first Hermes 450s went operational. The Hermes 450 was several generations in advance of the venerable Phoenix. It had four times the endurance on station, was far more airworthy and unlike Phoenix could be safely flown over Iraqi towns and cities. Whereas a whole Phoenix battery was lucky to fly some 500 hours during a six month tour in Iraq, a single Hermes 450 air vehicle could run up that many flight hours in a month of operations. The new UAV's sensors had longer range and generated far sharper images that allowed intelligence analysts to identify even the type of small arms being carried by insurgents. Crucially, the imagery from the Hermes 450 could be downloaded directly onto laptop-sized remote viewing terminals so frontline troops could watch the imagery in real-time. At first a bespoke receiver was in use, but by the end of 2007, Hermes 450 imagery could be received by the L-3 Communications ROVER terminals that were becoming standard issue across the US and British armed forces. ROVER terminals could receive imagery from multiple types of aircraft and UAVs, dramatically enhancing its usefulness. A simple dial allowed them to tune into which ever helicopter, aircraft or unmanned aerial vehicle was broadcasting imagery of their target.

The British UAV force in Iraq was now put on a firm footing with 32 Regiment providing half a battery's worth of personnel, around 50 troops, to run the Hermes 450 detachment. The responsibility for manning Desert Hawk fell to air defence troops from 47 Regiment Royal Artillery, who were temporarily re-roled as mini-UAV operators. Until Hermes 450 was up and running in the summer of 2007, the mainstay of airborne surveillance over Basra had been the Royal Navy Sea King HC4s of Joint Helicopter Force (Iraq), equipped with L-3 Communications MX-15 thermal imaging camera systems. Known as the Broadsword fit, these video cameras were able to monitor events in real-time by both day and night. A similar system, known as P4, had been fitted to RAF Pumas, but it been plagued with technical problems and was no longer in use in southern Iraq by 2005.[45]

The Broadsword-equipped Sea Kings had been an instant hit with British troops, because the video imagery they collected could be broadcast live to small laptop-sized video receiver terminals. For the first time, very junior army commanders had access to live video imagery of targets that previously had only been available to senior commanders in remote headquarters. In the summer of 2005, when two British Special Air Service soldiers were captured by Iraqi militia fighters, a Broadsword Sea King kept them under surveillance during the period of their captivity and provided vital intelligence to allow a successful rescue to be organised. In May 2006, insurgents brought down a Royal Navy 847 Squadron Lynx with a man-portable surface-to-air missile over central Basra, killing all five British personnel on board, including an AAC exchange pilot. The event was a major challenge to British air supremacy over Basra. Helicopter flights over Basra city in daylight had to be curtailed except in very exceptional circumstances. A crash programme was set in train to enhance the defensive systems on the Lynx.[46]

The growing intensity of the war in Afghanistan in 2006 meant that the Broadsword Sea King were scheduled to be transferred to Helmand province in early 2007, so a UOR programme was launched to equip four Lynx AH.9s in Basra with Broadsword equipment. This was taken to Iraq in the spring of 2007 and was an immediate success. For the next two years, it meant the Lynx detachment had a key ISTAR role in southern Iraq. Whenever a high priority operation was being planned or undertaken, the Lynx detachment was invariably in the thick of the action, conducting pre-mission intelligence gathering or providing commanders with a real-time eye-in-the-sky as the operation unfolded.

The MX-15 was relatively simple to use and reliable, making it far more popular than the P4 system it replaced. When fitted to the Lynx it allowed them to stand-off targets by up to 6,000 metres, and fly at heights that meant they could rarely be heard by insurgents on the ground, giving it the ability to carry out covert surveillance of targets. The system comprised an externally-mounted camera, a datalink antenna mounted under the helicopter's tail boom and an operator station in the rear cabin. This was manned by the Lynx's air trooper and he/she could either select video imagery to be recorded for later analysis, or download it in real-time to a viewing terminal. There was also a tablet screen that allowed the helicopter's commander to view the imagery while he sat in the helicopter's front seat.[47]

The MX-15/Lynx combination proved very popular, not only because it gave ground commanders a similar imagery to that provided by unmanned aerial vehicles, but also because it had a door-mounted 7.62mm GPMG for offensive action and, in extreme situations, the helicopter could land and pick up casualties or move small groups of troops around the battlefield. The arrival of MX-15 in early 2007 put Lynx back in the ISTAR game over Basra, and allowed it to carry out stand-off surveillance of urban targets without bringing the helicopter within range of heavy militia weapons.

One major equipment issue that the British Army grappled with during its six-year long engagement in Iraq was the provision of radio communications to frontline troops. The army initially deployed with the 1970s vintage Clansman radio system, which was in the process of being replaced by the Bowman system produced by the US company General Dynamics. Clansman was a good radio in its time, but the equipment was virtually worn out, spares were in short supply and only a small percentage of the radios could be fitted with electronic encryption equipment. Bowman was supposed to rectify these problems, but it was late entering service and when the first troops entered Iraq in 2003, the first army brigade had not been equipped with the new radios.

The Clansman radio network just about held together during the invasion phase, but during the occupation, the size of the British controlled zone in Iraq meant the old radios did not have the range to provide effective communications. In Maysan province this was a particularly problem, and troops in remote locations therefore were issued with satellite radios to overcome the range issue. The Royal Military Police patrol that was fatally attacked at Marjar Al Kabir in June 2003 had no satellite radio; this was judged by a subsequent board of inquiry to have contributed to them not being able to summon assistance.[48]

Rolling out Bowman across the British armed forces was a huge logistic exercise, involving 41,498 Bowman HF and VHF Combat Net Radios, 3,458 High Capacity Data Radios, 10,669 Local Area Sub-system or network installations and 26,498 computers, worth nearly £1.9 billion. Element of Bowman equipment also had to be installed in 133 naval vessels, 239 aircraft and 22,832 vehicles.[49]

A programme of conversion got under way in 2005 and 12 Mechanised Brigade took the first Bowman radios to Iraq later that year. However, even when Bowman was in service, it was not the answer to all the British Army's communications problems. The proliferation of electronic counter measures or jammers to defeat the militia IED threats resulted occasionally in what was termed 'electronic fratricide'. This in effect meant that the British jamming equipment was jamming their own radios. Troops learnt to get around the problem by only using their radios when their vehicles were stationary.[50]

One area where the British Army never seemed to gain any momentum was in the provision of modern computer networks and other information technology. Throughout the campaign, senior commanders repeatedly complained that there was no working intelligence database that troops across Iraqi could access and thereby cross reference information about the identity or location of militia fighters and groups.

"The computers available at sub-unit or company level were woeful and the only way to make operations work was for the commanders to use their own stuff," commented a 7 Brigade staff officer in 2006. "The guys doing the strike operations against the insurgents kept asking for more digital cameras to make records of arrests and searches, but for whatever reason this was ignored".[51]

Repeated requests for funding to set up and run an intelligence data base and other supporting computer systems were turned down by the Treasury because the Ministry of Defence already had a programme underway known as Dabinett, which was supposed to do the same job even though it would not be ready until later in the decade. Dabinett was eventually cancelled in 2010 before any of its equipment or systems was ever delivered. Using UOR funding to buy early equipment and systems that were already being purchased fell fowl of the Treasury's rules. "It was a question of the Treasury refusing to fund something under UOR procedures where there was already an equipment programme in place," commented one frustrated officer involved in this project. "A typical Catch 22 situation deliberately engineered by the Treasury."[52]

While the British Army's challenges with equipment procurement received most scrutiny during the Iraq campaign, the loss of a Hercules near Baghdad in January 2005 illustrated that the Royal Air Force also had problems. The coroners inquest into the crash that left 10 crew and passengers dead revealed that senior RAF officers had ignored recommendations by experts to fit fuel inerting systems, known as ESF, which might possibly have prevented the aircraft's wing fuel tank exploding after it had been hit by anti-aircraft fire.

A document trawl for the coroner unearthed a UK tactical analysis team (TAT) research report, which in 2002 advised RAF commanders to fit ESF. A further report, released just before the Iraq war in 2003, repeated the recommendation but the advice was not heeded, the inquest heard.[53]

The biggest criticism was that the UOR system was essentially reactive and that the 'system' did not always listen to the troops on the frontline. The consequence was that British troops were never able to get ahead of the insurgents in the race to field new and more effective weapons or deliver better protected vehicles. This was due in a large part to a lack of intelligence on Iraqi insurgent weapons and IED manufacturing capabilities for much of the campaign. The RAF was able to bid for and receive UOR equipment in the run up to the invasion in late 2002 and 2003 because they had been conducting a very active 'no-fly' zone operation over southern Iraq since the end of the first Gulf War. "The Iraqi air defence network was a known entity and it was possible to quantify what was needed to defeat the threat," recalled Torpy.[54] As a result, the RAF was able to secure funding to bring the Storm Shadow cruise missile and improvements to its aircraft's missile defence systems into service early, before the start of Operation Telic in March 2003.

As the campaign progressed, it became impossible to achieve this type of procurement and an arms race developed against the Iraqi militia groups. Insurgent weapon designers and tacticians studied British vehicles for weaknesses, but British Treasury rules prevented new equipment being purchased until the enemy had employed their latest weapons. Once the UOR system was activated, with few exceptions, it produced effective equipment that made a difference in the field. Unfortunately, it could only kick-in once soldiers had been killed or seriously injured – only latterly in the campaign were officers like Applegate allowed to develop an element of anticipation in the procurement process.

"The UOR system was designed for short-duration operations and not an enduring campaign," said Applegate.

"But as the army is routinely at the end of the queue for resources within the core peacetime defence programme, the UOR system was the only way of making good known short-falls, plus responding to the intrinsically dynamic nature of warfare, and the constant struggle between threat and counter-threat."[55]

Short-termism dominated this process throughout the Iraqi campaign, and there was a deep reluctance to spend time or money when the operation was theoretically due to wind up in a few months time.

"No one was willing to say what was likely to happen in six months time or what our pattern of operations might be," said Applegate. "So you couldn't be pro-active."[56]

According to General Dutton, "there was an element of 'you have got what you have got'. So you might have to use them, even if you know they are not the vehicle optimised for that particular [operation] -- and then you ask for different ones and, over time, they appear."[57]

The Iraq campaign raised serious questions about the interest of the British Army's senior leadership in equipment and technology. "Make do and mend" was too ingrained in their approach to make them raise their ambitions. The six-month tour cycle and systemic equipment under-funding reinforced these attitudes and created the view that commanders had more important things to concentrate on during their brief time in command.

"With a few exceptions, divisional and brigade commanders in Iraq passed stuff [about future equipment] down to the junior staff and did not consider it to be their job – we had also forgotten the lessons of Northern Ireland" said Applegate.

"People were too busy doing what they were doing to think about six months ahead, beyond their own tour. This was most obvious in the desperately slow development of our tactical intelligence capability and organisation. Too frequently, they paid insufficient attention to the contribution that equipment could make to success on the battlefield and how it could help to underpin the morale of one's own troops, their relatives and the support of the nation. Those that did understand this then had to work through the bureaucracy of the approvals system for UORs, including the choke-point of PJHQ. The Special Forces understood the need for new equipment, imagination and speed, using experimentation and rapid prototyping to seek new solutions, discarding equipment that could not be improved. It is hugely difficult to get the same approach in a large organisation like the British Army, and even worse in the Ministry of Defence. It took a huge amount of time to change attitudes and processes, and it is only latterly in Afghanistan that we now see a system that is anywhere close to being fit for purpose."[58]

Chapter 22

THE DUEL

During the afternoon of 6th May 2006, a small Royal Navy Lynx AH7 utility helicopter lifted off from the helipad at Basra Palace, and headed out over the Shatt-al-Arab waterway. Two Royal Air Force officers were on board carrying out a routine inspection of bases in the city, before taking up jobs in the headquarters controlling British helicopter operations in southern Iraq. It was a routine flight, on what seemed like a normal day. Along Basra's waterside thoroughfares traffic was flowing normally, and the city was its usual bustling self.

As the helicopter turned to head inland, sentries at British bases around the city saw it explode in a fireball. Seconds later it was falling to earth near the Old State Building in the centre of Basra. A group of insurgents had just fired a Soviet-era 9K34 Strela-3 shoulder-launched heat-seeking missile, or Manpad, at the British helicopter. The weapon, which NATO coded named the SA-14 Gremlin, worked perfectly, but more importantly it completely confounded the flares that were supposed to decoy away in-bound missiles. It hit the rear of the helicopter and blew its tail off, causing the Lynx to plummet to earth.[1]

Across the city, British troops started rushing to the scene to rescue their comrades and protect them from the expected mob of civilians who would swarm over the wreckage. They might kidnap the wounded crew members, creating a *Blackhawk Down*-like situation by parading them for propaganda purposes on Arab satellite news channels. In the worse case, if the crew were already dead, mobs of Iraqi civilians might loot their bodies of weapons, ammunition, wallets, personnel effects, jewellery and rings, as happened after British vehicles were blown up by improvised road-side bombs.

Sergeant N.S Reeder, of the Royal Anglian Regiment, was in one of the first patrols to reach the scene, and he set his dozen men the job of pushing back the three hundred-strong crowd that had already gathered and starting to grow rapidly.

"We knew that the integrity of the cordon was our main effort due to the fact that we did not know the situation at the crash site, and other agencies had to get in and take evidence away," he recalled.

"We could all see the crowd on the southern side of the bridge and we knew that we had to get them on the other side of the bridge to protect the crash site. We carried out what's known as a rapid advance with vehicles leading. The vehicles we had at our disposal were two Warriors and a number of Snatch Land Rovers; these would drive at the crowd with the troops to the rear of the Warriors ready to pounce. On the order we rushed the crowd; they did not want to fight toe-to-toe. They were on the back foot, and we got them on the other side of the bridge where we then blocked it with Warriors. When the crowd dispersed our next task was to wait for the other agencies to do their job; this took some time. We had been on the ground and in position for not much more than

45 minutes, when we took a barrage of mortars which landed about a hundred metres to the west of my men."[2]

For the rest of the night, and into the following morning, troops from Lieutenant Colonel Johnny Bowron's Basra City Battlegroup fought off hundreds of rioters and insurgents; they needed to allow the city's fire brigade to damp down the burning wreckage and military crash investigators to inspect the scene. They were able to confirm that the five personnel in the helicopter, including two RAF officers, pilots from the Army Air Corps and Royal Navy, as well as a Royal Marine crewman were dead. The incident escalated into what Bowron described as "protected street battles" in the heart of Basra's commercial district. Insurgents took aimed shots at the troops in the cordon and then mounted seven mortar barrages and ten rocket propelled grenade attacks through the night. The nearby base of the Light Infantry in the Old State Building was also targeted with mortars and small arms. Six British soldiers were wounded in the engagements, before the wreckage was recovered from the scene. Several insurgents and rioters were killed. Yet only a couple of streets away from the scene of mayhem around the crash site, the people of Basra were going about their business as if nothing had happened.[3]

The incident was a major jolt for the British forces in southern Iraq. Five personnel been killed and a helicopter shot down in public view of the whole of Basra. It was a major propaganda coup for the insurgents. The attack, however, highlighted that the insurgents now had access to modern weapons that could defeat the sophisticated countermeasures on British helicopters. A few weeks before, the 1st Battalion, The Royal Regiment of Fusiliers had seized a contingent of manpad missiles as they were being smuggled across the Iranian border to the east of Basra. More importantly, it was now clear that the insurgents knew how to use them. Equally worrying was the ability of the insurgents to rapidly mass fighters around the crash scene, and fight a determined battle with more than 300 heavily-armed British troops for a protracted period.[4]

Troops of 20 Armoured Brigade had just taken over from 7 Armoured Brigade two weeks before the Lynx incident. Units such as Bowron's 1st Battalion, The Light Infantry (1 LI), the 1st Battalion, The Princess of Wales's Royal Regiment (1 PWRR) and the Queen's Own Hussars had all been heavily engaged putting down the Sadr revolt in 2004, and they quickly worked out that they were up against more formidable opponents on this Iraq tour.

One veteran of the Operation Telic 4 tour in 2004 commented that then they "were faced with a fledgling insurgency that had a limited operating capability and an erratic leadership". At that time, insurgent attacks in Basra city were often restricted to small arms and RPG ambushes with a scattering of indirect fire onto base locations.

"These attacks would usually be conducted by no more than ten to 20 men at a time, who would seek to engage all our troops up closer and out in the open during both day and night" he said. "At [that] time there appeared to be no real method or constructive plan to their somewhat sproradic activities. The

[IED threat] at this stage was proving ineffective due to the lack of experience, equipment and expertise available to the insurgents."[5]

Arriving in Basra in the spring of 2006, the returning 1 Brigade soldiers found that their freedom of movement in Basra was now significantly restricted by the increased IED threat.

"The huge increase in the IED threat and the level of command and control that has appeared within the insurgents in the last 24 months is remarkable," wrote Sergeant Terry Thompson of the PWRR in an assessment of insurgent tactics.

"No longer are they a sporadic accumulation of men at a given time and place, they are a formed body, with a plan of action and co-ordinated movements of men and material. With the clear external influence and experience gained from insurgents who have migrated south from Baghdad, the sophistication of both the IED device and its method of operation have dramatically increased. This has meant the insurgents can defeat [our troops] on the ground without putting themselves at significant risk. Subsequently the small arms fire and RPG attacks have reduced but not disappeared, and are used in concert with, rather than in preference to, IED strikes."[6]

"The leadership of the insurgents appears to be more rigid with a clear delineation between fighters and planners" continued Thompson.

"This was clear for all to see when a prominent figure within the Basra insurgency was detained. The response from the insurgents was to revert back to the previous tactics of small arms and RPG ambushes on a larger scale of perhaps 100 men. Whilst noisy, their actions were fairly ineffective due to the lack of planning and preparation. The insurgents also suffered casualties as the presented us with an opportunity to hit back directly; a luxury not normally afforded during IED attacks. There is no doubt that the insurgents have become far more sophisticated in their modus operandi and are constantly looking for ways to defeat [our troops] on the ground. These methods range from kidnapping to sophisticated and specifically designed roadside mines; all previously unheard of during Operation Telic 4. While the Basra of 2004 appeared to be a much more violent city, the soldiers of Operation Telic 8 face an arguably more deadly, invisible enemy unwilling to allow himself to be engaged by troops on the ground."[7]

Sergeant Thompson's assessment may have been a very 'street level' view, but at the British command in Basra and at the high levels of the armed forces in London, similar reassessments were underway. The situation was clearly very serious. The death of two more British soldiers on 13th May in another IED attack added to the gloomy mood.

At the British divisional headquarters at Basra airport, Major General John Cooper was still leading the operation. He was not having much success re-engaging the local political and police leadership after the breakdown in relations since the January raids, that had resulted in several rogue police officers being arrested by British troops. Training of the local police in Basra had ground to a halt. A political vacuum had also developed in Baghdad, after the January parliamentary elections resulted in a six month-long political hiatus that ensued as the Iraqi political parties scrabbled to form a coalition government. This prevented Cooper from trying to get the Baghdad government to put pressure on the Basra politicians to re-engage with the British.

More dangerously, the political vacuum threatened to plunge Iraq into a sectarian civil war. Sunni extremists, allied to the al Qaeda in Iraq leader Abu Musab Al-Zarqawi, blew up the iconic Al-Askari shrine in Samarra in February. Baghdad and neighbouring cities were convulsed by sectarian massacres. Muqtadr al Sadr mobilised his Jaish al Mahdi (JAM) militia to defend Shia communities from Sunni insurgents and lead the fight back against them.

Iraq's Shia heartland in the south, around Basra and al Amarah, was largely spared this sectarian blood letting, but another dangerous dynamic was at work. The political infighting between the Shia parties to form the Baghdad government set off a new round of inter-Shia violence. As every Iraqi politician seemed to have their own militia or be allied to parties with militias, this political rivalry was soon being expressed through political assassinations and violent attacks on rivals. Some 174 people died in violence in Basra during April and May 2006, according to Basra police reports. Sadr was unwavering in his opposition to the presence of foreign troops. For the JAM fighters the way to enhance the political standing of the leader and his party was to launch attacks on British and US troops, to demonstrate that they were leading the resistance to the foreign occupation. Rival politicians who sought compromise with the US and British could be portrayed as lackeys of the occupiers. This resonated with the population of Basra, with 63% of the population wanting foreign troops to leave Iraq in six months, according to opinion polls conducted by British forces in April 2006. This was a 15% rise since the polling organisation asked the same question a year earlier.[8]

The British 'disengagement' with Basra's politicians and police during the first half of 2006 provided a vacuum for the JAM and other militias to expand their power base in the city. Recruitment and training rocketed. Neighbourhood militia units operated openly. Many were described by British intelligence officers as sort of 'home guard' units who patrolled their neighbourhoods to protect them from what was seen as a looming civil war. They also provided protection against the militias of rival political leaders and British troops who ventured out of their bases. By the spring of 2007 there would be three main Shia religious militia organizations in the city, with a combination of more than 20 different combat units, described as companies, battalions or regiments.[9]

These local units were backed up by more hard-core units, mostly from the JAM, who conducted offensive operations against the British with IEDs, mortars and rockets. They also routinely carried out assassinations of political rivals or people who they accused of collaborating with the British, including interpreters, local government officials and politicians.

The police was heavily infiltrated by the militia, and across the city had effectively begun to merge with pro-JAM groups.

British intelligence officers remained convinced that there was not a central militia command in Basra, but they described JAM as a 'brand'. As long as it was seen as being the most heavily-armed, best-trained and most successful militia group, then the others would follow its lead. The shooting down of the Lynx set the stock of JAM sky high on the streets of Basra, creating a spiral of escalating violence as the group's leaders sought to capitalise on their success and mount even more audacious attacks, with bigger and better weapons, to keep the flow of volunteers into their ranks.

Just 12 days after the loss of the Lynx, the new British defence secretary, Des Browne, and the new chief of defence staff (CDS), Air Chief Marshal Sir Jock Stirrup, arrived in Basra to make their own assessments of the situation. For Browne, the visit was his first taste of visiting war zones, but many of the officers who met him recorded that he was a "sharp political operator" who only two weeks before had been senior minister in Treasury.

"He was clearly on a steep learning curve," said one officer who met him during the visit.[10]

While Browne was running to catch up about Iraq, Stirrup was the exact opposite. He had visited Basra on several occasions after he became head of the RAF in 2003, and participated in all the chiefs of staff operations committee meetings that determined British strategy in Iraq since then. The appointment of Stirrup would prove a decisive turning point in the Iraq campaign. Some senior army officers in the Ministry of Defence were concerned that an RAF officer was leading the armed forces at the time when the British military was engaged in two major land operations; they were making comments along the lines of "what does a fighter pilot know about street fighting?"

But they seriously under-estimated him.

During his visit to Basra in May 2006, it soon became apparent that Stirrup was quick to make his mark on the Iraq campaign. Through his RAF career, Stirrup had earned a reputation for being able to quickly make a decision and then ensure it got carried out. This was a quality that some army officers and senior MOD civil servants found difficult to master. He was also considered ruthless with under-performing subordinates, with one senior officer in the MOD being unceremoniously moved from his job when he failed to live up to Stirrup's exacting standards.

This change in style was an abrupt shock for some senior army officers, who had become used to General Sir Mike Walker's 'collegiate and consensual' style as chief of the defence staff. It was rare for General Walker to overturn the collective recommendations of senior staff officers, leading to one senior officer who worked in the MOD at this time to describe the 2003-05 period as being marked by "strategic drift", with "little original thinking".

"We had to get used to Stirrup issuing directives and then having to make sure it happened," said the officer.[11]

According to one army officer who participated in briefing Stirrup during his visit to Basra, it was very clear he was not happy with what was happening. Some quick decisions were made to improve the security in Basra, including moving an extra British battlegroup into the city. Then an extra battlegroup was added to the order of battle of 19 Light Brigade, which was due to deploy to Basra in the autumn, reversing previous plans to draw down the force in Iraq to four battlegroups by the end of 2006.[12] The need to provide improved armoured vehicles for the British forces was fast-tracked in June, breaking paralysis inside the army over which new vehicles to buy.[13]

One his return to London, Stirrup also set about preparing a strategy document for the Cabinet that proposed a major switch of Britain's military main effort from Iraq to Afghanistan. This would see the overwhelming majority of the deployable forces and resources of the British armed forces committed to Afghanistan.

"He had already made his decision during the visit to Iraq," said officer who worked closely with Stirrup during this time.

"He very quickly took the view that we were loosing in Iraq. Iran and the Shia militia wanted to be seen to kick us out. Stirrup thought we had lost and needed to retreat. He believed we needed to get out and that we would need to conduct a withdrawal in contact [with the enemy]. Stirrup beefed up the brigade heading to Basra but it was not a long-term fix, that was clear."[14]

"In his paper, Stirrup used military logic, pushing that we lost consent in Iraq and we had consent in Afghanistan," commented a senior officer working in the Ministry of Defence at the time who saw it.

"He argued that we would get better return on our military investment in Afghanistan than Iraq. The terrain in Afghanistan was different from Iraq, it was largely rural, not urban like Basra. Maybe Stirrup thought that airpower could used to greater effect".[15]

Stirrup presented his paper to the Cabinet in June 2006, and it was quickly agreed. There was no political resistance to Stirrup's plan. The US was following a similar strategy to drawdown in Iraq. To the Prime Minister and other senior ministers, Afghanistan offered the prospect of an operation not tainted by the political poison that hung around the Iraq campaign. For the rest of the year Stirrup worked to put in place the plans to make the accelerated drawdown happen. There had been various targets for withdrawals from Iraq before, but they had come and gone. Now the atmosphere changed and across the British military, there was a clear understanding that drawdown was going to happen very soon.

Air Chief Marshal Sir Glenn Torpy, who had just been promoted and moved from Permanent Joint Headquarters (PJHQ) to be head of the RAF, replacing Stirrup, recalled that the new CDS' more directive approach did have impact but the changing strategic circumstances had more impact.

"When General Sir Richard Dannatt [who had just taken over as head of the army] said that we were part of the problem in Basra, he was intellectually right," said Torpy.

"We had trained the Iraqi army and police and then politics intervened. The Iraqis wanted to take control of the own destiny. We became the focus for violence. Beyond a certain point we overstayed our welcome. At that point we became an irritant, rather than adding value."[16]

"This was the opportune moment to leave," said Torpy.

"We needed to force the pace of transition, but in a controlled manner. The view collectively was that whilst it would be a bit messy, we had provided the Iraqis with the wherewith all to manage their own security and it now time for them to take responsibility for their own future. The transition plan was agreed to by the US, and dovetailed with their broader plans for provincial transition. Jock [Stirrup] made sure we stuck to it. You could say he forced the army to face up to the fact they would never get a perfect solution [in Iraq]. It was not a question of getting out because the going was getting tough. Other dynamics were also at play."[17]

At this time, the senior leadership of the British Army had been enthusiastic supporters of the switch to Afghanistan. This was before the escalating of fighting in Afghanistan, when it looked like operations in Helmand province would be a classic peacekeeping and nation state-building operation that the British Army believed it excelled at. The continued inability of the US military to craft a winning strategy to defeat the insurgency in Baghdad also made senior British Army officers keen to scale down their role in Iraq and become the masters of their own fate in Afghanistan. One commented to the author in the summer of 2006, "we are now playing for a draw in Iraq and playing to win in Afghanistan."[18]

Using the political authority granted by the Cabinet, Stirrup set in train the necessary operational planning to make the drawdown happen. Operation Plan G was developed, which envisaged a six-month period for setting the conditions for the drawdown of the British forces. They would first withdraw from the centre of Basra and al Amarah, to bases outside the urban areas. This would allow a cut in troop numbers by nearly half by the time the brigades rotated through Basra in the spring of 2007. From then on the majority of deployed British military combat power would be in Afghanistan. Stirrup's decision to switch effort to Afghanistan was not universally popular in the Ministry of Defence and across Whitehall.

"The new CDS provided command - which was good and had been lacking up to then - but his geo-strategic vision was lacking in political direction," commented one senior officer close to Stirrup, who worried that his boss' withdraw plan could eventually upset the Americans.

"The issue of Iraq's long term strategic importance as a major oil producer and potential as a trading partner for the UK, its linkages to the Gulf and implications for relations with Iran were never really considered in any depth in the rush to get to Afghanistan" " he said.

"Overriding all this, the key thing was the relationship with the Americans. That was why we went in to Iraq and eventually we reneged on it, the decision was not right in the long term. This is the heart of it, really – we got this bit wrong, and it proved very costly, as a result, and with no obvious long term strategic benefit."[19]

As these debates were unfolding in London, in Basra Brigadier James Everard, 20 Brigade's commander, was trying to regain the initiative and put a lid on the escalating violence, with a surge mission dubbed Operation Tyne. He ordered Bowron's Basra battlegroup to lead the offensive and in late May it began a two week-long series of strike operations to capture insurgent leaders and bomb makers. Raids were mounted by the Light Infantry, supported by the brigade operations company of Royal Anglians and the reserve battlegroup, 1 PWRR. In Operation Ouse, the Light Infantry claimed to have made the biggest find of bomb-making equipment in a raid on an insurgent safe house, which led to a marked decrease in IED attacks against British troops.[20]

Some good news came in June, when newly-appointed Iraqi prime minister, Nouri al Maliki, was at last able to form a government. Maliki had lived in exile for almost all of Saddam Hussein's rule, spending much of his time in Damascus as a senior official of the Shia Dawa. This was his most redeeming factor in the eyes of the Americans, who were struggling to find a suitable Iraqi Shia politician who did not appear to be under Iranian influence. Unfortunately for the British, Maliki's grandfather had played a leading part in a revolt against British rule in the 1920s, and the Iraqi prime minister seemed to harbour lingering resentment against Iraq's old imperial rulers.

Later in the month, he made a flying visit to Basra and declared a state of emergency. An emergency committee was set up, a night-time curfew was declared, which was to be enforced by Iraqi troops and police. To reinforce this apparent success, Brigadier Everard quickly moved to re-organise his forces to bring more troops into the heart of Basra. The operations area of the British Basra battlegroup was divided in two, with the Light Infantry being morphed into the Basra North battlegroup and the 2nd Battalion, The Royal Anglian Regiment being re-roled from security sector reform, to be the Basra South battlegroup. This added 25% more British infantry to back up the Iraqi security forces in the city.[21] General Cooper also managed to get Iraqi politicians in Basra to agree to allow the police to co-operate with the British again. To kick off the re-engagement, a survey of police reform requirements was launched. British troops began to be sent to visit police stations again but the effort was soon in trouble. Local officers still refused to go out on patrol with the British soldiers, no matter what their political masters said.

The spring of 2006 also saw a major increase in rocket and mortar attacks on British bases in Basra. Insurgent attack teams now boasted an arsenal of 240mm mortars, 107mm and 122mm rockets, and they were in action on a nightly basis across the city. In response the British began to speed up the fortification of their bases. At Basra airport, contractors from the UK-arm of the US military services company KBR started to build reinforced concrete buildings to house the main division and brigade headquarters, as well as the central dining facilities. Soldier's beds started to be surrounded with concrete breeze blocks, creating so-called 'Baghdad beds', to provide protection against shrapnel.

These attacks started to cause major disruption to British operations, with fuel dumps, vehicle parks and equipment stores regularly going up in smoke. The growing threat from the long-range 122mm rockets had already prompted improved defences at Basra airport, with 20 Brigade deploying with a detachment of Royal Artillery Cobra artillery location radars, to give warning of incoming rockets to allow troops to take cover, augmenting the shorter-range MAMBA radars and ASP sound detecting system.[22] The radars also allowed the rockets' launch points to be identified, so RAF Regiment security patrols could be sent to try to catch the perpetrators of the attacks.

"Indirect fire (mortars and rockets) was perhaps the threat that most affected our lives," recalled one British company commander.

"We were routinely attacked in the Palace throughout the tour. At times it was only once or twice a week in the late evening. At other times it was two or three times a day both in daylight and darkness. Some attacks were one or two rounds only; one consisted of fifteen rockets. Such attacks became almost the norm for us and caused little excitement. These attacks were a barometer of the feeling of the enemy towards us and following successful operations the threat would increase. One major effect of indirect fire attack was to disrupt rest, as head checks and clearances had to be completed. The fact that such attacks often followed a long night time operation would compound issues of fatigue."[23]

The IED campaign continued with a vengeance. Colour Sergeant Andy Roberts, of the Royal Anglians, described the experience of reaching the scene of an IED attack on a Snatch Land Rover in Qarmat Ali district of Basra on 28th May. It has been "peeled open like a tin can". One soldier was dead, another was dying and other wounded. A crowd of Iraqis were massing around the damaged vehicle, and C/Sgt Roberts realised that his small force could not hold them at bay while an ambulance or rescue helicopter arrived to pick up the wounded. He threw a phosphorous grenade into the devastated Land Rover to set it on fire to prevent it being captured, and then loaded the survivors in his own vehicles. The convoy then raced back across Basra to the Shatt-al-Arab Hotel.

"We moved at best speed through 'Five-Mile Market' which was blocked with traffic," he recalled.

"God knows how, but Private Briggs, my driver, got us through, his driving skills were fantastic. We got to base, which seemed to take forever, but in fact only took ten minutes. We moved complete as a multiple to the medical centre to get the injured to aid as quickly as possible, carrying the injured past the medical staff and the padre. The thing that sticks in my mind is seeing the dead on the stretchers and the faces of the people helping. Also, the unknown privates and NCOs shaking my hand and saying 'Cheers mate, for getting us here'; we lost two men that night. I looked at my [troops] and some of them had a look of despair on their faces; I think some grew up that night and realised that it was no video game and that they had seen it for real."[24]

The arrival of the Iraqi summer heat added a new dimension to the threats facing British troops, with the heat making it an ordeal for soldiers driving around Basra in armoured vehicles. Soldiers complained they were enduring "death by tracks" and the American journalist Michael Yon, who spent many months with British troops in Basra, commented that their vehicles never seemed to have functioning air conditioning.[25]

The commander of the Royal Anglian's A Company, Major Stuart Nicholson, described in graphic detail what it was like to work inside armoured vehicles in the summer temperature in excess of 50 degrees.

"You sweat the moment you step from an air-conditioned room," he recalled.

"After several hours on the ground not only are shirts soaked, but so are trousers, webbing and even boots. Temperatures in the back of a Snatch, or worse a Warrior, would be in the 60s. It can be frightening sitting in the back of a vehicle in such temperatures, wondering how long you can stand it and what will happen to you. Every time we went onto the ground we were wearing helmets and Osprey body armour. Osprey offered welcome protection, but was significantly heavier than previously used body armour. Soldiers carried full scales of ammunition and grenades. Moving in this equipment in any weather would be hard work; in the 50s it pushes the limits of endurance."[26]

Heat injury was an ever present threat, said Nicholson. "This does not just mean 'getting a bit hot and bothered', but rather permanent damage being done to organs" he commented.

"Heat exhaustion was almost routine. Following a patrol, speech would be slurred, concentration lowered and co-ordination impaired. Often in the back of a Warrior for several hours a soldier, teetering on the edge of heat injury, would have water poured over him, only to find that the water was actually uncomfortably hot. Heat limited operations, it prevented walking any distance in equipment, it made every movement a huge effort and it hospitalised many soldiers; thankfully none were in A Company."[27]

The scale of problems the environment was causing to British troops can be gauged from the fact that some 1,209 soldiers - or just under 10% of all the troops deployed to Iraq - had to be hospitalized due to no-battle injuries and health problems during 2006, compared to 93 who were wounded in action. Some 701 soldiers – 5% of the force - had to be evacuated back to Britain.[28]

As these events were unfolding a new British commander was preparing to take over in Basra. Major General Richard Shirreff was a dynamic cavalry officer with a taste for action, and supreme confidence in his ability to use the force of his personality to shape events. He led a squadron of tanks into action in the 1991 Gulf War. In June 2000 he was in command of a British-led multi-national NATO brigade in Kosovo when rioting broke out in a Serb enclave. He headed to the incident with his bodyguards to remonstrate with the crowd and calm the situation. Some 300 Serbs surrounded Shirreff and threatened to bundle him away. His bodyguards then intervened, shooting and wounding three Serbs to rescue their commander.[29] He had a ringside seat to the build up to the invasion to the Iraq war, as personal staff officer to the-then chief of defence staff, Admiral Sir Mike Boyce.

In the spring of 2006, he began preparing for this tour of command and made a brief reconnaissance visit to Basra in May to develop his plans. To fulfill his conditions shaping the mission to open the way for drawdown, Shirreff was determined to adopt an aggressive approach and make a decisive impact on the situation. According to his evidence to the Chilcot inquiry, some senior officers, including the new Chief of Joint Operations, Lieutenant General Nick Houghton, at PJHQ, which controlled all British overseas operations, were not happy at the aggressive nature of his plans.[30] They might stir up Basra and threaten to derail the withdrawal schedule. As an operational commander in the field, Shirreff had considerable freedom of action and he was determined to push the envelope of his delegated authority.

Ultimately PJHQ signed off on Operation Salamanca/Sinbad, and backed it with almost all of the available reserve of troops available in the British armed forces. It was in effect the main British military effort at this time, even if it was not formally designated as such. According to a senior officer involved in planning the operation, it was intended to be the UK's 'surge' to show the British Army had made a final effort to clear up Basra and having done so could withdraw without dishonour - it was one of the enabling conditions for Operation Zenith, the final pull-out of British troops from downtown Basra.

"Basra itself seemed to me to be the key issue, the second city of Iraq, and it was in Basra that the British reputation was going to stand or fall," he said at his appearance before the inquiry.

"What I found when I arrived was effectively no security at all. Any movement required deliberate operations to conduct -- to get around the city. There was a significant lack of troops on the ground. The result of all that was what I call a cycle of insecurity. No security meant no reconstruction and development, it meant a loss of consent, the militia filled the gap and, effectively, the militia controlled the city. So my objective was to re-establish security in Basra."[31]

The General's plan, codenamed Operation Salamanca, envisaged a series of systematic sweeps, or pulses, through Basra's neighbourhoods to clear out rogue police, conduct public works and economic regeneration projects to win over the population from the militia and Iraqi army units would then be posted to prevent insurgents returning. At the same time, British forces were to systematically target the militia leadership and logistics infra-structure, particularly its bomb making, rocket and mortar teams, to reduce their ability to regenerate.

After this battering, Shirreff believed the British could pull out their troops to bases outside Basra unhindered and with their heads held high.

The first call was to ask PJHQ for reinforcements, and he requested the use of the Middle East theatre reserve in Cyprus, 2nd Battalion, The Royal Regiment of Fusiliers (2 RRF). He was given most of the battalion, except for one infantry company, which was diverted to Afghanistan.[32] This was on top of the commitment of the Spearhead Lead Element battalion to 19 Brigade's deployment in the autumn, so Shirreff was soon to have more than 80% of the British Army's deployable reserve infantry companies. A special forces contingent, Task Force Spartan, was also sent to Basra to assist Shirreff. For the next six months, Shirreff would have the most powerful British force committed to Basra in the post-invasion period at his disposal. The troops were also soon to get some new equipment, such as the Bulldog tracked armoured vehicle, Mastiff mine-protected vehicle, and Osprey body armour.

To further concentrate his forces in Basra, Shirreff began to prepare to reduce the forces operating in Maysan, in a move he dubbed the "indirect approach". The province's political environment remained implacably hostile to the British and militia fighters resisted fiercely any incursions into al Amarah city. It was just more trouble than it was worth. Not only did it tie down 1,000 troops at Camp Abu Naji outside al Amarah, but weekly re-supply convoys needed more than a battalion's worth of troops to guard them. Thus by folding Task Force Maysan, Shirreff would effectively gain just over another battalion's worth of troops to operate inside Basra city. A light force of 400 troops would remain in Maysan to patrol the Iranian border to try to interdict arms smuggling, but half of them would come from the troops that were being freed up from the handing over of Muthanna province to the Iraqis in July. The move from al Amarah was potentially controversial, within both the British and US chains of command, leading to accusations that he was 'cutting and running', but Shirreff thought the situation was so serious in Basra that the risks were worth taking.

On his arrival in Basra in early July, Shirreff began working to get the necessary backing from the Iraqi government, the Americans and PJHQ to put his plan into action. The US commander in Baghdad, General George Casey, and his corps commander, Lieutenant General Peter Chiarelli, were both supportive, the concept chimed with their own plans to use Iraqi troops to hold areas cleared of insurgents, to allow US troops to pull back to bases outside major cities, and then hand over security to local troops, as a precursor to withdrawal.

The American generals gave Shirreff strong support, putting a company of eight AH-64 Apache attack helicopters at his disposal to support strike operations into Basra, as well as high-level MQ-1 Predator drone support. Counter-Rocket and Mortar (C-RAM) guns to shoot down incoming heavy weapons fire were sent to Basra Palace. Casey allocated $80 million to Shirreff for reconstruction projects to 'buy consent' from the population.[33] The American General also offered a US Army battalion to help Shirreff, but he was ordered by PJHQ to decline the offer because it would have implied British forces were unable to cope and needed to be bailed out by their allies.

Shirreff's plan to pull back from al Amarah worried the Americans, who were starting to become increasingly concerned by Iranian Revolutionary Guard Quds Force support for Shia insurgents. To beef up the effectiveness of the British desert patrols, US Navy P-3 Orion patrol aircraft with night-vision surveillance cameras were assigned set up a co-ordinated monitoring effort along the border.[34] US special forces commanders and intelligence chiefs were also becoming increasingly concerned about the role of Quds Force operatives in Iraq and moved to support the forthcoming British operation, sending people and specialist equipment to Basra Palace. These assets, including an advanced computer system to monitor and track mobile telephone traffic, so as to build up maps of insurgent networks through their telephone conversations, were positioned to support the British. It would be able to exploit material captured during raids on insurgent bases.[35]

Perhaps most importantly, Casey became heavily involved in lobbying Prime Minister Maliki to give Shirreff's plan political top cover. The Iraqi's leader's coalition government was dependent on the votes of Sadr's party, so he vehemently opposed the offensive or kinetic aspects of Operation Salamanca that were aimed at targeting the JAM in Basra.

Shirreff spent most of August trying to persuade Maliki, the Basra police chief Major General Mohammed Hamadi al-Mousawi, and the city security committee. As he was lobbying for Operation Salamanca, the Sadrists were conducting their counter effort, making repeated death threats against Hamadi and security committee members. At the same time Sadrists in the government pressurised the prime minister to not go along with the British plan to protect their allies in Basra. Ultimately, Maliki refused to sanction the kinetic element of Operation Salamanca, and Sherriff had repackaged his plans to keep the Iraqi prime minister happy, with the reconstruction effort separated from proposed strike operations. The new plan was now dubbed Operation Sinbad and it was scheduled to kick off in September.[36]

While Shirreff was making his preparations for Operation Salamanca/Sinbad, fighting in Basra and al Amarah continued at a pace. The small British special forces contingent in the city had spent several weeks building up intelligence on a suspected leading JAM member, Sajjad Badr Adal Saeed. Days after Shirreff's arrival in Basra, the special forces team thought they had enough intelligence to plan a raid to capture Sajjad in the centre of Basra. Not surprisingly, the General did not need much convincing and he swiftly authorised a raid to capture the target. A major operation was planned because significant resistance was expected.

Operation Test began in the early hours of 16th July, with C Company of the Royal Anglians, backed by the Brigade Surveillance Company from the Devonshire and Dorset Light Infantry (DDLI) and a special forces team. The strike force found Sajjid at home in his house just before 2am and quickly bundled him into the back of a Warrior. Intelligence officers then set about searching the premises and recovering documents, mobile phones and computers. During the search, it emerged that he owned two other houses, and racing against the dawn, the strike force moved off to raid the other premises. Three other men were arrested during the searches, but the militia units in the neighbourhood were now stirring. Resistance was being mobilised.

Private McCrae of the Royal Anglians was part of the outer cordon, "as we were filling out search documentation we heard a loud bang which was the sound of a grenade going off, and shots being fired at the inner cordon" he recalled.

"Unfortunately two of the attached soldiers were wounded in the contact. A few C Company soldiers opened fire on to the gunman. We rapidly moved out of the area as a hostile crowd developed. The two casualties were evacuated by helicopter immediately after receiving first aid from the team medics, although Corporal Cosby of the DDLI sadly died of his wounds."[37]

Another soldier was also wounded in the incident. Private D Maclean, DDLI, recalled as he was driving back to base after the incident, "I felt extremely angry and wanted revenge on every insurgent but my professionalism kicked in."

The intelligence haul from Sajjad's properties was immense, and during the following day the location of a major insurgent IED making facility was identified. Operation Harlequin was now ordered to take it down during the early hours of 18th July. A Warrior company was dispatched to lead the Company of the PWRR into the heart of Basra to raid the site but this time the militia were waiting in ambush. The assault force received heavy fire en route to the target. As assault and search teams did their work, more heavily armed militiamen started appearing and engaging the outer cordon. All the time the British troops were on their objective, they were under fire with small arms and RPGs. When mortar fire started to land around the British troops, an Army Air Corps Lynx AH7 was called up to try to locate the offending mortar team. Two snipers on the helicopters were ready to engage targets when the helicopter was hit by heavy machine gun fire, causing heavy damage to control cables and forcing the pilot to make a very precarious flight back to Basra airport as he struggled to control the machine. More militiamen began arriving in a convoy of cars, and trying to set up road blocks to cut off British vehicles. Some insurgents were using their car headlights to try to blind the night vision equipment of their British troops, before they were destroyed by 30mm cannon fire from the Warriors. As the strike force withdrew, it came under heavy fire along its route.[38]

When the strike force extracted back to Basra airport, it took a huge quantity of booty with it, including 50 rockets, about ten rocket-propelled grenades and 150 mortars, as well as fully-assembled IEDS, mines and other weapons. British commanders and government ministers were quick to boast about the haul, but the two day-long operation showed that in future the British would have to fight hard during strike operations to capture prisoners and intelligence.

A major plank in General Shirreff's plans for the autumn, centred around pulling out of Camp Abu Naji to free up its troops for Operation Sinbad. The arrival of the Queen's Royal Hussars (QRH) in May had been greeted by an upsurge in violence against the British presence. The main camp outside al Amarah was subjected to prolonged rocket and mortar fire never before experienced. Until the final pull out in August, 289 rockets and mortar rounds hit the camp, causing dozens of injuries, including one barrage of 54 rounds in an 11 minute period on 15th May. Another daylight attack struck the base with 14 120mm heavy mortars, setting on fire the helicopter fuel store and sending 79,000 litres of fuel up in smoke, and seriously injuring a soldier.[39]

To try to dampen this rain of shrapnel, Lieutenant Colonel David Labouchere, the commanding officer of the QRH, ordered a major raid into the centre of al Amarah on 11th June to try to capture the rocket firers. Eight targets would be raided simultaneously across the city by C Company of the PWRR, and platoons from the Grenadier Guards, backed by QRH Challenger tanks. As soon as the strike force entered the town, it came under heavy fire. When the Warriors dropped off the assault teams, they soon got pinned down and were trading fire with all their weapons. As dawn started to approach, the strike force was ordered to pull out. At this point one of the Warriors slid into a huge drainage ditch. Hundreds of militiamen and civilians started to gather around the vehicle in a bid to prevent its recovery and win a propaganda triumph over the British. A Warrior recovery vehicle, and then a Challenger tried to pull the vehicle free but it was stuck fast.[40]

A major operation was now launched to free the Warrior, with A Company of the Light Infantry being scrambled from Camp Abu Naji, with seven more Challengers, to set up a cordon around the incident in the very centre of town. Insurgents were dropping blast bombs and grenades on the roofs of British vehicle as the approached the scene and one Warrior took nine RPG hits. A PWRR sergeant was shot in the face. To try to drive back the crowds, a pair of US Air Force F-15E Strike Eagle was called up to provide a show of force. The jet made a supersonic pass over the incident at 200 feet which momentarily provided a breathing space. It was now five hours since the start of the operation, and there was no sign of the Warrior being freed. Colonel Labouchere was not willing to give the militia their prize, and he ordered the camp's cooks, clerks and truck mechanics to be mustered into an improvised company to go into town. The colonel was on the verge of ordering a Challenger to destroy the stricken vehicle, when a young Royal Electrical and Mechanical Engineer (REME) corporal was able to dodge past the insurgent fire, and jump into sewage up to his chest to oversee the attachment of a towing cable, which allowed the Warrior to be towed free, allowing the troops to return to base. In the six hour long battle the British troops had fired 7,000 rounds.[41]

At the end of July, General Shirreff was ready to give the final orders for the withdrawal from Camp Abu Naji. This gave QRH logistic echelon commanders eighteen days to clear out 900 soldiers, 200 ISO containers, 70 tracked armoured vehicles, 150 wheeled vehicles, 30 Corrimec temporary buildings, two prefabricated heli-pads and anything else of value. Mortar attacks continued at a renewed intensity and with increasing accuracy, hitting the helicopter fuel supply dump again.[42] Four large convoys carried all the material down to Shaibah Logistic Base over the next two weeks, as well as bringing up all the vehicles and supplies needed for Colonel Labouchere to begin his new desert patrol operations. Although the exact date of the closure was a closely held secret, the convoys were an unmistakable sign that the British were leaving al Amarah, and not surprisingly they were repeatedly ambushed and harassed as they moved down Route 6 to Basra. During this period, the precarious nature of British influence in the province was highlighted when two Iraqi army battalions mutinied, when their soldiers heard they were to be transferred to Baghdad. Order was only restored by the Iraqi 10th Division Reserve Company, which was moved to al Amarah to pacify the two units.

When the Queen's Dragoon Guards (QDG) had handed over the Muthanna province in the last week of July, their camp had been looted by civilians four days after the last British convoy left. The prospect of Camp Abu Naji being ransacked live on Arab satellite television news channels had to be avoided at all costs, to protect the reputation of the 'transition' policy. Unfortunately for General Shirreff and Colonel Labouchere the final days of the British operation in al Amarah did not go smoothly.[43]

To set the tone, on the day before the final withdrawal one last battlegroup operation was planned into al Amarah, to try to arrest a relative of the JAM leader in Maysan, Ahmed al Gharawi. In the early hours of 22nd August, the Light Infantry Warriors and QRH Challengers drove into town carrying a special forces assault team. The approach to the objective went relatively smoothly, but once the assault team went into action the operation started to unravel.

"Sadly the intended target of the operation was not found, and the tanks and Warriors were subject to a frenzied attack as they withdrew from the town," recalled the commander of C Squadron, QRH, Major R.C Martin.

"Rocket propelled grenades and mortars were being fired with abundance, with numerous impacts on the majority of the tanks. As the tanks regrouped on the outskirts of the town, there were further attacks on the vehicles and this sadly led to Trooper Chance having to be evacuated from the scene with an injury to his foot."[44]

A QRH Challenger commander and another QRH soldier were also injured in the heavy fighting. As well as having to co-ordinate the evacuation under fire of the wounded, Colonel Labouchere now had to deal with recovering an immobilised Challenger from downtown al Amarah. By mid-morning the tank was still stuck and heavy mortar fire was preventing REME repair teams getting to work. An estimated 300 militiamen were trading fire with the cordon protecting the tank and USAF F-16s circled over head ready to provide close air support. Two of the REME soldiers, sometimes regarded dismissively (and wrongly) by some frontline soldiers as only working in the 'rear echelons,' eventually dodged through mortar fire to hook up the Challenger to allow it to be towed away. Subsequent examination of Trooper Chance's tank revealed that its armour had been penetrated by a Russian-made RPG-29 shoulder launched anti-tank rocket. This boasted a tandem charge, with the first charge being designed to detonate a vehicle's reactive armour and so the secondary charge can punch through the steel armour underneath. This was the first recorded incident of a Challenger 2 being penetrated by an enemy weapon, and raised the prospect of the militia now being able to defeat every type of British vehicle.[45]

The troops withdrew back to their base and spend just over 24 hours enduring more mortaring, with no air conditioning in 60 degree heat, no showers and nothing more than ration packs to eat. On the morning of 24th August, the second in command of the QRH battlegroup, Major Matthew Cocup, finally told the Colonel who controlled the small Iraqi contingent at the base that the British were leaving for good later that day. The battlegroup commander had already headed out into the desert with his mobile border patrol force.[46]

After a brief flag lowering ceremony, the QRH and PWRR convoy headed south.[47] Five hours later, a crowd of several hundred civilians approached the camp and demanded that the Iraqi troops let them in. The guards did not fire a shot to stop the mob ransacking the place. Unlike in Muthanna, this time the events were filmed and subsequently broadcast on Arab television channels. The Iraqi 10th Division's Reserve Company were then sent to clear out the mob but the damage had been done. The prospects for an orderly transition of other British bases did not look good.

Out in the desert, the newly renamed Borders North Battlegroup was set to patrol the east of Maysan province for another 11 months. To prevent resupply convoys being ambushed, RAF Hercules transport aircraft flew in supplies to improvised airstrips on roads or Merlin helicopters landed supplies. The patrols moved every night to prevent the insurgents being able to prepare attacks.

"The manpower and material costs of a fixed base were behind us and we released our infantry back to the Brigade to reinforce Basra," recalled a relieved Lieutenant Colonel David Labouchere.

"Suddenly we were free of convoys, enemy mortar attacks and predictability. Our soldiers relished the freedom of mobility. Commanders had to survive on guile and fieldcraft."[48]

The QRH, supported by a squadron of the QDG, spent some ten more weeks on desert patrol, or Operation Vedette, before being replaced by the Queen's Royal Lancers.

In Basra during August 2006, as preparations mounted for the launching of Operation Sinbad, militia attacks continued on British bases in the city. The Old State Building in the heart of the city centre was the focus of mortar fire for several weeks, injuring several soldiers. This culminated on 1st August in an attack that left one Light Infantryman dead, the first British soldier to be killed by indirect fire since the start of the occupation. Militia attacks were becoming increasingly bold, including large and complex daytime ambushes. B Company of the Light Infantry was scrambled from the Old State Building in its Warriors to protect a large group of Royal Anglian troops, who were ambushed during a recovery from a strike operation, resulting in what some of the participants described as a 'Mogadishu Run' through the streets under rocket propelled grenade fire.[49]

A militia attempt to storm the provincial governor's building in the centre of Basra resulted in another daylight battle, with the Light Infantry sending Warriors to fight off the attack, and troops in the Old State Building spent several hours trading heavy fire down the street at the attackers.

Then the first reinforcements from the theatre reserve battalion started to arrive from Cyprus, in the second week of September, in preparation for Operation Sinbad, as the two armoured infantry companies released from al Amarah moved into Basra city to prepare for the coming operation. Cavalrymen from the QDG released from Muthanna were also put through a crash course in Warrior driving at Shaibah Logistic Base, to put more of the heavily-armoured vehicles on the streets. To beef up co-ordination with the Iraqi army and police, the commanding officer of 2 RRF and his headquarters team moved into the Provincial Joint Command Centre (PJCC), at the old Iraqi security headquarters a few streets away from the Old State Building. Working with the Iraqi police, security and army headquarters was a central element of General Shirreff's plans, and it was intended they would take over security duties once British troops had driven away rogue police and militiamen.[50]

The first pulse of Operation Sinbad was launched by the Light Infantry near Basra port on 28th September. A column of British vehicles moved to secure the target district's police station, where a detachment of Royal Military Policemen set about taking a roll call of the policemen, making an inventory of their weapons, checking pay records, searching the station and logging any prisoners held. The policemen were then finger-printed and photographed, which did not produce a very positive response. Other troops moved around the area looking for schools to repair, children's playgrounds to clear up, and other good works. Local people were hired to pick up rubbish and Iraqi building contractors were paid to repair electricity and water infra-structure.[51]

Several dozen Iraqi soldiers accompanied the British and helped set up the outer cordon to protect the reconstruction and police reform activities. The British and Iraqi troops maintained a continuous presence for two to four days to try to prevent militia fighters interfering, before they returned to base to begin preparations for the next 'pulse'. So through October and into November, a rolling series of pulses, one every five days, was carried out across the city's main residential neighbourhoods and suburbs. The two Basra city battlegroups took turns to launch the pulses, so each was carrying out one each fortnight with one or two company sized group of troops, which put around 150-200 British soldiers and the same number of Iraqis out on the ground in the target area.

The posting of British and Iraqi troops out on the ground for sustained periods was a new tactic, that the militia took some time to react to, but by late

October, firefights were soon a regular occurrence during Operation Sinbad pulses. Mortar attacks, IED attacks and ambushes remained routine. The Royal Anglian fought another intense battle, firing 3,000 rounds and calling in tank fire and fast jet support, to help extract a Danish patrol on the Qamat Ali Bridge on 6th October.[52] In early November, the first 19 Brigade units started arriving to take over from the Light Infantry and Royal Anglians in the city. The newly arrived C Company of the 1st Battalion, The Staffordshire Regiment carried out its first Operation Sinbad pulse in the Shia Flats area, a noted base for JAM fighters. According to the company commander, the reception they received was far from friendly, recording, "the small arms contacts and RPGs mounted up as two days of operations went in. On the first day Captain Mark Carnaghan and his multiple found themselves in an Alamo style situation pinned down on the roof of the police station engaging [militia] in the streets below."[53]

Captain Carnaghan recalled the "exhilarating" incident, writing that the "threat of indirect fire was considered low but the terrorists proved, as ever, how little they cared about their own people by sending a couple of rounds our way that sent everyone scuttling for cover. Forty minutes later they followed up with a couple of small arms and RPG contacts that allowed our [troops] the opportunity to get a few rounds down; Private Chambers especially relished the chance to use his General Purpose Machine Gun having exchanged his rifle for it the previous day. No hits were claimed but it did not matter, everyone had their bit of fun, came away with a good war story without casualties, and now looked forward to a quiet rest of tour."[54]

As an exercise in winning hearts and minds Operation Sinbad did not have much of an impact. Major Paul Leslie of the Royal Anglians recalled, "the Divisional plan sought to overcome the insurgents by stealth. Paint fumes to be precise; mass frenzied painting and pot hole filling; we would DIY them to death through re-generating local infrastructure and repairing schools. B Company's role was to clear and secure the insertion and extraction route into the target area; a hazardous task. An initial requirement was to test the 'atmospherics' at Green 18, the Al Jezaizah [district]. Advised by Captain Ding, Colour Sergeant Roberts and Sergeants Kirk and Groom that there was no need and that 'it was hostile and dangerous', the Divisional Staff insisted. The sound of small arms fire and rocket propelled grenade attack was drowned only by the sound of the Divisional clipboard being dropped! 'Atmospherics' had been successfully tested."[55]

A contingent of the QRH was sent to the town of Imam Annas which was just outside Shaibah Logistic Base.

"Its population was somewhere between 5,000 and 15,000, and they live in the usual Iraqi squalor that, for whatever reason, seems to surprise us," commented one Hussar.

"Getting sent into a village with open sewers and rubbish strewn across the street to clear it up is unlikely to produce anything other than a minor and short-lived cosmetic effect. Short of moving the people away, the village would return to its previous state in a very short period. We spent several days in the town, cleaning up rubbish and taking away over forty sewage trucks full of raw waste. The tragedy remains that the local young people in the village refused to help clear up their mess unless we paid them. We can clear up a small village, but we can't change the mindset of the people who simply aren't used to doing things for themselves."[56]

General Shirreff's troops continued with strike operations throughout Operation Sinbad, although to assuage the Iraqi prime minister they could not be carried out in proximity of the pulse locations. The threat of resistance and heavy fighting during these raids prompted commanders to adopt deception measures to disguise their approach and extraction. When the DDLI launched Operation Citadel on 24th October to capture Sameer Sangu, one of Basra Province's five 'most wanted' militia leaders, the strike group main body arrived simultaneously from three directions, with low loaders being taken along to make the insurgents think it was a routine British supply convoy movement, to confuse Sangu's experienced look-outs.[57] The slow progress of Operation Sinbad was blamed by the General and his battlegroup commanders on lack of both British and Iraqi troops.

"I did not have the force levels to actually hold on to an area and to maintain troops on the ground in a sort of framework operation format once we had -- once we had moved into an area," General Shirreff told the Chilcot inquiry.

"So we would pulse in, set the conditions for projects and then we would have to move on to another area with much the same concentration of force. Initially, I had planned to use the Iraqi army in order to do the holding piece. Now, they improved in terms of confidence, in terms of training, immeasurably, I think, during the period of Sinbad, but they were not up to holding in security terms, because, ultimately, however confident they got, you have to remember that the Iraqi army in south-east Iraq were Shia-recruited, locally recruited, they lived on the ground amongst the militia, and they were not prepared to fight the militia, because they knew that, if they did, they would come off worse."[58]

In his evidence, he continued, "I mean, I remember Governor Wa'ili saying to me, "This operation sounds fine, but you are going to need another brigade in order to do it, aren't you?", and I said, "Well, we probably will, but we haven't got it, so we have to make use of what we have got".[59]

The commanding officer of the 2nd Battalion, The Rifles, Lieutenant Colonel Justin Maciejewski, blamed the Ministry of Defence and PJHQ for not reinforcing Operation Sinbad and diverting troops and resources to Afghanistan.[60] Many other British officers in Iraq believed that the operation did not achieve any decisive effect because of the ambivalence of the Iraqi prime minister, and the inability of the Iraqi army to generate sufficient troops to make it a success. They compared the situation to 18 months later, during Operation Charge of the Knights when 10,000 Iraqi troops were on the streets of Basra, under the enthusiastic - if amateurish - direct command of Maliki himself. That operation involved less than half the number of British troops that were on the streets of

Basra in 2006. Operation Sinbad did not work because the Iraqis were unable to make it work or did not want to it to succeed.

Shirreff's enthusiasm for the operation was not shared by other senior officers in PJHQ and London. One recalled hearing an officer in PJHQ calling it "Operation Spinbad", however, the Chief of Joint Operations let Shirreff's operation continue through into 2007.

Shirreff's command in Basra has become very controversial, with some senior officers in PJHQ and the Ministry of Defence in London claiming that the General was overly ambitious or acting on his own accord. One senior officer in the MOD complained that Shirreff had a "we know how to do this mentality, which did not turn out in practice."[61]

His defenders say all his operations were endorsed or directed by senior officers back in the UK and such criticism are attempts to disassociate these officers from the operation. Shirreff's officers and soldiers are universally loyal to their commander and say his aggressive approach helped sustain morale in difficult circumstances. The General clearly cared deeply about the soldiers under his command and subsequently heavily involved in focusing British government efforts to help wounded soldier being treated at the Sellyoak hospital.

Although Operation Sinbad was scheduled to run until the end of January 2007, in mid November PJHQ promulgated the planning directive for Operation Zenith to General Shirreff. This instructed him to begin the planning to "re-position" the British forces outside Basra city. This followed on from weeks of negotiations and planning with the American command in Baghdad. At this point in the campaign, US and British aims coincided with General Casey keen to get foreign troops out of Iraqi cities and into bases far from the population. The close US-British co-operation was reinforced by the fact that the formal orders for Operation Zenith were issued by the US corps headquarters in Baghdad and the US agreed to provide extensive intelligence, special forces, artillery and attack helicopter support for the move. "It simply could not have been conducted without US agreement and support," commented a senior British officer who was heavily involved in planning Operation Zenith.[62]

The main British bases in the city, the Shatt-al-Arab Hotel, the PJCC, Old State Building and the Basra Palace, were all to be handed over to Iraqi force by the end of April. The replacement for 20 Brigade, 19 Light Brigade would still have just over 7,000 troops to execute Operation Zenith but the follow-on headquarters, 1 Mechanised Brigade would have to deploy with only 5,500 troops and for the first time more British soldiers would be in Afghanistan than Iraq.[63] Ordering Operation Zenith was the first concrete step by Air Chief Marshal Stirrup to put into action the switch of main effort to Afghanistan. The pressure of running two wars simultaneously was starting to impact on the RAF's ageing fleet of Tristar strategic transport aircraft and Hercules tactical airlifters. There were just not enough aircraft to carry out simultaneous Iraq and Afghanistan force rotations, so the troops taking part in Operation Telic 8 had to spend another month in Basra while the troops in Helmand were switched over first.

Not surprisingly, Shirreff was not happy at the accelerated withdrawal plan telling the Chilcot inquiry, "the point I made very strongly [to PJHQ and the MOD]......was that, in order to avoid being seen to have been -- been pushed out of the city, we needed to establish the right conditions to withdraw on our own terms at the right time, and the two areas that I felt we needed to ensure -- the two critical pre-conditions were, number 1, that we had removed the running sore of the [rogue police] Serious Crimes Unit, and, number 2, that we had done -- we had reduced the -- we had got the indirect fire threat under control. Now, the latter, of course, we did not do. It was quite clear to me that, once Sinbad had run its course, there was no appetite for any further plan, any further surge. Operation Zenith was the only show in town. So in a sense that was the direction from London, so that is what I got on with."[64]

General Shirreff was not going to go out with a whimper. As Christmas approached he ordered a series of operations to smash the Serious Crime Unit (SCU) based in the infamous Jamiat Police Station. This was seen as a safe haven for insurgents and pro-Sadr death squads. The Staffords, who had been bloodied during the famous 2005 hostage incident, were in the forefront of these actions and they launched into them with some gusto.

The British General in Basra had been pressing Maliki, ministries in Baghdad, the Basra emergency committee and provincial council to approve action against the SCU for several weeks. Reports that it was running a secret prison inside the Jamiat containing hundreds of illegally held inmates and suspected links to the death squads eventually won round the Iraqi politicians.

A spike in attacks on British troops after the arrival of 19 Light Brigade in November 2006 also prompted Shirreff and the new Brigade Commander, Tim Evans, to decide to take the fight to the militia. "The Brigade had a baptism of fire on its arrival, with six killed in action in the first three weeks," commented Evans in a post tour report. As a result, there was a conscious decision to raise the tempo of operations, to strike early and exploit any intelligence opportunity in order to disrupt the militia and ensure we seized the initiative. We could not afford to loose our reputation and be driven from Basra or the provinces, Transition to Iraqi control had to be at a time of the Iraqi government's and our choosing, not the militia."[65]

Captain Jaffar, the head of the SCU, and five of his senior side kicks were seized in a raid on 22nd December, but Shirreff saved the best for Christmas Day. He knew the Iraqi politicians would have leaked details of his intentions to the militia so achieving surprise would be difficult. One way to do this was launch Operation Thyme on 25th December, when the militia would have expected the Staffords to be tucking into their Christmas roast turkey dinner at Shatt-al-Arab Hotel.

Two weeks before a Staffords patrol has made a brief police mentoring visit to the Jamiat and this allowed them to plan the raid with great precision. C Company of the Staffords led a convoy of 19 Warriors through the streets of Basra towards the station in broad daylight, which attracted the usual barrage of small arms and RPG fire. When the column turned into the road outside the station, a watch tower opened fire on it resulting in a Warrior returning fire. Resistance silenced, a Royal Engineers armoured bulldozer smashed through the outer compound wall to allow the Staffords to charge inside. Wisely the SCU had fled, leaving still warm meals on tables.[66]

A systematic six hour long search followed and netted a huge trawl of 49 AK-47s and sniper rifles, 19 grenades, seven 122 mm shells and other components used in the manufacturer of IEDs, four RPGs, body armour, drugs, a container of whisky, as well as mobile phones and computers full of intelligence on militia operations. The material had to be loaded in two ISO containers to be removed from the site. In the basement cells some 178 prisoners were recovered and freed from medieval conditions. As a finale, the Royal Engineers planted demolition charges throughout the building and blew the roof 50 feet in the air as the Staffords pulled out. The raid was a pretty emphatic statement of British resolve. Morale among the British force in Basra was high as the Staffords returned to base feeling like "conquering heroes" but it did not strike a decisive blow against the JAM.

Three days later a Warrior of the 2nd Battalion, The Duke of Lancaster's Regiment was hit by an IED, killing the commander. The surviving soldiers spotted Iraqi police cars parked nearby the incident with their blue lights flashing, as if signalling to the bombers to set off the device.

Within days, Maliki had disowned the Christmas Day raid as an infringement of Iraqi sovereignty and soon the Basra provincial council broke off relations with the British military. British relations with all levels of Iraqi politicians and institutions seemed to hit a new low.

Chapter 23

THE ACCOMMODATION

The officer selected to complete the execution of Operation Zenith was Major General Jonathan Shaw. He was a former Parachute Regiment officer, who had led a platoon during the heavy fighting on the Falklands islands in 1982. He had been immersed in operations in Iraq for more than three years as Director of Special Forces. General Shaw had been to Iraq many times, knew the human, political and physical geography of the place, and was firmly of the view that success would only come from crafting a political strategy as well as fighting a tactical battle against the militias on the streets of Basra.

Unlike many of his predecessor who had commanded in Basra, he had the luxury of nearly six months to prepare for his mission, being selected in July 2006 for his posting. Air Chief Marshal Sir Jock Stirrup's intentions to switch the main effort away from Iraq to Afghanistan were quickly made known to Shaw.

"I knew my job was to pull our troops out," he recalled. "I did not know when or how. Shirreff was to set the conditions. I did not yet have specific orders, just intent. The methodology was left to me."[1]

General Shaw spent the next six months visiting Iraq, speaking to American generals in Iraq and the US, and researching the country's politics. He visited brigadiers like Tim Evans of 19 Light Brigade and James Bashall of 1 Mechanised Brigade, and the troops he would have under his command during his period in command from January to August 2007. From the point of being appointed as commander designate to taking up his post in Basra, Shaw had to deal with a fundamental change in US strategy in Iraq, which would come to be a major factor in how he conducted the operation to pull British troops out of downtown Basra.

In the summer and autumn of 2006, the US commander in Iraq, General George Casey, was still pushing hard on the transition strategy to hand over security to the Iraqis, followed by the repositioning of US troops outside major cities as a first step to their eventual withdrawal from the country. Unfortunately for General Casey, his strategy was not working. It was set against a background of a cycle of sectarian civil war between Iraq's Shia and Sunni communities.

In September 2006, Iraqi civilian deaths spiked to 3,500, and some hundred US soldiers were killed that month, with hundreds seriously wounded. US President George Bush ordered a re-think of strategy. The controversial US defense secretary Donald Rumsfeld, the architect of the old Iraq strategy, had just been 'let go' by the president in November. A panel of elder statesmen proposed a phased withdrawal, but a retired US general, Jack Keane, and a group of senior army officers who had served in Iraq, led by General David Petraeus, persuaded the president that the war could be won by surging reinforcements.

What winning meant was always a bit nebulous, but the main aim seemed to be to convince US public opinion that Iraq was not a lost cause, and persuade Congress to keep funding the war by demonstrating that the US military was no longer bogged down. A British officer, who attended planning meetings in Baghdad with Petraeus in early 2007, had noted, that this was also tied in with securing an extension to the UN Security Council resolution that gave legal cover to the US and British presence in Iraq, which was due to expire at the end of 2007.

"It was all about molding perceptions," said the officer.

By pushing troops into Iraq's cities, Petraeus hoped that they would provide street level protection for the country's civilians and win them over. This became known as population-centric counter-insurgency operations. At the same time as conventional US Army units were setting up bases across Baghdad to take the fight the insurgents on their home turf, special forces would step up their raids or strike operations to decapitate the leadership of the insurgent groups. This was a bold strategy and Keane used the title 'Choosing Victory' for his pitch to President Bush.

Keane and Petraeus both stressed that a retreat under fire from Iraq would be portrayed by America's enemies, inside and outside of the country, as a strategic defeat on a par with the debacle of Vietnam. The two generals also feared the psychological impact on the US Army and US public opinion of a defeat in Iraq after so much US blood had been shed. The surge, as the offensive became known, would be the main effort of the US armed forces. This would be a go-for-broke effort, with units already in Iraq having their tours of duty extended, while five additional combat brigades were flown to Iraq, tens of thousands of extra reservists being mobilised and additional air power sent to support the troops. Petraeus proved adept at not only at crafting his strategy and tactics but building political support for it across the US government, military bureaucracy, Congress and with public opinion.

He looked and sounded like a winner, and was compared to General Douglas MacArthur, who had turned around the Pacific campaign in World War Two. President Bush decided to send Casey home early and Petraeus was ordered to Baghdad to put his strategy into action in January 2007.[2]

This reversal of US strategy placed the British government and senior military leadership in a very difficult position. The switch to Afghanistan was well under way, and there was no appetite among the British public, political class or even with the leadership of the armed forces for joining Petraeus' surge.

"Iraq had become such a toxic topic in UK politics by 2007 that there was no political appetite to discuss it or make public statements; the sense was that no one would believe the government and no good could come of any attempt at explanation so no attempt would be made," recalled Shaw, who described a mood of defeatism as taking hold of large sections of the British political and military leadership at this time.[3]

Prime Minister Tony Blair's foreign and defence policy advisor, Sir Nigel Elton Sheinwald, held a series of meeting with senior British officers in late 2006 and told them to prepare to accelerate withdrawal plans. The Prime Minister was building up to leave office during the coming year and what to have all British troops out of Iraq by the end of 2007.

"It was to be his legacy", commented a witness to one of these discusions.[4]

The Chief of Defence Staff was equally unimpressed by the proposed US surge, telling General Shaw before he flew out to Iraq in the middle of January 2007 to take command that it was of "no relevance to us".[5]

According to one of the Air Chief Marshal's advisors at this point, "Stirrup was not having anything to do with the surge."[6]

Operation Zenith would go ahead as planned, and General Shaw left for Iraq still with instruction to move ahead with it.

"The intent was to pull out of Basra Palace by the end of May," he said.

"I learnt from the sacking of bases at al Amarah that it would not look good if the place was over run by rioters or militiamen, so we needed to pull out without a shot being fired. We had to work with the Iraqis. My definition of success was that we did not exist [in Iraq]. We judged that success had to be defined in a context that did not include us; success had to be defined in Iraqi not British terms, as it was the Iraqis that would have to sustain it when we were gone. Any success that depended on our being there was by definition transient and illusory. So we had to work out what a sustainable Iraqi end state was and enable the Iraqis towards it as far as we could. It was an un-heroic start point for the British Army, which has an addiction to heroes."[7]

"All base handovers were to be negotiated with the Iraqi police and army," said Shaw. "They would be done to a timetable so the Iraqis could take them over properly."[8]

Two days after landing in Basra, General Shaw headed up to Baghdad to meet General Casey and brief him on the proposed British re-positioning and the intention to hand Basra and Maysan provinces to Iraqi security control during 2007. The American General, who would be leaving Baghdad within days, warned Shaw that his plans were not likely to find favour with Petraeus and the new US defense secretary Robert Gates, who were due in Iraq in a few days after passing through London to speak to Blair.

"Gates arrived in Basra and we gave him our briefing" said the British general.

"We trotted out our lines that we were part of the problem, that there was no civil war in south, 80% of the violence was against us because we were occupiers, etc. He was very polite and just sat there. He did not engage in open debate. One thing his team flashed up was when we mentioned Iranian influence, and whether the Jaish al Madhi (JAM) militia were rented or bought by Iran. I said this did not mean they wanted to be run by Iran. This did not compute with the Americans, who just did not get it when I said not all Iranian influence was malign, and that they understood about making money and had invested heavily in Basra. The Iranians did not want to see it go up in flames."[9]

"I don't know if Gates went back to Blair to complain?" recalled Shaw.

"That loop was never closed all through the period I was in Basra."

General Shaw said diverging policies of the UK surging into Afghanistan, while the US ramped up its effort in Iraq were never really publicly reconciled at the highest levels of the British and US governments.

The incoming US commander was also not happy with Operation Zenith, and after he took over from Casey, Petraeus telephoned the British prime minister to ask him to reconsider it, so as not to undermine the psychological and propaganda impact of the surge. Blair had to appease both his own people and the US. He did not feel able to turn down a direct request from the US General, so in February he told the House of Commons that force levels in Iraq would drop by 3,000 soldiers to keep his backbenchers happy but that British troops would remain in Basra Palace until the "late summer". British troops would remain in Iraq into 2008 providing training and advice to Iraqis, monitoring the Iranian border and securing the US supply lines.[10]

Brigadier Evans commented in his end of tour report, "[my Brigade's] tour coincided with the US surge and this did create tension with [the US command in Baghdad] over the timing of any reduction or repositioning of UK forces, due to the political ramifications of any perceived difference between UK-US policies in Iraq."[11]

General Petraeus was mollified by Blair's announcement, as well as commitments that the British forces in Basra would continue aggressive strike operations against the JAM militia and to interdict the Iranian border. He was also pleased that the UK special force in central Iraq would continue to work alongside the US Joint Special Operations Command (JSOC) in high-tempo strike operations against al Qaeda leaders. As a result, Petraeus continued to provide US support for Operations Sinbad and Zenith, with American intelligence, special forces and attack helicopter assets remaining committed to help the British through into the summer.

General Shaw now had to spend the next six months straddling the steadily diverging fault line between US and British policies, particularly as the surge appeared to be working in Baghdad, and the situation in Basra progressively appeared to be worsening in the early summer of 2007.

Over the next eight months, US attitudes to Britain's Operation Zenith ebbed and flowed. US and UK forces in Iraq were dependent on a United Nations Security Council mandate for much of their legal authority to be in Iraq, and this had to be renewed at the end of 2007. British efforts to hand over Maysan and Basra provinces to Iraqi security control helped with building the diplomatic case to renew the mandate. So the US continued to back the handing of provinces to the Iraqis, even if they did not want the repositioning of British troops from Basra city to progress at the same rate.

"This lasted until the summer of 2007 when the surge was judged as being effective and US domestic support for the Iraq operation began to rise," said Shaw.

"Petraeus now became optimistic that the UN mandate could be extended and started to be less keen on us repositioning. It was only late in the day, in June 2007, that it became clear that the surge was working," said Shaw.

"So only then does the British pull out start to look off message, but it is too late, we had already handed over everything put Basra Palace. We were committed."[12]

It was not just the American command in Baghdad which was unhappy with the British plans. Iraqi Prime Minister Nouri al-Maliki was still fuming over the Christmas Day Jamiat police station raid. He continued to insist on political control of all British strike operations against high value targets within the militia, and he repeatedly vetoed raids against militia targets who were associated with his political allies in Basra. His attitude to British strike operations would also shift considerably in the autumn and winter of 2007, as his new coalition government became less dependent on the parliamentary votes of Muqtada al Sadr's party. In early 2007, the Shia cleric was morphing into a political rival of the prime minister, so Maliki was starting to take a very close interest in what was happening in Basra. He sent a new army commander to Basra to take a tough line with the militia loyal to rival political parties, but distrust and tension between the British and Maliki would grow over the next year.

As the political and strategic manoeuvring was underway to finesse the execution of Operation Zenith, on the streets of Basra the troops of 19 Light Brigade were locked in steadily escalating battles with the militias around Basra. Estimates varied but between 5,000 and 7,000 fighters were inside the city's main residential neighbourhoods. A significant number of the city's 5,000 or so policemen also regularly joined in fighting with British troops. They were heavily armed with small arms, machine guns, rocket propelled grenades, mortars and long range rockets, as well as sophisticated 'Explosively-Formed Improvised Explosive Devices' that could penetrate the armour of British Warrior vehicles.[13]

"Over 90% of attacks were against Multi-National Force [British troops] and the majority of the population were at best ambivalent about our presence," said Brigadier Evans. "Many thought we had outstayed our welcome".[14]

The violence in Basra produced strange effects, with the population of the city going about normal business for most of the time, yet when British vehicles appeared in a neighbourhood, within minutes scores of armed men would appear and firefights would break out that could last several hours. This switch from peace to war could occur in a very short time.

Ranged against the militias were the 7,100 troops of Brigadier Evans' force, who were some of the most battle-hardened and best-equipped troops to be deployed to Iraq. The 1st Battalion, The Staffordshire Regiment, based in the Shatt-al-Arab Hotel, had already served in Iraq in the summer of 2005.

It was picked specifically to go back to Iraq because of its combat experience. The division reserve or 'strike' battlegroup, the 2nd Battalion, The Duke of Lancaster's Regiment (2 Lancs) also contained a wealth of Iraq expertise. It had recently been formed from soldiers from the King's Own Royal Border Regiment, The King's Regiment and the Queen's Own Lancashire Regiment. The Basra South battlegroup, 1st Battalion, The Royal Green Jackets, soon to be the 2nd Battalion, The Rifles, had briefly served in southern Iraq in the autumn of 2003, so was not as experienced. The battlegroup outside Basra, the 1st Battalion, The Yorkshire Regiment had not served in Iraq before.[15]

During its tour, the Brigade received the first heavily-armoured Mastiff patrol vehicles, and the armoured Bulldog troop carriers. General Shirreff may have bemoaned the lack of artillery, attack helicopters and fast air to counter militia rocket attacks on Basra airport and other bases, but 19 Brigade was soon provided with these very capabilities. It received half a battery of 105mm Light Guns manned by 6/36 Battery of the Royal Artillery. It would soon be returning counter-battery fire for the first time since the 2003 invasion.[16]

The Americans had put an Apache attack helicopter company from the Texas National Guard's 1st Battalion, 149th Aviation Regiment on call to support British strike operations in Basra. In the spring of 2007, the 2nd Battalion, 159th Aviation Regiment replaced the Texas Apache unit for the rest of the year.[17] Occasional sorties by Hellfire missile-armed MQ-1 Predator drones were also committed to overfly Basra. The counter-rocket campaign was also boosted when the Americans sent a battery of M109 155mm howitzers, with Excalibur laser-guided artillery shells and long range locating radars to help defend the airport.[18]

"All [our] bases in MND(SE) were targeted by both rockets and mortars throughout the tour and resulted in 67 [British and coalition] casualties," said Brigadier Evans.

"To counter the threat, our counter-indirect fire operations were refined and the [Royal Artillery] surveillance and target acquisition battery and C-RAM, were well integrated into the Brigade operations room to provide early warning. These systems alongside our surveillance assets facilitated 17 strike operations, five deliberate operations 20 gun engagements and two fast air engagements with guided munitions, as well as an engagement from a Predator UAV. However, we were never going to be able to prevent all the rocket attacks and it was something we had to get used to."[19]

The two Basra city battlegroups were in the thick of the battle with the militia, running multiple operations each day. Major Greg Bayliss, the Staffords' battlegroup warfare officer, recalled that on the week his unit took down the infamous Jamiat police station, he was also preparing four other smaller strike operations, two Operation Sinbad reconstruction pulses, two protection operations for re-supply convoys, a search mission in an insurgent-held district, as well several small patrols to sweep expected rocket and mortar firing points. On the same day, there were several mortar attacks that inflicted three casualties.

Commanders, watchkeeping officers and radio operators in battlegroup operations rooms had to constantly juggle never-ending streams of uncontrollable events and still stay calm. But tension in battlegroup operations rooms was replicated, and multiplied, five times at the main Brigade operations room at Basra airport, or contingency operating base (COB) as it was now known.[20]

"The constant juggling of resources was at the heart of the Brigade operations team's daily business," recalled one former 19 Brigade staff officer.

"The five major units within the Brigade were always extremely busy, and were often conducting widely varied operations over a wide geographical spread. At any given time Brigade headquarters might have to monitor a sustainment convoy, another from Basra Palace to the Provincial Joint Co-ordination Centre (PJCC), a routine casualty evacuation from Maysan and a covert surveillance operation involving ground troops to deter indirect fire attacks on the COB. At the same time we may have been monitoring the progress of a private security company convoy somewhere within the province."[21]

"All these operations come with a significant degree of risk and could at anytime be subject to insurgent attack," said the major.

"It was not unusual in the summer of 2007 for the duty Brigade G3 operations staff to be dealing with multiple simultaneous contacts, some involving [recovering] causalities, necessitating the constant re-allocation of assets and prioritisation of information requirements. While this was going on the COB and Brigade operations room might well be coming under rocket fire. Rapid assessment of the situation and prioritisation of incidents was the key, as well as the ability to assimilate a mass of information from a range of sources."

Even the arrival of the 105mm Light Guns did not put a stop to the rocket attacks on the airport, which rose from 18 in January to 64 in April, 77 in May, 76 in June and 74 in July. This prompted one soldier at the COB to describe the experience as "buttock-clenching fear as we played rocket lottery". Troops who served at the airbase were soon generating what were called 'splat maps', showing locations of rockets strikes during their tours of duty. After General Shaw got permission from ministers in London in February, the 105mm Light Guns of 6/36 Battery started returning fire, firing 74 rounds in that month.[22]

The locations in Basra received similar treatment, with mortars thrown in for good measure. The Staffords at the Shatt-al-Arab Hotel were hit by over 100 rocket and mortar attacks, as well as 169 small arms and rocket propelled grenade attacks. Chindit Company of 2 Lancs, in the Old State Building, was on the receiving end of 350 attacks during its tour including 50 RPG and mortar strikes. In Basra Palace, the Green Jackets claimed to be holding the most mortared camp in the world, receiving 578 in-coming rounds in the course of 166 attacks during their first four months in the city centre base alone. The Americans subsequently moved one of their C-RAM Phalanx guns into the Palace to counter the rocket and mortar fire, but the militia mortar teams soon worked out that it had a two kilometre minimum engagement distance, so if they fired from under that distance the American weapon would not be able to intercept their fire.[23]

Brigadier Evans was a former Special Air Service troop commander, and he was determined that his troops would not just be made to sit tight in his bases and be targets. According to General Shaw, 19 Brigade became highly efficient at organising strike operations and generated an operational tempo that had not been reached by any previous brigade in Basra.

"19 Brigade conducted over two hundred operations, averaging one every two days," said Brigadier Evans.

"With the improvement in intelligence fusion and ISTAR assets, it led to a series of highly successful [intelligence] targeted strike operations that seriously undermined the enemy."[24]

He wanted to take the fight to the enemy using intelligence gathering by the small SAS contingent based in Basra Palace, as well as the Field Human Intelligence Team (FHT), who regularly ventured out into Basra to cultivate agents, or on occasions to don civilian clothes to try to get eyes on to potential targets for strike operations. So-called strategic agencies, including the US Central Intelligence Agency and the British Secret Intelligence Service (SIS) both had teams in the palace which worked closely together, and also had technical surveillance means, but this information was often not enough to plan a raid. According to one senior British officer, militia commanders were well aware the British and Americans were trying to monitor their communications and would rarely talk about sensitive information in telephone conversations. So the SAS and FHT had to try to build a more detailed picture and package it for military users. They had an on-call Warrior platoon of infantry to transport them into heavily defended insurgent areas of the city.[25]

The militia, meanwhile, were well aware the British and Americans were trying to penetrate their organisations and tried to target the intelligence operatives on several occasions. A speed boat carrying members of the FHT was targeted by an IED hanging under a bridge over the Shatt-al-Arab waterway in November, and a few days later a SAS sergeant was killed leading a raid on an insurgent base in Basra.[26]

Resistance to British strike operations was now at a level never before experienced in Basra, and even the heavily-protected Warriors were starting to take heavy losses. Major Andrew Maskall, a company commander with the reserve battlegroup, 2 Lancs, said that his regiment lost 14 Warriors to EFP IEDs during their tour up to April 2007. The militia had learned to position the weapons so they would fire up through the road wheels of the vehicle and hit a weak spot on the side of the hull. Militia IED tactics were starting to improve as well.

"Dependent on the time of year Warrior may be limited to metalled roads as opposed to the salt flats that surround the city," said Maskall. "This of course channels [our vehicles] into potential killing areas, there being only three routes into Basra from the COB. On occasions it is necessary to 'fight your way through' on an insertion or extraction [from strike operations]. Striking troops will seek to breach the perimeter defences with IEDs and RPG teams in order to secure a house, and detain insurgent leaders, and in these circumstances little can stop a Warrior. A commander must be decisive and the effect on urban infrastructure will not always be of primary concern. The 'break in battle' must be won."[27]

A crash programme was launched to up-armour the Warriors, which had new protection designed and fitted in a matter of weeks. In April, a Royal Tank Regiment Challenger 2 tank was badly damaged by a new type of explosively-formed penetrator IED during a strike operation in Basra, resulting in the driver losing his leg. This prompted an upgrade to the vehicle's armour-protection package.[28]

In battles with insurgents between November 2006 and the end of May 2007, offensive operations were considered essential to keep up the morale of troops in 19 Brigade. In the words of one officer who served in the city at the time, "we needed to let the troops get their frustration off their chests after we took a loss."[29]

Major Maskall described Operation Rattlesnake, which the battlegroup launched on 13th April, after the death of four of its soldiers in an IED strike on a Warrior.[30]

"Following the loss of our personnel on 5th April it was important that the battlegroup seized the initiative back from the insurgents in the Hyall Shuala [district]," he said.

"Operation Rattlesnake was our response to this and Arnhem Company with elements of Egypt Squadron [of the Royal Tank Regiment] acted as the lure for a battlegroup ambush. The target was the site where recce platoon had lost the Warrior. Targets were drawn into the 'killing area' and engaged with indirect fire from [105mm Light] guns [at the COB] and direct fire from Challenger 2, Warrior and Javelin. Our own Sergeant Harker and Lance Corporal Allen formed one of the Javelin sections and inserted by foot to a firing line with C Company 1 Yorks. The Javelin section identified a car-based IED team and fired three missiles, destroying the car and four insurgents. The tanks confirmed another group setting up a further two IEDs, the tanks fired five HESH rounds killing all eight insurgents and destroying both cars. The operation was a tactical success. The Company returned safely."[31]

Corporal Paul Fearnley fired the Javelin missiles during Operation Rattlesnake.

"The final analysis was eight insurgents killed with minimum collateral damage, a successful patrol, with a positive end state," he said. "The battlegroup had had a tough couple of weeks, returning to an offensive posture and thus reminding the [militia] of our capabilities, resolve and stance was a great boost to morale."[32]

The use of ambushes, or 'lurks' as they were nicknamed, became an increasingly common tactic in the first months of 2007, as 19 Brigade tried to inflict casualties on the insurgents and disrupt their freedom of movement. They grew in size and often involved multiple platoons moving out of British bases to set up ambushes, using their night-vision equipment to give them a tactical advantage. These ambushes soon escalated into major fire fights, with dozens of insurgents being killed.

Penetrating the JAM and its allied militias in Basra was a constant challenge for the British. The most prized information related to any links to Iran and the so-called 'JAM special groups'. The US JSOC was very keen to help in this effort because of growing concern among senior commanders, including General Petraeus, that the Iranians were using Basra to move advanced weapons and personnel up to Baghdad. In late 2006, the JSOC formed its own unit dedicated to countering Iranian influence, dubbed Task Force 17. The unit soon joined the British SAS in Basra, and began try to build up actionable intelligence on the special groups' leadership. The haul of prisoners and intelligence from 19 Brigade's strike operations generated a huge quantity of leads that the US and British special operators were keen to exploit.[33]

Major Bob Driver, commander of 2 Lancs Blenheim Company, was assigned to work with the new players in the battle for Basra.

"From early 2007 onwards, US Special Forces and US-led Iraqi Special Forces started to operate within Basra. These were strikes against specific targets with the troops coming down from Baghdad for the operation. Blenheim Company were chosen to lead the special forces onto the targets and then provide the 'ring of steel' around the target location. The first strikes went extremely well with the company; on a rapid learning curve, having to operate out of normal modus operandi, and with a concept of a mobility command [commander of Blenheim company] and ground command [commander of the special forces], this included operating with an AC-130 [Spectre gunship] and resulted in special forces elements detaining the targets. Meanwhile B Company isolated the position, fighting back insurgents as they tried to assist the target, who would invariably be a high ranking member of the insurgency; whilst this all occurred AC-130s would be providing depth and engaging targets further out."[34]

In March 2007, Basra got its own dedicated Iraqi Special Forces company, who were highly trained by the Americans, and directly paid by the US military rather than the Baghdad Ministry of Defence, to ensure their loyalty. They carried out raids for Task Force 17 for the remainder of the summer, including participating in a rare raid into downtown al Amarah in June.

A JSOC raid in January 2007 had captured a number of Iranian Quds Force operatives and the intelligence trail led to Basra, where two leading special group operatives, the Khazali brothers, Qais and Laith, were believed to be based. Task Force 17 and a large contingent from G Squadron of the SAS flew down to Basra from their base at Balad outside Baghdad on 20th March. Then 2 Lancs transported them to the target near the city port for the take down, which was being personally monitored by the JSOC commander, Major General Stanley McChrystal, via a Predator video link in his command post in Balad.[35]

The assault force successfully captured their targets, along with several other men, including one who later turned out to an operative of the Lebanese Hizbollah group. A huge haul of documents and computers was also gathered up, including ID passes of US soldiers kidnapped and executed by a special groups assault team in Karbala a few weeks before. The US and British special force had hit the jackpot, or so they thought. They had in fact stirred up a hornets' nest.

Three days later the Iranians struck back. Iranian Revolutionary Guards' speed boats surprised two Royal Navy patrol boats, who were protecting Iraq's off shore oil terminal. They captured 15 sailors and marines and swiftly extracted them to Tehran, where they were paraded on television for maximum propaganda effect. The incident spiraled into a public relations disaster for the British government. Deft diplomacy by the Foreign and Commonwealth Office secured the prisoners' release.

But when Ministry of Defence spin doctors allowed the only female captive sailor to sell her story to a tabloid newspaper, it unleashed a frenzy of demands in almost every national newspapers for ministerial resignations and the sacking of anyone involved in the incident.[36]

At the time the Iranian government did not explicitly link the capture of the sailors to the Khazali raid, with the Iranian President Mahmud Ahmedinejad quickly becoming more interested in using the incident to publicly humiliate the British. Another incident occurred in May when a British computer expert, and his four British civilian bodyguards were seized from a ministry building in Baghdad by special group operatives linked to the Khazali brothers. Dressed in police uniforms, they stormed the building in broad daylight and made off with their hostages to Iran. Direct demands were made to swap the Khazali brothers for the British hostages. Negotiations dragged on for two years and the four bodyguards were subsequently killed by their captors, with the only the computer expert returning alive.[37]

During a five-week period beginning on 21st March, General Shaw began handing over the first British bases in downtown Basra to the Iraqi military. The build up to Operation Zenith had been under way for several weeks, with huge truck convoys removing containers of stores from the bases to the COB. At the same time, General Shaw and his senior commanders had been making detailed preparations to build up the Iraqi units designated to take over the bases, to prevent a repeat of the rioting that followed the hand over of Camp Abu Naji the previous summer. This would have discredited the whole transition process, seriously embarrassed the British Army and caused major political problem for the Blair government.

The Iraqi army brigade based in Basra was strongly suspected of being infiltrated by militia supporters, or at least to be susceptible to intimidation by the JAM. Prior to the handover process starting, the Iraqi brigade commander and his officers refused to participate in a planned rotation to Baghdad, raising further questions about its reliability and prompting the British to accelerate the formation and training of the Iraqi 10th Division's new fifth brigade. Recruits and officers from outside the Basra region were used to man the new brigade to ensure its loyalty. Even the best trained Iraqi units were still not keen to take part in offensive operations against Shia militia fighters, prompting the British to suspect that a series of unspoken non-aggression pacts had been struck up between many army units and local militia commanders. The fact that Iraqi army bases were not subject to the relentless rocket and mortar fire experienced by British bases reinforced this suspicion.

A few Iraqi units, particularly those that served away from Basra, were picked for their reliability and efficiency to take over the British bases, and they were sent to their new posts in the weeks before the handover to receive additional training. To try to build up the Iraqi army and police across the city, 19 Brigade launched Operation Troy, to deploy 1,000 British troops to reinforce vehicle checkpoints and encourage the Iraqis to be more thorough in searches of suspect cars and their occupants. This led to a series of running battles with militia fighters who tried to engage the checkpoints.[38]

The training exercise worked, with the Old State Building being handed over to an Iraqi military police company on 21st March. There was a brief ceremony, and even Governor Waeli turned up to share the glory. There was no looting. On 8th April, the Staffords left the Shatt-al-Arab Hotel after a very peaceful handover parade. Sixteen days later, the British left the huge camp complex at Shaibah, leaving the Basra Palace and the PJCC as the only British bases in the centre of the town.[39] The draw-down considerably reduced the number of British troops in the centre of the city, leading to fears that small groups of soldiers could be overwhelmed. A group of 24 Danish soldiers who were helping to withdraw their forces from their base to the north of the city were ambushed in the Al Hartha district, and pinned down under heavy fire, with nine soldiers wounded. As 40 heavily-armed JAM fighters moved to join the battle, Blenheim Company of 2 Lancs were scrambled from the COB to rescue the beleaguered allies.[40]

The move from Shaibah Logistics Base was a huge undertaking, involving the removal of all the British Army's fuel, food, ammunition and other supplies to ports in Kuwait or to the COB at Basra airport. New logistics installations had to be replicated at the COB to continue to sustain the British mission in southern Iraq. One other important facility to be rebuilt was the British prison, that held some 200 insurgents who had been captured in strike operations over the past four years. Until the move to the airport, it was known as the Division Temporary Detention Facility, and was then resurrected as the Divisional Internment Facility (DIF). It played a key role in British strike operations by removing militia fighters from the battlefield pending their transfer to the Iraqi legal system for prosecution.

The holding of prisoners was a deeply controversial aspect of the British occupation, both in Iraq and in Britain. For the Iraqis, continued British detention of prisoners without them being tried in front of local courts was a symbol of a hated foreign occupation. While in Britain, the use of the phrase "internment" in the title of the facility had shades of the controversial arrest without trial of hundreds of Irish prisoners during Ulster's Troubles in the 1970s. When 11 Iraqi prisoners escaped from the prison at Shaibah in March 2007, by simply swapping their clothes with visiting relatives, it also became a laughing stock.[41]

Even within the British Army, the holding of hundreds of Iraqi prisoners for prolonged periods was not universally popular. Major Spencer took his company from the 1st Battalion, The Royal Welsh Regiment, to guard the DIF in the summer of 2007.

He described how "nothing could disguise the sheer desperation of the state of the new building". Despite being open for only 12 days, the sewage system had failed, the air conditioning had failed, turning the prison cells into saunas. Then the clean water pipes failed, causing the guards to have to distribute 500 bottles of water each day. Major Spencer said the experience of the Military Provost Staff prison experts, who advised the guard force, simply did not "equate" to the needs of holding over a hundred Muslim men, who had "nothing left to loose". Not surprisingly, the Welsh soldiers nicknamed the facility "the asylum".[42]

In his regimental journal, Major Spencer questioned whether the resources and potential for political embarrassment of keeping the DIF open were worthwhile. He said they caused enormous resentment among the local population, and doubted if the inmates were truly out of action because visits by relatives allowed the prisoners to communicate with their comrades still at large. Not only was a company of troops diverted from combat duty, but the "extensive staff hours of very senior commanders" was involved in the "legally required targeting and reviewing process", taking them away from other tasks. This distracted from other critical areas of the operation. He also said the operation was high-risk, with the "very real daily potential of an international incident involving an internee".[43]

Major Spencer's views only gained limited traction from the senior military leadership of the British armed forces, despite briefing the Chief of the Defence Staff and other senior officers during visits to the prison. The prisoners were a valuable source of intelligence on militia groups and the threat of being captured undermined the morale of militia fighters. And the morale of British troops would also have been damaged if enemy prisoners were allowed to walk away immediately after capture.[44]

There was also another important reason to hold onto the prisoners, although this was not really apparent at the time, or part of the thinking of senior British officers until well into 2007. They were one of the few bargaining chips the British held in any negotiations they might have to indulge in with the militias. Very soon the British would be able to play this card.

With the Iraqi forces now in charge of the majority of Basra, the British troops were confined to one major base and a smaller outpost in the centre of the city, occupied by the newly-arrived 4th Battalion, The Rifles. This was one of the British Army's new 'super regiments,' formed from the amalgamation of the Royal Green Jackets, the Light Infantry, Devon & Dorsets, and the Royal Berkshire, Gloucestershire & Wiltshire Regiment on 1st February 2007. Its commanding officer, Lieutenant Colonel Patrick Sanders, and his 800 soldiers spent the next three and half months under virtual siege in their bases.

"[Our last locations in the city] became the centre of attention for the militia attacks," said Brigadier Evans. "It reinforced the point that once the decision had been made towards provincial Iraqi control (PIC) and to start the transfer of security of Basra to the Iraqi security forces, it would be untenable to hold just one battlegroup in the city. However, with the US surge occurring in Baghdad, [US corps command] would not authorise PIC in Basra at this stage."[45]

Re-supplying 4 Rifles was turning into a major pre-occupation of the new British brigade, 1 Mechanised, and its youthful commander, James Bashall, a Parachute Regiment officer who replaced Brigadier Evans at the end of May. At the end of its tour, 19 Brigade had suffered 27 soldiers killed in action and over 150 wounded, including 47 very or seriously injured. The fatalities were up by five over those suffered by the brigade's predecessors but the number of wounded was nearly double. This spike in casualties was attributed to increased and sustained rocket and mortar fire, as well as the increased intensity of firefights, prompting Major Mike Foster-Brown of the departing 2 Rifles battlegroup to comment that "the levels of violence and casualty rates within the city have been more akin to general warfare."[46]

The convoys of food, fuel, ammunition and spare parts to 4 Rifles were quickly to come to dominate 1 Brigade's operations during May, June and July. These soon required deliberate operations needing most of 4 Rifles troops working from the Palace, and a new reserve battlegroup. This was now renamed the manoeuvre battlegroup, the 2nd Battalion, The Royal Welsh Regiment (2 Royal Welsh) operating into the city from the airport. At least two convoys were required each week, with the inbound leg taking one day, another day for unloading and re-organisation inside the Palace and then a third day to extract the convoy. These convoys could be made up of a mix of 80 to 100 civilian and military trucks carrying ISO containers, and low-loaders transporting vehicles. A protection force of 20 to 30 Warriors and Bulldogs escorted the convoy on its route, while several other units were positioned along the route to control key road junctions and possible ambush points. So, for a good part of each week, two or three battlegroups-worth of troops were tied up fighting to get the convoys through and back from Basra Palace.[47]

Every convoy operation resulted in a major battle along its route, as IED detonations, machine-gun, RPG ambushes and mortar barrages were sprung by multiple militia groups along the few routes to the Palace. As the convoys got nearer to their final destination, the options to vary the route narrowed considerably, making it very easy for the militia to set up attacks. This led to the escort troops quickly nicknaming the final stretch of road into the Palace 'Mogadishu Mile,' after the ambush made famous in the Hollywood film version of *Black*

Hawk Down. The convoys needed to be pushed into Basra Palace regularly, because not only were they bringing in supplies, they also had to bring out all of 4 Rifles stores, vehicles and anything that might be looted if the site was ransacked after the withdrawal in August.[48]

Invariably, vehicles broke down or were immobilised by IEDs, bringing the convoys to a halt at vulnerable points, exposing the convoys and their escorts to even more danger. The Pakistani drivers who drove the civilian contract trucks were not surprisingly terrified by the experience, and many had to fortify themselves with strong alcohol before making the journey to and from the Palace, prompting a series of crashes.[49] The American war correspondent, Michael Yon, who spent much of the summer of 2007 embedded with 4 Rifles, said the troops escorting the convoys experienced traumatic conditions spending up to 13 or 14 hours at a time inside their armoured vehicles.

"As temperatures approached 70° C (around 150° F) inside the armoured vehicles, soldiers poured water down their body armour," he wrote from Basra.

"A driver was naked other than his body armour and helmet, while soldiers in the back literally pulled down their pants. This was more than a mere attempt to keep cool. They were trying not to die. Thick clouds of dust baked the putrid Basra odours until they could gag a goat; although by then the soldiers inside the Bulldogs and Warriors could offer serious competition in a stink contest. With their heavy body armour and helmets, laden with ammunition, rashes erupted on their skin and their goggles and ballistic glasses were filthy. The place is like a toilet used as an oven. The people on the septic streets were flushed with hostility."[50]

Colonel Sanders and his men did not even have a chance to gently break themselves into this ordeal, with their first ever convoy operation turning into a two-day-long running battle through Basra's city centre area. He commented that, "we have been warned by 2 Rifles that the convoys would be gut-wrenching emotional experiences".

In a matter of hours the Colonel would find out for real what they meant.[51]

The evening convoy run, on 20th May, soon turned into an ordeal of endurance for the Riflemen and Royal Welsh soldiers of the escort force as it was dogged by breakdowns, IED strikes, ambushes, a Warrior got stuck in a ditch, and some of the drunken civilian drivers took a wrong turn, breaking up the convoy near a militia strong hold. The extraction of the convoy the following day turned out to be far worse. A night-time run to the PJCC to drop off supplies and escort Brigadier Evans on a farewell visit to the beleaguered outpost went smoothly, but as the convoy weaved its way back to the Palace to reform for the final trip out to the airport it came under sustained attack.

"There was intelligence that JAM was waiting ahead," recalled Yon.

"In fact, there apparently were about 100 enemy waiting to ambush. The convoy was just near the Martyr Sadr building when the enemy attacked with small arms and RPGs. Corporal Jez Brookes, a Bulldog vehicle commander, was shot in the head and died on the spot. Others were wounded. Some enemy concentrated fire on a fuel transporter driven by a Pakistani contractor whose son worked on base in Basra. His body slumped and fell from the burning truck; orange flames and black smoke filling the sky. Many enemies here shamelessly exploit women and children as cover—which sometimes works and sometimes backfires. This time an armed crowd surged into the street, including what appeared to be women dressed in black, and dragged away the body of the Pakistani man. British soldiers tried to get to the Pakistani, but with all the combat, it was too late: the man disappeared and was never seen again."[52]

A low loader carrying a Snatch Land Rover and Saxon armoured personnel carrier was immobilised blocking a bridge, the fuel tanker exploded and a Bulldog had a track blown off by an IED. For the rest of the day, the escort force put a cordon around the stricken vehicles and tried to get them moving again, to deny the JAM a propaganda victory from seizing them. The bulk of the convoy was able to weave its way back to the Palace in safety, including Brigadier Evans who spent several hours under fire in his vehicle. Despite the bravery of a Royal Electrical Mechanical Engineer (REME) recovery crew in an unarmoured Foden tow truck, the low loader could not be moved, so a Royal Welsh Warrior ended up blasting the vehicles with its 30mm cannon to deny them to the militia.[53]

In a classic piece of understatement, Colonel Sanders commented, "It was not a situation that any of us had hoped for on the first day of our tour, and there is little doubt that we were all shocked by the speed with which the situation unravelled so quickly, and of course, by Corporal Brooke's death."[54]

As the fighting intensified in Basra during the first months of 2007, it became increasingly difficult for the British government to portray it as a success. Transition to Iraqi control was supposed to be a sign that things were going well, but key attacks on British troops were reaching a new level. This placed British commanders in Iraq in an invidious position with the media, who during visits to Basra could witness the intense violence being directed at 19 and 1 Brigades. Commanders were keen to give their troops credit for their bravery in the face of unprecedented levels of violent, but this ran against the grain of instruction from London to play down militia attacks.

Captain Christopher Salmon, who worked in Basra Palace at this time as an army media minder, commented in an after-action report that the government's official message was "diverging from reality".[55]

"Given the political controversy around the Iraq war perhaps we should not be surprised that control of messages has remained with Ministry of Defence and ministerial press offices," he said.

"In reality, however, this control extends beyond general 'messages' to particular topics and precise wording of statements. Lower down the food chain the result is diminished credibility and paralysis. Instead of serious thought about how to use the media to challenge the militias, we are reduced to archaic discussions about whether enemy first-round hits should be described as coming from a 'sniper', a 'sharpshooter' or just a 'gunman'," said Salmon.

"A similar discussion occurred over the correct description of the enemy: 'insurgent' was ruled out, there being no insurgency in the south of Iraq; leaving 'militia' (the favoured option); anti-Iraqi forces (not very media-friendly), or 'terrorist' (a difficult term for the media to use)."

Captain Salmon described how he became "a sort of Political Commissar, reporting up a secondary chain of command to a civilian press office and advising his Commanding Officer on what to say, what not to say, and how to say it."[56]

Senior officers were under intense pressure not to rock the boat, and Brigadier Bashall sparked a major fissure with the government in London when he revealed in a newspaper interview the details of US pressure that led to 4 Rifles remaining in Basra Palace. After that it became increasingly difficult for senior officers to get authorisation from London to give media interviews.

Basra Palace and the PJCC did not offer much sanctuary to Colonel Sanders and his men. The battlegroup was on the receiving end of 1,750 mortars and rockets, in some 311 barrages, during its time inside Basra city. In July, there were 48 casualties from rocket and mortar fire across 1 Brigade.[57] Meanwhile detailed intelligence work by the special forces tracked down the leader of the JAM in Basra, Wissam Abu Qader, and gave General Shaw a chance to seize him. Task Force 17's Iraqi special forces company was teamed up with 2 Lancs, who were just in the process of handing over to the Royal Welsh, to capture him in the middle of the afternoon on 25th May, as he left a meeting at the Sadr organisation in central Basra.

Operation Chester was a highly unusual strike operation against a moving target in the centre of Basra, with 16 Warriors being positioned along his expected route to intercept Wissam's car. According to Major Maskall, of Arnhem Company, once the Warriors had closed off his escape routes, the Iraqi special forces moved in for the kill.[58]

"[The Iraqis] engaged the target car and the driver and passenger (the target) jumped out as the car exploded," said Maskall.

"The driver was chased down a side street and the passenger ran straight into the Iraq [special forces] who engaged and killed him."

The response of the JAM was very swift, and later that night they launched a concerted attack to overrun the PJCC building, where a platoon of 24 Riflemen were on guard duty. Commanded by a junior lieutenant, fresh out of the Royal Military Academy Sandhurst, the soldiers had only been in Basra for four days when militiamen opened up on the building from 20 different fire positions. The Riflemen fired 9,000 rounds to repel the attack, and when they ran out of gun oil to lubricate their weapons, they resorted to using cooking oil to keep up their fire. Two soldiers were wounded in the firefight that lasted more than four hours. Then a 200-strong force of militiamen edged closer to the building, when a US Predator drone and a pair of RAF Tornado GR4 bombers arrived overhead to deliver precision ordnance on the attackers. The employment of close air support proved decisive and the JAM fighters quickly withdrew, but the need to use airpower within the city limits showed how the precarious nature of 4 Rifles' toehold in Basra had become.[59]

The PJCC was now subjected to sustained mortar attacks over the next month that seriously wounded several Rifleman. Its isolated position meant that the only way to evacuate seriously-wounded soldiers quickly was by RAF Merlin helicopter. However, the helicopter landing site in the complex was easily observed from surrounding buildings, making its use only possible at night time, and then it was still a high risk manoeuvre. On 1st June, a Rifleman was seriously injured by mortar shrapnel while manning a fortified sanger or firing post on the PJCC roof. To get his man out, Brigadier Bashall asked Flight Lieutenant Michelle Goodman and her Merlin crew if they would fly the mission. The soldier was close to death and needed immediate surgery at the airport's field hospital. There was a high risk the helicopter would be shot down, but all the crew and a medical team volunteered straight away to go. An Army Air Corps Lynx escorted the big Merlin to the PJCC trying to divert attention from the evacuation helicopter. Four mortar rounds landed around the helicopter as his comrades loaded the wounded Rifleman on board, with more rounds landing around the helicopter, it lifted off and headed for safety.[60]

"It was an awesome bit of flying," commented Brigadier Bashall, "and it was important that [Rifleman] Stephen [Vause] was rescued. The soldiers needed to know that if they were badly injured we would come and get them out - no matter what."[61]

The PJCC continued to attract heavy JAM fire, and the Rifles' luck ran out on 19th June when Major Paul Harding, the most senior army officer to be killed in action in Iraq for four years, was hit by mortar shrapnel while manning a firing position on the roof of the building.

Colonel Sander's defence plan now involved the launching of strike operations to try to hit the JAM before they could attack. Some 30 strike operations were planned, many with the help of the small special forces detachment still in Basra Palace, and in the end ten were executed involving Rifles companies manoeuvring at night through Basra's streets on foot, or in vehicles.

The Rifles had built up their own network of intelligence sources across central Basra, people who were still willing to give the British detailed information on the militia on a daily basis. Divisions with the various militia groups prompted rival factions to pass on information to the British about their enemies. The Rifles also still had a budget for aid funding to distribute.

"With thousands of dollars to spend on local civil military aid [CIMIC] projects, [the battlegroup CIMIC officer] possessed sufficient leverage to gain useful information from important local leaders who could describe atmospherics and incidents within their tribal areas", commented a Rifles intelligence officer.

"These contacts provided specific and timely information both on pattern of life and atmospherics, and also gave warnings of planned indirect fire attacks and the locations of IEDs and ambushes. A couple of contacts had good access to militia groupings, which allowed them to give detailed order of battles, insights into attack modus operandi and names and addresses of insurgent leaders. This was all collated into Target Packs and passed up to Brigade Joint Targets Cell and other key stakeholders for further action."[62]

Until the final days before the withdrawal, the US and British strategic intelligence agencies remained in Basra Palace and fed some information to 4 Rifles to help in their defence. The new manoeuvre battlegroup, 2 Royal Welsh, soon joined this battle to disrupt the JAM attacks. They quickly found out that they would face a summer of heavy fighting, when they launched Operation Pandora on 6th June.

"[We] deployed after sunset to strike into a hardline estate on the city interface; the mission required us to push about five hundred metres into the city and conduct a near simultaneous entry of five houses to secure munitions and bomb making equipment," was how Major Didi Wheeler, second in command of the Royal Welsh, described the start of his unit's first deliberate battlegroup operation.

"As ever the intelligence was poor, information was scant and the enemy did not conform to the laid out plan we had derived! D Squadron (the King's Royal Hussars) punched into the City supported by Challenger tanks, and secured our route in as we encountered at least ten improvised explosive devices along the road side. [Our] C Company threw an outer cordon around the target area and A Company of the Rifles and A Company Royal Welsh struck the five houses. For the next two hours the battlegroup was embroiled in a most violent street fight against determined groupings of insurgents fighting their way along alley ways and roof tops to dislodge our positions around the houses. This was certainly not the scenario we had rehearsed in training!"[63]

The Major said as a result numerous insurgents were killed or wounded, and munitions had been seized in the greatest haul seized by the British for at least the proceeding year. Several soldiers were injured, including one seriously, after Rifles soldiers attached to the Royal Welsh were pinned down by heavy fire.

"Sadly, on our first operation we suffered a number of casualties and the loss of Corporal Wilson, killed in action," said Major Wheeler.

"Our reactions to this baptism of fire on our return were unsurprisingly mixed; some were elated at the 'buzz' that this action brings to a professional soldier; others were struck by the ferocity of the insurgent attack and his adaptability, all were saddened by the loss of Corporal Wilson. Importantly we were all determined to learn from our experiences and prepare to deploy the following night for the next operation. So it went on for the next three months."[64]

General Shaw continued with the operation to patrol the Iranian border in Maysan through to June, in part to reassure the Americans he was still working to intercept arms ships heading to the JAM. Maysan became the third province in the British divisional area to pass to provincial Iraqi control of security in March.

The Queen's Royal Lancers (QRL) battlegroup spent six months on border patrol duty up to May 2007, but the insurgents eventually found a way to track its patrols and it lost two soldiers to an IED attack. On 12th February 2007, a pair of RAF Hercules were tasked to fly in supplies and personnel to an abandoned Iraqi air force runway in the desert five miles from Iranian border, which was being used as a forward base by the QRL. A security sweep by the cavalrymen failed to detect two arrays of explosive-formed projective IEDs position along the runway. When the first aircraft touched down and started to roll to a halt the IEDs were detonated, spraying the aircraft with super hot molten jets of metal. It slewed off the runway and ground to a halt.[65] Miraculously none of the RAF crew or 58 soldiers on board, who were mostly members of a reconnaissance party from the King's Royal Hussars (KRH) were due to replace the QRL in a few weeks, suffered more than cuts and bruises. The £50 million aircraft was judged to be beyond repair, without a major operation to being in engineers and replacement parts. Senior army officers in Basra were worried that the JAM would use the incident as a propaganda victory and they ordered the carcass of the aircraft to be destroyed by 30mm cannon fire from the QRL's CVR(T) armoured vehicles but its tail section with a RAF roundel prominently displayed remained intact. The image was reminiscent of the Desert One debacle in Iran in 1980, according to a senior British Army officer involved in controlling the incident from the headquarters in Basra. To finish off the remains of the C-130, a RAF Tornado was then called up to bomb and destroy its carcass as dawn was breaking.[66]

Once the KRH replaced the QRL, they continued the mission for two more months, before the increasing burden of sustaining the force prompted General Shaw to pull the troops back to Basra airport. After the runway IED attack, the RAF resorted to parachuting supplies to the QRL, making 28 air drops to deliver 252,000 litres of water and 36,000 ration packs to the troops. The 250 kilometre long supply line to the borders' north battlegroup was now increasingly difficult to protect, and with heavy fighting now needed to punch through convoys to Basra palace, the manpower could not be spared for the desert re-supply runs. The KRH battlegroup also did not seem to be collecting any actionable intelligence on Iranian weapon smuggling efforts.[67] The last straw was a re-supply mission in June, dubbed Operation Octavia, that had to be protected by a company-sized force of Warriors. It was ambushed 14 times in what one KRH officer, called a "five day running battle".

"What was meant to be a forty-eight hour operation turned into a five day extravaganza. If there was a final nail in the coffin of the Maysan BG this was it," recalled Captain W.D Hodgkinson, the KRH operations officer.

"The Nomadic Hawks had become too expensive to maintain; resources, personnel and lack of actionable intelligence all added to our demise in the desert. I don't need tangible results to feel like we succeeded; we all made differences to each other and we are still here."[68]

In the midst of the withdrawal of the KRH from Maysan, US and Iraqi special forces mounted a series of raids against insurgent cells near Majar Al Kabir and al Amarah. The targets were suspected of having links to the smuggling of arms and EFP warheads from Iran. The raids immediately met heavy resistance. To extract themselves from the fighting around Majar Al Kabir, Task Force 17 called in US helicopter gunships to put down covering fire. Local people complained that this battle left 36 dead and more than a 100 wounded.

The main British base at Basra airport was now coming under increasing attention from the JAM rocket teams, with 150 107mm, 122mm and 240mm rockets landing there in June and July, with 745 rockets and mortars falling during 441 attacks over the summer.[69] This was despite the arrival of additional British C-RAM Phalanx guns, and 155mm AS-90 self-propelled guns; the rocket teams continued this unrelenting barrage that killed three RAF Regiment gunners and a REME technician in July. The RAF Regiment pushed regular patrols out into the desert around the air base in a bid to intercept the rocket teams before they could fire. They fought several engagements with militia, including a big battle on 7th/8th August at al Waki against a 50-strong group of fighters. A platoon of Warriors had to be called out from the airport to drive off the attackers.[70]

The summer of 2007 was proving to be most bloody yet faced by the British Army in Iraq. Some 17 of 1 Brigade's soldiers were killed in the fighting and hundreds wounded, including dozens seriously injured. Officers and soldiers across the Brigade were wondering where it would end. Movement in the centre of Basra could now only be conducted by large numbers of troops and armoured vehicles. The scale of what was required was illustrated by a visit to the PJCC by Brigadier Bashall on 16th July, that required eight Warriors to carry him and his staff. When militia opened fire on the vehicles with 38 RPGs and then detonated 12 IEDs, a pair of US Apache attack helicopters had to be called up to drive them off and open a route out of the city.[71]

Lieutenant Colonel Michael O'Dwyer, the commanding officer, 1st Battalion, The Irish Guards, described the situation as a cycle of violence that saw a constant fight in downtown Basra.

"Simply re-supplying the [troops in Basra Palace] from the Contingency Operating Base (COB) had become a deadly operation requiring pretty much the rest of the Brigade, supported from the air, deploying into the city," he recalled.

"The Manoeuvre Battle Group based in the COB was striking into the city nightly in an attempt to capture the perpetrators of the attacks against us. The more we were attacked, the more we struck. The result was unprecedented violence and the highest levels of casualties from enemy action seen during the Iraq campaign. The levels of violence took their toll. Vehicles from the battlegroup were hit countless times by roadside bombs and the near constant barrage of indirect fire also caused immeasurable death and destruction."[72]

General Shaw was actively looking for a way out of the violence that appeared to be spiralling out of control.

"The re-supply convoys were sitting ducks and resulted in a series of epic formulaic battles, with the troops moving along established routes across what were in effect pre-laid minefields," said Shaw.

"Every convoy was horrific. Imagine what would have happened to an opposed withdrawal. There would have been untold suffering and loss of life."[73]

From before his appointment, General Shaw had been curious about who was actually controlling the militia, and what were their motivations. There was little hard information about how they were organised, who were their leaders and to whom did they owe their loyalty. He was also keen to work with Foreign and Commonwealth Office diplomats in Basra, to build a plan to build up the political arrangements necessary to sign off control of security to the Iraqis.

In Central Iraq, Lieutenant General Graeme Lamb, the SAS veteran who was now General Petraeus's deputy, was heading up an effort to win over Sunni tribes and insurgents from al Qaeda. During January he received two approaches from JAM commanders complaining about "evil interference" from Iran. This raised the prospect of the potential to split the Iraqi nationalist elements of JAM from the Tehran loyalists in the special groups. US intelligence operatives in Task Force 17 shared the view that it might be possible to execute a split in the JAM, in the same way that Lamb was trying to peel local Sunni tribes away from supporting al Qaeda in Iraq.[74]

On his arrival in Basra in January, General Shaw found British intelligence-gathering efforts were focused on tactical deployments of militia groups, rather than their high level command and political allegiances. General Shaw tasked the local SIS team to get a better understanding of who was really pulling the leavers of control within the militia. According to Colonel Ian Thomas, Shaw's chief of staff, the headquarters staff generated an analysis that suggested linkages between the militias and all levels of Iraqi political life.

"In 2007 Iraq was still re-building itself after the dismantling of its official organs of state by Saddam and then the Coalition," wrote Thomas in a study of this phase of the Iraq campaign published in British Army Review

"It was happening from the bottom up, consistent with Arab cultural dynamics, whereby loyalty is to blood not institutions; it goes from the inside out and official/state allegiances attract the weakest loyalty. In a fractured society militias were potentially a cohering force: every militia had its political party (not vice versa), and also its violent wing, forming a three layered polity of the state institutions (the official state), and the militias split between their social organisations (the shadow state) and their violent henchmen (the dark state). Understanding these official/shadow/dark dynamics was key to plotting a way forward."[75]

General Shaw described Basra as "being more like Palermo than Beirut", to highlight the importance of control of economic resources, revenues from government-owned enterprises and smuggling rings. The British suspected that JAM controlled Basra's electricity supplies and scammed off a cut from its revenue. While the city's governor had a controlling interest in oil smuggling. There was a suspicion that rival Iraqi politicians were trying to manipulate the

British to take out their opponents in strike operations to allow them to move in on their financial interests.

He then started to begin pitching the idea for a political solution to the Basra problem with the US command in Baghdad. General Petraeus, his corps commander, Lieutenant General Ray Odierno, and the US Ambassador Ryan Crocker were utterly focused on the surge, and their interest in what the British were doing in Basra revolved around its impact on events in Baghdad, and how they were portrayed back in the US. They were keen on what was termed engagement and reconciliation efforts, to build support for the surge, ahead of crucial Senate and Congressional hearings in September; then Petreaus would have to persuade sceptical American politicians and public that the war in Iraq had been turned around.

Petraeus tentatively gave General Shaw permission to move ahead with an effort to engage with what were termed "reconcilable" elements in the JAM, which the American General now started to describe as an "irritant". An engagement and reconciliation staff officer was appointed in the British headquarters in Basra on 1st June, to begin working up the necessary contacts with the JAM to begin negotiations. Brigadier Bashall was brought into the loop at an early stage, and ordered to begin calibrating his strike operations so "irreconcilable" elements in the JAM received priority for elimination or capture.

"James Bashall bought into my political way," said General Shaw.

"Killing had to have a political purpose."[76]

This was the genesis of what became known as the "accommodation" with the militia in Basra.

"This was a positive response to a political challenge, how to create a sustainable Iraqi polity in Basra, it was not a life and face-saving dodgy deal," said Shaw.

"We began with a recognition that this was a political problem and that success had to be defined in a context that did not include us. Our job was to use our military instrument to shape the political environment to allow them to achieve their self-sustainable political stability. The Iraqis owned the end state, which had to be defined within the context of their cultural parameters. And they had to reach this end state in their own way. We turned the UK Iraqi approach on its head, by making us enablers of the Iraqi end state not imposers of our solution." [77]

The difficultly in bringing this about became apparent on 3rd to 4th March when the 19 Brigade and Iraqi special forces launched Operation Pegasus against a high value target in Basra.

British staff officer who served in Basra in early 2007 described this as "a defining strike operation", which revealed much about the realities of the operational environment and political context in Basra.

The Iraqi government had cleared the initial target for attack but once the strike force searched the building they found intelligence indicating that another senior militia leader was in a nearby Iraqi police headquarters. The strike force commander decided to seize the opportunity and exploit onto a new objective. According to a staff officer involved in monitoring the operation they were just too late to apprehend the target. During the raid, Iraqi special forces allegedly found an Iraqi policeman physically abusing a local woman.

The Iraqi troops reportedly intervened aggressively, beating the policemen and then shot up some of the Iraqi police vehicles before extracting. Also during the raid some of the prisoners held in the headquarters' jail escaped.

"That the strike force targeted the police headquarters, [an Iraqi government] institution, and force entry into it, was considered a violation of Iraqi sovereignty," recorded Colonel Thomas, the divisional chief of staff, in a study of the campaign subsequently published by a US defence academy. "Angry at this affront, the [Basra] provincial council refused to 're-engage' with Multi-National Division (South East). Ironically the provincial council was due to have restored formal engagement with the [division] on the day following the raid. Their refusal to do so prolonged the political paralysis in Basra."[78]

This was even though the operation had been cleared politically, was focused against an approved target and had Iraqi troops in the vanguard.

"The [police] headquarters that was raided belong to the National Intelligence and Information Agency (NIIA), which was some observers speculated was the personal fiefdom of a senior member of the [Iraqi government in Baghdad] who would have taken particular umbrage at the violation," wrote Thomas. "This might explain the extreme reaction to it."

For General Shaw and his senior staff, the incident highlighted the limits of the possible in Basra and that without a political 'buy-in' from the Iraqi government in Baghdad the British operation in Iraq would soon run into the sands, threatening a total break down in relations and the premature end of the British mission.

Within days General Shaw issued revised guidance to his commanders and staff, which re-emphasised that all our operations must be conducted in support of the political process and he put in place even more rigorous target-clearance procedures. Several subsequent strike operations against high-value targets had to be cleared via Maliki's office, via the US corps headquarters and Petreaus's staff. Some were vetoed and tight restrictions placed on Iraqi special forces operations in Basra.

"Subsequent operational planning re-emphasised the primacy of the political line of operation (LOO)," wrote Thomas. "Even if a particular individual was identified by intelligence to be an imperative threat to security, and thus designated as a legitimate target for arrest, the political ramifications of an arrest operation were carefully weighed. If it might provoke an adverse reaction, which could disrupt the political process, then risk might be taken against force protection rather than against the political LOO."[79]

British intelligence operatives now managed to get an insight into JAM thinking, finding out that the organisation's leader in Basra, Wissam Abu Qader, had held a secret meeting with the city provincial council on 23rd May in which he had proposed a "non-aggression pact". He said the JAM had no desire to attack the Iraqi army and police, and declared that the only purpose of the militia's existence was to attack the British and American occupation forces. He then went on to talk about rebuilding Basra and making it rival Dubai as a Gulf port. Two days later, but several days before this report was available to him, Shaw had authorised the attack on Wassim, which is recounted earlier in this chapter, that resulted in militia leader's death.[80]

Air Chief Marshal Stirrup arrived in Iraq at the beginning of July, and reiterated to General Shaw about the need to pull out from the Palace by the end of August. The Chief of Defence Staff said this would force the Iraqis to take responsibility for security in the city. He then flew up to Baghdad and confirmed the withdrawal timetable to Petraeus. According to one British officer who was present, the American commander's main reservation seemed to be that any announcement of a final British troop withdrawal from Iraq, rather than tactical repositioning, should not happen until he had made his big report to Congress in September. The 'buy-in' by Petreaus was vital because the British withdrawal would not have been possible without US sanction. Plans were now agreed with the Iraqis for Prime Minister Maliki's own personnel guard force to take over Basra Palace at the end of August. Senior UK and US officers knew that once the Iraqis 'owned' the plans for taking over the palace, there was no going back, and their focus became to enable the Iraqi handover. The new Iraqi general in Basra, Mohan, was meanwhile talking tough and was keen for the British to pull out of the city, to remove the major justification of the JAM for continuing to fight. Mohan told Shaw at a conference on 1st July that he was working on a plan to split to the bulk of the JAM rank and file from the pro-Iranian special groups.

With British, Iraqi and US military leaderships seemingly aligned in their intent, General Shaw now actively stepped up his hunt for someone within the JAM to negotiate with. His local SIS station head proved unable to find anyone to fill the role inside Basra, and attention then switched to the prisoners held in the DIF at the airport. General Shaw went to see one of the prisoners, Ahmed Fartosi, who had been the main JAM commander in Basra until he was captured in September 2005. He described Fartosi as "a strong leader, an Iraqi nationalist, not an Iranian puppet".[81]

The General, SIS agents and the militia leader had several meetings to try to work out what each other wanted and see if a deal was possible.

"My talks with Fartosi were based on each of us understanding what the other's end state was," recalled General Shaw.

"We both wanted the same thing - prosperity, girls going to school - he has two daughters -, no religious extremism, Iraqi not Iranian rule..... Graham Binns put it best: Fartosi attacking us made as little sense as the Warsaw uprising: where the real victors were the Russians! I told Fartosi that in the context of Basra, the only victors from the militia attacking us were the Iranians."[82]

"Keep strong to fight the Iranians, meanwhile recognise how we can help you achieve your goals and help us, was my line to Fartosi," said Shaw.

"Once he agreed this, he stopped the bombing. If he was not bombing us, he was not a threat because being a member of JAM was not illegal. If he was not a threat, we had no reason to detain him and his men. This may sound like ex post facto justification but I assure you it was the real logic and local justification for what we believed we were doing."[83]

At the heart of General Shaw's approach was splitting off the rump of the locally-recruited JAM commanders and fighters from Iranian-backed special groups, who were dubbed "irreconcilables". This was seen as potentially the nascent start of a peace process that would see the militias demobilised and their leaders becoming "normal" politicians. The Americans had their "Awakening" efforts in central Iraq to win over Sunni tribes from al Qaeda influence, and the British saw their "accommodation" as a way to end the fighting in Basra and de-escalate the situation.

An engagement and reconciliation cell in the British divisional headquarters was to oversee this exercise to drive a wedge into the JAM in Basra. The first stage was to make sure fighting did not break out again, and give the irreconcilable JAM commanders an excuse to mobilise the mass of the movement against the British again. The fracturing of the JAM would then provide the opportunity to neutralise the special groups.

"The one thing that united all the elements of the JAM was the hatred of the foreign troops," commented one British officer involved in this effort.

"We did not want to give them back their common enemy, without us to fight they were bound to fall out amongst themselves."[84]

Under the accommodation, both sides would agree to de-escalate combat operations. The British would not launch strike operations against JAM fighters into the city and in return the militia would not fire rockets at British bases at the airport, Shaibah Logistic Base and nearby Umm Qasr port. The British could use transit routes to bridges to get access to the Iranian border but otherwise no British vehicles were allowed to move to Iraqi army bases in the city, requiring any visits to be made by helicopter.

In return, the British agreed to progressively release the 120 JAM prisoners still held at the DIF at the airport. Fartosi was subsequently given access to a cell phone and fax machine in his cell, to allow the subsequent releases to be choreographed. This culminated in Fartosi being the last JAM prisoner to be freed at the end of December 2007.

By the start of August, it looked like Fartosi was up for a deal. It could not have come soon enough as the deadline to withdraw from Basra Palace was approaching and the prospect of a battle during a British retreat looked highly likely.

The commander officer of 2 Lancs, Lieutenant Colonel Mark Kenyon, claimed "[British] operations brought the enemy to the negotiating table by demonstrating to him that we would not be forced out of Basra, but rather would seek out and bring to account those who sought to subvert the rule of law."[85]

The troops of 19 and 1 Brigades had been involved in the most violent period of fighting ever experienced in Iraq. According to Brigadier Evans, his Brigade was involved in over 2,100 significant incidents during its tour. This tempo of combat continued into the summer after 19 Brigade left Iraq in May. But this had not been enough to inflict a decisive defeat on the militias, or even reduce the scale of violence being launched against British troops.

"Small arms contacts doubled and rocket attacks tripled over the period of [Operation] Telic 9," said Evans.[86]

Both sides now had a strong interest in pushing ahead with the accommodation. The potential to end the fighting in Basra and begin a political process was too great. Many commentators have specifically linked the accommodation to the withdrawal of the Rifles from Basra Palace, but General Shaw and his team had wider ambitions to make major political progress.

So, Shaw allowed Fartosi to contact his associates in Basra, while he made some final co-ordinating arrangements with Stirrup, Odierno, the Iraqi government and the FCO. General Odierno was initially not enthusiastic in the end he accepted Shaw's judgement, as did Petraeus. The Chief of the Defence Staff was very supportive. Prime Minister Maliki and his advisors were initially outraged by the prospect of the British doing a deal with people who were now becoming to be seen as their political opponents, even though only a few months previously they were allied with Maliki. The Iraqi leadership were eventually won round by the new British senior officer in Baghdad, Lieutenant General Bill Rollo, on 10th August. Few of the details of these discussions were put down in formal reports or distributed through the British military chain of command, because of the fear of leaks.

Events now moved up a gear as the 'accommodation' was about to be sealed. In one of his final acts before he left Basra on 15th August at the end of his six-month tour in command, General Shaw visited Fartosi in the DIF to complete the deal. One of Shaw's senior staff officers travelled into Basra to pass on details of the deal to militia contacts identified by Fartosi. The following week, four senior prisoners would be released, and the rocket ceasefire would come into effect for a trial period of three days. This was just in time to allow 4 Rifles to pull out of Basra Palace.

"We subsequently received intelligence that said the JAM had big plans to rip the hell out of the withdrawal convoy if the deal had not been agreed," recalled Shaw.

"It would have looked terrible, they would have trashed the place and we would have been humiliated."[87]

On the agreed day the first prisoners were released, the rockets stopped falling on the airport. There was some muttering at PJHQ about dishonourable deals, but General Shaw got support from his officers and troops. He recalled an infantry battlegroup commanding officer telling him that, "this was his third time in Iraq and commented 'it was getting repetitive. I am glad to be doing something different because my people can see the futility of carrying on as we are.'"[88]

Chapter 24

CHARGE OF THE KNIGHTS

After a brief flag-lowering ceremony on 2nd September 2007, Lieutenant Colonel Patrick Sanders led his battlegroup out of Basra Palace. Later that morning the column of Warrior and Bulldog vehicles arrived at the main British base outside the city without a shot being fired. An earlier operation to extract the small British contingent from the Provincial Joint Co-ordination Centre (PJCC) at the Warren in the downtown district had also gone without a hitch.

The final extraction of the 4th Battalion, The Rifles (4 Rifles), from its two downtown bases was the culmination of a summer of fighting that saw the British troops in Basra engaged in the most intense combat of the Iraq campaign. The British Army took it heaviest losses of the campaign with some 26 soldiers being killed in the city since the beginning of April and more than a hundred wounded in action. Several hundred militia fighters had been killed in the battles that raged across the city.[1]

Colonel Sanders and his men had fully expected to have to fight their way out of the city to meet the target of the end of August for their withdrawal back to the airport. Heavy air and artillery support was on call to cover their retreat. This would undoubtedly have gone down as a classic military retreat under fire, but senior British officers in Basra and London were convinced it would have been a political disaster. The militia commanders and their political supporters could have portrayed it as a victory over the hated occupiers, and allowed them to claim they had driven out the British. While in London, the impact of British troops retreating from Basra under fire would have been seen as an ignominious end to a highly unpopular war. Perhaps more importantly, it would have led to widespread loss of life among the British troops, the militia and Basra's civilian population. In the end, both British and militia commanders had a common interest in seeing the battle for Basra end in a whimper, not a bloody denouement.

"Throughout this time [we] expected to come under fire at any moment, but the Jaish al Mahdi (JAM) were under orders to leave us alone, and amazingly they obeyed, " recalled Colonel Sanders during the operation to move a convoy on 25th August into the city to extract the PJCC force.

"We left the PJCC and were back in the COB [Contingency Operating Base at Basra airport], over taking the unmanned aerial vehicles that were covering us en route. We found ourselves back at the COB, relieved to have got away with it, but not quite believing what had just taken place. It must have been at least two years since someone had driven so far into the city and back out without a single shot being fired."[2]

A week later, the Colonel's men handed over Basra Palace to the Iraqi Prime Minister's Palace Protection Force, to bring Operation Highbridge to a close. The significance of who took control of the palace was probably lost on the departing Riflemen, but the arrival of the paramilitary protection force signalled that the Iraqi Prime Minister, Nouri al Maliki, was taking a close interest in the city's future and wanted forces loyal to him in Basra.

The 'accommodation' reached by the outgoing British divisional commander, Major-General Jonathan Shaw and the JAM leader Ahmed Fartosi had allowed the extraction operation to go ahead peacefully and this new reality transformed the situation in southern Iraq. It fell to General Shaw's successor, Major General Graham Binns, to see through the accommodation, which was envisaged as being the equivalent of the 'awakening' exercise being undertaken by the Americans in central Iraq.

General Shaw and his close advisors, as well as the head of the British Secret Intelligence Service in Basra, were keen to split off the rump of the locally recruited JAM commanders and fighters from Iranian-backed special groups, who were dubbed 'irreconcilables'.[3] This was seen as potentially the nascent start of a peace process that would see the militias demobilised and their leaders becoming 'normal politicians'. An engagement and reconciliation cell in the British divisional headquarters was to oversee this exercise to drive a wedge into the JAM in Basra. The first stage was to make sure fighting did not break out again and give the irreconcilable JAM commanders an excuse to mobilise the mass of the movement against the British again.

"The one thing that united all the elements of the JAM was the hatred of the foreign troops" commented one British officer involved in this effort.

"We did not want to give them back their common enemy, without us to fight they were bound to fall out amongst themselves."[4]

The fracturing of the JAM would then provide the opportunity to neutralise the 'special groups', as the pro-Iranian hardliners were described by the US and British, although there was little idea in September and October of 2007 about how this would actually be achieved. Under the accommodation, both sides agreed to de-escalate combat operations. The British would not launch strike operations against JAM fighters into the city and in return the militia would not fire rockets at British bases at the airport, Shaibah Logistic Base and nearby Umm Qasr port. The British could use transit routes to bridges to get access to the Iranian border, but otherwise no British vehicles were allowed to move to Iraqi army bases in the city, requiring any visits to be made by helicopter.

In return, the British agreed to progressively release the 120 JAM prisoners still held at the Divisional Internment Facility at the airport. The first four prisoners were released prior to the extraction of 4 Rifles, and then Fartosi was given access to a cell phone and fax machine in his cell to allow the subsequent releases to be choreographed. This culminated in Fartosi being the last JAM prisoner to be freed at the end of December 2007.[5]

This was a tense time as the stand-off started to fray during the last three months of 2007. There were occasional rocket attacks on Basra airport, with five falling in September, nine in October, 11 in November and 12 in December. This was portrayed by Fartosi as the actions of rogue groups, and he claimed to be still committed to making the accommodation work.[6]

The existence of the accommodation and its full scope were not immediately made public in the autumn of 2007, with the British, Americans and the Iraqi government all having their own reasons for not wanting much scrutiny of General Shaw's deal with the JAM. The British government and army leadership were sensitive to accusations that it was negotiating with men with the blood of scores of British soldiers on their hands. The Americans were themselves trying to negotiate with militia groups across Iraq and did not want to make the issue controversial. General David Petreaus, the top US commander in Iraq, was also due to testify to the US Congress on the progress of his surge and needed to project an image of coalition unity, so did not want to get into a public row with his ally. And Prime Minister Maliki did not want the JAM to be able to claim credit for the withdrawal of the British, and played down the whole issue. The attitude of the key players in Iraq to the accommodation would change over the next six months as circumstances changed.

Binns, who led 7 Armoured Brigade during the 2003 invasion and then been involved in preparing troops for deployment to Iraq at the army's Land Command headquarters, was well versed in British operations in Basra. He took a similar view to his predecessor to the accommodation, and his tour of command was dominated by making it work so the British could formally hand over responsibility for security in Basra province to the Iraqi government, under a process know as Provincial Iraqi Control or PIC. General Binns recalled that during his time in command in Basra up to mid-January 2008, US commanders in Baghdad appeared content with the direction of British strategy in southern Iraq.

"We did nothing that US corps commander [Lieutenant-General Ray Odierno] was not happy with," said Binns.

"He was content with what we were doing. He told me what were doing with the JAM provided an example of how the Americans could deal with Shia militias in the Sadr city area of Baghdad".[7]

Although the withdrawal of 4 Rifles from the Basra Palace had in effect made the Iraqis responsible for security, the British government was keen to formally move to PIC as soon as possible. This would trigger a new round of troop withdrawals and free up more forces for the escalating war in Afghanistan.

General Binns said the switch to PIC would be an important psychological development, forcing the Iraqis to either make a political deal with the militias or take them on. How to help the Iraqi army and security forces in the build-up to PIC, and then afterwards, was the subject of intense debate within the British military. The old policy of training Iraqi troops at big depots and then sending them to fight on their own was criticised in a report written in late 2007 by 4 Mechanised Brigade staff.

During the summer, two battalions from the Iraqi 10th Division, based in the south, had been deployed to Baghdad and taken British advisors with them. These so-called 'embedded advisors' had co-ordinated air support, medical evacuations and logistics for the Iraqis with considerable success. Permanent Joint Headquarters (PJHQ) in Northwood, however, was not impressed. It ran against the aim of running down troop numbers and also was considered too dangerous because it would put small groups of British soldiers at risk of kidnapping or assassination.[8]

"Our mistake was not investing enough in transition, mentoring and training the Iraqi army," said General Binns.

"We were not standing side by side and fighting with the Iraqis. We trained them and send them out to fight. We had not thought through this to the finish. We did not finish until Iraqis were in charge."[9]

As the end of the year approached, Iraqi politicians and the western media began to criticise the British for leaving the militia in control of large parts of Basra, with reports of death squad murders rapidly escalating, and 45 Iraqi women being murdered for alleged un-Islamic behaviour.

"I would say we were withdrawing to counter attack" said Binns.

"We had to have a change of mindset among the population and their leaders. The Iraqis had to have this fight. It was too convenient for them to blame [us] for not securing Basra. We had to switch to the Iraqi army and police. The only way a mindset switch would take place would be if they were responsible. It was not easy to articulate that in public. People did not like the thought of it."[10]

"[Our troops] wanted to go down town and do stuff," he said.

"Night time raids by battlegroups into Basra made us feel better but they were counter-productive. Not everyone in the British Army liked what we did in 2007. Targeting had become an obsession. It was not working. We had to do something different. Many people preferred to slug it out and fight. That was not my thinking."[11]

The strike operations were feeding the feeling of occupation, fuelling resistance and violence, said Binns.

"In my view the situation did not improve until the Iraqi army were seen to be on the first foot," he said.

"It was the right decision to move as quickly to PIC. That was the only way for the situation to get better. It got worse before it got better, it was a price worth paying."

Major Hamish Cormack, a company commander in the 1st Battalion, The Duke of Lancaster's Regiment (1 Lancs), describe the mood as 4 Mechanised Brigade arrived to take over from 1 Mechanised Brigade in November 2007.

"[Our] ears [were] ringing to the parting words of the outgoing brigade 'not to start a fight and mess up all that we've achieved.' The message was clear, 'don't rock the boat'" recalled Major Cormack.

"In the words of one senior officer this was a 'mission in defence', which at the time could mean doing nothing was achieving the task. It seems to have achieved the aim and set in a chain of events that started with the sacrifices made by soldiers before us; we did not fail their memory. While to a man we would have preferred to be kicking in doors down town, the situation needed a steady hand if past sacrifices were not to be in vain. Yes, it was frustrating to face the daily rocket barrage but our time would come."[12]

Guardsman Graeme Boyd, of the 1st Battalion, The Scots Guards, recalled the excitement of deploying to Iraq in November expecting to go on strike operations after months of training for this role in Germany. When he got to Basra he found plans had changed. "Instead due to the upcoming handover of Provincial Iraqi Control (PIC) of MND South-East we would be scaling down our presence on the ground," said Boyd. This meant our role had changed from Strike to Manoeuvre Battle Group. This caused massive disappointment among us but we used our usual morale boosting methods and turned to our usual comedians to keep our spirits high."

The death of a Scots Guardsman in an accident at Basra airport in December "affected all of us deeply," said Boyd. "[It] caused our disappointment and frustration to soar to new levels."[13]

The operations and deployment of the British brigade evolved considerably during the last three months of 2007. After Colonel Sanders and Riflemen moved back from Basra Palace, they were re-roled to provide security along the Iranian border. The 4 Rifles Battlegroup launched ten patrols along the border in Basra province, under the code-name Operation Certain Shield.

Another battlegroup was assigned to patrol the roads of southern Iraq to protect US and British convoys heading up from Iraq, as well as guarding the airport and a base for training Iraqi navy personnel in Umm Qasr. This battlegroup and the RAF Regiment field squadron at the airport launched a major drive to deliver humanitarian aid and civilian reconstruction projects, in villages in the rural area between the airport and Basra city. There were several ambushes and IED strikes in this no-man's land area, with the British playing a cat and mouse game with militia men on operations outside Basra city limits.

A third battlegroup concentrated on training Iraqi army units at the Divisional Training Centre at Shaibah Logistic Base. One more battlegroup was held at high readiness to move to the assistance of British and Iraqi troops under threat. All four British battlegroups contributed to a rolling programme of mentoring visits to Iraqi units around Basra province, to assess their performance and training needs. Movement to the Iraqi bases outside Basra city was undertaken by helicopter or in large convoys of armoured vehicles to prevent attacks on the small groups of advisors. The training of the Iraqis was designated as the divisional main effort by General Binns. Lieutenant Colonel Michael O'Dwyer, Commanding Officer, 1st Battalion, The Irish Guards, used a sporting analogy to sum up the period of calm after the evacuation of Basra Palace.

"Half-time, however, was not an opportunity to sit down in the dressing room with the oranges and admire the achievements of the first half, rather it was the opportunity for us to focus on developing the Iraqi Army through monitoring, mentoring and training (M2T), something we had not really had the opportunity to focus on up until this point", he commented.[14]

In the build-up to the formal handover to the Iraqi forces, there was little consideration to planning any new operation to clamp down on the militia in the city. After the PIC ceremony at Basra airport on 16th December, this was the Iraqis' problem, and they did not seem to be in a hurry to decide what to do.

"At this stage there was no Iraqi planning," recalled Binns.

"So it was extremely difficult to work out how to attach ourselves to the Iraqis if or when they decided to moved back in. If we went back in [to the city] it would have been in support of the Iraqi army. We were not thinking of any unilateral drive. We had just got to Iraqi control so it would always have been a joint decision."[15]

As part of the PIC agreement, the British had pledged to provide military assistance to the Iraqi Basra Operational Command, led by Lieutenant General Mohan al-Firayji, but the circumstances which would warrant a return of General Binns' troops to the streets of downtown Basra were unclear. Under the overwatch agreement, the British could only re-intervene at the specific request of the Iraqi prime minister. This was different from the overwatch arrangements with the Americans, who could be called back into action by local Iraqi military commanders.[16]

The Iraqi general was increasingly frustrated at the British reluctance to take on the militia, whom he often railed against with considerable rhetorical flush. Capt James Bullock-Webster, the British aide de camp to Lieutenant General Mohan al-Firayji, recalled the new Basra security commander's appearance at a briefing in Baghdad in the summer of 2007.

"To our amazement General Mohan referred to an anecdote favoured by Saddam Hussein."

"Controlling the nation of Iraq is like placing three mice, one on top of each other. Virtually an impossible task, as the mice will run around and cause chaos. The solution is to place the mice in a bag, swing it around your head several times, and then smash the bag onto the floor. The mice are then taken from the bag, half dead and very dazed. It is then easy to tower the mice on top of each other. General Mohan went on to state that he intends to be the bag and bring order to Basra."[17]

Constricting General Binn's freedom of action was the accommodation with the militia but also the clear determination of the London government to draw down troop numbers rapidly during 2008. The new British Prime Minister Gordon Brown had signalled his intent to drop the strength of the force in Basra to 2,500, when 4 Brigade was rotated out in May 2008 and then to close Operation Telic by the end of year. Anything that endangered this schedule would have to be referred up the chain of command, via PJHQ, for a decision from the government. After the release of Fartosi at the end of 2007, the incentive of the militia to stick to the accommodation was seriously weakened, and during January rocket attacks on the airport steadily edged back up to the levels of the previous summer, with two or three attacks a day.

The C-RAM Phalanx guns manned by the Royal Artillery and Royal Navy intercepted many of the in-bound rockets, but on 28th February two rockets got through and killed a RAF sergeant. He would be the last UK serviceman to be killed in action in Iraq. Not surprisingly, this made it difficult for the British commanders and troops on the receiving end to continue to have much faith in Fartosi's commitment to peace.

It was also becoming increasingly obvious that the Iraqi government of Premier Maliki saw Muqtada al Sadr and his militia not as potential political partners but as a threat that required to be neutralised. In the 18 months since assuming office, Maliki had gone from relying on Sadr's party for votes in parliament to keep his coalition government in power to seeing them as rivals for leadership of Iraq's Shia. The success of General Petraeus' surge had also effectively neutralised the Sunni insurgency as a threat to Maliki's government, making the prime minister increasingly self-confident and determined to solidify his political base. The British, by continuing to play lip service to the accommodation with the militia in Basra, were putting a brake on Maliki's ambitions to deal with Sadr. He would repeatedly refer to the British deal with Fartosi in public speeches criticising London for not supporting his government, saying the British were in league with "criminals" undermining Iraq. It was a relationship that appeared to be heading for a crisis.

The reaction of the British to a militia attack on Mohan's headquarters in the Shatt-al-Arab Hotel in January did not help the tension. Mohan invoked the PIC agreement and asked the British to send troops to defend him. The Iraqi general and his prime minister were not happy when the British used their 'hot line' to Fartosi to arrange for tribal sheikhs to broker a ceasefire. As far as the Iraq government in Baghdad was concerned, they were not interested in any reconciliation with Sadr and his militia.

"The agreement with the militia for no British troops to be in Basra infuriated Maliki and he questioned our intentions", recalled Major General Barney White-Spunner, who took over from General Binns as the British commander in Basra in early February 2008.[18]

Although White-Spunner, with his interest in country pursuits and career in the Household Cavalry Regiment, appeared like chalk and cheese to the down-to-earth Binns, who hailed from an northern infantry regiment - the Prince of Wales's Own Regiment of Yorkshire - , both officers felt the divergent pressures facing the British contingent in southern Iraq.

White-Spunner, who had led peacekeeping forces in Macedonia and Afghanistan and just completed a tour as chief of staff of the army's Land Command, said when he arrived in Basra it was not immediately clear how long the British force would remain in Iraq.

"There were jobs to do, but there was little flexibility in how we could carry them out," he said.

"The political track was to stay with the Americans but we lacked the political will to do anything more than just sit there."[19]

Prime Minister Brown had already set in train the draw-down plan but the British government was loath to give up its divisional command in southern Iraq, even though it was now providing just a small brigade, of only three battlegroups, which were confined to operating only in Basra province. White-Spunner arrived a couple weeks after the Royal Dragoon Guards (RDG) battlegroup began returning to its base in Germany as part of a 1,000 troop draw-down announced by the Prime Minister the previous October. The departure of the 500-strong RDG battlegroup set the tone and created an atmosphere among the troops at Basra airport that the government was soon to pull the plug on the mission. It was far from welcome among many of the regiment's soldiers, who took the news that they were being sent home as a slight to their military prowess.

According to their commanding officer, Lieutenant Colonel James Carr-Smith. "On the one hand [my troops] were delighted to be returning to loved ones sooner than expected; but on the other – as you would expect – professional pride meant they would have wished to remain in Iraq until the end of 4 Mechanised Brigade's tour in May 2008."[20]

Carr-Smith told his troops that they had been selected because the RDG battlegroup contained the required number of infantry companies and armoured squadrons to be sent home, as set down by PJHQ.

"This was not a decision based on relative ability within the brigade," Carr-Smith wrote to his regiment.

"In fact the brigade commander [Brigadier Julian Free] stated publicly that in sending home the Regimental Battlegroup he would be 'sending home some his best first'."[21]

PJHQ instructed White-Spunner to prepare Basra airport for hand-over to the Iraqis and to continue to train local troops. Yet his American superiors in the coalition chain of command were starting to raise concerns about the disturbances in Basra city, and wanted the border with Iran monitored, while the Iraqi government and military were pressing White-Spunner to do something about the militia problem.

"The strategic guidance I was getting from London was that at the end of my tour we would still be in Basra, but with only 2000 people, not 4000, and that we would have no remit in Basra city," he said.

"The Americans were surprised about this. This is why we [in the divisional headquarters] said in February that we can't carry on like this. We have got to help the Iraqis get back into Basra".[22]

"There was no buy-in yet from the government in London," he commented. "We could have just continued doing what we were doing but it would have had no apparent purpose. I went around the battlegroups after I arrived and got some pointed questions from the troops about what was the point of them being here? The real purpose for us to stay was so Britain could be in tune with the Americans politically and strategically but we were not in tune with them tactically. London said, 'just stay put'."

"What really bothered me was when people in Basra came up to me and said the city was falling to bits" he said.

"They said no one was protecting them. I discussed this with the Iraqi army. It was obvious things were untenable and we could not maintain this charade."[23]

White-Spunner went to a multi-national corps conference in Baghdad on 5th March with General Petraeus, General Odierno, the Iraqi prime minister's national security advisor, Mowaffak Baqer al-Rubaie and General Mohan. This was to discuss the plans for the coming campaign across Iraq, not just in Basra. Mohan used a Power-Point presentation to brief the conference on his outline plans to sweep Basra of the militia. It laid out the phases of the operation, required Iraqi reinforcements, as well as US and British support. He envisaged a six-month-long campaign that would involve Iraqi troops sealing and clearing specific neighbourhoods of militia fighters. The finale would be a drive to take al Amarah from the Sadrists. The top US generals in Iraq were happy that Mohan had come up with his ideas for taking the initiative but they felt the strategic main effort should be finishing off of the al Qaeda enclave in Mosul first. Once that was done, then the US would swing its resource southwards to deal with Basra's militias.

"The view was the D-Day for the start of the Basra operation would be late May at the earliest once Mosul was finished," said White-Spunner.[24]

Iraqi troops would lead this operation and White-Spunner said he was keen to help provide advisors for the Iraqi units currently being trained by the British, as well as forward air controllers to direct air strikes, as well as intelligence and logistics support.

"We did some rough planning," said White-Spunner. "We profiled what the Iraqis wanted but we wanted to do it in a way that would not put Brits back on the streets of Basra. We had not yet got into full tactical planning."

White-Spunner then talked to the Chief of Joint Operations at PJHQ, Lieutenant-General Nick Houghton about the idea. "He said 'lets see how it goes'".

When the Defence Secretary Des Browne visited Basra in the second week of March, White-Spunner pitched the idea to him and he seemed supportive, but there was no apparent rush to push it up to the prime minister and cabinet for approval.

"What I was saying was clearly unwelcome, and there was no plan to discuss it in cabinet at that stage. However, I took from that meeting that London would consider our plan in due course although we would have to push very forcefully for it," said White-Spunner.[25]

During a visit to the 1st Battalion, The Royal Regiment of Scotland (1 SCOTS), at Shaibah in early March, Browne got a more down-beat assessment, with the commanding officer, Lieutenant-Colonel Charlie Herbert, telling the defence secretary that he "could barely envisage a scenario whereby UK forces would redeploy back into Basra City".[26]

The apparent lack of imminent action meant White-Spunner decided the following week to combine his two-week-long leave period with a briefing to the staff of 7 Armoured Brigade, who were due to replace 4 Brigade in May. He also allowed his liaison officer to General Mohan, Colonel Richard Iron, to go on his leave at the same time. The neat plan of Generals Petraeus and White-Spunner for a sequenced series of offensive operations over the next six months would soon be thrown into disarray by Iraq's prime minister. Not surprisingly, given Iraq's recent bloody political history, Maliki was emerging as a rather paranoid leader who was becoming increasingly pre-occupied with his own survival. With the war against the Sunni al-Qaeda insurgents now appearing to be almost won as a result of General Petraeus' surge, Maliki was increasingly pre-occupied with the upcoming election in June and was determined to neutralise his Shia political rivals. Ending the dominance of Sadr's allies in Basra was his main objective.

From US diplomatic cables and situation reports of the British divisional headquarters published by the WikiLeaks website, it is possible to build up a very detailed picture of Maliki's behaviour in the run-up to the Iraqi military offensive in Basra, which became known as Operation Charge of the Knights, or Saulat al-Fursan. The Iraqi prime minister can only be described as "erratic", "rash" and "completely out of his depth". In the end Maliki's closest advisors had to create a means of redeeming their prime minister's reputation from the disaster of his own making. The planning for the Iraqi operation was seriously lacking in detail, forcing US and British commanders to rapidly improvise a solution to recover the situation. Nothing about Operation Charge of the Knights was pre-ordained or pre-planned.

The origins of Maliki's determination to take action in Basra lay in a February visit to Umm Qasr port, south of Basra, by his deputy and his national security advisors. Pro-Sadr banners were all around the port, which was controlled by Facilities Police Force operatives loyal to the cleric. Maliki ordered his interior minister to prepare a plan to take back the port and disperse the pro-Sadr security personnel, to prevent his rival having control over Iraq's only deep water port and its large revenue. This would allow Maliki to make a high profile visit to the port and give out jobs and economic aid to the local population. Subsequently, Maliki's advisors provided him with a list 500 Sadr supporters in Basra city who needed to be purged to rid the province of 'criminals'. This coincided with the efforts by General Mohan to develop plans to defeat the militia in Basra, prompting the prime minister to take over the military operation.[27]

During a series of meetings in the third week of March, Mohan's plans were discussed with senior American and British officers in Baghdad. Also present at one of these meetings on 16th March was Lieutenant General Bill Rollo, now back in Iraq as Britain's senior military representative and Petraeus' deputy. He pushed for the development of a comprehensive counter-insurgency strategy with cross-ministerial security, economic and social development plans.[28]

At a 22rd March meeting with Petraeus and senior US officers, Maliki told the American commanders that he had decided to go to Basra in two days' time to lead the operation against the militias. He railed against the British for letting the militia run out of control in Basra. More detail of his intentions were given to the Americans at a meeting of the Iraqi security council the next day, and Maliki declared he would be heading to Basra to "show the people of southern Iraq that they were part of the country and that the central government would act for their security".[29]

Orders had already been issued to two Iraqi paramilitary police units, a special forces company and two battalions of the Iraqi Army's 1st Division to move to Basra from Baghdad. Another army battalion and police reinforcement were en route to Basra from Karbala. The first unit to leave its base to the west of Baghdad was the 2nd Battalion, 1st Division, which left on 23rd March for its three day-long drive south to Basra. It took with it an embedded team of US Marine Corps advisors and forward air controllers.[30]

General Petraeus had little choice but to go along with the Iraqi move, although the Americans had no real idea about what Maliki would actually do once he got to Basra. Maliki said he did not require any assistance from the Americans or British beyond some airlift capability to move troops southward. The American officers at the meeting urged Maliki to be cautious because of the poor logistical support available to the Iraqi troops. Petraeus advised the prime minister to take plenty of cash with him to buy food and fuel for his troops from civilian companies in Basra, as there was not enough time to move supplies from depots in Baghdad.[31]

Ryan Crocker, the US Ambassador in Baghdad, described Maliki as "impulsive", said that "the planning and execution of the operation left much to be desired", adding that the prime minister "probably bit off more than he could chew". But the American ambassador expressed relief that the Shia prime minister was at last moving against the JAM militia and its backers in the Iranian sponsored special groups.[32]

On 24th March, Maliki flew to Basra airport in his Prime Ministerial Airbus airliner, with Interior Minister Jawad Bolani, Defence Minister Abdul Qadar and Minister of State for National Security Sherwan al-Waeli. He then flew into Basra Palace on one of the Iraqi air force's Mil Mi-17 helicopters. The arrival of Maliki and his entourage at the airport created a flurry of activity in the nearby British headquarters. They had been warned by the Americans the night before that something might happen but until Maliki turned up no one knew for sure what would it would be Brigadier Free started phoning around Iraqi officers in the city to try to find out what the prime minister had planned. Maliki made a point of not asking the British to help.

The Americans had begun mobilising the embedded training teams of the remaining units from the 1st Division that was heading south, but it would be another three days before they could get to Basra. The Iraqis would be fighting on their own, except for small teams of a dozen advisors with the 1st Division's 2nd Battalion, including five forward air controllers. To try to get some 'ground truth', the brigadier ordered Colonel Carr-Smith and a small protection team to fly to the Shatt-al-Arab Hotel on a RAF Merlin helicopter to work with Mohan and co-ordinate any support he might need.[33]

During the day General Petreaus requested the combined air operations centre at al Udeid airbase in Qatar to begin ramping up patrols over Basra by armed MQ-1 Predator drones and fast jets, including RAF Tornado GR4s. The air operations centre inside the British headquarters at Basra airport became the focal point for all this air activity, using live video feeds from the US Predators and British Hermes 450 drones to identify targets for air strikes, and determine if civilians or friendly troops were at risk from collateral damage. Many of the US and British fast jets overflying Basra were also fitted with advanced targeting pods that had video downlinks, and these could also be viewed in headquarters and by forward air controllers on laptop computer-like video terminals called ROVERS. This allowed the jets to be used in the same way as the drones to look at what was happening on the ground.

The air co-ordination staff were situated right next to the US and British artillery commanders, so their fire could also be co-ordinated. Within seconds of militia mortars and rocket teams opening fire anywhere in Basra city the British COBRA and Giraffe radars, as well as American AN/TPQ-37 radars at the airport, could pin point their location and direct strike aircraft, drones or artillery fire against them in a matter of seconds. The surveillance capability available to British and US commanders during Operation Charge of the Knights was significantly better than anything that existed in Basra before and was a major factor in the success of the unfolding battle.

The first Predator arrived over Basra during the evening of 24th March, and it was soon put to good use by the British headquarters.[34] Since before Christmas 2006, the Reconnaissance Platoon of the Scots Guards had been sent out every night to set up covert observation patrols along the Basra canal to watch the edge of the city, and to provide early warning of movement by rocket teams trying to set up their weapons to attack the airbase. Late that evening they spotted ten men attempting to plant an IED near the Hayaniyah district. They called in the newly-arrived Predator and it fired two Hellfire missiles, killing five of the bomb makers and injuring several others.

The Scots Guards observation teams remained in position all through the night and into the following day, giving them what they called "a front row seat" on the unfolding battle between the Iraqi army and the militias. Their reports were some of the few accurate first-hand pieces of reporting of the evenings during the opening hours of Operation Charge of the Knights.[35]

At first light the following morning, some 10,000 Iraqi troops and police began moving across the city in convoys of lightly-armoured Humvees, unarmed trucks and jeeps. The operation was essentially a large scale cordon and search mission, with the 50, 51 and 52 Brigades of the Iraqi 14th Division, backed up by the army and police reinforcements from Baghdad, moving into the Tamaymiyah, Dakeer, Jamhoriyah and Hayaniyah districts to raid suspected militia bases and hideouts. The numerous militia informants in the police and army, of course, had let them know what was about to happen and thousands of fighters were ready and waiting. Maliki had asked for the US Air Force to put on three low-level shows of force over the city to coincide with the start of the operation.[36]

According to American diplomats in Basra, Maliki had developed a list of 28 targets that he believed could be quickly neutralized. He described these as JAM-affiliated criminal elements, that were responsible for the wave of oil smuggling, political killings, kidnappings and crimes against scientists, doctors, academics and women. As the Iraqi columns neared their objectives they were hit by withering small arms and mortar fire. Dozens of vehicles were destroyed or damaged by multiple IED ambushes. No British or American troops were with the Iraqis so they could not ask the F-16 jets flying overhead to hit the militia fighters, or organise casualty evacuation helicopters to pick up wounded troops. General Mohan's command centre consisted of little more than a map board and eight mobile telephones so he quickly lost control of events on the ground. His headquarters was so out of touch that it notified the British at the airport at 8am that its forces had "killed a number of terrorists and chased the remaining [militia] after disposing of their weapons in the al Jamiat area and the al Khadarah market."[37]

Maliki, according to his close advisors who briefed US diplomats, was wholly surprised by the entrenched and organised resistance by the JAM cells. He did not appreciate the extent to which JAM fighters either had already emplaced IEDs or were able to quickly set them up. The combination of IEDs, combined with heavy RPG7 and accurate mortar fire, had stymied Iraqi army movements all over the city.

Arab satellite news channels began broadcasting pictures of burning Iraqi Humvees with crowds of jubilant militiamen firing their AK-47s in the air in celebration at their victory. Several Iraqi army and police units were pinned down and were taking heavy losses. The 52nd Brigade, which had only been formed a couple of months before, lost hundreds of men dead and wounded, before it fled back to the safety of Shaibah Logistic Base. Mohan and the brigade commander had warned Maliki that their troops were not ready for action, but the prime minister thought Mohan was simply not being aggressive enough. The general was told to obey his orders. The arrival of panic-stricken Iraqi troops at Shaibah was the first Colonel Herbert and the 1 Scots battlegroup knew of the unfolding events in the city centre. An Iraqi Mi-17 helicopter was forced to make an emergency landing at the airport after being hit by machine gun fire.[38]

Colonel Carr-Smith and his team at Mohan's headquarters began passing reports of dozens of badly wounded Iraqi soldiers streaming into the base, screaming in pain because no morphine was available. Maliki was soon aware that things were not going well when Basra Palace started to be hit by a steady stream of mortar bombs, forcing him and his entourage to seek cover for hours on end. Maliki then announced he had sacked Mohan, blaming him for the disaster and replaced him with Major General Abdul Aziz, the commander of the 14th Division.

The 6,000 JAM militiamen in the city were soon on the offensive, seizing control of provincial government offices and several police stations. Several hundred policemen openly sided with the militia and joined the battle against Maliki's troops. Initial reports suggested that 50 Iraqi troops were killed and 120 wounded. Some 40 militia fighters were killed during the first day of fighting.[39]

In the evening a representative of the militia offered Maliki a ceasefire, but the beleaguered prime minister in turn demanded the surrender of wanted militia commanders. In Baghdad, General Petraeus was becoming increasingly concerned by the stream of reports from the British, and a couple of colonels he had sent to Basra Palace, that Maliki was in serious trouble. He telephoned the prime minister to warn him to be ready to evacuate the palace to prevent Maliki being killed or captured. Fortunately for Maliki, in Washington President Bush was so impressed by the Iraqi's determination to take on the militia that later that day he ordered Petraeus to do everything possible to make Operation Charge of the Knights succeed.[40]

During the night of 25th/26th March, a US special forces officer, US Navy Rear Admiral Ed Winters, and a small team of Central Intelligence Agency paramilitary operatives managed to infiltrate into Basra Palace by road to establish a forward command post to co-ordinate support to the Iraqi prime minister. Another small team of American special forces made its way to the Shatt-al-Arab Hotel to link up with General Mohan.[41]

A US Army airborne weapons team of four AH-64D Apache attack helicopters and two UH-60 Blackhawks at Tallil airbase outside Nasiriyah were placed on standby to fly to support Maliki. At Basra airport, Brigadier Free put the Scots Guard on 60-minute notice to move to be ready to intervene with a squadron of Challenger 2 tanks and three companies of armoured infantry. Maliki was still determined not to ask for direct assistance so the British and Americans commanders had little idea how to intervene.[42]

The fighting continued across Basra through the night and into 26th March, but still the Iraqis could make little serious progress. A large force of militiamen traded mortar fire with government forces in the main police station in the centre of Basra. JAM militiamen overran two more police stations and besieged an army ammunition depot in the north of the city. Basra Palace and the

Shatt-al-Arab Hotel were repeatedly mortared and sniper fire kept their defenders pinned down. A RAF Merlin helicopter was scrambled to rescue wounded Iraqi soldiers from Basra Palace. While the three casualties were being loaded the landing pad came under mortar fire but the helicopter was able to get the men to safety at the airport. Over the next two days the RAF helicopters flew five more rescue missions to lift out 30 wounded Iraqis. Fighting spread to Zubayr where two police stations were overrun by militiamen, and two western security contractors were killed by an IED in the nearby oil fields. Shaibah Logistic Base came under rocket and small arms fire in the afternoon.[43]

During the night, US airpower made its first intervention in the battle, being called into action by one of the CIA teams in the city centre after a JAM technical vehicle engaged a group of police. A US Air Force AC-130 Spectre gunship tracked the technical and destroyed it, killing ten fighters.[44] During the evening the US Army planned to launch Apache patrols over the city but strong winds at Talill grounded the helicopters.

With reports of Maliki's unbalanced behaviour continuing, General Petraeus sent the US corps commander, Lieutenant-General Lloyd Austin down to Basra to try to talk some sense into the prime minister. The 6 foot four-inch-tall general had led the US tank column that seized Baghdad in April 2003. He liked to get a personal feel for the sound and smell of a battlefield so was keen to get into the centre of the city to see what was going on.

Austin flew into the palace on the morning of 27th March with Brigadier Free, who was still in command of British operations until General White-Spunner got back, in the hope of being able to pull together a co-ordinated operation involving US, British and Iraqi forces. The Iraqi prime minister refused to see the British brigadier, who had to drum his heels outside Maliki's officer while General Austin tried to make him see sense. According to a US State Department report of the meeting, Maliki blamed the British and Americans for his predicament, criticizing the UK for letting militias take control of Basra and [US] for not doing enough to help in the present conflict.

"Providing Iraqi-requested support is problematic," said the report. "The Iraqis do not provide accurate coordinates or conduct intelligence surveillance, make last-minute requests, and do not bear in mind rule-of-engagement requirements."[45]

Now finally realising the seriousness of his position, Maliki agreed to let the American general to begin to co-ordinate support for his beleaguered troops.

"Julian Free had a frightful time with Maliki," said General White-Spunner.

"There was no planning, it was back-of-a-fag packet stuff. Maliki was asking for air strikes to be called onto streets with no specific target information or co-ordinates."[46]

The British Prime Minister Gordon Brown fared little better than Brigadier Free, with Maliki ignoring his calls. The American general and the British brigadier returned to the headquarters at the airport to try to develop a plan to redeem the situation. First of all they needed to get British, American and Iraqi special forces teams and forward air controllers into Basra city to find the location of the beleaguered Iraqi army units, and then help them call down air strikes on the militia. Once the situation had been stabilised, the plan called for intensive strike operations to neutralise militia commanders and arms depots. Then a concerted drive would push militia fighters out of Basra, and Iraqi troops would be positioned throughout the city to prevent the militia returning, to allow real police reform and reconstruction projects to get under way. This was how Operation Salamanca/Sinbad had meant to play out and was similar to the tactics being used in central Iraq by US surge troops.

Crucial to the success of the operation would be the use of Iraqi troops on the frontline, to give it an 'Iraqi face' so local people would not see it as a return of foreign occupation.

To make it work, British and American embedded advisor teams needed to be assigned to every Iraqi battalion to bring coherence to the operation, as well as organising essential logistics support to keep the Iraqi troops fighting. The first US Marine Corps advisors arrived during the day, but the bulk were still a few days behind, and a company of paratroopers from the US 82nd Airborne Division would arrive soon afterwards.[47]

The British forces were to provide the key support to the operation. First of all, the British-run Basra airbase was the key launch pad for offensive missions into the city, and the gateway for reinforcements from Baghdad. Secondly, the British had the only heavy armour in southern Iraq, which would be crucial to the break-in battle. Thirdly, British Hermes 450 drones, AS-90 155mm howitzers and Tornado GR4 jets made a significant contribution to the surveillance and strike power available for the operation. British infantry and special forces would also act as embedded advisors.

Although the subsequent US and British-directed operation bore the name Charge of the Knights, it was in fact very different from the one started by Maliki two days earlier. Pulling this plan together, in the middle of a confused battle, would not be easy and would take time to execute. The presence of a US three-star general in Basra, who was organising the arrival of hundreds of US ground troops into what, up to now had been a British patch, was highly sensitive. On a number of occasions, the British government had turned down offers of assistance from the US Army to send troops to Basra due to the political sensitivities. With the fate of the Iraqi prime minister at stake, there was little choice available to the British but to go along with the American plans.

When General Austin's deputy, Major-General George Flynn, arrived at Basra airport the next day with a tactical headquarters to co-ordinate the deployment and operations of the American reinforcements, the tension grew. General Flynn was a tough, no-nonsense US Marine Corps officer who was not afraid to ruffle feathers to get things done.[48] He would eventually be in charge of the base in 2010-11 where the Wikileaks suspect, Private Bradley Manning, was held in harsh conditions prior to his trial. When Flynn's staff officers arrived and started setting up shop inside the British headquarters it looked like a takeover. One officer complained that the new arrivals appeared to be 'mentoring' the British as well as the Iraqis. The insistence of the Iraqi prime minister on only working through the Americans, because of the British army's previous dealing with the militias, created an added complication, even though during the tense meeting with General Austin on 27th March, Maliki demanded that the British send ground troops into Basra to fight the militia. This initial tension soon passed, and the British and Americans began to get things moving. The Americans in Basra who had met the irrational Maliki were largely sympathetic to the British, with one US diplomat commenting that one of Flynn's tasks was to "assist in rebuilding the relationship between Maliki and [the British]."[49]

Fighting between the militia and Iraqi army continued throughout the 27th March in the centre of the city, with the British divisional intelligence assessment described as being "in contention," as it predicted continued strong resistance from the militia. Two police stations in al Maqil fell to the militia, and they drove off Iraqi troops sent to secure Camp Apache ammunition depot. Hundreds of policemen continued to defect to the militia, and the city's police chief narrowly escaped death when his convoy was hit in an IED ambush. The British suffered their first casualty of the operation when mortar fire wounded a member of the Royal Dragoon Guards liaison team at the Shatt-al-Arab Hotel. A US Army UH-60 Blackhawk picked up the wounded soldier, while a Apache gunship carried out three strafing runs to keep the militia mortar teams heads' down.[50]

The first US Marine Corps joint terminal attack controller (JTAC), or forward air control team, had linked up with Iraqi troops under mortar fire near the Gates of Basra, not far from the Shatt-al-Arab hotel. This five-strong team was soon bringing down air strikes across northern Basra. Near the Qarmat Ali Bridge it controlled two US Navy FA-18s to make three strafing runs against the militia fighters. A pair of RAF Tornado GR4s were called in to make low-level shows of force later in the evening. Then a pair of US Army Apaches were also called to intervene in a firefight between militia fighters and the Iraqi police Tactical Support Unit, with the American gunships claiming six JAM fighters killed.[51]

Overnight, and during the morning of 28th March, British and American efforts to build their plan gathered momentum. According to US diplomatic reports at the Multi-National Division South East headquarters morning briefing, Brigadier Free expressed concern about Maliki's governments' perceptions that the British were not providing adequate support.

"Free said the central government views the UK as "pariahs" that had indiscriminately released criminals who are now engaging Iraqi Security Forces (ISF) in Basra. Despite an ISF operation that has been described as random and poorly planned, Free stressed the importance of MND-SE support, saying 'don't let them fail, they must not fail.'"[52]

The US report continued that "according to MND-SE officers at the Basra Operations Center (BOC), General Mohan seems to be back in control of operations. However, ongoing problems remain between Mohan and General Aziz. MND-SE officers at the BOC believe Aziz wants to take control of operations but has been sidelined by Mohan. They add that Aziz speaks very good English and has a better understanding of the MND-SE support role. He also has been instrumental in sharing information from planning meetings that MND-SE [officers are] are no longer authorized to attend."

Flynn and Free flew by helicopter into the Shatt-al-Arab Hotel on 28th March to speak to Mohan and then Aziz, who was controlling the 14th Division at Shaibah Logistic Base, to try to find out what was happening, and to work out how to insert advisors into their units. Later that day General White-Spunner arrived back after being picked up by an Army Air Corps Lynx helicopter from Kuwait airport.

"It was clear it was going to take a long time to sort things out," he recalled.

"The US had started putting teams into Basra. We were then not authorised to do that, our training was all done in the camp at Shaibah. The Iraqi brigades we trained were not performing well. The [advisors] needed to deploy with them. The Iraqis were brave but they had no enablers with them [to co-ordinate air, medical and logistic support]."[53]

"I said to London, you have got to let us do this," said General White-Spunner.

"I wrote the ministerial submission with PJHQ and this went to the junior duty minister. It was Easter. Everyone in London was on holiday. Everything was done overnight. We got permission the next day to completely re-role our battalions. We should have done this a long time before. Maybe because of the Majar al-Kabir incident in 2003 we had been reluctant to do this. It was the only way to do it."[54]

Later that evening Colonel Herbert, the commanding officer of 1 Scots, was warned off to be ready to move back into Basra in 48 hours. He was told to re-organise his battle group from the old style monitoring, mentoring and training (M2T) at Shaihab, into a unit that could directly advise Iraqi units in combat, which was dubbed MiTTs (Military Transition Teams). His Rhine Company and D Squadron of the RDG were to move into Basra to work with the 14th Division, while Colonel Herbert would work alongside General Aziz.[55]

"[This was] based on the sound model developed by US MiTTs in Baghdad, and with some help from our sister company (Mons), we split the company into three distinct MiTTs of roughly platoon-size; three of them in direct support of 50, 51 and 52 Brigades" recalled Major Thomas Gilbert Scot Perkins, Rhine Company's commander.[56]

Each MiTT was to be a heavily armed force, boasting 24 infantrymen, a detachment armed with Javelin anti-tank guided missiles, a pair of snipers and two JTACs, or forward air controllers. The 1 Scots troops were to operate in the new big Mastiff for its first combat mission into downtown Basra, and the cavalry troopers of the RDG, who were already working as armoured infantry, took their Warriors. According to Perkins, the MiTTs were expecting to be engaged in serious fighting.

"My company sergeant major and I conducted a rough ammunition estimate, and then decided to triple it at the last minute," he said.

"Food and water sufficient for five days was crammed both inside and on top of the vehicles; every square inch was used. Our mission was threefold and pretty straightforward; thoroughly embed ourselves within respective Iraqi army units as quickly as possible within the city, rapidly establish ground truth and situational awareness on behalf of Headquarters MND(SE), and provide as much high-profile mentoring assistance and [artillery, air support and surveillance] support as possible, all in order to ensure the Iraqi Army leadership re-established the necessary confidence within itself to re-commence offensive operations against JAM in Basra."[57]

Major Ben Ryan, the commander of the RDG's Squadron, said his men had to work "round the clock to train and prepare" for the new mission.

"We knew it was serious when the personnel locator beacons (in case of kidnap) were issued to all," he recalled.[58]

As this frantic preparation was underway, the Scots Guards and RDG began to support strike operations by the Iraqi special forces and their US special forces mentors.[59] Their job was to deliver the Iraqi assault teams to their target and then safely extract them when the operation was over. The first mission during the early hours of 28th March took the Scots Guards Warriors to the edge of the Hayaniyah neighbourhood, which was the main JAM stronghold on the southern edge of Basra, for a three hour-long battle between the Iraqi special forces and militiamen. Subsequently, the Scots Guards battlegroup would support 17 US and Iraqi strike operations over the next three weeks.[60]

"The Squadron found itself in a pre-eminent role but now marching to the unfamiliar beat of the Iraqi Army and their 'Special' US mentors' drum," commented a RDG officer.

"The operational surge lasted the best part of three weeks and regularly involved the squadron leading US and Iraqi special forces units into Basra, primarily to act as bullet catchers or, more specifically, the 'IED sponge'."

The officer summed this up succinctly, as "deliver some men to the door of the target and more importantly, to take the enemy's punches and come up fighting".[61]

The JAM and Iraqis continued to trade fire across Basra, with neither side apparently gaining the upper hand. US F-16s and Hornets made two low level passes to try to scare off militia fighters attacking Iraqi bases. Shaibah Logistic Base and an Iraqi army base in Zubayr came under mortar and rocket fire. As this stand-off continued, Iraqi army and police units continued to suffer from mass desertions as they ran out of ammunition and food. One American colonel at Basra Palace reported Iraqi soldiers were resorting to dropping hand grenades in ornamental lakes to try to kill fish to eat.

The US diplomats in Basra were reporting the Iraqi government leadership in the palace were becoming increasingly desperate, with the Basra Police Chief Abdul Jalil Khalaf, "almost shouting that if US troops did not intervene in a matter of days, the city would be lost". Maliki's national security advisor Rubaie told another US official, "that his prime minister would remain in Basra until there was a clear perception that he had won a victory. Rubaie admitted that "he was thinking of 'creating' such a victory, but that nothing had yet come to mind. The problem was that some of the targets which the prime minister had set, such as all weapons in the hands of criminals being given up, were not achievable."[62]

Another US diplomat at the Palace assessed that "a military defeat for the militias is unlikely and would take at least days and probably weeks."[63]

Basra's civilian population had spent the past four days hiding in their homes, with shops and public utilities shut down. The hospitals remained open, but they were only treating emergency cases as it was too dangerous to move around the city. As food and water shortages began to take hold, General White-Spunner's headquarters began to develop plans to work with aid agencies to address how to deliver humanitarian aid. Accurate casualty numbers were extremely difficult to assess, but according to US reports, the 14th Division were reporting 15 killed in action and 91 wounded, along with 88 civilians dead.[64]

US and British troops were now poised to ramp up their offensive operations in the north west of Basra, in a bid to lessen pressure on General Mohan's headquarters in the Shatt-al-Arab Hotel. The Scots Guards supported a raid on a militia base in this area during the early hours of 29th March, that culminated in a AC-130 strike on the target. A Predator drone was called in to hit mortar teams firing at a US advisor team in the area, after being detected by a Royal Artillery MAMBA radar at the airport.[65]

Units of the Iraqi 1st Division pressed their attack during the day across the north of the city, but made little progress despite heavy US and British support, controlled by the US Marine JTAC team. A Royal Artillery Hermes 450 drone overflew an Iraqi army unit under machine gun and small arms fire during the afternoon. This battle lasted most of the afternoon and grew to involve the first employment of D Battery, 1st Royal Horse Artillery's AS-90 155mm guns during the operation. A pair of US Army Apaches then joined the battle and fired a Hellfire missile at a group of militia fighters.[66]

In the biggest US air strike to date, US Marine air controllers with 1st Division units, pinned down in the centre of the city by militia snipers, called up a giant B-1B bomber. It made two passes over Basra dropping two satellite guided 500lb Joint Direct Attack Munitions and the air controllers reported 16 militiamen were killed in the strikes.[67]

US F-16s and Predators were heavily involved during the day in the search for militia teams that fired four rockets at the airport. The British base at Umm Qasr also came under sniper fire, prompting fears of a militia mobilisation in the area close to the port.

The Iraqi prime minister and his advisors were now escalating their efforts to find a way out of the crisis, which had spread to several cities in southern Iraq. It had resulted in the Green Zone in Baghdad, which housed the Iraqi government and US military command centre, coming under sustained rocket fire from the Shia stronghold of Sadr city. During 29th March, a delegation of senior Iraqi Shia politicians travelled to Tehran and the holy city of Qom to try to get the Iranian government to broker a cease fire with Sadr.[68]

The national security advisor Rubaie also persuaded Maliki to adopt his plan to generate an 'artificial success and face-saving formula', and then "declare victory", allowing the prime minister to return to Baghdad in triumph. Rubaie told Maliki that "a military victory was impossible and that even Saddam Hussein could not control Basra's neighbourhoods".

The solution was to give Maliki "a graceful way out of the predicament".[69] The plan was for an Iraqi police column to make a highly publicised visit to the port at Umm Qasr to claim its recapture, even though it had never been a scene of fighting during the previous week. At the same time the Iraqi army would stage a symbolic advance into the Hayaniyah militia stronghold. Word had not yet come back of the success of the negotiators in Iran, and General Flynn and White-Spunner had to intervene firmly with Maliki to stop him sending Iraqi troops to storm the Iranian consulate in Basra.

"Maliki's relations with the Iranians were at best confused during the early stages of Charge of the Knights," commented General White-Spunner.[70]

Operation Lightning Anvil kicked off at just after 11.45am on 30th March. British artillery fired smoke to cover the advance of two Iraqi battalions, as British Hermes 450 and US Predator drones provided a live video feed of the action to the headquarters at the airport, and forward air controllers with the assault troops. Two F-16s were overhead, ready to strike. Once the smoke screen was in place, the AS-90s switched to firing high explosive shell to neutralise militia strong points as the troops started to advance.[71]

RDG Challengers led the attack to smash through militia barricades blocking roads into the built-up area, while shooting up a car suspected of containing a large IED.

"Sergeant Robert's Challenger was hit by three separate IEDs with a further two detonating but missing," recorded the commander of the tank troop leading the assault.

"He and his crew continued with their task of leading Iraqi forces onto their objectives. Within the same operational period, Lieutenant Troy demolished the insurgent's barricade with 120mm training ammunition (but main armament rounds, none the less,) even if Corporal Edward's [armoured recovery tank] did have to do a bit of 'sweeping up'."[72]

For nearly an hour the Iraqi troops battled with the militia fighters in the district before a withdrawal was ordered and the government forces pulled back, covered by the British Warriors and Challengers. Further south, in Umm Qasr the 300 strong police task force met no resistance. Maliki had his symbolic victories, even if in the rest of Basra the situation was little changed.[73] And as Operation Lightning Anvil was underway, F-16s and Hornets had to bomb militia mortar teams firing on the Shatt-al-Arab Hotel.

The first British embedded MiTT team headed into Basra during the night, with a column of Warriors and Bulldogs from Arnhem Company, the Duke of Lancaster's Regiment heading to the Shatt-al-Arab hotel to deliver an enhanced co-ordination and communications team to General Mohan's headquarters. Other British units deployed along the route to secure key road junctions. Operation Wilden went largely without a hitch, beyond one of the Warriors scoring a first-round hit on a suspected IED with its 30mm cannon. This allowed the column to keep moving to safely reach its destination.

Major Cormack, Arnhem Company's commander described how the upsurge in the operational tempo had an exhilarating effect on his troops.

"There were tumultuous days with the outcome on a real knife-edge for some time," he recalled.

"At times the only sign of momentous events happening a matter of kilometres away was Sky news, or more vividly brought home when we were on duty at permanent vehicle check points [PVCPs] [around the airport] where casualties from the fighting would arrive. In hindsight nothing was going to mess with us. We had a clear intent, robust rules of engagement, more aviation, air and ISTAR than we had seen before. The company was buzzing and thoroughly up for it, as we deployed on Operation Wilden to deliver support to the Basra Operations Centre."[74]

In Qom, the Iranians were now putting heavy pressure on Sadr to calm the situation. The last thing they wanted was a full-blown civil war within Iraq's Shia community. A deal emerged during 30th March in which Sadr and the Iranians effectively pulled the plug on the JAM militia. Sadr declared that the JAM would hand over its heavy weapons to the government and anyone who disobeyed would be considered a 'criminal', open to arrest by the army and police. The militia were ordered to stop patrolling Basra's streets. In return the Iraqi government would allow Sadr's political party to continue to participate in up-coming elections.

The next day, Maliki announced he would agree to go along with the ceasefire, which created a new political dynamic in Basra. There was great relief when it appeared, as if the fighting was over. Public opinion now seemed to turn against the militia, who were becoming unpopular for turning their guns and IEDs on poorly-trained Iraqi soldiers. The change in attitude from the Iranian government proved decisive in undermining the morale of the special groups supported by the Quds Force.

In a matter of hours after the cease fire was announced, the mortar and rocket fire on Basra Palace and the Shatt-al-Arab Hotel ceased. Across the city, militia fighters and Iraqi army soldiers stopped trading fire. Basra's citizens came out onto the streets to buy food, take their sick to hospital and celebrate an end to the fighting. These developments came as something of a surprise to the British and Americans, who were not party to Maliki's dealings with the Iranians and Iraqi Shia politicians.

"I don't know if Maliki did a deal with the Iranians himself," commented General White-Spunner.

"It's an interesting idea. Maybe there is something in it. Clearly it was more than the military operation caused JAM to collapse. Resistance in Basra just went away."[75]

General White-Spunner said the British Army later tracked a number of Quds force operatives working with the JAM, moving back over the border after the ceasefire, and they seemed to stayed out of Iraq for a long time. This exodus deprived the JAM of its best and most effective leaders, who co-ordinated its operations across Basra. Some British officers talked about the JAM leadership being "effectively decapitated".

"We later picked off fifty of them as they moved back into the country," he said. The JAM leader Ahmed Fartosi decamped to Beirut and the infamous Captain Jafar fled to Iran.[76] On 1st April, Maliki quietly boarded a Mi-17 helicopter and flew out of Basra Palace. He left behind a group of relieved British, American and Iraqi senior officers, who could now get on with the task of clearing up the mess. Maliki was determined to keep up the pressure on his Sadrist rivals, and use the small print of the ceasefire agreement to mop up the militia strongholds across southern Iraq. Operation Charge of the Knights would not stop. It was now re-packaged for public consumption as a law enforcement operation to round up criminal elements that were not abiding by the terms of the ceasefire. Maliki wanted the JAM and their Sadrist allies kept on the run.

The prominent role given to Iraqi troops was having an important impact, with local civilians cheering them on the streets in many parts of Basra. To prevent the key role of British and US troops in the operation being exposed, international journalists were forbidden from joining these troops during the next month.

Rather than halt the offensive, on 1st April US, Iraqi and British reinforcements were streaming into Basra and fighting continued on a localised basis. A militia rocket team was discovered by a RAF Tornado during the afternoon setting up to fire at the airport. After a Predator drone took a closer look, the Royal Horse Artillery fired six 155mm shells before the RAF put down a 1,000lb bomb.[77] A British Hermes 450 drone spotted a militia RPG team firing on Iraqi troops in the north of Basra, prompting a pair of US Apache gunships to be called in to attack the target with their 30mm cannons.[78] The Scots Guards continued with its patrols along the outskirts of Basra, where they were repeatedly engaged by militia snipers. Militia fighters in the Five Mile Market area were still putting up strong resistance, driving back two Iraqi battalions that tried to enter the district.

As darkness fell, at Shaibah Logistic Base Colonel Herbert's troops were ready to roll.

"At 2230, following a pretty sombre church service with the Battle Group Padre in the Mastiff vehicle park, and what I hoped was a few inspiring words of encouragement to the boys from myself, we set off into the city," said Major Perkins, Rhine Company's commander.

"Basra had effectively become the Bogeyman for 4 Brigade during Operation Telic 11," he said.

"G2 [intelligence] briefs had consistently warned of layered IED screens on the city outskirts, and of insurgents having had months of ambush rehearsals to counter any hostile incursions; a pretty daunting prospect then to be leading that incursion into a city that we as a company didn't know well, on a moonless night, with multiple [firefights] still obviously occurring all around us."[79]

"We slipped back into Basra as the lead element of the 1 Scots Battlegroup MiTT mission," said Major Ryan.

"The insertion by Warrior was completed under the cloak of darkness, with US Apache gunships riding as overhead outriders, acting on our request, as well as F/A-18 jets and Predator unmanned aerial vehicles prowling above the route ahead. Once inserted by first light into Iraqi army bases in the heart of Basra, there were some slightly sleepy faces as they greeted their new guests. However, pleasantries exchanged, it was down to the serious business of taking forward the next stage of the Iraqi Army's Operation Charge of the Knights".[80]

As 1 Scots and the RDG were moving into the city centre, the Scots Guards were supporting another Iraqi special forces raid into the Hayyaniyah district. Ten rounds of 155mm fire were put down by the Royal Horse artillery before the Iraqi troops raided their target. Militia men on roof-tops engaged the Iraqis as they moved in. The British and American advisor units found the Iraqi army units they were to lead into battle were in poor shape.

"The first 48 hours were pretty memorable," said Major Perkins.

"The MiTTs having linked up successfully with respective elements of 50 and 51 Brigades, who were themselves holed up in desperately unprotected strongholds, spent the time constructively by conducting localized joint reassurance patrols. In our case the battalion commander was reluctant to allow his men to patrol more than twice a day in vehicles let alone on foot, but soon saw the benefit of our presence following a series of demonstrations of air cover intent over his area of responsibility, orchestrated by the [forward air controllers]. We came under small arms contact several times during these patrols, but chose not to retaliate due to population density."[81]

Major Perkins began working in a temporary MiTT base in an abandoned school in al Jubaylah alongside the headquarters of 51 Brigade. He said it had an experienced commander who had been drafted in on a temporary basis three days previously, following the death of Brigadier Wessam in an remote controlled IED attack on the northern edge of 5-Mile Market.

"[The new commander] appeared delighted to see us, and almost immediately called an orders group to introduce me to his obviously exhausted staff and battalion commanders," said Perkins.

"Collectively at that stage they had been under almost continuous contact for ten days, were clearly suffering logistically, medical and vehicle resupplies in particular, and appeared to have settled for a very unsatisfactory stalemate with JAM."[82]

Even though the ceasefire had been called two days earlier, all over Basra militia fighters were still putting up spirited, if unco-ordinated, resistance in several neighbourhoods where support for Sadr was still strong. They were beginning to realise that Maliki was moving against them and the ceasefire was going to be ignored by the Iraqi government forces. A militia technical vehicle carried out a drive-by shooting of the Shatt-al-Arab Hotel during 2nd April, and a Predator on patrol overhead knocked it out with a Hellfire missile. Iraqi army units were urged by the new advisors to begin local patrolling around their improvised bases in the city centre, to build up their confidence and stop the militia operating outside their local areas. One of these patrols arms caches were discovered, with an Iraqi battalion finding 22 122mm rockets, seven 107mm rockets, one Iranian made EFP IED, 21 anti-tank mines, sixty boxes of plastic explosives, five RPGs and a mortar tube hidden in the Tunnumah district.[83]

"The continuing operation in the city involved a series of slightly haphazard forays into nasty areas to advertise the fact that we meant business," said Major Ryan.

"Our main function included the provision of military planning advice, passing information on Iraqi intentions and enabling access to coalition artillery, surveillance and aircraft. We were also to coerce the enemy, who we probably confused to some degree. However, apart from some small arms fire, we were surprised not to be taken on at all. The ever present Apaches and other coalition aircraft probably helped in this regard!"[84]

To sustain the MiTT teams in the city, the Duke of Lancaster's escorted daily supply convoys out from the airport, protected British bases and supported General Mohan's headquarters. The Scots Guards remained committed to Operation Lightning Anvil, the mission to support US, British and Iraqi special forces, helping them mount nightly raids on the suspected hideouts of JAM leaders. RDG Challengers led the columns of Warriors that carried the special forces teams deep into militia neighbourhoods. These met resistance as they neared their targets, with one Guardsman being injured by an IED during a raid on 2nd April. British Special Forces reinforced their Task Force Spartan in Basra to support Operation Lightning Anvil, working in downtown neighbourhoods to stake out militia targets and guide in strike teams.

"The Battle Group operations conducted under the banner of 'Charge of the Knights' were the most exciting and adrenalin-filled part of Telic XI," commented a Scots Guards reconnaissance platoon officer.

"However, a huge amount of respect must be shown to both Iraqi Special Forces as night after night they ran the gauntlet through Basra City in their [lightly armoured] Humvee's."

"Lance Sergeant Baines deserves a special mention for his role on one such operation where he dismounted and led his team to marry up with the Task Force Spartan Liaison Officer, in order to extract an accurate situation report and commence a casualty evacuation. He was not helped in the least by Iraqi Special Forces standard operating procedures of speculatively firing at everything!"[85]

General Mohan was now in the forefront of efforts to kick-start the delivery of humanitarian aid and reconstruction across Basra. He led a convoy of Iraqi vehicles through Hayaniyah on 2nd April, and surprisingly it was not engaged by the militia. The next day, he was back again with 1st Division troops to deliver food and water. The same day Maliki announced $100 million to fund improvements in Basra.[86] Ten days later the British and American advisors were confident enough that they had got the Iraqi army into some sort of shape to enable it to begin large-scale operations. The first major cordon and search operation began in Qibla district on 12th April, and lasted five days. Iraqi troops knocked down barricades, searched houses for arms and helped distribute aid to civilians. Although this phase went relatively smoothly, when the Iraqi army moved into Hayaniyah district on 19th April it met initial resistance, which culminated in an early morning missile strike from a Predator on a militia RPG team.[87]

During daylight eight Iraqi battalions, operating under the control of three brigades, conducted the largest cordon and search operation to date in Basra. They found ten large arms caches containing tons of weapons and ammunition, which required a convoy of trucks to remove. This included a huge quantity of IED components, explosives, man-portable surface-to-air missiles, 122mm rockets and enough mortars, RPGs, AK-47s, machine guns and other weapons to equip a small army.[88] The following week, the Iraqi army repeated the exercise in the north west to complete its sweep of Basra city.

"Charge of the Knights was a series of logical and progressive district by district cordon and search operations within Basra, led by the Iraqi army, with UK and US MiTTS in direct support at both brigade and battalion level," said Major Perkins.

"I had not been more convinced of our worth at this stage than when the commanding officer of 51 Brigade's second battalion requested our assistance, to neutralise a JAM mortar team harassing one of his company cordon positions to the east of the Hayaniyah late on 10th April. My [forward air controllers] in conjunction with the FIRES Cell at Headquarters MND(SE) conjured up a Hellfire strike from a circling Predator, and with a sinister countdown in front of this commander and approximately forty of his men, spectacularly dealt with their problem right there."[89]

Operations Charge of the Knights 2, 3, 4, 5 and 6, cleared militia from the critical districts of Al Quibla, Al Hayyaniyah, Al Jazazer, Five Mile Market, Al Latif and Al Jumhuriyah over the next three weeks, said Perkins. The rejuvenated 51 Brigade was heavily involved in the discovery and subsequent rescue of the British journalist Richard Butler from a militia compound in the Al Jubaylah district on 14th April.

"By the end of April the large-scale cordon and search phase was complete. JAM had effectively imploded, leaving the Iraqi Army suddenly and very prominently in a position of complete authority within Basra."[90]

By the end of April, police and health workers said at least 236 people were killed and 600 wounded in the fighting in districts of central and northern Basra, with at least 50 civilians among the dead. Among the fatalities were at least 30 members of the security forces, including 15 soldiers and 15 policemen. The Iraqi interior ministry claimed 210 militiamen killed, 600 wounded and 155 captured since the beginning of the operation. British casualties were remarkably light, with only seven soldiers wounded in action. One US Marine Corps lieutenant was killed in fighting in Basra on 21st April, being the only non-Iraqi fatality during Operation Charge of the Knights.

This success resulted in the UK Defence Secretary, Des Browne announcing that the size of the British force would not be reduced when the next brigade rotated in May. This was not the time to draw down troops, just as the Iraqis were on a roll across Basra. So during May, 7 Armoured Brigade rotated with Brigadier Free's troops, and some 4,000 British personnel remained in Iraq over the summer.[91]

Browne visited Basra the following month and was taken out to a café in the centre of the city by Colonel Herbert's Scottish troops. He sat in the café without his body armour and spent an hour talking to local people. It was a dramatic change of fortunes from a year earlier, when only a few hundred metres away the determined Colonel Sanders and his Rifles battlegroup were fighting for their lives.[92]

But Operation Charge of the Knights was not quite finished. The final cordon and search missions took place in al Qurnah, to the north of Basra, in late May and early June. These were then followed by Operation Yarborough in Maysan province. US and Iraqi special forces first launched a series of helicopter raids and Predator missile strikes on JAM bases around al Amarah during late May, before the US MiTT teams moved into the Iraqi Army base outside the city to re-invigorate the 10th Division's 4th Brigade. By the second week of June, the Americans and Iraqis were ready to move into al Amarah, and began a series of cordon and search operations, similar to those carried out in Basra.[93]

According to US military reports, between 19th and 22nd June, a total of 117 weapons caches were captured and more than 63 criminal personalities were arrested. This involved the seizure of over 1,700 mortar rounds, 873 mines, 445 artillery rounds, 347 rocket propelled grenades, 267 rockets, 227 missile launchers, 109 improvised explosive devices, 74 grenades, 27 EFPs, and 14 missiles. As in Basra, the JAM militia in Maysan were decimated as a fighting force. The US IED task force recorded the seizure of some 144 Iranian manufactured EFPs across southern Iraqi during April and May 2008.[94]

Within days of the arrival of the US-backed Iraqi units, they had arrested Adel Muhoder al Maliki, the governor of Maysan province; Abdul Jabar Wahied al Ukeli, the chief of the provincial council; Fadel Neaama, the deputy chief of the security committee; and Abdul Latief Jawad, the head of the health committee. These were all leading members of pro-Sadr parties and over the past five years they had been instrumental in making life very difficult for the British in Maysan province. It was also the first time Maliki had used his security forces to arrest elected political leaders, an exercise he would repeat on a number of later occasions.[95]

"By the time I left Basra [in July] I was walking in the city with General Mohammed Jowad Hameidi [who had replaced Mohan] with bodyguards, but no body armour, eating on the cornice, and you could buy alcohol and hear music," recalled General White-Spunner.

"By then there was huge confidence in Iraqi army."[96]

Operation Charge of the Knights remains highly controversial. Iraqi, American and British participants all portray it in different ways. Competing political narratives were all at play. Prime Minister Maliki was desperate to blame everyone else for his own failings and dumping on the British and to a lesser extent on the Americans proved very convenient. British dealings with the 'criminal militia' during 2007 and early 2008 are a constant theme of Maliki's public and private rants. His subsequent clampdown on political opponents, and use of his security forces to arrest rivals, can clearly be seen in his behaviour during Operation Charge of the Knights. The British were trying to reach an accommodation with his political opponents, and Maliki was determined to prevent this. He conveniently forgot his alliance with Sadr's political movement in 2006 and 2007, and his ban on British troops arresting militia leaders at this time.

For many British and American officers, as well as diplomats, the ability of Maliki and other Iraqi politicians to scheme and switch allegiances with great rapidity was a source of constant amazement. No one was really sure whether Maliki was an ally of the Iranians, in their pay or just unable to grasp what they were doing.

"Maliki's loyalty had always been in question," commented Major General Jonathan Shaw in 2013.

"Given the lack of any Sunni (eg. Saudi and Gulf Arab) support for their fellow Arabs, it is in retrospect no surprise that Maliki should have become increasingly in the pocket of the Iranians, as he now clearly is. When this became starkly obvious was in Operation Charge of the Knights. This showed that Maliki could only control the Iraqi Shia with Iranian help, and that they should both work together to keep Iraqi Shia against a Sunni resurgence. This ties them at the hip. Maliki would never admit this, so dumped on the Brits."[97]

For senior Americans officers who participated in the operation, their main criticism of the British was not the deal with Fartosi, or the supposed delay in committing troops to Operation Charge of the Knights, but the failure to build up the 14th Division. The collapse of the division's 52nd Brigade during the first day of the operation was blamed by Americans on the British not embedding advisors with it. This then meant there was a delay of some two days in getting MiTT teams ready to go back into the city to work with the 14th Division's units.

"We should have been more proactive than we were," said General White-Spunner.

"The Americans thought the way we trained the Iraqis was wrong and they were right. Our model was flawed and they did it much better than us, especially the US Marine Corps. The British approach goes back to this central theme of short termism, of trying to minimise risk whilst retaining political influence. Once we did get permission to deploy teams along the US model it was win-win both politically and tactically; the Iraqis were in the lead, which is what the people in Basra wanted, and we were in support providing those capabilities they lacked. Charge of the Knights started as a muddle. We were caught short by Maliki starting the operation two months early, but once Basra had stabilised, we realised that we had a real opportunity".[98]

British participation in General Mohan's originally proposed May offensive was by no means certain, given the desire of the London Government in the February and early March period to drawn down the force from 4,000 to 2,500 troops. It was not certain that government ministers and senior commanders at PJHQ would have agreed to the embedded MiTT-ing that subsequently proved so effective. General White-Spunner was not confident what would have happened if Operation Charge of the Knights had not created a political dynamic. There was huge pressure to make sure Maliki was not seen to fail.

"Would we have got permission from London [without the crisis created by Maliki's offensive]?" commented White-Spunner.

"The way it happened meant London had no choice to do what we recommended and they did not have time to come up with restrictions [on what we could do]."[99]

There was a media controversy over whether the British had moved fast enough to support the Iraqis, with unflattering comparisons being drawn with the speed at which US forward air controllers and advisor teams arrived in Basra. This is not borne out by the involvement of British artillery, strike aircraft, drones and the Scots Guards battlegroup in the days after the start of the offensive. The main hindrance to both British and American participation in the operation was the stubborn refusal of Maliki to accept any help, from both of his allies, for two days, until the arrival of General Austin. Only then did allied help begin to come on line, with British forces some of the first units to be involved. Once this was under way, embedded international reporters were not allowed to visit British and American units, so as to give the mission an 'Iraqi face', ensuring the British role had limited prominence.

Even the small American force in Basra in the first five days of the operation, some 150 personnel, was not yet having a decisive effect. There were never more than half a dozen air strikes a day up to the 31st March ceasefire, and the Iraqi units that had American advisors made little progress against the militia. The much-trumpeted offensive into the militia stronghold into the

Hayaniyah district on 30th March was little more than a face-saving exercise for Maliki, and the troops pulled out after an hour or so of fighting. Maliki was saved by the intervention of the Shia politicians from Baghdad, who went to Iran to broker a deal with the Iranians and Sadr. This fractured the political and public support for the JAM in Basra, as well as leading the Iranians to pull their key 'special group' operatives from the city and breaking the militia's leadership open. This eventually allowing the Iraqi security forces to advance. Undoubtedly there was some friction between the British and Americans in the opening days of the operation. It was a tense and confusing situation, with high stakes involved, so it is not surprising.

General White-Spunner described General Flynn, the supposed "mentor of the British headquarters" as "a good friend".

"Some Brits felt the US were tipped off about what Maliki was doing, I don't believe that," commented White-Spunner.

"It is clear General Austin, would have rather finished Mosul before Basra."[100]

Unflattering comparisons are also made by some commentators between the British-led Operation Sinbad in 2006-07, and the post cease-fire phases of Operation Charge of the Knights. General White-Spunner was clear the reason why Operation Sinbad failed was that "the Iraqis were not in the lead. Sindad was a good operation and a good concept but it was seen as foreign interference by Iraqis. In 2008 when the Iraqis appeared Sadr's militia left".[101]

Also, for Operation Charge of the Knights, the Iraqis were eventually able to muster elements of seven army brigades and numerous paramilitary units for the cordon and search missions, compared to around 100 soldiers for each of Operation Sinbad's pulses. This increased troop ratio meant Iraqi units could be left to hold areas cleared of militia fighters, to prevent them returning to re-establish their positions.

Despite the controversies, Operation Charge of the Knights meant the British Army could leave Iraq on something of a high. All the battlegroups of 4 Brigade had seen plenty of action and were at the centre of events. There was some satisfaction in seeing the JAM leaders who had caused the British so much trouble over the previous five years effectively run out of town. This was a big difference from the mood after the withdrawal from Basra Palace, and the accommodation with the militia in 2007. Then there was a feeling the British army had not prevailed, particularly after so much effort and many lives had been lost in the offensive operations by 19 and 1 Mechanised Brigades during the winter of 2006 and spring of 2007.

"Most British soldiers are mature enough to know the reason for this", said White-Spunner.

"But there were some units that did feel aggrieved. In February 2008 there was a feeling of 'What are we still doing here now?' The Army was annoyed when I arrived - the boys were asking me 'Why are we here?' Charge of the Knights got them moving again; it was a huge fillip to morale."[102]

Chapter 25

TIME TO GO

During May 2008, the troops of 4 Mechanised Brigade who had participated in Operation Charge of the Knights went home, to be replaced by 7 Armoured Brigade.

Many of the Desert Rats flying out for their last tour of Operation Telic were veterans of the brigade's two previous tours in Iraq. They found Basra to be transformed, with the militia in retreat and the Iraqi army at last taking control of the city. The British mission in Basra was also now very different, with troops spread out across the city working and living alongside the Iraqi army. American troops were also now on the ground in Basra. The British were no longer the dominant military player in southern Iraq, and the clock was clearly ticking before Prime Minister Gordon Brown ordered Operation Telic to be wrapped up.

Many of Brigadier Sandy Storrie's troops had not even expected to go to Iraq at all, instead being warned off to prepare to go to Afghanistan. When defence secretary Des Browne cancelled the troop drawdown in April, rapid re-planning for Iraq had to be organised.[1] Brigadier Storrie was just about to organise his final mission rehearsal exercise, when news of Operation Charge of Knights filtered through, and his staff had to rapidly re-jig the exercise to focus on military transition team (MiTT) operations.

The relief in place, or RIP, saw 7 Brigade's units now moving out across Basra to take over from 4 Brigade's units, which were deployed in more than a dozen Iraqi bases. While the British divisional and brigade headquarters, and a reserve or strike battlegroup remained at the RAF-run airport, the rest of the British troops were broken down into 19 platoon sized MiTT teams, of around 30 or 40 soldiers, and they were paired up with Iraqi battalions or brigade headquarters. These MiTT teams were based across the city in areas where only a year ago militia groups held sway, such as the Hayyaniyah district.[2]

A new headquarters, known as the MiTT Group, co-ordinated this advisory operation with the command group of the Royal Scots Dragoon Guards in charge. There were also three US Army MiTT teams working in the city, supported by Apache attack and Blackhawk transport helicopters at the airport. US special forces were working with Iraqi troops in Maysan province, where a continued drive against the pro-Sadr militia was underway. A battalion of US Army Military Police was sent to Basra to mentor the Iraqi police and 15 senior police officers selected for their loyalty to Prime Minister Maliki were posted to the city from Baghdad to root out pro-Sadr supporters.

According to Brigadier Storrie, progress over the summer was dramatic as the Iraqi 14th Division was declared fit for purpose and "capable of overmatching any insurgent capability it is likely to face". The Iraqi army and police, supported by their British and American mentors, arrested 300 suspected militiamen during the six months of 7 Brigade's tour and seized 2,000 weapons. The brigade was only subject to 14 rocket and mortar attacks, as well as 12 IED attacks. In July 2008 there were 31 violent deaths in Basra, and this dropped to six in November. There were also observable rises in economic activity, said Brigadier Storrie, with Umm Qasr port operating at full capacity from the middle of summer onwards. Crucially, his Brigade suffered no fatalities during its tour.

"The first Op Telic on which this was achieved," he said.[3]

On 1st September, much reduced force protection measures were introduced, because of the diminished threat of a JAM revival. Challenger tanks and Warriors were removed from urban areas, the C-RAM rocket defence battery at the airport was taken off continuous alert and British advisors were given permission to travel in Iraqi vehicles and helicopters. Symbolically, for the first time in four years troops were allowed to patrol in 'soft hats'.[4]

General White-Spunner left Iraq in July, at the end of his tour, commenting that "now was the time for us to go."

"I then went back to London and made myself unpopular," he said.

"There was clearly no point in retreating back to the airport. The Prime Minister came out in July, and I told him we had to be honest with the Americans. We couldn't go back to controlling Basra and could not commit to further MiTTing. We should re-configure the mission as a training mission, not as a ground holding division, and given the numbers, we should come under command of US 10th Mountain Division. I wanted to change the name of the mission and declare an end to Operation Telic. That was unpopular. There was political desire to be seen as a major player with Americans - it would have been very difficult to portray it to the public. You could say there was not a meeting of ideas with me and the Ministry of Defence. They needed to be seen on the world stage."[5]

The result was that the British continued providing MiTTs in Basra province, but also remained in command of Multi-National Division South East, even though British troops were still banned from operating in Maysan and other provinces. It resulted in rather unsatisfactory parallel command arrangements, with rival British and US chains of command operating across southern Iraq. A request for the British advisors to travel with their Iraqi brigade when it was posted to Baghdad was turned down by London. Fortunately the relatively benign security environment meant this command construct was not put under any strain.[6]

Prime Minister Gordon Brown was not yet prepared to break with President George Bush, before he concluded his own negotiations with the Iraqis over the timetable for a withdrawal of US troops. It would have played very badly with the Americans if the British had pulled out their remaining troops from Basra before the US had set its own exit strategy.

The escalating fighting in Afghanistan was making senior officers, such as the Chief of Defence Staff, Air Chief Marshal Sir Jock Stirrup and the head of the army's Land Command, General David Richards, keen to wind up Iraq to allow resources to be switched to Afghanistan. This pressure was already apparent in 7 Brigade's order of battle, with a number of units deploying under strength because companies and platoons had been detached to Afghanistan, bringing force levels a couple of hundred men below the declared 4,300 troop level. The force in Iraq was progressively hollowed out to move resources to Afghanistan, with funding for urgent operational requirement equipment effectively being stopped, as the threat to lives of British soldiers had been reduced significantly.

In October, Washington and Baghdad concluded their negotiations, and announced that US troops were to stay in Iraq until the end of 2011. The mood in the US changed dramatically with the election in November of the Democratic contender, Barack Obama, who was proposing to pull out American troops ahead of President Bush's timeline. The British government had been hedging its bets during this time, with work under way to keep troops in Iraq all through 2009. These plans involved 12 Mechanised Brigade replacing 20 Armoured Brigade in May 2009, on Operation Telic 14. This brigade had spent a tough summer fighting in Afghanistan and the prospect of sending it to Iraq less then a year after it returned home showed the pressure the British Army was under to sustain a war on two fronts.[7]

At the same time, in August, Permanent Joint Headquarters in Northwood set up a planning team to prepare for what became known as Operation Brockdale, the total withdrawal of British forces and their equipment from Iraq.[8] The start date for this operation was still a matter of considerable uncertainty. General White-Spunner's successor, Major General Andy Salmon, arrived in Basra in August not knowing exactly how the next six months would play out. On the ground, 7 Brigade continued with the support to the Iraqi army established by its predecessors until it handed over to 20 Brigade at the end of its tour. The defining moment came in the first week of November with the election of President Obama. Britain was no longer bound by its commitments to President Bush, and Prime Minister Brown decided to accelerate the withdrawal of British troops. The die was cast and Brown travelled to Baghdad in December, to meet with Prime Minister Nouri al Maliki and senior US commanders to confirm the details of the withdrawal. He announced on 16th December that British combat troops would end their operations in Iraq at the end of March and they would be out of the country within two months.[9]

The Americans wanted a 200-strong Royal Navy training team to remain to work with the Iraqi navy and marines, a frigate to participate in off-shore security of Iraq's oil export platforms, and a force protection company of troops was also offered to provide security for the NATO run-military academy in Baghdad, where Britain had some 44 instructors. It was proposed that 400 British personnel would remain in Iraq for at least another year. The clock was now ticking to wrap up Operation Telic. General Salmon was to stay in place to oversee the final withdrawal, as the Joint Force Logistic Headquarters for

Operation Brockdale set up shop at Camp Buerhring in northern Kuwait, under Brigadier Paul Sterns. He began deploying with the Royal Logistic Corps' 4 Logistic Support Regiment and some 1,300 specialist troops, who would pack up all the British equipment in southern Iraq.[10]

The Divisional Internment Facility at the airport was emptied of its last two prisoners, Faisal Attiyah Nassar Khalaf Hussain Al-Saadoon and Khalef Hussain Mufdhi, who were accused of the execution of two Royal Engineers in Zubayr in March 2003. The men were ex-Ba'ath Party officials, so had not been released as a result of the accommodation with Shia militias in 2007. The RAF flew the two prisoners to Baghdad where they were handed over to the Iraqi legal authorities. Lieutenant Kennedy-Lunde, of the Queen's Royal Hussars described the landmark event. "New Year 2009 on Op Telic was rung in with the closure of the dreaded Divisional Internment Facility. The two guests who had spent five years at Hotel COB were sorry to leave the hospitality of the Queen's Royal Hussars, but their spirits were soon lifted when they learned that they were flying to Baghdad in the style and comfort that only the Royal Air Force could provide. We watched as the Hercules took off from the airfield with a sense of relief, knowing that the drudgery of guarding a facility with only two internees was soon to end."[11]

American troops were to stay in Iraqi for at least a further year to continue to train the Iraqis and pack up their equipment. Hence it was agreed that US forces would take over British bases around Basra, to cover the south until their final withdrawal. The US assumed control of coalition military forces across all of southern Iraq on 31st March 2009, after the UK stood down its divisional headquarters in the region, with a symbolic flag-lowering ceremony at Basra airbase.

The standing down of the UK-led Multi-National Division (South East) Headquarters and its merger with the US-led Multi-National Division (Centre) to create the new Multi-National Division (South) left 20 Armoured Brigade under US command for the last month of its tour of duty. Several large facilities, including extensive troop accommodation and a hardened command-post building at the airport, was handed over to the US military for $40 million and its new management also took over catering contracts from the British.[12] There was considerable pressure for the withdrawal to be conducted in what was termed 'good order'. There was a desire to not to upset the Americans by leaving behind abandoned facilities that they could not use, and fuelling a new round of "Brits cut and run" media headlines. Also much of the equipment in Iraq was needed for use in Afghanistan, and had to be recovered in good condition to allow it to be sent to the new operational theatre.

Once General Salmon handed over command to his counter-part from the US 34th Division, the commander of 20 Brigade, Brigadier Tom Beckett began moving his troops to Kuwait in a series of convoys. The Queen's Royal Hussars escort force protected these convoys as they moved south from Basra airport. In Basra city, US troops took over the MiTT facilities and tasks officially ended on

30th April, after a ceremony in which the names of the 179 British personnel, 55 coalition allied soldiers and civilian contractors killed in south-eastern Iraq since 2003 were read aloud. It took 55 minutes to read out all the names of the dead.[13]

The Basra Wall memorial, which recorded names of all the British and coalition dead, was then dismantled brick by brick and shipped to Britain to be rebuilt as a permanent memorial to the sacrifice during Operation Telic. Then all British troops began concentrating at the airport as final preparations for the departure accelerated. The final convoys of 20 Brigade's combat troops left for the border on 11th May, and degenerated into almost a comic moment as three units – the QRH, C Company of 1st Battalion, The Princess of Wales's Royal Regiment (PWRR) and T Squadron of 1st Royal Tank Regiment – all vied to be the last unit to leave Iraq.

Captain Kieron Lyons, the second-in-command of the PWRR's C Company, recounted the incident.

"The officer commanding T Squadron was organising a parade through the border crossing point, complete with pipes, and a Combat Camera Team filming the event as the 'final troops leaving Iraq,' although of course C Company was still firmly inside Iraq," recalled Lyons.

"We finally reached the border at 0130 hours on 11th May to find the commanding officer of the QRH's tactical headquarters group just driving off, trying to be the last troops. Headquarters T Squadron RTR were moving off, having been filmed as the last troops, and then we simply drove through, as the actual last troops. We had the Mastiff commanded by Sergeant Sean Robson MC, being the final vehicle out, with the distinctive blue/yellow/blue of the regimental flag flying from the rear of his vehicle. As I swung into the Kuwaiti border crossing point and watched Sergeant Robson cross the line I made the radio call to the [company commander], Major Giles Francke, "All Tigers now clear of Iraq".[14]

British special forces remained in Baghdad until 30th May when they concluded Operation Crichton, in support of the US Joint Special Operations Command. A pair of RAF Tornados GR4 of 13 Squadron made their symbolic last mission the following day.

In Kuwait, Brigadier Stearns and his logistics troops were still receiving the convoys of cargo from Basra. British-run convoys stopped running at the end of May and US contractors moved the remainder during June and July. Six of the Ministry of Defence's contracted roll-on, roll-off ferries carried 5,000 containers of equipment and more than 500 vehicles back to Britain, with the last ship leaving in August.[15]

Plans for the residual training mission did not go as smoothly as the withdrawal of 20 Brigade from the south. Prime Minister Maliki still held a grudge against the British and he set about derailing the exercise. A Company of the 3rd Battalion, The Yorkshire Regiment had arrived in Baghdad in May to act as the protection force of the Iraqi Military Academy Ar Rustamiyah and the

Senior British Military Representative in Baghdad, Lieutenant-General Chris Brown. They were planning to stay for at least a year, until Maliki decided he did not want an "enduring bilateral relationship" with Britain. General Brown and the Yorkshire soldiers were out of Baghdad by the end of July. The British trainers at the academy remained, as they were under the auspices of NATO.[16]

The 150-strong Royal Navy training team based at Umm Qasr similarly had to beat a retreat in Kuwait for five months, until Maliki relented to American pressure and the British sailors and marines returned. A Royal Navy frigate also returned to take turns with the US Navy to patrol around the off shore Iraqi oil export platforms. In public, the hiatus was blamed on a backlog of business in the Iraqi parliament, but it took intense diplomacy by the US Navy leadership to get Maliki to agree to let the Royal Navy back into Umm Qasr. The US Navy wanted the British to share the burden, and went out on something of a limb to lobby Maliki, according to senior US officers involved in the discussions. The naval training and security mission finished on 22nd May 2011 and the last Royal Navy sailors left Umm Qasr.

While off shore, the Type 23 frigate HMS Iron Duke sailed south leaving the Iraqi navy to secure the Al Basrah Oil Terminal.[17] The final British military personnel left Baghdad in December 2011, just hours before the last US troops pulled out of Iraq. NATO had hoped to keep its training academy operating until 2013, but Maliki decided he wanted to end all foreign military presences, so he terminated the agreement with the alliance. An RAF Hercules flew to Baghdad to pick up the British trainers, ending nearly eight years of British military operations in Iraq.

OPERATION TELIC: LOOKING BACK

The re-building of the Basra Wall at the National Arboretum has provided an opportunity for relatives of the Britain's war dead from the 2003 to 2009 Iraq campaign, former comrades and ordinary members of the public to pay their respects.

Its location in the lush Staffordshire countryside could not be more removed from its original home outside the British divisional headquarters building at Basra airport. It is not a very scientific way to gauge public opinion, but talking to the visitors engenders a range of responses. A group of army veterans from Northern Ireland's Troubles in the 1970s and 1980s were dismissive, branding Iraq as "Blair and Bush's war". "Why did we get involved in that? It was just politics", said one old soldier. A visiting group of young army officers from a nearby military barracks were more reflective. One officer was able to pinpoint several of his comrade's names on the wall and recount how they died in great detail. The experience of serving in Iraq had clearly troubled him.

The reactions at the Basra Wall illustrated how Operation Telic left major scars on the British armed forces, its soldiers, sailors, marines and airmen, as well as their families and Britain's military and political establishments. Much the trauma caused by the Iraq experience was never fully explored or faced immediately after the withdrawal from Iraq because of the immediate escalating of the British role in Afghanistan meant there was little time to dwell on Operation Telic.

As can be expected, the senior British officers who oversaw the capture of Basra and then handed back the city to the Iraqis have very mixed emotions about the experience. A phrase many of them use is that the campaign "did not end on the terms we wanted". I found no senior officers involved in the Iraq campaign were was prepared to say it was a resounding success. All the ones I have spoken to say the campaign could have been conducted in a better way. Graham Binns, who led 7 Armoured Brigade into Iraq and they handed the city back to the Iraqi military in 2007, in his usual blunt Yorkshire fashion, summed it up this way. "If we do it again we should do it differently."

The perception that Iraq did not end in a way that could be easily defined as a British success has seeped into public and political consciousness, creating a suspicion and caution about future foreign military engagements. This culminated in the August 2013 House of Commons vote against military engagement in the Syria crisis.

How Britain senior military officers inter-acted with their political masters during the Iraq campaign clearly left a lot to be desired.

General Brims expressed concerned that many senior officers, including himself, were not forceful enough in communicating the problems that the British Army was facing in Iraq to government ministers.

"Not all of us communicated as well as we could. Did we engage successfully with Secretary of State for Defence [Geoff Hoon]?" recalled Brims. "We gave him huge briefing notes but not pithy points to make recommendations to cabinet."

"The majors and lieutenant colonel of today's British army say that senior officers are too often seen as military toadies of politicians and that we did not dig our feet in," he said. "They may have a point."

He wondered if the politicians of the 2003 to 2005 era really understood what they were told by commanders in Iraq. "The politicians did not understand us." He said. "Nor did the senior civil servants and special advisors understand us. It is all about communications."

The role of senior British officers in the decision to go war and subsequent prosecution of the occupation has largely gone unexamined. They are largely considered figures of little influence, with blame for the failures in Iraq being squarely directed at the "neocon" Americans such as the Coalition Provisional Authority administrator Paul Bremer and hawkish defence secretary Donald Rumsfeld, who directed the war and occupation. Blair, Gordon Brown and other British politicians are blamed for leading Britain into an illegal war, telling lies about weapons of mass destruction, not having a plan to rebuild Iraq, not buying enough equipment to protect the troops and then not looking after wounded soldiers when they returned home. Faceless Ministry of Defence bureaucrats get more blame for not supporting frontline troops by delaying the purchase of life saving equipment, not granting asylum to loyal Iraqi interpreters and treating the families of dead and wounded soldiers as "legal threats to public money" rather that human beings.

It is indeed correct to say that the views of Britain's generals had little sway on Donald Rumsfeld and Bremer's decision to disband the Iraqi army and ban former Ba'ath party officials from government jobs. British generals also played no role in Blair's political calculation to join President George Bush's invasion of Iraq. The leadership of the British armed forces, however, did play a crucial role in deciding how the war would be fought and how the occupation was conducted. In these aspects they were not hapless bystanders to a car crash but key players in Whitehall debates and eventual decision making in the field.

In the wake of the Argentine invasion of the Falklands in 1982, there was as crucial meeting in the House of Commons office of the then Prime Minister Margaret Thatcher. A gaggle of government ministers and senior civilian advisors all seemed to be in total despair and were struggling to come up with any response. The First Sea Lord Admiral Henry Leach arrived in his uniform, radiating confidence and calmly told Thatcher that a task force could sail to recapture the islands in a matter of days and that Britain needed to respond firmly the Argentine invasion to recover its honour and place in the world. The die was cast and the following day, Thatcher told the House of Commons that the fleet was to sail to the South Atlantic.

In the summer and winter of 2002, there was no "Leach Moment" but once it became clear the Prime Minister was minded to get involved in US-led military action, the heads of Britain's armed services were pushing the Blair to send the largest force possible. One officer involved in this process described the mood in this way, "when you get invited to the World Cup Final, everyone wants to be in the team even if you known you are going to get smashed six nil by Germany or Brazil - you just don't want to miss the chance for your ninety minutes of fame and glory, even if you know it is going to end in tears."

The last half of 2002 saw this push to maximise their role being played out by service chiefs and their staffs in London. The Royal Navy were pretty blatant in their push to get a large naval task force included in the operation, against the wishes of the Chief of Joint Operations, Lieutenant General John Reith. While the army's keenness for the Turkey operation to give it a leading role in the northern front ultimately ended in tears and led to the short notice, switch to the southern option. This had serious consequences, including making the logistic preparations sub-optimal, consigning the British Army to a supporting role in the operation, fixing Britain in the so-called "Basra Box" for the subsequent occupation and compressing dangerously preparations for the occupation phase.

Once the final decision was made in January 2003 to begin deploying British forces to Kuwait to execute the 'southern option', it unleashed a head long rush to get 46,000 troops, their equipment and supplies to start line in the desert in time to go to war with the Americans. In less than two months, three brigades, a naval task force, special forces and the air component were all dispatched from their homes bases. This was a major logistic exercise, which just about succeeded. All the major combat units arrived in time, along with their main weapon systems and ammunition but risks had to be taken with large amounts other equipment and supplies. The British commanders and logistic planners played a very poor hand well but shortcomings in the distribution of body armour and chemical weapon protection equipment meant frontline troops did not have enough of these items at the start of the war. Fortunately, the British Army's luck held out and the Iraqis never had chemical weapons and only one soldier was killed because of a lack of body armour. The army's Challenger tanks and Warrior armoured fighting vehicles were up armoured in time so British frontline troops in Basra were largely protected from Iraqi fire and none of these vehicles were penetrated by enemy fire.

During the combat phase of the invasion of Iraq, British commanders and troops achieved almost all of the objectives set for them by their political masters in London and their American allies. British officers and troops were able to secure themselves senior positions across the US-led invasion force, with commanders, staff officers and troop contingents assigned to every part of the US military hierarchy in the Middle East. This was a major feat and was aimed at fulfilling Prime Minister Blair's overarching objective of gaining "influence" within the American military machine. How much influence was actually achieved is open to question and was largely dependent on the relationships between individuals on the ground and the contribution British forces could make to the US war effort. British air, naval, chemical weapons detection and special forces gained high levels of influence on their American counter-parts but relations between the British and US land commands was problematical. The British Army and US Marine Corps had a strong relationship because 1 (UK) Armoured Division was working directing for I Marine Expeditionary Force (I MEF), which highly valued the work the British were doing screening the eastern flank of the Marines drive on Baghdad. The US Army's V Corps had little to do the British Army, so senior British officers had little influence on the decisive battle for Baghdad in April and its chaotic aftermath that ended up defining the course of the occupation. This was the price of the delays in committing to the Turkey option.

Once committed to action, British commanders and troops fought hard and in almost all engagements came off better than their Iraqi opponents. The British battlegroups fought aggressively and they succeeded in their aims of keeping the Iraqis off balance. Throughout the combat phase, there was considerable tension between battlegroup commanding officers, back by their brigade commanders, and the division commander, Major General Robin Brims, over the tempo of the drive into southern Iraq. The frontline commanders wanted to push forward aggressively and exploit the success their troops were having against the poorly armed and disorganised Iraqi resistance. While General Brims and other senior officers were more cautious and thought that the British division could achieve its objectives, as set by I MEF commander, by just being in place outside Basra. Brims was also concerned about preventing his division getting bogged down in street fighting in Basra until the outcome of the US drive on Baghdad was certain. The General had delegated authority to decide on the timing of the final assault on Basra, making this a classic case of the "loneliness of command".

The role of the Royal Air Force and Special Forces in supporting the US-drive on Baghdad and operations in western Iraq are often overlooked by the Basra-centric nature of much media coverage of the war. British officers were involved in planning and directing the air and special forces elements of the campaign. These operations had significant impact on the outcome of the US drive on Baghdad, with the push into western Iraq from Jordan undermining the Iraqi defence of their capital at a critical moment in the battle.

The British Army must also face questions over its planning and preparations for the occupation of southern Iraq. Event leading up to the occupation were out of the army's hands – US policy in Baghdad and British government decisions limiting the size of the garrison – but it was responsible for the preparation, training and deployment of the follow-on British occupation force in Basra. This force was thrown together at a few weeks notice despite the army having six months notice to prepare and 19 Mechanised Brigade ended up being the least prepared, equipped and trained of any of the British brigades to deploy to Basra. Many of the army's problems were self-inflicted. Perhaps the biggest failing was the unwillingness of senior officers to question the line from London limiting the size of the garrison. Commanders in Iraq were told the size of the force they were getting, not asked what they needed to do the job. It was only after Basra was ablaze in August did commanders feel confident to ask for more troops.

Once the occupation got underway, it was more than two years until the army seemed to get a handle on what was really happening in southern Iraq. Much of what it did was templated from its successful operations in Kosovo. Nothing summed up the army's lack of focus on making the operation a success than its attitude to the appointment of commanders and the deployment of headquarters. From the autumn of 2003 ad hoc divisional headquarters were routinely deployed and so generals had to command staff whom they had no experience work with. This was not rectified until 2005. For a key period in 2003 and 2005, British brigadiers were lucky to have three months in command in Basra. The army seemed to think it was more important to give its senior officers vital ticks for their promotion, rather than ensure continuity in command. There has been much criticism of the British Army's six month tour policy and recommendations that senior officers should spend a year in post in operational theatres. In Iraq - at the crucial point in the campaign – only two brigadiers completed six month long command tours in Basra, with six more brigadiers only serving three month long tours.

The centre piece of British strategy in Iraq was the training and mentoring of the country's security forces. Although British Army had run training programmes for foreign armies successfully in many countries, the scale of the task in Iraq was of a magnitude that had never been faced before. While the political and social environment this training effort was being conducted in had also never been faced before. Not surprisingly there was never a considered view of how to approach this problem, even within the British Army, let along across the British government. Largely by default, the military in Basra ended up running the project and it never seemed to get any traction or momentum. Frustration at lack of progress meant that when every new British general and brigadier arrived in Basra, they could not resist the temptation to tinker and turn the training programme on its head. Consistency was lacking. It was not until 2007-2008 that British operations in Basra had any consistency across six month-long brigade tours.

When the political situation changed in mid 2006 and the Iraqis started to re-assert their political independence, the training requirements changed but the British military were slow to move from providers of basic training to military partners, working side by side, with the Iraqis. The debate over embedding advisors crystallised this and show that some senior British policy makers could not adjust to the new environment.

The first eighteen months of the British participation in the occupation of Iraq also saw considerable tension among senior officers over the degree to which UK forces should support their American allies in their growing fight against the Sunni insurgency in central Iraq. There was a feeling among many officers, including several of the senior British Military Representatives in

Baghdad that campaign success could only come if the American effort in the infamous Sunni Triangle was successful. This was ran headlong into the reluctance of Blair's government to become deeper involved in Iraq. The war was being sold to an unhappy public and disgruntled members of parliament as the successful handing over to local Iraqi security forces to allow the rapid withdrawal of British troops. Getting deeper into Iraq and sending troops to fight in Baghdad just ran against this narrative. This tension reared its head first in May when General Sir Mike Jackson pitched for the dispatch of 16 Air Assault Brigade to Baghdad try to put a lid on the looting engulfing the Iraqi capital. The Chief of the General Staff, General Sir Mike Wakler, did not even put the idea to ministers because he knew the result would be negative.

The same tensions came to a head in October 2004 when the Americans requested British help in the assault on the insurgent held town of Fallujah. Blair reluctantly agreed to insistent requests from field commanders in Baghdad and Basra to allow the Black Watch to deploy to central Iraq. The political, media and public back lash meant senior service chiefs were told in no uncertain terms that there would be no more British military excursion outside of the Basra box.

This was the root of the growing divergence of British and US policies in Iraq. The Americans were now aware in no uncertain terms that the British would not be joining them in what they considered the decisive phase of the Iraq war. Low profile special forces and RAF air support continued to be provided to the Americans in Baghdad and this was very welcome but it was not the same as the public presence of large numbers of conventional troops on the ground. The messy British exit from Iraq began here.

On the streets of Basra during 2005 and into 2006, the British Army struggled to come up with a response to growing Iraqi political sovereignty. A line of British generals never really got a handle on how to deal with the increasingly complex and confused political landscape of post-sovereignty Basra and Maysan. The Shia population of southern Iraq were overwhelmingly opposed to the presence of British troops in their country and the elected Iraqi politicians reflected this view with considerable vigour, repeatedly refusing to co-operate with what they termed "occupying forces". Many of southern Iraq's political leaders were in league the militia groups that were starting to take an increasing toll on British troops. When British commanders used their powers of self defence to strike back at the militia, it only fuelled the unpopularity of the British and spurred Iraqi politicians to distance themselves even more from the occupiers.

Into this toxic situation, came the new Iraqi prime minister Nouri al-Maliki who had a visceral hatred of the British because of his grandfather's involvement in resistance to British occupation of Iraq in the 1920s. He was closely allied with many of the anti-British politicians and militia groups in Basra and in 2006 and 2007 he repeatedly used his power of veto over British strike operations against high profile militia commanders. When a British operation raided a police station linked to his militia allies, Maliki went ballistic and threatened to withdrawal all co-operation with British forces in Basra.

Due to this political context any idea that British forces could launch a US-style 'surge' to root out Basra's militia fighters was a non-starter, as a succession of frustrated British generals and brigadiers discovered during 2006 and into the spring of 2007. The reluctance of senior commanders take an aggressive stance against the militia through out this period caused much resentment among British troops in Basra and led to many of these generals being branded appeasers, or worse, for not being willing to strike decisively against those responsible for the deaths of so many British soldiers. The high level linkages between Maliki and the Basra militia was so sensitive that intelligence about it was - and still is - highly sensitive that senior commanders were not allowed to distribute it to their troops. Even today, senior officers who served in Basra are heavily restricted by the Ministry of Defence from making reference to this information in public. This issue has left many senior officers who served in Iraq at this time bitter that they are unable to articulate and justify decisions, such as withdrawing forces from downtown Basra and negotiating with militia commanders, that were controversial at the time and appeared to tarnish the reputation of the British Army.

In such circumstances, the policy of British disengagement from downtown Basra could not come soon enough. The fact that the prime minister of Iraq, who the British were nominally supporting with so much blood and treasure, was then in cahoots with the militia who were waging a war against the British Army in Basra was not a sustainable situation or one that could have been sold to the British public, if it had ever emerged at the time.

At this time, the growing British involvement in Afghanistan led to service chiefs in London to recommend to the Prime Minister that the UK's main military effort be switched to the new theatre of war.

The lack of British appetite to remain in Iraq, however, ran up against the new US 'surge 'policy that was rolled out during the first months of 2007. As a result to maintain good relations with the new American commander in Baghdad, General David Petraeus, the British remained in downtown Basra for another four months and sustained heavy casualties.

A number of American retired generals and commentators with close links to Petraeus, such as Jack Keane, Bing West and Michael Gordon, have characterised the British retreat from Basra as a 'defeat'. Senior British officers who served in Iraq at this time strike back, saying that a surge type 'victory' as eventually achieved by Petraeus in Baghdad was just not possible in Basra. Given that 'enemy' who the British were supposed to 'defeat' were the allies of the Iraqi Prime Minister who the Americans were supporting in Baghdad, a military solution to Basra was a non-starter. This situation was understood by US commanders in Iraq at the time, who were equally frustrated by Maliki's sabotaging of British operations in Basra. General George Casey and his successor, Petraeus, both provided US troops and specialist assets, including attack helicopters, drones, special forces and intelligence operatives, to help the British execute Operations Sinbad and Zenith to pull out of downtown Basra.

The involvement of Maliki's allies in Basra in running death squads and torture prisons and his sabotaging of British attempts to close them down, made many British officers cynical about the Iraqi prime ministers claims that he launched Operation Charge of the Knights in March 2008 to free Basra from the militia's "reign of terror".

How did the British armed forces perform in Operation Telic? Iraq was Britain's longest and most costly overseas campaign since Malaya emergency in the 1950s. It is clear that the government ministers, service chiefs and military bureaucracy did not appreciate how long the campaign would drag on or its intensity. The potential for the Iraq campaign to irrevocably damage the reputation of the British armed forces was also not fully appreciated. The US military had seen how defeat in Vietnam had impacted on their reputation and hence willingness of politicians to fund them, as well as the public appetite to support foreign wars, and were determined to avoid a similar situation as a result of Iraq. The US military leadership turned to Petreaus' surge as a way to avoid 'defeat' in Iraq. Britain's senior military leadership, saw the possibility of success in Afghanistan as the way to compensate for the lack of an apparent success in Iraq. Victory in Afghanistan eventually proved to be just as elusive as success in Iraq.

In the first two years of the occupation there was not really any understanding about how British forces could extract themselves from Iraq. Senior military commanders were working on the basis that they would be pulling their troops out of Iraq in a matter of months. This attitude pervaded all thinking about how the campaign should be conducted, preventing long-term thinking or serious campaign planning being undertaken until into late 2004 or early 2005. As a result, the main drive was to accelerate troops withdrawals, the purchase of better equipment and the building of infra-structure to allow troops to better operate in Iraq's extreme climate was never considered a priority. Deploying to Iraq became an end-in-itself for many officers and their units, as a means to demonstrate their military prowess, get their subordinates promoted, sustain funding of pet projects and attract new recruits. Mission success seemed to be a secondary issue.

The spring of 2006 and the arrival of the new Chief of Defence Staff, Air Chief Marshal Sir Jock Stirrup, seemed to shake the Ministry of Defence out of its lethargy. The British armed forces were placed on a campaign footing, money was found for improved training, new vehicles, hardened buildings, drones and other protective equipment. Reinforcements were sent to temporarily cover the withdrawal of troops from their city centre bases. The rising casualties and the determined resistance being put up by the militia was a real reality check for many in the British Army.

By late 2006 and early 2007, British units in Basra were fighting an all out war with the militia, using innovative tactics and equipment that was a generation ahead of those available only a year before. Drones, attack helicopters, C-RAM anti-rocket weapons, electronic jamming equipment and surveillance balloons were all being used by British battlegroups in a complex urban battlefield, against an elusive and highly skilled enemy.

In 2007 and 2008, the British Army leadership in southern Iraq were forced to innovate and overhaul their operations at pace that was not present in the early phases of the occupation. The British Army changed how it operated but it took a long time for this process to gain any momentum and many soldiers were killed or wounded in the process.

The response to the chaotic start to Operation Charge of the Knights showed the new capabilities of the British Army in action during a high pressure crisis. It eventually proved to be a major turning point, with the British eventually working hand-in-hand with the Americans to rescue Iraqi forces caught in a debacle of Maliki's own making. This operation saw a few hundred British troops using US-style embedded mentoring teams, special forces raids, drone, close air support and artillery fire to operate across Basra in a way that only a year before would have required several thousand British troops. The political context of the operation had been transformed by Maliki's decision to dump his militia allies, but it also showed that the tactics and technology of the British Army of 2008 had progressed dramatically over the previous four years.

During the course of Operation Telic, almost every member of the British Army and Royal Air Force served in Iraq in some capacity or deployed to a neighbouring country to support the operation.

As a result, the participating individuals and units amassed a huge amount of combat experience. Many individuals experienced more violence in the space of a six-month long Operation Telic tour than in the whole of their previous military careers. Many units severed multiple Operation Telic tours. Although the level of casualties was at the time seen as high, the subsequent operation in Afghanistan, made those experienced in Iraq seem modest. The psychological impact of the sustained exposure to combat in Iraq has left a legacy of post-traumatic stress disorder (PTSD) on veterans.

A major issue for many Iraq veterans is the perception, common amongst the public and politicians that the campaign was not a success and that the hardships they endured and fatalities suffered by their units were in vain or have been forgotten.

The Ministry of Defence and the British Army have not helped this issue by their refusal to date to grant battle honours to units that participated in major combat actions during the occupation period. The fierce battles fought by the Princess of Wales's Royal Regiment (PWRR) in Maysan in 2004, the Black Watch in Operation Bracken and the Rifles in Basra Palace in 2007 were all classic actions that warrant recognition.

The ham-fisted legalistic reaction of the Ministry of Defence to court cases brought by human rights activists adds to the feeling that the British government is ashamed of the actions of British troops in Iraq. The fact that British government is even considering a claim for compensation brought by the leader of the Basra militia - a man with the blood of dozens of British troops on his hands - for alleged ill treatment while in British custody cannot be understood by many Iraq veterans.

These legal actions against the British government have only gained momentum and credibility because of failings by the military legal authorities to establish a functioning system of redress for ordinary Iraqis injured or killed by the actions or British troops. A lack of candour and willingness to promptly pay small amounts of compensation just stored up trouble. These disputes are now being played out in the on-going inquiries into Iraq abuse.

There is no doubt that many of these alleged abuses did in fact occur. Baha Mousa was beaten to death in British custody. So-called 'street punishments' occurred in 2003 and 2004. Civilians were wounded by British fire on many occasions. The British Army is sometimes described as a 'blunt instrument' and some of its actions in southern Iraq reinforced this perception. Several incidents can be attributed to sadistic or psychologically damaged individuals loosing control, but the vast majority are the result of the 'friction' that inevitably arises from using military force in close proximity to a civilian population, such as road traffic accidents, collateral damage from heavy weapons or mis-identification of targets during confused fire-fights.

In such circumstances, the use of a legalistic approach to apportion guilt to individual soldiers must be questioned. Other countries have adopted truth commissions as a means of getting participants in conflicts to opening talk about their role as a means of reconciliation. This way the relative's abuse victims could get what is termed 'closure' over what happened to their relatives without the alleged perpetrators being branded 'war criminals'. It would seem to be too late to adopt this approach in Iraq but it might have some validity as the British campaign in Afghanistan draws to a close.

Many British veterans of Iraq are highly critical of the decision by the Blair government in 2006 to switch its main effort from Iraq to Afghanistan, saying it spread Britain's limited military resources too thinly which prevented success in either theatre. How this decision was made is subject of much controversy within the British military and the process is criticised for being based on short term motives, such as the tactical situation in Afghanistan and the need to give the Blair government a political quick fix to the unpopularity of the war in Iraq.

For Britain, the financial, political and human costs of the Iraq war were staggering. By the time last combat troops left in 2009, it had cost the British taxpayer some £8 billion for military operations and £250 for economic, humanitarian and other civilian aid. Iraq crippled the British Prime Minister Tony Blair's political career and effectively drove him out of Westminster politics. The war cost the death of 179 British military personnel and another 222 seriously injured, including many who lost limbs. Some 315 British personnel were admitted to field hospitals after being wounded in action and a further 3,283 suffered non-battle injuries or serious illness in Iraq.

The number of Iraqi casualties caused by British operations is far harder to gauge due to the chaotic nature of medical services in the country. It is possible to piece together some figures from a variety of sources. From the kills claimed by British units across Iraq during March and April, it would appear that somewhere between 1,000 and 2,000 Iraqi soldiers and para-military militia fighters must have lost their lives and hundreds more were wounded. Civilian casualties during the first Battle for Basra in 2003 are hard to estimate but the respected non-government organisation, Human Rights Watch, presented credible evidence that several dozen civilians were injured and handful killed in British artillery fire and US air strikes in and around Basra.

During the occupation period it is equally difficult to track Iraqi casualties. In answer to a British parliamentary question, the defence minister Adam Ingram reported that 200 "enemy combatants" were killed and another 80 injured by British troops between 1st May 2003 and 26th November 2004. A further 17 combatants died and another 22 were injured in other incidents, for example being killed when roadside bombs they were planting prematurely detonated. Ingram then said some 144 civilians were killed and 192 injured during incidents involving British troops, which included people caught in cross fire or run over in accidents involving British vehicles.

During Operation Charge of the Knights in 2008, police and health workers in Basra reported said at least 236 people were killed and 600 wounded in the fighting, with at least 50 civilians among the dead.

These two periods saw the heaviest fighting of the occupation but there was also a steady drip of Iraqi casualties between 2004 and 2008. On top of these figures must be added the insurgents killed in central Iraq by Special Forces raids, RAF Tornado GR4 air strikes and drone engagements controlled by RAF personnel. The SAS are alone attributed with killing some 350 to 400 insurgents during their operations in and around Baghdad.

This results in a cumulative total of Iraqi militia and civilian casualties than can be attributed to British forces during the occupation that must run towards or even exceed 2,000, with at least as many wounded.

For the old soldiers at the Basra Wall and many other critics of Britain's involvement in the Iraq war, this cost was clearly not worthwhile. From even before the start of the war, their voice has been dominant one in British public discussions about the conflict. A decade on few British politicians and media commentators are now prepared to support the Iraq war, even through both the country's two major political parties supported the war and 412 members of parliament voted in favour in the 18th March 2003 vote authorising military action.

When the final British troops left Iraq in 2009, British political, economic and military engagement with the country came to an abrupt end as the London government switched all its focus to Afghanistan. This reinforced the view among Iraq veterans that their efforts and the sacrifices were being forgotten. Many also saw this as being short sighted and not in Britain's long term political, economic and military interests in the Middle East. Iraq's oil wealth, with its linkages to important Gulf allies and strategic position near to Iran all offered long term benefits to the Britain. Iraq had the potential to generate a return on all the investment Britain made in it, whereas Afghanistan in effect was nothing more than a drain on money, resources and lives, say military critics. What ever the political controversy over the decision of Tony Blair's decision to back the US invasion of Iraq, the rush to disengagement from the country in the end undermined Britain's long term interests and locked directed Britain up a blind alley in Afghanistan.

General Brims and Binns, who played such a decisive role in the occupation of Basra in 2003, by quirks of fate turned out to have second careers working in Iraq after their retirement from the British Army. Their continued engagement in Iraq, is unlike many of their military contemporaries, government officials or journalists who found themselves moving rapidly on to the war in Afghanistan.

After retiring from the army in 2008, Brims went on to be vice chancellor of Irbil university in Kurdistan. He is up beat about the country's future prospects. "Iraq has changed a lot," Brims said in 2012. "At long last the oil is flowing and they have a huge amount of money. Whether everyone will stop squabbling over how to share it out is another matter. Iraq could be prosperous, definitely a good opportunity, it has got wealth."

"[Britain's military engagement in] Iraq ended in a way we did not wish, but our presence was not wholly bad," he said . "It ended when the Iraqis took control, that was a good thing."

The former commander of the Desert Rats, Binns, went on to be chief executive of Aegis Defence Services and regularly travelling to Basra to oversee security in the Rumaylah Oilfield outside the city. He had no doubt that the citizens of Basra are better off than they were under Saddam Hussein's rule. "The removal of Saddam was worthwhile," Binns said. "Basra now is a vibrant, energetic, dirty, chaotic, Middle East city, where people are making a life for themselves. There is a huge amount of development in oil fields. Had we been able to put Iraqis in charge of process in charge more speedily this would have happened sooner."

In October 2014, Philip Hammond, the then defence secretary, told the House of Commons Defence Committee that the "public appetite for expeditionary warfare is pretty low, based on the experience of 10 years in Iraq and Afghanistan. It would be realistic of me to say that I would not expect, except in the most extreme circumstances, a manifestation of great appetite for plunging into a prolonged period of expeditionary warfare any time soon."

Mr Hammond compared Britain's attitude with that of the US public following the Vietnam War, when America undertook a "clear disengagement" from international affairs.

The Vietnam comparison is also been drawn by many senior officers who served in Iraq, particular in reference to public, media and political concern about casualties.

"This is a problem for us," commented Robin Brims, who led 1 (UK) Armoured Division into Basra in 2003. "Force protection takes over the mission. We are now casualty averse, like the Americans were in Bosnia. This is a problem for the next generation of military commanders. How do we persuade politicians to have the political stamina if we are prepared to use the military?"

The Iraq campaign has also seen an undermining of the concept of mission command within the British military. This relied on commanders on the ground being given general instructions and then left to work out for themselves what to do. It had been a bed rock of the British Army's way of war for many generations but the inability of army to craft a consistent strategy in Iraq has led to the Ministry of Defence in London, via the Permanent Joint Headquarters, to draw back more responsibility and control from field commanders. The proliferation of video conferencing, drone imagery and email communications have given ministers and senior officers in London the ability to interfere in minor tactical decisions. This micro-management has been evident in Afghanistan, Libya and in Indian Ocean counter piracy operations in recent years. The moves by Mr Hammond and his successor to prevent senior military officers to talk in public or to the media without his personal permission is a further indication that mission command has fallen out of fashion in the British military.

The aftermath of the Iraq campaign, however, suggests the British government and military establishment is not good at learning lessons from the experience. The British Army has carried out four studies into its performance during the war. All of them were classified secret to ensure they would never be published. The first two, which covered the invasion period and first two years of the occupation period, were leaked to the media and were used in research for this book. A third was de-classified under the Freedom of Information Act only after a long campaign by a newspaper. The final and most comprehensive study - based on a major exercise of hundreds of participants of all ranks and the complication of thousands of documents, led by a senior brigadier - still remains classified secret and it will probably never be made public.

Senior Ministry of Defence officials made deliberate attempts to prevent serving and retired members of the armed forces and ministry civilian officials speaking to me during the preparation of this book. The Secretary of State for Defence Philip Hammond personally banned me from interviewing senior serving officers.

These are hardly the action of an institution trying to learn from its experiences. The continued delay in publishing the Chilcot Inquiry adds to the feeling that British government and military establishment just wants to forget the Iraq campaign. I hope this book goes some to the way to keeping interest in Operation Telic alive and informs future generations so the mistakes of the past are not repeated.

OPERATION TELIC COMMANDERS, HEADQUARTERS AND MAJOR UNITS 2003 TO 2009

(detailed orders of battle, down to company group level for each Op Telic tour are posted and downloadable at www.operationtelic.co.uk)

Doha, Qatar
UK National Contingent
Commander Air Marshal Brian Burridge (Jan to May 2003)
Chief of Staff Brig Wall (Jan to Apr 2003)/Brig Barney White-Spunner (May to June 2003)

Baghdad
Senior British Military Representative/Deputy Commander Multi-National Force, Iraq
Maj Gen Freddie Viggers (May to Nov 2003)
Lt Gen Andrew Figgures (Dec 2003 to Apr 2004)
Lt Gen John McColl (May to Sept 2004)
Lt Gen John Kiszely (Oct 2004 to Mar 2005)
Lt Gen Robin Brims (Apr to Sept 2005)
Lt Gen Nick Houghton (Oct 2005 to Feb 2006)
Lt Gen Rob Fry RM (Mar to Aug 2006)
Lt Gen Graeme Lamb (Sept 2006 to June 2007)
Lt Gen William Rollo (Jul 2007 to Feb 2008)
Lt Gen John Cooper (Mar 2008 to Feb 2009)
Lt Gen Chris Brown (Mar to Jul 2009)

Strategic Forces
US CJSOTF-West (January to Jun 2003) (Jordan/Western Iraq)
Deputy Commander, Brigadier Adrian Bradshaw
Task Group HQ, 22 SAS Regiment
B and D Squadrons, 22 SAS Regiment
M Squadron, Special Boat Service
45 Commando RM
II Squadron, Royal Air Force Regiment
7 Squadron, RAF (Chinook HC.2 helicopters)
657 Squadron, Army Air Corps (Lynx AH.7 helicopters)
3 Squadron, RAF (Harrier GR.7 strike jets)
39 Squadron, RAF (Canberra PR.9 reconnaissance aircraft)
Detachment Joint NBC Regiment
264 Signals Squadron, Royal Signals

US Joint Special Operations Command (Baghdad/Balad) (May 2003 to May 2009)
Squadron, *22 SAS Regiment* on four to six month rotations
Detachments *33 and 230 Squadrons RAF* (Puma HC.1 helicopters)
Company Group, *1st Battalion, The Parachute Regiment* (Special Forces Support Group) on six month rotations
264 Signals Squadron, Royal Signals
Airborne ISTAR support
Nimrod MR2 (*120, 206, 201 Squadrons*, on rotation)
Predator/Reaper UAV (*1115 Flight* at Creech AFB Nevada and at Balad AB)
Britten Norman Defender AL.1 (*651 Squadron, Army Air Corps*)
Diamond DA42 MPP (RAF)

Combat Forces Deployed into Southern Iraq 2003 to 2009
Op Telic 1 (Jan to Jul 2003)
(46,000 personnel at peak in April 2003)
Headquarters 1 (UK) Armoured Division
(26,000 in division)
Commander Maj Gen Robin Brims (Jan to May 2003)
Maj Gen Peter Wall (May to July 2003)

7 Armoured Brigade
Commander Brig Graham Binns
Battlegroups
Royal Scots Dragoon Guards (Scots DGs)
2nd Royal Tank Regiment (2 RTR)
1st Battalion, Royal Regiment of Fusiliers (1 RRF)
1st Battalion, Black Watch (1 BW)

16 Air Assault Brigade
Commander Brig Jacko Page
Battlegroups
2nd Battalion, Parachute Regiment (2 PARA)
3rd Battalion, Parachute Regiment (3 PARA)
1st Battalion, Royal Irish Regiment (1 R IRISH)
3 Regiment Army Air Corps (3 Regt AAC)

3 Commando Brigade RM
Commander Brig Jim Dutton RM
Battlegroups
40 Commando RM
42 Commando RM
15th Marine Expeditionary Unit (24 MEU) (US Marine Corps)

102 Logistics Brigade (Brigadier Shaun Cowan)

Op Telic 2 (Jul to Nov 2003)
(9,500 troops)
Headquarters Multi-National Division (South East)
Commander Maj Gen Grame Lamb
(July 2003 to May 2009 logistic support was provided via a tri-service National Support Component headquarters at Shaibah Logistic Base/Umm Qasr/ Basra Airport)

19 Mechanised Brigade
Commander Brig Bill Moore
Ground Holding Battlegroups
1st Battalion, King's Own Scottish Borders Regiment (1 KOSB)(TF Maysan)
1st Battalion, King's Regiment (1 KINGS)
1st Battalion, Queen's Lancashire Regiment (1 QLR)
40 Regiment Royal Artillery
Surge/Reinforcement Battlegroups
1st Battalion, Royal Green Jackets (1 RGJ)
2nd Battalion, Light Infantry (2 LI)

Op Telic 3 (Dec 2003 to May 2004)
(8,500 troops)
Headquarters Multi-National Division (South East)
Commander Maj Gen Andrew Stewart
20 Armoured Brigade
Commanders Brig David Rutherford-Jones/Nick Carter
Ground Holding Battlegroups
1st Battalion, Light Infantry (1 LI) (TF Maysan)
1st Battalion, Royal Regiment of Wales (1 RRW)
Queen's Royal Hussars
26 Regiment Royal Artillery
Surge/Reinforcement Battlegroups
2nd Battalion, Parachute Regiment (2 PARA)
1st Battalion, Argyll and Sutherland Highlanders (1 A&SH)

Op Telic 4 (May to Nov 2004)
(8,900 troops)
Headquarters Multi-National Division (South East)
Commander Maj Gen William Rollo
1 Mechanised Brigade
Commander Brig Andrew Kennett
Ground Holding Battlegroups
1st Battalion, Princess of Wales's Royal Regiment (1 PWRR) (TF Maysan)
1st Battalion, Cheshire Regiment (1 Cheshire)
1st Battalion, Royal Welch Fusiliers (1 RWF)
1st Royal Horse Artillery
Surge/Reinforcement Battlegroups
40 Commando RM/1st Battalion, Royal Highland Fusiliers (1 RHF)
1st Battalion, Black Watch (1 BW)

Op Telic 5 (Nov 2004 to Apr 2005)
(8,000 troops)
Headquarters Multi-National Division (South East)
Commander Maj Gen Jonathon Riley
4 Mechanised Brigade
Commanders Brig Paul Gibson/Chris Deverell
Ground Holding Battlegroups
1st Battalion, Welsh Guards (1 WG) (TF Maysan)
1st Battalion, The Duke of Wellington's Regiment (1 DWR)
Royal Dragoon Guards (RDG)
4 Regiment Royal Artillery
Surge/Reinforcement/Battlegroups
1st Battalion, The Scots Guards
2nd Battalion, Princess of Wales's Royal Regiment (2 PWRR)
1st Battalion, Royal Highland Fusiliers (1 RHF)
1st Queen's Dragoon Guards (QDG)

Op Telic 6 (May to Oct 2005)
(8,000 troops)
Headquarters Multi-National Division (South East)
Commander Maj Gen Jim Dutton RM
12 Mechanised Brigade
Commanders Brig Chris Hughes/John Lorimer
Ground Holding Battlegroups
1st Battalion, Royal Irish Regiment (1 R IRISH)
1st Battalion, Staffordshire Regiment (1 STAFFS) (TF Maysan)
1st Battalion, Coldstream Guards (1 CLD GUARDS)
19 Regiment Royal Artillery
Surge/Reinforcement/Reserve/Rear Ops Battlegroups
1st Battalion, Royal Regiment of Wales (1 RRW)
Light Dragoons (LD)
King's Royal Hussars (KRH)

Op Telic 7 (Nov 2005 to Apr 2006)
(8,000 troops)
Headquarters Multi-National Division (South East)
Commander Maj Gen John Cooper
7 Armoured Brigade
Commander Brig Patrick Marriott
Ground Holding Battlegroups
1st Battalion, Highlanders (1 Highlanders)
Royal Scots Dragoon Guards (Scots DGs) (TF Maysan)
3rd Royal Horse Artillery
Reserve/Rear Ops Battlegroups
1st Battalion, King's Own Royal Border Regiment (1 KORBR)
1st Battalion, Royal Regiment of Fusiliers (1 RRF)
9/12th Royal Lancers
2nd Battalion, Parachute Regiment (2 PARA)

Op Telic 8 (May to Oct 2006)
(7,000 troops)
Headquarters Multi-National Division (South East)
Commander Maj Gen Richard Shirreff
20 Armoured Brigade
Commander Brig James Everard
1st Battalion, Light Infantry (1 LI)
2nd Battalion, Royal Anglian Regiment (2 R ANGLIAN)
1st Battalion, Devonshire and Dorset Light Infantry (1 DDLI)
1st Battalion, The Princess of Wales's Royal Regiment (1 PWRR)
Queen's Royal Hussars (QRH) (TF Maysan)
Surge/Reinforcement/Reserve/Rear Ops Battlegroups
12 Regiment Royal Artillery
1st Queen's Dragoon Guards (QDG)
2nd Battalion, Royal Regiment of Fusiliers (2 RRF)
1st Battalion, Grenadier Guards (1 GN GUARDS)

Op Telic 9 (Nov 2006 to May 2007)
(7,100 troops)
Headquarters Multi-National Division (South East)
Commander Maj Gen Jonathan Shaw
19 Light Brigade
Commander Brig Tim Evans
Ground Holding Battlegroups
2nd Battalion, Duke of Lancaster's Regiment (2 LANCS)
1st Battalion, Staffordshire Regiment (1 STAFFS)
1st Battalion, Royal Green Jackets (1 RGJ)/2nd Battalion, The Rifles (2 Rifles)
1st Battalion, The Yorkshire Regiment (1 YORKS)
Reserve/Rear Ops Battlegroups
Queen's Royal Lancers (QRL) (TF Maysan)
40 Regiment Royal Artillery

Op Telic 10 (June to Dec 2007)
(5,500 troops)
Headquarters Multi-National Division (South East)
Commander Maj Gen Graham Binns
1 Mechanised Brigade
Commander Brig James Bashall
Ground Holding Battlegroups
4th Battalion, The Rifles (2 Rifles)
Reserve/Rear Ops Battlegroups
1st Battalion, Irish Guards (1 I GUARDS)
2nd Battalion, Royal Welch Regiment (2 RWR)
1st Royal Horse Artillery
King's Royal Hussars (KRH) *(TF Maysan)*

Operation Telic 11 (Dec 2007 to May 2008)
(5000 troops)
Headquarters Multi-National Division (South East)
Commander Maj Gen Barney White-Spunner
4 Mechanised Brigade
Commander Brig Julian Free
Strike/Manoeuvre Battlegroups
1st Battalion, The Scots Guards (1 SG)
2nd Battalion, Duke of Lancaster's Regiment (2 LANCS)
Reserve/Rear Ops Battlegroups
1st Battalion, Royal Regiment of Scotland (1 SCOTS)
1st Battalion, The Mercian Regiment (1 Mercian)

Operation Telic 12 (May to Dec 2008)
(4000 troops)
Headquarters Multi-National Division (South East)
Commander Maj Gen Andy Salmon
7 Armoured Brigade
Commander Brig Sandy Storrie
Battlegroups
2nd Battalion, Royal Anglian Regiment (2 R ANGLIAN)
4th Battalion, Royal Regiment of Scotland (4 SCOTS)
1st Battalion, Royal Regiment of Fusiliers (1 RRF)
3rd Royal Horse Artillery

Op Telic 13 (Jan to May 2009)
(4,000 troops)
Headquarters Multi-National Division (South East)
Commander Maj Gen Andy Salmon
20 Armoured Brigade
Commander Brig Tom Beckett
Battlegroups
1st Battalion, The Yorkshire Regiment (1 YORKS)
1st Battalion, The Princess of Wales's Royal Regiment (1 PWRR)
5th Battalion, The Rifles (5 RIFLES)
26 Regiment Royal Artillery

Operation Brockdale (December 2008-August 2009)
Joint Force Logistic Headquarters
Camp Buerhring in northern Kuwait
Commander Brig Paul Sterns
4 Logistic Support Regiment RLC (1,300 specialist troops)

UK Air and Naval Deployments, Operation Telic 1
Total 206 aircraft and helicopters
(all squadrons/units RAF except where marked)

Incirlik, Turkey: 4 Jaguar GR3, 1 VC10 (10/101 Sqn)
Akrotiri, Cyprus: 1 VC10 medivac, 8 C130K/J (LTW)
Iraq, Jordan/Western Iraq: 8 Harrier GR7 (3 Sqn), 2 Canberra PR9 (39 Sqn), 8 Chinook (7 Sqn), 6 x Lynx AH.7 (657 Sqn AAC)
Kuwait, Ali al Salem: 18 Tornado GR4 (II Sqn, 9 Sqn, 31 Sqn, 617 Sqn)
Kuwait, Ahmed al Jaber: 12 Harrier GR7 (IV Sqn)
Kuwait/Iraq (1 UK Armd Div); 4 Pheonix UAV launcher and 29 air vehicles (32 Regt RA)
Saudi Arabian Prince Sultan AB: 14 Tornado F3 (43, 111 Sqns) 2 HS125 (32 Sqn), 4 E3D AWACS (8/23 Sqn), 4 Nimrod MR2 120/201/206 Sqn), 7 VC10 (10/101 Sqn), 1 Nimrod R1 (51 Sqn)
Bahrain, Muharraq: 4 Tristar (216 sqn)
Qatar, Al Udeid: 12 Tornado GR4 (II Sqn, 12 Sqn, 617 Sqn) 1 HS125 (32 Sqn)
UAE: 4 C130K/J (LTW)
Oman, Seeb: 2 Nimrod MR2 (120/201/206 Sqn)
Kuwait, Ali al Salem and Iraq FOB (Joint Helicopter Force): 6 Chinook (18 Sqn), 7 Puma (33 Sqn), 12 Lynx AH.7/9 and 10 Gazelles AH.1 (3 Regt AAC – Attached 16 Air Assault Brigade)
HMS Ocean (Commando Helicopter Force): 10 Sea King HC.4(845 NAS), 6 Lynx AH.7 and 6 Gazelle AH.1 (847 NAS)
HMS Ark Royal: 5 Chinook (18 Sqn - Joint Helicopter Force), 4 Sea King AEW.7 (849 NAS)
RFA Fort Victoria: 4 Merlin HMA.1 (814 NAS)
RFA Argus, RFA Austin and RFA Rosalie: 6 Sea King HAS.6 (820 NAS) in hack role.MS Liverpool, HMS Edinburgh, HMS York, MS Marlborough HMS Richmond, HMSChatham (2 x Lynx), HMS Cardiff: Total 9 Lynx HAS3/HMA8 (all 815 NAS)

UK Maritime Component
Commander - Rear Admiral David Snelson (succeeded by Major General Tony Milton 16 April 2003)

Commander Amphibious Task Group - Commodore Jamie Miller
HMS Ark Royal (flag ship/helicopter carrier)
HMS Ocean (helicopter carrier)
HMS Edinburgh (Type 42 destroyer)
HMS Liverpool (Type 42 destroyer)
HMS York (Type 42 Destroyer)
HMS Chatham (Type 22 frigate)
HMS Richmond (Type 23 frigate)
HMS Marlborough (Type 23 frigate)
HMS Splendid (Trafalgar class Tomahawk cruise missile firing submarine)
HMS Turbulent (Trafalgar class Tomahawk cruise missile firing submarine)

Mine Counter Measures Force
RFA Sir Bedivere (support and repair vessel)
HMS Bangor
HMS Blyth
HMS Brocklesby
HMS Grimsby
HMS Ledbury
HMS Sandown
HMS Shoreham
HMS Ramsey
HMS Roebuck (survey vessel)

Support vessels of the Royal Fleet Auxiliary
RFA Sir Galahad
RFA Sir Percivale
RFA Sir Tristram
RFA Argus
RFA Bayleaf
RFA Brambleleaf
RFA Orangeleaf
RFA Grey Rover
RFA Fort Austin
RFA Fort Rosalie
RFA Fort Victoria
RFA Diligence
RFA Sea Crusader

Strategic Ro-Ro Vessels
MV Hurst Point
MV Eddystone
MV Longstone
MV Beachy Head
MV Hartland Point
MV Anvil Point

May 2003-2009 UK Air Component
UK Detachment at US-run Combined Air Operations Centre (Prince Sultan Airbase, Saudi Arabia/Al Udeid Airbase, Qatar)
Tornado Detachment (TORDET): Ali Al Salem Airbase, Kuwait/Al Udeid Airbase, Qatar) (8 x Tornado GR4, with squadrons rotating every two months)
Hercules Detachment: Basra Airport, Iraq/Al Udeid Airbase, Qatar (5-6 Hercules, with squadrons rotating every two months)
VC-10 Detachment: Muharraq International Airport, Bahrain/Al Udeid Airbase, Qatar (2 x VC-10 with squadrons rotating every two months)
Nimrod Detachment: Basra Airport, Iraq/Seeb International Airport, Oman (2-4 Nirmod MR2, with squadrons rotating every two months)
32 (The Royal) Squadron Detachment: Muharraq International Airport, Bahrain/ Al Udeid Airbase, Qatar (BAe-125 and BAe 146)
Squadrons and crews rotated back to home bases every two months)

Within southern Iraq, Royal Navy, RAF and Army Air Corps helicopters were assigned to the tri-service Joint Helicopter Force (Iraq) organisation at Basra Airport, which was under the operational command of the UK-run divisional headquarters.

May 2003 to 2010 UK Maritime Component
UK Detachment at US Central Command Naval Component Headquarters, Manama, Bahrain
UK provided command of CTF 158.1 in northern Arabian Gulf for four months at a time, in rotation with US and Australia.
Force elements provided included a Type 22 or 23 frigate on a near continuous basis, as well as boarding parties from Fleet Protection Group RM and 539 Assault Squadron RM. Occasionally a Royal Fleet Auxiliary vessel was present in northern Arabian Gulf support CTF 158.1
Royal Navy and Royal Marines personnel provided Training Team at Umm Qasr throughout Operation Telic. A force protection company of Royal Marines was provided at Umm Qasr between May 2009 and the end of the training mission in May 2011.

WITH THANKS TO

This book has only been possible thanks to the help of scores of members of the British and allied armed forces who have recounted their experiences or provided assistance to the author on his numerous visits to Iraq and neighbouring countries. Many are named below but many others asked to remain anonymous, to avoid falling victim of the Ministry of Defence's draconian rules preventing serving members of the armed forces contributing to publication such as this. They know who they are - many thanks to you all.

Many retired British military personnel who served in Iraq or had a detailed knowledge of Operation Telic provided invaluable assistance, providing interviews, contacts and commenting on my drafts. They include Dick Applegate, Ben Barry, Brian Burridge, Graham Binns, David Eadie, and Nicholas Mercer, Jonathon Riley, Jonathan Shaw, Glenn Torpy and Barney White-Spunner. A particular thank you must go to Robin Brims whose insights and wisdom at key points were vital during the writing of this book.

Journalistic colleagues Robert Fox, Andrew Gilligan and Thomas Harding were instrumental in providing informative insights and contacts with many interesting people involved in Operation Telic. A big thank you to all of you.

My colleagues at the now defunct Centre for Defence and International Security Studies (CDISS) at Lancaster University, Professor Martin Edmonds, Pauline Elliott and Richard Connaughton provided excellent advice and support during the early work in this study.

The final production was ably assisted by Keith Simpson and the crew at Pageast in Lancaster who designed my book cover, Bonnie Craig did stirling work on the layout and John Freeman generated the book's website, www.operationtelic.co.uk.

Air Vice Marshal Andrew Vallance and his deputy at the Defence Advisory-Notice Secretariat also provide invaluable advice and assistance to ensure I did not give away any secret information that might put British forces at risk in future conflicts.

In the end, any errors of omissions are entirely my responsibility.

Regimental Headquarters and Museums

A large part of this work has involved drawing on the journals and other material held by regimental museums of the British Army. Universally, they were keen to help and honour the work of the comrades during Operation Telic. These include: Cheshire Regiment, Sue Weston; Duke of Lancaster's Regiment and Lancashire Infantry Museum, Jane Davies and Roger Goodwin; Grenadier Guards RHQ; Irish Guards, Capt R.J. Wilmont; King's Own Museum, Peter Donnolly; King's Own Scottish Borders RHQ; King's Regiment, Capt MR Hunt; King's Royal Hussars, Maj Boone; Lancashire Country Museum Service, Dr Stephen Bull; The Highlanders, Maj MRM Gibson; The Light Infantry; Maj Hugo White, Maj TW Stipling; Mercian Regiment, Jim Massie, Helen Rayson; Queen's Royal Hussars, Maj David Innes-Lumesden; Queen's Royal Lancers, Lt Col Joe Adkin; Princess of Wales's Royal Regiment; Maj Steve Bream; The Rifles, Danielle Goodchild; Royal Anglian Regiment, Capt Tom Green; Royal

Dragoon Guards, Mark Barrowby; Royal Irish Regiment, Regimental Clerk; 9th/12th Royal Lancers, Maj PA Watkins; Royal Marines, Captain J Hillier, LCpl Lee Whitfield; Royal Regiment of Fusiliers, Capt ARG Harris, Fusilier Mackintosh; Royal Regiment of Scotland, Janine Cashmore; Royal Scots Dragoon Guards, Capt Springthorpe; Royal Tank Regiment, Angie King; Royal Welsh, Col PL Gooderson; Royal Welsch Fusiliers, Roger Owen; Staffordshire Regiment, Jeff Elson; Welsh Guards, Maj Keith Oultram; Corporate and Forces Publishing, Ron Pearson and Joanna Barnes.

During my travels to Iraq and around the Middle East, the following people provided assistance and insights. Many thanks for your understanding.

2003 Invasion Period

Ahmed Al Jaber AB: LTC Jennifer Cassidy USAF PAO, LTC Tom Bergy, 524th Fighter Squadron, LTC 'Skeeter' Gus Kohntopp, 190th FS, Boise, Idaho ANG

Ali Al Salem AB: PAO Capt John Sheets, Tsgt Neely; LTC Gary Fabricius, 15th Expeditionary Reconnaissance Squadron.

Camp Doha ACCC: Major General Dan Leaf, Major Dan Snyder, Executive Officer

Ahmed al Jaber AB: Major TV Johnson, 3 MAW PAO, LTC Ed Hebert 3 MAW staff, Major Mark Butler VMA 214, Major Bruce Laughlin 3 MAW staff, Major Jim Wolfe, 3 MAW ground liaison officer;

London DCC(RAF): WCO Ian Tofts,

UK PIC Qatar: Simon Wren, Gp Captain Al Lockwood, Maj Will MacKinnley;

RAF PIC Kuwait: Spokesman Gp Captain John Fynes, WCO Mike Cairns and Steve Dargan, Paul Bernard

Ali Al Salem AB: Gp Captain Andy Pulford, JHF, WCO Paul Lyall, 33 Sqn, WCO David Prowse, WCO Andy Lawless, Sqn Steve Carr, 18 (Bomber) Squadron, WCO Dave Robertson, 617 Sqn

Ahmed Al Jaber AB; Gp Captain Mike Harwood, Flt Lt John Gunther.

Royal Marines PIC Kuwait, Maj Ray Tonner,

Royal Navy – Bahrain and HMS Ark Royal: Cdr Nick Chatwin, Lt Cdr Steve Tatam, Lt Cdr Ken Sprowlres RNR, Lt Cdr 'Mac' Mackenzie, 849 Naval Air Squadron.

2003 to 2009 Occupation Period

Basra CPA: Dominic D'Angio, press spokesman, Political Director, CPA South Robert Wilson,

MND(SE): Lt Cdr Richard Whalley, Div media advisor, Sgt Jon Priestley, RAF 5131 Sqn, Gp Cpt Tony Gunby, RAF Deployed Operation Base Commander, Sqn Ldr Bob Pedard, RAF Basra Air Ops, Sqn Ldr Gary Lane, JHF(I), Major Sid Seymour, OC HQ Coy 1 KOSB,

Lt Cdr Charlie Mahoney, DCC(RN), Major Charlie Mayo LD Spokesman, Nigel Sargeant Div Media Advisor, Lt Cdt Tim Watkins, Det Commander 846 NAS Lt Alastair Jenkins, RNTT, Lt Col Andrew Cuthbert, CO QRH, Cdr Tony Ratakan, CO HMS Norfolk, Lt Tim Olivey and Lt Jack Gibbs, 815 NAS.

RAF Air Staff: CAS ACM Sir Glenn Torpy, WCO Jon Agar,

Al Udeid AB, Qatar: UK PIO Flt Lt Ian Heath, UK PIO, Sqn Ldr Andy Arnold and WO Sam McMillan 31 Squadron, C130 Det Command, Sqn Ldr Rich

Waller, XXIV Sqn, Wing Commander Nick Laird, 230 Sqn, Air Commodore Clive Bairsto, AOC 83 EAG and UK Air Component Commander Op Telic and Op Herrick . Air Commodore Bryan Collins, NATO/ISAF LO TO CAOC, WCO Alisa Gough RAF Strike Command DCC, WCO Nick Laird MOD, Sqn Ldr Martin Balshaw, OC C-130 Det, WCO Trevor Field, RAF DCC MOD

JHC/AAC: AVM David Niven, Maj Gen Gary Coward, Lt Col Paul Beaver

CAOC Al Udeid: CAOC Director Major General Dutch Holland USAF, CAOC Deputy Director BG Tony Haires USAF, Captain Bill Reavey, USN, Wing Commander Mason Fenlon,SO1 Senior UK Representative, RAF

The Media:

I would also like to thank my media colleagues who have provided help and assistance during my travels around Iraq and the Middle East, including:

The Scotsman, Andrew McLeod, Tim Cornwall, James Hall, Gethin Chamberlain; Daily Telegraph, Michael Smith, Jack Fairweather, Neil Tweedie; Sky News, Tim Marshall, Francis Tusa, Geoff Mead, James Forlong; DPL; Dave Reynolds, Dil Bannerjee; BBC Michael Voss, Paul Adams; Reuters; Peter Graff; Air Forces Monthly; Alan Warnes; Flight International; Stewart Penny, Jane's Defence Weekly, Cliff Beale, Marion Childs, Peter Felstead, Patrick Allen; City Forum Ltd: Marc Lee, Veronica Scott

Photographic Credits:

The author has made every effort to trace the copyright owners of all the images but if any are incorrectly attributed this will be corrected in subsequent editions.

Finally, a special thank you must also go to Dr Amanda Cahill, AKA Mrs Ripley, for her support and understanding during the long process of writing this volume. It would not have been possible without her.

REFERENCES

Chapter 1 – Telic Tour
[1] Robin Brims Interview, 13th November 2012
[2] Meeting with General Sir David Richards, 22nd April 2009
[3] Jonathan Shaw Interview, 8th November 2012
[4] Interviews RAF personnel al Udeid Airbase, 23rd September 2006
[5] p.30, 2003 edition, The Borderers Chronicle, King's Own Scottish Borders

Chapter 2 – The Commanders
[1] 1 PWRR BG Lessons Report Operation Telic, October 2004
[2] Daily Mail, 9th June 2007
[3] www.theguardian.com/politics/blog/2011/feb/16/curveball-confession-dent-iraq-conspiracy-theory

Chapter 3 - The Iraqis
[1] CFLCC OPPLAN Cobra II Southern Oil field Seizure Mission Analysis 19 Nov 2002
[2] Comprehensive Report of Special Advisor to the Director Central Intelligence on Iraq's Weapons of Mass Destruction (Iraq Survey Group Report), 30th September 2004
[3] Robin Brims Interview 13th November 2012
[4] Iraq Perspective Report, Kevin Woods and others, US Joint Forces Command, November 2007
[5] Iraq Perspective Report, Kevin Woods and others, US Joint Forces Command, November 2007
[6] 32nd Army Air Missile Defense Command, Operation Iraqi Freedom report
[7] Iraq Perspective Report, Kevin Woods and others, US Joint Forces Command, November 2007
[8] Iraq Perspective Report, Kevin Woods and others, US Joint Forces Command, November 2007
[9] Iraq Perspective Report, Kevin Woods and others, US Joint Forces Command, November 2007
[10] Basra Post Saddam Governance, Defence Intelligence Staff, 11th March 2003

Chapter 4 - Planning the War
[1] p.331, *Alistair Campbell Diaries: Countdown to Iraq*, Alistair Campbell (Hutchinson) 2012
[2] Op Telic Lessons for the Secretariat, David Johnson, 6th July 2004
[3] Op Telic Lessons for the Secretariat, David Johnson, 6th July 2004
[4] Author Interview with participant in the meeting
[5] Op Telic Lessons for the Secretariat, David Johnson, 6th July 2004
[6] Brian Burridge Interview, 24th May 2013
[7] Anthony Piggott evident to Chilcott Inquiry, 4th December 2009
[8] Op Telic Lessons for the Secretariat, David Johnson, 6th July 2004
[9] John Reith evidence to Chilcott Inquiry, 15th January 2010
[10] John Reith evidence to Chilcott Inquiry, 15th January 2010
[11] Brian Burridge Interview, 24th May 2013

[12] Hoon to Blair UK Military Options, 15th October 2002
[13] p.269, *The New Machiavelli: How to Wield Power in the Modern World*, Jonathan Powell, (The Bodley Head) 2010
[14] p. 331,*Alistair Campbell Diaries: Countdown to Iraq,* Alistair Campbell (Hutchinson) 2012
[15] Brian Burridge Interview, 24th May 2013
[16] p.2, *War Without Consequences,* Terence McNamee (editor), (RUSI) 2008
[17] Flight International Magazine, 14th August 2000
[18] Glenn Torpy Interview, 20th June 2013
[19] 32nd Army Air Missile Defense Command, Operation Iraqi Freedom report
[20] Interview senior RAF officer.
[21] Brian Burridge Interview, 24th May 2013
[22] Presentation for US-UK Integration Conference, Camp Pendleton, 3-5 Jan 2003
[23] p.63-64, *Target Barsa*, Mark Rossiter, (Corgi), 2009
[24] Brian Burridge Interview, 24th May 2013
[25] Presentation for US-UK Integration Conference, Camp Pendleton, 3-5 Jan 2003
[26] Robin Brims Interview 13th November 2012
[27] p.348, *Alistair Campbell Diaries: Countdown to Iraq,* Alistair Campbell (Hutchinson) 2012
[28] John Reith evidence to Chilcott Inquiry, 15th January 2010
[29] Brian Burridge Interview, 24th May 2013
[30] Robin Brims Interview 13th November 2012
[31] Post Operational Tour Report, Operation Telic, Headquarters 16 Air Assault Brigade, May 2003
[32] Statement to Chilcott Inquiry, Major General Albert Whitley
[33] Statement to Chilcott Inquiry, Major General Albert Whitley
[34] John Reith evidence to Chilcott Inquiry, 15th January 2010
[35] Michael Walker, evidence to Chilcott Inquiry, 1st February 2010
[36] Post Operational Tour Report, Operation Telic, Headquarters 16 Air Assault Brigade, May 2003
[37] April 2004 edition of the Vedette, Queen's Royal Lancers Journal
[38] Post Operational Tour Report, Operation Telic, Headquarters 16 Air Assault Brigade, May 2003
[39] Op Telic Lessons for the Secretariat, David Johnson, 6th July 2004

Chapter 5 – To Kuwait
[1] Robin Brims Interview 13th November 2012
[2] Author witnessed the ships being loaded
[3] Presentation for US-UK Integration Conference, Camp Pendleton, 3-5 Jan 2003
[4] p.93, Amphibious Assault; Manoeuvre from the Sea, Tristan Lovering, (Seafarer Books), 2007
[5] Author visit to HMS Ark Royal off Kuwait, 13th March 2003
[6] Author visit to HMS Ark Royal off Kuwait, 13th March 2003
[7] Author visit to Centcom Forward Headquarters, Doha, Kuwait, 8th March 2003
[8] Brian Burridge Interview, 24th May 2013

9. Robin Brims Interview 13th November 2012
10. Senior British Land Advisor to PJHQ Decision Imperatives dated 5 January 2003
11. Brian Burridge Interview, 24th May 2013
12. Brian Burridge Interview, 24th May 2013
13. Robin Brims Interview 13th November 2012
14. Robin Brims Interview 13th November 2012
15. Witness to CDS Briefing to Prime Minister 15th January 2013
16. p.122, *US Marines in Iraq 2003: Barsah, Baghdad and Beyond,* Colonel Nicholas E. Reynolds (United States Marine Corps), 2007
17. p.2-3, Operations in Iraq – An Analysis from a Land Perspective, British Army 2003
18. Michael Walker, evidence to Chilcott Inquiry, 1st February 2010
19. Op Telic Lessons for the Secretariat, David Johnson, 6th July 2004
20. Post Operational Tour Report, Operation Telic, Headquarters 16 Air Assault Brigade, May 2003
21. Post Operational Tour Report, Operation Telic, Headquarters 16 Air Assault Brigade, May 2003
22. p.705, June 2003 edition, The Fusilier, Royal Regiment of Fusiliers
23. p.8, 2004 edition, Eagle and Carbine, Royal Scots Dragoon Guards
24. p.26, 2004 edition of Vedette, Queen's Royal Lancers
25. p.5-2, Operations in Iraq – An Analysis from a Land Perspective, British Army 2003
26. p.2-7, Operations in Iraq – An Analysis from a Land Perspective, British Army 2003
27. p.14, 2004 edition, Eagle and Carbine, Royal Scots Dragoon Guards
28. p.20, November 2003, The Red Hackle, Black Watch
29. p.2-12, Operations in Iraq – An Analysis from a Land Perspective, British Army 2003
30. 7 Armoured Brigade, Operation Telic Presentation 27th April 2003, Major Peter Langford Deputy Chief of Staff
31. p.5-3, Operations in Iraq – An Analysis from a Land Perspective, British Army 2003
32. p.705, June 2003 edition, The Fusilier, Royal Regiment of Fusiliers
33. Graham Binns Interview, 24th October 2012
34. Post Operational Tour Report, 7 Armoured Brigade
35. Author interview, Ali Al Salem Airbase, Kuwait, 15th March 2003
36. Author interview, Ali Al Salem Airbase, Kuwait, 15th March 2003
37. p.148, *Tornado F3,* Wg Cdr Justin Reuter, Mark McEwan, Gill Howie, Berry Vissers, Geoffrey Lee, (Squadron Prints), 2011
38. Major Combat Operations: Iraq at the Operational Level, ACM Sir Brian Burridge, ASC 16, 17 April 2013
39. Glenn Torpy Interview, 20th June 2013
40. Brian Burridge Interview, 24th May 2013
41. Operation Telic Aircraft Movement Analysis, Peter Foster
42. p.90-91, *Gulf War II,* Jamie Hunter, (TomCat) 2003
43. p.47, Operations in Iraq: First Reflections, UK Ministry of Defence, 2003
44. Glenn Torpy Interview, 20th June 2013
45. Glenn Torpy Interview, 20th June 2013

[46] Author interview with witness in Kuwait, March 2003
[47] Author interview with member of media operations staff, UK National Component Headquarters, Doha, Qatar, 18th March 2003

Chapter 6 – The Battle Plan

[1] 1 (UK) Armoured Division, Operations Order 001/03 for Operation Telic, 7th March 2003
[2] Annex 1 to 1 (UK) Armoured Division, Operations Order 001/03.
[3] Graham Binns Interview, 24th October 2012
[4] Graham Binns Interview, 24th October 2012
[5] Brian Burridge Interview, 24th May 2013
[6] p.5-6, Op Telic Special Edition, Tank, The Royal Tank Regiment
[7] Author interview with member of media operations staff, UK National Component Headquarters, Doha, Qatar, 18th March 2003
[8] p.23, November 2003, The Red Hackle, Black Watch
[9] FRAGO 003 1 (UK) Armoured Division, Operations Order 003/03 for Operation Telic, 19th March 2003
[10] p.154, *All Roads Lead to Baghdad,* Charles Briscoe and others, (Paladin Press) 2007
[11] p.185, *Cobra II,* Michael Gordon and Bernard Trainor, (Atlantic Books) 2006
[12] Graham Binns Interview, 24th October 2012, Brain Burridge Interview, 24th May 2013
[13] 1 (UK) Armoured Division, Operations Order 001/03 for Operation Telic, 13th March 2003
[14] Author visit to HMS Ark Royal off Kuwait, 13th March 2003
[15] p.37, *US Marines in Iraq 2003: Barsah, Baghdad and Beyond,* Colonel Nicholas E. Reynolds (United States Marine Corps), 2007
[16] Author visit to HMS Ark Royal off Kuwait, 13th March 2003
[17] Robin Brims Interview 13th November 2012
[18] p.14, 2004 edition, Eagle and Carbine, Royal Scots Dragoon Guards
[19] Glenn Torpy Interview, 20th June 2013
[20] Glenn Torpy Interview, 20th June 2013
[21] Glenn Torpy Interview, 20th June 2013
[22] Glenn Torpy Interview, 20th June 2013
[23] Brian Burridge Interview, 24th May 2013
[24] Lieutenant Colonel Nick Mercer statement to Baha Mousa Inquiry, 9 September 2009
[25] Robin Brims Interview 13th November 2012
[26] www.qdg.org.uk/pages/Op-Telic-Headquarters-Squadron-124.php
[27] Statement to Chilcott Inquiry, Major General Albert Whitley
[28] Robin Brims Interview 13th November 2012
[29] Robin Brims Interview 13th November 2012
[30] Op Telic Lessons for the Secretariat, David Johnson, 6th July 2004
[31] Op Telic Lessons for the Secretariat, David Johnson, 6th July 2004
[32] p.164, *Cobra II,* Michael Gordon and Bernard Trainor, (Atlantic Books) 2006
[33] p.29, *Challenger 2 Main Battle Tank 1987-2006,* Simon Dunstan (Osprey), 2006
[34] Robin Brims Interview 13th November 2012

[35] Brian Burridge Interview, 24th May 2013
[36] Robin Brims Interview 13th November 2012
[37] p.123, p.37, *US Marines in Iraq 2003: Barsah, Baghdad and Beyond*, Colonel Nicholas E. Reynolds (United States Marine Corps), 2007
[38] p.706, June 2003 edition, The Fusilier, Royal Regiment of Fusiliers

Chapter 7 – Across The Border

[1] p.149, *Tornado F3, Wg Cdr Justin Reuter, Mark McEwan, Gill Howie, Berry Vissers, Geoffrey Lee,* (Squadron Prints), 2011
[2] 32nd Army Air Missile Defense Command, Operation Iraqi Freedom report
[3] Brian Burridge Interview, 24th May 2013
[4] Author Interview with senior RAF officer in Kuwait, April 2003
[5] p.83, *F-15E Strike Eagle Units in Combat 1990 to 2005,* Steve Davies (Osprey) 2005
[6] p.227, *Cobra II,* Michael Gordon and Bernard Trainor, (Atlantic Books) 2006
[7] p.176, May-June 2003edition, Global & Laurel Journal
[8] Author interview with senior British officer, Kuwait, April 2003
[9] 1 (UK) Armoured Division, Operations Order 001/003 for Operation Telic, 7th March 2003
[10] Glenn Torpy Interview, 20th June 2013
[11] p.5-6, Op Telic Special Edition, Tank, The Royal Tank Regiment
[12] 32nd Army Air Missile Defense Command, Operation Iraqi Freedom report
[13] p.32, *US Marine Corps and RAAF Hornet Units of Operation Iraqi Freedom,* Tony Holmes, (Osprey) 2005
[14] p.187, *Cobra II,* Michael Gordon and Bernard Trainor, (Atlantic Books) 2006
[15] p.5-6, Op Telic Special Edition, Tank, The Royal Tank Regiment
[16] p.170, *With the 1st Marine Division in Iraq, 2003,* Lieutenant Colonel Michael S. Groen and Contributors (Marine Corps University), 2006
[17] Author visit to HMS Ark Royal off Kuwait, 13th March 2003
[18] Author Interview with Wing Commander David Prowse, Kuwait, 16th April 2003
[19] Author Interview with Wing Commander David Prowse, Kuwait, 16th April 2003
[20] Author Interview with Squadron Leader Steve Carr, 10th September 2004
[21] Author Interview with Squadron Leader Steve Carr, 10th September 2004
[22] Author Interview with Peter Graff, July 2003
[23] p.196-7, *Cobra II,* Michael Gordon and Bernard Trainor, (Atlantic Books) 2006
[24] Author Interview with David Bowden, Sky News Correspondent, 20th October 2003
[25] p.189, May-June 2003, edition of Globe & Laurel
[26] Board of Inquiry Report into loss of Sea Kings XV650 and XV704, 19th April 2003
[27] www.qdg.org.uk/pages/Op-Telic-C-Squadron-127.php
[28] www.qdg.org.uk/pages/Op-Telic-C-Squadron-127.php
[29] p.178, May-June Edition, Globe Laurel 30 Robin Brims Interview 13th November 2012
[31] Post Operational Tour Report, Operation Telic, Headquarters 16 Air Assault Brigade, May 2003

[32] Operations Lessons for Operation Telic, 3 Regiment Army Air Corps, 7 May 2003
[33] p.862-863, December 2003 edition, The Fusilier, Royal Regiment of Fusiliers
[34] p.862-863, December 2003 edition, The Fusilier, Royal Regiment of Fusiliers
[35] p.14, 2004 edition, Eagle and Carbine, Royal Scots Dragoon Guards
[36] p.864, December 2003 edition, The Fusilier, Royal Regiment of Fusiliers
[37] p.865, December 2003 edition, The Fusilier, Royal Regiment of Fusiliers
[38] www.qdg.org.uk/pages/Op-Telic-A-Squadron-125.ph
[39] p.30, November 2003, The Red Hackle, Black Watch
[40] Robin Brims Interview 13th November 2012
[41] p.140, 2004 edition, Eagle and Carbine, Royal Scots Dragoon Guards
[42] p.140, 2004 edition, Eagle and Carbine, Royal Scots Dragoon Guards
[43] Graham Binns Interview, 24th October 2012
[44] www.qdg.org.uk/pages/Op-Telic-Headquarters-Squadron-124.php
[45] www.qdg.org.uk/pages/Op-Telic-Headquarters-Squadron-124.php
[46] Lt Col Nick Mercer evidence to Baha Mousa Inquiry, 9 September 2009 and correspondence with author November 2012
[47] Lt Col Nick Mercer evidence to Baha Mousa Inquiry, 9 September 2009 and correspondence with author November 2012
[48] Lt Col Nick Mercer evidence to Baha Mousa Inquiry, 9 September 2009 and correspondence with author November 2012
[49] Robin Brims Interview 13th November 2012
[50] Graham Binns Interview, 24th October 2012

Chapter 8 - Taking Down Zubayr
[1] Brian Burridge Interview, 24th May 2013
[2] Robin Brims Interview 13th November 2012
[3] Graham Binns Interview, 24th October 2012
[4] Graham Binns Interview, 24th October 2012
[5] Graham Binns Interview, 24th October 2012
[6] http://news.bbc.co.uk/1/hi/uk/5399052.stm
[7] Graham Binns Interview, 24th October 2012
[8] p. 23-34, November 2003, The Red Hackle, Black Watch
[9] p. 23-34, November 2003, The Red Hackle, Black Watch
[10] www.independent.co.uk/news/uk/politics/the-betrayal-of-a-soldier-coroner-in-blistering-attack-on-ministers-at-inquest-429222.htm
[11] p.69-77, *Main Battle Tank,* Niall Edworthy, (Penguin), 2010
[12] p.87, *Main Battle Tank,* Niall Edworthy, (Penguin), 2010
[13] p.90, *Main Battle Tank,* Niall Edworthy, (Penguin), 2010
[14] p.31, November 2003, The Red Hackle, Black Watch
[15] p.31, November 2003, The Red Hackle, Black Watch
[16] p.31, *Challenger 2 Main Battle Tank 1987-2006,* Simon Dunstan (Osprey), 2006
[17] p.31, November 2003, The Red Hackle, Black Watch
[18] http://news.bbc.co.uk/1/hi/uk/5399052.stm
[19] Robin Brims Interview 13th November 2012

[20] Graham Binns Interview, 24th October 2012

Chapter 9 - Holding the Basra Canal
[1] 16 Air Assault Brigade War Diary, Mar-Apr 2003
[2] 16 Air Assault Brigade War Diary, Mar-Apr 2003
[3] Brian Burridge Interview, 24th May 2013
[4] Author was present at Brigadier Peter Wall's Briefing
[5] Graham Binns Interview, 24th October 2012
[6] Robin Brims Interview 13th November 2012 Robin Brims Interview 13th November 2012
[7] UK Tactical UAV Operations Iraq 2003/4, Presentation to Shephard UAV Conference, June 2003, Major Charles Barker Royal Artillery, 2IC 32 Regiment RA
[8] UK Tactical UAV Operations Iraq 2003/4, Presentation to Shephard UAV Conference, June 2003, Major Charles Barker Royal Artillery, 2IC 32 Regiment RA
[9] UK Tactical UAV Operations Iraq 2003/4, Presentation to Shephard UAV Conference, June 2003, Major Charles Barker Royal Artillery, 2IC 32 Regiment RA
[10] Brain Burridge Interview, 24th May 2013
[11] Author interview with RAF Harrier pilots Ahmed Al Jaber Air Base, Kuwait, 13th April 2013
[12] p.867, December 2003 edition, The Fusilier, Royal Regiment of Fusiliers
[13] p.943, December 2003 edition, The Fusilier, Royal Regiment of Fusiliers
[14] p.944, December 2003 edition, The Fusilier, Royal Regiment of Fusiliers
[15] p.943, December 2003 edition, The Fusilier, Royal Regiment of Fusiliers
[16] p.33, April 2004 edition of Vedette, Queen's Royal Lancers
[17] p.33, April 2004 edition of Vedette, Queen's Royal Lancers
[18] p.25, November 2003 edition, The Red Hackle, Black Watch
[19] Board of Inquiry into the circumstances surrounding the deaths of Cpl Allbutt and Tpr Clarke, 23rd July 2003
[20] Operations Lessons for Operation Telic, 3 Regiment Army Air Corps, 7 May 2003
[21] Operations Lessons for Operation Telic, 3 Regiment Army Air Corps, 7 May 2003
[22] Operations Lessons for Operation Telic, 3 Regiment Army Air Corps, 7 May 2003
[23] Operations Lessons for Operation Telic, 3 Regiment Army Air Corps, 7 May 2003
[24] p.11, 2004 edition, Eagle and Carbine, Royal Scots Dragoon Guards
[25] p.17, 2004 edition, Eagle and Carbine, Royal Scots Dragoon Guards
[26] p.185, *Main Battle Tank,* Niall Edworthy, (Penguin), 2010
[27] Graham Binns Interview, 24th October 2012
[28] p.28, *Main Battle Tank,* Niall Edworthy, (Penguin), 2010
[29] Brian Burridge Interview, 24th May 2013
[30] Robin Brims Interview 13th November 2012
[31] 16 Air Assault Brigade War Diary, Mar-Apr 2003
[32] 16 Air Assault Brigade War Diary, Mar-Apr 2003
[33] 16 Air Assault Brigade War Diary, Mar-Apr 2003

Chapter 10 - Royal Marines vs T-55 Tanks
[1] Robin Brims Interview 13th November 2012
[2] p.163, May-June 2003 edition, Globe & Laurel
[3] www.qdg.org.uk/pages/Op-Telic-C-Squadron-127.php
[4] p.157, *Armed Action,* James Newton, (Headline) 2007
[5] www.qdg.org.uk/pages/Op-Telic-C-Squadron-127.php
[6] p.163, May-June 2003 edition, Globe & Laurel
[7] p.173, May-June 2003 edition, Globe & Laurel
[8] Board of Inquiry into the circumstances surrounding death of Marine Maddison, 1st February 2006
[9] p.194, May-June 2003 edition, Globe & Laurel
[10] p.221, *Armed Action,* James Newton, (Headline) 2007
[11] p.167, May-June 2003 edition, Globe & Laurel
[12] Robin Brims Interview 13th November 2012
[13] Robin Brims Interview 13th November 2012
[14] Operations Lessons for Operation Telic, 3 Regiment Army Air Corps, 7 May 2003
[15] p.117, *Main Battle Tank,* Niall Edworthy, (Penguin), 2010
[16] p.145, *Main Battle Tank,* Niall Edworthy, (Penguin), 2010
[17] Robin Brims Interview 13th November 2012
[18] p.168, May-June 2003 edition, Globe & Laurel
[19] p.168, May-June 2003 edition, Globe & Laurel
[20] p.219 *Armed Action,* James Newton, (Headline) 2007
[21] p.214, *Armed Action,* James Newton, (Headline) 2007
[22] p.242, *Main Battle Tank,* Niall Edworthy, (Penguin), 2010
[23] p.165, May-June 2003 edition, Globe & Laurel
[24] p.165, May-June 2003 edition, Globe & Laurel
[25] Robin Brims Interview 13th November 2012

Chapter 11 – To the Gates of Baghdad
[1] 16 Air Assault Brigade Planning Document
[2] 1 (UK) Armoured Division, Operations Order 001/003 for Operation Telic, 7th March 2003
[3] 16 Air Assault Brigade War Diary, Mar-Apr 2003
[4] Robin Brims Interview 13th November 2012
[5] Post Operational Tour Report, Operation Telic, Headquarters 16 Air Assault Brigade, May 2003
[6] Post Operational Tour Report Op Telic, 7 RHA, May 2003
[7] Post Operational Tour Report Op Telic, Pathfinder Platoon, May 2003
[8] p.9, December 2003 edition, Soldier Magazine
[9] p.6, December 2003 edition, Soldier Magazine
[10] Post Operational Tour Report, Operation Telic, Headquarters 16 Air Assault Brigade, May 2003
[11] p.7, December 2003 edition, Soldier Magazine
[12] Post Operational Tour Report, Operation Telic, Headquarters 16 Air Assault Brigade, May 2003
[13] 16 Air Assault Brigade War Diary, Mar-Apr 2003

[14] http://news.bbc.co.uk/1/hi/uk/6449227.stm
[15] 16 Air Assault Brigade War Diary, Mar-Apr 2003
[16] http://www.wsws.org/en/articles/2003/04/brit-a04.html
[17] Post Operational Tour Report, Operation Telic, Headquarters 16 Air Assault Brigade, May 2003
[18] Robin Brims Interview 13th November 2012
[19] p.94, *Gulf War II,* Jamie Hunter, (TomCat) 2003
[20] p.93, *Gulf War II,* Jamie Hunter, (TomCat) 2003
[21] Brian Burridge Interview, 24th May 2013
[22] p.71, *All Roads Lead to Baghdad,* Charles Briscoe and others, (Paladin Press) 2007
[23] Lt Gen Bradshaw, ISAF Biography
[24] p.2, *Desperate Glory,* Sam Kiley, (Bloomsbury), 2009
[25] p.53-54, Stanley McChrystal, My Share of the Task,(Penguin), 2013
[26] Author interviews, UNSCOM weapons inspectors, New York, 1992
[27] p.127, *All Roads Lead to Baghdad,* Charles Briscoe and others, (Paladin Press) 2007
[28] p.17, Relearning Air-Land Co-operation, Wing Commander Harvey Smyth, in Volume 10 Number 1 Spring 2007
[29] p.71, *All Roads Lead to Baghdad,* Charles Briscoe and others, (Paladin Press) 2007
[30] p.17, Relearning Air-Land Co-operation, Wing Commander Harvey Smyth, in Air Power Review, Volume 10 Number 1 Spring 2007,
[31] Author interview with senior RAF Officer in Kuwait, April 2003
[32] p.8, RAF News, 14th November 2003
[33] Author interview with senior RAF Officer in Kuwait, April 2003
[34] Author interview with senior RAF Officer in Kuwait, April 2003
[35] p.171, May-June 2003 edition, Globe & Laurel
[36] Author Interview Wing Commander Ken Smith, 24th October 2003
[37] Author Interview Wing Commander Ken Smith, 24th October 2003
[38] p.93, *Gulf War II,* Jamie Hunter, (TomCat) 2003
[39] p.163, *Zero Six Bravo,* Damien Lewis, (Quercus), 2013
[40] p.71, *F-16 Fighting Falcon Units of Operation Iraqi Freedom,* Steve Davies and Doug Dilby (Osprey) 2006
[41] p.306, *Zero Six Bravo,* Damien Lewis, (Quercus), 2013
[42] Iraq Perspective Report, Kevin Woods and others, US Joint Forces Command, November 2007
[43] p.6-7, Task Force Black, *Mark Urban (Little & Brown) 2010*
[44] Author Interview Wing Commander Ken Smith, 24th October 2003
[45] Brian Burridge Interview, 24th May 2013
[46] *Comprehensive Report of Special Advisor to the Director Central Intelligence on Iraq's Weapon of Mass Destruction (Iraq Survey Group Report),* 30th September 2004
[47] Author Interview Group Captain Mike Harwood, Ahmed Al Jaber Air Base, 13th April 2003
[48] Author Interview with RAF Harrier pilots, Ahmed Al Jaber Air Base, 13th April 2003
[49] Glenn Torpy Interview, 20th June 2013
[50] Glenn Torpy Interview, 20th June 2013

[51] Author Interview with RAF Harrier pilots, Ahmed Al Jaber Air Base, 13th April 2003
[52] Author Interview with RAF Harrier pilots, Ahmed Al Jaber Air Base, 13th April 2003
[53] p.48, Operations in Iraq: First Reflections, UK Ministry of Defence, 2003
[54] Author interview Group Captain Mike Harwood, Ahmed Al Jaber Air Base, 13th April 2003
[55] Author interview Group Captain Mike Harwood, Ahmed Al Jaber Air Base, 13th April 2003
[56] Author Interview with RAF Harrier pilots, Ahmed Al Jaber Air Base, 13th April 2003
[57] Brian Burridge Interview, 24th May 2013
[58] Author Interview with RAF Harrier pilots, Ahmed Al Jaber Air Base, 13th April 2003
[59] Author Interview with RAF Harrier pilots, Ahmed Al Jaber Air Base, 13th April 2003
[60] Author Interview with Major General Dan Leaf USAF, Kuwait, 16th April 2003
[61] Author Interview with RAF Harrier pilots, Ahmed Al Jaber Air Base, 13th April 2003
[62] Author interview Group Captain Mike Harwood, Ahmed Al Jaber Air Base, 13th April 2003
[63] p.26, Summer 2003 edition Pegasus, Parachute Regiment
[64] p.3-18, Operations in Iraq – An Analysis from a Land Perspective, British Army 2003
[65] p.328, *Cobra II*, Michael Gordon and Bernard Trainor, (Atlantic Books) 2006
[66] p.5-6, Op Telic Special Edition, Tank, The Royal Tank Regiment
[67] p.5-6, Op Telic Special Edition, Tank, The Royal Tank Regiment
[68] Author interview with member of media operations staff, UK National Component Headquarters, Doha, Qatar, 18th March 2003

Chapter 12 - Fall of Basra

[1] Brian Burridge Interview, 24th May 2013
[2] Brian Burridge Interview, 24th May 2013
[3] Intelligence summary, 1 (UK) Armoured Division, 2 Apr 2003
[4] 16 Air Assault Brigade War Diary, Mar-Apr 2003
[5] Brian Burridge Interview, 24th May 2013
[6] 16 Air Assault Brigade War Diary, Mar-Apr 2003
[7] Operations Lessons for Operation Telic, 3 Regiment Army Air Corps, 7 May 2003
[8] p.33, April 2004 edition of Vedette, Queen's Royal Lancers
[9] 16 Air Assault Brigade War Diary, Mar-Apr 2003
[10] p.173, May-June 2003 edition, Globe & Laurel
[11] 16 Air Assault Brigade War Diary, Mar-Apr 2003
[12] p.16, 2004 edition, Eagle and Carbine, Royal Scots Dragoon Guards
[13] Iraq Perspective Report, Kevin Woods and others, US Joint Forces Command, November 2007
[14] Robin Brims Interview 13th November 2012

[15] UK Tactical UAV Operations Iraq 2003/4, Presentation to Shephard UAV Conference, June 2003, Major Charles Barker Royal Artillery, 2IC 32 Regiment RA
[16] Brian Burridge Interview, 24th May 2013
[17] p.66-68, *F-16 Fighting Falcon Units of Operation Iraqi Freedom,* Steve Davies and Doug Dilby (Osprey) 2006
[18] Robin Brims Interview 13th November 2012
[19] Author was present at these briefings
[20] Brian Burridge Interview, 24th May 2013
[21] p.24, September 2003 Edition, Tank, The Royal Tank Regiment
[24] I am almost certain that Chemical Ali is still alive, says senior Army officer, By Charlotte Edwards, Daily Telegraph, 18 May 2003
[23] Graham Binns Interview, 24th October 2012
[24] p.17, 2004 edition, Eagle and Carbine, Royal Scots Dragoon Guards
[25] Graham Binns Interview, 24th October 2012
[26] p. 272, *Main Battle Tank,* Niall Edworthy, (Penguin), 2010
[27] Gethin Chamberlain, Iraqis point out Fedayeen hiding-spots to British Troops, April 7, 2003, The Scotsman
[28] Gethin Chamberlain, Iraqis point out Fedayeen hiding-spots to British Troops, April 7, 2003, The Scotsman
[29] Graham Binns Interview, 24th October 2012
[30] Graham Binns Interview, 24th October 2012
[31] p.868, December 2003 edition, The Fusilier, Royal Regiment of Fusiliers
[32] Graham Binns Interview, 24th October 2012
[33] p.4-11, Operations in Iraq – An Analysis from a Land Perspective, British Army 2003
[34] 16 Air Assault Brigade War Diary, Mar-Apr 2003
[35] Graham Binns Interview, 24th October 2012
[36] p.17, 2004 edition, Eagle and Carbine, Royal Scots Dragoon Guards
[37] p.17, 2004 edition, Eagle and Carbine, Royal Scots Dragoon Guards
[38] Fusilier killed by friendly fire, coroner rules, Kim Sengupta, The Independent, 20th October 2006
[39] p.173, May-June 2003 edition, Globe & Laurel
[40] p.139, 2004 edition, Eagle and Carbine, Royal Scots Dragoon Guards
[41] p.11, 2004 edition, Eagle and Carbine, Royal Scots Dragoon Guards
[42] p.31-32, Summer 2003 edition, Pegasus, The Parachute Regiment
[43] Graham Binns Interview, 24th October 2012
[44] Robin Brims Interview 13th November 2012
[45] p.52, Summer 2003 edition, Pegasus, The Parachute Regiment
[46] p.22, Summer 2003 edition, The Silver Bugler, The Light Infantry
[47] Robin Brims Interview 13th November 2012
[48] Graham Binns Interview, 24th October 2012
[49] Graham Binns Interview, 24th October 2012
[50] Graham Binns Interview, 24th October 2012
[51] p.869, December 2003 edition, The Fusilier, Royal Regiment of Fusiliers

Chapter 13 – Military Judgement

[1] UK Military Contribution to post Conflict Iraq, to PM by SOS Defence and and FS, 19th March 2003, declassified by Chilcot Inquiry.
[2] Warning Order for Recovery of 1 (UK) ARMD DIV, 19 Apr 03
[3] Author Interview with senior British officer, Kuwait, April 2003
[4] Brian Burridge Interview, 24th May 2013
[5] p.869, December 2003 edition, The Fusilier, Royal Regiment of Fusiliers
[6] Graham Binns Interview, 24th October 2012
[7] p.869, December 2003 edition, The Fusilier, Royal Regiment of Fusiliers
[8] Robin Brims Interview 13th November 2012
[9] Post Operational Tour Report, Operation Telic, Headquarters 16 Air Assault Brigade, May 2003
[10] Robin Brims Interview 13th November 2012
[11] Robin Brims Interview 13th November 2012
[12] 16 Air Assault Brigade War Diary, Mar-Apr 2003
[13] 16 Air Assault Brigade War Diary, Mar-Apr 2003
[14] 16 Air Assault Brigade War Diary, Mar-Apr 2003
[15] 1 (UK) Armoured Division, Operations Order Phase IV for Operation Telic, 17 Apr 2003
[16] p.14, September 2003 Edition, Tank, The Royal Tank Regiment
[17] p.11, 2004 edition, Eagle and Carbine, Royal Scots Dragoon Guards
[18] p.14, March/April 2005 edition, Military Logistics International
[19] p.165, May-June 2003 edition, Globe & Laurel
[20] p.11, 2004 edition, Eagle and Carbine, Royal Scots Dragoon Guards
[21] p.5-9, Operations in Iraq – An Analysis from a Land Perspective, British Army 2003
[22] Robin Brims Interview 13th November 2012
[23] p.34-35, November 2003 edition, The Red Hackle, Black Watch
[24] p.34-35, November 2003 edition, The Red Hackle, Black Watch, Operations in Iraq – An Analysis from a Land Perspective, British Army 2003 and p.33. Stability Operations in Iraq (Op Telic 2-5), An Analysis from a Land Perspective, Major General W R Rollo, British Army, 2006
[25] p.35, November 2003 edition, The Red Hackle, Black Watch
[26] Brian Burridge Interview, 24th May 2013
[27] p.26-35, *Bank Rolling Basra,* Andrew Alderson, (Robinson) 2005
[28] Brian Burridge Interview, 24th May 2013
[29] p.870, December 2003 edition, The Fusilier, Royal Regiment of Fusiliers
[30] p.870, December 2003 edition, The Fusilier, Royal Regiment of Fusiliers
[31] Nicholas Mercer witness statement to Baha Mousa Inquiry, 9th September 2009
[32] p.47. Stability Operations in Iraq (Op Telic 2-5), An Analysis from a Land Perspective, Major General W R Rollo, British Army, 2006
[33] p.26, November 2003 edition, The Red Hackle, Black Watch
[34] Posters in 1 (UK) Division Headquarters seen by author during visit in September 2003
[35] Nicholas Mercer witness statement to Baha Mousa Inquiry, 9th September 2009
[36] Robin Brims Interview 13th November 2012
[37] Robin Brims Interview 13th November 2012

38 Author visit to 49 Joint Force EOD Group Shaibah Logistic Base, 29th September 2003
39 Author visit to 49 Joint Force EOD Group Shaibah Logistic Base, 29th September 2003
40 Robin Brims Interview 13th November 2012
41 Robin Brims Interview 13th November 2012
42 Author visit to al Amarah, 30th September 2003
43 16 Air Assault Brigade War Diary, Mar-Apr 2003
44 16 Air Assault Brigade War Diary, Mar-Apr 2003
45 16 Air Assault Brigade War Diary, Mar-Apr 2003
46 Author visit to al Amarah, 30th September 2003
47 Robin Brims Interview 13th November 2012
48 Michael Jackson evidence to Chilcot Inquiry, 28th July 2010
49 Michael Jackson evidence to Chilcot Inquiry, 28th July 2010
50 Brian Burridge Interview, 24th May 2013
51 p.12, September 2003 Edition, Tank, The Royal Tank Regiment
52 p.143, 2004 edition, Eagle and Carbine, Royal Scots Dragoon Guards
53 p.12, September 2003 Edition, Tank, The Royal Tank Regiment
54 Lieutenant General Adrian Bradshaw biography posted on www.isaf.nato.int, 2009
55 EPW Incident ARF – Fri 11 Apr 02, II Squadron RAF Regiment, 7 Sep 2004
56 Robin Brims Interview 13th November 2012
57 Robin Brims Interview 13th November 2012
58 HQ 16 Air Assault Brigade, Op Telic Chronology, 29 May 03
59 Board of Inquiry Regarding the Circumstances Surrounding the Deaths of Sergeant Simon Hamilton-Jewell, Corporal Russell Aston, Corporal Paul Graham Long, Corporal Simon Miller, Lance-Corporal Benjamin John McGowan Hyde, and Lance-Corporal Thomas Keys, 19 Oct 2004
60 Board of Inquiry Regarding the Circumstances Surrounding the Deaths of Sergeant Simon Hamilton-Jewell, Corporal Russell Aston, Corporal Paul Graham Long, Corporal Simon Miller, Lance-Corporal Benjamin John McGowan Hyde, and Lance-Corporal Thomas Keys, 19 Oct 2004
61 Author interviews during 22nd June 2003 with a senior army officer based in MOD
62 Board of Inquiry Regarding the Circumstances Surrounding the Deaths of Sergeant Simon Hamilton-Jewell, Corporal Russell Aston, Corporal Paul Graham Long, Corporal Simon Miller, Lance-Corporal Benjamin John McGowan Hyde, and Lance-Corporal Thomas Keys, 19 Oct 2004
63 SAS 'beat Iraqi policemen with rifles in hunt for Red Caps killers', Mark Nicol, 3rd November 2012 Daily Mail

Chapter 14– Basra Summer
1 p.13, 2003 Edition, The Borderers Chronicle, King's Own Scottish Borders
2 Lesson Capture Process Interview, Maj Gen Graeme Lamb, 23 Feb 04
3 Lesson Capture Process Interview, Maj Gen Graeme Lamb, 23 Feb 04
4 Bill Moore evidence to Baha Mousa Inquiry, 3rd January 2010
5 Post Operations Report and Lessons Identified, 19 Mech Brigade, Op Telic 2
6 Post Operations Report and Lessons Identified, 19 Mech Brigade, Op Telic 2
7 Bill Moore evidence to Baha Mousa Inquiry, 3rd January 2010

[8] Post Operations Report and Lessons Identified, 19 Mech Brigade, Op Telic 2
[9] p.4, 2003 Edition, The Borderers Chronicle, King's Own Scottish Borders
[10] Post Operations Report and Lessons Identified, 19 Mech Brigade, Op Telic 2
[11] Lesson Capture Process Interview, Maj Gen Graeme Lamb, 23 Feb 04
[12] Post Operation Tour Report, Operation Telic 2/3 Headquarters Multinational Division (South East), 30 Jan 04
[13] Lesson Capture Process Interview, Maj Gen Graeme Lamb, 23 Feb 04
[14] Graeme Lamb evidence to Baha Mousa Inquiry, 2nd October 2009
[15] Post Operations Report and Lessons Identified, 19 Mech Brigade, Op Telic 2
[16] p.17, 2003 Edition, The Borderers Chronicle, King's Own Scottish Borders
[17] Post Operation Tour Report, Operation Telic 2/3 Headquarters Multinational Division (South East), 30 Jan 04
[18] Post Operation Tour Report, Operation Telic 2/3 Headquarters Multinational Division (South East), 30 Jan 04
[19] Graeme Lamb evidence to Chilcot Inquiry, 9th December 2009
[20] Graeme Lamb evidence to Chilcot Inquiry, 9th December 2009
[21] 19 Mech Brigade Chronology, Op Telic 2
[22] 19 Mech Brigade Chronology, Op Telic 2
[23] Post Operations Report and Lessons Identified, 19 Mech Brigade, Op Telic 2
[24] Lesson Capture Process Interview, Lt Col Richard Nugee
[25] Lesson Capture Process Interview, Colonel Cairan Griffin
[26] Lesson Capture Process Interview, Brig Bill Moore, 26 Mar 04
[27] Lesson Capture Process Interview, Brig Bill Moore, 26 Mar 04
[28] Post Operations Report and Lessons Identified, 19 Mech Brigade, Op Telic 2
[29] Post Operations Report and Lessons Identified, 19 Mech Brigade, Op Telic 2
[30] Graeme Lamb evidence to Baha Mousa Inquiry, 2nd October 2009
[31] 19 Mech Brigade Chronology, Op Telic 2
[32] 19 Mech Brigade Chronology, Op Telic 2
[33] Post Operation Tour Report, Operation Telic 2/3 Headquarters Multinational Division (South East), 30 Jan 04
[34] Lesson Capture Process Interview, Maj Gen Graeme Lamb, 23 Feb 04
[35] Post Operations Report and Lessons Identified, 19 Mech Brigade, Op Telic 2
[36] Post Operations Report and Lessons Identified, 19 Mech Brigade, Op Telic 2
[37] Post Operations Report and Lessons Identified, 19 Mech Brigade, Op Telic 2
[38] p.30, 2003 Edition, The Borderers Chronicle, King's Own Scottish Borders
[39] http://news.bbc.co.uk/1/hi/uk/3979645.stm
[40] Post Operations Report and Lessons Identified, 19 Mech Brigade, Op Telic 2
[41] http://www.bahamousainquiry.org
[42] Post Operation Tour Report, Operation Telic 2/3 Headquarters Multinational Division (South East), 30 Jan 04
[43] Post Operations Report and Lessons Identified, 19 Mech Brigade, Op Telic
[44] p.19, Summer 2004 edition, The Silver Bugler, The Light Infantry
[45] Post Operation Tour Report, Operation Telic 2/3 Headquarters Multinational Division (South East), 30 Jan 04
[46] Post Operations Report and Lessons Identified, 19 Mech Brigade, Op Telic 2
[47] Post Operation Tour Report, Operation Telic 2/3 Headquarters Multinational Division (South East), 30 Jan 04
[48] Graeme Lamb evidence to Baha Mousa Inquiry, 2nd October 2009

[49] Graeme Lamb evidence to Baha Mousa Inquiry, 2nd October 2009
[50] Lesson Capture Process Interview, Brig Bill Moore, 26 Mar 04
[51] Lesson Capture Process Interview, Maj Gen Graeme Lamb, 23 Feb 04
[52] Post Operation Tour Report, Operation Telic 2/3 Headquarters Multinational Division (South East), 30 Jan 04
[53] Post Operations Report and Lessons Identified, 19 Mech Brigade, Op Telic
[54] Post Operations Report and Lessons Identified, 19 Mech Brigade, Op Telic
[55] Post Operations Report and Lessons Identified, 19 Mech Brigade, Op Telic
[56] Post Operations Report and Lessons Identified, 19 Mech Brigade, Op Telic
[57] Major John Clark, Interview with US Combat Studies Institute, Fort Leavenworth, Kansas, 7th February 2007
[58] Post Operations Report and Lessons Identified, 19 Mech Brigade, Op Telic
[59] Post Operation Tour Report, Operation Telic 2/3 Headquarters Multinational Division (South East), 30 Jan 04

Chapter 15 – A Mature Theatre?

[1] Iraq Theatre Brief, PJHQ, 22nd November 2004
[2] p.7, 2004 edition, The Crossbelts, Queen's Royal Hussars
[3] Post Operation Tour Report, Operation Telic 2/3 Headquarters Multinational Division (South East), 30 Jan 04
[4] Post Operation Tour Report, Operation Telic 2/3 Headquarters Multinational Division (South East), 30 Jan 04
[5] p.12, 2004 edition, p.7, 2004 edition, The Crossbelts, Queen's Royal Hussars
[6] Post Operation Tour Report, Operation Telic 2/3 Headquarters Multinational Division (South East), 30 Jan 04
[7] p.11, 2004/2005 Edition, Quis Separabit: The Journal of the Royal Dragoon Guards
[8] Lesson Capture Process Interview, Col JK Tanner, 8 Sept 2004
[9] Lesson Capture Process Interview, Col JK Tanner, 8 Sept 2004
[10] p.37, *Bank Rolling Basra,* Andrew Alderson, (Robinson) 2005
[11] p.118, Muqtada Al-Sadr and the Future Battle for Iraq, Patrick Cockburn (Scribner) 2008
[12] p.33 & p.50, *The End Game,* Michael Gordon and Bernard Trainor, (Atlantic Books) 2012
[13] p.226, *Bank Rolling Basra,* Andrew Alderson, (Robinson) 2005
[14] p.99, *Occupational Hazards,* Rory Stewart (Picador) 2006
[15] p.20, Summer 2004 edition, The Silver Bugle, The Light Infantry
[16] p.23, Summer 2004 edition, The Silver Bugle, The Light Infantry
[17] p.26-27, Summer 2004 edition, The Silver Bugle, The Light Infantry
[18] p.26, 2004 edition, The Crossbelts, Queen's Royal Hussars
[19] Lesson Capture Process Interview, Lt Col AC Cuthbert, 6 Jul 04
[20] p.30-31, Summer 2004 edition, The Silver Bugle, The Light Infantry
[21] p.20, Summer 2004 edition, The Silver Bugle, The Light Infantry
[22] p.60-61, *The End Game*, Michael Gordon and Bernard Trainor, (Atlantic Books) 2012
[23] p.32, Winter 2004 edition, Men of Harlech, Royal Regiment of Wales
[24] p.41-42, Winter 2004 edition, Men of Harlech, Royal Regiment of Wales
[25] p.42, Winter 2004 edition, Men of Harlech, Royal Regiment of Wales
[26] Lessons Capture Process Interview, Maj Gen Andrew Stewart, 31 Aug 2004

[27] p.32, Winter 2004 edition, Men of Harlech, Royal Regiment of Wales
[28] Lessons Capture Process Interview, Maj Gen Andrew Stewart, 31 Aug 2004
[29] Lessons Capture Process Interview, Maj Gen Andrew Stewart, 31 Aug 2004
[30] Lesson Capture Process Interview, Brig Nick Carter, 23 June 04
[31] p.42-43, Winter 2004 edition, Men of Harlech, Royal Regiment of Wales
[32] p.42-43, Winter 2004 edition, Men of Harlech, Royal Regiment of Wales
[33] p.34, Winter 2004 edition, Men of Harlech, Royal Regiment of Wales
[34] 1 RWF Post Operational Report for Op Telic 4, 18 Oct 04
[35] 1 RWF Post Operational Report for Op Telic 4, 18 Oct 04
[36] Lesson Capture Process Interview, Lt Col JR Free, 22 Jun 04
[37] p.34, Winter 2004 edition, Men of Harlech, Royal Regiment of Wales
[38] 1 BW Post Operation Report – Operation Bracken, 9 Dec 04
[39] 1 PWRR BG Lessons Report Operation Telic, October 2004
[40] 1 PWRR BG Lessons Report Operation Telic, October 2004
[41] p.353, *Dusty Warriors,* Richard Holmes (Harper Collins) 2007
[42] 1 PWRR BG Lessons Report Operation Telic, October 2004
[43] 1 PWRR BG Lessons Report Operation Telic, October 2004
[44] p.226-246, *Dusty Warriors,* Richard Holmes (Harper Collins) 2007
[45] 1 Cheshire Post Operational Report for Op Telic 4, 19 Oct 04
[46] p.9, The Oak Tree, The Cheshire Regiment
[47] p.16, 2004 Edition, Journal of The Princess of Wales's Royal Regiment
[48] Multinational Division (South East) Commander's War Diary 16 Jun to 30 Nov 04
[49] Why you don't hear about our brave boys, Stephen Grey in News statesman magazine, 31st May 2004
[50] Lessons Capture Process Interview, Maj Gen Andrew Stewart, 31 Aug 2004

Chapter 16 – Street Fighting Summer

[1] Multinational Division (South East) Commanders War Diary 16 Jun to 30 Nov 04
[2] Board of Inquiry (BOI) into the death of Fusilier Gordon Gentle
[3] http://news.bbc.co.uk/1/hi/scotland/4444118.stm
[4] p.104, p.154 to 156, *The End Game*, Michael Gordon and Bernard Trainor, (Atlantic Books) 2012
[5] Author interview with senior British staff officer in Basra 2004
[6] Multinational Division (South East) Commanders War Diary 16 Jun to 30 Nov 04
[7] p.17-20, 2004 Edition, Journal of The Princess of Wales's Royal Regiment
[8] 1 PWRR BG Lessons Report Operation Telic, October 2004
[9] 2005 Edition, Vedette, Queen's Royal Lancers & Journal of The Princess of Wales's Royal Regiment
[10] 1 PWRR BG Lessons Report Operation Telic, October 2004
[11] 1 PWRR BG Lessons Report Operation Telic, October 2004
[12] p.305, *Sniper One,* Dan Mills, (Penguin) 2007
[13] p.20-22, 2004 Edition, Journal of The Princess of Wales's Royal Regiment
[14] Multinational Division (South East) Commanders War Diary 16 Jun to 30 Nov 04
[15] p.39, 2005 Edition, Vedette, Queen's Royal Lancers

[16] 1 Cheshire Post Operational Report for Op Telic 4, 19 Oct 04
[17] p.40, 2005 Edition, Vedette, Queen's Royal Lancers
[18] p.16-17, 2004 Edition, The Oak Tree, The Cheshire Regiment
[19] p.25, November 2004 Edition, The Red Hackle, The Black Watch
[20] p.25, November 2004 Edition, The Red Hackle, The Black Watch
[21] p.17, 2004 Edition, The Oak Tree, The Cheshire Regiment
[22] Author interview with senior British staff officer in Basra 2004
[23] p.9, 2004 Edition, The Oak Tree, The Cheshire Regiment
[24] Multinational Division (South East) Commanders War Diary 16 Jun to 30 Nov 04
[25] Multinational Division (South East) Commanders War Diary 16 Jun to 30 Nov 04
[26] p.9, 2004 Edition, The Oak Tree, The Cheshire Regiment
[27] p.29, November 2004 Edition, The Red Hackle, The Black Watch
[28] p.9, 2004 Edition, The Oak Tree, The Cheshire Regiment
[29] Multinational Division (South East) Commanders War Diary 16 Jun to 30 Nov 04
[30] Multinational Division (South East) Commanders War Diary 16 Jun to 30 Nov 04
[31] Robin Brims Interview 13th November 2012
[32] Post Operational Tour Report, Operation Telic, Headquarters 1 Mechanised Brigade, January 2005
[33] p.6, 2004 Edition, The Crossbelts, Queen's Royal Hussars
[34] Post Operation Tour Report, Operation Telic 4/5, Headquarters Multinational Division (South East), 4 Dec 04
[35] Post Operation Tour Report, Operation Telic 4/5, Headquarters Multinational Division (South East), 4 Dec 04
[36] Multinational Division (South East) Commanders War Diary 16 Jun to 30 Nov 04
[37] Multinational Division (South East) Commanders War Diary 16 Jun to 30 Nov 04
[38] Post Operation Tour Report, Operation Telic 4/5, Headquarters Multinational Division (South East), 4 Dec 04
[39] Lessons Capture Process Interview, Maj Gen Andrew Stewart, 31 Aug 2004
[40] Lesson Capture Process Interview, Brig Nick Carter, 23 June 04
[41] Post Operation Tour Report, Operation Telic 4/5, Headquarters Multinational Division (South East), 4 Dec 04
[42] Lesson Capture Process Interview, Lt Col PML Napier, 6 Jul 04
[43] 1 PWRR BG Lessons Report Operation Telic, October 2004
[44] Post Operation Tour Report, Operation Telic 4/5, Headquarters Multinational Division (South East), 4 Dec 04
[45] Lesson Capture Process Interview, Lt Col JR Free, 22 Jun 04
[46] Lesson Capture Process Interview, Brig Nick Carter, 23 June 04
[47] Lesson Capture Process Interview, Brig Nick Carter, 23 June 04
[48] Lesson Capture Process Interview, Maj AJ Aitkin, 22 Jun 04
[49] Lesson Capture Process Interview, Maj AJ Aitkin, 22 Jun 04
[50] Lessons Capture Process Interview, Maj Gen Andrew Stewart, 31 Aug 2004
[51] Lessons Capture Process Interview, Maj Gen Andrew Stewart, 31 Aug 2004
[52] Lesson Capture Process Interview, Colonel RD Marshall, 3 Sept 2004

[53] Post Operation Tour Report, Operation Telic 3/4, Headquarters, Multinational Division (South East), 13 Jul 04
[54] Post Operation Tour Report, Operation Telic 4/5, Headquarters Multinational Division (South East), 4 Dec 04
[55] Lesson Capture Process Interview, Col JK Tanner, 8 Sept 2004
[56] Lesson Capture Process Interview, Col JK Tanner, 8 Sept 2004
[57] Lessons Capture Process Interview, Maj Gen Andrew Stewart, 31 Aug 2004
[58] Lesson Capture Process Interview, Col JK Tanner, 8 Sept 2004
[59] Post Operation Tour Report, Operation Telic 3/4, Headquarters, Multinational Division (South East), 13 Jul 04
[60] Lesson Capture Process Interview, Colonel RD Marshall, 3 Sept 2004
[61] Post Operation Tour Report, Operation Telic 4/5, Headquarters Multinational Division (South East), 4 Dec 04
[62] Post Operation Tour Report, Operation Telic 4/5, Headquarters Multinational Division (South East), 4 Dec 04
[63] p.196, *Muqtada Al-Sadr and the Future Battle for Iraq*, Patrick Cockburn (Scribner) 2008
[64] Multinational Division (South East) Commanders War Diary 16 Jun to 30 Nov 04
[65] p.39, p.40, 2005 Edition, Vedette, Queen's Royal Lancers

Chapter 17 – Buying Influence

[1] p.18, *The End Game*, Michael Gordon and Bernard Trainor, (Atlantic Books) 2012
[2] https://www.gov.uk/government/fatalities/corporal-ian-plank-royal-marines
[3] John Hutton, Hansard, 26th February 2009
[4] Lesson Capture Process Interview, Lt Col JR Free, 22 Jun 04
[5] John McColl evidence to Chilcot Inquiry, 8th February 2010
[6] 1 BW Post Operation Report – Operation Bracken, 9 Dec 04
[7] p.223, *Leading from the Front,* Richard Dannatt, (Bantam) 2010
[8] Lessons Capture Process Interview, Maj Gen Andrew Stewart, 31 Aug 2004
[9] Barney White-Spunner, 29th January 2013
[10] Barney White-Spunner, 29th January 2013
[11] p.222, *Leading from the Front,* Richard Dannatt, (Bantam) 2010
[12] p.27, May 2005 Edition, The Red Hackle, The Black Watch
[13] Multinational Division (South East) Commanders War Diary 16 Jun to 30 Nov 04
[14] 1 BW Post Operation Report – Operation Bracken, 9 Dec 04
[15] p.29, May 2005 Edition, The Red Hackle, The Black Watch
[16] John McColl evidence to Chilcot Inquiry, 8th February 2010
[17] Glenn Torpy Interview, 20th June 2013
[18] Michael Walker, evidence to Chilcot Inquiry 1st February 2010
[19] Glenn Torpy Interview, 20th June 2013
[20] Robin Brims Interview 13th November 2012
[21] Geoff Hoon, Hansard, 19th October 2012
[22] Geoff Hoon, Hansard, 21st October 2012
[23] p.65. Task Force Black, *Mark Urban (Little & Brown) 2010*
[24] 1 BW Post Operation Report – Operation Bracken, 9 Dec 04

[25] p.30-31, May 2005 Edition, The Red Hackle, The Black Watch
[26] 1 BW Post Operation Report – Operation Bracken, 9 Dec 04
[27] p.33, May 2005 Edition, The Red Hackle, The Black Watch
[28] 1 BW Post Operation Report – Operation Bracken, 9 Dec 04
[29] 1 BW Post Operation Report – Operation Bracken, 9 Dec 04
[30] Multinational Division (South East) Commanders War Diary 16 Jun to 30 Nov 04
[31] p.37, May 2005 Edition, The Red Hackle, The Black Watch
[32] 1 BW Post Operation Report – Operation Bracken, 9 Dec 04
[33] p.44, May 2005 Edition, The Red Hackle, The Black Watch
[34] p.45, May 2005 Edition, The Red Hackle, The Black Watch
[35] p.46, May 2005 Edition, The Red Hackle, The Black Watch
[36] John Kiszley evidence to Chilcot Inquiry, 14th December 2009
[37] Robin Brims Interview 13th November 2012
[38] Robin Brims Interview 13th November 2012

Chapter 18 – The Trainers

[1] p.5, 2005/06 Edition, Welsh Guards Regimental Magazine
[2] p.16, 2005/06 Edition, Welsh Guards Regimental Magazine
[3] p.17, 2005/06 Edition, Welsh Guards Regimental Magazine
[4] Sgt Paul Connolly inquest verdict Oxfordshire Coroner 17th May 2006 and Pte Mark Dobson inquest verdict Oxfordshire Coroner 14th December 2005
[5] Brian Burridge Interview, 24th May 2013
[6] p.22, 2006 Edition, The Lion and the Dragon, King's Own Royal Border Regiment
[7] p.11, 2004/05 Edition, Quis Separabit: The Journal of the Royal Dragoon Guards
[8] p.11, 2004/05 Edition, Quis Separabit: The Journal of the Royal Dragoon Guards
[9] p.10, 2005/06 Edition, Welsh Guards Regimental Magazine
[10] p.29, 2006 Edition, The Lion and the Dragon, King's Own Royal Border Regiment
[11] p.43, 2006 Edition, The Highlander, The Highlanders
[12] MOD Op Telic troop rotation announcements, 2003 to 2006
[13] Author Interview with senior Ministry of Defence-based military officer
[14] Glenn Torpy Interview, 20th June 2013
[15] Glenn Torpy Interview, 20th June 2013
[16] Correspondence with Jonathon Riley, 24-29 July 2013
[17] p.34-35, February 2005 Edition, Scots Guards Magazine, The Scots Guards
[18] Correspondence with Jonathon Riley, 24-29 July 2013
[19] p.34-35, February 2005 Edition, Scots Guards Magazine, The Scots Guards
[20] p.34-35, February 2005 Edition, Scots Guards Magazine, The Scots Guards
[21] Security Sector Reform (SSR), Op TELIC 7, Lieutenant Colonel I G Harrison MBE RHA, Commanding Officer, 3rd Regiment Royal Horse Artillery, 27 Sept 2005
[22] Security Sector Reform (SSR), Op TELIC 7, Lieutenant Colonel I G Harrison MBE RHA, Commanding Officer, 3rd Regiment Royal Horse Artillery, 27 Sept 2005

[23] Security Sector Reform (SSR), Op TELIC 7, Lieutenant Colonel I G Harrison MBE RHA, Commanding Officer, 3rd Regiment Royal Horse Artillery, 27 Sept 2005
[24] Security Sector Reform (SSR), Op TELIC 7, Lieutenant Colonel I G Harrison MBE RHA, Commanding Officer, 3rd Regiment Royal Horse Artillery, 27 Sept 2005
[25] Glenn Torpy Interview, 20th June 2013
[26] Correspondence with Jonathon Riley, 24-29 July 2013
[27] p.43, 2006 Edition, The Highlander, The Highlanders
[28] Security Sector Reform (SSR), Op TELIC 7, Lieutenant Colonel I G Harrison MBE RHA, Commanding Officer, 3rd Regiment Royal Horse Artillery, 27 Sept 2005
[29] Glenn Torpy Interview, 20th June 2013
[30] Glenn Torpy Interview, 20th June 2013
[31] p.100-102, 2004/05 Edition, Quis Separabit: The Journal of the Royal Dragoon Guards
[32] Major Johnny Austin, Interview with US Combat Studies Institute, Fort Leavenworth, Kansas, 7th May 2008
[33] p.4, 2005/06 Edition, Welsh Guards Regimental Magazine
[34] p.43, 2006 Edition, The Highlander, The Highlanders
[35] p.100-102, 2004/05 Edition, Quis Separabit: The Journal of the Royal Dragoon Guards
[36] p.29, 2006 Edition, The Lion and the Dragon, King's Own Royal Border Regiment
[37] p.29, 2006 Edition, The Lion and the Dragon, King's Own Royal Border Regiment
[38] p.35, 2005 Edition, The Stafford Knot, Staffordshire Regiment
[39] p.100-102, 2004/05 Edition, Quis Separabit: The Journal of the Royal Dragoon Guards
[40] Jim Dutton Evidence to Chilcot Inquiry, 12th July 2010
[41] Security Sector Reform (SSR), Op TELIC 7, Lieutenant Colonel I G Harrison MBE RHA, Commanding Officer, 3rd Regiment Royal Horse Artillery, 27 Sept 2005
[42] p.159-161, *The End Game*, Michael Gordon and Bernard Trainor, (Atlantic Books) 2012
[43] Security Sector Reform (SSR), Op TELIC 7, Lieutenant Colonel I G Harrison MBE RHA, Commanding Officer, 3rd Regiment Royal Horse Artillery, 27 Sept 2005
[44] Security Sector Reform (SSR), Op TELIC 7, Lieutenant Colonel I G Harrison MBE RHA, Commanding Officer, 3rd Regiment Royal Horse Artillery, 27 Sept 2005
[45] Glenn Torpy Evidence to Chilcot Inquiry, 18 January 2011
[46] Jim Dutton Evidence to Chilcot Inquiry, 12th July 2010

Chapter 19 – The Divorce
[1] p.418-420, *Occupational Hazards*, Rory Stewart (Picador) 2006
[2] p.418-419, *Occupational Hazards*, Rory Stewart (Picador) 2006
[3] Glenn Torpy Interview, 20th June 2013

[4] p.155-156, *The End Game*, Michael Gordon and Bernard Trainor, (Atlantic Books) 2012
[5] Author interview with 7 Armoured Brigade officers, 2006
[6] Author interview with 7 Armoured Brigade officers, 2006
[7] We will spill British blood, warns Sheikh Ahmad Fartusi, Hala Jaber, Sunday Times, 14th September 2008
[8] Major Johnny Austin, Interview with US Combat Studies Institute, Fort Leavenworth, Kansas, 7th May 2008
[9] Major Johnny Austin, Interview with US Combat Studies Institute, Fort Leavenworth, Kansas, 7th May 2008
[10] Author interview with 7 Armoured Brigade officers, 2006
[11] p.33, 2005 Edition, The Stafford Knot, Staffordshire Regiment
[12] p.33, 2005 Edition, The Stafford Knot, Staffordshire Regiment
[13] p.34, 2005 Edition, The Stafford Knot, Staffordshire Regiment
[14] p.34, 2005 Edition, The Stafford Knot, Staffordshire Regiment
[15] p.4, 2006 Edition, King's Royal Hussars Regimental Journal
[16] Author interview with 7 Armoured Brigade officers, 2006
[17] p.30, 2005 Edition, The Stafford Knot, Staffordshire Regiment
[18] p.32, 2005 Edition, The Stafford Knot, Staffordshire Regiment
[19] p.34, 2005 Edition, The Stafford Knot, Staffordshire Regiment
[20] http://www.shinycapstar.com/optelsitrep_d.htm
[21] p.34, 2005 Edition, The Stafford Knot, Staffordshire Regiment
[22] Basrah City BG Brief, 1 Coldstream Guards 2005
[23] http://www.shinycapstar.com/basrahbulletin_aug05.htm
[24] Basrah City BG Brief, 1 Coldstream Guards 2005
[25] p.23, p.30, 2005 Edition, The Stafford Knot, Staffordshire Regiment
[26] Major Johnny Austin, Interview with US Combat Studies Institute, Fort Leavenworth, Kansas, 7th May 2008
[27] Author interview with 7 Armoured Brigade officers, 2006
[28] p.36, December 2005, Edition, The Castle, Royal Anglian Regiment
[29] p.28-29, 2005 Edition, The Stafford Knot, Staffordshire Regiment
[30] p.28-29, 2005 Edition, The Stafford Knot, Staffordshire Regiment
[31] p.5, 2006 Edition, King's Royal Hussars Regimental Journal
[32] Who dares mutinies: How the SAS defied orders to launch the most audacious rescue of the Iraq war, Tony Rennell, Daily Mail, 15th May 2010
[33] Ronnie Flanagan evidence to Chilcot Inquiry, 26th July 2010
[34] Author interview with 7 Armoured Brigade officers, 2006
[35] p.42, 2006 Edition, The Highlander, The Highlanders
[36] p.47, 2006 Edition, The Highlander, The Highlanders
[37] p.42, 2006 Edition, The Highlander, The Highlanders
[38] p.23, 2006 Edition, The Vedette, Queen's Royal Lancers
[39] p.17, 2006 Edition, The Lion and the Dragon, King's Own Royal Border Regiment
[40] p.43, 2006 Edition, The Highlander, The Highlanders
[41] p.43, 2006 Edition, The Highlander, The Highlanders
[42] Major Johnny Austin, Interview with US Combat Studies Institute, Fort Leavenworth, Kansas, 7th May 2008

[43] Major Johnny Austin, Interview with US Combat Studies Institute, Fort Leavenworth, Kansas, 7th May 2008
[44] Major Johnny Austin, Interview with US Combat Studies Institute, Fort Leavenworth, Kansas, 7th May 2008
[45] Op Telic 7 Commanders Study Period Briefing 27th September 2005, Brigadier P C Marriott
[46] Author interview with 7 Armoured Brigade officers, 2006
[47] Op Telic 7 Commanders Study Period Briefing 27th September 2005, Brigadier P C Marriott
[48] Op Telic 7 Commanders Study Period Briefing 27th September 2005, Brigadier P C Marriott
[49] Op Telic 7 Commanders Study Period Briefing 27th September 2005, Brigadier P C Marriott
[50] Major Johnny Austin, Interview with US Combat Studies Institute, Fort Leavenworth, Kansas, 7th May 2008
[51] Major Johnny Austin, Interview with US Combat Studies Institute, Fort Leavenworth, Kansas, 7th May 2008
[52] p.47, 2006 Edition, The Highlander, The Highlanders
[53] p.49, 2006 Edition, The Highlander, The Highlanders
[54] Author interview with former member of 1 KORBR
[55] p.43, 2006 Edition, The Highlander, The Highlanders
[56] Author interview with 7 Armoured Brigade officers, 2006
[57] p.43, 2006 Edition, The Highlander, The Highlanders
[58] Author interview with 7 Armoured Brigade officers, 2006
[59] p.43, 2006 Edition, The Highlander, The Highlanders
[60] Author interview with 7 Armoured Brigade officers, 2006
[61] p.18, 2006 Edition, The Lion and the Dragon, King's Own Royal Border Regiment
[62] p.44-45, Letters from Amarah, The Iraq Tour Oct 05 to Apr 06, Royal Scots Dragoon Guards
[63] John Cooper evidence to Chilcot Inquiry, 15th December 2009
[64] British troops out of Iraq in two years, Oliver Poole, Daily Telegraph, 7th March 2006
[65] p.269-271, *My Share of the Task,* Stanley McChrystal, (Penguin), 2013
[66] p.132, Task Force Black, *Mark Urban (Little & Brown) 2010*
[67] A Strategic Review of the Puma Helicopter Force, Air Commodore CW Dixon and Colonel NJW Moss, 15th May 2008
[68] p.92-93, Task Force Black, *Mark Urban (Little & Brown) 2010*
[69] Author interview with senior military officer who served in Ministry of Defence in 2006

Chapter 20 – RAF Against Insurgents

[1] 1 (UK) Armoured Division, Operations Order Phase IV for Operation Telic, 17 Apr 2003
[2] 8th August Edition, RAF News
[3] Post Operations Report and Lessons Identified, 19 Mech Brigade, Op Telic 2
[4] Author Interview at al Udeid Airbase, 24th September 2006
[5] Author Interview at al Udeid Airbase, 24th September 2006
[6] Author Interview at al Udeid Airbase, 24th September 2006

[7] Author Interview at al Udeid Airbase, 24th September 2006
[8] Author Interview at al Udeid Airbase, 24th September 2006
[9] Author Interview at al Udeid Airbase, 24th September 2006
[10] p.2, *War Without Consequences,* Terence McNamee (editor), (RUSI) 2008
[11] Flight International, 15th August 2000
[12] http://www.14sqn-association.org.uk/14_Squadron_Association/Issue_8.html
[13] Author Interview at al Udeid Airbase, 23rd September 2006
[14] Author Interview at al Udeid Airbase, 23rd September 2006
[15] Author Interview at al Udeid Airbase, 23rd September 2006
[16] Author Interview at al Udeid Airbase, 23rd September 2006
[17] Author Interview at al Udeid Airbase, 23rd September 2006
[18] Author Interview at al Udeid Airbase, 23rd September 2006
[19] http://www.14sqn-association.org.uk/14_Squadron_Association/Issue_9.html
[20] Eagles Over the Desert' The RAF and Iraq, 1990-2009, RAF Air Staff, 16th March 2009
[21] Author Interview at al Udeid Airbase, 24th September 2006
[22] Author Interviews at RAF Kinloss, 10th March 2010
[23] Post Operation Tour Report, Operation Telic 3/4, Headquarters, Multinational Division (South East), 13 Jul 04
[24] Post Operation Tour Report, Operation Telic 3/4, Headquarters, Multinational Division (South East), 13 Jul 04
[25] Nimrod Operational Hours, released by RAF Air Command, 14th April 2010
[26] Author Interviews at RAF Kinloss, 10th March 2010
[27] Author Interviews at RAF Kinloss, 10th March 2010
[28] Author Interviews at RAF Kinloss, 10th March 2010
[29] Author Interviews at RAF Kinloss, 10th March 2010
[30] Author Interviews at RAF Kinloss, 10th March 2010
[31] Author Interviews at RAF Kinloss, 10th March 2010
[32] Nimrod Operational Hours, released by RAF Air Command, 14th April 2010
[33] Author Interviews at RAF Kinloss, 10th March 2010
[34] Author Interview Creech AFB, 19th March 2009
[35] Author Interview Creech AFB, 19th March 2009
[36] Author Interview Creech AFB, 19th March 2009
[37] Author Interview Creech AFB, 19th March 2009
[38] Author Interview at al Udeid Airbase, 24th September 2006

Chapter 21 – Good Kit? Crap Kit?

[1] Board of Inquiry in Death of Sgt Roberts, 31st July 2006
[2] p.2-12, Operations in Iraq – An Analysis from a Land Perspective, British Army 2003
[3] Dick Applegate Interview, 23rd October 2012
[4] p.143, 2004 Edition, Eagle and Carbine, Royal Scots Dragoon Guards
[5] p.52-12, Operations in Iraq – An Analysis from a Land Perspective, British Army 2003
[6] Dick Applegate Interview, 23rd October 2012
[7] Dick Applegate Interview, 23rd October 2012
[8] David Eadie correspondence, 25th September 2013
[9] David Eadie correspondence, 25th September 2013

[10] Hansard, 20 July 2006
[11] Author interview with MOD EOD official
[12] Dick Applegate Interview, 23rd October 2012
[13] Project Locksmith Overview, PJHQ Briefing 2005
[14] Project Locksmith Overview, PJHQ Briefing 2005
[15] Project Locksmith Overview, PJHQ Briefing 2005
[16] Post Operational Tour Report, Operation Telic, Headquarters 1 Mechanised Brigade, January 2005
[17] The cost-effective delivery of an armoured vehicle capability, National Audit Office, 2011
[18] Post Operational Tour Report, Operation Telic, Headquarters 1 Mechanised Brigade, January 2005
[19] Dick Applegate Interview, 23rd October 2012
[20] 7 Armoured Brigade IED Briefing 2005
[21] Senior MOD official in 2006
[22] Interview 7 Armoured Brigade Officer, 2006
[23] Jim Dutton evidence to Chilcot Inquiry, 15 July 2010
[24] Glenn Torpy evidence to Chilcot Inquiry, 18 January 2011
[25] Richard Dannatt evidence to Chilcot Inquiry, 28th July 2010
[26] Glenn Torpy evidence to Chilcot Inquiry, 18 January 2011
[27] Lord Drayson Witness Statement to Chilcot Inquiry on Protected Patrol Vehicles, 15th December 2010
[28] Dick Applegate Interview, 23rd October 2012
[29] Dick Applegate Interview, 23rd October 2012
[30] Lord Drayson Witness Statement to Chilcot Inquiry on Protected Patrol Vehicles, 15th December 2010
[31] Glenn Torpy evidence to Chilcot Inquiry, 18 January 2011
[32] Dick Applegate Interview, 23rd October 2012
[33] Dick Applegate Interview, 23rd October 2012
[34] Dick Applegate Interview, 23rd October 2012
[35] p.30, *British Next Generation Armour*, Carl Schulze, (Tankograd) 2008
[36] p.10, *British Next Generation Armour*, Carl Schulze, (Tankograd) 2008
[37] BAE Systems Briefing on Warrior 26th June 2013
[38] UK deploys Phalanx C-RAM system to protect forces in Iraq, Jane's Defence Weekly, 30th May 2007
[39] UK deploys Centurion to counter insurgent attacks on Basra, Jane's Defence Weekly, 24th September 2009
[40] 7 Armoured Brigade Commander's Study Period, UAV Support to Operations in Iraq Major P Tombleson RA, Battery Commander 57 (Bhurtpore) Battery Royal Artillery
[41] http://www.michaelyon-online.com
[42] Richard Shirreff evidence to Chilcot Inquiry, 11th January 2010
[43] Author interview with Thales UK executive 2006
[44] Author interview with Thales UK executive 2006
[45] Post Operation Tour Report, Operation Telic 3/4, Headquarters, Multinational Division (South East), 13 Jul 04
[46] Author interview with Vector Aerospace executive, 25th November 2008
[47] Author visit to 9 Regiment Army Air Corps, 14th June 2010

[48] Board of Inquiry Regarding the Circumstances Surrounding the Deaths of Sergeant Simon Hamilton-Jewell, Corporal Russell Aston, Corporal Paul Graham Long, Corporal Simon Miller, Lance-Corporal Benjamin John McGowan Hyde, and Lance-Corporal Thomas Keys, 19 Oct 2004
[49] British Army holds 'census' to locate Bowman kit, Jane's Defence Weekly, 2nd May 2008
[50] Bowman Experience from OP Telic ,WO2 S J Harris - RSWO 4 RIFLES , The Infantryman, 2007
[51] Author interview with 7 Armoured Brigade officer in 2006
[52] Comments of MND (SE) staff officer in 2007
[53] http://www.theguardian.com/uk/2008/oct/22/hercules-inquest-verdict
[54] Glenn Torpy Interview, 20th June 2013
[55] Dick Applegate Interview, 23rd October 2012
[56] Dick Applegate Interview, 23rd October 2012
[57] Jim Dutton evidence to Chilcot Inquiry, 15 July 2010
[58] Dick Applegate Interview, 23rd October 2012

Chapter 22 – The Duel

[1] Board of Inquiry of Aircraft Crash Lynx AH Mk.7 (XZ614) of 847 NAS In Basra, Iraq, 20 June 06
[2] p.42, December 2006 Edition, The Castle, Royal Anglian Regiment
[3] p.18, Winter 2006 Edition, The Silver Bugler, The Light Infantry
[4] Major Johnny Austin, Interview with US Combat Studies Institute, Fort Leavenworth, Kansas, 7th May 2008
[5] p.17, 2006-07 Edition, Journal of The Princess of Wales's Royal Regiment
[6] p.17, 2006-07 Edition, Journal of The Princess of Wales's Royal Regiment
[7] p.17, 2006-07 Edition, Journal of The Princess of Wales's Royal Regiment
[8] Attitudes in Iraq – Apr/May 2006 Wave 6, Iraq Polling Data, June 2005 to December 2006, PJHQ
[9] The 4 RIFLES Battle Group Operations in Basra, Summer 2007, Patrick Sanders, RUSI Presentation, 9th March 2009
[10] Author interview with close advisor to Air Chief Marshal Sir Jock Stirrup
[11] Author interview with close advisor to Air Chief Marshal Sir Jock Stirrup
[12] p.139, *The Rifle's Chronicle 2007,* (RHQ The Rifles) 2008
[13] Author interview with close advisor to Air Chief Marshal Sir Jock Stirrup
[14] Author interview with close advisor to Air Chief Marshal Sir Jock Stirrup
[15] Author interview with close advisor to Air Chief Marshal Sir Jock Stirrup
[16] Glenn Torpy Interview, 20th June 2013
[17] Glenn Torpy Interview, 20th June 2013
[18] Author Interview with senior British officer September 2006
[19] Author interview with close advisor to Air Chief Marshal Sir Jock Stirrup
[20] p.19, Winter 2006 Edition, The Silver Bugler, The Light Infantry
[21] p.19, Winter 2006 Edition, The Silver Bugler, The Light Infantry
[22] p.18, September 2009 edition of The Gunner, Royal Artillery
[23] p.42, 2006-07 Edition, Journal of The Princess of Wales's Royal Regiment
[24] p.51, December 2006 Edition, The Castle, Royal Anglian Regiment
[25] http://www.michaelyon-online.com
[26] p.40-41, December 2006 Edition, The Castle, Royal Anglian Regiment

[27] p.40-41, December 2006 Edition, The Castle, Royal Anglian Regiment
[28] Op Telic Casualty and Fatality Tables, 31st July 2009, DASA
[29] Author interview with witness to events
[30] Nick Houghton evidence to Chilcot Inquiry, 5th January 2010
[31] Nick Houghton evidence to Chilcot Inquiry, 5th January 2010
[32] p.67 December 2006 Edition, The Fusilier, Royal Regiment of Fusiliers
[33] Richard Shirreff evidence to Chilcot Inquiry, 11th January 2010
[34] p.316-317, *The End Game*, Michael Gordon and Bernard Trainor, (Atlantic Books) 2012
[35] p.257, *My Share of the Task,* Stanley McChrystal, (Penguin), 2013
[36] Richard Shirreff evidence to Chilcot Inquiry, 11th January 2010
[37] p.58, p.40-41, December 2006 Edition, The Castle, Royal Anglian Regiment
[38] p.34, 2006-07 Edition, Journal of The Princess of Wales's Royal Regiment
[39] p.18 2006 Edition, Grenadier Gazette, The Grenadier Guards
[40] p.18-19, 2006 Edition, Grenadier Gazette, The Grenadier Guards
[41] p.19, 2006 Edition, Grenadier Gazette, The Grenadier Guards
[42] p.32, 2006 Edition, The Crossbelts, Queen's Royal Hussars
[43] p.27, 2006 Edition, The Crossbelts, Queen's Royal Hussars
[44] p.27, 2006 Edition, The Crossbelts, Queen's Royal Hussars
[45] MoD kept failure of best tank quiet, Sean Rayment, Daily Telegraph, 13th May 2007
[46] p.28, 2006 Edition, The Crossbelts, Queen's Royal Hussars
[47] p.28, 2006 Edition, The Crossbelts, Queen's Royal Hussars
[48] p.4, 2006 Edition, The Crossbelts, Queen's Royal Hussars
[49] p.22, Winter 2006 Edition, The Silver Bugler, The Light Infantry
[50] p.73, December 2006 Edition, The Fusilier, Royal Regiment of Fusiliers
[51] p.194-5, Task Force Black, *Mark Urban (Little & Brown) 2010*
[52] p.48, December 2006 Edition, The Castle, Royal Anglian Regiment
[53] p.38, Winter 2006 Edition, The Silver Bugler, The Light Infantry
[54] p.19, The Basra Knot, Staffordshire Regiment
[55] p.49, December 2006 Edition, The Castle, Royal Anglian Regiment
[56] p.13, 2006 Edition, The Crossbelts, Queen's Royal Hussars
[57] p.234, *The Devonshire and Dorset Regiment: 11th, 29th and 54th of Foot, 1958 - 2007,* (Pen & Sword) 2007
[58] Richard Shirreff evidence to Chilcot Inquiry, 11th January 2010
[59] Richard Shirreff evidence to Chilcot Inquiry, 11th January 2010
[60] p.163, *British Generals in Blair's Wars,* Jonathan Bailey, Richard Iron and Hew Strachan, (Ashgate) 2013
[61] Author interview with close advisor to Air Chief Marshal Sir Jock Stirrup
[62] Author interview with member of MND(SE) staff
[63] p.139, *The Rifle's Chronicle 2007,* (RHQ The Rifles) 2008
[64] Richard Shirreff evidence to Chilcot Inquiry, 11th January 2010
[65] p.142, *The Rifle's Chronicle 2007,* (RHQ The Rifles) 2008
[66] p.59-64, The Stafford Knot, Staffordshire Regiment

Chapter 23 – The Accommodation
[1] Jonathan Shaw Interview, 8th November 2012

[2] p.223-226, *The Strongest Tribe,* Bing West, (Random House) 2008
[3] Jonathan Shaw Interview, 8th November 2012
[4] Author interview to witness to these meetings
[5] Jonathan Shaw Interview, 8th November 2012
[6] Author interview with close advisor to Air Chief Marshal Sir Jock Stirrup
[7] Jonathan Shaw Interview, 8th November 2012
[8] Jonathan Shaw Interview, 8th November 2012
[9] Jonathan Shaw Interview, 8th November 2012
[10] Author interview with member of MND(SE) staff officer
[11] p.141, *The Rifle's Chronicle 2007,* (RHQ The Rifles) 2008
[12] Jonathan Shaw Interview, 8th November 2012
[13] The 4 RIFLES Battle Group Operations in Basra, Summer 2007, Patrick Sanders, RUSI Presentation, 9th March 2009
[14] p.141, *The Rifle's Chronicle 2007,* (RHQ The Rifles) 2008
[15] p.140-143, *The Rifle's Chronicle 2007,* (RHQ The Rifles) 2008
[16] p.18, September 2009 edition of The Gunner, Royal Artillery
[17] Unit Photograph on display in the Lancashire Infantry Museum, Fulwood Barraks, Preston
[18] Armed Forces seek WLR connect, Rupert Pengelley, Jane's International Defence Review, January 2009
[19] p.143, *The Rifle's Chronicle 2007,* (RHQ The Rifles) 2008
[20] p.59, 2007 Edition, The Stafford Knot, Staffordshire Regiment
[21] p.100, Summer 2008 Edition, Y Cymro (The Welshman), The Regimental Journal of The Royal Welsh, The Royal Welsh Regiment
[22] Adam Ingram, Hansard, 18th February 2008
[23] p.24, 2007 Edition, The Stafford Knot, Staffordshire Regiment
[24] p.142, *The Rifle's Chronicle 2007,* (RHQ The Rifles) 2008
[25] Author interview with member of MND(SE) staff officer
[26] p.200, Task Force Black, Mark Urban (Little & Brown) 2010
[27] p.70, 2007 Edition, The Kingsman, The Duke of Lancaster's Regiment
[28] p. 2, *British Next Generation Armour,* Carl Schulze, (Tankograd) 2008
[29] Author interview with member of MND(SE) staff officer
[30] p.81, 2007 Edition, The Kingsman, The Duke of Lancaster's Regiment
[31] p.81, 2007 Edition, The Kingsman, The Duke of Lancaster's Regiment
[32] p.75, 2007 Edition, The Kingsman, The Duke of Lancaster's Regiment
[33] p.351, *The End Game,* Michael Gordon and Bernard Trainor, (Atlantic Books) 2012
[34] p.86-87, 2007 Edition, The Kingsman, The Duke of Lancaster's Regiment
[35] p.257, *My Share of the Task,* Stanley McChrystal, (Penguin), 2013
[36] http://news.bbc.co.uk/1/hi/6765903.stm
[37] p.231, Task Force Black, Mark Urban (Little & Brown) 2010
[38] p.25, The Basra Knot, Staffordshire Regiment
[39] p. 144, *The Rifle's Chronicle 2007,* (RHQ The Rifles) 2008
[40] p.87, 2007 Edition, The Kingsman, The Duke of Lancaster's Regiment
[41] http://news.bbc.co.uk/1/hi/world/middle_east/6458173.stm
[42] p.71-72, Summer 2008 Edition, Y Cymro (The Welshman), The Regimental Journal of The Royal Welsh, The Royal Welsh Regiment

[43] p.71-72, Summer 2008 Edition, Y Cymro (The Welshman), The Regimental Journal of The Royal Welsh, The Royal Welsh Regiment
[44] p.71-72, Summer 2008 Edition, Y Cymro (The Welshman), The Regimental Journal of The Royal Welsh, The Royal Welsh Regiment
[45] p.141, *The Rifle's Chronicle 2007,* (RHQ The Rifles) 2008
[46] Company Operations Around Basra, Maj M E Foster-Brown - OC C Coy 2 RIFLES The Infantryman 2007
[47] The 4 RIFLES Battle Group Operations in Basra, Summer 2007, Patrick Sanders, RUSI Presentation, 9th March 2009
[48] p.53, Spring 2008 Edition, The Bugle, The Rifles
[49] p.56, Autumn 2007, The Bugle, The Rifles
[50] http://www.michaelyon-online.com/men-of-valor-part-ii.htm
[51] The 4 RIFLES Battle Group Operations in Basra, Summer 2007, Patrick Sanders, RUSI Presentation, 9th March 2009
[52] http://www.michaelyon-online.com/men-of-valor-part-ii.htm
[53] p.57, Autumn 2007, The Bugle, The Rifles
[54] p.57, Autumn 2007, The Bugle, The Rifles
[55] Who's Afraid of Fleet Street?, Capt C T R Salmon, RSO and Media Offr 2 RIFLES, The Infantryman 2007
[56] Who's Afraid of Fleet Street?, Capt C T R Salmon, RSO and Media Offr 2 RIFLES, The Infantryman 2007
[57] The 4 RIFLES Battle Group Operations in Basra, Summer 2007, Patrick Sanders, RUSI Presentation, 9th March 2009
[58] p.83, 2007 Edition, The Kingsman, The Duke of Lancaster's Regiment
[59] p.58, Autumn 2007, The Bugle, The Rifles
[60] p.58, Autumn 2007, The Bugle, The Rifles
[61] Basra's last battle: the untold story, Sean Rayment, Sunday Telegraph, 2nd March 2008
[62] ISTAR at BG level in Peace Support Operations, 4 Rifles Experience from Op Telic 10, Capt A N L Boardman and Capt A B L Price, The Infantryman 2007
[63] p.88, Summer 2008 Edition, Y Cymro (The Welshman), The Regimental Journal of The Royal Welsh, The Royal Welsh Regiment
[64] p.89, Summer 2008 Edition, Y Cymro (The Welshman), The Regimental Journal of The Royal Welsh, The Royal Welsh Regiment
[65] Board of Inquiry into Accident involving Hercules C130 Mk4 ZH876
[66] Author interview with senior MND(SE) staff officer
[67] p.67, 2007 Edition, King's Royal Hussars Regimental Journal
[68] p.32, 2007 Edition, King's Royal Hussars Regimental Journal
[69] Des Browne, Hansard, 18th February 2008
[70] p.32, *History of 1 Squadron,* (The Royal Air Force Regiment) 2011
[71] p.23, 2007 Edition, King's Royal Hussars Regimental Journal
[72] p.46, 2008 Edition, The Irish Guards Journal
[73] p.46, 2008 Edition, The Irish Guards Journal
[74] CJTSOF(I) and TF17 Intelligence summaries, 20 & 21 January 2007
[75] Colonel Ian Thomas, 'Pointing the Way Out: The Utility of Force and the Basra Narrative. January-August 2007', *British Army Review,* issue 148, 2010 and p.45, The British Experience in Iraq, 2007: A Perspective on the Utility of Force, Colonel Ian N. A. Thomas, School of Advanced Military

Studies, United States Army Command and General Staff College, Fort Leavenworth, Kansas
[76] Jonathan Shaw Interview, 8th November 2012
[77] Jonathan Shaw Interview, 8th November 2012
[78] The British Experience in Iraq, 2007: A Perspective on the Utility of Force, Colonel Ian N. A. Thomas, School of Advanced Military Studies, United States Army Command and General Staff College, Fort Leavenworth, Kansas
[79] The British Experience in Iraq, 2007: A Perspective on the Utility of Force, Colonel Ian N. A. Thomas, School of Advanced Military Studies, United States Army Command and General Staff College, Fort Leavenworth, Kansas
[80] MND(SE) Intelligence summary 23rd May 2007
[81] Jonathan Shaw Interview, 8th November 2012
[82] Jonathan Shaw Interview, 8th November 2012
[83] Jonathan Shaw Interview, 8th November 2012
[84] Author interview with senior MND(SE) staff officer
[85] p.68, 2007 Edition, The Kingsman, The Duke of Lancaster's Regiment
[86] p.142, *The Rifle's Chronicle 2007,* (RHQ The Rifles) 2008
[87] Jonathan Shaw Interview, 8th November 2012
[87] Jonathan Shaw Interview, 8th November 2012

Chapter 24 - Operation Charge of the Knights
[1] The 4 RIFLES Battle Group Operations in Basra, Summer 2007, Patrick Sanders, RUSI Presentation, 9th March 2009
[2] p.58, Spring 2008 Edition, The Bugle, The Rifles
[3] p.53, Spring 2008 Edition, The Bugle, The Rifles
[4] Author interview with MND(SE) staff officer
[5] Author interview with MND(SE) staff officer
[6] Author interview with MND(SE) staff officer
[7] Graham Binns Interview, 24th October 2012
[8] p.51, 2008 Edition, The Irish Guards Journal
[9] Graham Binns Interview, 24th October 2012
[10] Graham Binns Interview, 24th October 2012
[11] Graham Binns Interview, 24th October 2012
[12] p.16, 2008/9 Edition, The Kingsman, The Duke of Lancaster's Regiment
[13] p.23, 2008 Edition, The Scots Guards Magazine
[14] p.46, 2008 Edition, The Irish Guards Journal
[15] Graham Binns Interview, 24th October 2012
[16] Author interview with MND(SE) staff officer
[17] p.50, 2008 Edition, The Irish Guards Journal
[18] Barney White-Spunner, 29th January 2013
[19] Barney White-Spunner, 29th January 2013
[20] p.13, 2009 Edition, Quis Separabit: The Journal of the Royal Dragoon Guards
[21] p.13, 2009 Edition, Quis Separabit: The Journal of the Royal Dragoon Guards
[22] Barney White-Spunner, 29th January 2013
[23] Barney White-Spunner, 29th January 2013
[24] Barney White-Spunner, 29th January 2013
[25] Barney White-Spunner, 29th January 2013
[26] p.32, March 2009 Edition, Royal Regiment of Scotland Journal

[27] US State Department Cable, 04/02/2008 IRAQI OFFICIALS ON MALIKI'S BASRAH CAMPAIGN POL-MIL MINISTER-COUNSELOR MARCIE B. RIES
[28] US State Department Cable, MCNS MARCH 16 DISCUSSES BASRAH SECURITY, Ambassador Ryan C. Crocker
[29] US State Department Cable, MCNS ON MARCH 23 REVIEWED RECENT BAGHDAD ATTACKS, BASRAH SECURITY, AND STAFFING THE IRAQI ARMY Ambassador Ryan C. Crocker
[30] p.338-339, *Victory in Iraq*, Duncan L.Hunter, (Victory in Iraq), 2010
[31] p.472, *The End Game*, Michael Gordon and Bernard Trainor, (Atlantic Books) 2012 US State Department Cable, 03/31/2008 HELPING THE NEGIHBORS MAKE SENSE OF BASRAH Ambassador Ryan C. Crocker
[33] p.41, 2009 Edition, Quis Separabit: The Journal of the Royal Dragoon Guards
[34] MND(SE) Significant Event Report, 24th March 2008
[35] p.43, 2009 Edition, The Scots Guards Magazine
[36] p.474, *The End Game*, Michael Gordon and Bernard Trainor, (Atlantic Books) 2012
[37] MND(SE) Significant Event Report, 25th March 2008
[38] p.474, *The End Game*, Michael Gordon and Bernard Trainor, (Atlantic Books) 2012
[39] US State Department Cable, 03/26/08 BASRAH/BAGHDAD SITUATION REPORT: MARCH 25-26, Ambassador Ryan C. Crocker
[40] It's Hell Mr President, Episode 3, The Iraq War, broadcast on BBC2 14 August 2013
[41] p. 476, *The End Game*, Michael Gordon and Bernard Trainor, (Atlantic Books) 2012
[42] US State Department Cable, 03/26/08 BASRAH/BAGHDAD SITUATION REPORT: MARCH 25-26, Ambassador Ryan C. Crocker
[43] US State Department Cable, 03/26/2018 SOUTHERN IRAQ SITUATION REPORT: MARCH
[44] MND(SE) Significant Event Report, 26th March 2008
[45] US State Department Cable, 03/30/2008 SOUTHERN IRAQ SITUATION REPORT: MARCH 28, 1300, Political-Military Minister-Counselor Marcie B. Ries
[46] Barney White-Spunner, 29th January 2013
[47] p.348, *Victory in Iraq*, Duncan L.Hunter, (Victory in Iraq), 2010
[48] Author interview with MND(SE) staff officer
[49] US State Department Cable, 03/30/2008 SOUTHERN IRAQ SITUATION REPORT: MARCH 28, 1300, Political-Military Minister-Counselor Marcie B. Ries
[50] MND(SE) Significant Event Report, 27th March 2008
[51] MND(SE) Significant Event Report, 27th March 2008
[52] US State Department Cable, 03/30/2008 SOUTHERN IRAQ SITUATION REPORT: MARCH 28, 1300, Political-Military Minister-Counselor Marcie B. Ries
[53] Barney White-Spunner, 29th January 2013
[54] Barney White-Spunner, 29th January 2013
[55] p.36, March 2009 Edition, Royal Regiment of Scotland Journal
[56] p.36, March 2009 Edition, Royal Regiment of Scotland Journal

[57] p.36, March 2009 Edition, Royal Regiment of Scotland Journal
[58] p.42, 2009 Edition, Quis Separabit: The Journal of the Royal Dragoon Guards
[59] MND(SE) Significant Event Report, 28th March 2008
[60] p.478, *The End Game*, Michael Gordon and Bernard Trainor, (Atlantic Books) 2012
[61] p.27, 2009 Edition, Quis Separabit: The Journal of the Royal Dragoon Guards
[62] US State Department Cable 03/29/2018 MILITARY AND POLITICAL DEADLOCK IN BASRAH Political Counselor Matt Tueller
[63] US State Department Cable 03/29/2018 MILITARY AND POLITICAL DEADLOCK IN BASRAH Political Counselor Matt Tueller
[64] US State Department Cable, 03/29/2018 MILITARY AND POLITICAL DEADLOCK IN BASRAH Political Counselor Matt Tueller & 03/30/2018 SOUTHERN IRAQ SITUATION REPORT: MARCH 28, 1300 Political-Military Minister-Counselor Marcie B. Ries
[65] MND(SE) Significant Event Report, 29th March 2008
[66] MND(SE) Significant Event Report, 29th March 2008
[67] MND(SE) Significant Event Report, 29th March 2008
[68] US State Department Cable, 08/04/08: DAWA PARTY OFFICIAL ON BASRAH OPERATION AND UIA-SADR NEGOTIATIONS IN IRAN Political Counselor Matt Tueller (28th March visit)
[69] US State Department Cable, 03/30/2018: PM'S ADVISORS DISCUSS BASRAH EXIT STRATEGY Political-Military Counsellor Ambassador Marcie Ries
[70] Barney White-Spunner, 29th January 2013
[71] MND(SE) Significant Event Report, 30th March 2008
[72] p.28, 2009 Edition, Quis Separabit: The Journal of the Royal Dragoon Guards
[73] p.481, *The End Game*, Michael Gordon and Bernard Trainor, (Atlantic Books) 2012
[74] p.18, 2008/9 Edition, The Kingsman, The Duke of Lancaster's Regiment
[75] Barney White-Spunner, 29th January 2013
[76] We will spill British blood, warns Sheikh Ahmad Fartusi, Hala Jaber, Sunday Times, 14th September 2008
[77] MND(SE) Significant Event Report, 1st April 2008
[78] MND(SE) Significant Event Report, 1st April 2008
[79] p.36, March 2009 Edition, Royal Regiment of Scotland Journal
[80] p.42, 2009 Edition, Quis Separabit: The Journal of the Royal Dragoon Guards
[81] p.36, March 2009 Edition, Royal Regiment of Scotland Journal
[82] p.36, March 2009 Edition, Royal Regiment of Scotland Journal
[83] MND(SE) Significant Event Reports, 1st –20th April 2008
[84] p.42, 2009 Edition, Quis Separabit: The Journal of the Royal Dragoon Guards
[85] p.44, 2009 Edition, The Scots Guards Magazine
[86] US State Department Cable, 04/05/2018 APRIL 2 MEETING BETWEEN THE AMBASSADOR, GENERAL PETRAEUS AND PM MALIKI Charge d'Affaires Patricia A. Butenis
[87] MND(SE) Significant Event Report, 19th April 2008
[88] MND(SE) Significant Event Report, 1st April 2008
[89] p.37, March 2009 Edition, Royal Regiment of Scotland Journal

[90] Barney White-Spunner, 29th January 2013
[91] http://news.bbc.co.uk/1/hi/uk/7365147.stm
[92] p.32, March 2009 Edition, Royal Regiment of Scotland Journal
[93] p.18-19, The Road to Al Amarah:Operation Yarborough and U.S. Army Special Forces in Southern Iraq (January – June 2008), Duane L. MosierDuane L. Mosier, Small Wars Journal, 2010
[94] Iranian Strategy in Iraq: Politics and "Other Means", Joseph Felter and Brian Fishman, Combating Terrorism Center at West Point, Oct 13, 2008
[95] Iraqi forces detain Sadrist leaders, uncover Special Groups headquarters in Amarah, Bill RoggioJuly 2nd July 2008, Long War Journal
[96] Barney White-Spunner, 29th January 2013
[97] Jonathan Shaw Interview, 8th November 2012
[98] Barney White-Spunner, 29th January 2013
[99] Barney White-Spunner, 29th January 2013
[100] Barney White-Spunner, 29th January 2013
[101] Barney White-Spunner, 29th January 2013
[102] Barney White-Spunner, 29th January 2013

Chapter 25 - Time to Go

[1] p.4, 2009 Edition, The Highlanders, The Royal Regiment of Scotland
[2] p.30, First Do No Harm: 7 Armoured Brigade in Southern Iraq, Brigadier Sandy Storrie, Summer 2009 Edition, British Army Review
[3] p.32, First Do No Harm: 7 Armoured Brigade in Southern Iraq, Brigadier Sandy Storrie, Summer 2009 Edition, British Army Review
[4] p.31, First Do No Harm: 7 Armoured Brigade in Southern Iraq, Brigadier Sandy Storrie, Summer 2009 Edition, British Army Review
[5] Barney White-Spunner, 29th January 2013
[6] p.31, First Do No Harm: 7 Armoured Brigade in Southern Iraq, Brigadier Sandy Storrie, Summer 2009 Edition, British Army Review
[7] p.13, September/October 2009 Edition, Military Logistics International
[8] p.7, September/October 2009 Edition, Military Logistics International
[9] Hansard, 16th December 2008
[10] p.7-8, September/October 2009 Edition, Military Logistics International
[11] p.6, 2009 Edition, The Crossbelts, Queen's Royal Hussars
[12] p.11, September/October 2009 Edition, Military Logistics International
[13] http://www.telegraph.co.uk/news/worldnews/middleeast/iraq/5253656/British-legacy-in-Iraq-remembered-in-Basra.html
[14] p.39-40, 2009-2010 Edition, The Journal of The Princess of Wales's Royal Regiment
[15] p.20-21, September/October 2009 Edition, Military Logistics International
[16] p.16, Autumn 2008, The Yorkshire Regiment Journal
[17] https://www.gov.uk/government/news/operations-in-iraq-finish-with-completion-of-royal-navy-training-mission

BIBLIOGRAPHY

British Army Regimental Journals
The Infantryman, Director of Infantry
The Delhi Spearmen, 9th/12th Lancers
The Red Hackle, The Black Watch
The Oak Tree, The Cheshire Regiment
The Kingsman, The Duke of Lancaster's Regiment
Grenadier Gazette, The Grenadier Guards
The Irish Guards Journal, The Irish Guards
The Lion and the Dragon, King's Own Royal Border Regiment
The Borderers Chronicle, King's Own Scottish Borderers
The Kingsman, The King's Regiment
King's Royal Hussars Regimental Journal, King's Royal Hussars
The Highlander, The Highlanders
The Light Dragoons Journal, The Light Dragoons
The Silver Bugle, The Light Infantry
Mercian Eagle, Mercian Regiment
Sandy Times & QDG Newsletter, 1st The Queen's Dragoon Guards
Lancashire Lad, Queen's Lancashire Regiment
The Crossbelts, Queen's Royal Hussars
Vedette, Queen's Royal Lancers
Pegasus, The Parachute Regiment
Journal of The Princess of Wales's Royal Regiment, The Princess of Wales's Royal Regiment
The Bugle, The Rifles
The Castle, Royal Anglian Regiment
The Gunner & The Journal of the Royal Artillery, Royal Artillery
Quis Separabit, The Royal Dragoon Guards,
Blackthorn, Royal Irish Regiment
The Sustainer, Royal Logistic Corps
The Globe & Laurel, The Royal Marines
The Fusilier, The Royal Regiment of Fusiliers
The Royal Regiment of Scotland Journal, The Royal Regiment of Scotland
Men of Harlech, Royal Regiment of Wales
Y Cymro (The Welshman), The Royal Welsh Regiment
Eagle and Carbine, Royal Scots Dragoon Guards
The Wire, Royal Signals
Op Telic Special Edition, Tank, The Royal Tank Regiment
Y Ddraig Goch, Royal Welch Fusiliers
Scots Guards Magazine, The Scots Guards
The Stafford Knot, The Staffordshire Regiment
Welsh Guards Regimental Magazine, The Welsh Guards
The Yorkshire Regiment Journal, The Yorkshire Regiment

UK Documents

Hoon to Blair UK Military Options, 15th October 2002
1 (UK) Armoured Division, Operations Order 001/003 for Operation Telic, 7th March 2003
Basra Post Saddam Governance, Defence Intelligence Staff, 11th March 2003
FRAGO 003 1 (UK) Armoured Division, Operations Order 003/003 for Operation Telic, 19th March 2003
Intsum, 1 (UK) Armoured Division, 2 Apr 2003
16 Air Assault Brigade War Diary, Mar-Apr 2003
1 (UK) Armoured Division, Operations Order Phase IV for Operation Telic, 17 Apr 2003
Warning Order for Recovery of 1 (UK) ARMD DIV, 19 Apr 03
7 Armoured Brigad e, Operation Telic Presentation 27th April 2003, Major Peter Langford MBE RE Deputy Chief of Staff
Post Operational Tour Report, 7 Armoured Brigade
HQ 16 Air Assault Brigade, Op Telic Chronology, 29 May 03
Operations Lessons for Operation Telic, 3 Regiment Army Air Corps, 7 May 2003
Post Operational Tour Report Op Telic, 7 RHA, May 2003
Post Operational Tour Report Op Telic, Pathfinder Platoon, May 2003
Post Operational Tour Report, Operation Telic, Headquarters 16 Air Assault Brigade, May 2003
Post Operations Report and Lessons Identified – Operation Telic 2, 12 February 04*19 Mech Brigade Chronology*, Op Telic 2
Post Operations Report and Lessons Identified, 19 Mech Brigade, Op Telic 2
UK Tactical UAV Operations Iraq 2003/4, Presentation to Shephard UAV Conference, June 2003, Major Charles Barker Royal Artillery, 2IC 32 Regiment RA
Operations in Iraq: First Reflections, UK Ministry of Defence, 2003
Operations in Iraq – An Analysis from a Land Perspective, British Army 2003
Post Operation Tour Report, Operation Telic 2/3, Headquarters Multinational Division (South East), 30 Jan 04
Post Operation Tour Report, Operation Telic 3/4, Headquarters, Multinational Division (South East), 13 Jul 04
Op Telic Lessons for the Secretariat, David Johnson, 6th July 2004
EPW Incident ARF – Fri 11 Apr 03, II Squadron RAF Regiment, 7 Sep 2004
1 PWRR BG Lessons Report Operation Telic, October 2004
1 RHA Post Operational Report, 2004
1 RWF Post Operational Report for Op Telic 4, 18 Oct 04
1 Cheshire Post Operational Report for Op Telic 4, 19 Oct 04
Post Operation Tour Report, Operation Telic 4/5, Headquarters Multinational Division, (South East), 4 Dec 04
Multinational Division (South East) Commander's War Diary 16 Jun to 30 Nov 04, Headquarters
Multinational Division (South East
1 BW Post Operation Report – Operation Bracken, 9 Dec 04
Project Locksmith Overview, British Army Briefing, 2005
Operation Telic 4 Chronology, Headquarters Multinational Division (South East), 25 Jan 05

Post Operational Tour Report, Operation Telic, Headquarters 1 Mechanised Brigade, January 2005
1st Battalion, The Royal Regiment of Wales, Div Res AI BG, Capt K D Taaffe, 2005
7 Armoured Brigade Commander's Study Period, *UAV Support to Operations in Iraq*, Major P Tombleson RA, Battery Commander 57 (Bhurtpore) Battery Royal Artillery
Operation Telic Briefing, ACM Sir Glenn Torpy, ICSC, 21 Apr 2005
Security Sector Reform (SSR), Op TELIC 7, Lieutenant Colonel I G Harrison MBE RHA, Commanding Officer, 3rd Regiment Royal Horse Artillery, 27 Sept 2005
Basrah City BG Brief, 1 Coldstream Guards 2005
Op Telic 7 Commanders Study Period Briefing 27th September 2005, Brigadier P C Marriott
Letters from Amarah, The Iraq Tour Oct 05 to Apr 06, Royal Scots Dragoon Guards
Stability Operations in Iraq (Op Telic 2-5), An Analysis from a Land Perspective, Major General W R Rollo, British Army, 2006
The Rifle's Chronicle 2007 (RHQ The Rifles) 2008
Eagles Over the Desert' The RAF and Iraq, 1990-2009, RAF Air Staff, 16th March 2009
History of 1 Squadron (The Royal Air Force Regiment) 2011
The cost-effective delivery of an armoured vehicle capability, National Audit Office, 2011
Iraq Polling Data, June 2005 to December 2006, PJHQ
A Strategic Review of the Puma Helicopter Force, Air Commodore CW Dixon and Colonel NJW Moss, 15th May 2008
Major Combat Operations: Iraq at the Operational Level, ACM Sir Brian Burridge, ASC 16, 17 April 2013
Lesson Capture Process Interview, Colonel Cairan Griffin
Lesson Capture Process Interview, Maj Gen Graeme Lamb, 23 Feb 04
Lesson Capture Process Interview, Brig Bill Moore, 26 Mar 04
Lesson Capture Process Interview, Brig Nick Carter, 23 June 04
Lesson Capture Process Interview, Brig David Rutherford-Jones, 21 June 2004
Lessons Capture Process Interview, Maj Gen Andrew Stewart, 31 Aug 2004
Lesson Capture Process Interview, Col JK Tanner, 8 Sept 2004
Lesson Capture Process Interview, Lt Col PML Napier, 6 Jul 04
Lesson Capture Process Interview, Lt Col AC Cuthbert, 6 Jul 04
Lesson Capture Process Interview, Lt Col JR Free, 22 Jun 04
Lesson Capture Process Interview, Maj AJ Aitkin, 22 Jun 04
Lesson Capture Process Interview, Colonel RD Marshall, 3 Sept 2004
Lesson Capture Process Interview, Lt Col Richard Nugee

UK Service Inquiry Reports
Board of Inquiry Report into loss of Sea Kings XV650 and XV704, 19th April 2003
Board of Inquiry into the circumstances surrounding the deaths of Cpl Allbutt and Tpr Clarke, 23rd July 2003

Board of Inquiry into the death of Fusilier Gordon Gentle, 8 September 2004
Board of Inquiry Regarding the Circumstances Surrounding the Deaths of Sergeant Simon Hamilton-Jewell, Corporal Russell Aston, Corporal Paul Graham Long, Corporal Simon Miller, Lance-Corporal Benjamin John McGowan Hyde, and Lance-Corporal Thomas Keys, 19th October 2004
Board of Inquiry into the loss of Hercules XV179, 13th January 2006
Board of Inquiry into the circumstances surrounding death of Marine Maddison, 1st February 2006
Board of Inquiry in Death of Sgt Roberts, 31st July 2006
Board of Inquiry of Aircraft Crash Lynx AH Mk.7 (XZ614) of 847 NAS In Basra, Iraq, 20 June 06
Board of Inquiry into Accident involving Hercules C130 Mk4 ZH876, 17th May 2008

US Documents

CFLCC OPPLAN Cobra II Southern Oilfield Seizure Mission Analysis, 19 Nov 2002
Presentations for US-UK Integration Conference, Camp Pendleton, 3-5 Jan 2003
Operation Iraqi Freedom, 32nd Army Air Missile Defense Command, September 2003
Comprehensive Report of Special Advisor to the Director Central Intelligence on Iraq's Weapons of Mass, (Iraq Survey Group Report), 30th September 2004
Major John Clark, Interview with US Combat Studies Institute, Fort Leavenworth, Kansas, 7th February 2007
Major Johnny Austin, Interview with US Combat Studies Institute, Fort Leavenworth, Kansas, 7th May 2008
Iraq Perspective Report, Kevin Woods and others, US Joint Forces Command, November 2007

Books

Bank Rolling Basra, Andrew Alderson, (Robinson) 2005
In the Company of Soldiers, Rick Atkinson, (Little & Brown) 2004
British Generals in Blair's Wars, Jonathan Bailey, Richard Iron and Hew Strachan, (Ashgate) 2013
An Ordinary Soldier, Doug Beattie, (Simon & Schuster) 2008
AH-64 Apache Units of Operations Enduring Freedom and Iraqi Freedom, Jonathan Bernstein (Opsrey) 2005
A Journey, Tony Blair, (Hutchinson) 2010
Pathfinder, David Blakeley, (Orion) 2012
All Roads Lead to Baghdad, Charles Briscoe and others, (Paladin Press) 2007
Army Field Manual, Vol 1:10, Countering Insurgency (British Army) 2010
The Middle East Military Balance, 1999-2000, Broom and Shapir, (BCSIA) 2000
Reform and Reconstruction of the Security Sector, Alan Bryden, Heiner Hanggi (editors), (DCAF), 2004

Alistair Campbell Diaries: Countdown to Iraq, Alistair Campbell (Hutchinson) 2012
CIA World Fact Book, (CIA) 2003
Muqtada Al-Sadr and the Future Battle for Iraq, Patrick Cockburn, (Scribner) 2008
Rules of Engagement, Tim Collins, (Headline) 2005
A Brief History of Modern Warfare, Richard Connaughton, (Robinson) 2008
Iran & Iraq: The Threat from the Northern Gulf, Anthony Cordesman (Westview)
Leading from the Front, Richard Dannatt, (Bantam) 2010
F-16 Fighting Falcon Units of Operation Iraqi Freedom, Steve Davies and Doug Dilby, (Osprey) 2006
F-15E Strike Eagle Units in Combat 1990 to 2005, Steve Davies, (Osprey) 2005
F-15C/E Eagle Units of Operation Iraqi Freedom, Steve Davies, (Osprey) 2004
Back from the Brink, Alistair Darling,(Atlantic) 2011
Inside Centcom, Michael De Long, (Regnery) 2004
The King's Own in Mesopotamia, Peter Donnolly, (King's Own Museum) 2005
Hide and Seek, Charles Duelfer, (Public Affairs) 2009
Challenger 2 Main Battle Tank 1987-2006, Simon Dunstan, (Osprey), 2006
Lions and Dragons, Stuart Eastwood, (Silver Link Publishing) 2006
Main Battle Tank, Niall Edworthy, (Penguin), 2010
War of Choice, Jack Fairweather, (Jonathan Cape) 2011
On Point I, Gregory Fontenot, EJ Degen, David Tohn, (US Army), 2004
On Point II, Dr. Donald P. Wright, Colonel Timothy R. Reese, with the Contemporary Operations Study Team (US Army), 2008
Operation Telic Aircraft Movement Analysis, Peter Foster (unpublished)
American Soldier, Tommy Franks, (Regan) 2004
Iraq Campaign, Robert Fox, (Agenda Publishing) 2003
Cobra II, Michael Gordon and Bernard Trainor, (Atlantic Books) 2006
The End Game, Michael Gordon and Bernard Trainor, (Atlantic Books) 2012
With the 1st Marine Division in Iraq, 2003, Lieutenant Colonel Michael S. Groen and Contributors, (Marine Corps University), 2006
Chain of Command, Seymour Hersh, (Penguin) 2004
Dusty Warriors, Richard Holmes, (Harper Collins) 2007
US Navy Hornet Units of Operation Iraqi Freedom, Part 1, Tony Holmes, (Osprey) 2004
US Navy Hornet Units of Operation Iraqi Freedom, Part 2, Tony Holmes, (Osprey) 2005
US Marine Corps and RAAF Hornet Units of Operation Iraqi Freedom, Tony Holmes, (Osprey) 2005
US Navy Tomcat Units of Operation Iraqi Freedom, Tony Holmes, (Osprey) 2005
Victory in Iraq, Duncan L.Hunter, (Victory in Iraq), 2010
Gulf War II, Jamie Hunter, (TomCat) 2003
Soldier, Mike Jackson, (Bantam), 2007

Midnight in Some Burning Town, Christian Jennings, (Wiedenfeld & Nicolson) 2004
Blair's Wars, John Kampfner, (Free Press) 2003
Desperate Glory, Sam Kiley, (Bloomsbury), 2009
Zero Six Bravo, Damien Lewis, (Quercus), 2013
The Third Man, Peter Mandleson, (Harper Press) 2010
Predator, Matt Martin (Zenith) 2010
My Share of the Task, Stanley McChrystal, (Penguin), 2013
War Without Consequences, Terence McNamee (editor), (RUSI) 2008
Special Forces in Iraq, Eric Micheletti, (Histoire & Collections) 2006
Sniper One, Dan Mills, (Penguin) 2007
Eyes on the Horizon, Richard Myers, (Threshold) 2009
Armed Action, James Newton, (Headline) 2007
Last Round, Mark Nicol, (Wiedenfeld & Nicolson) 2005
Ministry of Defeat, Richard North, (Contiunum) 2009
The Devonshire and Dorset Regiment: 11th, 29th and 54th of Foot, 1958 - 2007, (Pen & Sword) 2007
Ambush Alley, Tim Pritchard, (Ballantine) 2007
The New Machiavelli: How to Wield Power in the Modern World, Jonathan Powell, (The Bodley Head) 2010
Tornado F3, Wg Cdr Justin Reuter, Mark McEwan, Gill Howie, Berry Vissers, Geoffrey Lee, (Squadron Prints), 2011
Fiasco, Thomas E.Ricks, (Penguin) 2006
The Gamble, Thomas E.Ricks, (Penguin) 2009
US Marines in Iraq 2003: Barsah, Baghdad and Beyond, Colonel Nicholas E. Reynolds, (United States Marine Corps), 2007
Air War Iraq, Tim Ripley (Pen & Sword) 2003
16 Air Assault Brigade, Tim Ripley, (Pen & Sword) 2008
Operation Enduring Freedom, Tim Ripley, (Pen & Sword) 2011
Middle East Airpower in 21st Century, Tim Ripley, (Pen & Sword) 2010
British Army Aviation in Action, Tim Ripley, (Pen & Sword) 2012
Target Barsa, Mark Rossiter, (Corgi), 2009
Rumsfeld's War, Rowan Scarborough, (Regnery) 2004
British Next Generation Armour, Carl Schulze, (Tankograd) 2008
British Armour Evolution, Carl Schulze, (Tankograd) 2007
The Wars Against Saddam, John Simpson, (MacMillan) 2003
Occupational Hazards, Rory Stewart, (Picador) 2006
Hammers from Above, Jay Stout, (Ballantine Books) 2006
At the Centre of the Storm, George Tenet, (Harper Luxe) 2007
Task Force Black, Mark Urban, (Little & Brown) 2010
The Conduct of the Persian Gulf War, (US DoD) 1991
First in the Field, Guy Warner, (Pen & Sword) 2011
March Up, Bing West and Ray Smith, (Pimlico), 2003
The Strongest Tribe, Bing West, (Random House) 2008
B-1B Lancer Units in Combat, Thomas Withington, (Osprey) 2006
Plan of Attack, Bob Woodward, (Simon & Shuster) 2004
State of Denial, Bob Woodward, (Simon & Shuster) 2006
The War Within, Bob Woodward, (Simon & Shuster)2008

On Point II, Donald P. Wright, Timothy R. Reese, (US Army), 2008

Magazines and Journals
Airforces Monthly
Air Force
Air Force, Army, Navy Times
Air Power Review (RAF)
Combat Aircraft
Defense News
Flight International
Jane's Defence Weekly
Jane's International Defence Review
Jane's Intelligence Review
Jane's Sentinel
Military Logistics International
Navy News
RAF News
RUSI Journal
Soldier Magazine
Strategic Assessments (US National Defence University)
The Hook
World Air Power Journal/International Air Power Journal

Websites
www.bahamousainquiry.co.uk
www.googleearth.com
www.globalsecurity.org
www.iraqinquiry.org.uk (Chilcot inquiry evidence)
www.longwarjournal.org
www.understandingwar.org
www.mod.uk
www.michaelyon-online.com
www.operationtelic.co.uk

GLOSSARY

AAC: Army Air Corps (British Army)
AB: Air Base
ASTOR: Airborne Stand Off Radar (UK)
Avn: Aviation (US Army)
AWACS: Airborne Warning and Control System
Bn: Battalion
Bde: Brigade
BG: Battlegroup
CAB: Combat Aviation Brigade (US Army)
CAOC: Combined Air Operations Centre (USAF)
CJSOTF: Combined Joint Special Operations Task Force (US)
CDS: Chief of Defence Staff (UK)
CENTCOM: US Central Command
CIA: Central Intelligence Agency (USA)
CPA: Coalition Provisional Authority
CSAR: Combat Search and Rescue
Det: Detachment
ELINT: Electronic intelligence
FAC: Forward Air Controller
FARP: Forward Arming and Refuelling Point
Flt: Flight
FCO: Foreign and Commonwealth Office
FOB: Forward Operating Base
GOC: General Officer Commanding
IADS: Integrated air defence system
IA: Iraqi Army
ING: Iraqi National Guard
IPS: Iraqi Police Service
ISOF: Iraqi Special Operations Forces
JAM: Jaish al Madhi militia
JHF(I): Joint Helicopter Force (Iraq) (UK)
JSFAW: Joint Special Forces Aviation Wing (UK)
JSOC: Joint Special Operations Command (US)
JTAC: Joint Terminal Attack Controller (US)
LTW: Lynham Transport Wing (RAF)
MANPAD: Man-portable surface-to-air missile
MND(SE): Multi National Division (South East)
Multi National Force – Iraqi (MNF-I)
NAEWF: NATO Airborne Early Warning Force
NATO: North Atlantic Treaty Organisation
NAS: Naval Air Squadron (UK)
RAF: Royal Air Force (UK)
Regt: Regiment
RM: Royal Marines
RN: Royal Navy
SAM: Surface-to-air missile

SAS: Special Air Service (UK and Australia)
SF: Special Forces (UK)
SOAR: Special Operation Aviation Regiment (US Army)
SOF: Special Operations Forces (US Army)
SOG: Special Operations Group (USAF)
SOS: Special Operations Squadron (USAF)
SOW: Special Operation Wing: (USAF)
Sqn: Squadron
TACP: Tactical Air Control Party (UK)
TF: Task Force
TORDET: Tornado Detachment (UK RAF)
USAF: US Air Force
USMC: US Marine Corps
USN: US Navy
UN: United Nations

British Army Regimental Abbreviations
Cavalry
HCR: Household Cavalry Regiment
KRH: King's Royal Hussars
LD: Light Dragoons
9/12 Lancers: 9/12th Royal Lancers
QDG: 1st Queen's Dragoon Guards
QRH: Queen's Royal Hussars
QRL: Queen's Royal Lancers
RDG: Royal Dragoon Guards
Scots DG/RSDG: Royal Scots Dragoon Guards
1 RTR: 1st Royal Tank Regiment
2 RTR: 2nd Royal Tank Regiment

Royal Artillery
1 RHA: 1st Royal Horse Artillery
3 RHA: 3rd Royal Horse Artillery
RA: Royal Artllery

Infantry Battalions/Regiments
1 A&SH: 1st Battalion, The Argyll and Sutherland Highlanders
1 BW: 1st Battalion, The Black Watch
1 Cheshire: 1st Battalion, The Cheshire Regiment
1 Coldstream: 1st Battalion, The Coldstream Guards
DDLI: The Devonshire and Dorset Light Infantry
1 Lancs: 1st Battalion, The Duke of Lancaster's Regiment
2 Lancs: 2nd Battalion, The Duke of Lancaster's Regiment
1 DWR: 1st Battalion, The Duke of Wellington's Regiment
1 Grenadier: 1st Battalion, The Grenadier Guards
1 IG: 1st Battalion, The Irish Guards
The Highlanders: 1st Battalion, The Highlanders
1 LI: 1st Battalion, The Light Infantry

2 LI: 2nd Battalion, The Light Infantry
1 Kings: 1st Battalion, The King's Regiment
1 KORBR/King's Own Border: 1st Battalion, The King's Own Royal Border Regiment
1 KOSB: 1st Battalion, The King's Own Scottish Borders
1 QLR: 1st Battalion, The Queen's Lancashire Regiment
1 PARA: 1st Battalion, The Parachute Regiment
2 PARA: 2nd Battalion, The Parachute Regiment
3 PARA: 3rd Battalion, The Parachute Regiment
1 PWRR: 1st Battalion, The Princess of Wales's Royal Regiment
2 Rifles: 2nd Battalion, The Rifles
4 Rifles: 4th Battalion, The Rifles
1 Royal Anglian: 1st Battalion, The Royal Anglian Regiment
2 Royal Anglian: 2nd Battalion, The Royal Anglian Regiment
1 RRF: 1st Battalion, The Royal Regiment of Fusiliers
2 RRF: 2nd Battalion, The Royal Regiment of Fusiliers
1st Battalion, The Royal Green Jackets
2nd Battalion, The Royal Green Jackets
1 Royal Irish: 1st Battalion, The Royal Irish Regiment
1 RHF: 1st Battalion, Royal Highland Fusiliers
1 Scots: 1st Battalion, The Royal Regiment of Scotland
1 RRW: 1st Battalion, The Royal Regiment of Wales
1 RS: 1st Battalion, The Royal Scots
1 Royal Welsh: 1st Battalion, The Royal Welsh Regiment
1 RWF: 1st Battalion, The Royal Welch Fusiliers
1 SG: 1st Battalion, The Scots Guards
1st Battalion, The Staffordshire Regiment
1 Staffs: 1st Battalion, The Yorkshire Regiment
1 WG 1st Battalion, The Welsh Guards

Corps
RLC: Royal Logistics Corps
RAMC: Royal Army Medical Corps
RMP: Royal Military Police

INDEX

British Politicians and Civilian Officials
Bob Ainsworth 300
Tony Blair 3, 10, 11, 22,23, 38, 39, 40,41, 42, 45, 47, 50, 51, 53, 54, 67, 72, 73, 74, 75, 137, 165, 166, 169, 184, 191, 195, 227, 231, 233, 234, 236, 237, 260, 276, 293, 335, 336, 343, 396, 397, 401, 405, 422, 454, 456
Des Browne 300, 301, 314, 368, 386, 390, 448
Gordon Brown 23, 301, 363, 367, 374, 390, 391, 392, 397
Lord (Paul) Drayson 300, 301, 444
Dr David Kelly 20, 166, 191, 229
Geoff Hoon 38, 39, 40, 41, 45, 46, 47, 49, 50, 51, 53, 54, 57, 72, 234, 396, 422, 438, 454
Rory Stewart 259, 435, 440, 458
Kevin Tebbitt 53

British Army Officers
Jonny Austin 261, 266, 270, 271, 272, 440, 441, 442, 445, 456
Richard Barrons 171
James Bashall 333, 346, 349, 350, 353, 355, 413
Tom Beckett 168, 169, 175, 393, 414
Graham Binns 27, 57, 60, 66, 69, 70, 75, 87, 91, 94, 96, 97, 101, 103, 106, 108, 140, 143, 144, 145, 147, 149, 154, 168, 255, 357, 361, 362, 363, 364, 365, 366, 396, 407, 411, 413, 418, 423, 424, 426, 427, 431, 449
Adrian Bradshaw 27, 126, 166, 255, 409, 429, 433
Robin Brims, 3, 12, 25, 26, 32, 41, 45, 46, 52, 53, 54, 57, 65, 67, 69, 70, 72, 73, 75, 86, 90, 91, 92, 93, 94, 95, 96, 101, 102, 103, 109, 110, 11, 114, 115, 118, 120, 124, 125, 138, 139, 140, 141, 142, 143, 144, 145, 147, 148, 149, 151, 152, 153, 154, 156, 157, 160, 162, 164, 167, 168, 170, 218, 233, 237, 238, 255, 270, 396, 399, 402, 407, 409, 410, 418, 421, 422, 423, 424, 425, 426, 427, 428, 429, 431, 432, 433, 437, 438, 439
Chris Brown 394, 409
Mark Carlton-Smith 126
Nick Carter 27, 195, 196, 202, 221, 223, 258, 411, 435, 437, 455
Tim Collins 28, 86, 145, 198, 457
John Cooper 26, 174, 258, 270, 271, 274, 275, 312, 313, 317, 409, 412, 442
Hamish Cormack 363, 381
James Cowan 29, 331, 232, 234, 235, 236, 277
Jonny Crook 269, 275
Tim Cross 73
Chris Deverell 412
Tim Evans 331, 333, 336, 337, 338, 339, 340, 346, 347, 348, 358, 359, 413
James Everard 317, 413
Andrew Figgures 409
Julian Free 27, 222, 367, 370, 373, 374, 376, 414, 436, 437, 438, 455, 457
Paul Gibson 29, 412, 418
Andrew Kennett 196, 207, 214, 215, 217, 411
Matt Kenyon 358
John Kiszely 233, 237, 238, 409
Nick Houghton 24, 25, 276, 300, 320, 368, 409, 445
Chris Hughes 412
Richard Iron 396, 446, 456
Mike Jackson 73, 163, 164, 165, 167, 401, 433, 457
Graeme Lamb 25, 41, 126, 131, 166, 167, 171, 172, 174, 175, 177, 180, 181, 183, 184, 185, 186, 189, 258, 354, 409, 411, 433, 434, 455
John Lorimer 27, 266, 267, 268, 412
Patrick Marriott 270, 271, 412, 441, 442, 455
Jorge Mendonca 28, 184

John McColl 213, 214, 230, 232, 233, 409, 438
Bill Moore 172, 173, 174, 175, 176, 177, 179, 180, 181, 182, 183, 184, 185, 189, 258, 300, 411, 433, 434, 455
David Paterson 60, 76, 88, 104, 144, 151
Antony Piggott 40, 421
John Reith 24, 39, 40, 41, 44, 45, 46, 47, 52, 53, 54, 166, 167, 172, 177, 182, 202, 211, 255, 398, 421, 422
Mike Riddell-Webster 59, 97, 98, 99, 144
Jonathon Riley 26, 242, 243, 244, 245, 247, 251, 252, 412, 418, 439, 440
Bill Rollo 26, 159, 195, 210, 211, 212, 213, 214, 214, 217, 218, 219, 220, 221, 222, 224, 225, 232, 234, 236, 259, 369, 409, 411, 432, 455
David Rutherford-Jones 195, 199, 411, 45
Patrick Saunders 19, 28, 29, 345, 347, 348, 349, 360, 364, 386, 445, 386, 445, 447, 448, 449
Jonathan Shaw 3, 26, 162, 258, 333, 334, 375, 336, 337, 339, 343, 349, 351, 352, 353, 354, 355, 356, 357, 359, 361, 387, 413, 418, 446, 447, 448, 449, 452
Richard Shirreff 304, 319, 320, 321, 322, 324, 325, 329, 330, 331, 333, 338, 413, 444, 446
Andrew Stewart 26, 185, 195, 198, 199, 202, 203, 204, 205, 208, 209, 219, 220, 221, 223, 224, 230, 231, 259, 286, 411, 420, 435, 436, 437, 438, 455
Sandy Storie 390, 414, 452
Freddie Viggers 409
Mike Walker 23, 47, 54, 164, 165, 202, 229, 233, 251, 277, 314, 422, 423, 438
Barney-White Spunner 27, 231, 366, 367, 368, 369, 374, 377, 380, 381, 387, 388, 389, 409, 414, 418, 438, 449, 450, 451, 452

Richard Williams 169, 263, 265, 268, 277,

Royal Air Force Officers
Andy Arnold 282, 283, 419
Stuart Atha 127
Brian Burridge 25, 41, 42, 44, 52, 53, 61, 67, 69, 71, 71, 75, 95, 102, 104, 131, 135, 138, 142, 143, 157, 164, 240, 255, 281, 409, 418, 421, 422, 423, 424, 425, 426, 427, 429, 430, 433, 439, 455
Steve Carr 83, 84, 419, 425
Andy Pulford 121, 419
Dave Robertson 60, 61, 132, 419
Ken Smith 129, 429
Harvey Smyth 128
Jock Stirrup 23, 24, 26, 314, 315, 316, 330, 335, 357, 359, 391, 403, 445, 446
Glenn Torpy 24, 25, 41, 43, 61, 63, 71, 72, 80, 128, 131, 133, 134, 233, 343, 247, 248, 252, 255, 260, 299, 300, 308, 315, 316, 418, 419, 422, 423, 424, 425, 429, 438, 439, 440, 444, 445

Royal Navy Officer
Mike Boyce 22, 138, 40, 41, 45, 47, 53, 73, 151, 167, 320
David Snelson 41, 44, 255, 415

Royal Marines Officers
James Dutton 26, 50, 51, 70, 82, 84, 111, 112, 113, 114, 115, 140, 158, 251, 252, 258, 266, 269, 299, 309, 410, 412, 440, 444, 445
Rob Fry 23, 24, 202, 251, 409
Buster Howes 84, 113
Gordon Messenger 29, 82, 118
Andy Salmon 27, 292, 293, 414

US Officers, Politicians and Civilian Officials
Lloyd Austin 374, 375, 388, 389
Paul Bremer 161, 162, 186, 191, 197, 200, 201, 202, 203, 229, 230, 397

George W Bush 39, 40, 41, 63, 74, 75, 77, 78, 137, 191, 200, 203, 234, 33, 334, 373, 391, 391
George Casey 230, 232, 242, 251, 321, 322, 330, 333, 334, 335, 336, 402
Tommy Franks 25, 41, 45, 36, 52, 62, 63, 74, 78, 126, 134, 151, 457
Timothy Keating 44
Stanley McChrystal 276, 342, 429, 442, 446, 447, 457
Buzz Moseley 43, 61, 63, 77, 125, 126, 127, 132, 133
Barack Obama 392
Ray Odierno 355, 359, 362, 368
David Petreaus 334, 336, 355, 357, 362, 371, 402, 403
Donald Rumsfeld 71, 72, 231, 333, 397

Iraqi Officers, Politicians and Officials

Ahmed Fartosi 210, 216, 260, 261, 266, 267, 357, 358, 359, 361, 365, 366, 282, 387
Saddam Hussein 10, 30, 31, 32, 33, 34, 35, 36, 37, 43, 55, 67, 74, 77, 78, 82, 86, 87, 95, 98, 106, 108, 115, 119, 131, 137, 141, 148, 150, 162, 163, 167, 190, 194, 196, 228, 260, 285, 317, 354, 365, 365, 380, 407, 421, 454, 458
Ali Hassan al-Majid (Chemical Ali) 34, 35, 37, 95, 108, 141, 142, 143, 148, 150, 152, 431
Nouri al Malaki 317, 322, 329, 331, 337, 359, 361, 362, 366, 369, 370, 372, 373, 374, 376379, 380, 381, 382, 383, 384, 386, 387, 388, 389, 390, 392, 394, 395, 401, 402
General Mohan 357, 365, 366, 368, 369, 371, 372, 373, 376, 384, 386
Muqtada Al Sadr 26, 28, 37, 190, 196, 197, 198, 200, 201, 203, 204, 207, 208, 211, 213, 216, 218, 217, 219, 222, 224, 225, 226, 230, 231, 232, 240, 250, 257, 260, 262, 266, 267, 268, 279, 286, 297, 311, 313, 331, 347, 349, 366, 369, 374, 381, 383, 386, 388, 390, 435, 438, 456

British Military Units Divisions/Brigades

1 (UK) Armoured Division 3, 45, 52, 58, 60, 65, 67, 68, 75, 84, 85, 86, 92, 93, 102, 103, 110, 119, 120, 125, 138, 142, 148, 151, 169, 171, 173, 174, 175, 186, 229, 255, 339, 407, 410, 424, 425, 428, 430, 432, 442,
3 (UK) Division 167, 171, 172
1 Mechanised Brigade 192, 200,205, 214, 218, 220, 297, 312, 330, 333, 363, 365, 349, 411, 413, 437, 444, 455,
4 Mechanised Brigade 363, 369, 382, 390, 412, 414
7 Armoured Brigade 27, 46, 48, 57, 59, 65, 66, 68, 73, 75, 87, 88, 90, 95, 96, 102, 103, 105, 108, 109, 113, 114, 140, 143, 145, 147, 148 150, 151, 153, 155, 156, 167, 173, 174, 195, 214, 255, 269, 271,274, 275, 307, 311, 362, 369, 386, 389, 392, 396, 410, 412, 414, 423, 440, 441
12 Mechanised Brigade 307, 392, 412
16 Air Assault Brigade 48, 49, 54, 55, 56, 57, 58, 63, 66, 70, 86, 87, 102, 107, 114, 119, 120, 122, 123, 124, 125, 136, 139, 140, 145, 153, 155, 162, 163, 164, 167, 168, 229, 253, 255, 266, 410, 422, 423, 425, 426, 427, 428, 430, 431, 432, 433, 454, 458
19 Light Brigade 315, 328, 330, 331, 333, 337, 338, 339, 340, 341, 344, 346, 355, 359, 413
19 Mechanised Brigade 42, 54, 172, 174, 177, 180, 186, 187, 191, 192, 258, 399, 411
20 Armoured Brigade 184, 191, 192, 195, 196, 200, 258, 311, 318, 330, 392, 394, 411, 413, 414,

Royal Armoured Corps
Household Cavalry Regiment 56, 122, 124, 366, 461
King's Royal Hussars 126, 263, 265, 351, 352, 412, 413, 418, 441, 448, 453, 461
Light Dragoons 43, 176, 195, 412, 453, 461, 419
9/12th Royal Lancers 412, 418, 461
Queen's Dragoon Guards 46, 72,84, 85, 86, 88, 90, 92, 111, 112, 114, 116, 117, 234, 325, 326, 327, 412, 413, 453, 461,
Queen's Royal Hussars 199, 204, 219, 304, 324, 325, 326, 328, 392, 393, 411, 413, 418, 419, 435, 437, 446, 452, 453, 461
Queen's Royal Lancers 87, 89, 105, 106, 107, 139, 144, 145, 146, 205, 206, 207, 209, 211, 2014, 215, 220, 226, 269, 326, 351, 352, 413, 418, 423, 427, 430, 436, 438, 441, 455, 461
Royal Dragoon Guards 14, 241, 249, 250, 367, 377, 378, 380, 383, 384, 412, 418, 435, 439, 440, 449, 450, 451, 453, 461
Royal Scots Dragoon Guards 46, 57, 59, 70, 71, 88, 90, 98, 100, 106, 108, 114, 115, 139, 140, 143, 146, 155275, 390, 410, 412, 418, 423, 424, 426, 427, 430, 431, 432, 433, 442, 443, 453, 455, 461
1st Royal Tank Regiment 67, 80, 81, 137, 165, 394, 461
2nd Royal Tank Regiment 57, 67, 80, 90, 98, 100, 106, 107, 118, 139, 144, 146, 148, 163, 175, 293, 341, 410, 419, 424, 425, 430, 431, 432, 433, 453, 461

Royal Artillery
1st Royal Horse Artillery 204, 214, 220, 411, 413, 454, 461,
3rd Royal Horse Artillery 87, 412, 414, 461

7th Parachute Regiment Royal Horse Artillery 56, 120, 212, 123, 125, 428, 454
4 Regiment 412
5 Regiment 56
12 Regiment 413
16 Regiment 303
19 Regiment 412
26 Regiment 411, 412
29 Commando Regiment 51, 85, 116, 117
32 Regiment 305, 427, 430, 454
40 Regiment 176, 177, 179, 181, 411, 413

Army Infantry Battalions
The Argyll and Sutherland Highlanders 206, 220, 411, 461
The Black Watch 29, 57, 59, 68, 88, 90, 98, 100, 101, 104, 106, 107, 108, 109, 139, 143, 144, 146, 154, 156, 157, 159, 165, 205, 209, 210, 211, 212, 215, 217, 220, 226, 230, 231, 232, 233, 234, 235, 236, 237, 238, 297, 401, 404, 410, 411, 423, 424, 426, 427, 432, 436, 437, 438, 439, 453, 461
The Cheshire Regiment 207, 214, 215, 216, 217, 411, 436, 437, 453, 461
The Coldstream Guards 263, 264, 267, 268, 269, 412, 441, 455, 461
The Devonshire and Dorset Light Infantry 322, 323, 329, 413, 446, 458
The Duke of Lancaster's Regiment 332, 337, 339, 340, 342, 344, 349, 359, 363, 380, 413, 414, 418, 447, 448, 449, 451, 453, 461
The Duke of Wellington's Regiment 72, 92, 109, 412, 461
The Grenadier Guards 324, 413, 418, 446, 453, 461
The Irish Guards 90, 109, 126, 146, 147, 154, 165, 353, 364, 413, 418, 448, 449, 453, 461
The Highlanders 171, 242, 247, 249, 262, 266, 268, 269, 271, 273, 412,

418, 439, 440, 441, 442, 452, 453, 461
The Light Infantry 98, 100, 148, 182, 198, 199, 200, 201, 203, 204, 311, 317, 324, 325, 326, 327, 411, 413, 418, 401, 431, 434, 435, 445, 446, 453, 461
1st Battalion, The King's Regiment 175, 176, 177, 178, 179, 180, 181, 184, 338, 411, 418, 453, 462
The King's Own Royal Border Regiment 240, 241, 249, 271, 274, 412, 439, 440, 441, 442, 453, 462
The King's Own Scottish Borders 19, 174, 175, 176, 178, 181, 183, 411, 419, 453, 462
The Queen's Lancashire Regiment 28, 176, 178, 180, 181, 182, 183, 184, 411, 453, 462
The Parachute Regiment 13, 48, 55, 66, 74, 86, 119, 120, 122, 123, 139, 147, 152, 160, 164, 167, 168, 169,175, 196, 266, 333, 346, 410, 411, 412, 430, 431, 453, 462
The Princess of Wales's Royal Regiment 28, 204, 205, 206, 207, 208, 209,210, 211, 212, 213, 215, 217,220, 225, 239, 264, 311, 312, 317, 323, 324, 326, 394, 404, 411, 412, 413, 414, 421, 436, 437, 448, 449, 453, 454, 462
The Rifles 19, 28, 29, 329, 338, 346, 346, 347, 350, 351, 359, 360, 361, 364, 386, 404, 413, 418, 445, 446, 447, 448, 449, 453, 455, 462
The Royal Anglian Regiment 267, 310, 317, 318, 322, 323, 328, 413, 414, 418, 441, 445, 446, 453, 462
The Royal Regiment of Fusiliers 57, 60, 76, 87, 88, 89, 90, 104, 105, 106, 107, 145, 146, 151, 154, 157, 158, 159, 249, 253, 261, 265, 269, 270, 272, 274, 311, 321, 327, 410, 411, 412, 413, 414, 418, 423, 425, 426, 427, 432, 445, 462
The Royal Green Jackets 182, 338, 345, 411, 413, 462

The Royal Irish Regiment 28, 55, 139, 145, 152, 163, 410, 412, 418, 543, 462
Royal Highland Fusiliers 209, 411, 412, 462
The Royal Regiment of Scotland 362, 414, 418, 449, 449, 450, 451, 453, 462
The Royal Regiment of Wales 199, 201, 202, 203, 204, 205, 207, 222, 263, 267, 268, 411, 412, 413, 435, 436, 455, 462
The Royal Welsh Regiment 345, 346, 447, 448, 453, 462
The Royal Welch Fusiliers 204, 211, 213, 220, 411, 453, 462
The Scots Guards 209, 244, 245, 264, 371, 378, 379, 382, 384, 388, 412, 414, 439, 449, 450, 451, 453, 462
The Staffordshire Regiment 250, 257, 262, 264, 265, 266, 267, 268, 275,331, 332, 328, 337, 338, 339, 344, 412, 413, 419, 440, 441, 446, 447, 453, 462,
The Yorkshire Regiment 338, 394, 413, 414, 453, 462
The Welsh Guards 239, 241, 249, 259, 262, 263, 412, 419, 439, 440, 453, 462

Special Forces
Special Air Service (SAS) 17, 27, 68, 77, 78, 81, 89, 99, 100, 102, 108, 125, 126, 127, 128, 129, 131, 141, 142, 143, 148, 166, 169, 171, 183, 228, 229, 233, 234, 263, 264, 267, 268, 271, 276, 277, 305, 339, 340, 342, 354, 406, 409, 410, 433, 441, 461,
Special Boat Service (SBS) 78, 125, 130, 147, 152, 163, 229, 277, 409

Army Air Corps
3 Regiment 48, 55, 86,120, 410, 425, 427, 428, 430, 454
662 Squadron 99, 107
657 Squadron 409

Other Units, Regiments and Corps
Royal Electrical and Mechanical Engineers 324, 325, 353, 348
Royal Logistic Corps 14, 17, 46, 124, 183, 392, 414, 453, 462
Royal Military Police 158, 159, 168, 169, 178, 207, 248, 307, 433, 462

Royal Marines and Royal Navy
3 Commando Brigade 21, 44, 45, 48, 50, 51, 52, 70, 78, 82, 83, 85, 111, 113, 114, 115, 116, 125, 145, 153, 158, 230, 231, 410
40 Commando 44, 50, 51, 65, 70, 83, 84, 85, 86, 113, 114, 116, 117, 118, 140, 220, 230, 234, 410, 411
42 Commando 51, 65, 84, 113, 114, 118, 140, 146, 462
45 Commando 78, 125, 129, 154, 409
847 Naval Air Squadron 112, 113, 114, 117, 305

Royal Air Force
RAF Regiment 78, 80, 165, 178, 181, 303, 304, 318, 353, 364, 433, 454
II (Army Co-operation) Squadron 126, 278
3 (Fighter) Squadron 62
7 Squadron 126, 130, 409
9 Squadron 285
13 Squadron 278, 394
14 Squadron 282, 283, 442, 443
18 (Bomber) Squadron 83, 120, 419
31 Squadron 282, 283, 4319
39 Squadron 126, 129, 409
47 Squadron 126, 130, 136
51 Squadron 285
120 Squadron 126
617 Squadron 60, 132

Equipment
Aircraft – US sourced
A-10 104, 112, 122
AC-130 206, 214, 286, 342, 374, 379
B-1B 72
B-52 379, 458
C-17 62, 209
CH-47 Chinook 44, 62, 83, 120, 124, 126, 129, 140, 166, 168, 179, 235, 415
Desert Hawk 303, 304, 305
E-3D 43, 126, 128
F-15E 77, 109, 134, 212, 324, 425, 457
F-16 112, 127, 212, 372, 429, 430, 457
F-117 78
F/A-18 Hornet 66, 81, 100, 425, 457
Hercules 12, 17, 56, 66, 67, 126, 136, 239, 308, 330, 351, 393, 395, 417, 448, 456
MQ-1 Predator 28, 43, 82, 127, 286, 290, 321, 338, 371
MQ-9 Reaper 28
Tristar 14, 60, 330, 415

Aircraft – UK sourced
Gazelle 51, 56, 112, 113, 120, 172, 415
Harrier 42, 43, 61, 62, 63, 66, 104, 126, 128, 131, 132, 133, 134, 135, 136, 255, 409, 415, 427, 429, 430
Lynx 48, 51, 56, 85, 107, 112, 113, 114, 116, 1230, 122, 139, 147, 234, 236, 300, 305, 306, 310, 314, 323, 350, 377, 409
Phoenix 53, 56, 85, 91, 99, 103, 104, 105, 111, 122, 142, 187, 224, 253, 293, 303, 304, 305
Puma 84, 234, 288, 410, 415, 442, 455
Tornado F3 60, 62, 415, 423, 425, 458
Tornado GR4 133, 135, 136, 142, 206, 228, 233, 234, 253, 278, 280, 281, 283, 284, 285, 291, 349, 352, 371, 375, 376, 406, 415, 417, 461
VC-10 134, 228, 278, 417

Ground Equipment and Vehicles
AS-90 16, 56, 58, 66, 87, 91, 103, 105, 123, 139, 353, 375, 379
Bulldog 299, 301, 302, 321, 338, 347, 348, 360
Challenger 2 46, 57, 58, 59, 60, 74, 87, 89, 91, 97, 98, 99, 105, 106, 107, 108, 114, 115, 116, 117, 139, 143, 146, 148, 176, 192, 199, 204, 205, 206, 208, 214, 221, 226, 293, 301, 325,

326, 341, 351, 373, 380, 390, 398, 424, 426, 457
CVR(T) Scimitar 56, 86, 94, 117, 122, 198, 237, 352,
Mastiff 301, 321, 338, 377, 382, 394
MAMBA 56, 123, 310, 379
Snatch Land Rover 192, 201, 205, 206, 209, 212, 213, 215, 218, 248, 256, 257, 263, 264, 269, 271, 274, 275, 292, 296, 297, 298, 299, 300, 310, 318, 319, 349
Vector 299
Warror 58, 88, 91, 97, 100, 107, 109, 139, 147, 148, 175, 181, 192, 198, 201, 203, 204, 206, 207, 208, 209, 210, 213, 215, 217, 221, 230, 232, 235, 236, 237, 257, 262, 265, 267, 269, 274, 293, 297, 299, 310, 302, 319, 322, 323, 324, 327, 331, 332, 337, 340, 341, 347, 348, 360, 383, 398, 444
105mm Light Gun 51, 56, 120, 121, 123, 303, 338, 339, 340

Warships

HMS Ark Royal 65, 70, 84, 84, 85, 415, 419, 422, 424, 425
HMS Ocean 65, 70, 88, 415

16383666R00266

Printed in Poland
by Amazon Fulfillment
Poland Sp. z o.o., Wrocław